Praise for Richard Taruskin's *The Oxford History of Western Music*

"There is not a page without insight, and not a chapter that does not fundamentally change the reader's perspective on its subject matter. . .. It is a visionary addition to our understanding of our culture." – Roger Scruton, *Times Literary Supplement*

"Readable, provocative, endlessly challenging and informative, his narrative account of more than a millennium's worth of musical activity represents a virtuoso display of the historian's craft." — Joshua Kosman, *San Francisco Chronicle*

"The most important publishing event in classical music since The New Grove Dictionary of Music and Musicians." — *The New York Times*

"Expresses the magnificence and melancholy of its age. . .. Singular in every possible way." — Paul Griffiths, *The Nation*

"If you want to know how brilliant Richard Taruskin's *Oxford History of Western Music* is, just open the first of its five long volumes and start reading right from page one. I found myself on the edge of my seat, as Mr. Taruskin begins his journey of a thousand years." — Greg Sandow, *The Wall Street Journal*

"Erudite, engaging, and suffused throughout with a mixture of brilliance and delirium. . .a highly personal (and often delightfully prickly) take on musical history from an original and eccentric mind — a mind to which anybody interested in the art of music should be exposed." — Tim Page, *The Washington Post*

"[Taruskin's] analyses are generally both cogent and entertaining, written in a rambunctious style that conveys technical information with great lucidity." — Charles Rosen, *The New York Review of Books*

"Taruskin has created a corpus of scholarship of breathtaking scope and crushing weight." – *Lingua Franca*

"[Taruskin is]. . .one of the most fluent writers on music in modern scholarship." – *The Musical Times*

"Entertaining. Provocative." – *The New York Times Book Review*

"Taruskin's magnum opus is a must-read, and in its way, a real page-turner of detective non-fiction. It's a cinch to become the most discussed music title of the year, if not of the decade." — Robert Everett-Green, *The Globe & Mail*

"It's a must-read for people who love or are curious about what we call western classical music. . .. Suddenly there is a coherent, irresistible narrative, full of delightful, sometimes disturbing surprises that leave you thinking for days. Suddenly, music history lives and breathes." — Tamara Bernstein, *CBC Online*

"Erudite, biased and persuasive; an irresistible survey of a millennium of music. Its ideas, a brillliant distillation of contemporary cultural attitudes, will likely percolate across music studies and other cultural histories." — Pierre Ruhe, *Atlanta Journal-Constitution*

"He is an elegant storyteller whose gifts of explication lead the reader to new levels of understanding, if not always agreement. . .his history is destined to remain intriguing and influential for years to come." — Don Rosenberg, *Cleveland Plain Dealer*

"It isn't likely that anyone, anytime soon, will challenge or replace this huge effort of Taruskin's. . .it is a staggering accomplishment." — Alan Rich, *LA Weekly*

"The book is nothing short of spectacular. . .stellar, worthwhile reading. — Daniel Felsenfeld, *New Music Box*

"One of the liveliest and most remakable books about music. . .. It will give real pleasures and revelations to any music lover, amateur or professional." — Raphael Mostel, *The Forward*

"It is difficult to arrive at a final opinion of so vast and multifarious a work other than to say that few people in the field could have encompassed it with the thoroughness and knowledge of Richard Taruskin." — Patrick J. Smith, *The New Criterion*

"Musicians, students, historians, and other readers wishing a detailed narrative about the career, patronage, musical influences, reception, and creative production of western composers, as well as the development of musical styles, will find this a fascinating and satisfying resource." — *Reference & Research Library Book News*

"Richard Taruskin, the most authoritative controversialist in modern musicology, has written an *Oxford History of Western Music* to rival Gibbon's *Decline and Fall* in ambition, literary distinction and sheer bulk. " — David Gutman, *The Independent*

"There's no doubt. . .that *The Oxford History of Western Music* is an important model of music historiography for some years to come." — Rob Haskins, American Record Guide

"There's no place else to look for such a comprehensive, entertaining overview of this immense subject." — John W. Freeman, *Opera News*

"It's likely to be remembered as the magnum opus of the most stimulating and insightful English-languge writer on music at work today." — Claude Bustard, *Richmond Times-Dispatch*

"A towering achievement." — Melinda Bargreen, *The Seattle Times*

"Taruskin has suceeded in writing a stimulating overview of Western society, setting a standard that will not be surpassed for a very long time." — Timothy J. McGee, *Library Journal starred review*

"Wickedly brilliant." — *BBC Music Magazine*

MUSIC IN THE

LATE TWENTIETH CENTURY

THE OXFORD HISTORY OF WESTERN MUSIC

The Oxford History of Western Music is a continuous narrative, in five volumes (originally issued with a sixth containing indices and other back matter), covering the history of literate music making in Europe and (eventually) North America from inception, with the introduction of music notation in the ninth century CE, to the dawn of the third millennium. This book, corresponding to Volume 5 of the whole, has been lightly revised for the sake of greater accuracy and self-sufficiency. The indices and back matter have been divided among the several volumes in this edition.

The Earliest Notations to the Sixteenth Century

The Seventeenth and Eighteenth Centuries

The Nineteenth Century

The Early Twentieth Century

The Late Twentieth Century

MUSIC IN THE LATE TWENTIETH CENTURY

Richard Taruskin

THE OXFORD HISTORY OF WESTERN MUSIC

OXFORD
UNIVERSITY PRESS

2010

OXFORD
UNIVERSITY PRESS

Oxford   New York

Auckland   Bangkok   Buenos Aires   Cape Town   Chennai
Dar es Salaam   Delhi   Hong Kong   Istanbul   Karachi   Kolkata
Kuala Lumpur   Madrid   Melbourne   Mexico City   Mumbai   Nairobi
São Paulo   Shanghai   Taipei   Tokyo   Toronto

Copyright © 2005, 2010 by Oxford University Press, Inc.

Published by Oxford University Press, Inc.
198 Madison Avenue, New York, New York 10016
http://www.oup.com/us

Oxford is a registered trademark of Oxford University Press

Library of Congress Cataloging-in-Publication Data
Taruskin, Richard.
[Oxford history of western music. 5, Late twentieth century]
Music in the late twentieth century/by Richard Taruskin.
p.cm. — (The Oxford history of western music; v. 5)
Originally published as: Oxford history of western music. Vol. 5, Late twentieth century.
Oxford; New York : Oxford University Press, 2005.
ISBN 978-0-19-538485-7 (alk. paper)
1. Music – 20th century – History and criticism. I. Title.
ML197.T28 2009
780.9'04 – dc22
2008045161

1   3   5   7   9   8   6   4   2
Printed in the United States of America

Contents

Introduction:
The History of What?

The argument is no other than to inquire and collect out of the records of all time what particular kinds of learning and arts have flourished in what ages and regions of the world, their antiquities, their progresses, their migrations (for sciences migrate like nations) over the different parts of the globe; and again their decays, disappearances, and revivals; [and also] an account of the principal authors, books, schools, successions, academies, societies, colleges, orders — in a word, everything which relates to the state of learning. Above all things, I wish events to be coupled with their causes. All this I would have handled in a historical way, not wasting time, after the manner of critics, in praise and blame, but simply narrating the fact historically, with but slight intermixture of private judgment. For the manner of compiling such a history I particularly advise that the matter and provision of it be not drawn from histories and commentaries alone; but that the principal books written in each century, or perhaps in shorter periods, proceeding in regular order from the earliest ages, be themselves taken into consultation; that so (I do not say by a complete perusal, for that would be an endless labour, but) by tasting them here and there, and observing their argument, style, and method, the Literary Spirit of each age may be charmed as it were from the dead.

— Francis Bacon, *De Dignitate et Augmentis Scientiarum Libri IX* (1623)[1]

Mutatis mutandis, Bacon's task was mine. He never lived to complete it; I have — but only by dint of a drastic narrowing of scope. My *mutanda* are stated in my title (one not chosen but granted; and for that honor I extend my thanks to the Delegates of the Oxford University Press). For "learning and the arts" substitute music. For "the different parts of the globe" substitute Europe, joined in Volume 3 by America. (That is what we still casually mean by "the West," although the concept is undergoing sometimes curious change: a Soviet music magazine I once subscribed to gave news of the pianist Yevgeny Kissin's "Western debut" — in Tokyo.) And as for antiquities, they hardly exist for music. (Jacques Chailley's magnificently titled conspectus, *40,000 ans de musique*, got through the first 39,000 years — I exaggerate only slightly — on its first page.[2])

Still, as the sheer bulk of this offering attests, a lot was left, because I took seriously Bacon's stipulations that causes be investigated, that original documents be not only cited but analyzed (for their "argument, style, and method") and that the approach should be catholic and as near exhaustive as possible, based not on my preferences but on my estimation of what needed to be included in order to satisfy the dual requirement of causal explanation and technical explication. Most books that call themselves histories of Western music, or of any of its traditional "style periods," are in fact surveys, which cover—and celebrate—the relevant repertoire, but make little effort truly to explain why and how things happened as they did. This set of books is an attempt at a true history.

Paradoxically, that means it does not take "coverage" as its primary task. A lot of famous music goes unmentioned in these pages, and even some famous composers. Inclusion and omission imply no judgment of value here. I never asked myself whether this or that composition or musician was "worth mentioning," and I hope readers will agree that I have sought neither to advocate nor to denigrate what I did include.

But there is something more fundamental yet to explain, given my claim of catholicity. Coverage of all the musics that have been made in Europe and America is obviously neither the aim of this book nor its achievement. A glance at the table of contents will instantly confirm, to the inevitable disappointment and perhaps consternation of some, that "Western music" here means what it has always meant in general academic histories: it means what is usually called "art music" or "classical music," and looks suspiciously like the traditional canon that has come under so much justified fire for its long-unquestioned dominance of the academic curriculum (a dominance that is now in irreversible process of decline). A very challenging example of that fire is a fusillade by Robert Walser, a scholar of popular music, who characterizes the repertoire treated here in terms borrowed from the writings of the Marxist historian Eric Hobsbawm. "Classical music," writes Walser,

> is the sort of thing Eric Hobsbawm calls an "invented tradition," whereby present interests construct a cohesive past to establish or legitimize present-day institutions or social relations. The hodgepodge of the classical canon—aristocratic and bourgeois music; academic, sacred and secular; music for public concerts, private soirées and dancing—achieves its coherence through its function as the most prestigious musical culture of the twentieth century.[3]

Why in the world would one want to continue propagating such a hodgepodge in the twenty-first century?

The heterogeneity of the classical canon is undeniable. Indeed, that is one of its main attractions. And while I reject Walser's conspiracy-theorizing, I definitely sympathize with the social and political implications of his argument, as will be evident (for some—a different some—all too evident) in the many pages that follow. But that very sympathy is what impelled me to subject that impossibly heterogeneous body of music to one more (perhaps the last) comprehensive examination—under a revised definition that supplies the coherence that Walser impugns. All of the genres he mentions, and all of the genres that are treated in this book, are literate genres. That is, they are genres that have been disseminated primarily through the medium of writing. The sheer abundance and the generic heterogeneity of the music so disseminated in "the West" is a truly distinguishing feature—perhaps the West's signal musical distinction. It is deserving of critical study.

By critical study I mean a study that does not take literacy for granted, or simply tout it as a unique Western achievement, but rather "interrogates" it (as our hermeneutics of suspicion now demands) for its consequences. The first chapter of this book makes a fairly detailed attempt to assess the specific consequences for music of a literate culture, and that theme remains a constant factor — always implicit, often explicit — in every chapter that follows, right up to (and especially) the concluding ones. For it is the basic claim of this multivolumed narrative — its number-one postulate — that the literate tradition of Western music is coherent at least insofar as it has a completed shape. Its beginnings are known and explicable, and its end is now foreseeable (and also explicable). And just as the early chapters are dominated by the interplay of literate and preliterate modes of thinking and transmission (and the middle chapters try to cite enough examples to keep the interplay of literate and nonliterate alive in the reader's consciousness), so the concluding chapters are dominated by the interplay of literate and postliterate modes, which have been discernable at least since the middle of the twentieth century, and which sent the literate tradition (in the form of a backlash) into its culminating phase.

This is by no means to imply that everything within the covers of these volumes constitutes a single story. I am as suspicious as the next scholar of what we now call metanarratives (or worse, "master narratives"). Indeed, one of the main tasks of this telling will be to account for the rise of our reigning narratives, and show that they too have histories with beginnings and (implicitly) with ends. The main ones, for music, have been, first, an esthetic narrative — recounting the achievement of "art for art's sake," or (in the present instance) of "absolute music" — that asserts the autonomy of artworks (often tautologically insulated by adding "insofar as they are artworks") as an indispensable and retroactive criterion of value and, second, a historical narrative — call it "neo-Hegelian" — that celebrates progressive (or "revolutionary") emancipation and values artworks according to their contribution to that project. Both are shopworn heirlooms of German romanticism. These romantic tales are "historicized" in volume III, the key volume of the set, for it furnishes our intellectual present with a past. This is done in the fervent belief that no claim of universality can survive situation in intellectual history. Each of the genres that Walser names has its own history, moreover, as do the many that he does not name, and it will be evident to all readers that this narrative devotes as much attention to a congeries of "petits récits" — individual accounts of this and that — as it does to the epic sketched in the foregoing paragraphs. But the overarching trajectory of musical literacy is nevertheless a part of all the stories, and a particularly revealing one.

* * * * *

The first thing that it reveals is that the history narrated within these covers is the history of elite genres. For until very recent times, and in some ways even up to the present, literacy and its fruits have been the possession — the closely guarded and privileging (even life-saving) possession — of social elites: ecclesiastical, political, military, hereditary, meritocratic, professional, economic, educational, academic, fashionable, even criminal. What else, after all, makes high art high? The casting of the story as the story of the literate culture of music turns it willy-nilly into a social history — a contradictory social history in which progressive broadening of access to literacy and its attendant cultural perquisites (the history, as it has sometimes been called, of the democratization of taste), is accompanied at every turn by a counterthrust that seeks to redefine elite status (and its attendant genres) ever upward. As most comprehensively documented by Pierre Bourdieu, consumption of cultural goods (and music, on Bourdieu's showing, above all) is one of the primary means of social classification (including self- classification) — hence, social division — and (familiar proverbs notwithstanding) one of the liveliest sites of dispute in Western culture.[4] Most broadly, contestations of taste occur across lines of class division, and are easiest to discern between proponents of literate genres and nonliterate ones; but within and among elites they are no less potent, no less heated, and no less decisively influential on the course of events. Taste is one of the sites of contention to which this book gives extensive, and, I would claim, unprecedented coverage, beginning with chapter 4 and lasting to the bitter end.

Indeed, if one had to be nominated, I would single out social contention as embodied in words and deeds — what cultural theorists call "discourse" (and others call "buzz" or "spin") — as the paramount force driving this narrative. It has many arenas. Perhaps the most conspicuous is that of meaning, an area that was for a long time considered virtually off limits to professional scholarly investigation, since it was naively assumed to be a nonfactual domain inasmuch as music lacks the semantic (or "propositional") specificity of literature or even painting. But musical meaning is no more confinable to matters of simple semantic paraphrase than any other sort of meaning. Utterances are deemed meaningful (or not) insofar as they trigger associations, and in the absence of association no utterance is intelligible. Meaning in this book is taken to represent the full range of associations encompassed by locutions such as "If that is true, it means that ...," or "that's what M-O-T-H-E-R means to me," or, simply, "know what I mean?" It covers implications, consequences, metaphors, emotional attachments, social attitudes, proprietary interests, suggested possibilities, motives, significance (as distinguished from signification)... and simple semantic paraphrase, too, when that is relevant.

And while it is perfectly true that semantic paraphrases of music are never "factual," their assertion is indeed a social fact — one that belongs to a category of historical fact of the most vital importance, since such facts are among the clearest connectors of musical history to the history of everything else. Take for example the current impassioned debate over the meaning of Dmitry Shostakovich's music, with all of its insistent claims and counterclaims. The assertion that Shostakovich's music reveals him to be a political dissident is only an opinion, as is the opposite claim, that his music shows him to have been a "loyal musical son of the Soviet Union" — as, for that matter, is the alternative claim that his music has no light to shed on the question of his personal political allegiances. And yet the fact that such assertions are advanced with passion is a powerful testimony to the social and political role Shostakovich's music has played in the world, both during his lifetime and (especially) after his death, when the Cold War was playing itself out. Espousing a particular position in the debate is no business of the historian.

(Some readers may know that I have espoused one as a critic; I would like to think that readers who do not know my position will not discover it here.) But to report the debate in its full range, and draw relevant implications from it, is the historian's ineluctable duty. That report includes the designation of what elements within the sounding composition have triggered the associations — a properly historical sort of analysis that is particularly abundant in the present narrative. Call it semiotics if you will.

But of course semiotics has been much abused. It is an old vice of criticism, and lately of scholarship, to assume that the meaning of artworks is fully vested in them by their creators, and is simply "there" to be decoded by a specially gifted interpreter. That assumption can lead to gross errors. It is what vitiated the preposterously overrated work of Theodor Wiesengrund Adorno, and what has caused the work of the "new musicologists" of the 1980s and 1990s — Adornians to a man and woman — to age with such stunning rapidity. It is, all pretenses aside, still an authoritarian discourse and an asocial one. It still grants oracular privilege to the creative genius and his prophets, the gifted interpreters. It is altogether unacceptable as a historical method, although it is part of history and, like everything else, deserving of report. The historian's trick is to shift the question from "What does it mean?" to "What has it meant?" That move is what transforms futile speculation and dogmatic polemic into historical illumination. What it illuminates, in a word, are the *stakes*, both "theirs" and "ours."

Not that all meaningful discourse about music is semiotic. Much of it is evaluative. And value judgments, too, have a place of honor in historical narratives, so long as they are not merely the historian's judgment (as Francis Bacon was already presciently aware). Beethoven's greatness is an excellent case in point because it will come in for so much discussion in the later volumes of this book. As such, the notion of Beethoven's greatness is "only" an opinion. To assert it as a fact would be the sort of historians' transgression on which master narratives are built. (And because historians' transgressions so often make history, they will be given a lot of attention in the pages that follow.) But to say this much is already to observe that such assertions, precisely insofar as they are not factual, often have enormous performative import. Statements and actions predicated on Beethoven's perceived greatness are what constitute Beethoven's authority, which certainly is a historical fact — one that practically determined the course of late-nineteenth-century music history. Without taking it into account one can explain little of what went on in the world of literate music-making during that time — and even up to the present. Whether the historian agrees with the perception on which Beethoven's authority has been based is of no consequence to the tale, and has no bearing on the historian's obligation to report it. That report constitutes "reception history" — a relatively new thing in musicology, but (many scholars now agree) of equal importance to the production history that used to count as the whole story. I have made a great effort to give the two equal time, since both are necessary ingredients of any account that claims fairly to represent history.

* * * *

Statements and actions in response to real or perceived conditions: these are the essential facts of human history. The discourse, so often slighted in the past, is in fact the story. It creates new social and intellectual conditions to which more statements and actions will respond, in an endless chain of agency. The historian needs to be on guard against the tendency, or the temptation, to simplify the story by neglecting this most basic fact of all. No historical event or change can be meaningfully asserted unless its agents can be specified; and *agents can only be people.* Attributions of agency unmediated by human action are, in effect, lies — or at the very least, evasions. They occur inadvertently in careless historiography (or historiography that has submitted unawares to a master narrative), and are invoked deliberately in propaganda (i.e., historiography that consciously colludes with a master narrative). I adduce what I consider to be an example of each (and leave it to the reader to decide which, if any, is the honorable blunder and which the propaganda). The first comes from Pieter C. Van den Toorn's *Music, Politics, and the Academy,* a rebuttal of the so-called New Musicology of the 1980s.

> The question of an engaging context is an aesthetic as well as an historical and analytic-theoretical one. And once individual works begin to prevail for what they are in and of themselves and not for what they represent, then context itself, as a reflection of this transcendence, becomes less dependent on matters of historical placement. A great variety of contexts can suggest themselves as attention is focused on the works, on the nature of both their immediacy and the relationship that is struck with the contemporary listener.[5]

The second is from the most recent narrative history of music published in America as of this writing, Mark Evan Bonds's *A History of Music in Western Culture.*

> By the early 16th century, the rondeau, the last of the surviving *formes fixes* from the medieval era, had largely disappeared, replaced by more freely structured chansons based on the principle of pervading imitation. What emerged during the 1520s and 1530s were new approaches to setting vernacular texts: the Parisian chanson in France and the madrigal in Italy.
>   During the 1520s, a new genre of song, now known as the Parisian chanson emerged in the French capital. Among its most notable composers were Claudin de Sermisy (ca. 1490–1562) and Clément Jannequin (ca. 1485–ca. 1560), whose works were widely disseminated by the Parisian music publisher Pierre Attaingnant. Reflecting the influence of the Italian frottola, the Parisian chanson is lighter and more chordally oriented than earlier chansons.[6]

This sort of writing gives everybody an alibi. All the active verbs have ideas or inanimate objects as subjects, and all human acts are described in the passive voice. Nobody is seen as *doing* (or deciding) anything. Even the composers in the second extract are not described in the act, but only as an impersonal medium or passive vehicle of "emergence." Because nobody is doing anything, the authors never have to deal with motives or values, with choices or responsibilities, and that is their alibi. The second extract is a kind of shorthand historiography that inevitably devolves into inert survey, since it does nothing more than describe objects, thinking, perhaps, that is how one safeguards "objectivity." The first extract commits a far more serious transgression, for it is ideologically committed to its impersonality. Its elimination of human agency is calculated to protect the autonomy of the work-object and actually prevent historical thinking, which the author evidently regards as a threat to the universality (in his thinking, the validity) of the values he upholds. It is an attempt, caught as it were in the act, to enforce what I call the Great Either/Or, the great bane of contemporary musicology.

The Great Either/Or is the seemingly inescapable debate, familiar to all academically trained musicologists (who have had to endure it in their fledgling proseminars), epitomized in the question made famous by Carl Dahlhaus (1928–89), the most prestigious German music scholar of his generation: Is art history the *history* of art, or is it the history of *art*? What a senseless distinction! What seemed to make it necessary was the pseudo-dialectical "method" that cast all thought in rigidly—and artificially—binarized terms: "Does music mirror the reality surrounding a composer, OR does it propose an alternative reality? Does it have common roots with political events and philosophical ideas; OR is music written simply because music has always been written and not, or only incidentally, because a composer is seeking to respond with music to the world he lives in?" These questions all come from the second chapter of Dahlhaus's *Foundations of Music History*, the title of which—"The significance of art: historical or aesthetic?"—is yet another forced dichotomy. The whole chapter, which has achieved in its way the status of a classic, consists, throughout, of a veritable salad of empty binarisms.[7]

This sort of thinking has long been seen through—except, it seems, by musicologists. A scurrilous little tract—David Hackett Fischer's *Historians' Fallacies*—that graduate students of my generation liked to read (often aloud, to one another) behind our professors' backs includes it under the rubric "Fallacies of Question-Framing," and gives an unforgettable example: "Basil of Byzantium: Rat or Fink?" ("Maybe," the author comments, "Basil was the very model of a modern ratfink."[8]) There is nothing *a priori* to rule out both/and rather than either/or. Indeed, if it is true that production and reception history are of equal and interdependent importance to an understanding of cultural products, then it must follow that types of analysis usually conceived in mutually exclusive "internal" and "external" categories can and must function symbiotically. That is the assumption on which this book has been written, reflecting its author's refusal to choose between *this* and *that*, but rather to embrace this, that, and the other.

Reasons for the long if lately embattled dominance of internalist models for music history in the West (a dominance that in large part accounts for Dahlhaus's otherwise inexplicable prestige) have more than two centuries of intellectual history behind them, and I shall try to illuminate them at appropriate points. But a comment is required up front about the special reasons for their dominance in the recent history of the discipline—reasons having to do with the Cold War, when the general intellectual atmosphere was excessively polarized (hence binarized) around a pair of seemingly exhaustive and totalized alternatives. The only alternative to strict internalist thinking, it then seemed, was a discourse that was utterly corrupted by totalitarian cooption. Admit a social purview, it then seemed, and you were part of the Communist threat to the integrity (and the freedom) of the creative individual. In Germany, Dahlhaus was cast as the dialectical antithesis to Georg Knepler, his equally magisterial East German counterpart.[9] Within his own geographical and political milieu, then, his ideological commitments were acknowledged.[10] In the English-speaking countries, where Knepler was practically unknown, Dahlhaus's influence was more pernicious because he was assimilated, quite erroneously, to an indigenous scholarly pragmatism that thought itself ideologically uncommitted, free of theoretical preconceptions, and therefore capable of seeing things as they actually are. That, too, was of course a fallacy (Fischer calls it, perhaps unfairly, the "Baconian fallacy"). We all acknowledge now that our methods are grounded in and guided by theory, even if our theories are not consciously preformulated or explicitly enunciated.

And so this narrative has been guided. Its theoretical assumptions and consequent methodology — the cards I am in process of laying on the table — were, as it happens, not preformulated; but that did not make them any less real, or lessen their potency as enablers and constraints. By the end of writing I was sufficiently self-aware to recognize the kinship between the methods I had arrived at and those advocated in *Art Worlds*, a methodological conspectus by Howard Becker, a sociologist of art. Celebrated among sociologists, the book has not been widely read by musicologists, and I discovered it after my own work was finished in first draft.[11] But a short description of its tenets will round out the picture I am attempting to draw of the premises on which this book rests, and a reading of Becker's book will, I think, be of conceptual benefit not only to the readers of this book, but also to the writers of others.

An "art world," as Becker conceives it, is the ensemble of agents and social relations that it takes to produce works of art (or maintain artistic activity) in various media. To study art worlds is to study processes of collective action and mediation, the very things that are most often missing in conventional musical historiography. Such a study tries to answer in all their complexity questions like "What did it take to produce Beethoven's Fifth?" Anyone who thinks that the answer to that question can be given in one word — "Beethoven" — needs to read Becker (or, if one has the time, this book). But of course no one who has reflected on the matter at all would give the one-word answer. Bartók gave a valuable clue to the kind of account that truly explains when he commented dryly that Kodály's *Psalmus Hungaricus* "could not have been written without Hungarian peasant music. (Neither, of course, could it have been written without Kodály.)"[12] An explanatory account describes the dynamic (and, in the true sense, dialectical) relationship that obtains between powerful agents and mediating factors: institutions and their gatekeepers, ideologies, patterns of consumption and dissemination involving patrons, audiences, publishers and publicists, critics, chroniclers, commentators, and so on practically indefinitely until one chooses to draw the line.

Where shall it be drawn? Becker begins his book with a piquant epigraph that engages the question head-on, leading him directly to his first, most crucial theoretical point: namely, that "all artistic work, like all human activity, involves the joint activity of a number, often a large number, of people, through whose cooperation the art work we eventually see or hear comes to be and continues to be." The epigraph comes from the autobiography of Anthony Trollope:

> It was my practice to be at my table every morning at 5:30 A.M.; and it was also my practice to allow myself no mercy. An old groom, whose business it was to call me, and to whom I paid £5 a year extra for the duty, allowed himself no mercy. During all those years at Waltham Cross he was never once late with the coffee which it was his duty to bring me. I do not know that I ought not to feel that I owe more to him than to any one else for the success I have had. By beginning at that hour I could complete my literary work before I dressed for breakfast.[13]

Quite a few coffee porters, so to speak, will figure in the pages that follow, as will agents who enforce conventions (and, occasionally, the law), mobilize resources, disseminate products (often altering them in the process), and create reputations. All of them are at once potential enablers and potential constrainers, and create the conditions within which creative agents act. Composers will inevitably loom largest in the discussion despite all caveats, because theirs are the names on the artifacts that will be most closely analyzed. But the act of naming is itself an instrument of power, and a propagator of master narratives (now in a second, more literal, meaning), and it too must receive its meed of interrogation. The very first chapter in Volume I can stand as a model, in a sense, for the more realistic assessment of the place composers and compositions occupy in the general historical scheme: first, because it names no composers at all; and second, because before any musical artifacts are discussed, the story of their enabling is told at considerable length—a story whose cast of characters includes kings, popes, teachers, painters, scribes and chroniclers, the latter furnishing a *Rashomon* choir of contradiction, disagreement and contention.

Another advantage of focusing on discourse and contention is that such a view prevents the lazy depiction of monoliths. The familiar "Frankfurt School" paradigm that casts the history of twentieth-century music as a simple two-sided battle between an avant-garde of heroic resisters and the homogenizing commercial juggernaut known as the Culture Industry is one of the most conspicuous and deserving victims of the kind of close observation encouraged here of the actual statements and actions of human agents ("real people"). Historians of popular music have shown over and over again that the Culture Industry has never been a monolith, and all it takes is the reading of a couple of memoirs—as witnesses, never as oracles—to make it obvious that neither was the avant-garde. Both imagined entities were in themselves sites of sometimes furious social contention, their discord breeding diversity; and paying due attention to their intramural dissensions will vastly complicate the depiction of their mutual relations.

If nothing else, this brief account of premises and methods, with its insistence on an eclectic multiplicity of approaches to observed phenomena and on greatly expanding the purview of what is observed, should help account for the extravagant length of this submission. As justification, I can offer only my conviction that the same factors that have increased its length have also, and in equal measure, increased its interest and its usefulness.

R. T.
El Cerrito, California
16 July 2008

Preface

Many believe that all history is about the present, in that our present dilemmas are what impel our interest in the past. I would not necessarily go that far. I see no need to insist that no one studies the past — especially the remote past — for its own sake. When I lived to perform medieval and Renaissance music, I was not conscious of any ulterior purpose (other than wealth, fame and power). But when my interests began to turn toward the more recent past, I was very much aware that I was motivated by my discontent with the present and my wish to understand its sources as a first step toward amelioration.

If one accepts the premise that the more recent the past, the less disinterested our curiosity about it, then one has an additional explanation for a phenomenon with which all teachers of music history must contend. At the front end of the narrative, everyone seems to teach the same material, but by the time one reaches the twentieth century, and particularly the later twentieth century, one has to cut one's own swath through the jungle, and no two treatments of the period ever duplicate one another's choice of topics or examples. This situation is usually attributed to the increasing, eventually bewildering, abundance of sources as one moves through time or to the relative stability of consensus about the early phases. But, in fact, consensus has been significantly destabilized in recent years, even for the early periods, and noting the proliferation of sources does nothing to account for the swath one has chosen to cut through them.

The theme governing this volume's coverage is the cold war and its as yet insufficiently acknowledged (not to say tendentiously minimized) impact on the arts. The cold war was a period of political and cultural polarization — a polarization that is all too readily apparent in terms of musical style, but one that is rarely explained in any way other than by appealing to what Leonard B. Meyer called "fluctuating stasis" or "delight in diversity." Yet even as pluralism took hold, significant evolution continued, and the late-twentieth-century diversity was not generally experienced as delightful. No period was ever more contentious, be it the late nineteenth century, with its Brahms versus Wagner brawling, or the early twentieth, with its Schoenberg–Stravinsky rows. The contention has by no means abated even now, which turns any attempt to treat the last fifty years of music history into a polemic or at the very least something that will attract polemical responses. The reception of *The Oxford History*, following its original (2005) publication in six volumes, is sufficient evidence of that.

Among the factors that made for contention was the emphasis — the willfully exaggerated emphasis, in the eyes of British and Western European reviewers — on events in America and their musical repercussions. I, of course, acknowledge the obvious prominence of matters American in this account, but it is hardly exaggerated. The United States unquestionably inherited musical leadership during this period from

Europe — at first by default, as a gift from Adolf Hitler, thanks to whom Schoenberg, Stravinsky, Bartók, Hindemith, Krenek, Korngold, Milhaud, and many others had, by 1945, joined Rachmaninoff, Varese, and Bloch in America, many of them remaining and becoming citizens. The conditions that stimulated the rise of the postwar European avant-garde were largely created by the Office of Military Government, United States (OMGUS), the American occupying force that, for one particularly telling example, financed and at first administered the Darmstädter Ferienkurse, at which total serialism, European-style, was born — in far more direct response to Soviet arts policy than has ever been publicly admitted. Thereafter, it was the music of the American avant-garde, chiefly represented by John Cage and Morton Feldman, and enthusiastically propagated by lavishly subsidized West German radio stations (which, in the words of Björn Heile, "competed for prestige but not for resources"), that set the tone for European experimentation. (This unprecedented, much vaunted public support for avant-garde music lasted, of course, only — and exactly — as long as the cold war; it came to an abrupt end with German reunification.) Still later, minimalism became the first style of literate music making originating in America to have the same transformative impact on European musicians that earlier European innovations had previously had on Americans, especially those studying abroad. Even here, there was a significant postwar cross-current, with many European composers coming to the United States for training as well as employment. The main impetus, moreover, for the countervailing trends toward eclecticism, postmodernism, and rapprochement with commercial genres came likewise from the United States, having originated in American youth culture and the social turbulence of the 1960s, which spread from America to Europe rather than the other way round. My emphases have been predictably ascribed to chauvinism by Europeans, but I am sooner inclined to see chauvinism in their resistance, for their accusations have not been accompanied by rebuttals or counterexamples.

American leadership in directions musicians in the West have regarded as progressive (and therefore worthy of claiming by others) is offset, of course, by Soviet leadership in directions the same musicians tend to stigmatize as reactionary. But the very use of such terminology is the best proof that esthetic judgments during the period of the cold war had been tacitly politicized. It is one of the missions of the present account to make that politicization explicit, to force it into consciousness as a necessary prelude to exorcism. That the national protagonists of this account should, in fact, turn out to be the postwar superpowers, rather than the older musical leader nations left fatigued and impoverished at war's end, only confirms the truer correspondence of this account to historical realities.

Thus, the present account is offered not in a spirit of contention, but rather one of corrective. That, of course, is the most contentious claim of all.

R. T.
November 2008

MUSIC IN THE

LATE TWENTIETH CENTURY

CHAPTER 1

Starting from Scratch

MUSIC IN THE AFTERMATH OF WORLD WAR II: ZHDANOVSHCHINA, DARMSTADT

"I can't go on. I'll go on."

—SAMUEL BECKETT, *THE UNNAMABLE* (1953)

A NEW AGE

The Second World War ended with a bang the likes of which the world had never seen. The atomic bombs dropped by the United States Army Air Forces on the Japanese cities of Hiroshima and Nagasaki in August 1945 instantly reduced them to rubble. Between them they ended some 114,000 lives in seconds. Those who justified the bombing cited the far greater number of casualties that would have inevitably followed upon an Allied invasion of the Japanese home islands; those who condemned it held that balancing military casualties against civilian ones was a barbarian calculation that wiped out the moral superiority of the Allied cause.

What everyone had to recognize, and somehow cope with, was the fact that the history of humanity had entered a new and potentially terminal phase. People living in the atomic age could no longer believe in the permanence of anything human. Individual human lives and destinies were irrevocably marked as fragile, and as expendable. Living with the constant threat of annihilation was the war's lasting legacy. It cast a long shadow over the second half of the twentieth century. It was that period's dominant fact of life. No aspect of human existence or activity could possibly escape its impact.

The nervous strain of mid-twentieth-century existence in the shadow of the bomb is perhaps best summarized in the

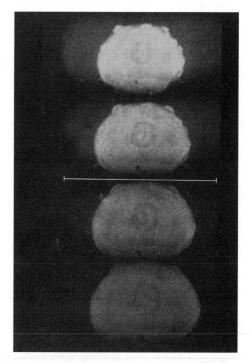

FIG. 1-1 Nuclear bomb test, three weeks before the bomb was dropped.

harsh but highly influential philosophy of existentialism put forth by Jean-Paul Sartre (1905–80) and other French writers in the aftermath of the war, according to which man's freedom is a curse from which there can no longer be any refuge in faith. Cut adrift from all moral certainty in an amoral and indifferent universe, man is nevertheless morally responsible; but one's choices, however dreadful (like the decision to drop the bomb), can be justified only on the basis of one's voluntary, fallible, and constantly threatened personal principles, principles in which one can have no a priori faith. We have no choice but to choose.

One can never invoke external legal or ethical standards that absolve oneself from the onus of personal responsibility (as many who served the Nazis tried to do). One cannot look to others for validation, for they, too, are fallible and corruptible. Only by shouldering the risks of choice can one hope (against hope) to achieve *essence*: authentic, rather than merely contingent, being. A pitiless and puritanical philosophy, it offered some small comfort in the face of perceived helplessness, but only at the price of all moral security and easy pleasure. No wonder, as the title of the psychoanalyst Erich Fromm's best-selling existentialist primer proclaimed, people sought "Escape from Freedom."

These shattering perceptions and the ensuing malaise were somewhat delayed, especially on the victorious side, by the immediate exhilaration of triumph. The triumph, moreover, was of a novel character. For it was not force of arms per se that finally decided the outcome of the war in the Pacific; it was superior technology. Science had won the war and saved mankind from the fascist threat. J. Robert Oppenheimer (1904–67), the American physicist who directed the atomic energy research project at Los Alamos, New Mexico, where over the years 1942–45 the bombs that would vanquish Japan were designed and produced, was widely regarded as a war hero, and thereafter as a culture-hero. His later political disgrace, over issues of national security, fairly epitomizes the neurotic suspicions that eventually came to the fore as the ghastly price of victory was realized; but in the immediate postwar period, science and technology enjoyed an unprecedented prestige.

That prestige was symbolized by the figure of Albert Einstein (1879–1955), the outstanding German physicist whose presence in the United States as a refugee from the Nazis was seen as indirectly responsible for the Allied victory, since it was his letter to President Roosevelt that first brought the military potential of atomic power to the attention of the government. Einstein became a household name, synonymous with intellect, and his grandfatherly, bushy-haired, walrus-mustached

FIG. I-2   Albert Einstein.

countenance became a household icon. His status, and that of science itself, was symbolized and enhanced by the folk saying, "In all the world only twelve men understand Einstein." The reconditeness of "advanced" modern science was taken as an implicit proof of its value; the winning of the war on the basis of arcane formulas like $E = mc^2$ (which also, in its way, became a folk saying) was more tangible proof.

The contradictory or "dialectical" themes broached in these introductory paragraphs — triumph vs. insecurity, responsibility vs. escape, science-as-savior vs. science-as-destroyer, esotericism vs. utility, intellect vs. barbarism, faith in progress vs. omnibus suspicion — will be the cantus firmi of the next several chapters, along with the all-pervading image of rubble and waste, and the paralyzing (or inspiring) prospect of rebuilding. All of the bizarre and contradictory musical events and phenomena to be recounted must be understood as counterpoints against these intractable and irresolvable dilemmas that unbalanced the world's mind.

A foretaste of the ambivalences to come can be read in the story of Aaron Copland's Third Symphony. Written between the summer of 1944, right after the American landing in Normandy ("D day"), and the summer of 1946, it was the Great American Symphony to end all great American symphonies. Third Symphonies by American composers had always inclined Beethovenishly toward the "heroic"; in Copland's case that tendency (already heightened, perhaps, by his rivalry with Roy Harris) was abetted by the mood of euphoria that accompanied the end of the war.

That mood is embodied in hymns and fanfares. The scherzo (second movement) is based on a marchlike idea Copland discarded on the way to the *Fanfare for the Common Man*, his 1942 contribution to wartime morale; and the finale is based on the *Fanfare* itself, developed in the coda into a grandiose peroration (Ex. 1-1) that some commentators have compared with the climax of the "Ode to Joy" in Beethoven's Ninth. A huge orchestra with triple and quadruple winds, augmented by a piano, two harps, and a clangorous percussion section manned by six players, reaches full tilt with a sudden halving of the tempo in every way comparable to the climax that capped the first movement of *Copland's Music for the Theater* some twenty years before — in every way, that is, except context. For whereas the earlier climax had scandalized the Boston Symphony audience by evoking a sexy bump-and-grind, the new one brought the very same audience to its feet at the premiere (under Serge Koussevitzky, Copland's longstanding patron) on 18 October 1946. One critic immediately ranked it with Harris's Third as "the two finest works in the form by American composers."[1] Koussevitzky himself broke the tie by flatly declaring Copland's symphony the greatest.[2] Virgil Thomson showed his envy in a mixed review titled, somewhat sardonically, "Copland as Great Man."[3]

But something festered beneath the praise. Copland's composer friends were uncomfortable with the overly triumphant tone, or became so as the euphoric mood of 1946 gave way to a somewhat hung-over sobriety in 1947 (the year in which Sartre's *L'existentialisme* was published in English translation). Leonard Bernstein (1918–90), Koussevitzky's main conducting protégé, led the European premiere at the World Youth Festival in Prague on 25 May 1947; two days later he wrote to Copland, "Sweetie, the end is a sin."[4] Arthur Berger (1912–2003), another fellow composer, who was also

EX. 1-1   Aaron Copland, Symphony no. 3, IV, climax (original version)

EX. I-I (continued)

Copland's first biographer, complained in a 1948 review of the finale's "pomp and overstatement."[5] Bernstein wrote again, from the newborn state of Israel in November 1948, to say that he now thought the work "quite magnificent," but then confessed that he had "made a sizable cut near the end and believe me it makes a whale of a difference."[6]

In fact he had taken out the first eight measures of Ex. 1-1. Copland was at first as miffed by Bernstein's "nervy"[7] deed as one might have expected. "Being a careful and slow worker," he told an interviewer, "I rarely felt it necessary to revise a composition after it was finished, and even more rarely after it was published." But amazingly enough, he went on to say that "I came to agree with Lenny and several others about the advisability of shortening the ending," and had the publisher remove the offending passage from subsequent printings of the score; it has never been recorded commercially. Even in its toned-down form, the finale is an effective memento of its euphoric time; but the squeamishness that so swiftly forced revision (little noticed or commented on at the time, since the publisher never announced the change and the small first printing was quickly sold out) is perhaps a more significant token.

By the end of 1946, victors' euphoria had given way to mutual suspicion among the erstwhile Allies. The United States and Soviet Russia, united during the war by a common enemy, now saw their foreign policies diverge irreparably into antagonism. The Soviet Union, which had suffered betrayal and invasion in 1941, and sustained heavy losses in the war (as many as twenty million lives), had insisted at the Yalta Conference, held shortly before the German surrender, and the Potsdam Conference shortly afterward, on a buffer of friendly states (that is, Communist-dominated governments) along the length of its European frontiers.

The compromise reached at the conferences fell short of these demands, and the Soviets felt justified in sealing off the areas of the former German Reich that were occupied by the Red Army, and fomenting coups d'état in other Eastern European countries. As early as March 1946, less than seven months after the war's end, former British Prime Minister Winston Churchill could speak, in a speech delivered in the United States, of an "Iron Curtain" that had descended over Europe dividing East from West. The coining of this famous phrase was a defining moment. The Cold War had begun.

COLD WAR

The Cold War, which lasted at full terrifying strength at least until the early 1970s, and remained a major factor in Euro-American foreign policy and internal politics until the collapse of the Soviet Union in 1991, was a period of intense political and ideological rivalry between the United States and its European allies, on the one hand, and the Soviet Union and its "satellites," on the other. After the Soviets successfully tested an atom bomb of their own in 1949, the Cold War constantly threatened to erupt into an actual military engagement with the potential to destroy civilization. In a widely used phrase of the time, the world was permanently poised on "the brink of World War III." It was widely assumed in "the West" that the Soviets had been aided toward their scientific achievement by espionage, some of it carried on not by the Soviets themselves

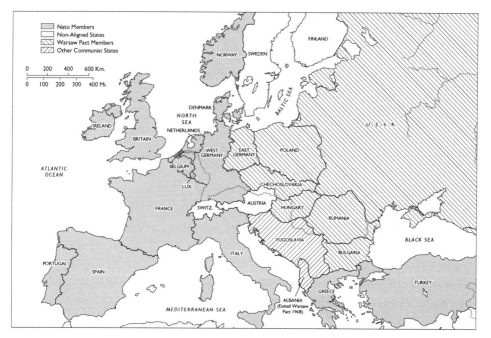

FIG. 1-3 Cold War military alignments.

but by Westerners under Communist discipline. (Some, indeed, were detected: in the United States Julius and Ethel Rosenberg were convicted and executed for passing "atomic secrets"; in Great Britain, Guy Burgess and Kim Philby were exposed but escaped to the USSR.) Political suspicion, directed not only at the potential enemy, but at fellow citizens, now became a fact of life in East and West alike.

The same year that the Soviets exploded their atomic bomb, "the West" collectively adopted and implemented the policy of "containment"[8] (so named after a famous memo by the American diplomat George F. Kennan). To check any further Soviet expansionist efforts in Europe the North Atlantic Treaty Organization (NATO) was established, the members of which were pledged to consider an armed attack on any one of them an attack against them all. Despite its name, the North Atlantic Treaty's guarantee of mutual defense extended far beyond the North Atlantic. Its signatories included Italy and Denmark, countries without an Atlantic seacoast, and (after 1952) Greece and Turkey as well (where Communist coups had nearly succeeded in the Cold War's early days).

Needless to say, the Soviet Union regarded the formation of NATO as an act of aggression and countered with the Warsaw Pact, a mutual defense treaty signed in 1955 by the USSR and the countries that by then formed the "Soviet bloc" of buffer states: Albania, Bulgaria, Czechoslovakia, Hungary, Poland, Romania, and the German Democratic Republic or "East Germany," namely the part of Germany that had been assigned to the Soviet Army of occupation at Yalta, and that Stalin refused to give up when the rest of Germany was united under a demilitarized government called the Federal Republic of Germany.

Naturally, "West Germany" was admitted, in retaliation, to NATO, thus putting the border between East and West right in the middle of the old common foe. A decade after the war, all of Europe and North America was a virtual armed camp—or rather, two hostile armed camps, each with the power of "mutual assured destruction" (MAD) against the other. Local conflicts—over the political status of Berlin, over a border clash in divided Korea that was interpreted by NATO as a Soviet-inspired invasion, over the political status of newly independent states in Africa—were all magnified into superpower confrontations that threatened world destruction.

The mutual threat of annihilation, it was widely agreed, was the only effective deterrent against deployment of thermonuclear weapons, and so the United States and the Soviet Union became embroiled in an economically draining and psychologically intolerable arms race, stockpiling weapons of mass destruction that now included hydrogen bombs with many times the annihilative power of the bombs dropped on Japan. When a 1959 revolution in Cuba put that island neighbor of the United States in the Soviet camp, tensions reached their peak. The "Cuban missile crisis" of October 1962, brought on when a Soviet missile base was detected in Cuba (installed as a countermeasure to NATO installations in Turkey), was the closest the "nuclear superpowers" actually came to the well-named MAD-point.

DENUNCIATION AND CONTRITION

Amid the kind of chronic anxiety to which Cold War tensions gave rise, triumphant rhetoric in the arts took on an air of saber-rattling, producing not euphoria but heightened apprehension. It was to the beginnings of that mood that Copland's critics, and eventually the composer himself, were surely reacting when he allowed himself to be persuaded to tone down the end of his Third Symphony. The effects of incipient Cold War anxieties were felt much more directly by artists in the Soviet Union, the surviving (and spreading) totalitarian state, where the government saw the regulation of all society as its proper responsibility.

The war itself (known in Russia as the "Great Patriotic War of 1941–1945") had, paradoxically enough, been a period of relatively free expression in the Soviet Union. The early and easy victories of Hitler's armies in White Russia and the Ukraine, where the local populations often greeted the invaders as liberators, had frightened Stalin into a relaxation of censorship and political repressions in an effort to regain the good will of intellectuals and mobilize them for war propaganda. Dmitry Shostakovich's Seventh Symphony, dedicated to the city of Leningrad, with a first movement that graphically portrayed the fascist invasion and its heroic repulsion, had been microfilmed and sent via Tehran and Cairo to America, where it was broadcast by Toscanini and the NBC Symphony in the summer of 1942 in a frenzy of media publicity.

Shostakovich became the recipient of high state honors. His Eighth Symphony (1943), a monumental work without program, but unquestionably grim, was received with equal fervor and praise, even though its implied "dramaturgy" was far from the sort of optimistic, "life-affirming" declaration normally demanded by the doctrine of socialist realism. It was accepted on the basis of its "truthful" reflection of the horrors and losses of war, as were some ponderous works of Sergey Prokofieff, like his Seventh (1942) and Eighth (1944) Sonatas for piano, and his Sixth Symphony, in the dark key of E-flat minor, composed immediately after the war and first performed on 25 December 1947.

Full Stalinist controls were reimposed, and with a vengeance, as the Cold War gathered impetus. Responsibility for taming the arts was delegated to Andrey Zhdanov, the old theorist of socialist realism. Now the Leningrad Party leader and a full member of the ruling Politburo, Zhdanov was one of the main architects of the Soviet Union's paranoically anti-Western postwar foreign policy, and the chief organizer of the Cominform (Communist Information Bureau), the successor to the Comintern (dissolved by Stalin in 1943 in a gesture to the wartime Allies) as the central agency that managed and coordinated the activities of communist parties abroad. Next to Stalin himself, Zhdanov was the most powerful politician in the growing Communist world.

Working through the creative unions managed by the Ministry of Culture, Zhdanov convened a series of extraordinary conferences at the headquarters of the Central Committee of the Soviet Communist Party. They amounted to political hearings at which charges were brought against deviant artists in the fields of literature (1946), film (1947), and finally music. The conference on music opened on 10 January 1948. The immediate pretext was discussion of the shortcomings of an opera, *Velikaya druzhba* ("The great friendship"), by Vano Muradeli (1908–70), a minor composer of Georgian birth, which was accused both of historical inaccuracies in its portrayal of events connected with the Russian Revolution, and of an excessively modernistic musical style that rendered it inaccessible to nonprofessional audiences.

Over the next three days, however, the designated scapegoat was forgotten as twenty-seven musical figures took the floor in a frightening ritual of denunciation and contrition. The chief targets were the so-called "Big Four" of Soviet music: Prokofieff, Shostakovich, Nikolai Myaskovsky (a prolific composer of symphonies), and Aram Ilyich Khachaturian (1903–78), a composer of Armenian heritage and Georgian birth, famous in the West for some colorful concertos and a ballet suite containing a rousing "Sabre Dance" that had become a jukebox hit. All were charged with "formalism," a vague term with a checkered history, defined in a post-1948 Soviet music encyclopedia as "an esthetic conception proceeding from an affirmation of the self-sufficiency of form in art, and its independence from ideological or pictorial content."[9] In practice it was code for elite modernism, something that the doctrine of socialist realism expressly forbade.

Shostakovich, who had already been singled out for political attack in 1936, received the roughest treatment. Vladimir Zakharov, the director of the leading Russian professional ensemble for folk song and dance, rose on the first day to render judgment on behalf of "the people." Never mind *The Great Friendship*, he told the assembled musicians and political functionaries:

> That's not the point. Muradeli's opera is actually one of the more intelligible pieces. But if you look at our symphonic music, you'll see that some big names have gradually arisen among us, very famous both here and abroad. But I must say that the works of these composers are altogether alien and unintelligible to our

Soviet people. Debate continues among us about whether Shostakovich's Eighth Symphony is good or bad. In my opinion, the question is meaningless. I reckon that from the people's point of view the Eighth Symphony is not a musical work at all, but a "work" that has nothing whatever to do with the art of music.[10]

As Zakharov's remarks continued, they led into even more sinister terrain. "We read in the papers about the heroic deeds that are being accomplished by the workers in our factories, on our collective farms, and so forth," he reminded his listeners. "Ask these people whether they really like the Eighth or Ninth Symphonies of Shostakovich." And after thus insinuating that Shostakovich, in his "formalism," was an "enemy of the people," the most dangerous of all Soviet epithets, Zakharov went on to impugn his loyalty to the Soviet state:

> Several of these composers think that they enjoy success abroad, or even that they are taken there to represent the highest achievements of Soviet musical culture. But let's take a look at the question. Let's say that, for example, the Eighth, the Ninth or the Seventh Symphonies of Shostakovich are looked upon abroad as works of genius. But who, exactly, is looking upon them? There are lots of persons living abroad. Besides the reactionaries whom we struggle against, besides the bandits, the imperialists, and so on, there are also the people. It would be interesting to know with whom these compositions are having such success. With the people? I can answer that wholly categorically: no, it cannot be.

After hearing all these calumnies, after being branded alien to the people but congenial to reactionaries, bandits, and imperialists, Shostakovich was obliged to mount the podium and express his thanks for the constructive critique he had received. "In my work I have had many failures," he admitted to the meeting,

> even though, throughout my career, I have always thought of the people, of my listeners, of those who reared me; and I always strive that the people should accept my music. I have always listened to criticism, and have always tried to work harder and better. I am listening to criticism now, and shall continue to listen to it and shall accept critical instructions.[11]

Since his death, Shostakovich's friends have disclosed that in the aftermath of the "Zhdanov flap" (*Zhdanovshchina*), as it became popularly known, the composer had contemplated suicide. To many observers, however, particularly those abroad, the most dreadful humiliation was not Shostakovich's; it was Prokofieff's. For Prokofieff, unlike any other major Soviet composer, was a former émigré. He had had a brilliant cosmopolitan career and had many friends in the West who esteemed his talent and achievements, and who had assumed (as Prokofieff himself must have assumed) that his international reputation would insulate him from bureaucratic meddling. The presumption that he was promised immunity is the only way to make sense of Prokofieff's decision to return home in 1936, the very year in which Shostakovich was disgraced and threatened for the first time, thus the year that ushered in the most draconian period in Soviet arts policy.

Even at that, Prokofieff's powers of denial were impressive. In 1939, for example, the famous director Vsevolod Meyerhold, who had already collaborated indirectly with the composer on the opera *The Love for Three Oranges*, disappeared (that is, was arrested and condemned) just as he and Prokofieff were working intensively on the staging of *Semyon Kotko*, Prokofieff's first Soviet opera. Yet Prokofieff was untouched, just as he had not been mentioned in the attacks on Shostakovich, and his opera's production proceeded on schedule (albeit with big disfiguring changes in the libretto made necessary by the infamous Hitler-Stalin pact). Crazy as it seems in retrospect, Prokofieff had read good omens in all of these events. The Zhdanovshchina took him completely by surprise.

But now, less than three weeks after the brilliant premiere of his Sixth Symphony, Prokofieff heard himself denounced at the headquarters of the Communist Party's Central Committee as a composer "who has even now not yet outgrown the childish dogma of innovation for the sake of innovation, who still practices artistic snobbism, who still suffers from a mistaken fear of the commonplace or ordinary." As for the Sixth Symphony, "it was quaint to hear the way one Prokofieff struggled with another in it: the penchant for broad melody and vivid thematic development is constantly interrupted and overthrown by the crude, unprovoked intrusion of the nasty, antisocial Prokofieff."[12] In particular, Prokofieff was faulted for spurning the resources of folklore — not only an unpatriotic move, but one bound to lessen the accessibility of his music to ordinary listeners.

Prokofieff, too, was obliged to make a public recantation and express his thanks to the Party for its "precise directives," which "will help me in my search of a musical language accessible and natural to our people, worthy of our people and of our great country."[13] Owing to his greater age and his precarious health, he was spared the ignominy of a personal appearance before his judges. Instead, he wrote (or at least signed) a letter that was published as a response to the "Resolution on Music" that the Communist Party issued on 10 February 1948.

This Resolution decreed that Soviet composers henceforth favor vocal music over instrumental; program music over "absolute"; shun the use of modernistic techniques that shut out nonprofessional listeners; make liberal use of folklore; and actually emulate the styles of the great Russian composers of the nineteenth century. Never before, not even in Nazi Germany, were composers ever enjoined so literally to isolate themselves from the rest of the musical world and turn back the stylistic clock. But style was not the main issue. The Resolution's demands, especially for concrete musical "content" embodied in texts and programs, were at bottom an attempt to render musical compositions more easily censorable.

The Zhdanovite directives were quickly disseminated to the "fraternal republics" that were forming in Eastern Europe. The Resolution was paraphrased, if anything in even stronger terms, in a proclamation drafted in German by Hanns Eisler at the Second International Congress of Composers and Music Critics, held in Prague in May 1948, three months after the Communist coup d'état in Czechoslovakia. The crisis in "the music and the musical life of our times" it was there declared, can only be overcome if composers renounce "bourgeois individualism" once and for all, so that "their music becomes the expression of the great new progressive ideas and feelings of the masses."[14]

Works by the Soviet Big Four, not to mention countless lesser fry in all the countries of the burgeoning Soviet empire, that were not considered to be in conformity with the Resolution (and that meant most of them) were banned from performance. Many composers suffered reprisals. Shostakovich, ever the main scapegoat, was fired from his post as professor of composition at the Moscow Conservatory. All were required to make propitiatory offerings. Shostakovich's included an oratorio, *Pesn' o lesakh* ("Song of the forests," 1949), and a cantata, *Nad rodinoy nashey solntse siyayet* ("The sun shines over our motherland," 1952), both to texts by the poet Yevgeniy Dolmatovsky (1915–94), a dependable Party hack who was best known for writing lyrics for "mass" (propaganda) songs.

Both works feature a children's chorus, as do two of Prokofieff's offerings, a suite called *Zimniy kostyor* ("Winter bonfire," 1949–50) and an oratorio called *Na strazhe mira* ("On guard for peace," 1950), both to texts by Samuil Marshak (1887–1964), a poet and translator best known for his children's verse. Prokofieff's last symphony, the posthumously performed Seventh (1952), a work in which he expressly simplified his style to a point that privately embarrassed him as "childish," won a government prize that formally rehabilitated his name, but only after an even more "optimistic" ending (fast and jolly instead of dreamy and nostalgic) had been demanded and supplied.

The Soviet music of what might be called the post-Zhdanov half-decade, lasting from the 1948 Resolution until the death of Stalin (the same day as Prokofieff's) in 1953, is the work of gifted and extremely well trained composers. Much of it is highly palatable stuff that compares favorably with the 50- to 100-year-old Russian "classics" it forcibly imitated. But of course when one knows its actual date, and the fear and trembling that stood behind its folksy pleasantries and its smooth or stirring platitudes, it can turn quite indigestible. As always, inevitably, subtexts of a kind not intended either by the composers or by those who compelled their output have grown into the works over the course of their histories.

But their immediate and intended subtext, now grown faint perhaps, is no less historically significant. The emphasis on childhood themes — themes of reassurance, innocence, and calm bright futures — is clearly a response to the same anxieties of the early Cold War that we have so far examined mainly from the "Western" side. In Russia, too, the triumphant mood of the immediate postwar moment had modulated into one of insecurity. Where in 1945 Prokofieff could compose an "Ode to the End of the War" for wind band (including six flute and six trumpet parts), four pianos, eight harps, four saxophones, and augmented percussion (and Khachaturian could outdo him with a *Simfoniya-Poèma* for orchestra, organ, and twenty-three obbligato trombones), his oratorio of 1950 included a Lullaby for a solo mezzo-soprano who croons to her child (and to the country at large), "Sleep, don't be afraid, your life and quiet home are guarded by a great friend who lives above us all in the Kremlin." Shostakovich, for his part, had shown a squeamishness about "Ninth Symphony" rhetoric even earlier than Aaron Copland did. At the end of the war he was up to his own Symphony no. 9, but found he could not bring himself, after Hiroshima, to compose the glorious choral symphony, replete with personal praise of Stalin, that many were awaiting from him.

Instead, his cold feet sent him in the opposite direction: his Ninth Symphony is for the most part a slight and whimsical opus in the spirit, the composer suggested, of Haydn. It became another point against him at the Zhdanov conference.

The mood of calm and comfort that Shostakovich and Prokofieff were now seeking, at the Party's behest, to communicate was not so far, ironically enough, from that of Shostakovich's unexpectedly good-humored and diverting Ninth. Yet not everybody was consoled. Prokofieff's former colleagues in the West were appalled. As we know from letters and memoirs, composers like Francis Poulenc and Arthur Honegger, who had known Prokofieff in Paris, were dismayed at his mistreatment and disillusioned with the society for the sake of which he had forsaken them, and which until then had continued despite everything to be for many idealists a beacon of hope. Stravinsky, who was under no illusions where Soviet totalitarianism was concerned, was nevertheless shocked out of his complacency about "benevolent despotisms." The former admirer of Mussolini, now living in Hollywood, remarked to a friend about the Europeans, "As far as I am concerned, they can have their Marshals and Fuehrers; leave me Mr. Truman and I'm quite satisfied."[15]

BREAKING RANKS

One of the most poignant reactions was that of the German composer Stefan Wolpe (1902–72). An ardent Communist in "Weimar" Berlin, he followed the example of Hanns Eisler in renouncing his elite training for the sake of political activism, conducting choruses at demonstrations and rallies, and composing militant mass songs (*Kampflieder*) and revolutionary cantatas and oratorios. He first became famous in 1931 as the composer of the incidental score for *Die Mausefalle* ("The mousetrap"), the maiden production of Die Truppe 31, a workers' theater collective led by the director Gustav von Wangenheim. It was scored for a shoestring cabaret "jazz" ensemble of trumpet, saxophone, piano, and percussion. Wolpe was actively promoted as an activist composer by the Comintern. His *Kampflied* "Ours Is the Future" (also known as *Rote Soldaten* or "Red Soldiers") appeared in the New York Composers Collective's *Workers Song Book No. 2* and many other Communist publications of the 1930s.

When Hitler came to power in 1933, Wolpe fled to Vienna, where he took some lessons in orchestration from Webern. In 1934 he went to Jerusalem to head the theory and composition faculty at the newly founded Palestine Conservatory. But Wolpe's continued, flamboyant commitment to leftist politics (flaunting red bandanas and preaching revolution to his pupils) cost him his job there and helped precipitate his move, in 1938, to the United States, where he was no longer in demand as a revolutionary. Instead, he carried on as a much sought-after private composition teacher. His works, too, grew more "private" and abstract (although they still often embodied tacit political programs).

After the war, Wolpe's retreat into abstraction continued, now in response to the suspicion with which left-leaning artists were held in America with the coming of the Cold War, but also in response to something else. Wolpe was painfully disillusioned by the postwar political crackdown in the Soviet Union and horrified by the persecution and humiliation of Prokofieff. In a sense his disillusion only confirmed and intensified his commitment to political and artistic avant-gardism; but the status quo he now opposed encompassed all entrenched power, which, he now saw, was by definition reactionary and intolerant of difference.

And so when he went back on a visit to his native Berlin, now the capital of "East Germany," in 1957, Wolpe found himself unable to comply with an invitation from his old collaborator Wangenheim (now a decorated state-subsidized artist) to play over his old Kampflieder. In the postwar context such music no longer seemed to represent protest, but instead political hegemony and repression. And so, feigning forgetfulness, he played his host instead a recording of his two-movement Quartet (1950) for trumpet, saxophone, piano, and drums, and was met with incomprehension.

Although the performing ensemble was the very same as the combo that used to accompany the Truppe 31 plays, which made the Quartet to that extent nostalgic, the musical content was altogether different. The jazz it now echoed was be-bop, a postwar New York elite or "avant-garde" style that many jazz lovers found as incomprehensible as their "classical" counterparts found twelve-tone music. And sure enough, the Quartet, like most of the music Wolpe had written in America (and would continue to write until his death) was composed using a modified twelve-tone technique, formerly the bête noire of all socially committed musicians.

Whether the lively second movement of Wolpe's Quartet (Ex. 1-2) was composed with a specific program in mind is open to question. Wolpe gave it two different story lines in conversation with different interviewers. On one occasion he said that it had been inspired by Henri Cartier-Bresson's famous photograph of children playing amid the rubble of the Spanish Civil War, a famous metaphor of optimism in the face of political catastrophe. On another, he said that it celebrated the victory of the Chinese Communists in 1949 over the regime of Chiang Kai-shek (and that the grim first movement memorialized Mao Tse-tung's famous Long March, an equally potent symbol of resolution in the face of privation).

Either or both stories could be true, and there is no reason to doubt the sincerity of the composer's inspiration. But the music no longer communicates with the directness of a Kampflied. A listener would be hard pressed to paraphrase its "message," or guess its precise motivation, with any confidence. But if it thus frustrated willing listeners, it also frustrated would-be censors, and that may well have been the point. The hermeticism of Wolpe's postwar — or rather, Cold War — music was a deliberate and demonstrative refusal to comply with the directives of the Zhdanovshchina. And yet, the question nags, how did an artist with Wolpe's social conscience feel about a decision, however honestly arrived at, to insulate his artistic integrity within a music that eventually became so abstract that its content would be a riddle, its style so advanced that few except fellow musicians could take pleasure in it, and so demanding of its performers that almost no one could play it?

ZERO HOUR

The tension and frustration inherent in Wolpe's position was characteristic of the time, and contributed to many a strange turn of events that could never have been

EX. 1-2 Stefan Wolpe, Quartet (1950), II, mm. 1–5

predicted before the war's end. The most noteworthy was the unexpected resurgence of twelve-tone composition—or "serialism," to use the postwar term—from what many considered to be a moribund, sectarian status into something that began to look like stylistic dominance among "serious" composers in Western Europe and America. (The word *serious*, now widely recognized as an invidious standard and an enforcer of conformity, is nevertheless the word to use in this context, for it was the word then used: it derived from German usage, in which the distinction between "classical" and "popular" music was couched as one between *ernste Musik* or "E-Musik"—that is, "serious music"—and *Unterhaltungsmusik* or "U-Musik," meaning "entertainment music.") For such a thing to happen, a complex and remarkable convergence of circumstances and personalities was required.

Perhaps the best place to begin surveying it would be with a book that appeared in Paris in 1946, bearing a most un-Parisian message. *Schönberg et son école: L'état contemporaine du langage musical* (*Schoenberg and His School: The Contemporary Stage of the Language of Music*), by René Leibowitz (1913–72), was the first extended treatment on the work of the Viennese atonalists to appear in a language other than German, and the first anywhere since the rise of Nazism. The author was a Polish-born musician — equally active and significant as composer, conductor, and teacher — who had lived in Paris since 1929 but claimed to have studied in the early 1930s with Schoenberg in Berlin and Webern in Vienna. He spent the war years hiding from the Nazis in unoccupied (Vichy) France. A widely admired figure, he had many pupils who went on to important careers.

Schönberg et son école was a militant reprise of the neo-Hegelian position first asserted ninety years before by the historian-spokesmen of the New German School. The subtitle already said it all, simply in the way it used the definite article. *The* language of music is a universal language that has undergone a single historical development, of which *the* most advanced contemporary stage is perforce *the* only historically valid and viable language at any given time. That stage, as of 1946, was the stage reached by the Schoenberg school; any music not at that level of historical evolution was of no historical account and consequently of no serious interest. As Leibowitz put it at the very outset, twelve-tone serial music was "the only genuine and inevitable expression of the musical art of our time." Indeed, unless one has recognized this basic fact, he went so far as to allege, one had no right to call oneself a composer at all.

> If the activity of composing or making music is carried on with the intention of solving those profound problems which have confronted the consciousness of the individual, that individual has a chance to become a composer, a true musician. In the case of the composer, this sudden consciousness comes at the moment when, in the work of a contemporary musician, he discovers what seems to him to be the language of his epoch, the language which he himself wants to speak. Up to that point, he may have assimilated, in more or less accurate fashion, the language of the past; he may have believed that he has profited from certain excursions into a style which seems to him to furnish fresh possibilities. But his real consciousness of *being a composer* cannot be foursquare and unshakable until some master of our time brings him the assurance, the irrefutable evidence of the necessity and authenticity of his personal language.[16]

Aaron Copland, asked to review Leibowitz's book on its publication in English translation in 1949, was shocked at its "dogmatic" and "fanatical"[17] tone; indeed, the authoritarian subtext is palpable, and in stark contradiction to the lip service the text paid (in good existentialist fashion) to the responsible "individual." Phrases like "master of our time" had disquieting resonances, to put it mildly, in a world just rid of Hitler, and one where Stalin's ascendancy was still encroaching. And yet the book's message was heard and widely obeyed — even by Copland, who only a year later, and against his own expectations, began sketching his first twelve-tone composition (see chapter 3 for details). Clearly, it was not just Leibowitz's authoritarianism that invested his words with authority.

There was also the fact that in territories under Nazi control, the work of Schoenberg and his school had been banned. That gave it not only the aura of forbidden fruit, but something more as well. Twelve-tone music became a symbol of resistance (embodied, too, in Leibowitz's wartime activities, which included the making of a clandestine recording of Schoenberg's Wind Quintet, an early twelve-tone piece), and, by extension, a symbol of creative freedom. As it happened, this last perception was based on a historical error: Schoenberg's music was banned by the Nazis because it was "Jewish," not because it was twelve-tone. In fact, there had been an officially tolerated Nazi school of twelve-tone composers; nor were all twelve-tone composers anti-Nazi. But factual accuracy is never the decisive factor in the creation of a legend.

Serial music was also viewed by many as a symbol of incorruptible purity, precisely because it was (to use the Soviet term) so "formalist." Because it seemed to deal only with "purely musical" relationships of structure rather than with "extramusical" considerations of expression, it was a music that seemed incapable of being commandeered for purposes of propaganda. Its only political stand seemed to be the rejection of politics and the affirmation of the right of the individual to turn away from the coercive public sphere. What Theodor Wiesengrund Adorno called its "dialectics of loneliness"[18] made twelve-tone music seem an embodiment of Sartre's existentialism.

Adorno made his famous remark in *Philosophie der neuen Musik* ("Philosophy of new music"), a book he published in 1949, shortly after returning to Germany from his wartime exile in the United States. This book, which added an existentialist argument to the older doctrine of progress, proved even more influential than Leibowitz's. If, as the existentialists argued, authenticity can only be personal and justified from within, never collectively asserted or justified from without, then a music that by virtue of its difficulty shunned popularity had to be a more authentic music than one that potentially spoke for the many. Responding only to what Adorno called "the inherent tendency of musical material"[19] rather to any call from the wider world, twelve-tone music seemed to embody a perfect artistic "autonomy." That autonomy easily translated into personal and political autonomy — that is, individual integrity — in the minds of many who were emerging from decades of oppression, an oppression that was still going on in the East.

There was a telling difference between Adorno's idea of musical value and Leibowitz's. Adorno's ideal of "autonomy" clearly owed a lot to romanticism and its glorification of subjective feeling. He regarded the autonomy of Schoenberg's twelve-tone music as a sublimation of the composer's earlier Expressionism; that is why, despite its abstractness, it remained for Adorno the most humane of all contemporary musics. For Leibowitz, his sincere reverence for Schoenberg notwithstanding, the culmination was Webern. Indeed, his book was for most readers their first exposure to the work of a composer who during his lifetime had remained an obscure and esoteric name, and whose music was still, much of it, unpublished.

Leibowitz emphasized Webern's radicalism and his purity. Obviously, he had no idea (and neither did anyone else at the time) of Webern's actual political sympathies, which would have sorely disconcerted him and undermined his argument. Nor was he (or anyone else at the time) inclined to reflect on the relationship between radical artistic purisms and their political cousins. He was content to celebrate Webern's "projection of the Schoenbergian acquisitions into the future," which made him "the incarnation of the most radical side of Schoenberg,"[20] implying the rejection of what remained conservative in Schoenberg's outlook (particularly the useless "subjective" component). According to Leibowitz, Webern alone understood that the proper task of a composer was to "attack the most fundamental and radical problems of the evolution of music." To understand Webern is to understand "the *necessity* of such purity," and the "necessity of carrying an experience so far"[21] that it cannot be carried further. It is on Webern, Leibowitz argued, that hopes of a "great renewal" of music must be pinned, although "it is evident that such a renewal cannot take place without a violent reaction." The words are chilling; substitute politics for music, and they might have been written by Joseph Goebbels, Hitler's Minister of Propaganda.

But they chimed ideally with the dislocated, amnesiac mood of the times, particularly in Germany and the other parts of Western Europe, like Leibowitz's northern France, that had been occupied by the Nazis. Those who looked to the future in the defeated parts of Europe saw the present as a *Stunde Null*, a "zero hour," meaning a time without a past. The necessity to start from scratch, to reject the past in its totality as something tainted if not actually destroyed in the Holocaust of World War II, was a watchword. "During those immediate postwar years," wrote Hans Werner Henze (b. 1926), a leading German composer then just beginning his career,

> no one believed how it could have been possible for a nation to have sunk so low—into a disgrace that centuries could not wash clean. We were assured by senior composers that music is abstract, not to be connected with everyday life, and that immeasurable and inalienable values are lodged in it (which is precisely why the Nazis censored those modern works which strove to achieve absolute freedom) . . . .
>
> Everything now had to be stylized and made abstract: music regarded as a glass-bead-game, a fossil of life. Discipline was the order of the day. Through discipline it was going to be possible to get music back on its feet again, though nobody asked what for. Discipline enabled form to come about; there were rules and parameters for everything. Expressionism and Surrealism were mystically remote; we were told that these movements were already obsolete before 1930, and had been surpassed. The new avant-garde would reaffirm this. The audience, at whom our music was supposed to be directed, would be made up of experts. The public would be excused from attending our concerts; in other words, our public would be the press and our protectors.[22]

Thus the "Webern cult" became the musical expression of an anxious age. "We realized," wrote Henze, "that dodecaphony and serialism were the only viable new techniques: fresh, and able to generate new musical patterns"[23] without recalling the dead disgraceful past. Willed amnesia, however, is not quite the same as amnesty, which implies contrition and forgiveness. It can be a dangerous game: it offers solace, but it can also offer cover. And repressed memory, not only psychoanalysts but countless playwrights and novelists have warned, is the breeding ground of phobias.

POLARIZATION

All of this can be seen in the ultimate statement of the *Stunde Null* position: "Schoenberg est mort" ("Schoenberg is dead"), a manifesto published in February 1952, seven months after Schoenberg's death, by Pierre Boulez (b. 1925), a young French composer who had studied officially with Messiaen, and with Leibowitz on the side. The violence that Leibowitz had predicted certainly came to the fore in Boulez's frantically coercive and intolerant rhetoric. No one who has read the article has ever forgotten its frightening climax, expanded in a somewhat later squib into a battle cry: "Since the Viennese discoveries, any musician who has not experienced — I do not say understood, but truly experienced — the necessity of the dodecaphonic language is USELESS. For his entire work brings him up short of the needs of his time."[24]

Not even Zhdanov had ever voiced a judgment more categorical or intransigent (and indeed it is obvious that Boulez's rhetorical model was the Communist journalism of his day). There were Nazi resonances as well. Herbert Eimert (1897–1972), a once-persecuted member of the first generation of atonalists, declared a few years later, in response to a frequent complaint, that "if we say that only composers who follow Webern are worthy of the name, it is no new 'totalitarian order' but a simple statement of fact." Nazi race theory, too, had once been a simple fact by similar decree. In any event, it was clear that, conventional "esthetic" opinion notwithstanding, musicians were not going to be exempt from the world's dire postwar polarization; on the contrary, like everyone else they were to be participants in it and contributors to it.

The most vivid early symptom of musical polarization was the fierce postwar controversy about Bartók, who had died in New York in September 1945, only a month after the end of the war. Over the next few years, Bartók's legacy, like Europe itself, was ruthlessly partitioned into Eastern and Western zones. In his native Hungary, as in the rest of the Soviet bloc, those of his works in which folklorism seemed to predominate over modernism were touted by the cultural politicians as obligatory models and the rest were banned from public performance or broadcast. Since Bartók's modernist peak came in the middle of his career, he became (for one often joked-about example) the composer of two quartets, the First and the Sixth.

The Western avant-garde, meanwhile, made virtual fetishes out of the banned works, particularly the Fourth Quartet, which some critics, including Leibowitz, tried to read as proto-serial. The rest they rancorously consigned to the dustbin of history, sometimes in very sinister terms, as when Leibowitz (writing in *Les temps modernes*, a journal edited by Jean-Paul Sartre himself) attacked Bartók in 1947 for having "compromised" himself during the war with stylistically accessible pieces like the popular *Concerto for Orchestra*.[25] That was the undisguised language of political denunciation, a cruel insult to Bartók's principled antifascist commitment and the bitter sacrifices it had entailed.

Bartók's alleged moral failure was held against him in exactly the way that "passive collaborators" with the Nazis were blamed in the wake of the so-called Nuremberg trials. "The very fact that our purity or compromise in matters of composition depend only on our choice implies that it is our duty to create the one and avoid the other," wrote Leibowitz.[26] Bartók, looking for social approval rather than facing his lonely historical obligation, had not met this challenge, his stern posthumous accuser now asserted, very much in the spirit of the new existentialism.

But the most shocking provocation (and the most potent) remained Boulez's. For the violence that Leibowitz had somewhat smugly foreseen in the form of reaction had instead taken the form of a slander addressed to the new revolution's very figurehead. There was logic in the position: if all the past had to be rejected, then Schoenberg had to be rejected too. (Had he not advertised himself as an upholder of the great tradition?) But Boulez exaggerated the difference between Schoenberg and Webern into one of kind rather than degree, and this gave him a pretext to dismiss Leibowitz along with Schoenberg and displace him as the leader of the young serialists. Danton had given way to Robespierre.

"Schoenberg is open to bitter reproach for his exploration of the dodecaphonic realm," Boulez alleged, "for it went off in the wrong direction so persistently that it would be hard to find an equally mistaken perspective in the entire history of music."[27] The great mistake had been the effort to reconcile the new means of tonal organization with traditional "classic" forms and traditional "expressive" rhetoric: "all those endless anticipations with expressive accent on the harmony note, those fake appoggiaturas, those arpeggios, tremolandos and note repetitions that sound so terribly hollow."[28] Thus Schoenberg was lumped together with the other neoclassicists of the interwar period as a practitioner of what Adorno called the "*gemässigte Moderne*," or "moderate modernism,"[29] and tainted with the dishonor of the "moderate liberals" who could not stave off the rise of Nazism. It was Webern who pointed the way, in works like his Symphony and his Piano Variations to actual "serial structures" based on "serial functions." Forgetting Schoenberg, Boulez advised,

> we might, like this Webern, investigate the musical *evidence* arising from the attempt at generating structure from material. Perhaps we might enlarge the serial domain with intervals other than the semitone: micro-intervals, irregular intervals, noises. Perhaps we might generalize the serial principle to the four constituents of sound: pitch, duration, dynamics/attack, and timbre. Perhaps . . . perhaps . . .[30]

DARMSTADT

Although Boulez cast them all as hypotheticals, some of the new extensions of serialism he was proposing had already been put into practice by 1952, both by Boulez himself and by some of the other musicians who had been meeting every summer at a unique institution that had been set up in 1946 in Darmstadt, a town located in the state of Hessen in central Germany, which is to say in the American zone of occupation. These International Summer Courses for New Music (*Internationale Ferienkurse für Neue Musik*) were founded by Wolfgang Steinecke (1910–61), a music critic, and Wolfgang Fortner (1907–87), a composer, first with the permission, later with the active financial backing of the United States military government as channeled through Everett Helm (1913–99), an American composer and musicologist who held the position of chief music officer with the Theater and Music Branch of the American Military Government. (Fortner, who had been active and successful throughout the Nazi period but was now an ardent "post-Schoenbergian," was perhaps the most conspicuous of those seeking cover in the "zero hour" myth.) The courses had two main goals: first, to propagate American political and cultural values as part of the general Allied effort to reeducate the German population in preparation for the establishment of democratic institutions; and second, to provide a meeting place where musicians from the former fascist or fascist-occupied areas of Europe — chiefly Germany/Austria, France, and Italy — might further their musical reeducation through exposure to (and instruction in) styles and techniques that had been prohibited or otherwise silenced during the fascist years. The first of these aims was mainly that of the American backers. The Summer Courses, in their earliest phase, have been compared with the Congress for Cultural Freedom, an anti-Communist organization headed by the composer Nicolas Nabokov, which was secretly funded by the United States government's Central Intelligence Agency as an instrument of American foreign policy. (The difference was that the source of the Summer Courses' financial support was never a secret.) The second aim, more insularly professional, was primarily that of the Germans. Each took advantage of the other's interests — a classic case of mutual "co-option." During the first few years, the American presence was strongly pronounced at the "Darmstadt school" (as the Courses quickly became known). Lectures by American musicians were frequent, as were those by Germans who had fled to America such as Leo Schrade, a famous musicologist who, though primarily a medievalist, spoke at Darmstadt about Charles Ives, and Stefan Wolpe, whose leftist commitments had been muted in the wake of the Zhdanovshchina. Music by Ives, Harris, Copland, Walter Piston, Wallingford Riegger, and other "Americanist" composers were performed at Darmstadt, as was the music of Paul Hindemith, who had become an American citizen.

During the first session, in 1946, Henze conducted a performance of Brecht and Hindemith's *Lehrstück vom Einverständnis* ("Lesson in Acquiescence"), a work that had been banned under Hitler for political rather than stylistic reasons. The fact that Hindemith's music was not all that different, stylistically, from the music played under Hitler eventually made it seem superfluous at Darmstadt. It did not further the politically important purposes of the "zero hour" myth. But the most decisive change of course came after (and as a result of) the Zhdanovshchina, news of which was followed at Darmstadt with horrified fascination.

The urgent wish, especially after 1949 when administration of the courses passed from the American occupying force to the new West German government, was to provide the musicians of the avant-garde with a protected space free from all social or political pressures

FIG. 1-4 Pierre Boulez, Bruno Maderna, and Karlheinz Stockhausen at Darmstadt, 1956.

("avant-garde" now being defined entirely in esthetic rather than political terms — in other words, no more Brecht!). It became imperative, in short, to foster at Darmstadt, in the name of creative freedom, exactly that which was subject to repression in the Soviet bloc. And that made, as if in obedience to some Newtonian law of culture, for equal and opposite repressions.

Henze has left a vivid recollection of Darmstadt in 1955 that well captures the grim irony whereby the very thing most feared was reproduced. The dominating presences by then were three young composers who had first come in 1951–1952. One was Boulez; the others were Karlheinz Stockhausen (1928–2008), a German who had moved to Paris early in 1952 to study with Messiaen, and Bruno Maderna (1920–73), an Italian composer and conductor who had originally come as a member of the paid faculty, teaching conducting and analysis in addition to composition. In 1955, the composition class was taught by Henze, Maderna, and Boulez. "Things had become pretty absurd," Henze recalled:

> Boulez, who saw himself as the supreme authority, was sitting at the piano, flanked by Maderna and myself — we must have looked like reluctant assistant judges at a trial, as young composers brought their pieces forward for opinion. Anything that wasn't Webernian, he brusquely dismissed: "If it isn't written in the style of Webern it's of no interest."
>
> My antipathy was directed not against Webern's music, but against the misuse and misinterpretation of his aesthetic and, indeed, of his technique and its motivation and significance. Thanks to the initiative of Boulez and Stockhausen this had become institutionalized as official musical thinking, whose maxims the body of lesser mortals now had to put into practice with religious devotion, *esprit de corps* and slavish obedience. . . . There was constant talk of law and order. Just imagine: it was being bureaucratically determined how people should compose, in which style and according to which criteria.[31]

It was an irony that was being played out in all walks of life during the early cold war. (Just to cite the most obvious example, it was paranoiac antagonism to expanding Soviet totalitarianism that led to the most serious breaches of democratic process in the United States during the so-called "McCarthy" period, named after Senator Joseph McCarthy, who in pursuit of traitors led aggressive and destructive investigations into the lives of many innocent Americans.) But this particular irony, while revealing, is far from all-explaining. Some investigation of the actual music produced at or for Darmstadt during the years 1949–54 will show another irony: its considerable actual distance from Webern, whose meticulous control over his materials was now systematically sacrificed in the interests of something more urgent that Webern, in his prewar or wartime world, never thought to seek. Identifying and assessing this discrepancy will shed the sharpest light on the world the war's survivors inherited.

FIXATIONS

The earliest actual piece of music that can be securely identified as belonging to the "Darmstadt school" was not by any of the composers recalled by Henze, nor was it even a twelve-tone piece. It was a work for piano by Messiaen called *Mode de valeurs et d'intensités* (roughly, "Scheme of note values and dynamics"), which he composed (or began composing) during the summer of 1949 while engaged as an instructor at the Summer Courses. Published the next year as the second in a set of four *Études de rhythme*, it is in fact a study in "hypostatization," the total determination ("fixing") of a limited assemblage of sonic elements or events. This idea had a direct precedent in Webern, who in his Symphony, his String Quartet, and his Piano Variations had experimented with the fixed assignment of particular pitches to particular registers. As his title suggests, Messiaen thrust this principle of fixed assignment into three additional domains.

EX. 1-3   Olivier Messiaen, *Mode de valeurs et d'intensités*, prefatory table

This piece uses a scheme of 36 pitches, 24 note values, 12 attacks, and 7 dynamic levels. It is written entirely according to the scheme.

Attacks:

(with the neutral, unsigned attack, this makes 12.)

Dynamics: *ppp pp p mf f ff fff*

Tones: The scheme comprises 3 Divisions, or melodic groupings of 12 tones, each extending through several octaves, with overlaps. Tones of the same name differ in pitch, duration and loudness.

Division I: chromatic degrees from 1 to 12 (etc.)

Division II: chromatic degrees from 1 to 12 (etc.)

Division III: chromatic degrees from 1 to 12 (etc.)

24 durations in all:

Here is the scheme:

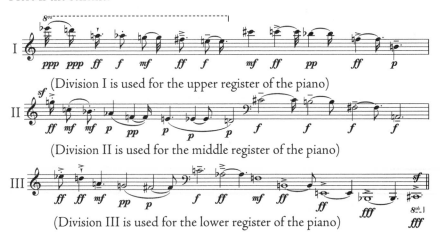

(Division I is used for the upper register of the piano)

(Division II is used for the middle register of the piano)

(Division III is used for the lower register of the piano)

The material out of which Messiaen assembled the composition consisted of thirty-six different notes, each characterized by a unique combination of pitch, duration, loudness, and attack. They are all systematically catalogued in a table (Ex. 1-3) that precedes the score. The thirty-six pitches are laid out in three overlapping registral domains (or "divisions," as Messiaen calls them) containing all twelve notes of the chromatic scale, each represented once. In the score, of which the first page is given in Ex. 1-4, each division has a staff to itself. No pitch appears in the same register in more than one division. Within each division, a given pitch is assigned a duration from another set of three overlapping "divisions." The first consists of all the durations between a thirty-second note and a dotted quarter (= twelve thirty-seconds), laid out in thirty-second-note increments: a sort of "chromatic scale" of thirty-seconds. The second division doubles everything: a chromatic scale of sixteenths, from one to twelve (= a dotted half); and the third doubles everything again: a chromatic scale of eighths, from one to twelve (= a dotted whole note).

EX. 1-4   Olivier Messiaen, *Mode de valeurs et d'intensités*, mm. 1–10

Within each domain there is thus a fixed correspondence between pitch and duration, and a systematic lengthening of durations as pitches descend. The highest note in the piece is also the shortest, and the lowest the longest. In addition, each note is assigned a mode of attack from an arbitrary list of twelve (the number corresponding again with the number of elements in the chromatic scale) and a loudness from an incremental list of seven. Thus every "pitch-class" (or "note-name," e.g. A, B♭, B, etc.) is represented in three different registers, each time with a different duration, loudness, and mode of attack. But since no combination of pitch, duration, loudness, and attack ever recurs within the scheme, every note is a completely discrete element. No special significance attaches to octave equivalency; the texture is utterly "atomized." The only notes that recur in melodic conjunction are the ones that come under slurs (the first two in Division I; nos. 2–3, 4–5 and 6–8 in Division II; nos. 4–5 in Division III). To be fastidiously exact, then, the number of "elements" in the piece is thirty: twenty-five single notes, four two-note groups, and one three-note group.

The music consists of a ceaseless "counterpointing" of elements drawn from the stringently limited menu just described, individual hypostatized objects in seemingly fortuitous relationships. Stockhausen called it "a mosaic of sound." Calling it a sonic "mobile" might come even closer to its effect. Some sense of overall progression emerges from the general tendency of all three domains to descend and slow down; the thundering low C♯ at the end of Division III comes three times and seems to divide the piece into three sections, the last time (in the words of the critic Paul Griffiths) effectively "stopping the music in its tracks."[32] (Not much of a surprise, really; ending a piece with a long loud low note is not exactly unheard of.) Different registers, regardless of "division," have characteristic attack and loudness features as well, as may be seen in Ex. 1-5, a summary devised by the pianist and Messiaen scholar Robert Sherlaw Johnson, in which the complete array of "particles" is laid out in a single succession. Finally, the middle staff, with its three slurred groups,

EX. 1-5 Olivier Messiaen's scheme reduced to a single succession (after R. S. Johnson)

possesses in consequence a certain amount of "motivic consistency," so that despite the arbitrariness of its constituent elements and its atomized texture, the music never sounds entirely random.

Still, one may fairly wonder why Messiaen would have wished to court an impression of randomness; or (perhaps more to the point) why one would wish to plan such an apparently haphazard outcome in such meticulous detail. (Even when the three staves line up on a plain old diminished triad, as happens in m. 56, it's just a "happening," and more likely to be spotted by eye than by ear; see Ex. 1-6.) In the case of Messiaen himself, answers are probably to be sought in his religious philosophy, in which the incomprehensible results of unknowable plans can symbolize the relationship of man and God.

EX. 1-6   Olivier Messiaen, *Mode de valeurs et d'intensités*, mm. 54–56

Arcane structures, reminiscent of medieval speculations in sound, were an old story with Messiaen. They conveyed the "charm of impossibilities"—sublime truths that we may apprehend only with our minds, not our senses. Shortly after composing the *Mode de valeurs et d'intensités*, Messiaen wrote an organ piece called "Soixante-quatre durées" ("Sixty-four durations," the seventh and last item in his *Livre d'orgue* or Organ Book); its title refers to a "chromatic" series of note values, increasing from one thirty-second all the way to a breve (or "double whole note"), which makes the divisions in *Mode de valeurs* seem like child's play. Is a listener expected to distinguish a duration of 57 thirty-seconds from one of 56 or 58? Or is all the elaborate rational calculation a "theological" ploy to boggle (yet somehow comfort) the mind?

But *Mode de valeurs et d'intensités* was special in its obsession with the number twelve; and that made it a sign of the times. As laid out in the preliminary table, the three pitch "divisions" looked like tone rows, even though in practice they were unordered rather than ordered sets. Moreover, by conceiving the durations as "chromatic scales," and mapping them onto the pitches in a one-to-one relationship, Messiaen seemed (or could seem) to be doing something about that perceived gap between serial pitch structure and garden-variety "classical" rhythm that so bothered his pupil Boulez.

"TOTAL SERIALISM"

That is how the Darmstadt "class of 1951" chose to interpret Messiaen's purpose, at any rate, when he played them his recording of the piece. Boulez in particular found the work inspiring, not only for the way in which it seemed to integrate "the four constituents of sound" as he listed them (surely under the influence of Messiaen's "divisions") in "Schoenberg Is Dead," but also for the way in which the whole piece arose out of a set of axioms, or what Messiaen scholar Peter Hill called its "fantastically detailed set of a priori rules."[33] It promised a new utopia: "total" or "integral" serialism.

All one had to do was introduce strict serial ordering into the four Messiaenic domains. And that is just what Boulez did in *Structures* for two pianos (1951). He paid tribute to Messiaen's example, and declared his intention to realize explicitly what Messiaen had been content merely to imply, by adopting the pitch succession of Division I in *Mode de valeurs* as an actual tone row in *Structures*, turning what had been for Messiaen a quarry of "stones" for a mosaic into a rigorously ordered pitch and intervallic sequence. Next, Messiaen's twelve chromatically graded durations were likewise put in a definite and rigorously maintained order, derived from the pitch order but operating independently. The method of derivation is what mathematicians call "mapping," that is, a system of one-to-one correspondences. The starting point, as before, is Messiaen's Division I of note values, in which each successive pitch is assigned the next successive "degree" of the "chromatic scale of thirty-second notes." Thus E♭ (pitch 1) is associated with the thirty-second note, D (pitch 2) with the sixteenth note, A (3) with the dotted sixteenth, A♭ (4) with the eighth note, and so on.

But where Messiaen maintained this pitch/duration association as a constant throughout *Mode de valeurs*, Boulez related the pitch-classes and durations independently to the order positions (the numbers in parentheses). This allowed him to create twelve "permutations" of the rhythm series that corresponded demonstrably (if only numerically) to the twelve possible transpositions of the pitch series, and to deploy the pitch and rhythm series independently of one another, like the color and talea in a medieval "isorhythmic" motet. The result is a truly fantastical set of a priori rules — fantastical in that the principle of correspondence is purely conceptual, devoid of any aurally perceivable relationship to the principle of pitch transposition on which it was based.

Here is why. As we know, when any twelve-tone pitch series is transposed — down, say, by one semitone — the result is a new ordering of pitch classes that preserves the same intervallic relationships as the original one. (One of the most basic aspects of twelve-tone technique, then, is that a "tone row" is really an "interval row" since it is the succession of intervals — the all-important motivic *Grundgestalt* — that remains constant when the row is subjected to its various transformations.) In Ex. 1-7a, the stated transformation of the *Structures* row (transposition down a semitone) is set down twice, each time both in terms of letter names and in terms of the reordering of the pitch numbers:

EX. I-7A   Transformation of Pierre Boulez's *Structures* row

E♭	D	A	A♭	G	F♯	E	C♯	C	B♭	F	B
(1)	(2)	(3)	(4)	(5)	(6)	(7)	(8)	(9)	(10)	(11)	(12)

down a semitone, becomes

D	C♯	A♭	G	F♯	F	E♭	C	B	A	E	B♭
(2)	(8)	(4)	(5)	(6)	(11)	(1)	(9)	(12)	(3)	(7)	(10)

and down another semitone, becomes

C♯	C	G	F♯	F	E	D	B	B♭	A♭	E♭	A
(8)	(9)	(5)	(6)	(11)	(7)	(2)	(12)	(10)	(4)	(1)	(3)

In Ex. 1-7b, the same mapping operation is shown for the durational "scale," each time maintaining the original assignment of durations to pitch numbers:

EX. I-7B   Transformation of Pierre Boulez's *Structures* durational "scale"

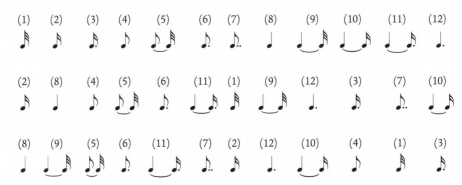

Boulez's whole "precompositional strategy" can be represented as a pair of "magic squares" (Ex. 1-8). Running across the top and down the left side of the first square are the numbers corresponding to the original pitch/duration order of Messiaen's "Division I" as set forth in the preceding example. Note that in these squares, the number 1 always refers to E♭ (pitch 1 of the original series) and to a thirty-second note (the first "degree" of the chromatic scale of durations); the number 2 always refers to D (pitch 2 of the original series) and to a sixteenth note (the second "degree" of the durational scale); the number 3 to A (pitch 3) and a dotted sixteenth (the third "degree"), and so on. Thus the "transpositions," reading down the left-hand column, are not by successive semitones (as in the explanatory example) but by the actual order of intervals in the row.

If the twelve columns in the first square, reading from left to right across or down from top to bottom, represent the twelve possible transpositions of the original row, then the same columns read from right to left or bottom to top represent the twelve possible retrogrades. The columns of numbers in the second square (from left to right

EX. I-8 Pierre Boulez, *Structures Ia*, "O" and "I" matrices

1	2	3	4	5	6	7	8	9	10	11	12
2	8	4	5	6	11	1	9	12	3	7	10
3	4	1	2	8	9	10	5	6	7	12	11
4	5	2	8	9	12	3	6	11	1	10	7
5	6	8	9	12	10	4	11	7	2	3	1
6	11	9	12	10	3	5	7	1	8	4	2
7	1	10	3	4	5	11	2	8	12	6	9
8	9	5	6	11	7	2	12	10	4	1	3
9	12	6	11	7	1	8	10	3	5	2	4
10	3	7	1	2	8	12	4	5	11	9	6
11	7	12	10	3	4	6	1	2	9	5	8
12	10	11	7	1	2	9	3	4	6	8	5

1	7	3	10	12	9	2	11	6	4	8	5
7	11	10	12	9	8	1	6	5	3	2	4
3	10	1	7	11	6	4	12	9	2	5	8
10	12	7	11	6	5	3	9	8	1	4	2
12	9	11	6	5	4	10	8	2	7	3	1
9	8	6	5	4	3	12	2	1	11	10	7
2	1	4	3	10	12	8	7	11	5	9	6
11	6	12	9	8	2	7	5	4	10	1	3
6	5	9	8	2	1	11	4	3	12	7	10
4	3	2	1	7	11	5	10	12	8	6	9
8	2	5	4	3	10	9	1	7	6	12	11
5	4	8	2	1	7	6	3	10	9	11	12

or top to bottom) represent the twelve inverted row forms, and (from right to left or bottom to top) the retrograde-inversions. The relationship between these pitch rows and their associated durational rows is again mediated by the numbers. Under these rules a given series of durations can be called the "inversion" of another only by this arbitrary set of numerical correspondences — that is, only by an ad hoc definition or convention.

The remaining "constituents of sound" for which Messiaen had provided unordered "modes" are serialized in Boulez's composition according to a procedure that is even more arcane (so arcane, in fact, that it was not detected until 1958). Messiaen's collection of seven degrees of loudness was easily expanded to twelve, simply by making the gradations finer:

1	2	3	4	5	6	7	8	9	10	11	12
pppp	*ppp*	*pp*	*p*	*quasi p*	*mp*	*mf*	*quasi f*	*f*	*ff*	*fff*	*ffff*

And Messiaen's collection of twelve attacks could also be taken over (albeit with slight modifications for reasons that will soon become apparent).

The deployment of loudnesses and attacks was geared not to the individual notes, as in Messiaen's *Mode de valeurs*, but to the overall "structure" of *Structures*, which consisted of a single complete traversal of the pitch and durational "matrices" contained within his magic squares. Each section would contain forty-eight row statements, twenty-four for each piano. Boulez derived a series of twenty-four loudnesses for each piano by taking the right-to-left diagonals of each square. The diagonal from the square based on Messiaen's original series (the "O" matrix) governed the loudnesses for piano I, and the diagonal from the other square (the one based on inversions, or the "I" matrix) governed the loudnesses for piano II.

These diagonals formed "Webernian" palindromes, which must have been Boulez's reason for selecting them. To arrive at a full forty-eight elements Boulez constructed additional palindromes by taking the identical left-to-right diagonals from the seventh order position both at the top and along the side of each square, and running them back-to-front then front-to-back. Thus (for the "O" matrix):

Right-to-left diagonal across:

12	7	7	11	11	5	5	11	11	7	7	12
$fff\!f$	mf	mf	fff	fff	quasi p	quasi p	fff	fff	mf	mf	$fff\!f$

Left-to-right diagonals from 7th place:

$\leftarrow \mid \rightarrow$

2	3	1	6	9	7	7	9	6	1	3	2
ppp	pp	$pppp$	mp	f	mf	mf	f	mp	$pppp$	pp	ppp

The series of attacks is coordinated with the pitch/duration series by taking the opposite diagonals (full across from upper left to lower right and, from the sixth position, from upper right to lower left). What Boulez apparently did not foresee is that the numbers 4 and 10 happen to be absent from all the diagonals he selected. In the case of the dynamic series he fudged a bit to incorporate the levels in question (p and ff). In the case of the attack series he simply left them out, resulting in a "row" of only ten members.

The only decisions that remained concerned the order of presentation of the concurrent (but independent) pitch and durational series. With the magic squares in hand these choices could be planned in fairly mechanical fashion, after which the composer could sit back, as it were, and let the music write itself. The real work, in short, was all "precompositional." Thus, at the beginning of *Structures* (Ex. 1-9), Piano I simply goes through the twelve transpositions of the basic pitch series in the order given by the numbers read from left to right across the top of the "I" matrix as they match up with Messiaen's old Division I: 1 (= E♭) 7(= E) 3(= A) 10(= B♭) 12(= B) 9(= C) 2(= D) 11(= F) 6(= F♯) 4(= A♭G♯) 8(= C♯) 5(= G). (The pitches in parentheses are the starting pitches for Piano I's row forms through m. 64; Ex. 1-9 shows only the first two row forms.) Then, in similar mechanical fashion not shown in the example, Piano I goes through the twelve transpositions of the retrograde in an order determined by the numbers read from right to left across the bottom of the same magic square: 12(= B) 11(= F) 9(= C) 10(= B♭), and so on.

Piano II performs exactly the "opposite" (that is, reciprocal) set of operations. First it goes through the twelve inversions in an order determined by the numbers read from left to right across the top of the "O" matrix (i.e., Messiaen's original series), and then (from m. 65) it traverses the twelve retrograde inversions in an order determined by the numbers read from right to left across the bottom of the same magic square: 5 (= G) 8 (= C♯) 6(F♯) 4(G♯A♭), and so on.

As for the durational series, their order is determined, first, by taking the rows or columns in sequence according to their positions in the squares, and then (from m. 65) in an order determined by the size of their first components. Again each piano reciprocates the other's operations. The first durational series in Piano I, as shown in Ex. 1-9, is ♩. ♩ ♪ ♩ ♩ ♪ ♩ ♪ ♪ ♪ ♪. ♪ ♩ ♪ ♪ ♪, which corresponds to the numbers either read from bottom to top along the right edge of the "I" matrix or from right to left across the bottom; the second, ♩ ♪ ♩. ♪ ♪. ♩ ♪ ♩ ♪ ♪ ♪ ♪ ♪ ♪, corresponds to the next column to the left (or the next row from the bottom); the third (no longer shown in Ex. 1-9 but easily predictable, i.e., ♩ ♪ ♩ ♪ ♩ ♩ ♩ ♪ ♪ ♩ ♪ ♩ ♪ ♪ ♪ ♪ ♩), corresponds to the next column or row in the same direction and so on. (When the articulation is staccato, the durations are measured from attack to attack rather than in sustained sound.)

EX. 1-9   Pierre Boulez, *Structures Ia*, mm. 1–15

EX. 1-9 (*continued*)

At m. 65 (Ex. 1-10), Piano I shifts over to a contrapuntal combination of three row forms. The one marked *ppp* uses the "I" matrix series that begins with 12 (the fifth column from the left or the fifth row from the top); the one marked *pp* uses the series that begins with 11 (eighth column from the left or row from the top); the one marked *pppp* uses the series that begins with 10 (fourth column from the left or row from the top). At m. 73, the single line played by Piano I uses the series that begins with 9 (sixth column from the left or row from the top), and so it goes, all the way down to 1.

Piano II, meanwhile, has started with the sequence of durational series beginning with the right-hand column (read bottom to top) or bottom row (read right to left) in the "O" matrix, and progressing thereafter across to the left or up to the top. At m. 65

(Ex. 1-10), the pattern reverses: now Piano II's durational series are chosen from the left-to-right rows or top-to-bottom columns. But the order of selection is no longer governed by a simple predetermined rule (or "algorithm," to use the mathematical word). Here, and only here, in other words, Boulez seems to have chosen the order of presentation "freely"—that is, spontaneously, in the act of composing. (For the record, the order, counting the rows from top down, is 5/8, 6/4, 2/11, 12/9, 10, 7/1/3, with numbers grouped by slashes representing row forms that are played simultaneously, in counterpoint.) Boulez never acknowledged this spontaneous choice, but he did acknowledge others. One was "density," as he called it, meaning the number of row

EX. 1-10   Pierre Boulez, *Structures Ia*, mm. 65–81

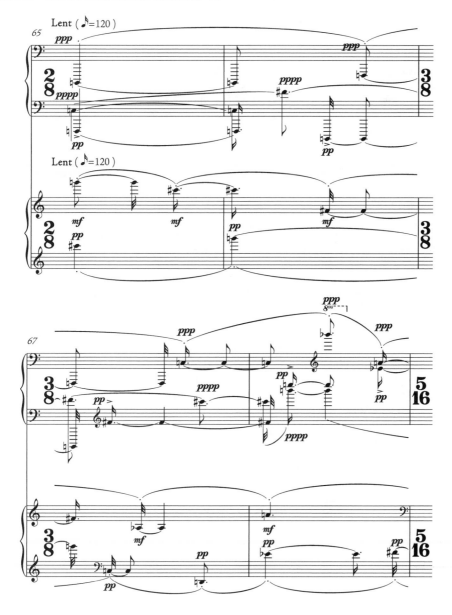

forms deployed simultaneously in any given subsection of the piece. The number of contrapuntal lines varies from one to three in each piano (which means, potentially, four to six in toto). Even here, Boulez seems to have followed "rules" where he could. Consecutive row forms that are assigned by the "diagonals" to the same dynamic level are often played together. But not always; and the inconsistency must count as a "liberty." The other conspicuous "liberty" is registral distribution. Although the score seems to be notated like conventional piano music, there is no a priori assignment of

EX. I-IO   (*continued*)

the players' right and left hands to the top and bottom staves, nor does the assignment of a note to the upper or lower staff imply anything about its register. Instead, the contrapuntal lines so frequently cross, and leap so capriciously from register to register (often extreme ones) that it is impossible to hear the texture as consistently linear, the way one can hear the texture of Messiaen's *Mode de valeurs*. Thus Boulez's composition is not at all like Messiaen's, its putative model, in aural effect. There is no consistent "hypostatization" to which the ear can grow accustomed. Since Boulez treats his "four constituents of sound" as independent variables, any pitch can occur in any register at any loudness and with any duration or attack.

EX. 1-10   (*continued*)

EX. 1-10   (*continued*)

Not only that, but whereas Messiaen clearly imagined his musical "atoms" or "particles" as sounds, and took acoustical factors (like the greater loudness and sustaining power of the low end of the keyboard) into account in devising his algorithms, Boulez's are entirely abstract or "conceptual." Boulez's series of twelve dynamic gradations, in particular, is entirely utopian, both in its assumption that the twelve levels can be manipulated as discrete entities on a par with pitches and durations, and also in the way levels are assigned to pitches regardless of register.

When the texture becomes dense, moreover, so much interference is caused by the mixing of registers that there can be no hope of grouping the individual notes into contrapuntal lines by ear, hence no way of perceiving by listening the relationship between the sounds heard on the "surface" of the music and the axioms that motivated their choice. In bluntest terms, then, the paradox created by "total serialism" is this: once the algorithms governing a composition are known (or have been determined), it is possible to demonstrate the correctness of the score (that is, of its component notes) more decisively and objectively than is possible for any other kind of music; but in the act of listening to the composition, one has no way of knowing (and, no matter how many times one listens, one will never have a way of knowing) that the notes one is hearing are the right notes, or (more precisely) that they are not wrong notes.

Indeed, by excluding beams from the notation, Boulez makes it difficult to gain this knowledge even by eye. (Hence, too, not only the arduousness but also the tediousness of the foregoing explanation; the reader is forgiven for skimming.) The extreme fragment-ation of the texture into atomic particles insures that, paradoxically, all the meticulous "precompositional" planning—the music's basic theoretical justification—is lost on the listener, and even on the score reader. The music yields its secrets—that is, its governing algorithms or a priori rules—to nobody's senses, only to the mind of a determined analyst (which is why so much of it remained secret for so long).

The value of technical analysis as a separate musical activity, therefore, experienced an unprecedented boom. (Boulez was overheard at Darmstadt to say that the age of the concert had passed; scores need no longer be played, just "read" — i.e., analyzed.) Along with the growth of integral serialism, then, there grew up a new musicological specialization, that of music analyst (sometimes loosely identified with the much older and broader calling of music theorist), and a number of outlets for the practice in the form of specialized journals. The first to appear was *Die Reihe* ("The row"), widely regarded as the unofficial Darmstadt house organ, issued between 1955 and 1962 by the Vienna publisher Universal Edition, and coedited by Stockhausen and the equally intransigent Herbert Eimert, who as early as 1924 had published a little practical method for twelve-tone music, the first of its kind. An English translation of *Die Reihe*, published in the United States between 1958 and 1968, retained the German title (though it might have been called *The Row* or *The Series*).

DISQUIETING QUESTIONS

But why was all this considered desirable, or if not desirable at least inevitable? To this question many different (often contradictory) answers have been given; over it many battles have been fought. Many resented on social grounds the idea of a music that disclosed so little to an ordinary listener, associating it with the arrogant rhetoric of manifestos like "Schoenberg Is Dead," with elitism (that is, the use of a willfully difficult style to create a social elite that excluded the noninitiated), and with the misappropriation of scientific prestige. (All of these criticisms could just as well have been leveled at the medieval troubadours, but they weren't, since the idea of social elites in those days required no apology, least of all in artistic circles.) On the other side, the music, the rhetoric, and the cult of difficulty were all upheld as necessary protections against those who would regulate art, and curtail the freedoms of artists, on social or commercial grounds. Back came the retort that there could be no greater regulation or regimentation of art than that of "total serialism" (or, more generally, any method of composing by algorithm). Yet a discipline one imposes on oneself, no matter how zealously one may exhort others to follow suit, ought not, perhaps, to be equated with a discipline imposed by political authority. Was it just puritanism, then?

Boulez's own answer, given long after the fact to a sympathetic interviewer (and long after he had given up the utopian dream of "total serialism"), invoked something milder: experimental curiosity. He wanted, he said, "to find out how far automatism in musical relationships would go."[34] The idea of taking things to their limits has always had an appeal to modernists, as we have known, so to speak, since the days of Mahler and Scriabin. We also know that Messiaen, Boulez's teacher, had been a rare keeper of the maximalist flame all through the reign of irony. But why should there have been such a resurgence of maximalism among so many young composers precisely at this time? And what was the appeal of algorithmic methods — what Boulez called "automatism," or what the Italian composer Luciano Berio (1925–2003), another important alumnus of Darmstadt, called "writing music without being personally involved"?

Boulez was not unaware of the paradox inherent in a process of composition that applied the most stringent controls, only to bring forth a product that, as far as even the most educated listener was concerned, might as well have been the product of chance. "From the prescriptions we have been examining in detail," he wrote toward the end of an article in which he gave a preliminary analysis of *Structures*, "there arises the unforeseen."[35] (Indeed, he went on, characteristically, to turn the remark into a dogma: "There is no creation except in the unforeseeable becoming necessary.") That begins to approximate the terms of existentialist thought, with its meditations on the relationship between free will and necessity, on the one hand, and between free will and contingency, on the other. Still, what did it mean (or could it mean) freely to decide, as the music theorist Roger Savage has put it, to "hand the work's structure over to the serial operations which control it"? What did that say about agency and responsibility?

DISQUIETING ANSWERS

An unusually frank and revealing answer to these difficult questions was given in 1960 by Ernst Krenek, a composer who won his first fame as the author of *Jonny spielt auf*, the most popular European opera of the "jazz age." Over the intervening decades, Krenek's career had gone through some intense vicissitudes, and so had his compositional approach. From having been the darling of a brash materialistic society, Krenek had become a political refugee, unexpectedly committed to twelve-tone composition as a symbol of "the loneliness and alienation of humanity,"[36] and regarding it, perhaps reluctantly, as the only morally valid form music could take.

Practically alone among his generation, Krenek was strongly attracted to the reconditeness and the rigors of "total serialism" as preached and practiced by the young composers at Darmstadt — all the more so when he found that they mistrusted his commercially successful past and, practicing some fairly brazen generational politics, rebuffed his friendly overtures during the summers of 1954 and 1956, shutting him out and making him feel doubly isolated. (In 1961 Darmstadt witnessed a little scandal when the students and staff of the summer course turned out in force to jeer a work of Krenek's that was being performed at the local opera house.) Personal hostility kept Krenek out of the "Darmstadt school" per se; by the time he got around to it, moreover, the official Darmstadt line was that total serialism was passé. Yet these circumstances made his embrace of total serialism all the more significant, for they showed

FIG. 1-5   Ernst Krenek.

that its appeal was not just a sectarian or a passing phenomenon but a genuine sign of the times.

Krenek's most rigorously organized serial composition was *Sestina* (1957) for soprano and ten instruments. The text, by the composer himself, was a meditation on the notorious philosophical problems we are now considering. It was cast in an elaborately organized medieval verse form, Krenek (a part-time musicologist) having noticed the similarity, alluded to above, between the hermeticism of the new music and the *trobar clus* or "exclusive poetry" of the troubadours. Krenek had learned about the sestina form from R. P. Blackmur, a literary critic on the faculty of Princeton University, who hosted a series of lectures the composer had been invited to deliver on "Recent Advances in Musical Thought and Sound." Supposedly invented by the troubadour Arnaut Daniel, the sestina consisted of six six-line stanzas in which the end-words of every stanza were the same, but presented each time in a different order.

The six orderings of the end-words were obtained through a process of permutation that, Krenek immediately saw, could be adapted to the permutations of a tone row. The order established in the first stanza (1 2 3 4 5 6) was rearranged in successive stanzas by continually pairing the last with the first, the next-to-last with the second, and the third- from-last with the third: $1\,2\,3\,4\,5\,6 \rightarrow 6\,1\,5\,2\,4\,3 \rightarrow 3\,6\,4\,1\,2\,5 \rightarrow 5\,3\,2\,6\,1\,4$ $\rightarrow 4\,5\,1\,3\,6\,2 \rightarrow 2\,4\,6\,5\,3\,1$; and here the process must stop because the next (seventh) permutation would reproduce the first. Instead, the poem ends with a three-line *tornada* or refrain that uses all six words, two to a line.

Krenek's poem, composed in his native German even though the performances were to take place in New York, ponders the esthetic and existential problems of "total serialism" by adopting a set of relevant terms for permutation at the line-endings: *Strom* (flow or stream), *Mass* (measure or measurement), *Zufall* (chance), *Gestalt* (shape), *Zeit* (time), and *Zahl* (number). The *tornada* summarized the issues:

Wie ich mit *Mass*	As I with measurement
bezwinge Klang und *Zeit,*	master sound and time,
entflieht *Gestalt*	Shape recedes
im unermessnen *Zufall.*	in unmeasured chance,
Kristall der *Zahl*	The crystal of number
entlässt des Lebens *Strom.*	releases the stream of existence.

To represent musically the endless or cyclic permutation symbolized as well as pondered in the poem, Krenek divided the tone row into its constituent hexachords, which he then modified (or as he put it, "rotated") numerically as shown in Ex. 1-11, the pitch numbers standing for the end-word numbers displayed above in the sestina scheme. The resulting stream of numbers, further permuted by the usual serial procedures (cancrizans, inversion, retrograde inversion), could then be adapted to the serialization of duration, loudness, and attack, according to a set of algorithms comparable to those that Boulez had employed in *Structures*. And just as in *Structures*, as the composer was well aware, the algorithms produced sound sequences that could not be parsed as relationships by a listening ear, only by an inquiring mind.

EX. 1-11 Cyclic permutation in Ernst Krenek, *Sestina*

Performed and recorded in March 1958 and published shortly afterward, Krenek's *Sestina* made little impression at first. But in 1959 the composer was invited back to Princeton to participate in a seminar in "advanced musical studies" and gave a paper there entitled "Extents and Limits of Serial Technique," in which, among other things, he commented on several of his recent works, including *Sestina*. His remarks, considered overly and even offensively candid by several in attendance, attracted wide attention when they were published (along with several others from the seminar) in a special issue of *The Musical Quarterly* (April 1960) that was reissued two years later as a book called *Problems of Modern Music*.

Recalling a statement made by Stockhausen at a Darmstadt lecture — "Boulez's objective is the product; mine is the process" — Krenek endorsed the implied emphasis on the composer (the maker) rather than the audience (the passive receiver) and as much as wrote the latter out of the picture. In describing one of his earlier experiments in total serialism, he asserted that "whatever occurs in this piece at any given point is premeditated and therefore technically predictable"; but immediately qualified the statement with what many regarded as a stunning admission. "While the preparation and the layout of the material as well as the operations performed therein are the consequence of serial premeditation," he allowed, "the audible results of these procedures were not visualized as the purpose of the procedures. Seen from this angle, the results are incidental."[37] It didn't matter, in other words, what the music sounded like.

After describing the algorithms employed in *Sestina*, Krenek made an admission even more alarming to those who had thought of total serialism as a means of securing maximum control over the musical material:

> If the succession of tones is determined by serial regulation (as is the case in the classical twelve-tone technique) and, in addition to this, the timing of the entrance into the musical process of these tones is also predetermined by serial calculation (as, for example, in the case of the *Sestina*), it is no longer possible to decide freely (that is, by "inspiration") which tones should sound simultaneously at any given point. In other words, the so-called harmonic aspect of the piece will be entirely the result of operations performed on premises that have nothing to do with concepts of "harmony," be it on the assumption of tonality or atonality or anything else. Whatever happens at any given point is a product of the preconceived serial organization, but by the same token it is a chance occurrence because it is as such not anticipated by the mind that invented the mechanism and set it in motion.[38]

This much had been acknowledged before, if not quite so forthrightly. But Krenek went on to answer the question posed above — "Why is this desirable?" — in equally forthright terms, and this had never been done before. He took as the "text" for his sermon a recent analysis of *Structures* in *Die Reihe* that had at last uncovered its algorithms, thus implying that his comments were not merely the personal reflections of an aging and isolated figure but characterized the attitudes of the younger European composers as well. (The author of the analysis, György Ligeti, was a Hungarian composer who had emigrated to Austria at the time of the Hungarian revolt against Communist rule in 1956.) Krenek began by explaining why he had put derisive quotation marks around the word "inspiration" in the passage just quoted:

> Actually the composer has come to distrust his inspiration because it is not really as innocent as it was supposed to be, but rather conditioned by a tremendous body of recollection, tradition, training, and experience. In order to avoid the dictations of such ghosts, he prefers to set up an impersonal mechanism which will furnish, according to premeditated patterns, unpredictable situations. Ligeti characterizes this state of affairs very well: "We stand in front of a row of vending machines ("Automaten") and we can choose freely into which one we want to drop our coin, but at the same time we are forced to choose one of them. One constructs his own prison according to his wishes and is afterwards freely active within those walls — that is: not entirely free, but not totally constrained either. Thus automation does not function as the opposite of free decision: rather free selection and mechanization are united in the process of selecting the mechanism." In other words, the creative act takes place in an area in which it has so far been entirely unsuspected, namely in setting up the serial statements (selecting the slot machines). What happens afterwards is predetermined by the selection of the mechanism, but not premeditated except as an unconscious result of the predetermined operations. The unexpected happens by necessity. The surprise is built in.[39]

On one level this looked like the *reductio ad absurdum* of the modernist attitude in its "zero hour" extremity: better a random or meaningless product than one that bears traces of the past. That truly seemed like pursuing novelty at all costs — specifically, at the exorbitant cost of "recollection, tradition, training, and experience," the very sources of consciousness, especially artistic consciousness, and of the capacity to act responsibly. The renunciation was so extreme, and so telling, as to attract the attention of contemporary philosophers. Stanley Cavell, a philosopher then on the faculty of the University of California at Berkeley (and a trained musician as well) responded almost immediately to Krenek's paper, in a paper of his own read in December 1960 and reworked into a celebrated essay, "Music Discomposed," that was published in 1965 and widely anthologized thereafter, becoming the subject of commentary and debate in its own right.

Cavell's immediate reaction to Krenek's position was an impulse to mock it: "This is not serious, but it is meant,"[40] was his much-repeated quip. Reading more widely in the professional arts literature of the day, he was forced to acknowledge the position as "symptomatic" of a "dissonant and unresolved emotion"[41] that was felt not just in music but in all the contemporary arts. He recognized the language, or jargon, of existentialism: "It is scarcely unusual," he observed, "for an awareness of determinism to stir philosophical speculation about the possibilities of freedom and choice and responsibility." But there was a big, unprecedented difference. "Whereas the more usual motivation has been to preserve responsibility in the face of determinism, these new views wish to preserve choice by foregoing responsibility (for everything but the act of 'choosing')."[42] It was the ultimate "escape from freedom." Cavell cast the paradox of total serialism in terms of a familiar antithesis. "In denying tradition," he observed, "Krenek is a Romantic, but with no respect or hope for the individual's resources; and in the reliance on rules, he is a Classicist, but with no respect or hope for his culture's inventory of conventions."[43] Exposing so fundamental an incoherence, the philosopher thought, would undermine such a music's claim to validity—or at least the validity of the justification now being offered for its existence. "Such philosophizing as Krenek's does not justify it," Cavell asserts, "and must not be used to protect it against aesthetic assessment."[44] But just as he delivers the intended deathblow, Cavell suddenly and, it seems, unwittingly identifies the source of the music's validity—or rather, identifies the reason why the practice proved so appealing (or consoling) and was so widely taken up by rational musicians in full awareness of the attendant paradoxes.

"What in fact Krenek has come to distrust," the philosopher alleges, "is the composer's capacity to feel any idea as his own."[45] Cavell calls this "nihilism,"[46] for it contradicts what he sees (in an argument that ultimately goes back to Immanuel Kant) as the ultimate value of any work of art: "A work of art does not express some particular intention (as statements do), nor achieve particular goals (the way technological skill and moral action do), but, one may say, celebrates the fact that men can intend their lives at all (if you like, that they are free to choose), and that their actions are coherent and effective at all in the scene of indifferent nature and determined society."[47] Total serialism, "by calling something musically organized (let alone totally organized) on grounds unrelated to any way in which it is, or is meant to be, heard," must therefore express "contempt for the artistic process"—and by extension, it expresses contempt for (or disbelief in) the "fact" that the artistic process is meant to celebrate. We cannot "intend our lives" any more, such music seems to say. "Nothing we now have to say, no *personal* utterance, has its meaning conveyed in the conventions and formulas we now share,"[48] it dispiritingly implies. Therefore, "taste must be *defeated*"[49] as a justification for art or indeed for any human action, since taste in any consensual sense must rest on beliefs that have become untenable.

Cavell decries this nihilistic defeatism. Yet rather than an expression of simple nihilism, or belief in nothing, the renunciation total serialism demanded might rather be seen as expressing existential despair. It was the passionately intense reaction of artists who could no longer believe in the supreme value of the individual self, the "autonomous subject" exalted by romanticism, at a time when a hundred thousand selves just as individual as theirs might vanish at the push of a button. There was no point in having intentions or expressing feelings at a time when the best laid plans seemed so futile, and personal feelings so trivial, in the face of such destructive power. That had to be what Boulez meant when he "decreed" that art had to transcend persons. The authoritarian manner was bravado in the face of impotence.

One took refuge instead in what Ligeti frankly called a "compulsion neurosis"[50] — elaborate mechanical methods that put one in touch with something less vulnerable than personal wishes and tastes, or subjective standards of beauty. The contempt that Stanley Cavell discerned in Krenek's pseudo-technical writing is even more evident in Boulez's determination "to strip music of its accumulated dirt and give it the structure it had lacked since the Renaissance." But it is also evident that the contempt is directed not merely at traditional art, or the traditional audience, but at the whole idea that art is for the sake of people. One's only solace was to strip away all personality, feelings, and expressive intention. That was the "dirt." And the artist's own personality and feelings were not exempted. After Hiroshima everyone felt like dirt. The only responsible decision left was to face that miserable contingency and find a way of composing that would stamp out the artist's puny person and allow something "realer" to emerge. And what could be realer than number?

The desperate antihumanism of the early atomic age, then, sought its consolation in an ancient prehumanism — something far older than what is usually called "the Renaissance." Behind that imprecise formulation, as we know, Boulez had the music of the fourteenth-century Ars Nova in mind, and the isorhythmic motets of Machaut and Du Fay. In one of his earliest manifestos, Boulez actually revealed as the source of his inspiration a passage from the foreword to a then recent edition of Du Fay's complete works (the author, Guillaume de Van, was actually a transplanted American, William Carrolle Devan, who had compromised himself by heading the music division of the Bibliothèque Nationale in Paris during the German occupation):

> Isorhythm was the finest expression of the fourteenth-century musical ideal, the *arcanum* which only the few could penetrate, and which constituted the supreme test of the composer's ability. . . . The limitations imposed by the rigid dimensions of a plan which determined beforehand the tiniest details of rhythmic structure, did not stint the composer's inspiration, for his motets give the impression of free, spontaneous compositions, while in fact the isorhythmic canon is strictly observed.[51]

But while Boulez called this elite *arcanum* "the most rational attitude to rhythm in our Western music," and cited it as "precedent for modern research,"[52] it rested on a Platonic (and before Plato, a Pythagorean) faith in number as the ultimate and imperishable reality, as memorably expressed in the ninth-century *Scholia enchiriadis*, the textbook that stands at the very wellspring of the continuous tradition of music theory in the west. "Notes pass quickly away," the book proclaimed; "numbers, however, though stained by the corporeal touch of pitches and motions, remain."[53]

SOLACE IN RITUAL

It was that faith that total serialism tried — vainly, of course — to revive, by excluding the corporeal (which is to say the perishable, threatened by time and doomed to eradication), and the all-too-human, as far as was humanly possible. In the end, for all its vaunted rationalism, it was at bottom something of a religious revival, and its roots in Messiaen's avowedly pious art no longer seem so anomalous. As religions find expression in ritual, it seems fitting to end our consideration of the Darmstadt "zero hour" with a look at *Kreuzspiel* ("Cross-play," or "Crossing game"), Stockhausen's immediate response to his experiences there in the summer of 1951.

Stockhausen had a traditional Catholic upbringing (as did both Krenek and Boulez) and from childhood was unusually devout. For him the Nazi years were above all a time of religious conflict, and his experience of "zero hour," colored by the loss of his father in the last days of the war, was one of religious rededication. It was now an unconventional religion to which he devoted himself, heavily influenced by a reading of the novel *Das Glasperlenspiel* ("The glass-bead game," or "Magister Ludi") by the pacifist author Hermann Hesse (1877–1962), whose writings were informed by an interest in Asian religions, especially Buddhism. Stockhausen identified strongly with Joseph Knecht, the protagonist of the novel, who like him was an orphan boy with musical gifts studying at the Cologne Musikhochschule (Conservatory), and who dedicates himself to the "glass bead game" of the title, a quasi-monastic exercise that combines the disciplines of "science, reverence for the beautiful and meditation." Such activity, Stockhausen came to believe, connected the callings of musician with that of "spiritual servant."[54] He had found his own path to a prehumanistic musical ideal, and became a zealous proselytizer for it. (The reference to "a glass-bead-game" in Henze's description of the zero-hour sensibility, quoted earlier, was surely an allusion to Stockhausen's exhortations.) Stockhausen's initial exposure to twelve-tone music came by way of Herbert Eimert, who lived in Cologne and gave him a copy of his 25-year-old textbook, banned by the Nazis. It was Eimert, too, who advised him to attend the 1951 Summer Courses at Darmstadt, where he heard the recording of Messiaen's *Mode de valeurs* and immediately sensed its kinship to Hesse's imaginary bead game. In his excitement over that discovery he found that the orgiastic "Dance of the Golden Calf" from Schoenberg's unfinished opera *Moses und Aron*, the sensation of the Darmstadt season, seemed altogether passé. For Stockhausen too, Schoenberg was dead.

He explained that impression to Adorno, who had taken over the composition class that Schoenberg was supposed to have taught himself but for his final illness, and who inquired about the development of motives in an embryonic total-serial piece that another student had submitted, by replying, "Professor, you are looking for a chicken in an abstract painting."[55] The remark became a Darmstadt legend, not merely for its sassiness but for its charisma. Attesting so impressively to the unknown young composer's self-assurance, it immediately attracted disciples to his side.

Like *Mode de valeurs* or *Structures*, Stockhausen's *Kreuzspiel* replaces "chickens" (conventional motives for development) with "sound atoms," to use Stockhausen's term. But whereas Messiaen's and Boulez's compositions displayed their component particles in static arrangements, Stockhausen's embodies a dynamic process of unfolding, in which the tones can be likened to actors, or participants in a ritualized action that has no other goal than its own completion—hence *spiel* ("game"). What is predetermined is not just how things *are*, but what they seem to *do*, and what they will *become*.

EX. 1-12 Karlheinz Stockhausen, *Kreuzspiel*, mm. 1–13

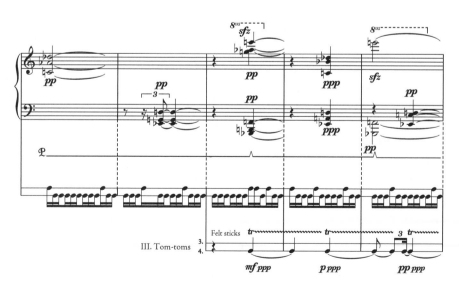

EX. I-I2   (*continued*)

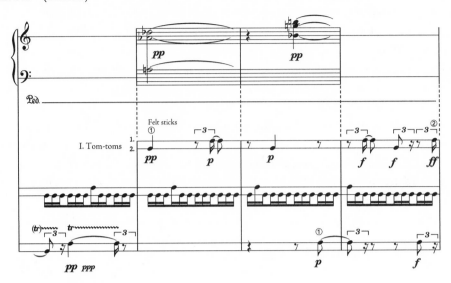

① Full value without *tr*; dampen drumhead with the hand at the end of the notated value.

② for ♪ or ♪, the stick should not leave the drumhead.

The work is scored for two woodwind players (on oboe and bass clarinet), a pianist (who also plays woodblock), and three percussionists who together play on eight tuned drums (pitched, like so much early modernist harmony, at intervals of alternating perfect fourths and tritones) and four suspended cymbals of varying size, for an obviously significant total of twelve instruments. Its temporal unfolding consists of three main parts, distinguished from one another by tempo changes and connected with transitional passages. During the first thirteen bars (the "slow introduction," Ex. I-I2), the piano and the percussion introduce their respective "chromatic" domains. The piano, concerned with pitches, gives out a series of twelve-tone aggregates arranged into three-note chords, of which the first, at the registral extremes, remains constant. The drums give out a pair of rhythmic series, expressed by alternations between the high and low tumbas (or conga drums): each time the higher drum is struck, a different number of pulses on the lower drum must intervene before the next time until all twelve "chromatic" degrees have been sounded. The second of these series (beginning in the middle of m. 7) is just a "chromatic scale" à la Messiaen: I pulse, then 2, then 3, and so on to I2. In the one given at the outset, the order has been scrambled: **2 8 7 4 11 1 12 3 9 6 5 10**. Counting pulse-groups throughout the first section would reveal that no two orderings are alike, but all are permutations of the full "chromatic" spectrum of durations. The same principle of constant permutation goes for the pitch series in the piano and, eventually, the winds. The "cross-play" of the title follows a complicated set of algorithms or precompositional rules, but its result is easily observed. In the piano's first "linear" statement of the pitch series, at m. I4 (Ex. I-I3a), the twelve pitches are associated by extreme registers into two hexachords: E♭, D, E, G, A, and A♭ in the high treble and D♭, C, B♭, F, B, and G♭ in the low bass. In the last statement of Part I, which begins precisely in the middle of m. 85 (Ex. 1-13b), the registral positions are reversed, the first hexachord now sounding in the bass and the second in the treble.

That is the most obvious of the "crossings"; there are many others, involving timbre, dynamics, and rhythm, to which only arduous analysis rather than sensory perception can give access. In this sense the workings of *Kreuzspiel* are just as arcane, just as mysterious and obscure, as those of *Structures*. But the constant pulse and the contrasting, obviously interacting timbres give the piece a sense of "narration" or progression through time that turns the algorithms into enactments. That, plus its

EX. 1-13A   Karlheinz Stockhausen, *Kreuzspiel*, mm. 14–20

exotic scoring and its "hockety" texture (reminiscent at times of jazz percussion), give the piece a somewhat less ascetic or forbidding aspect, even a "stain of the corporeal." Within the ascetic world of "total serialism," at any rate, *Kreuzspiel* counts as easy listening. That may be one reason why Stockhausen suppressed constant pulsation in the works that followed, and also withheld *Kreuzspiel* from publication for nearly a decade, despite positive audience reactions. We have seen that audience appeal could be

EX. 1-13B   Karlheinz Stockhausen, *Kreuzspiel*, mm. 85–91

stigmatized, in the tense political atmosphere of the early cold war, as "compromise." At the very least, a lapse of moral purity could cost an avant-garde composer his intellectual prestige, which is to say his political capital, and ultimately (paradoxically enough), his access to patronage and promotion.

POSTER BOY

"In the arts an appetite for a new look is now a professional requirement, as in Russia to be accredited as a revolutionist is to qualify for privileges,"[56] wrote Harold Rosenberg, a champion of avant-garde painting, in 1960. He was calling attention to some of the unintended ironies that resulted from the politics of the cold war, the chief one being the political and commercial exploitation of the very stance of apolitical and noncommercial unexploitability that was supposed to be the distinguishing feature of the "Western" side in the debate over the meaning and purpose of art.

If we wish to examine the musical side of this curious yet telling state of affairs, the focal figure for the 1950s would have to be György Ligeti (b. 1923), the Hungarian composer with whose widely heralded analysis of *Structures* we are already acquainted. The dynamics of his career will offer an ironic counterpoint, or perhaps provide an inverted mirror-reflection, to the tribulations that befell the legacy of his countryman Bartók around the same time.

Ligeti finished his musical education and began his composing career precisely at postwar Hungary's most stringently "Zhdanovite" moment. He graduated from the Liszt Conservatory in Budapest in 1949, the very year the Hungarian Communist Party gained absolute power and began regulating the arts in accord with its Soviet prototype's Resolution on Music. As a Jew, he had lived in terror and ultimately in hiding during the war, and greeted the arrival of the Soviet liberators in Hungary with joy. Like many formerly left-leaning Eastern European intellectuals, as he has told interviewers, he found that it took the experience of living under Soviet power to turn him into an anti-Communist. ("So many people believed in this utopia, and then they were so completely disappointed—more than disappointed."[57]) It also turned his composing predilections, in a spirit of defiance, away from Bartók and Stravinsky and toward the avant-garde, which in the Hungarian context still meant Schoenberg.

There was no possibility of performance or publication of such music in Hungary at the time, so Ligeti began doing as some Soviet composers also did—writing utilitarian music (folksong arrangements and school choruses) for pay and "serious" works for the drawer. One of them, in the composer's words, was "completely twelve-tone and rhythmically machine-like."[58] Even behind the "iron curtain," composers felt the paradoxical need to surrender their decision-making faculties to algorithms—in the name of freedom.

Ligeti seized his chance to leave Hungary in the wake of the failed 1956 rebellion, which briefly toppled the Communist regime before being crushed by the Soviet army. He crossed into Austria in December, and fetched up in Cologne in February 1957. He had been corresponding with Eimert and Stockhausen, and they arranged a stipend to pay his living expenses so that he could work at a new-music studio Eimert had set up at the state-supported radio station in that city. That year, too, Ligeti spent the first of seven summers at Darmstadt. The first item he produced in the West, however, was not a musical composition but the analysis of *Structures*, which his hosts, being the editors of *Die Reihe*, were eager to publish.

The ironies and ambivalences of the cold war situation — the simultaneous escape into and escape from freedom, about which existentialist philosophers and psychologists wrote interminably — is nowhere more poignantly summed up than in that essay, where the recent refugee from Soviet tyranny wrote happily about "choosing one's own prison according to one's wishes," and being "free to act within those walls." In an equally remarkable conclusion, the fugitive from the world of "historical materialism" — where the sacrifice of present happiness to future utopia was mandated by the state, and the independence of the "esthetic" and the "artistic" as autonomous categories was disputed in the name of social progress — called for just such a sacrifice in the name of technical progress.

> Since in music a pure structure can only be achieved through time, composition at the serial level has become work with time. Thus composition ceases to be essentially "art-work"; to compose now takes on an additional character of research into the newly-discovered relationships of material. This attitude may strike people as negative, "inartistic" — but there is no other way for the composer of today, if he wants to get any further.[59]

Certainly Ligeti's first year in Germany had the character of research. "I soaked things up like a sponge," he told an interviewer; "for several months I did nothing but listen to tapes and discs."[60] The Boulez analysis was in its way what in Germany is called a *Habilitationsschrift* or "inaugural thesis," a formal demonstration of mastery and a ticket of admission to an academy. The first few musical pieces were of a similar kind, in which the newcomer from the "backward" or "retarded" East demonstrated that he was no bumpkin. The big one was *Apparitions* for orchestra, a maximalist effort in every way, requiring a score with sixty-three staves. It was specifically, and consciously, a maximalization of the most radical aspects of Bartók's music as they were then understood by Hungarian musicians, and an adaptation of that view of Bartók to the reigning ideologies and methodologies of Darmstadt.

In 1955 two important books on Bartók were published in Budapest, both by a single author, Erno Lendvai (1925–93), a musicologist who lectured on analysis at the Liszt Academy of Music in Budapest, where Ligeti also worked up to the time of his emigration.[61] The books were systematic demonstrations of Lendvai's thesis that Bartók's works were formed according to what the architects of the Italian Renaissance called the Golden Section (or Divine Proportion), a ratio that supposedly governs the proportions of natural objects and is for that reason naturally pleasing to the mind.

(The two segments of a line divided according to the Golden Section will have the same ratio of length as the ratio between the larger segment and the whole line. Like "Pi," the ratio between the circumference and diameter of a circle, the Golden Section cannot be exactly expressed in the decimal system, but only approximated, usually as 1.618. It is progressively approached by the ratios produced by pairs of numbers along a Fibonacci series, the sequence formed by adding two successive members to find the next member: for example 1, 1, 2, 3, 5, 8, 13, 21, 34, etc. In other words, the values of the ratios 1/2, 2/3, 3/5, 5/8, etc. approach the Golden ratio.)

Lendvai analyzed many works of Bartók to show that Bartók transferred the ratios of the Fibonacci series and the Golden Section to the temporal domain in order to govern the length of the component sections in his works and thus generate their form. His theory has not gained wide acceptance among musicologists, but in 1956 it became the basis for an entirely inappropriate political denunciation (on grounds of "formalism") that led to Lendvai's dismissal from his position at the Academy. As a demonstration of solidarity with his former colleague, whose tribulations made the defense of a "formalist" view of Bartók seem more politically urgent than ever, Ligeti deliberately proportioned the first of the two movements in *Apparitions* on the Fibonacci series throughout, applying it as a typically Darmstadtian algorithm with far greater rigor than Lendvai ever suspected Bartók of doing (but, as it happened, in a way that another avant-garde musician, Iannis Xenakis, a Greek-born Parisian who had actually trained as an architect, was beginning to do).

The pitch material of the movement was developed from tone clusters, the harmonic effect that, as used in such works as the Fourth Quartet or the piano suite *Szabadban* ("Out of doors"), symbolized Bartók's radical extreme in another musical dimension. What was of greatest immediate importance was the way in which Ligeti developed the implications of Bartók's musical ideas, as he understood them, in a context completely devoid of folklore, siding decisively with those who wanted to see the great Hungarian composer as a universal modern master on a par (however difficult it might be for his German hosts to accept such an idea) with Schoenberg and Webern. In any event, it was a view that utterly opposed the image of Bartók that the Communist government was promoting back home, and was therefore a contribution in actual music to the ongoing debate about Bartók's legacy that was such a conspicuous aspect of the cold-war musical scene.

But the West, too, participated in cold-war image-making and promotions, and this was an important factor in Ligeti's own reception. In addition to *Apparitions*, during his first years in the "free world" Ligeti composed two short pieces in a new medium, "electronic music," that had only existed since the war, and was therefore enormously attractive to musicians who saw themselves as re-creating the art of music from scratch. Eimert had set up a studio for electronic music—the first in Europe—at the Cologne Radio, and Stockhausen had been busy there since 1953.

The early history of electronic music will be sketched in chapter 4, but it will be worthwhile, in the present context, to say a few words in advance about Ligeti's electronic studies of 1957–58. The medium attracted him long before he came West, he has said, because the composer of electronic music realizes the actual sounding composition in the act of creating it, so that there is no need for performers, publishers, or any social mediation at all. That could make it seem the misanthrope's delight, perhaps, but from Ligeti's perspective (or that of any composer growing up in the Soviet bloc) it promised a way of making music beyond the reach of bureaucratic interference.

Ligeti's second electronic composition, *Artikulation* (1958), arose out of a preoccupation shared by several of the musicians and technicians working at the Cologne studio: the age-old question of the relationship between music and speech. They approached it in characteristically "atomistic" fashion, not in terms of sentences or words but in terms of phonology — that is, individual phonetic units — according to a classification system for "sound signals" worked out by the communications theorist Werner Meyer-Eppler, whose lectures at the University of Bonn had been an inspiration to Stockhausen. Ligeti's piece was a collage of "sound atoms" selected from a big Meyer-Epplerish menu according to a set of algorithms that grouped forty-four sound-types into ten categories or "texts," thence modified into "words," thence into "languages," thence into "sentences" with intonational contours reminiscent of speech. Another set of algorithms divided the music among four antiphonal recorded tracks. The results were further mixed down to two stereophonic channels to enable publication in the form of a recording.

There was no score (and no possibility, therefore, for analysis of the result), for the composer had worked by ear on the basis of rough charts. There was no need for a prescriptive notation since electronic music, once fixed on tape, required no performers at all, just playback equipment. One of the most significant if initially unsuspected aspects of electronic music, it eventually dawned, was that it produced the first fundamental alteration of the relationship between composition and notation in a thousand years, pointing the way (not that anyone was looking for it then) toward musical "postliteracy." This will be a big theme, in fact the biggest, in the closing chapters of this book.

And yet a dozen years later, in 1970, the German publishing house of Schott, the most powerful firm in Europe, celebrated its "acquisition" of Ligeti by commissioning from a technician named Rainer Wehinger what it was pleased to call a "Hörpartitur" or "aural score" of *Artikulation*. Like any score, it could be followed while listening to the piece, but it served no other practical purpose — not even for analysis, since the sounds were not represented with enough specificity as to their exact frequency or duration. Instead, they were rendered impressionistically, by fancifully executed shapes of arbitrary design that corresponded with various timbres and attack characteristics.

These shapes appear from left to right in the order in which the little sounds in *Artikulation* are heard, their spatial frequency coordinated with a grid that marks elapsing seconds. The antiphonal effects are indicated by the little circles above the "score," which are divided into quadrants that stand for the four stereophonic tracks. Perhaps deliberately, Wehinger's shapes are reminiscent of the unidentified objects one might see in a modern painting, say by the Spanish painter Joan Miró (1893–1983), whose quirky surrealistic images Ligeti had in mind (according to his biographer Richard Toop) while composing the piece.[62] In that case, the peculiarly named "Hörpartitur" (which isn't actually required for hearing anything) is more a sort of parallel objet d'art — an impression that becomes all the stronger when one learns that, in addition to the conventionally bound score, Schott also published the Hörpartitur of *Artikulation* in the form of a large poster in bright colors, suitable for hanging on the wall. It was in effect a work of visual art founded on, or determined by, a piece of music.

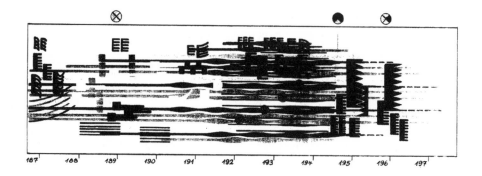

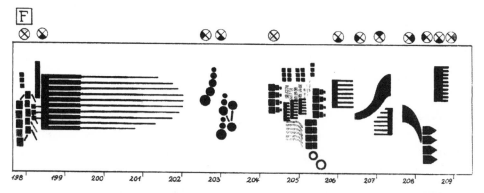

FIG. I-6   Page from the "Hörpartitur" by Rainer Wehinger for Ligeti's *Artikulation* (Mainz: B. Schott's Söhne, 1970).

Thus the score serves a decorative or celebratory purpose rather than a practical one. It is a "production value" meant to enhance the status of the work and its author, and reflect prestige on the publisher, evidence that Ligeti had become the focus of a "cult of personality" of a kind far more common in the marketing of commercial pop music than in the "serious" "classical" sphere. His emblematic status derived in large part from the dramatic circumstances of his career, with its spectacular move from East to West. To put it very crudely, Ligeti's fame had turned him into a sort of cold-war trophy or poster boy, a status that then fed back into his fame. And with that, we arrive back at our starting point, the political polarization of the cold war now yielding exploitable goods.

Ligeti could not have achieved such a position had he not joined forces with the Western avant-garde. Andrzej Panufnik (1914–91), a composer and conductor who made a comparable defection to the West from the Soviet bloc around the same time, sank like a stone. A much-honored figure in his native Poland, he sought asylum from the Communist regime in England during a 1954 concert tour, and, as he put it ruefully in retrospect, "leapt from my Polish position of Number One to no one at all in England."[63]

Compared with the Darmstadt avant-garde, Panufnik's music could be described as "gemässigte Moderne." Cast for the most part in traditional forms — overtures, symphonies, and the like — that had been anathematized at Darmstadt but not at home, it lacked propaganda value. By the 1970s, the cold war waning, Panufnik found some champions, most notably the veteran conductor Leopold Stokowski (1882–1977) who in 1973, after a long career in the United States, moved back to his native England. In 1991, near the end of his life, Panufnik was honored by his adopted country with a knighthood. But without the cachet of stylistic as well as political "dissidence," an Eastern European composer could not attract much sympathetic attention during the years of political stress.

Stockhausen, the most flamboyant of the Darmstadt avant-gardists, was the other charismatic figure of the age. His publisher, Universal Edition, gave him the same sort of star treatment as Schott gave Ligeti, posters and all, and he eventually became a minor cult figure in the pop world. His *Klavierstück XI* (1956), whose many component fragments could be played in many different orders, had to be custom-printed on a gigantic piece of heavy paper to eliminate the need for page turns. Not only did the publishing house accommodate with a beautifully engraved score packaged as a roll inside a cardboard cylinder, it also provided a custom-designed folding music-stand with clips that would hold the unwieldy thing in place atop the piano.

No other "serious" composers of the period could expect that kind of aggressive promotion from commercial publishers. It testified impressively to Stockhausen's and Ligeti's standing as culture heroes and to the publishers' willingness to take a loss for prestige purposes. But all that prestige, and the attendant "commodification" of the pieces so lavishly produced, did rather alter the status of the "Darmstadt school" as an avant-garde. When capitalist enterprises began engaging in cold-war cultural politics alongside governments, the cultural message could not remain unaffected. By the 1980s, Darmstadt had become a sleek establishment indeed; a book published in 1991 listed the sponsors of the famous summer courses as including "music publishers, automobile manufacturers, radio and television stations, and an impressive number of state and city officials." That co-opting of the enterprise will be something to keep in mind when it comes time to assess the inevitable reaction against it, widely billed as the "death of the avant-garde." Its demise was already implicit in the nature of its success.

CHAPTER 2

Indeterminacy

CAGE AND THE "NEW YORK SCHOOL"

MEANS AND ENDS

The American counterpart to the postwar avant-garde in Europe was a group of composers and performers gathered around the charismatic figure of John Cage (1912–92). Their methods differed so radically from those of the Europeans as to hide their basic affinities from many contemporary observers. What they shared, however, went much deeper than their differences, for both groups sought "automatism," the resolute elimination of the artist's ego or personality from the artistic product. It was a traditional modernist aim (compare Josè Ortega y Gasset's ideal of "dehumanization", enunciated in a celebrated essay of 1925), pushed to a hitherto unimaginable extremity.

The Americans went about the task with such stunning directness as to put themselves almost wholly outside what anyone could possibly think of as the musical mainstream. Cage in particular, an inveterate maverick, was long thought of as a joker — or at least a "dadaist" — on the margins of the legitimate musical world. The postwar existentialist mood, however, and especially the European "zero hour," brought the mainstream round to him, and he became for a while perhaps the most influential musician in the world.

Like Henry Cowell, his early mentor, Cage was born and grew up in California, far from the power centers of the Eurocentric mainstream. Almost his entire formal music education consisted of childhood piano lessons. He never attended a conservatory, and never acquired the basic skills in ear training and sight singing normally thought necessary for creative work in music. He audited some of Schoenberg's theory courses at UCLA and the University of Southern California beginning in the summer of 1935, and thereafter called himself a Schoenberg pupil,[1] but as a composer (except for some sporadic private lessons with Adolph Weiss, a genuine Schoenberg pupil who was the first American to use the twelve-tone system) he was self-taught — a "primitive." "The whole pitch aspect of music eludes me,"[2] he once cheerfully told an interviewer, no doubt exaggerating for effect. But it could be fairly said that his whole career was devoted to countering the supremacy of traditional pitch organization — harmony, counterpoint, and all the rest — as the basis for making music. A few unpromising apprentice works aside, his earliest original compositions, beginning with a Quartet composed in 1935, were for percussion ensembles that included pots and pans and other household items ("Living Room Music," as he actually titled one piece) in addition to more conventional percussion instruments.

In composing them, Cage was putting into practice a theory that he enunciated, in an astonishingly developed form, in a lecture called "The Future of Music: Credo," first delivered in Seattle in 1940, under the auspices of Bonnie Bird, a dancer who had hired him to accompany her classes, when he was a twenty-eight-year-old unknown. "The present methods of writing music, principally those which employ harmony and its reference to particular steps in the field of sound, will be inadequate for the composer, who will be faced with the entire field of sound."[3] Where Schoenberg had "emancipated the dissonance," in other words, Cage now proposed to complete the job and emancipate noise. This was the basis for his interest in percussion music.

But the implications went much further. Having envisioned a music that might include, as he put it, "a quartet for explosive motor, wind, heartbeat, and landslide," and anticipating objections from those for whom "the word 'music' is sacred and reserved for eighteenth- and nineteenth-century instruments," Cage suggested that the word be abolished for new creation and replaced with "a more meaningful term: organized sound." From this emerged an even more radical thought:

> The composer (organizer of sound) will be faced not only with the entire field of sound but also with the entire field of time. The "frame" or fraction of a second, following established film technique, will probably be the basic unit in the measurement of time. No rhythm will be beyond the composer's reach.[4]

So the music of the future, as Cage envisioned it, would not merely replace one type of sound with another on its sounding surface, but would entail an entirely new ordering of the musical elements, with duration rather than pitch as the fundamental organizing principle. Duration, Cage argued, was the fundamental musical element, since all sounds — and silence, too — had it in common. And therefore, he could aver, he was the only contemporary musician who was dealing newly with music on its root (i.e., "radical") level. Accordingly, most of Cage's early percussion pieces, like most of the music he would write forever after, were based on abstract durational schemes — "empty containers," he called them, to be filled with sounds — that replaced the abstract harmonic schemes of the classical tradition.

Imaginary Landscape No. 1 (Ex. 2-1), composed in 1939, was the first piece in which Cage filled an empty container with sounds. The container consisted of four sections each comprising fifteen (3×5) measures, separated by interludes that grow progressively in length from one to three measures, and followed by a four-measure coda to complete the growth progression. (Ex. 2-1 shows the first two sections and the first two interludes.) The sounds were furnished by a quartet consisting of a muted piano, a suspended cymbal, and two variable-speed turntables on which single-frequency radio test records were played at various steady speeds and also sliding between speeds in siren-like glissandos. The title came by its surrealist ring honestly; Cage had been commissioned to provide music to accompany a performance of Cocteau's *Les mariés de la tour Eiffel*, the very skit for which the composers of Les Six had a written a ballet in 1921. For Cage, the idea of the "imaginary landscape" was a striking spatial analogy for his preplanned temporal schemes; he used it as a title several times.

In later percussion compositions, Cage incorporated instruments or sonorities associated with various kinds of Asian and Caribbean repertoires, like the Indonesian *gamelan*, an orchestra of metallic percussion (compare Cage's two *Constructions in Metal*, composed in 1939 and 1940), or Afro-Cuban pop music, in which elements of West-African drumming were combined with the rhythms of syncopated Latin-American ballroom dances. An inventory of percussion instruments in Cage's collection, drawn up in 1940 when he formed a regular touring ensemble to perform his own percussion music

EX. 2-1   John Cage, *Imaginary Landscape No. 1*, beginning

EX. 2-1 (*continued*)

and that of other composers, included a large assortment of Afro-Cuban instruments (bongos, *quijadas* or rattles, *güiro* or scraped gourd, *marimbula, maracas, claves*, etc.).[5]

Cage's performances with his ten-piece percussion ensemble (whose members included his wife Xenia and Merce Cunningham, later a prominent modern dancer) culminated in a concert at the New York Museum of Modern Art on 7 February 1943. It was widely written up in the press, including a picture spread in *Life* magazine, and won him his first fame. The program on that occasion, which featured Cage's *Constructions* alongside works by the Cuban composer Amadeo Roldán (1900–39), was covered mainly for its exotic curiosity value. The musicians dressed formally and behaved with punctilious decorum. But it is already evident that, although his manner was polite and friendly, Cage had anticipated the intransigent renunciations of the postwar avant-garde, turning his back on virtually the whole European art-musical tradition while claiming a place within it.

Even before that concert, Cage had taken a step that would bring him additional notoriety, and see him creatively through the 1940s. One of Bonnie Bird's pupils, an African-American dancer named Syvilla Fort, had worked up a neoprimitivist dance solo called *Bacchanale* for her graduation recital in 1940 and asked Cage to provide an accompaniment for it. The performance space was too small to accommodate a percussion ensemble, so (recalling Cowell's experiments in extended piano technique) Cage ingeniously turned an ordinary piano into a one-man percussion band by inserting metal screws, pencil erasers and other homely devices between the piano strings to deaden the pitch or otherwise alter the timbre. He called his invention the "prepared piano"; skeptics called it the "well-tampered clavier."

A glance at the score (Ex. 2-2) is enough to verify that Cage's neoprimitivism was of the conventional, ostinato-driven sort established for all time (or so it seemed) by Stravinsky's *Rite of Spring*. What cannot be gleaned at all from the score is any idea of what the piece sounds like in terms of pitch or timbre, since the sounds of a prepared piano no longer have any predictable relationship to the keys that activate the strings. In this sense a prepared piano score is like an old "tablature" for lute or keyboard, of a kind widely used in the sixteenth and seventeenth centuries. It prescribes the player's actions directly, the resulting sounds only indirectly (based on the tuning of the lute or, in Cage's case, the specifications for piano-preparation that come with the sheet music).

Between 1940 and 1954 Cage produced some two dozen works for his new percussive medium. They constitute a major body of twentieth-century keyboard music. At first they were mainly orgiastic, rather patronizingly neo-Africanist dance pieces like the original *Bacchanale*—for example, *Primitive* or *Totem Ancestor* (both 1942)—but around 1944 Cage began using the medium to write pieces meant not for dance accompaniment but for "pure" concert use. The summit of his achievement in the medium was an hour-long set of *Sonatas and Interludes* (1946–48), in which the sonatas were of the Scarlattian type (single binary-form movements, with repeats) and the interludes consisted, very often, of very sparsely filled time-containers. It was Cage's single concession to then-fashionable neoclassicism.

In terms of its significance within his career, however, the most important of Cage's prepared-piano compositions was a six-movement suite called *The Perilous Night* (1944), which carried, and sought to convey, a strong emotional charge. Cage always referred to it as his "autobiographical"[6] piece, and his biographer David Revill has convincingly associated it with the traumas associated with Cage's sexual reorientation, culminating (1945) in divorce from his wife and the beginning of a monogamous homosexual partnership with Merce Cunningham that lasted to the end of his life.

It may be difficult in more tolerant times to recall the stigma once associated with homosexual liaisons, and the emotional trials that reordering one's life on less than socially respectable terms then entailed. At any rate, *The Perilous Night* was Cage's attempt to express, and thereby relieve, the anxieties he was experiencing in his private life. One can understand his distress, then, when a frivolous critic, who could not get over the shock of the novel prepared-piano timbres, dismissed this most intimately confessional of all Cage's works with the remark that it sounded like "a woodpecker in a church belfry."[7] The wounded composer talked about this experience for the rest of his life. Thenceforth, he once told an interviewer, "I could not accept the academic idea that the purpose of music was communication."[8] Another time, even more strongly, he said that after the *Perilous Night* fiasco, "I determined to give up composition unless I could find a better reason for doing it than communication." One might say that the bruise that Cage received from an uncaring philistine equipped him with the resentment and aggression that a truly avant-garde artist needs.

EX. 2-2   John Cage, *Bacchanale*, "piano preparation" chart and first page of musical notation

Piano Preparation

Tone	Material	String (left to right)	Distance From Damper
	small bolt	2-3	circa 3"
	weather stripping*	1-2	**
	screw with nuts & weather stripping*	2-3 1-2	** **
	weather stripping*	1-2	**
	weather stripping*	1-2	**
	weather stripping*	1-2	**
	weather stripping*	1-2	**
	weather stripping*	1-2	**
	weather stripping*	1-2	**
	weather stripping*	1-2	**
	weather stripping*	1-2	**
	weather stripping*	1-2	**

*fibrous

**determine position and size of mutes by experiment

EX. 2-2   (*continued*)

WHOSE LIBERATION?

What better reasons did he find? The one that he liked to offer was spiritualistic and vaguely "oriental," borrowed in the 1940s from an Indian friend, Gita Sarabhai, with whom he was exchanging music lessons, and from whom he learned about the Indian concept of *tala*, a predetermined rhythmic structure (comparable, as already observed in connection with Messaien, to the talea of the medieval motet) in which he saw reflected his own ideas about "containers." The purpose of music, she told him (quoting her own Indian music master) was "to sober and quiet the mind, thus making it susceptible to divine influences."[9]

Pressed by a skeptical interviewer, Cage produced a less "churchy" version: "The function of music is to change the mind so that it does become open to experience, which inevitably is interesting."[10] Stripped to its essentials, Cage's doctrine ultimately comes down to what philosophers call particularism or "naive realism": the resolute avoidance of theory, or any mental act of generalization, so as to experience and enjoy the "real" or external world as it is in all its variety, and to perceive things (sounds, for instance) in all their individuality.

Ultimate purposes, however, do not produce a program of action. For managing his creative career from day to day and work to work, Cage embraced the model—inherited, he said, from his father, an inventor—of experimental science. Rather than communication, then, Cage adopted the purposes of research: not the kind of theoretical research in which many modernist artists engaged, which resulted in the extension and rationalization of known techniques toward precisely envisioned aims (e.g., the development of twelve-tone technique to extend and rationalize the principle of *Grundgestalt*, or Webern's refinement of Schoenberg's twelve-tone methods) but truly experimental research in which the outcome of one's actions was unpredicted and, as far as possible, unplanned. Henceforth, Cage's abundant ingenuity would be lavished on strategies to frustrate the planning of results, so that the object he produced would be completely free of his own wishes, preferences, tastes. He envisioned, in short, and strove to achieve, the complete liberation of sound.

But the liberation of sound was in no sense the liberation of the composer, or of any other person. In fact it was more nearly the opposite. Although Cage often described the elaborate methods he devised to realize his new purposes as involving indeterminacy or chance, they were anything but anarchic. In seeming (but only seeming) paradox, the liberation of sound demanded the enslavement, indeed the humiliation, of all human beings concerned—composer, performer, and listener alike—for it demanded the complete suppression of the ego.

Cage came to these precepts, he claimed, through immersion in the quietistic philosophy of Zen Buddhism, a fashionable preoccupation among Euro-American intellectuals in the late 1940s and early 1950s. It seems clear enough in retrospect that the general fascination, just then, with Zen was related to the interest in existentialism described in the preceding chapter, and that both were indirect responses to the stresses of the atomic age and the emergent cold war. Cage was only one of many New Yorkers who flocked to Columbia University, beginning in 1945, to hear the American-educated Daisetz Suzuki (1869–1966), Zen's chief ambassador abroad, give his well-publicized, soothing lectures on the subject. Among Suzuki's other auditors was Jack Kerouac (1922–69), the author who by his example defined the "beat generation," a group of bohemian artists and intellectuals whose seemingly anarchic quest for artless authenticity through irrational behavior and unconsidered experience was also a self-declared adaptation of Zen thinking.

Japanese for "meditation," Zen is an anti-intellectual mental discipline that aims at sudden spiritual illumination by systematically rejecting the illusory safety of rational thought, which it regards as contrary to nature. Its chief methods are *zazen*, long sessions of ritualized contemplation with the mind cleared of all expectation, and *koan*, deliberately paradoxical riddles and sayings, sometimes accompanied by corporal punishments for incorrect (i.e., would-be logical) answers as a form of aversion therapy.

The principle of nonexpectation is clearly, if perhaps superficially, related to Cage's ideal of experimental music; and as some of the quotations from his writings and interviews may have already suggested, Cage loved to express his ideas in the baffling manner of a koan.

Around the same time that Cage was absorbing Zen, in 1950, an aspiring composer named Christian Wolff (b. 1934), the son of a well-known publisher, brought Cage (from whom he was taking lessons) a copy of his father's new edition of the *I Ching* or "Book of Changes," an ancient Chinese manual of divination, the art of reading portents to gain knowledge unavailable to reason. The user of the *I Ching* would toss three coins (or six sticks) six times to determine which of sixty-four possible hexagrams (combinations of six continuous or broken lines) to consult in answer to a question about the future or some other unobservable thing (see Fig. 2-1 for the first sixteen of the possible sixty-four). By associating the hexagrams with musical parameters (pitch, duration, loudness, attack, etc.) Cage was able to convert the coin-tossing method into a means of eliminating his habits or desires (or as he put it, "memories, tastes, likes and dislikes"[11]) as factors in making compositional decisions. Once he had decided how the coin tosses would determine the musical results, he could relinquish control of the process and compose "non-intentionally," as Zen prescribed.

Although it may look like some kind of esoteric religious syncretism, and although that may have been its justification in Cage's own mind, his mixture of Zen with *I Ching* was a practical stroke of genius. The predetermination of the relationships between the divination charts and the musical results was precisely the sort of music-producing algorithm that Boulez and Stockhausen and their Darmstadt colleagues had been seeking via the multiple application of the twelve-tone serial principle. The difference was simply that whereas Boulez, having determined the broad outlines of structure, handed the specific contents of his work over to the serial operations designed to control it, Cage handed the specific contents of his work over to Dame Fortune (alias Lady Luck). His was a much more direct route to the "automatism" that the times demanded.

Indeed, for all their differences in background and method, Cage and Boulez immediately recognized that they were kindred spirits. They met in Paris in 1949, when Boulez had just written his Second Piano Sonata, a sprawling work that deals at Schoenbergian length with tiny Webernian pitch cells, building up saturated but inchoate motivic textures that in their fragmented, "pointillistic" approach to pitch register, dynamics, and articulation never

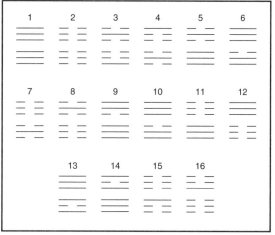

FIG. 2-1　Hexagrams from the I Ching. Each design is a combination of unbroken (*yin*) and broken (*yang*) lines.

coalesce into any recurrent or otherwise memorable thematic substance and never harden into any generic formal mold. It was in effect a fierce manifesto against neo-classicism, against all musical "business as usual." Cage, fresh from his *Sonatas and Interludes*, was left "trembling in the face of great complexity"[12] after hearing Boulez play it. Christian Wolff's fortuitous gift, the *I Ching*, gave him the means of equaling, in fact surpassing, Boulez's iconoclastic tour de force.

The first work Cage composed by tossing coins was titled, appropriately enough, *Music of Changes*. Like Boulez's Sonata, it was a huge, monumentally serious work for piano in several movements in an atomized or pointillistic style. Boulez and Cage kept up a lively, now published correspondence while Cage was at work on the *Music of Changes* and Boulez, partly under Cage's influence, worked on *Structures*, his most automatistic piece. Their letters contain joyously detailed technical descriptions of their elaborate methods, conveying tremendous excitement and providing a wonderful source for historians and analysts. Sometimes Cage would write a relatively skimpy letter, for which he would apologize by reminding Boulez, as he put it in one of them, "that I spend a great deal of time tossing coins, and the emptiness of head that that induces begins to penetrate the rest of my time as well."[13] The elegance of the phrasing shows how much personality and cultivated intellect Cage was willing to renounce in his quest for musical "reality." Boulez was respectful of that, and perhaps a little envious. It led eventually to a break. For whereas Boulez's serial operations established multifarious arbitrary relationships among the events that took place in the score, Cage's chance operations generated truly atomistic sequences in which every event was generated independently of every other. His methods explicitly destroyed relationships ("weeded them out,"[14] he crowed) because attention to the fashioning of relationships, being egoistic, defeated the impersonalism demanded not only by Zen but by the "zero hour" mood in which (as Boulez himself loudly insisted) everyone alive to the tenor of the times had to participate. Music that contained lots of significant abstract relationships defeated the whole nature (or "reality") of music, Cage declared. Instead of listening, one analyzed.

"Composers," he gibed, "are spoken of as having ears for music which generally means that nothing presented to their ears can be heard by them."[15] Boulez's product, being full of relationships, could be parsed in traditional ways. Its events could be reduced to general principles. Its methods could be rationally deduced. All of that gave reassuring evidence, despite the zero-hour rhetoric, of an "ear for music," a controlling intelligence, a respectable moral accountability. By incorporating chance operations into the composing process, Cage was issuing a challenge to really stand behind the rhetoric and give up all traditional artistic values. (In a way, the best proof that Cage practiced what he preached, unquestioningly accepting the gifts of chance, is the presence in *Music of Changes* of occasional triadic harmonies that a serial composer would have been sure to purge from the score—see the "d-minor triad in first inversion" in the first measure of Ex. 2-3.) That much renunciation was too much for the Europeans. Boulez and Stockhausen each made token gestures in the direction of Cageian "indeterminacy," Stockhausen with his *Klavierstück XI* (1956), described in the previous chapter, and

Boulez with the Third Piano Sonata (1955–57) a five-movement work in which the order of the movements (or "formants," as Boulez called them) could be rearranged around the central "Constellation," and in which the order of sections within movements were also subject to some limited variation. (Cage had anticipated this idea, too, in his *Music for Piano* 4–19 of 1953, consisting of *I Ching*-derived material notated on a sheaf of sixteen unbound and shuffleable pages that "may be played as separate pieces or continuously as one piece or:" [*sic*].)

Boulez published a manifesto of his own, called "Aléa" (from the Latin for dice), in which he described the "open form" concept his new Sonata exemplified, carefully tracing its origin not to Cage but to the French literary avant-garde from Stéphane Mallarmé to the contemporary novelist Alain Robbe-Grillet (1922–2008). His main contribution to the evolving theory of musical contingency was the word "aleatoric," now often used to describe music composed (or performed) to some degree according to chance operations or spontaneous decision. The degree of indeterminacy that Boulez and Stockhausen found admissible, however, never approached Cage's; and by thus exposing the limits to their avant-gardism (or, to put it the other way around, exposing their residual conservatism) Cage became for them a threatening presence.

The high point of their association came in 1958, when Cage and the pianist David Tudor (1926–96) visited Darmstadt, where they gave concerts and Cage directed a seminar on experimental music. (An earlier appearance, in 1954, at the old European new-music festival at Donaueschingen had been a jeered fiasco.) Cage proved a charismatic presence at Darmstadt. An oft-reproduced photograph, taken at the Brussels World Fair that summer (where the Philips audio company maintained a pavilion and commissioned some composers of the European avant-garde to create a sonic ambience that would show off its sound equipment) shows Cage comfortably at home in the presence of his European counterparts (Fig. 2-2). That fall he spent some months at Milan, at the invitation of Luciano Berio, a Darmstadt alumnus who made his experimental music studio at the state-subsidized radio station available to Cage.

Relations inevitably cooled thereafter. The Europeans, with their sense of inherited tradition (try as they might to repudiate it), could never reconcile themselves to the randomly generated sounds with which Cage, the innocent American, was happy to fill his time containers. Cage loved to tell the story of the Dutch musician who said to him, "It must be very difficult for you in America to write music, for you are so far away from the centers of tradition." Of course Cage replied, "It must be very difficult for you in Europe to write music, for you are so close to the centers of tradition."[16]

Cage's audience, both at home and abroad, was increasingly drawn from the tolerantly eclectic worlds of visual arts and modern dance rather than the tense musical establishment, even the established avant-garde. He was just too effortlessly further-out-than-thou, or so it seemed to them. "I like fun," the poet John Hollander sneered in an American new-music magazine, "but I shall resist the impulse to have as much fun being a critic as Mr. Cage has being a composer."[17] Yet Cage was not just having fun. His schemes were just as complicated, just as exacting, just as pitiless as a total serialist's.

EX. 2-3 John Cage, *Music of Changes*, II, fourth page of score (diamond note-heads indicate keys silently depressed)

Chance operations were anything but labor-saving. Cage's motives did not differ from those of the composers who were now writing him off, and his product (as long as he was writing for conventional instruments) resembled theirs far more than they were prepared to admit. All that differed were the means. But the means seemed, in the eyes of many, to outweigh motives and ends. And that says a lot about modernism.

FIG. 2-2   The assembled transatlantic avant-garde at the Philips pavilion, Brussels World's Fair, 1958: John Cage is supine on the floor. Kneeling above him are (left to right) Maricio Kagel (1931–2008), a German composer of Argentine birth; Earle Brown; Luciano Berio; and Stockhausen. Standing behind them are Henk Badings (1907–1987), a Dutch composer; André Boucourechliev (1925–1997), a Bulgarian-born French composer and writer on music; Bruno Maderna; Henri Pousseur (b. 1929), a Belgian composer and music theorist; Mlle. Seriahine of the Philips Company; Luc Ferrari (b. 1929), a French composer; and Pierre Schaeffer.

NE PLUS ULTRA (GOING AS FAR AS YOU CAN GO)

It also says a lot about Romanticism. Cage's activity, more than that of any other individual, reveals the latent continuity between the Romantic impulse and the impulses that drove modernism, even (or especially) its most intransigent, avant-garde wing. His unsettling presence on the scene replayed the esthetic battles of the nineteenth century, splitting the avant-garde all over again into what the German poet Friedrich Schiller had called "naive and sentimental poets" in a famous essay of 1795. Sentimental poets were the kind "whose soul suffers no impression without at once turning to contemplate its own play."[18] Such artists were egoists, forever proclaiming their purposes and analyzing their methods, even when consciously directing their purposes and methods toward the elimination of ego. Hence the need for magazines like *Die Reihe*, the organ of the "sentimental" Darmstadt school, full of scientific or pseudoscientific explanations, formal justifications and, above all, rationalizations.

Naive poets (in Schiller's words) celebrated "the object itself," not "what the reflective understanding of the poet has made." Or as Cage put it, "the division is between understanding and experiencing, and many people think that art has to do with understanding, but it doesn't."[19] To relinquish rational reflection, Schiller said, leads to "tranquillity, purity and joy." Or as Cage put it, "the highest purpose is to have no purpose at all. This puts one in accord with nature in her manner of operation."[20] In saying this Cage thought that he was expressing the main principle of Zen, even though the aphorism itself was a paraphrase of one he had come across in the writings of the Indian art scholar Ananda Coomaraswamy (1877–1947). But appropriating and paraphrasing "oriental" philosophy was nothing new. Cage was doing exactly what Arthur Schopenhauer, the German Romantic writer who had exerted such a decisive influence on Wagner a hundred years before, had done; Schopenhauer, too, had claimed that he was bringing the wisdom of Hinduism and Buddhism to the West, when in fact he was pioneering a new Romantic esthetic.

Cage's principle of "purposeful purposelessness," whatever its remote links to Hinduism or Buddhism, was the direct descendent (or, to put it musically, an inversion) of the "purposeless purposefulness" (*Zweckmässigkeit ohne Zweck*[21]) by which Immanuel Kant had defined the brand-new Western concept of "the esthetic" in his *Critique of Judgement*, published in 1790. Like Cage, Kant was after purity. The esthetic, in Kant's definition, was a quality of beauty that wholly transcended utility. Esthetic objects existed — that is, were made — entirely for their own sake, requiring "disinterestedness" and zealous application on the part of the maker, and a corresponding act of disinterested, self-forgetting contemplation on the part of the beholder. As we have known, so to speak, for two hundred years, autonomous works of art occupied a special hallowed sphere, for which special places were set aside (museums and concert halls, "temples of art"), and where special modes of reverent behavior were observed, or, when necessary, imposed.

As we have also long known, music, inherently abstract to some degree owing to its lack of an obvious natural model, quickly became the Romantic art of choice, the most sacred of the autonomous arts. Not only for that reason, but also because it was a performing art in which a potentially meddlesome middleman stood between the maker and the beholder, "classical" music developed the most ritualized and the most hierarchical social practices. Like many artists, especially in liberal and democratic America, Cage consciously opposed this notoriously oppressive social practice: "The composer," he told an interviewer, "was the genius, the conductor ordered everyone around and the performers were slaves."[22] (And the listener? An innocent bystander.) As we shall see, though, his work went on upholding it in spite of himself.

The composer's status was enhanced, and the performer's demeaned, precisely because the new romantic concept of the autonomous artwork sharply differentiated their roles and assigned them vastly unequal value. The composer created the potentially immortal esthetic object. The performer was just an ephemeral mediator. Musical works that were too closely allied with egoistical performance values (virtuoso concertos, for example), or that too obviously catered to the needs or the whims of an audience, or even that too grossly represented the personality of the composer, were regarded as sullied because they had, in Kant's terms, a *Zweck*, a utilitarian purpose that compromised their autonomy. The only truly artistic purpose was that of transcending utilitarian purpose.

The art that most fully met this prescription, as we have long known, was "absolute music." It fell to Cage to magnify and purify the notion of absolute music beyond anything the romantics had foreseen. In his compositions of the 1950s, romantic art reached the most astounding, self-subverting purism of its whole career. In this way, Cage's "Zen" period paradoxically represented a long-heralded, if little recognized, pinnacle of Western art. In so doing, it reexposed with unprecedented boldness the problematic and self-contradictory aspects of the idea of absolute music, the West's most cherished esthetic tenet.

Cage reopened all the old questions: How does an art form that is inherently temporal achieve transcendent objectification? What is the actual ontological status (i.e., the status as "object") of a musical work? How does "the work" as such (or as an idea) relate to its performances? To its written score? The Polish philosopher Roman Ingarden once teasingly summed up all of these pesky ontological questions when he asked, "Where is Chopin's B-minor Sonata?"[23] Cage provided the most cogent, and therefore the most unsettling, answers.

We have seen that the essential structure, the "workhood," of a formalistic composition like Boulez's *Structures* can have rather little to do with its aural experience. Cage's highly determined "containers" were even more arcane, because they had even less to do with the often wholly indeterminate sounds that now filled them. Cage was fully aware of these problems, and engaged with them both playfully and in deadly earnest in his "Lecture on Nothing" of 1959, which begins with a sort of Zen koan that on repetition becomes a mantra: "I have nothing to say and I am saying it and that is poetry."

The Lecture is not really a lecture, though; it is a typical Cage composition consisting of a predetermined time-container. The filling in this case consists of familiar words in grammatical sentences that chiefly concern the filling process itself. Here is an excerpt, which the reader is invited to recite aloud, pausing in accordance with the spatial layout:

Here we are now   at the beginning   of the
eleventh unit of the fourth large part   of this talk.
More and more   I have the feeling
            that we are getting
nowhere. Slowly   ,   as the talk goes on
,   we are getting   nowhere
            and that is a pleasure
.   It is not irritating   to be where one is
.   It is only irritating
to think that one likes   to be somewhere else.
            Here we are now
,   a little bit after the   beginning
of the eleventh unit   of the
fourth large part   of this talk .
    More and more   we have the feeling
    that I am getting   nowhere

Slowly   ,
as the talk goes on ,   slowly
,   we have the feeling
    we are getting   nowhere
.

        That is a pleasure
    which will continue   .
    If we are irritated   ,
    it is not a pleasure .
Nothing is not   a   pleasure
if one is irritated   ,   but suddenly
,   it is a pleasure   ,
and then more and more   it is not irritating
(and then more and more   and slowly   ).
Originally ,   we were nowhere   ;
If anybody is sleepy ,   let him go to sleep
.   Here we are now   at the beginning of the
thirteenth unit   of the fourth large part
of this talk.   More and more
I have the feeling   that we are getting
nowhere.

Cage's *Imaginary Landscape No. 3* (1942) is scored, in the manner of its time, for several audio-frequency oscillators, two variable-speed turntables, an electric buzzer, and several other pieces of audio equipment. Nine years later, after his encounter with Zen and the *I Ching*, Cage returned to the surrealistic genre he had invented and found a way, by tossing his coins, to compose a fully determined score that would produce a completely indeterminate, hence completely autonomous performance.

The work that accomplished this breakthrough was *Imaginary Landscape No. 4* (1951), scored for twenty-four players playing twelve radios under the direction of a conductor. Two players are assigned to each radio: one controls the volume knob, the other the tuner. The score, notated in fairly conventional notation that looks quite intricately contrapuntal, directs that the players turn the knobs at specified times to specified frequencies (where there may or may not be a broadcast signal) and amplitudes (many much softer than comfortable listening volume).

The conductor executes all kinds of tempo changes that relate only to the "work" as notated, not to the aural experience, which depends on entirely unpredictable and uncontrolled factors. His elaborately choreographed actions, often eliciting no discernable result, pointedly signal the abstractness and the autonomy of the work-concept. The first performance, which took place late at night when there was very little on the air, was an apparent fiasco, but its very sparseness illustrated all the more forcefully how unstable the ontological relationship between the prescribed work (as an ideal object) and the actual physical performance could be.

Any whiff of spoof—there is always nervous laughter at performances—is definitely an illusion. When Virgil Thomson told Cage he didn't think a piece like that ought to be performed before a paying audience, Cage took extreme umbrage and it caused a permanent rift in their relationship.[24] Perhaps needless to say, the piece has never been recorded. What would be the point?

Strangely enough, however, the celebrated 4'33" (1952), Cage's most extreme experiment in indeterminacy, has been recorded several times, icon that it has become. Its subtitle is "Tacet for any instrument or instruments," and Cage (who according to his biographer always spoke of it "reverentially"[25]) called it his "silent piece." But that is a misnomer. It is, rather, a piece for a silent performer or performers who enter a performance space, signal the beginnings and the ends of three movements whose timings and internal "structural" subdivisions have been predetermined by chance operations, but make no intentional sound. (Usually the performer is a pianist and the signals are given by most carefully and noiselessly closing and raising the keyboard lid.) The piece consists of whatever sounds occur within a listener's earshot during these articulated spans.

This might seem on the face of it the very antithesis of an autonomous work of art, since the sounds are wholly contingent, outside the composer's control. (Cage often maintained that his aim in composing the piece was to erase the boundary between art and life.) But sounds are not the only thing that a composer controls, and sounds are not the only thing that constitutes a musical work. Under the social regimen of modern concert life, the composer controls not just sounds but people, and a work is defined not just by its contents but also by the behavior that it elicits from an audience. As the philosopher Lydia Goehr has observed,

> It is because of Cage's specifications that people gather together, usually in a concert hall, to listen to the sounds of the hall for the allotted time period. In ironic gesture, it is Cage who specifies that a pianist should sit at a piano to go through the motions of performance. The performer is applauded and the composer granted recognition for the "work." Whatever changes have come about in our material understanding of musical sound, the formal constraints of the work-concept have ironically been maintained.[26]

And she comments tactfully, in the form of a question, "Did Cage come to the compositional decisions that he did out of recognition that people will only listen to sounds around them if they are forced to do so under traditional, formal constraints?"

It is a profound political point. A work that is touted as a liberation from esthetics in fact brings an alert philosopher to a fuller awareness of all the constraints that the category of "the esthetic" imposes. Sounds that were noise on one side of an arbitrary framing gesture are suddenly music, a "work of art," on the other side. The esthetic comes into being by sheer fiat, at the drop of a piano lid. The audience is invited — no, commanded — to listen to ambient or natural sounds with the same attitude of reverent contemplation they would assume if they were listening to Beethoven's Ninth.

That is an attitude that is born not of nature, but of Beethoven. By the act of triggering it, art is not brought down to earth in the least. On the contrary, "life" is brought up for the duration into the transcendent. 4'33" is thus the ultimate esthetic aggrandizement. Like any other musical "work," it has a published, copyrighted score. The space on its pages, measured from left to right, corresponds to the elapsing time. Most of the pages have vertical lines drawn on them, denoting the chance-calculated time articulations on which the duration of the piece depends. One of the pages, bypassed by these markers, remains blank. If copyrighting a blank page is not an act of esthetic grandiosity, what is?

FIG. 2-3   Marcel Duchamp, *Fountain* (1917); replica, 1964.

So Cage's radical conceptions were as much intensifications of traditional practices, including traditional power relations, as departures from them. And they kept up a tradition of art-as-philosophy that was wholly a phase of the Western romantic tradition. The most obvious predecessor to 4'33" was a work of visual rather than musical art: *Fountain* (1917) by the painter Marcel Duchamp (1887–1968), who later became a close friend and mentor to Cage. Asked to submit a work for a jury-free exhibition organized by an avant-garde artists' society of which he was a prominent member, Duchamp purchased a commercially manufactured porcelain urinal, signed it "R. Mutt," and sent it in. On its rejection he noisily resigned from the society, turning his "readymade" or found object into a much-exhibited cause célèbre, paradoxically one of the most famous artworks of the early twentieth century (Fig. 2-3).

The immediate effect of Duchamp's *Fountain* was similar to that of Cage's early chance pieces: it exposed the residual or "invisible" restrictions that continued to operate behind a self-advertised facade of liberation, forcing even the most extreme modernists to acknowledge their sentimental ties to the past or stand convicted of hypocrisy. Once exhibited, however, the work acquired a new meaning: a test, or limit-case, to define the nature of art not just according to the artist's intent but according to the mode of its reception.

If people walked by his signed urinal and, rather than using it as its manufacturer intended, looked at it the way they looked at the more conventional art works in the gallery, then their act of "disinterested" contemplation defined it as — or, more strongly, transformed it into — a work of art. Even if, as was sometimes claimed, it was Duchamp's signature (the signature of a recognized "genius") that turned a piece of plumbing into art, the act required the public's collusion. They were free to reject his gesture, but they did not. Art is defined, as in the case of 4'33", by the behavior that it induces. All that it takes to make art these days, cynics muttered (and philosophers admitted), was a frame.

But there was nothing as inherently provocative in 4'33" as the selection of something normally fouled by body waste for transformation into art. On the contrary, Cage's conception of the piece (and by now the reaction of most audiences as well) was entirely one of reverence — the reverence that was due not only to sacralized nature, but also to sacralized art in the Beethovenian tradition. In keeping with that tradition, it was left to a musician to achieve the ultimate transcendence of life into art. For music did not necessarily carry automatic "life" associations the way a urinal (or any other physical object) did.

Especially in the age of recordings, music had no necessary physical presence at all. (Was it a coincidence that the length of Cage's piece was exactly that of a 12-inch 78

RPM "side"?) Even if one exhibited an empty frame in a museum gallery, there would be a physical object, and a "normal" utilitarian association, to limit the viewer's reaction. Paintings and frames were not only art objects but life objects as well. *4′33″* was literally a blank, a void, on which anyone could inscribe anything. To an extent unavailable to any other art medium, Cage's silent performance was divorced from surrounding "life," which normally contains lots of music. But all of that music was specifically excluded by the "silence."

PURIFICATION AND ITS DISCONTENTS

That excluded music was the utilitarian music that accompanies our everyday lives and that does not require special temples for its contemplation, including all popular music. Cage's attitude in *4′33″* was just as purified of the popular as any other kind of midcentury sacralized art (say, a Beethoven symphony recorded by Toscanini), and it was an especially poignant purification in Cage's case since his early percussion and prepared-piano music had been so full of popular-music resonances. Once Cage became a prophet of purity, a "Beethoven," his earlier life was rewritten as myth, a myth that no longer contained any reference to the Asian or Afro-Cuban musics that had inspired Cage in his West Coast youth, although it did anachronistically prefigure his discovery of nonintention and chance.

Here, for example, is an abridgment of Cage's own account, published in 1973 and titled like a fable or a fairy tale, of his first prepared-piano composition:

HOW THE PIANO CAME TO BE PREPARED
In the late thirties I was employed as an accompanist for the classes in modern dance at the Cornish School in Seattle, Washington. These classes were taught by Bonnie Bird, who had been a member of Martha Graham's company. Among her pupils was an extraordinary dancer, Syvilla Fort. Three or four days before she was to perform her *Bacchanal*, Syvilla asked me to write music for it. I agreed.

At that time I had two ways of composing: for piano or orchestral instruments I wrote twelve-tone music (I had studied with Adolph Weiss and Arnold Schoenberg); I also wrote music for percussion ensembles: pieces for three, four, or six players.

The Cornish Theatre in which Syvilla Fort was to perform had no space in the wings. There was also no pit. There was, however, a piano at one side in front of the stage. I couldn't use percussion instruments for Syvilla's dance, though, suggesting Africa, they would have been suitable; they would have left too little room for her to perform. I was obliged to write a piano piece.

I spent a day or so conscientiously trying to find an African twelve-tone row. I had no luck. I decided that what was wrong was not me but the piano. I decided to change it.

Besides studying with Weiss and Schoenberg, I had also studied with Henry Cowell. I had often heard him play a grand piano, changing its sound by plucking and muting the strings with fingers and hands. I particularly loved to hear him play *The Banshee*. To do this, Henry Cowell first depressed the pedal with a wedge at the back (or asked an assistant, sometimes myself, to sit at the keyboard and hold the pedal down), and then, standing at the back of the piano, he produced the music by lengthwise friction on the bass strings with his fingers or fingernails, and by crosswise sweeping of the bass strings with the palms of his hands. In another piece he used a darning egg, moving it lengthwise along the strings while trilling, as I recall, on the keyboard; this produced a glissando of harmonics.

Having decided to change the sound of the piano in order to make a music suitable for Syvilla Fort's *Bacchanal*, I went to the kitchen, got a pie plate, brought it into the living room, and placed it on the piano strings. I played a few keys. The piano sounds had been changed, but the pie plate bounced around due to the vibrations, and, after a while, some of the sounds that had been changed no longer were. I tried something smaller, nails between the strings. They slipped down between and lengthwise along the strings. It dawned on me that screws or bolts would stay in position. They did. And I was delighted to notice that by means of a single preparation two different sounds could be produced. One was resonant and open, the other was quiet and muted. The quiet one was heard whenever the soft pedal was used. I wrote the *Bacchanal* quickly and with the excitement continual discovery provided. [. . .]

When I first placed objects between the strings, it was with the desire to possess sounds (to be able to repeat them). But, as the music left my home and went from piano to piano and from pianist to pianist, it became clear that not only are two pianists essentially different from one another, but two pianos are not the same either. Instead of the possibility of repetition, we are faced in life with the unique qualities and characteristics of each occasion.

The prepared piano, impressions I had from the work of artist friends, study of Zen Buddhism, ramblings in fields and forests looking for mushrooms, all led me to the enjoyment of things as they come, as they happen, rather than as they are possessed or kept or forced to be.[27]

Cage has given himself here an entirely European musical ancestry, one that included Schoenberg, of all contemporary composers the one who most insistently claimed a lineage from Beethoven, but whose influence actually had no bearing at all on Cage's neoprimitive *Bacchanale*. And of Cowell's magnificently eclectic legacy (one that encompassed all the "Music of the World's Peoples," to cite the title of Cowell's popular course at the New School and the once fairly big-selling record set that came out of it) Cage chose only the Irish mythological side, the most European side, to admit to his self-constructed narrative. In later life, Cage even replaced the Indian and Japanese sources of his spiritual philosophy with European and Euro-American ones, claiming a lifelong latent kinship with James Joyce and Henry David Thoreau. At the same time, Cage began to embrace aspects of mainstream culture he had formerly eschewed.

He became fascinated with "big science," the government-subsidized scientific projects of the cold war period, especially computer technology and the exploration of space. Enlisting the help of Lejaren Hiller, a computer engineer and early experimenter with music-writing programs at the University of Illinois, Cage devised a flamboyant mixed-media performance called *HPSCHD* (computerese for "harpsichord"). The piece had been commissioned by a Swiss harpsichordist, Antoinette Vischer, who had little idea of what she was letting herself in for. Her money enabled Cage to buy mainframe computer time and hire a programmer. Programming a computer to make the *I Ching* coin tosses for him enabled Cage to make enough random decisions — more than a million — to keep seven keyboard players (one of them Mme Vischer), fifty-two tape recorders playing random computer-generated "tunes" in fifty-two different tuning systems, fifty-two film projectors and sixty-four slide projectors (showing scenes of space travel, some from old science-fiction movies) constantly busy for four-and-a-half hours in a University of Illinois campus auditorium on the evening of 16 May 1969 (Fig. 2-4).

Another space-age extravaganza was *Atlas eclipticalis* (1962), in which Cage derived eighty-six instrumental parts that could be played in whole or in part, for any duration and in any combination from soloist to full orchestra, by projecting sidereal charts ("star maps") on huge sheets of music paper and inking in a note wherever there was a

FIG. 2-4   Premiere of *HPSCHD* by John Cage and Lejaren Hiller, University of Illinois at Champaign-Urbana, 1969.

heavenly body, later deciding with the aid of the *I Ching* which staves carried which clefs, and how they were to be assigned to the various instruments of the orchestra. Leonard Bernstein, then the conductor of the New York Philharmonic-Symphony Orchestra, selected *Atlas eclipticalis*, the only Cage piece as of then that could enlist his whole band, for a performance in February 1964 that would introduce the work of the avant-garde to an unprecedentedly large audience. (A piece by Cage's avant-garde colleague Earle Brown was also scheduled, together with Vivaldi's *Four Seasons* and Chaikovsky's *Pathétique* Symphony.)

The performance was a fiasco, compared by many to the scandalous first night of Stravinsky's *Rite of Spring*. There was a significant difference, however: the orchestra rebelled along with the audience. When Cage took his bows he heard their hissing behind him; and at the last performance they engaged in sabotage, playing scales or banal tunes instead of their prescribed parts, and singing or whistling into the contact microphones attached to their instruments. A few players were so enraged that they threw their microphones on the floor and stamped on them, obliging Cage to replace them out of pocket.

These were regrettable discourtesies, but their explanation may be something more than mere philistinism on the part of unimaginatively conservative musicians, as is usually alleged. Far more frequently than any other modernist composer, Cage got into confrontational situations with performers at various points over the course of his career, and with orchestral musicians in particular. After a performance of another Cage orchestral work by the Los Angeles Philharmonic in 1977, one of the members wrote to the *Los Angeles Times* to complain that "no musical training is necessary for this quasi-intellectual trash, only the ability to make noise for thirty embarrassing minutes. I felt ashamed to sit on stage and be a part of it."[28] As noted earlier, Cage himself has acknowledged, and at times decried, the way in which the social practices that have grown up around the sacralized work-object since the advent of Romanticism have tended to dehumanize performers, especially those who play under conductors. The only way in which such musicians are able to retain a sense of personal dignity is by believing in the esthetic of communication or self-expression (expanded to encompass a notion of collective self-expression), the very notion that Cage devoted his career to discrediting. When asked to perform works based on the principle of nonintention, the contradiction has been for many musicians unendurable, because such works present performers with a set of especially arbitrary, hence (potentially) especially demeaning, commands. They are intolerably deprived of their normal sense (or illusion) of creative collaboration.

The contact mikes in *Atlas eclipticalis*, which fed each player's sound into a mixing console that, operating on the usual chance principles, added an extra dimension of unpredictability to the proceedings, were a special outrage. As Earle Brown explained, "Even if you were making your choices with diligence, you might be turned off. Maybe you were heard, maybe you weren't."[29] The composer, though ostensibly (and, from his own perspective, sincerely) aiming to efface his ego — and ostensibly (and equally sincerely) opposed, as Cage put it, to "the conventional musical situation of a composer telling others what to do" — became more than ever the peremptory genius, the players more than ever the slaves. By forcing others to efface their egos along with his, he had become an oppressor. His effacement was voluntary; theirs wasn't.

Even soloists devoted to Cage have recognized the paradoxical reinforcement that his work has given to the old hierarchies. By the use of chance operations, Cage said, he was able to shift his "responsibility from making choices to asking questions."[30] When the work is finished, he said, he had the pleasure of discovering it along with the audience. The only one who cannot share the pleasure is the performer, to whom the buck is passed, who cannot evade the choices, but must supply laborious answers to the composer's diverting questions.

The pianist Margaret Leng Tan, an outstanding exponent of Cage's keyboard music (including the prepared-piano works), has complained of being cut out of the fun. Her freedom in performing "chance music" is not enhanced but diminished: "By the time you've worked out all this material, can you really give a spontaneous performance? It's a discovery for him [that is, Cage] if he's hearing it for the first time, but it's not a discovery for me."[31] Once again the composer's authority over the performer is paradoxically magnified. The grandiosity of genius is affirmed. If that is something to rebuke in Beethoven, it is something to rebuke in Cage as well. But the main paradox or contradiction is the one that maximalists have always faced. At some point quantity inevitably, and subversively, transforms quality. At some point — but what point? — the disinterestedness of the artist and the transcendence of the artifact inevitably metamorphose into indifference and irrelevance. That has been the fate and the tragedy of "purist" modernism, and Cage was (or became) the purest of the pure.

PERMISSION

The New Grove Dictionary of American Music (published in 1986) claimed flatly that John Cage "has had a greater impact on world music than any other American composer of the twentieth century."[32] That is certainly possible if his impact is measured by the number of artists (not just musicians) who have acknowledged Cage as an influence or an enabler. "He has immense authority," the art dealer Leo Castelli, an energetic promoter of avant-garde painters and sculptors, said of Cage. "He is, after all, a guru; and just the fact that he was there with his fantastic assurance was important to us all."[33]

The painter Robert Rauschenberg (b. 1925), one of Cage's closest friends, said it was Cage's example that "gave me license to do anything,"[34] especially when what he wished to do defied the established modernists of the day. The composer Morton Feldman (1926–87), a close associate of Cage who was also friends with many painters, claimed that Cage gave not only him but everybody "permission."[35] Cage's joyously accepting attitude, "naive" in the special philosophical sense discussed above, made him a charismatic facilitator, not to say a liberator. It was a role comparable in many ways to that played by Liszt a hundred years earlier with respect to the "New German" avant-garde.

Yet many if not most of the artists and musicians who venerated Cage and thought of themselves as his disciples seem to have misunderstood him in a very significant way. The art movement usually linked with the composers in Cage's orbit is the one called abstract expressionism, which flourished in New York from the mid-1940s until the 1970s, exactly the period of Cage's most intense activity, and which established New York as an international artistic center on a par with Paris. It was the first American school of painting to have a significant influence on European artists, and in this, too, it parallels the influence of Cage, who after his Darmstadt lectures had many European disciples.

But as the movement's very name suggests, abstract expressionist painters were primarily interested in freedom of personal expression and intensity of emotional communication, the very things Cage had renounced. The turbulent "action paintings" of Cage's exact contemporary Jackson Pollock (1912–56), in which the artist hurled and spattered pigments on a canvas stretched out on the floor, were often regarded as a "liberation of paint" in much the way Cage liked to speak of the "liberation of sounds." But the comparison was misguided. Pollock sought greater freedom of action, sometimes described as greater freedom from form, the better to express his individuality of feeling through the medium of color. To invoke Nietzsche's old Wagnerian dualism, Pollock's was the quintessential "Dionysian" art. Cage looked for the very opposite: ever more stringent ways of constraining his actions so as to free the sounds he produced from his own wishes and feelings and so achieve greater harmony with nature. His was "Apollonian" art at its most extreme.

A similarly Apollonian impulse, and a similar commitment to philosophical realism (or particularism) drove the work of Iannis Xenakis (1922–2001), one of the European composers most often compared with Cage. A Romanian-born Greek-speaking composer resident in France, Xenakis had a thorough training in mathematics and engineering before he decided on a musical career. His expertise in these technical fields was sufficient to land him a job as assistant to the celebrated modern architect Le Corbusier (real name Charles Jeanneret, 1887–1965). Xenakis strove to base his musical practice directly on classic mathematical formulas, the most impersonal and transcendent of all truth-concepts. It was he who, in collaboration with Le Corbusier, designed the Philips Pavilion at the 1958 Brussels World's Fair on principles already embodied in several of his compositions.

Xenakis is best known for what he called "stochastic music," deriving the adjective from mathematical probability theory. Rejecting the over-determined causality of "integral serialism"[36] (which, he alleged in an inflammatory article written in 1954 and published in 1961, only succeeds in sounding aimless and unintelligible) and the underdetermined contingencies of "aleatoric" music (which, he declared, was an abdication of creative responsibility), he sought a music that would create an intelligible shape out of a multitude of seemingly random musical events, much as a multiplicity of chance occurrences — like Cage's beloved flipped coins — makes a gradual approach to a predictable outcome (equal numbers of heads and tails).

It is the response of a composer who had spent the war years in the Resistance movement (and with a blind eye to show for his pains) to the dilemma of reclaiming free will and the possibility of meaningful action in the face of existential pessimism — a pessimism that, in music, had led to various kinds of abject submission, whether to voluntary regimentation (symbolized by total serialism) or to fatalism (symbolized by chance operations). The events in Xenakis's stochastic music are planned in the large but unpredictable in the small. Its individual elements are insignificant but they make a strong collective statement. Its governing political metaphor was expressed most directly in the dedication of one of Xenakis's works to the "unknown political prisoners" and "the forgotten thousands whose very names are lost," but whose uncoordinated and singly ineffectual contributions to the cause of freedom were collectively decisive.

Xenakis's *Metastasis* (first performed at the Donaueschingen Festival in 1955) consisted entirely of a complex texture of glissandos, interacting in time and space, in which every single member of the forty-four-piece string section had a separate part, so that nobody's line was individually conspicuous. All, however, contributed equally to an overall impression of smoothly rising and lowering curves of pitch. The same principle of endless curvature (or displacement — metastasis — from straightness) governed the shape of the Philips pavilion. In Fig. 2-5a – d, a page from the sketch score of *Metastasis* is juxtaposed with one of Xenakis's architectural sketches for the pavilion, and then both sketches are juxtaposed with their realizations (the finished score, the actual building). In the sketches it is especially noticeable how the curves are the overall product of an indeterminate multiplicity of straight lines, as the victory over fascism was the product of an indeterminable multiplicity of individual sacrifices.

Pithoprakta (1956) was the first composition in which Xenakis used the "cloud" effect that became synonymous with his name. The title means "actions through probabilities"; the goal on which all the seemingly random sounds converge is the emergence of conventionally recognizable musical tone out of "noise," as controlled by various mathematical formulas. The fifty-piece orchestra includes a couple of trombones that play glissandos as before, and a percussionist who contributes seemingly random and disruptive punctuations on xylophone and woodblock; but the main sonority is that of forty-six solo strings, now making extremely discontinuous sounds — pitchless tapping on the instruments, gradually giving way to pitched pizzicato — organized into processes of continuous change.

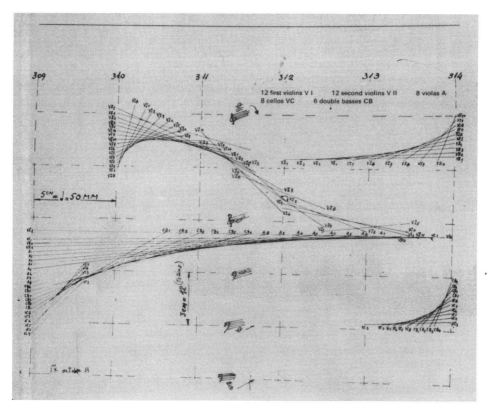

FIG. 2-5A   Iannis Xenakis, sketch for *Metastasis* (1953).

What gives a sense of progression through time is the variable density of these swarming musical particles, creating the impression of a shifting nebulous shape, calculated according to the so-called Maxwell-Boltzmann law, which predicts the behavior of gas molecules at various pressures and temperatures. The composer, as it were, adjusts conceptual pressure valves and thermostats, to which the musical molecules, individually maintaining what seem to be random trajectories, nevertheless "react" collectively according to the law's predictions.

Xenakis's music can be interpreted as a negative critique of "Darmstadt" serialism. Listening to it (as he put it to an interviewer in 1980),

our attention is unable to follow all the various events, so instead we form a general impression. That's simply

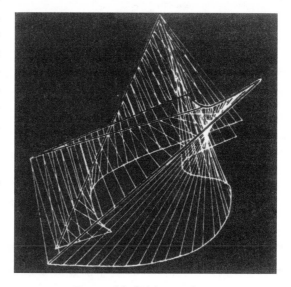

FIG. 2-5B   First model of Philips pavilion.

FIG. 2-5C   Corresponding page from the score of *Metastasis* (1954).

how our brain reacts to mass phenomena—there's no question of scientific computations. Our brain does a kind of statistical analysis! We have to reckon with the same thing as in the kinetic gas theory.[37]

Such a listening process, Xenakis asserted, is natural; a music that elicits it is a realistic (or scientifically "true") music. The impracticably detailed listening process presupposed by serialism was, by implication, utopian and (given the limitations of our mental processing) a falsehood. Not surprisingly, Xenakis was sym-

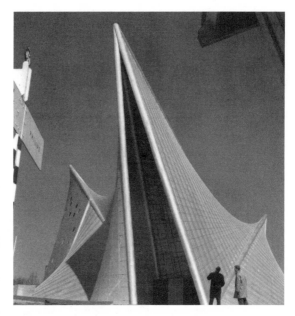

FIG. 2-5D   Philips pavilion (1958).

pathetic to Cage, who also appealed to nature (though more the nature we experience with our senses than nature as it is understood by scientific theory) to justify his version of avant-gardism. Xenakis, in fact, was one of the first Europeans to support Cage, whom he regarded as an amiable exotic: "I liked his thinking, which is of course a characteristic product of American society," he recalled to an interviewer. "I was attracted by the freedom and lack of bias with which he approached music." He thought the "mystical color" Cage claimed to have inherited from Asian philosophy naive, and his lack of overt political commitment all too typical of what Europeans often regard as American complacency, but "at least he tried to do something different and in opposition to the absolutist trend of the serialists."[38]
But then he went on:

> Cage's music can be interesting, until he relies too heavily on the interpreters, on improvisation. That's why I've kept aloof from this trend. In my opinion it is the composer's privilege to determine his works, down to the minutest detail. Otherwise he ought to share the copyright with his performers.

Xenakis had made the commonest, most obvious of all mistakes with regard to Cage, seeing him as a liberator of people rather than sounds, never realizing that Cage shared his horror of improvisation (if not for all the same reasons), and that Cage, too, determined his most influential works down to the minutest detail (although he sometimes sought to disguise the fact in conversation and interview). This misunderstanding was as typical of Cage's admirers and colleagues as of his critics and adversaries. As we are about to discover, even some of Cage's most ardent disciples made the same mistake about his aims. And yet misunderstandings of this kind are common in the history of art. They can be inspiring. Indeed, we often "need" to misunderstand those we follow, so that their authority can become an enabling rather than a restraining force.

MUSIC AND POLITICS REVISTED

Artists who justified their personal freedom by citing Cage's example managed to forget just what it was that Cage had liberated, and from whom. Not that this mattered in the long run. Messages sent are not always the ones received, and the history of art is full of examples of would-be followers who became innovators by misreading their predecessors' intentions. A celebrated theory of literary history advanced in the 1970s by the critic Harold Bloom (b. 1930) elevated creative misreading of this kind to the status of main determinant, or driving force, behind all creative evolution.[39] Nor does the fact that an artist misreads the example he claims to follow necessarily reflect in any way on the authenticity or value of his own work or that of his ostensible "guru." Nevertheless it is curious that the musician most interested in reining in the impulses of human beings so as to keep them out of the way of sounds, and who never gave performers (or listeners) any real freedom of choice, should have been regarded as a human liberator. It testifies to the power of suggestion, to the allure of liberation as concept for artists brought up with the rhetoric of American democracy ringing in their ears, and to the paradoxical need most artists share with the rest of humanity to justify their freedom on the basis of authority. By merely using the word liberation at a time when systems ruled, Cage gave those lacking his fantastic assurance permission to follow their own inclinations. It is a paradox that went all the way back to Rousseau's *Social Contract*, with its troubling call to liberate mankind, if necessary, against its will, forcing freedom on the comfortably enslaved.

Christian Wolff, for example, who inadvertently midwifed Cage's adoption of chance operations by presenting him with a copy of the *I Ching*, has been mainly concerned in his own compositions with giving performers what he called "parliamentary participation," the freedom to choose among alternatives, as opposed to the "monarchical authority" of the composer or conductor.[40] In his *Duo for Pianists II*, for example, the notation is deliberately left incomplete, so that the players (originally Wolff himself and the American pianist Frederic Rzewski) are forced to decide for themselves matters of detail usually decided by the composer: now exact duration, now exact pitch, now register. As in Stockhausen's *Klavierstück XI*, the music is written down in discrete chunks whose order of performance is left indeterminate. Each performer makes choices on the basis of what the other has last chosen.

The notation below from the *Duo* score is typical. Numbers before the colon indicate spans of time in seconds. Those after the colon indicate the number of notes to be played in the allotted time, selected from "source collections" of predetermined pitches, while the sign *x*, appearing above and/or below, directs the player to higher or lower keyboard registers. Thus, the configuration

$$\frac{1}{4} : \frac{\overset{x-}{3a}}{\underset{2b}{x-}}$$

means that in the space of a quarter of a second the pianist must choose three pitches from source collection **a** and two from source collection **b**, making sure to play them in a higher or a lower register than the last time the same pitches were chosen. Whether to play the pitches singly or in chords (and if singly, whether closely spaced like a melody or leaping "pointillistically" among far-flung registers), whether to play them loud or soft, and how their individual durations shall compare, are all decisions left to the quick-thinking performer.

Quick-reacting, too, since each player's choices are determined in part by cues given, according to a prearranged scheme, by the other player. The piece amounts to an exciting game for the players that allows (in the composer's words) for "precise actions under variously indeterminate conditions." Since "no structural whole or totality is calculated either specifically or generally in terms of probabilities or statistics," the outcome of the game is never predictable. "The score makes no finished object, [something regarded as] at best hopeless, fragile, or brittle. There are only parts which can be at once transparent and distinct."

In his later music, Wolff's notation became less and less determinate, the necessity of performer choice ever greater, to the point where the performers virtually improvise within loosely defined limits. Wolff has justified his practices on explicitly political grounds. A composition, in his view, must "make possible the freedom and dignity of the performer." Yet having declared that "no sound is preferable to any other sound or noise" (which sounds vaguely Cageian), Wolff allows performers to exercise their own preferences in choosing sounds, which is as un-Cageian as can be.

Unlike Cage, Wolff is interested in explicit political analogies. The unusual appearance of his scores, and the freedoms he delegates to performers, are intended "to stir up," as he has put it, "a sense of the political conditions in which we live and of how these might be changed, in the direction of democratic socialism." These convictions have led him back, in his most recent work, to the use of material borrowed from labor and protest songs in the manner of Hanns Eisler or the members of the New York Composers Collective in the period of the Great Depression. (Cage, by contrast, was resolutely consistent in his principle of quietism or noninterference. His most explicit political pronouncement has become notorious: "There is not too much pain in the world; there is just the right amount."[41]) A similar impulse led Frederic Rzewski (b. 1938), Wolff's sometime duo partner, out of the avant-garde altogether. Born in Massachusetts and educated at Harvard, Rzewski lived in Europe during the 1960s, at first in the orbit of Stockhausen, of whose *Klavierstück X* Rzewski (a virtuoso pianist) gave the first performance. The political upheavals of the later 1960s (to be considered in greater detail in chapter 7) convinced Rzewski of the irreconcilable contradiction between the private games of the avant-garde and the social purposes to which he was dedicated. The eventual result, in the early 1970s, was a series of virtuoso variation sets for piano on workers' songs in a traditionally "heroic" style modeled expressly on that of Beethoven's monumental "Diabelli" Variations.

Rzewski's *The People United Will Never Be Defeated*, 36 variations on the Chilean protest song "¡El pueblo unido jamás será vencido!" (1975, Ex. 2-4a), while obviously (and successfully) directed — as political exhortation — at the broad concert public that favors virtuoso piano recitals, nevertheless retains features of the composer's earlier avant-garde idiom, now smoothly integrated, in a fashion that the avant-garde had once declared impossible, into a politically — and, of course, commercially — exploitable idiom. The first variation adapts the simple melody of the song to the radically disjunct "pointillistic" texture by then long associated with the piano music of Stockhausen and Boulez (Ex. 2-4b).

INTERNALIZED CONFLICT

Rzewski's politically (or at least esthetically) efficacious "compromise" with tradition exposed a fault line within the politicized avant-garde of the late 1960s. On one side were those determined to remain true despite their political commitments to the esthetic principles of avant-gardism that had by then become a tradition in its own right; on the other were those for whom the political commitments of the so-called "new left" outweighed the esthetic. Sometimes the two commitments battled one another within the same unhappy creative personality.

The most extreme case was that of Cornelius Cardew (1936–81), an English composer who after a conventional elite training at the Royal Academy of Music went to Cologne and worked for three years (1957–60) as Stockhausen's assistant at the equally (though differently) elite electronic music studio maintained by the German Radio. In 1967 he was appointed to the faculty of the Royal Academy, but by 1969, under the influence of the Cultural Revolution instigated in China by Mao Tse-tung and his Red Guards, Cardew renounced his advanced musical techniques as "bourgeois deviationism." Together with some friends and like-minded musicians, he formed an organization called the Scratch Orchestra, "a gathering," as Cardew later put it, of "musicians, artists, scholars, clerks, students, etc, willing to engage in experimental performance activities."[42] The willingness in question meant readiness to submit to a

EX. 2-4A   Frederic Rzewski, "The People United Will Never Be Defeated!," theme

EX. 2-4B   Frederic Rzewski, "The People United Will Never Be Defeated!," first variation

radically egalitarian discipline, bordering on anarchy, in which no a priori standard of quality could be asserted. "No criticism before performance"[43] was the group's motto. Their main activity consisted of group improvisation, for which members prepared by writing and teaching to the rest of the group examples of Scratch Music, something "halfway between composing and improvising."[44]

It was defined in the Orchestra's draft constitution as "accompaniments, performable continuously for indefinite periods."[45] An accompaniment was defined as "music that allows a solo (in the event of one occurring) to be appreciated as such," notated "using any means — verbal, graphic, musical, collage, etc." The only condition was that a piece of Scratch Music "be performable for indefinite periods of time." A necessary proviso was that "the word music and its derivatives are here not understood to refer exclusively to sound and related phenomena (hearing, etc); what they do refer to is flexible and depends entirely on the members of the Scratch Orchestra."

For outsiders, further definition had to await the publication of *Scratch Music* (1972), an anthology edited by Cardew, containing examples by himself and fifteen other members of the Orchestra. Very few Scratch pieces employed musical notation as normally defined. Many consisted of drawings that, without oral explanation, could not readily be translated into the sort of continuous action the constitution specified. Some, however, consisted of verbal prescriptions that occasionally suggested vivid musical (or at least sonic) results. "Take a closed cylinder (empty pepsi-cola tin)," one began. "Bang it. Drop things through the holes the pepsi came out of."[46] A more elaborate recipe for action, entitled "Scratch Orchestral Piece with Gramophone" (i.e. phonograph or record player) read as follows:

> A gramophone record of an orchestral composition, known to have a scratch in it such as will cause infinite repetition of one groove, is taken and played. The (live) orchestra accompanies the record, repeating the music heard to the best of its ability. (What will come out is a sort of canon between the recorded and live performance.) The record should preferably not be a popular classic. The performers must play quietly to avoid losing touch with the record, which should not be played loudly.
>
> When the record arrives at the repeating groove, the performers should, after a few repetitions, be able to play in unison with the record. The general volume level will probably rise here. When a member loses touch with the record, he may go over to the gramophone and jerk the needle on. This action should be plainly visible to the other performers, who must immediately resume their low volume and follow the record as before. The performance ends a) (if the gramophone is automatic) when the gramophone switches itself off, b) (if the gramophone is manually controlled) at any time after the record has ended. The audible click which sometimes occurs as the needle moves around the innermost groove may be taken as part of the record, in which case a similar situation to the one described above may obtain.
>
> The piece could be played by any performer(s), in which case the record should match as far as possible the instrument(s) or voices(s) used.[47]

The book culminated in a list titled "1001 Activities, by members of the Scratch Orchestra" (Fig. 2-6). Some, perhaps most, are entirely "conceptual" in the sense that they can be more or less vaguely imagined but not literally realized. It is not clear whether the performable items in the list were actually performed as Scratch Music; but in any case, by the time the list was published the Scratch Orchestra had disbanded. It lasted only two years and is probably best categorized as one of the many failed experiments in utopian living that proliferated during the late 1960s.

"Did all this have to change? It changed," was Cardew's Samuel Beckett–like comment in retrospect. He went on to describe how

> the internal contradictions in the Scratch got sharper and sharper until, possibly triggered by the civic and press response (we had a concert banned on grounds of obscenity and the press went to town on the scandal) to our Newcastle Civic Centre concert on June 21 1971, I opened the doors to criticism and self-criticism. A collection of the resulting documents was circularized under the title "Discontent." . . . The Scratch was saved from liquidation by two communist members. At the August 23/24 discussions of the Discontent documents John Tilbury exposed the contradictions within the orchestra, and proposed the setting up of a Scratch Ideological Group. I and several others were glad to join this group, whose tasks were not only to investigate possibilities for political music-making but also to study revolutionary theory: Marx, Lenin, Mao Tse-Tung. Another aim was to build up an organizational structure in the Scratch that would make it a genuinely democratic orchestra and release it from the domination of my subtly autocratic, supposedly anti-authoritarian leadership.[48]

But the group was never reconstituted; its members escaped from freedom. The perennial political contradictions between anarchistic ideals and the realities of

554 Drop out
555 Put your foot in it
556 Be put out
557 Lose track of time
558 Lose face
559 Put your left leg in
560 Put your left leg out
561 In, out, in, out, shake it all about
562 Do as you would be done by
563 Be done by as you did
564 Eternalise
565 Dangle
566 Jangle
567 Wrangle
568 Tangle
569 Mangle
570 Spangle
571 Blow the gaff
572 Fall about laughing
573 Jump up and bang your head on the ceiling
574 Explode a hypothesis
575 Expound a theory
576 Make your blood boil
577 Imitate Che Guevara as a small badger
578 Change guard at Buckingham Palace
579 "You'll never go to heaven if you break my heart"
580 Who says?
581 Be Rife
582 Incline your head till it touches the ground
583 Break the large glass
584 Arrest a Policeman
585 Singing Balls to the Baker, arse against the wall
586 Climb every mountain
587 "Fuck my old Boots"
588 The two fingered sign of distaste in conjunction with something sweet and sugary, painted yellow, lusciously curving into the distance, taking her pants off, reaping the whirlwind and singing a twelve bar blues on the back seat of a tandem tricycle
589 Come to a pretty pass
590 Come to a pretty lass
591 Sweat like a pig
592 Burn the boats
593 Shiver me timbers
594 Splice the mainbrace
595 Drink like a fish
596 Swear like a trooper

677 Beg for mercy
678 Take yourself down a peg
679 Question your bank statement
680 Never say die
681 Do or die
682 Die the death
683 Become a dyed in the wool dogmatic
684 Unfrock a clergyman
685 Bat an eyelid
686 Turn the other cheek
687 Whippoorwill
688 Pursue a will o' the wisp
689 Make a bloomer
690 Rut
691 Split your difference
692 Turn up trumps
693 Give a light show to a heavy audience
694 Make a face at a tree
695 Give away the game
696 Let the cat out of the bag
697 Hunt the thimble
698 Make out a case for a logical bassoon
699 Syndicate every boat you row
700 Indicate every thing you see
701 Celebrate every thing you are
702 Dig a pony
703 Photograph the back of your head
704 Make a sculpture of the wind
705 Paint your anus
706 Fight the good fight,
    each and every night.
    Cor strike a light,
    with all thy might
707 "Know the male but keep to the role of the female"
708 Thank Lao Tzu for "707"
709 Thank D C Lau for translating "708" from the original Chinese
710 Conquer the ineluctable
711 Know the wisdom of refraining from action
712 Polish off a three-course breakfast at 3 o'clock in the afternoon
713 Leap before you look
714 Leak before you loop
715 Loop before you leak
716 Clean your teeth with a universal spanner
717 Knock your friends down with a feather
718 Swing a cat
719 Swing a Blue Whale

597 Arsenic and old lace
598 Be written off
599 Wreck yourself with a rusty mattock, the handle of which is exquisitely carved, inlaid with ivory and set with precious stones
600 Translate the Hsin-Hsin Ming into Medieval Russian
601 Write a précis of the Bible in words of not more than one syllable
602 Play the whale
603 Fish for compliments
604 Fish for fivers
605 Fish for the notes
606 Land a gigantic catch
607 Make a false entry and still hold back
608 Giver her/him satisfaction
609 Take it easy, but take it
610 Demonstrate the sound of one hand
611 Fall among thieves
612 Fall into arrears
613 Fall into disfavour
614 Fall into disgrace
615 Fall into a vat of boiling dung (or oil)
616 A little of what you fancy
617 Throw the world over, the white cliffs of Dover
618 Turn a Chinese Revolution
619 Make a Venetian blind
620 Make a Maltese Cross
621 Fly in the face of danger
622 Put on a brave face
623 Fly on the face of her Majesty the Queen
624 Pollute a bowl of custard
625 Dispute a Death sentence
626 Rumble the Popish plot
627 Give a detailed exposition as to the reasons for Titus not getting his oats
628 Make peace
629 Make war
630 Make love
631 Make friends
632 Make amends
633 Rake up your past
634 Dig up your potatoes, trample on your vines
635 "Gimme that thing"
636 A cat's lick and a promise
637 Grow younger from today
638 Make-up
639 Decree a repetition, of the Spanish Inquisition

720 Up, up and away
721 Help an old lady across the road against her will
722 Drink a yard of ale
723 Drink a yard of whisky
724 Hold a special service in the memory of anyone attempting "723"
725 Speak now or forever hold your peace
726 Commit perjury
727 Walk around London in Indian file
728 Have a picnic in Hammersmith Bridge
729 Say the unrepeatable
730 Ball the Jack
731 Touch the moon
732 Be a bit of a bastard (which bit is up to you(?))
733 Play with your friends
734 Play with your self
735 Cycle up the steps of the Eiffel Tower, then cycle down again
736 Walk backwards for a hundred yards then run backwards for a hundred yards
737 Collapse as if exhausted, dissimulation will not be permitted
738 Brush up your Shakespeare
739 Do something for Pete's sake
740 Part your hair from ear to ear
741 Grow a moustach in the small of your back
742 Run amok
743 Make some Holy smoke without a celestial fire
744 Take off your clothes before a paying audience sitting in total darkness
745 Perform a five card trick and amaze your friends
746 Execute a lithograph of a pig in a poke
747 Count the number of hairs on the back of each hand, and take down the number of the difference, climb the same number of trees with a chamber-pot and a small goat strapped to your back
748 Fiddle while Rome burns
749 Given an imitation of the Vienna Secession, blindfolded and standing in a bucket of pirana fish
750 Give a Royal Command Performance of Gavin Bryar's "Serenely beaming and leaning on a fivebar gate"
751 Turn topsy-turvy
752 Don't come that one
753 Knit your brows so that they keep your eyelids warm in winter
754 Perform "175" with your head tucked underneath your arms

640 Keep your head in the presence of a tiger
641 Make yourself a jacket out of National Velvet
642 Invest in squirrels
643 Go on for longer than you intended
644 Go on for longer than you expected
645 Go on for ever
646 Throw fifty fits, make allowance for the proximity of spectators
647 Laugh fit to bust
648 Laugh till you cry
649 Laugh till you break your jaw
650 Lie on the bottom of a swimming pool and breathe in deeply
651 Repeat 650 wearing an atomic powered kilt and seven league boots
652 Up an' give 'em a bla' a bla' Wi' a hundred pipers an' a' an' a'
653 Moonlight and roses and parsons' noses
654 Every lassie loves his laddie, coming through the rye (misquote)
655 "Someday my prince will come", Something with a pitch fork
656 Home, home on the range, where the people are acting so strange
657 Show them who's boss, then resign your position
658 Run the gauntlet
659 Be the object of a fugue subject
660 Give a tonal answer to a rhetorically insulting question
661 Be "cut to the quick"
662 Be quick to the cut
663 Do the dirty on somebody
664 Breeze it, bug it. easy does it
665 Lose your cool
666 Lose your virginity
667 Lose your self respect
668 Be caught with your trousers at the cleaners
669 Beat your wife with a damp squid
670 Pick your nose with a mechanical shovel
671 Feel glad all over. (How did "Glad" enjoy it?)
672 Be pipped at the post or (conversely) give somebody the pip
673 Get the pip or (conversely) give somebody the pip
674 Set the pips on a well known politician
675 Loop the loop
676 Squander your ill-gotten gains

755 Now for something completely different
756 Open up them Pearly Gates
757 Swim the Channel underwater
758 Fall asleep during page five of John Cage's "The Music of Changes", Book III
759 Fall awake during Group 139 of Stockhausen's "Gruppen"
760 Whistle to your hearts content
761 Take some coal to Newcastle
762 Kiss the Blarney Stone
763 Wipe your slate clean
764 Rape a canary
765 Construct a short way to Tipperary
766 Put off procrastinating till tomorrow
767 Regurgitate an eel pie
768 Put out a candle and apologise to it for so doing
769 Flush the lavatory with one almighty stroke of t pen
770 Drown one of larger types of rodent with the sweat of your brow
771 Shave the cat with a few sharp words
772 Confucan confusion
773 Be redundant
774 Learn to recognise St Peter's Square, and so is the Pope
775 Confine yourself to a wheel chair for the day and make a round tour of the bottoms of crowded staircases. (Be a nuisance!)
776 Remember something you had long since forgotten
777 Board and leave a tube train inbetween stations
778 Broadcast to the Nation
779 Paint your face in the dress tartan of the clan Macleod
780 Satire:– send up a balloon
781 Forfeit your right to live
782 Hold your own with one hand and someone else's with the other
783 Argue till you are black in the face (a coloured issue?)
784 Talk to a brick wall
785 Ask a ticket machine for your money back
786 Begin hesitantly, continue nervously, expound at great length and end in a blaze of glory
787 Finger pie
788 Suddenly become lop-sided
789 Grow on trees
790 Use your loaf
791 "You're no fun anymore" –-illustrate with

FIG. 2-6   Cornelius Cardew, pages from "List of 1001 Activities" (*Scratch Music*, 1972).

leadership were not the only factor. The Scratch Orchestra came up against the perennial dilemma of maximalism: they reached the limit. As one antagonist scoffed, "How can you make a revolution when the revolution before last has already said that anything goes?"[49] The thought was unkindly put, but the truth that it contained was one of the predicaments that led eventually to the eclipse of the avant-garde as a force in contemporary music.

Like Christian Wolff, Cornelius Cardew wound up writing mass songs to incite popular activism, and in 1974 published another, rather disillusioned book called *Stockhausen Serves Imperialism.* "Nowadays a Cage concert can be quite a society event,"[50] he noted sarcastically; and also, more wistfully, that Cage's "emptiness does not antagonize the bourgeois audience which is confident of its ability to cultivate a taste for virtually anything."[51] Even the avant-garde, he had found, could be commercially co-opted, consumed, commodified; the process (exemplified most dramatically by the New York Philharmonic's notorious experience with *Atlas eclipticalis*) had painfully exposed "the sharply antagonistic relationship between the avant-garde composer with all his electronic gadgetry and the working musician."[52]

As for Stockhausen, he had been tamed, his erstwhile disciple charged, by "repressive tolerance,"[53] the insidious and corrupting approval of the establishment. All that was left was shopworn romanticism, the old idealistic religion of art that Cardew now attacked the way Marx had denounced "the opium of the people" in the name of historical materialism.

"Salesmen like Stockhausen," he wrote,

> would have you believe that slipping off into cosmic consciousness removes you from the reach of the painful contradictions that surround you in the real world. At bottom, the mystical idea is that the world is illusion, just an idea inside our heads. Then are the millions of oppressed and exploited people throughout the world just another aspect of that illusion in our minds? No, they aren't. The world is real, and so are the people, and they are struggling towards a momentous revolutionary change. Mysticism says "everything that lives is holy," so don't walk on the grass and above all don't harm a hair on the head of an imperialist.[54]

CONFLICTS DENIED

There were those, however, who managed to maintain the frayed analogy between "revolutionary" politics and progressive esthetics and reconcile radical politics with radical art, though they did so by reverting to the nostalgic, by then fairly untenable ideal of what was known in the 1960s as the Old Left. The term referred to idealistic remnants of the revolutionary tide that had made the Russian Revolution, who refused to recognize or acknowledge the way in which that Revolution had been betrayed. At a time when the Soviet Union stood, for all the world to see, on the side of enforced artistic populism, these artists defended the old "revolutionary" ideal on both the political and the esthetic fronts.

Perhaps the most prominent was Luigi Nono (1924–90), who as a young partisan fighter courageously joined the Italian Communist Party during the last days of Mussolini's dictatorship, when membership was a crime, and who was eventually

(1975) elected to the Party's Central Committee. Nono, who married Schoenberg's daughter Nuria in 1955, was a committed twelve-tone composer, as convinced as was his father-in-law of the method's historical inevitability, just as he was convinced of the inevitability of Communist revolution. He never recognized a contradiction between his musical idiom, which appealed only to an elite coterie, and his commitment to egalitarian politics. Although he was a loyal upholder of Soviet economic and diplomatic policies to the end (paying his last official visit to the USSR as late as 1988), his music was of a kind anathematized in the Soviet Union in 1948 and never "rehabilitated." The contrast between Nono's political and esthetic commitments is particularly pointed, of course, in his most overtly political works, like *Ein Gespenst geht um in der Welt* ("A specter is abroad in the world"; 1971), a choral setting of words drawn from Marx and Engels's *Communist Manifesto*, accompanied by an orchestra with a colossal percussion section (and with the strings often "percussing" à la Xenakis) (Fig. 2-7). Despite the source of its text and its expressive purpose, entirely comparable to Rzewski's, the work was given its premiere in West Germany rather than the part of Germany where Marx and Engels were honored as founding fathers, but where music like Nono's was unperformable. Nor was the work ever performed in the Soviet bloc.

Nono defended his musical idiom in terms borrowed from Adorno, another Marxist who turned a blind eye to the actual historical consequences of Marxist philosophy. Its dissonance was to be interpreted "dialectically," like Schoenberg's, as a critique of bourgeois society's irreconcilable antagonisms ("disharmonies"). Such a metaphorical interpretation of a musical style was acceptable neither to the Soviets nor to the former avant-gardists of the New Left. To the former it smacked of self-indulgent hypocrisy; to the latter, of sterile utopianism. It was Nono's fate to be best appreciated musically where his ideological commitments were devalued, and vice versa. He had an important like-thinking exponent in the charismatic piano virtuoso Maurizio Pollini (b. 1942), whose concerts became Nono's best attended forum. But Pollini, too, has had to face the contradiction between leftist political sympathies and the realities of musical politics.

At the opposite, somewhat happier pseudo-political extreme were the outwardly carefree revolutionaries who created "happenings." These were minimally planned performance events, at the border between music and theater, that mixed Cage's "purposeful purposelessness" with the ideology of the "absurdist" theater in which playwrights like Beckett and Eugene Ionesco (1909–94) expressed the bewilderment, alienation, and despair of existentialist philosophy by abandoning all logical plot development, meaningful dialogue, or intelligible character delineation in favor of a gross unpredictable humor that mocked all efforts at making sense of incomprehensible reality. Or perhaps it would be more accurate to say that the perpetrators of happenings repressed their bewilderment and alienation and the rest in a great show of childish fun and aggression.

The first — typically solemn, typically misunderstood — happening was engineered by Cage himself at Black Mountain College, an avant-garde retreat in North Carolina, in 1952. It was a variation on the 4′33″ idea. Cage programmed some overlapping sound

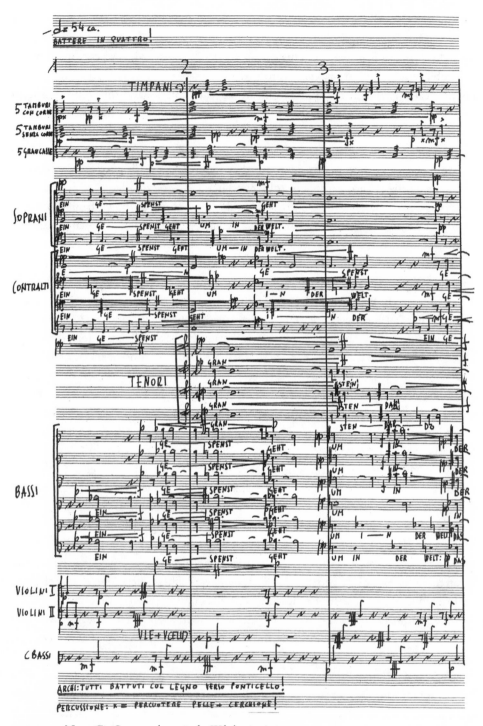

FIG. 2-7   Nono, *Ein Gespenst geht um in der Welt*, beginning.

containers (or "compartments," as he called them this time) in advance by the use of chance operations and allowed himself and his fellow performers to choose an activity to perform during their allotted compartments. Cage himself, standing on a ladder, read a lecture that contained some compartments of silence; some poets climbed other ladders when their time came and read; others ran a movie, projected slides, played phonograph records, danced, and played the piano, while Robert Rauschenberg suspended some paintings above the audience's heads. The idea, as in 4′33″, was to re-create utilitarian reality as autonomous art: "If you go down the street in the city you can see that people are moving about with intention but you don't know what those intentions are," Cage said, lecturing. "Many things happen which can be viewed in purposeless ways."[55] The music of life was a perpetual impersonal flux.

Between 1956 and 1960 Cage taught a class at the New School called Composition of Experimental Music. In 1958, the class included a number of poets, painters, and composers—George Brecht, Allan Kaprow, Jackson Mac Low, Dick Higgins—of whom some later participated in a loose performance association called Fluxus. Organized by George Maciunas in 1961–62, Fluxus provided a venue for what Kaprow was the first to call happenings. Brecht, the group's main theorist, disclaimed all theory. "In Fluxus, there has never been any attempt to agree on aims or methods," he wrote in 1964. "Individuals with something unnameable in common have simply naturally coalesced to publish and perform their work." And yet he did try to name it: "Perhaps this common something is a feeling that the bounds of art are much wider than they have conventionally seemed, or that art and certain long-established bounds are no longer very useful."[56] In contrast to Cage's original happening (and his later "musicircuses"), which sought to embrace the macrocosm, setting in motion an uncoordinated, ungraspable multiplicity of events that would create an esthetic analogy to the totality and complexity of life, Fluxus celebrated the microcosm, reflecting that totality and complexity in single, individual *actes gratuits* (as the existentialists would say), acts-without-purpose. At first their happenings were minimally prescribed and modestly executed. Brecht's *Organ Piece*, for example, consists of a single instruction: "organ."[57] *Piano Piece 1962* consists of another: "a vase of flowers onto a piano." The Brecht instruction most frequently cited by those seeking to define or illustrate happenings is "Discover or make on(to) a piano." His best-known composition, *Three Telephone Events*, consisted of the following:

- When the telephone rings, it is allowed to continue ringing, until it stops.
- When the telephone rings, the receiver is lifted, then replaced.
- When the telephone rings, it is answered.[58]

The conceptual kinship with 4′33″ is made explicit in a Performance Note, which reads, "Each event comprises all occurrences within its duration." It is Brecht's best known piece because Cage made seeming (and typically inaccurate) reference to it when asked to define music. "If the phone rings and you answer, that is not music," he replied. "If it rings and you listen, it is." Takehisa Kosugi, a Japanese composer who joined Fluxus a bit later, contributed a piece, *Anima 7*, whose instruction reads, "Perform any action as slowly as possible."[59] La Monte Young (b. 1935 in Idaho), the best-known

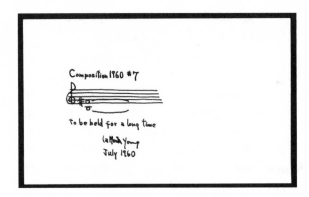

FIG. 2-8A   La Monte Young, *Composition 1960 #7*.

composer ever associated with the group, had a big influence on its style and esthetic with a set of instructions called *Compositions 1960*, which included one of the few such compositions to incorporate conventional musical notation (see Fig. 2-8a). Another from the set consists of the instruction, "push the piano to the wall; push it through the wall; keep pushing."[60] In *Composition 1960 #3*, specially designated performers are dispensed with. Instead, the audience is instructed that for a specified period of time they may do anything they wish.

Over time, the group's activities followed the usual maximalist course into flamboyance and aggression, and acquired notoriety. A Fluxus composer named Ben Vautier composed a number of *Audience Pieces* that came close to psychological abuse. One involved locking the audience into the theater; the piece was over when (if) they escaped. Richard Maxfield (1927–69) created the emblematic *Fluxus* happening, "Concert Suite from *Dromenon*," during which La Monte Young determined to set a violin on fire. The peak of aggression against the audience was reached by Nam June Paik (b. 1932), a Korean-born composer whose *Hommage à John Cage* consisted (as described by Al Hansen, a fellow Fluxian) of "moving through the intermission crowd in the lobby of a theater, cutting men's neckties off with scissors, slicing coats down the back with a razor blade and squirting shaving cream on top of their heads."[61] At one performance the recipient of Paik's attention was Cage himself, who, unamused, was led (in the words of the critic Calvin Tomkins, to whom he confided) "to wonder whether his influence on the young was altogether a good one."[62] Afterward, as Merce Cunningham recalled, "the piece went on for quite a while, and then Nam June disappeared. And we all sat and waited, and some time later, he telephoned from someplace to tell us the piece was over."[63] Cunningham, looking back on the experience, told a reporter that "it was wonderful." Others, sitting and waiting to no apparent purpose, may have been perplexed at their strange imprisonment by the rules of concert decorum. Exposing them may have been Paik's purpose. Or perhaps it was sheer aggression.

But aggression, too, is a purpose; and acts like Paik's, therefore, do not seem quite as innocent in practice as they do in

FIG. 2-8B   Nam June Paik.

theory. Dick Higgins faced up to the dilemma—meanwhile putting Fluxus, in its maximalist phase, into a historical perspective of sorts—when he commented, in terms that other members may not have approved, that the group had a purpose after all, and that purpose was (or had become) the reintroduction of a sense of danger that had been lost to modern music. "A sense of risk is indispensable," he wrote in 1966,

> because any simple piece fails when it becomes facile. This makes for all the more challenge in risking facility, yet still remaining very simple, very concrete, very meaningful. The composer is perfectly well aware of the psychological difficulties which his composition may produce for some, if not all, of the audience. He therefore finds excitement in insisting on this, to the point of endangering himself physically or even spiritually in his piece.[64]

The motivating emotion seemed to have become envy of the scandals of the past, which led composers actively to court the sort of hostile response from audiences of which legends (like that of *The Rite of Spring*) were made. One concert the author of this book remembers attending did succeed in provoking a violent counter-demonstration from its tiny audience. It was sponsored by a Fluxus spin-off group called Tone Roads, a name derived from a series of compositions by Charles Ives, and took place at the New School during the 1964–65 season. The last composition on the program, by Philip Corner (b. 1933), ended with a trumpet player and a trombonist standing at center stage, each unrelentingly emitting the highest and loudest note he could maintain steadily, until most listeners had fled.

The remaining spectators either watched in bemusement to see how and when the performance would end, or tried to interfere with it. Paper airplanes were launched in profusion. Audience catcalls began to rival in volume the noise the musicians were making. One sincerely irate patron jumped on stage and snatched the music off the players' stands, as if that would silence them; the trombonist pursued the would-be disrupter and snatched it back. The piece finally ended when the building custodian ordered everyone out of the hall. By then there were two on stage and five in the auditorium. (The author suspects that the intended ending was the departure of the last audience member.)

Paik produced the biggest scandal in 1967, with a happening called *Opéra sextronique*. The performance was heralded by a poster, proclaiming (in the spirit of the *Communist Manifesto*) that

> After three emancipations in twentieth-century music (serial, indeterminate, actional) I have found that there is still one more chain to lose. That is PRE-FREUDIAN HYPOCRISY. Why is sex, a predominant theme in art and literature, prohibited ONLY in music? How long can New Music afford to be sixty years behind the times and still claim to be a serious art? The purge of sex under the excuse of being "serious" exactly undermines the so-called "seriousness" of music as a classical art, ranking with literature and painting. Music history needs its D. H. Lawrence, its Sigmund Freud.[65]

The performance consisted of a cellist, Charlotte Moorman, appearing on stage "topless" (i.e., bare-breasted, in the media slang of the time). Paik, in Nicolas Slonimsky's untoppable description, "acted as a surrogate cello, his denuded spinal column serving as the fingerboard for Moorman's cello bow, while his bare skin provided an area for inter-mittent pizzicati."[66] Alerted by the poster, the police were on hand to arrest Moorman on a charge of public indecency. Instantly famous, she became the object of countless "news-maker" interviews (including an appearance—fully clothed—on the *Tonight Show*, a late-evening television "talk-show" hosted by Johnny Carson) in which she gamely defended the cause of new music as a "First Amendment" (i.e., free-expression) issue.

It was at this point that the artistic avant-garde appeared to meld in common cause with the demonstrations of civil disobedience (sparked by the "Free Speech Movement" at the University of California at Berkeley) that grew with the expansion of the unpopular Vietnam War. Serious political engagement, however, was not motivating Fluxus's or Tone Roads's acts of provocation. Suspected of frivolity at a time of severe political unrest, the avant-garde found its reason for being undermined, and it largely evaporated. Its political energy, as we will see in a later chapter, passed, for most part, into popular culture.

Looking back on his activities in the year 2000, Paik laughed them off as a "kind of stupid avant-garde," the antics of a "groupie" infatuated with Cage and the idea of liberation that he symbolized.[67] The avant-garde to which he had belonged, he now admitted, consisted for the most part of "lucky, middle-class people" who found that inventing meaningful applications of what seemed the easiest idea in the world, total freedom, was in fact bafflingly difficult. "We were just wondering how to be new," he conceded, at a time when novelty had become a debased currency.

But the movement was no laughing matter, really. Underlying it was a negative pathology, perhaps the most extreme artistic symptom of the period's widespread existential despair. Many of its members, having made renunciations just as impressive as Cage's, failed to find any positive outlet for their creative urge. Paik and Young, for example, were Darmstadt refugees with solid academic credentials. Paik had been a pupil of Wolfgang Fortner, the German serialist, while Young had studied in Los Angeles with Leonard Stein (b. 1916), who had served as Schoenberg's teaching assistant at UCLA.

Maxfield was perhaps the most dramatic case. He had worked with Roger Sessions at Berkeley and Milton Babbitt at Princeton before going to Italy on a Fulbright Fellowship to study with the leading Italian twelve-tone composers, Luigi Dallapiccola (1904–75) and Bruno Maderna (1920–73). By the time of his involvement with Fluxus he had already made a name for himself, having "acquired an excellent technique of com-position in the traditional idiom before adopting an extreme avant-garde style"[68] (as his entry reads in *Baker's Biographical Dictionary of Musicians*). He was also a skilled and highly paid recording engineer, employed by Westminster Records, one of the most active inde-pendent classical labels of the early LP era. Against this background, Higgins's *Danger Musics*, not to mention acts of outright destruction like violin burning (or taking an axe to a piano, as prescribed in Paik's *Hommage à John Cage*), do not seem merely "gratuitous" but sadomasochistic. Maxfield's final act was literally self-destructive. He committed suicide by jumping out of the window of a Los Angeles hotel room at the age of forty-two.

NEW NOTATIONS

Less obviously contradictory were the efforts of Earle Brown (1926– 2002), another early associate of Cage, to free performers from their usual constraints, and make them fully "aware" participants in the making of his music, by means of a "graphic notation" that eventually dispensed with conventional symbols. In *Synergy* (subtitled "November 1952"), conventional noteheads and dynamic markings were deployed on a sheet that was lined from top to bottom. Performers had

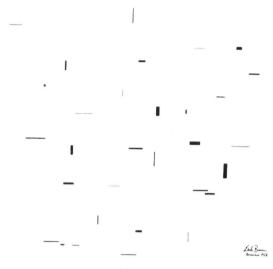

FIG. 2-9 Brown, *December 1952*.

to decide on instrumentation, place clefs where they wished, choose a mode of attack for each note, and decide both when to play it and how long it would be (within limits suggested by the use of empty and filled note-heads). A month later, in *December 1952*, Brown provided a score consisting of nothing but lines and rectangles on a white background (Fig. 2-9). The symbols represented "elements in space"; the score was "a picture of this space at one instant." It was for the performer "to set all this in motion," whether by "sit[ting] and let[ting] it move" or by "mov[ing] through it at all speeds."

December 1952 was written under the direct impact of Cage's *4′33″*, which had had its premiere (by David Tudor) in August of that year. In its vague and "conceptual" character it did resemble Cage's famous "tacet" piece; but in turning his notation into a kind of "inkblot test" to elicit the performer's associations, Brown was obviously letting back in all the "memories, tastes, likes and dislikes" that Cage had zealously sought to exclude (in keeping, one might note, with the original intention of Dr. Hermann Rorschach, the Swiss psychiatrist who devised the inkblot test on the theory that individuals will project their own unconscious attitudes into ambiguous situations.)

Brown was the first of many composers who, especially in the 1960s, employed "conceptual" notations to enlist the performers' imaginations (or their prejudices). The score page in Fig. 2-10 is from *The Nude Paper Sermon* (1969), a "music theater" piece by Eric Salzman (b. 1933), a composer and critic who studied at Darmstadt in the late 1950s. The musicians (vocal soloists, chorus, and Renaissance consort) are asked to "react" physically, on their instruments, to the unconventional graphic shapes, with little or no prompting from the composer. In Europe, the most prominent exponent of conceptual notations was Sylvano Bussotti (b. 1931), whose score pages were frequently hung by admirers as art prints. To reflect the trend toward conceptual notations, and perhaps to abet it, Cage published a compilation, *Notations* (1969), containing reproductions of score pages solicited from 269 composers to show "the many directions in which notation is now going."[69] The Bussotti page shown in Fig. 2-11, reproduced from Cage's compilation, was actually a New Year's greeting to the compiler.

FIG. 2-10   Score page from Eric Salzman's *The Nude Paper Sermon: Tropes for Actor, Chorus, and Renaissance Instruments* (words by John Ashbery), used by the author, who played bass viol at the premiere performance in New York, 20 March 1969.

Cage's own graphic notations, by contrast (and as might be expected), were always precisely specified and tightly controlled. Performers interpreting them found that the composer demanded extraordinary discipline of them, being intolerant of clichés

FIG. 2-11   Bussotti, score page reproduced in Cage's *Notations*.

and notoriously difficult to please. Among the many who misunderstood this aspect of Cageian "indeterminacy" was Leonard Bernstein, who prefaced the 1964 concert at which the New York Philharmonic played Cage's *Atlas eclipticalis* with four "improvisations" by the orchestra, redone later as a studio recording, that elicited mainly Kreutzer études from the strings, fanfares from the brass, and "Rite-of-Spring" arpeggios from the winds.

As for Earle Brown, his most widely performed pieces were "open form" compositions (a term of his coining, later applied to the work of many composers), in which sections were treated as "moving parts" like those of a mobile sculpture by Alexander Calder (1898–1976), his acknowledged inspiration. The score of *Available Forms I* (1961), for large orchestra led

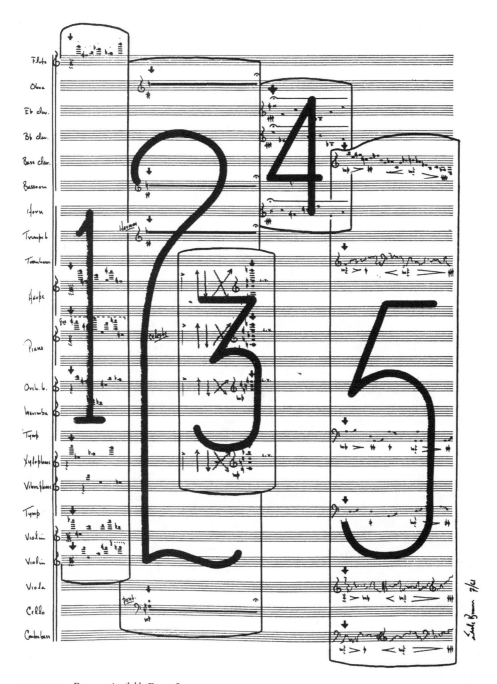

FIG. 2-12   Brown, *Available Forms I.*

by two conductors, consists of a sheaf of unbound pages (like the one given in Fig. 2-12) on each of which several "events" are notated, each calling upon a different group of instruments and exhibiting vastly differing characters (some static, others very active; some notated using conventional notes or note-heads, others "conceptually").

Every member of the orchestra has half of the full set of pages, as does each of the conductors. The order of pages is decided in advance by the two conductors independently. Whenever the page is turned, the conductors indicate by holding up the fingers of one hand which of the five events is to be played, and by their gestures regulate the speed (steady or variable, at their discretion) at which it is to be executed. Ideally, the work should be performed several times during a concert, to duplicate the effect of the mobile, whose finite set of parts can come into an infinite variety of alignments.

PRESERVING THE SACROSANCT

As always, the allowance for discretion (particularly discretionary tempo or *tempo rubato*) reintroduces personal interpretation, even self-expression, into an ideal realm from which Cage, the consummate Apollonian, had sought to exclude it. That realm, as we have seen, is the ideally autonomous artwork. Cage's most zealous competitor in the pursuit of esthetic autonomy was Morton Feldman. Their approaches were very different. Cage's involved a meticulous and demanding methodology. Feldman, who studied in the 1940s with Stefan Wolpe (not a Cageian by any means but also a sympathetic friend of surrealist and abstract expressionist painters), tried more spontaneously to achieve *l'acte gratuit*, the wholly unmotivated gesture.

His earliest pieces ("gestures") were of three kinds: *Projections* (five, 1950–51), *Extensions* (four, 1951–53), and *Intersections* (four, 1951–53). By "projection" Feldman meant an attempt "not to 'compose' but to project sounds into time, free from a compositional rhetoric that had no place here. In order not to involve the performer (i.e. myself) in memory (relationships), and because the sounds no longer had an inherent symbolic shape, I allowed for indeterminacies in regard to pitch."[70] His were in fact the first pieces to make such allowances.

Anticipating Earle Brown by a couple of years, Feldman developed a rudimentary graphic notation so as to avoid specifying exact pitches, which all too easily

fell into predictable patterns that reflected the conditioned responses of human beings in society rather than the autonomy of an esthetic object. Instead, he drew boxes of varying length on graph paper to indicate roughly defined high, middle, and low registers, from which the player was free to select any note. Each choice was supposed to be made "blind," or "from scratch," that is, without regard for logical sequence. Most notes were to be played softly, often "just about audible" (to cite a favorite Feldman direction), so that occasional loud notes might appear "for no reason." The composer exercised control over duration, hence overall shape, timbre, and (when the medium was polyphonic) texture. *Projection*

FIG. 2-13   Morton Feldman.

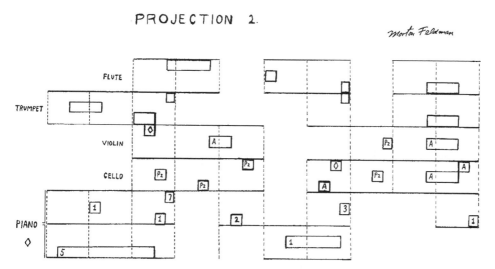

FIG. 2-14   Score page from Feldman, *Projections II*.

I (1950) was for solo cello. *Projection II* (1951), from which Fig. 2-14 is selected, is scored for an ensemble of five instruments.

"Intersections" were pieces in which the players were asked occasionally to make simultaneous attacks so that their individual "lines" intersected, as lines might do on a painted canvas. In the "Extensions" series, conventional notation was occasionally used to set up little repetitive phrases that might go on (extend themselves) for as many as fifty iterations, providing not a narrative or logical continuity but an ambience against which unpredictable events might unfold. These delicate ostinati must come and go, like the occasional loud eruptions, without apparent rhyme or reason. The listening ear must never be allowed to form expectations. Indeed, Feldman once wrote, his music should be listened to "as if you're not listening, but looking at something in nature,"[71] which exists for its own reasons, ignorant and independent of the observer.

Beginning in 1954, however, Feldman abruptly abandoned graphic notation and brought his various gestural series to an end. The reason was simple and significant. Hearing enough performances of his pieces convinced him that his method had an undesirable side effect. As he later put it, "I was not only allowing the sounds to be free — I was also liberating the performer."[72] As Cage had realized before him (and as the experience of the Scratch Orchestra would confirm), liberating people only frees them to follow their habits and whims, which once again deprives the music of its autonomy. Once again it became necessary to put limits on discretion, which meant reverting once again to conventional pitch notation. The difference in musical effect was not great; Cage wryly observed that "Feldman's conventionally notated music is himself playing his graph music."[73] But if performers were now to become the proxies of the composer's own master-rendition, then the paradoxical social elevation of the composer over the performer threatened to intrude anew.

Feldman tried to get around this by a process of automatic writing. In his *Piece for Four Pianos* (1957; Ex. 2-5), the bunch of chords prescribed and arbitrarily repeated seem to have been invented by an unpremeditated "laying on of hands" at the keyboard. The composer's seemingly random touch is then duplicated by four pianists, all playing at different (but not too different) tempos, and at different (but not too different) levels of soft volume. The music achieves a quality of shimmering reverberation during the more repetitive moments, of inscrutable disclosure during the unique events. The periodic general pauses allow the gathered echoes to disperse and a new set to begin.

Pieces from this phase of Feldman's career are written in what is sometimes called "free-rhythm notation," but that is a misnomer. The effect of the music depends on relative uniformity of action within a limited latitude of variation, the composer

EX. 2-5   Morton Feldman, *Piece for Four Pianos*

The first sound with all pianos simultaneously. Durations for each sound are chosen by the performer. All beats are slow and not necessarily equal. Dynamics are low with a minimum of attack. Grace notes should not be played too quickly. Numbers between sounds are equal to silent beats.

counting on his vague performance directions to activate a basically similar response in all performers. Performers and listeners with the capacity for making themselves passive often find the results ravishing; those without it can find the experience maddening. "What was great about the fifties," Feldman wrote, "is that for one brief moment—maybe say, six weeks—nobody understood art. That's why it all happened."[74]

In later years Feldman demanded ever greater reserves of passive endurance on the part of listeners. The music of his last two decades, fully and conventionally notated, entered a time scale unprecedented for "autonomously" conceived instrumental music, maximizing (and thus transforming) the whole centuries-old idea of esthetic autonomy. *For Philip Guston* (1984), a trio for a flutist (doubling alto flute), a pianist (doubling celesta), and a percussionist, dedicated to one of the composer's many artist friends, wends its quiet, basically uniform, yet wholly unpredictable way for four-and-a-half hours. The Second String Quartet (1983), Feldman's longest work, lasts more than six. When listening to one of these pieces, as the critic Paul Griffiths put it in a perceptive review, "all you can say is that you are there; and when it is over, that you were there." The music, "hovering in the rare space between what you can ignore and what you can understand," effectively ignores you.[75]

Yet it is anything but "furniture music." Complete performances of such pieces, in which the traditional concert format and its attendant etiquette are fully maintained, are necessarily infrequent. The Second String Quartet was not attempted complete during Feldman's lifetime. Its first uncut performance, by a young ensemble of Juilliard graduates called the Flux Quartet, took place in October 1999. It was treated by its audience (and heralded by the New York press) as a once-in-a-lifetime event. In this way Feldman managed, even more emphatically than Cage, to preserve the specialness of the esthetic experience during what the critic Walter Benjamin famously called "the age of mechanical reproduction,"[76] when art, by being rendered too easily accessible, had been effectively demystified (or, as Benjamin put it, had lost its "aura").

During a performance of *For Philip Guston*, Griffiths noted, not more than a dozen listeners managed to sit still all the way through. "Perhaps another 20 stayed and moved from place to place. A few others came and went, tiptoeing in and out, like visitors to a long religious ceremony."[77] And with that, the motivation hidden behind the *acte gratuit* is at last revealed. Only by dint of extreme measures could the romantic sacralization of art continue into the age of science. The avant-garde had become a conservative faction, perhaps (as Cornelius Cardew, had he lived, would certainly have charged) the most reactionary faction of them all.

CHAPTER 3

The Apex

BABBITT AND COLD WAR SERIALISM

CONVERSIONS

One effect of the postwar avant-garde, in both its "total serial" and its "indeterminate" phases, was to put the more moderate techniques of prewar twelve-tone music much nearer the middle of the stylistic road, making those who resisted them seem all the more embarrassably conservative. During the 1950s and 1960s nearly everyone experimented with twelve-tone methods, partly out of curiosity, partly in response to the constant pressure to keep stylistically abreast as mandated by the historicist ideology to which practically everyone, regardless of stylistic orientation or one's other artistic convictions, tacitly assented at the middle of the twentieth century.

Paul Hindemith, for example, had inveighed fiercely against the "unnaturalness" of Schoenberg's methods in *The Craft of Musical Composition*, a prewar textbook that was issued in English translation in 1942. "Nowhere," he asserted,

> does Nature give us any indication that it would be desirable to play off a certain number of tones against one another in a given duration and pitch-range. Arbitrarily conceived rules of that sort can be devised in quantities and if styles of composition were to be based upon them, I can conceive of far more comprehensive and more interesting ones. To limit oneself to home-made tonal systems of this sort seems to me a more doctrinaire proceeding than to follow the strictest diatonic rules of the most dried-up old academic . . . . But already a decline is noticeable in the interest manifested in this music based on rules dictated by fashion and contrary to nature.[1]

This was a common enough view in 1937, when Hindemith set it down. By 1955, however, even Hindemith was sketching fully chromatic twelve-tone themes or tone rows for use in a sonata for tuba and piano. As Ex. 3-1 shows, by the time the sonata was fully composed, Hindemith had worked the twelve-tone bug out of his system; the theme eventually chosen no longer exactly coincided with a tone row, even if it did contain representatives of all twelve pitch classes. And yet his fleeting susceptibility shows (all the more clearly, perhaps, for his fighting it off) that Soviet composers were not the only ones who felt pressure to conform to a decreed official style. Even Poulenc, surely the unlikeliest of prospects, gave in to it in his *Elégie* (1957) for horn and piano.

Beginning in 1956, the year in which the new Soviet leader, Nikita Khrushchev, launched a "de-Stalinization" campaign, young Soviet composers also wrote (clandestine) twelve-tone music. For them it was an act of symbolic nonconformism; for Poulenc it was nearer the opposite. (But nonconformism can itself become a form of conformist

EX. 3-1A Paul Hindemith, twelve-tone theme in Tuba Sonata, sketch

EX. 3-1B Paul Hindemith, twelve-tone theme in Tuba Sonata, sketch

EX. 3-1C Paul Hindemith, twelve-tone theme in Tuba Sonata, sketch

EX. 3-1D Paul Hindemith, twelve-tone theme in Tuba Sonata, sketch

EX. 3-1E Paul Hindemith, Tuba Sonata, opening theme as eventually worked out

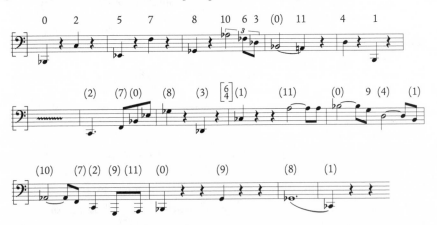

pressure when practiced by an elite group.) By the late 1960s, twelve-tone rows — or, to put it neutrally, successions of twelve nonrepeating pitch classes — had even surfaced in the work of Dmitriy Shostakovich, by then the dean of Soviet composers, as the opening of his Twelfth Quartet (1968) will illustrate (Ex. 3-2). Nor, occurring as they did in the plainly "tonal" context of D♭ major, did they occasion censure. The gesture, becoming commonplace, was losing its shock value.

Several composers, however, underwent more thorough and lasting — and historically significant — conversions to dodecaphonic techniques. One was Aaron Copland, the most prominent representative of the Americanist "populist" style, for whom the adoption of twelve-tone methods was more than a technical advance. It was also a calculated retreat from explicit Americanism and from populism, both of which had paradoxically become politically suspect in the tense early years of the cold war. Copland's unexpected turn to the elite and reputedly forbidding twelve-tone idiom paralleled Stefan Wolpe's, described in chapter 1. It represented the further progress, so to speak, of the cold feet that had led Copland to moderate the ending of his Third Symphony, as described in the same chapter.

Beginning in 1947, the American government, acting through the Committee on Un-American Activities of the U.S. House of Representatives, perpetrated a

EX. 3-2   Dmitriy Shostakovich, Quartet no. 12, Op. 133, I, opening

FIG. 3-1   Hanns Eisler and his wife, Louise, boarding a plane for Vienna in 1948 after the composer's subpoenaed appearance before the House Committee on Un-American Activities.

little "Zhdanovshchina" of its own—public hearings at which artists were politically disgraced (the musicians among them actually a little ahead of their Soviet counterparts). The first musical quarry was Hanns Eisler, who had fled Germany for his life in 1933 and had lived continuously in the United States (chiefly in Hollywood) since 1942. He appeared before the Committee in September 1947 and was deported in March 1948 for being, in the words of the Committee's chief counsel, "the Karl Marx of Communism in the musical field."[2] In the course of presenting evidence against Eisler, the chief counsel read excerpts from interviews the composer had given the Soviet press during a visit to Moscow in 1935. One of them called attention to Copland's mass song, "Into the Streets May First". Another reported "a considerable shift to the left among American artists," and added

> I do not believe it would be an exaggeration to say that the best people in the musical world of America (with very few exceptions) share at present extremely progressive ideas. Their names? They are Aaron Copland, Henry Cowell, Wallingford Riegger, the outstanding musical theoretician Charles Seeger, the greatest specialist on modern music Nicolas Slonimsky, and finally the brightest star on the American musical horizon, the great conductor, Leopold Stokowski.[3]

Copland's name had been named, to use the expression current at the time, in what had become a highly invidious context. More bad publicity followed the so-called Cultural and Scientific Conference for World Peace, held at the Waldorf Astoria Hotel in New York in 1949, where Copland, there as a member of the National Council of American-Soviet Friendship, a remnant of the wartime alliance, was photographed with the recently disgraced Shostakovich (now traveling as a Soviet cultural ambassador at Stalin's behest). Copland's picture was printed in *Life* Magazine under the headline "Dupes and Fellow Travelers Dress Up Communist Fronts."

That embarrassment was followed by more sinister events the next year, when Copland's close friend Clifford Odets, a famous playwright, was called to testify before the House Committee. In March of 1950, Copland was denounced by the American Legion, a veterans organization. In June, he was blacklisted in a notorious publication called *Red Channels: The Reports of Communist Influence in Radio and Television*, albeit without serious consequences to his income, which did not come by way of the entertainment industry. His reaction to the *Red Channels* listing was nevertheless nervous: he withdrew from the NCASF that very month and, over the course of the next few years, severed virtually all his connections with political organizations.

Political pressure on Copland reached its peak in 1953. *A Lincoln Portrait*, a much-promoted product of wartime patriotism, was scheduled for performance by the British-born film star Walter Pidgeon with the National Symphony Orchestra at a Washington concert to celebrate the inauguration of the newly elected President, Dwight David Eisenhower, formerly the Supreme Commander of the Allied military forces that had won the war. Fred Busbey, an Illinois congressman, assailed the choice of Copland's music in a speech delivered on the floor of the House of Representatives on 3 January:

> There are many patriotic composers available without the long record of questionable affiliations of Copland. The Republican Party would have been ridiculed from one end of the United States to the other if Copland's music had been played at the inaugural of a President elected to fight communism, along with other things.[4]

FIG. 3-2   President Dwight D. Eisenhower's inaugural parade, 20 January 1953. Aaron Copland's *Lincoln Portrait* was scheduled for, but later scratched from, a commemorative concert that evening. Copland testified before Senator Joseph McCarthy's Permanent Subcommittee on Investigations four months later.

The performance was canceled. The League of Composers, a promotional organization of which Copland had been the executive director from 1948 to 1950, sent a telegram protesting the ban to the *New York Times*, which reported it. Paul Hume, the music critic of the *Washington Post*, went further, defending Copland in an article that appeared under the title "Music Censorship Reveals New Peril," and ending his review of the sanitized concert (which now contained no American music at all) by taunting "the idea that music by various American-born composers is to be banned if Congressmen protest."[5] The American Civil Liberties Union sent a letter of protest to the inaugural committee, and the historian Bruce Catton published an essay that ridiculed the folly of exercising political censorship in the ostensible name of freedom.

The publicity had on the whole been favorable to Copland; but the little scandal had brought artistic matters to the attention of Senator Joseph McCarthy, whose dreaded Permanent Subcommittee on Investigations had assumed the leading role in exposing and punishing Americans for their "questionable affiliations." Copland's music, along with that of a long list of other American composers against whom "derogatory" allegations had been made, was excluded at Senator McCarthy's urging from promotion by the U.S. Information Agency or from the lending collections at the libraries maintained abroad by the U.S. State Department. Finally, Copland received a telegram summoning him to testify in person before Senator McCarthy's committee on 25 May 1953.

He actually appeared on 26 May, having been granted a day's extension to secure legal representation. He was required to comment on a long list of affiliations to organizations identified by the subcommittee as "Communist fronts," and in particular, to account for his participation in the notorious "Waldorf Conference" in 1949. He was also asked for the names of others with whom he had consorted in the course of his political activities. On the advice of counsel, Copland was a cooperative witness; on the delicate matter of "naming names," particularly of those participating in the Peace Conference, he prepared a statement attesting that, having reread newspaper accounts of the event, "I do not personally remember having seen anyone at the conference who is not listed in those published reports." He kept hidden his indignation (which he confided to his diary) at having, even for the sake of expediency or tactics, to make such admissions when "in a free America I had a right to affiliate openly with whom I pleased; to sign protests, statements, appeals, open letters, petitions, sponsor events, etc., and no one had the right to question those affiliations."[6]

It was during this stressful time that Copland turned to twelve-tone composition. On the one hand, it seemed an unexpected and (to many) even an incomprehensible withdrawal from the large audience that he had won against such heavy odds. Copland had become something of an emblem for that possibility of success (or, depending on how one looked at it, of compromise). In 1948, his commitment to audience appeal had led him into a rather uncomprehending (or even, depending on how one looked at it, a heartless) response to the plight of the Soviet composers under Zhdanov's attack. "They were rebuked," a reporter quoted him as saying, "for failing to realize that their musical audience had expanded enormously in the last several years (you have only to pass a record or radio shop to see that), and that composers can no longer continue to write only for a few initiates."[7] At the 1949 Peace Conference, however, he made a speech, "The Effect of the Cold War on the Artist in the U.S.," that may shed some light on his seemingly paradoxical course of action in the years to come. "Lately," he told the audience,

> I've been thinking that the cold war is almost worse for art than the real thing—for it permeates the atmosphere with fear and anxiety. An artist can function at his best only in a vital and healthy environment for the simple reason that the very act of creation is an affirmative gesture. An artist fighting in a war for a cause he holds just has something affirmative he can believe in. That artist, if he can stay alive, can create art. But throw him into a mood of suspicion, ill-will and dread that typifies the cold war attitude and he'll create nothing.[8]

The status of art as "affirmative gesture" became equivocal at a time when governments demanded conformism. That was the tiny kernel of justice in the otherwise preposterously prosecutorial case that the once-persecuted Leibowitz had mounted against Bartók's "compromises." For T. W. Adorno, the word "affirmative" had become almost tantamount to "fascist." It took the tensions of the cold war to drive the point home to American artists who had never before entertained the possibility that their government might adopt a comparable attitude, let alone try to control or influence their work except by giving them opportunities to receive payment for it.

Works like *A Lincoln Portrait* that affirmed political commitments, even commitments as seemingly uncontroversial as patriotism or identification with one's nation or its greatest president, could easily become political footballs, as the American saying went, when political alignments changed. The nation to which Copland proclaimed his impassioned adherence in wartime was a nation then allied with the Soviet Union ("our gallant Russian allies," as General Eisenhower himself had put it on D day). That all-too-easily forgotten fact tainted the sincere patriotism of many American artists in retrospect, and, as the cold war rewrote history, rendered their patriotic offerings politically ambiguous. At the very least, it was clear in retrospect that if Copland had not composed works with explicit patriotic or national themes, his music would not have been proposed for inclusion in the inaugural concert, and he would have been spared his frightening brush with censorship and possible repression. It was a tormenting dilemma.

While the ivory tower of "pure art" offered Soviet artists scant security, it could look like a haven to their American counterparts, accustomed not to the active support and promotion that totalitarian governments offered in return for cooperative service, but rather to an official attitude of laissez-faire ("leave them be," otherwise known in English as "benign neglect") toward artists, especially those involved in "high culture." When one learns that Copland began sketching his Piano Quartet, the first of his twelve-tone compositions, in March 1950, the same month in which he was targeted by the American Legion, the coincidence of dates prompts the reflection that the composer may have been seeking refuge in the "universal" (and politically safe) truth of numbers, rather than the particular (and politically risky) reality of a national or popular manner.

"MAINSTREAM" DODECAPHONY

The first movement of the Piano Quartet well exemplifies Copland's "mainstream" or "middle of the road" approach to twelve-tone composition. The row (Ex. 3-3) is used as a theme in the traditional sense, which means that it will be varied according to standard methods of thematic elaboration as well as according to specifically serial procedures. It is constructed on the principle of "whole-tone complementation"—that is, playing off the two mutually exclusive whole-tone scales against one another. Whole-tone scale segments, a familiar sound in music since before the turn of the century, are what the themes present most saliently to the listening ear, and what make them memorable.

EX. 3-3A   Aaron Copland, Piano Quartet, development of twelve-tone themes: complementary whole-tone scales

EX. 3-3B   Aaron Copland, Piano Quartet, development of twelve-tone themes: main theme of first movement

EX. 3-3C   Aaron Copland, Piano Quartet, development of twelve-tone themes: main theme as first heard

EX. 3-3D   Aaron Copland, Piano Quartet, development of twelve-tone themes: second theme (pitch content of Example 3-3c transposed and reversed)

EX. 3-3E   Aaron Copland, Piano Quartet, development of twelve-tone themes: opening of second movement (violin)

EX. 3-3F   Aaron Copland, Piano Quartet, development of twelve-tone themes: third movement, viola and cello in mm. 103–105

The structure of the theme already presents in microcosm the Quartet's chief form-generating procedure: the breaking and eventual completion of patterns. The initial whole-tone descent goes as far as the fifth degree out of six before being interrupted by the other whole-tone scale, ascending through four degrees. The withheld pitch from the first scale is then interpolated into the second, creating an intervallic sequence (perfect fourth followed by perfect fifth) suitable for a diatonic cadence. That traditional cadential resonance will of course be exploited in the music. But it raises a question: why go to the trouble of contriving special ingenious situations within a twelve-tone row only to achieve what would have been so much more easily obtainable using Copland's usual compositional techniques? The question confirms the impression that Copland's use of serial techniques may have been prompted less by the specific "purely musical" possibilities it offered than by the "purely abstract," hence politically neutral and unquestionable, musical context it provided.

The breaking of the initial whole-tone pattern by the intrusion of its complement within the theme is projected onto the "macrostructure" of the first movement by withholding the last note of the row on every occurrence of the theme except the last. Example 3-3b, which shows the complete theme, is taken from the piano part at the very end. Example 3-3c, the violin part at the outset, shows the theme as it is heard every other time, with the last pitch replaced by a repetition of the first, as if the theme had been based on an eleven-note row. It is this eleven-note version that is reversed, in "orthodox" twelve-tone fashion (but at an equally "orthodox" tonal transposition to the lower fourth or "dominant") to provide the second theme (ex. 3-3d).

The remainder of Ex. 3-3 is drawn from the second and third movements, to show how the thematic material of the whole quartet is drawn from the initial row (or at least its whole-tone complementation idea). The main theme of the second movement (Ex. 3-3e), close to a retrograde-inversion of Ex. 3-3c, is another eleven-tone melody with a redundant pitch, here at the beginning rather than the end. The withheld pitch (or "hidden pitch" — *note câchée* — as Nadia Boulanger's pupils tended to call it, it being an old idea of hers) does not make an appearance until the nineteenth measure. Ex. 3-3f, from the third movement's coda, shows how the two whole-tone scales are given a complementary summary in the inner parts to provide harmonic closure as the piece draws to its serene completion.

Returning to the first movement, the piano part midway (Ex. 3-4a), and the string parts at the very end (Ex. 3-4b), illustrate how Copland extracts harmonies, respectively, from the whole-tone and "diatonic" portions of his row-theme, and uses the contrast between them to regulate the harmony of the whole according to a traditional tension-and-release concept. Thus harmonic relations govern the emergent sense of the movement's form just as they had always done in "tonal" music. It was the kind of thing that drew fire from the "left" (that is, from Darmstadt) for representing "compromise" with tradition, and with the nonprofessional audience. It shows that Copland, despite his recourse to serial procedures, still regarded himself as a composer living in, and engaged with, a social network.

But the Piano Quartet was only the beginning of Copland's serial odyssey. Over the rough quarter-century remaining to his creative career (which ended in the early seventies, although he lived until 1990), he maintained two compositional approaches, one diatonic and the other twelve-tone. He called them his "popular" and "difficult" styles; on occasion he referred to them as his "public" and "private" manners. And yet his largest, most public works of the 1950s and beyond, the kind for which he had originally developed his "Americanist" idiom, were cast more and more dependably in the "difficult" style, with a musical content that tended conspicuously toward the abstract, even the "formalist." Except for the Third Symphony, Copland's lengthiest and in that sense most ambitious instrumental composition was the twelve-tone *Piano Fantasy* of 1957, cast in a single tightly woven movement that lasts over half an hour and makes a considerable demand on a listener's powers of concentration. The opening of the work (Ex. 3-5) lends striking support to Copland's slightly defensive contention that "twelve-tonism is nothing more than an angle of vision . . . . It is a method, not a style; and therefore it solves no problems of musical expressivity."[9] With its expansive intervallic leaps

EX. 3-4A   Aaron Copland, Piano Quartet, I, mm. 55–61

and its wide-open chord spacing, the music—to anyone who knows the composer's "Americanist" works—sounds palpably "Coplandesque." But what had once been in part a function of subject matter was now entirely a matter of "autonomous" style.

By far the most utterly and essentially "public" composition of Copland's late career was an orchestral piece commissioned by the New York Philharmonic for a 193 gala concert, conducted by Leonard Bernstein, to inaugurate the orchestra's new home at New York City's Philharmonic (now Avery Fisher) Hall, the first building to be completed in the immense complex of performance spaces known as the Lincoln Center for the Performing Arts. The concert, attended by a long list of public figures headed by Jacqueline Kennedy, the first lady of the United States, was televised live and broadcast to a nationwide audience of millions.

The honor of receiving such a commission was not only a testimonial to Copland's incontestable stature as a creative figure, but also a recognition of his special relationship to the American public. Perhaps needless to say, Copland's virtually unique status

EX. 3-4B   Aaron Copland, Piano Quartet, I, mm. 98–end

EX. 3-5   Aaron Copland, *Piano Fantasy*, mm. 1–22

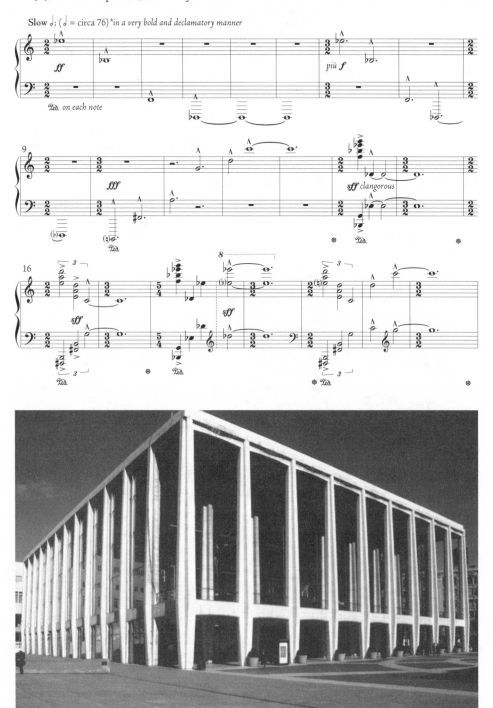

FIG. 3-3   Philharmonic (later Avery Fisher) Hall, Lincoln Center, New York, inaugurated in 1961.

among "serious" composers as a household name derived from his Americanist works of the 1930s and 1940s; and yet the work he produced for this most publicized moment of his career was an especially severe exercise in abstraction. Its very title, *Connotations*, suggested that its tight motivic "argument" — that is to say, its formal procedure — was tantamount to its content; and in the introductory remarks that preceded the broadcast performance, Copland emphasized the strictness with which the entire twenty-minute composition was derived from the "three harsh chords" (Ex. 3-6a) that opened the work (each containing four notes of the governing twelve-tone row). The ending was a series of strident "aggregates" — that is, twelve-note chords that the audience found perplexing, if not downright distasteful (Ex. 3-6b). The immediate reaction was embarrassing: "a confused near silence,"[10] as Copland recollected it.

EX. 3-6A Aaron Copland, *Connotations*, opening ("three harsh chords" and their immediate consequences)

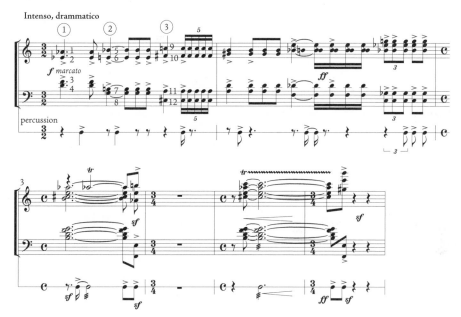

EX. 3-6B Aaron Copland, *Connotations*, ending

The dramatic fashion in which Copland had sacrificed his hard-won, well-nigh unique public appeal for the sake of what seemed (at least in the context of a glittering public gala) an "alienated" modernist stance, seemed to give credence to the idea that the triumph of twelve-tone music was the result of an inevitable and irresistible historical process. Copland himself accounted for his change of style, in a modest comment to Bernstein, by saying that he "needed more chords"[11] — implying, if not the "exhaustion of tonality" that more pretentious commentators had been proclaiming for decades, at least that his own technical or stylistic resources had needed renewal.

There is no reason to expect a composer to look beyond his conscious musical appetites for the sources of his musical behavior. But the corollary, that such appetites are stimulated only spontaneously ("from within"), is contradicted — at least in the present case — by the fact that the idiom Copland had adopted in search of new chords was not his alone, but part of an emergent "period style." It opened him up to charges, in the words of one disapproving critic in the Lincoln Center audience, of having "yielded to conformism."[12] Stated in such an unflattering way, the remark is hostile. But one can put the matter in a less invidious light by quoting a perceptive remark by Copland himself.

It was part of a lecture that Copland gave in 1952 at Harvard University, where he was occupying the same "chair of poetry" that had given Stravinsky a forum in 1939. The title of the lecture, "Tradition and Innovation in Recent European Music," may have been a deliberate attempt to deflect attention away from his own present creative concerns, or those of other American composers. But its contents were nevertheless pertinent to those concerns. "The twelve-tone composer," Copland declared (not letting on that he had lately become one himself), "is no longer writing music to satisfy himself; whether he likes it or not, he is writing it *against* a vocal and militant opposition."[13] The opposition Copland had in mind, of course, was the Communist (or Zhdanovite) opposition, which many former Soviet sympathizers now saw as a deadly threat. But the virtues that twelve-tone music seemed, in its wholly formal purity, to possess in contrast to the mandated political content of Stalinist art were no less attractive as a refuge from attempts to control art in the name of anti-Communism. "New chords" could come from many sources. That special sense of refuge in the discipline of one's art was something only twelve-tone music then seemed to guarantee so reliably.

THE GRAND PRIZE

Or as Igor Stravinsky put it to a Paris reporter, in response to what by 1952 had become an inevitable interviewer's question: "The twelve-tone system? Personally I have enough to do with seven tones. But the twelve-tone composers are the only ones who have a discipline I respect. Whatever else it may be, twelve-tone music is certainly pure music."[14]

Like Copland, Stravinsky left out the most newsworthy part: that he himself had begun to appropriate the system he had long opposed (or, as some grumbled, to be appropriated by it). The "conversion" or "capitulation" of the most celebrated living composer to the serialist cause was an enormous boost not only to the prestige of serial music, but to the whole deterministic view of history that supported its resurgence. Until Stravinsky's death in 1971, that doctrine would be virtually unassailable in the places where history was written. Moreover, the path Stravinsky took to the twelve-tone method was remarkably gradual, incremental, and orderly from a technical point of view. It provided, as if in microcosm, a model of the historical process it was said to embody, and has therefore become one of the most frequently retold stories in the recent history of music.

Between December 1947 and April 1951 Stravinsky wrote by far the longest work of his career: a three-act opera called *The Rake's Progress*, after a set of paintings (later engravings) by the English artist William Hogarth (1687–1764) that depicted the moral and material decline of a rich young wastrel. On the basis of Hogarth's painted scenes, the English poet W. H. Auden (1907–73) had worked out a scenario in collaboration with the composer, and worked it up into a libretto in collaboration with a younger poet named Chester Kallman (1921–75). The libretto, all about free choice and its consequences, was a very timely primer of post–World War II existentialism, turned out in an elegant "period" style to match the opera's eighteenth-century setting.

Striving in his music for a similar ironic parallel between the modern implications of the drama and its period setting, Stravinsky produced what was on the surface his most literalistically "neoclassical" score, replete with harpsichord-accompanied recitatives, strophic songs, da capo arias, and formal ensembles, including a moralizing quintet at the end to draw explicit lessons from the foregoing action, obviously modeled on the sextet at the end of Mozart's *Don Giovanni*. Although composed to an English text, the work had its premiere in Venice, before a cosmopolitan festival audience at the famous eighteenth-century Teatro La Fenice (Phoenix Theater), on 11 September 1951.

The Rake's Progress is now a much admired repertory opera, but it had at first a very problematic reception. The high-society audience that heard it on its first night received it warmly. Among musicians, however, it was widely written off as a trifling, fashionable pastiche. And no wonder: its archly pretty, stylistically retrospective music jarred cacophonously with the bleak "zero-hour" mood, described in chapter 1, that reigned in Europe. Its obsessive stylistic self-consciousness, now easily understood as consciousness of art in crisis, seems just as much a response to its uncertain times as the work of the Darmstadt avant-garde. At the time, though, it seemed the product of a composer blissfully out of touch with the contemporary requirements of his art. For the first time in his life, Stravinsky found himself rejected by the younger generation of European musicians. The effect of this rejection on his self-esteem was traumatic.

We know about this aftereffect of the *Rake* premiere thanks to Robert Craft (b. 1923), an aspiring conductor who had made Stravinsky's acquaintance, and impressed him very favorably, at the very start of work on the opera. Their first meeting, in fact, took place on the very day in March 1948 when Auden delivered to Stravinsky the completed libretto of the first act. Stravinsky hired Craft to join him at his California home as an assistant for the summer. One of his jobs was to make a catalogue of Stravinsky's manuscripts, which had just arrived from safekeeping in Europe. Another was to read the *Rake* libretto aloud to Stravinsky so that the composer, for whom English was a fourth language, could hear it idiomatically pronounced. (Craft was at first disconcerted that the composer did not hesitate to set it "wrong"[15] wherever he saw a musical advantage in doing so.) The young assistant never left, but remained a member of the composer's household until Stravinsky's death almost twenty-three years later.

Craft made himself indispensable to Stravinsky in any number of ways. He shared conducting duties on concert tours and rehearsed orchestras before recording sessions. He served as an interlocutor through whom Stravinsky published five volumes of memoirs in dialogue form. Craft's most important service to Stravinsky, however, was in enabling him to weather the post-*Rake* creative crisis by providing a conduit through which the seventy-year-old composer gained access to new modes of musical thinking and writing he had previously ignored, and even scorned. When Stravinsky suddenly felt the need to catch up, Craft (who knew the works of the Viennese atonalists, rehearsed and conducted them in Stravinsky's presence, and procured scores and even textbooks for his employer's instruction) stood ready to abet him. In so doing he made possible the last sixteen years of Stravinsky's active life as a composer.

Stravinsky's assimilation of serial technique, though orderly and eminently traceable, was actually (because it came so late in his career) quite idiosyncratic. In effect, he became a serial composer before becoming a twelve-tone one; indeed his example is what makes it possible to draw this very useful distinction. His first serial work was a "ricercar" for tenor and five accompanying instruments called "Tomorrow Shall Be My Dancing Day." It was part of a *Cantata* on anonymous fifteenth- and sixteenth-century English lyrics, the very next piece Stravinsky composed after *The Rake's Progress*, in 1951–52.

The first item in the *Cantata* in order of composition, a ricercar called "The Maidens Came," for mezzo-soprano and the same accompanying ensemble, was completed in July 1951, before the *Rake* premiere; the rest was written afterward. There is no premonition in "The Maidens Came" that other parts of the Cantata would use a serial technique (unless the eerie fact that Arnold Schoenberg, then Stravinsky's never-visited Los Angeles neighbor, happened to die while it was in progress counts as a premonition). But by the time it came to composing "Tomorrow Shall Be My Dancing Day," Stravinsky had become fascinated with the "discipline" his old rival had pioneered — although on this maiden outing he was content to apply it (recalling his repartee with the Paris reporter) to a "seven-tone" or diatonic context.

Stravinsky selected a little A-minor phrase, seemingly at random, from "The Maidens Came," transposed it to C major simply by substituting the bass clef for the treble, arbitrarily inserted a tiny chromatic inflection just for spice, and ended up with the eleven-note "row" shown in Ex. 3-7a. In terms of its contents it is very far from being a twelve-tone row, since it only contains eight different pitches, and two of the eight, C and E, are repeated in succession to give it a pronounced "tonal" focus. But Stravinsky's use of it is quite strictly "serial," for he maintained its intervallic order as a given throughout the new ricercar, which actually consists of a series of canons in which the eleven-note subject is treated the same way Schoenberg treated a twelve-tone row: as originally notated, in reverse, in inversion, and in reversed inversion.

Example 3-7b reproduces a chart Stravinsky jotted down to guide him in composing his ricercar, in which he designated the "classical" serial operations using his own idiosyncratic terms. The subject is immediately followed by its "cancricans" or retrograde. Below it is the "riverse" or inversion, followed by *its* "cancricans." The chart's most noteworthy aspect is the pitch level selected for the inversion, a downward transposition by a third that reproduces the opening pitches of the original subject in reversed order, thus insuring that the whole complex stays "in C" and makes its "final cadence" there.

The reason for the transposition is evident from Ex. 3-7c, a musical example that Stravinsky prepared for a program note distributed at the Cantata's premiere performance in the fall of 1952. It is the opening of the tenor part (or Cantus Firmus, as Stravinsky called it), encompassing the first three lines of the poem. The four "serial permutations" have been welded, by the use of overlapping pitches at the joins, into a single C-major melody. Stravinsky drew the brackets himself, to demonstrate the four permutations. What is more surprising, the published score contains similar brackets that call attention to the serial manipulations throughout the piece.

In Ex. 3-8, which shows the fourth canon in the ricercar, these brackets are preserved, and labels have been added to assist the reader in identifying the "row forms" according to standard nomenclature: P for prime, R for retrograde, I for inversion, RI for retrograde inversion. Subscripts indicate transpositions, always "upward" by semitones: 1 = a semitone up, 11 = a major seventh [eleven semitones] up or one

EX. 3-7A   Igor Stravinsky, *Cantata*, Ricercar II ("Tomorrow Shall Be My Dancing Day"), derivation of the subject

EX. 3-7B   Igor Stravinsky's table of serial permutations in *Cantata*, Ricercar II

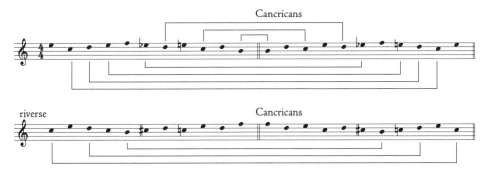

EX. 3-7C   Igor Stravinsky, *Cantata*, Ricercar II, beginning of the tenor part

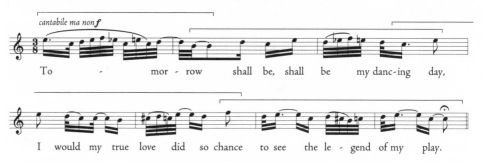

semitone down, and so forth. Stravinsky's relief at having managed, so late in the day, to assimilate an advanced compositional technique is evident in the pride with which he provided an analysis of the music to go along with the score. His 1952 program note, too, was wholly concerned with a technical description of how the music is made. Here is a sample, describing the music shown in Ex. 3-8:

> In the fourth canon the first oboe follows the second at the interval of a second while the voice transposes the Cantus in inverted form down a minor third to A. In the three last bars, the cello, which has been accompanying with a new rhythmic figure, plays the Cantus in F, original form, while the voice and the first oboe play it in A, original form. The fifth canon is identical with the first. The sixth begins with the Cantus in the voice in original form . . .[16]

This way of describing the piece, solely in terms of its technical procedures, again chimes with Stravinsky's remark to the Paris reporter ("Whatever else it may be, twelve-tone music is certainly pure music").

But is it quite fair to describe, or conceive of, the second ricercar from Stravinsky's *Cantata* as "pure music"? Can the fact (which Stravinsky never mentioned in his program note) that the piece has a text, and that the text poetically narrates the life of Christ, be considered irrelevant to an esthetic consideration of it? More uncomfortably yet, are the facts that the "fourth canon" (at 18) sets words reflective of an ancient libel against the Jews, and that the composer chose them for setting seven years after the Nazi Holocaust, likewise to be regarded as esthetically irrelevant (implying that to take offense at the act or its product was a philistine — or worse, a Zhdanovite — reaction to fine art)?

Going further yet, is there a correlation between the quest for musical purity that, Stravinsky said, motivated his recourse to the serial method, and the moral evasion at which all these uncomfortable questions seem to point? How shall we define or evaluate that relationship, and how does it compare with the political, social, and moral issues that motivated the adoption of serial technique by the young composers of Europe, as described in chapter 1? Was Stravinsky, too, practicing a willed amnesia? Was Copland? Under what circumstances do (or should) artists have the right to turn away from the cruel facts of life and attend only to "the inherent tendency of musical material"? Do they (or should they) always have social responsibilities?

THE PATH TO THE NEW/OLD MUSIC

These questions, always discomforting, achieved special poignancy after the war—and especially in America, where the sheer research and development of musical technique achieved a prodigious, institutionally supported acme that was never approached in Europe. Stravinsky's location in America colored his serial quest in ways he was probably unaware of, conditioning its slow, cumulative, evolutionary—and yes, somewhat academic—progress (in sharp distinction to the sweeping revolutionary gestures of the Darmstadt school, so reminiscent of Stravinsky's own early maximalist phase).

Stravinsky continued to work with "rows" of varying length and content for a while, before settling on the canonical twelve non-repeating pitch classes. The next work after the *Cantata* was a Septet for three woodwinds, three strings, and piano. Its middle movement, a Passacaglia, has a sixteen-note ground bass on which Stravinsky erected

EX. 3-8   Igor Stravinsky *Cantata*, Ricercar II, fourth canon

EX. 3-8   (*continued*)

an intricate canonic structure like the one in "Tomorrow Shall Be My Dancing Day," replete with inversions, retrogrades, and retrograde inversions. The last movement, called Gigue (but actually a multiple fugue), is obviously modeled on the Gigue in Schoenberg's Suite, op. 29 (1926), for an almost identical instrumental septet. (Craft prepared a performance of Schoenberg's Suite at UCLA while Stravinsky was at work on the piece, and Stravinsky attended all the rehearsals.) Each instrument in this contrapuntal tour de force has its own "row," as Stravinsky (misleadingly) put it in the score, meaning that every instrument employs an eight-note "unordered collection" or scale abstracted from the Passacaglia's ground bass, each at its own transposition.

"Musicke to heare" (Sonnet VIII), the first of *Three Songs from William Shakespeare* (1953), gives the serial treatment to a "row" of only four notes; *In Memoriam Dylan Thomas* (1954) uses a row of five. The two large-scale works that followed—*Canticum Sacrum* (1955), a cantata in honor of St. Mark composed for performance at the Venice Cathedral bearing his name, and *Agon* (1957), a "ballet for twelve dancers" commissioned for the choreographer George Balanchine by the New York City Ballet—contain Stravinsky's first compositions using twelve-tone rows of the usual sort. In each, however, the twelve-tone component consists of short, individual, self-contained episodes in what is otherwise a tonally centered, nonserial composition.

At last, with *Threni* (1958), a thirty-five-minute oratorio on texts from the biblical Lamentations of Jeremiah, Stravinsky turned out a work that was both serial and atonal, and that was composed using twelve-tone rows of standard design throughout. Stravinsky prepared for the task of writing it by working through the exercises in *Studies in Counterpoint*, a textbook on twelve-tone composition (the first in English), which the newly emigrated Ernst Krenek had published in 1940 while teaching composition at Vassar College. Krenek had completed a setting of verses from the Lamentations himself in 1942, and published it in 1957; Stravinsky studied that, too. From it, he appropriated a clever technique of serial manipulation that fascinated him, and that he would make peculiarly his own.

It was inspired by Webern's symmetrical row structures, which Krenek had been among the first to analyze. Krenek called the technique "rotation." More precisely, it was a process of cyclic permutation whereby one varied the intervallic structure of a row, or a portion thereof, by starting on each of its constituent notes in turn and transferring the previous starting note to the end. To gain an extra dimension of symmetrical design à la Webern, Krenek worked the technique on the two complementary halves (or "hexachords") of a row fashioned so that the hexachords were related symmetrically.

In the unusually scalar row Krenek adopted for his *Lamentations* setting, the intervallic sequence of the second hexachord reproduced that of the first in retrograde inversion. Ex. 3-9 shows Krenek's "rotation" technique applied to the *Lamentations* row. The process of cyclic permutation is accompanied in each case by a transposition that keeps the starting pitches for the two respective hexachords the same. In this way the hexachords become "modal scales," as Krenek put it, as one might derive the whole series of diatonic modes or octave species (Dorian, Phrygian, Lydian, and so on) on

EX. 3-9 "Rotation" (cyclic permutation and transposition) in Ernst Krenek, *Lamentatio Jeremiae prophetae*

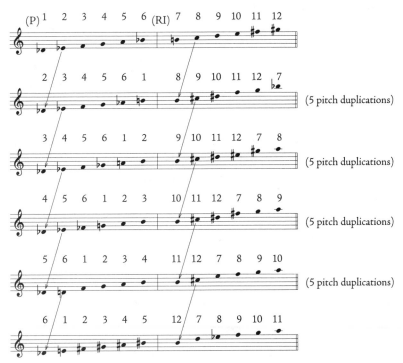

a given tonic by applying Krenek's rotation method to a major or minor scale. What evidently attracted him to the idea, when writing a modern version of sacred choral polyphony, was the apparent relationship of his "twelve-tone modal system" to the modal system of medieval music theory.

But in the process of transposition, Krenek's modal system stops being a "twelve-tone technique," strictly speaking; it introduces pitch duplications between the hexachords, whose sums therefore no longer necessarily exhaust the twelve pitch classes. As Krenek put it in the essay already quoted in chapter 1, "the purpose of the operation was not so much to make the serial design stricter, but rather to relax it, insofar as the wide variety of available six-note patterns made it possible to remain within the frame of reference of the twelve-tone serial technique without constantly having to use complete twelve-tone rows."[17] Indeed, the technique "relaxes" serial design far more than Krenek admits, since it produces a series of varied arrangements of intervals around a pair of constant pitches (here, D♭ and B), which are in a sense promoted to the level of tone centers. Minimizing this contradiction with the bland remark about remaining "within the frame of reference of the twelve-tone serial technique," Krenek has in effect (unwittingly?) readmitted tonal (or, more neutrally, "centric") relations into the purportedly serial domain.

Krenek may eventually have come to see this feature of his rotation technique as an experimental flaw, or perhaps a feature suitable only for writing updated Palestrina. In any case he did not pursue the method in later works. But it gave Stravinsky just what he was looking for, namely a strategy that enabled him to wangle from the twelve-tone technique a familiar sort of material that suited his longstanding creative predilections. We have seen Copland doing similarly: for both composers it was worth the trouble to find a new and tortuous way back to their customary terrain because for their varying reasons they each felt the need to operate, or to be seen as operating, "within the frame of reference of the twelve-tone serial technique." Beginning with *Movements* for piano and orchestra (1959–60), the next work after *Threni*, Stravinsky introduced a new wrinkle into the technique Krenek had pioneered. He began extracting the pitches from each successive vertical column in his hexachord arrays, and using the groups of pitches thus extracted — he called them "verticals" — as chords. Stravinsky once wrote out a demonstration of the method (shown in Fig. 3-4), using for the purpose the first hexachord in the inverted row of his *Variations* for orchestra (1964), and accompanied it with an idiosyncratic verbal explanation in his version of English:

> Some stressed octaves and fifths and doubled intervals which could be found in this score shouldn't contradict the serial (and not harmonical) basis of the composition; the origin of it lies not in a horizontal contrapunctical accord of different voices but in a vertical similtaneous [sic] sounding of several notes belonging to a certain number of forms played together.[18]

Despite the octave doublings on A and C♯, in other words, the chord shown below is not a traditional triad with double-inflected third, of a kind Stravinsky often used during his "neoclassical" period, but an authentic artifact of the serial system — at least *his* serial system — since both A and C♯ occur twice in the outlined column of which the chord is a summary.

Stravinsky's squeamishness is revealing, but also concealing. In fact his whole "verticals" technique was designed to give him access to chords like the one outlined in this demonstration. Fig. 3-4 is amplified in Ex. 3-10, which shows all the verticals that can be derived from the array. (Since the first column yields nothing but a single pitch, that column is customarily designated "zero" when doing analyses of this kind.) Ex. 3-11, from the *Variations*, shows the whole panoply of verticals deployed as chords in the actual composition, punctuating a counterpoint of three trombones that is derived from the rotations of the row's complementary hexachord. (Those looking closely will notice that the chord representing vertical [1] contains an A♯ instead of an

FIG. 3-4   Stravinsky's analytical demonstration of his "verticals" technique.

F♯; such discrepancies are often noted by analysts of Stravinsky's serial works; opinions differ as to whether they are adjustments for the sake of euphony or slips to be corrected by an editor.)

And what is the special property of all verticals (not just the ones that contain triads) that made them so attractive to Stravinsky? Another look at Ex. 3-9 or Ex. 3-10 will confirm that the successive transpositions of the hexachords exactly mirror the intervals between the consecutive pitches in the original form, or more simply, that the hexachord is being transposed by its own interval content, inverted. Because of this built-in inversional symmetry, the pitch-content of the verticals produced by any hexachordal "rotation" (permutation-plus-transposition) will invariably be disposed symmetrically around the generating ("zero") pitch, the latter thus assuming, in the most literal sense of the word, the role of a tone center.

Thus, in Ex. 3-10, verticals 1 + 5, 2 + 4, and 3 (which is necessarily self-inverting) can all be symmetrically displayed around D, the zero pitch. For Stravinsky, who had long ago cut his compositional teeth on symmetrically disposed harmonies mined from the whole-tone and octatonic scales, Krenek's rotation technique, when expanded to include the extraction of verticals, offered systematic access to a greatly expanded vocabulary of symmetrical harmonic constructions, including (but not limited to) all the Stravinskian perennials like the "major-minor triad," which shows up in the array in Ex. 3-10 not only in position 2 (as demonstrated by Stravinsky himself in Fig. 3-4), but also in position 4, the complementary location.

The same "center" pitches that function as axes of symmetry for the verticals, moreover, continually recur as the "tonics" of the "modal scales" produced by the rotations. By emphasizing these relations, Stravinsky was well aware that he was not abandoning the "tonal system" but rather (as he put it in an interview with Craft) composing in an alternative tonal system ("*my* tonal system") inspired by and related to, but not entirely congruent with, the more strictly contrapuntal twelve-tone idiom employed by Schoenberg or Webern.

For in an important sense the verticals technique is not a twelve-tone technique at all, or even a serial one. As harmonic constructs Stravinsky's verticals are only very tenuously related to the original row, or "series." In particular they have little or nothing to do with the series qua series — that is, a temporally unfolding sequence

EX. 3-10   Igor Stravinsky, *Variations*, full tabulation of "verticals" from the hexachord rotated in Fig. 3-4

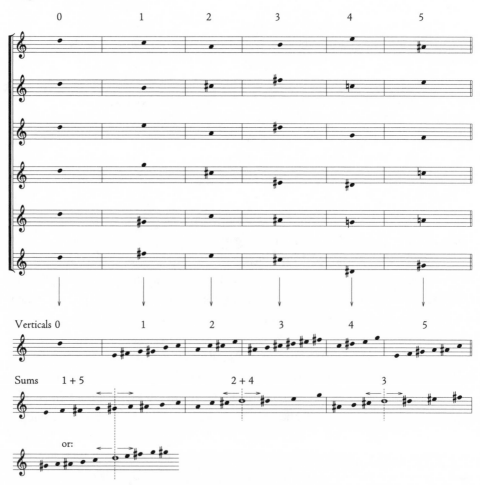

or succession of intervals. Instead, that temporal unfolding has been frozen (or "hypostatized") into a static vertical equilibrium, like so many of the harmonies in *The Firebird* or *The Rite of Spring*. In his serial music Stravinsky sought what he had always sought. The new technique made it more difficult to find, but that only added to the virtuousness of adopting the method. Working against greater resistance, according to the existentialist work ethic, gave one's creative products greater "authenticity." They had to be truly chosen from among consciously weighed alternatives, not merely inherited from unthinking adherence to habit, or dictated by conditioned reflex.

EX. 3-11   Igor Stravinsky, *Variations*, mm. 73–85

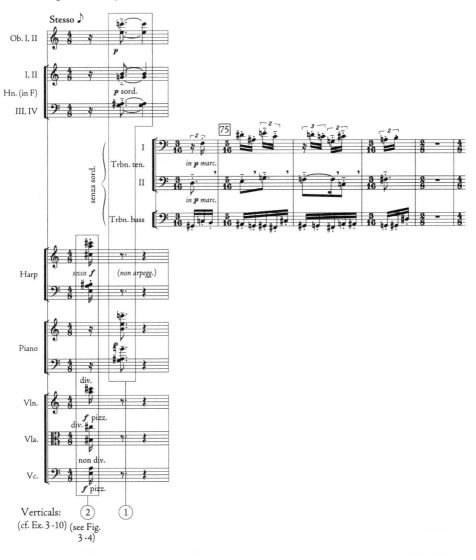

EX. 3-11 *(continued)*

REQUIEM FOR A HEAVYWEIGHT

Stravinsky's serial technique can be sampled at its ripest in his last major work, the *Requiem Canticles* of 1966. (Only one composition would follow in 1967, a cute but inconsequential setting for voice and piano of Edward Lear's children's poem, "The Owl and the Pussy-Cat.") This fifteen-minute setting—for contralto and bass soloists, small chorus, and small orchestra—of several short selections from the text of the Mass of the Dead, was completed when the composer himself was eighty-four years old and infirm, and expected that it would be his final work.

Nevertheless, its musical technique remained faithful to the questing spirit of modernism. Stravinsky actually tried a few novel devices out in it for the first time, and several aspects of the work made it at first an enigma for analysts. That was a point of pride for Stravinsky, as for most modernists, since it gave him the sense (particularly important to Stravinsky since his crisis of the early fifties) of being out in front again. "No theorist," Stravinsky boasted in published conversation with Robert Craft, "could determine the spelling of the flute solo near the beginning [of *Movements*], or the derivation of the three Fs announcing the last movement simply by knowing the original order"[19] of the series. The three Fs were just three "zero pitches" from an array like the one in Ex. 3-10; but of course when Stravinsky issued his challenge the only published analysis of such an array was in a long-forgotten (except by Stravinsky) article of Krenek's.

The riddle of the *Requiem Canticles* was why Stravinsky used two different series in alternation for the various sections of this short work, while many longer works (Schoenberg's evening-length opera *Moses und Aron*, for instance) managed to achieve all the variety they needed within the constraints of a single series. Sampling the last three sections of the work will suggest an answer. They sum up the three textures or media found within the *Requiem Canticles*. The Lacrimosa is an accompanied vocal solo; Libera me is choral and chordal; the Postlude, also chordal, is an instrumental commentary.

EX. 3-12   Igor Stravinsky, *Requiem Canticles*, Lacrimosa

EX. 3-12   (*continued*)

In the Lacrimosa (Ex. 3-12), the musical material is drawn almost entirely from a "rotational" array like the one in Ex. 3-10, constructed on the inverted retrograde of the second series (see Ex. 3-13). The contralto part begins at the lower right and simply snakes its way up the right-hand column, then across to the left-hand column and down, reading the cyclically permuted and transposed hexachords alternately right-to-left and left-to-right. Meanwhile, the sustained accompanying chords are simply the ten verticals, beginning with those of the second hexachord straightforwardly presented from 1 to 5,

EX. 3-12 *(continued)*

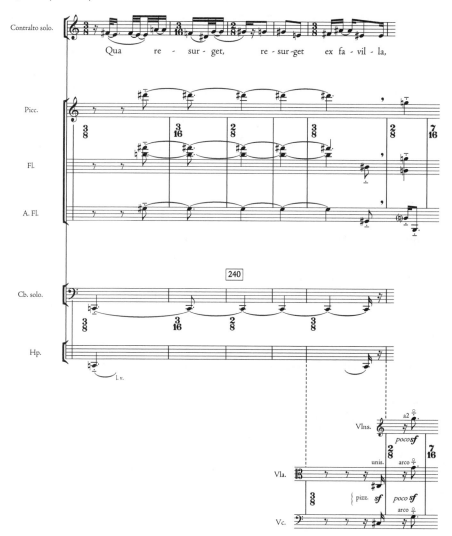

and continuing in similar fashion with those of the first. (The multiply doubled G that intervenes at the end of the example is nothing but the second hexachord's "zero" pitch.) The few remaining notes in the piece are derived from another row form, unrotated and untransposed.

The Libera me (Ex. 3-14) is derived from a similar rotational array based on the inverted retrograde of the first series, handled much more "freely" (that is, selectively) so as to generate the consonant harmonies that give this chorus, which simulates an actual Orthodox *panikhida* or service for the dead, its "antique" or "liturgical" effect. This movement is especially poignant, not only in its prefiguring the composer's own *panikhida*, five years later, where it was indeed performed, but also because it shows Stravinsky, by dint of an especially elaborate strategy, wresting from the serial method a kind of harmony he might have composed especially easily, without qualm or strain, at an earlier phase of his career. The harmony in the Lacrimosa, too, is ingeniously retrospective, Stravinsky having structured the second series so that five pitches in each of its hexachords are referable to a single octatonic scale—a feature that lends a peculiarly familiar color to the melodic writing and the supporting harmonies alike.

It is in the concluding Postlude (Ex. 3-15) that the two series are used concurrently, as if in synthesis. In a disarmingly artless maneuver, Stravinsky let the two series (Ex. 3-16) simply run side by side together with their inversions to generate the strings of four-part harmonies played by the "mallet percussion" instruments (celesta doubling tubular chimes and vibraphone). The horn F at the beginning is the "zero pitch" from which the four set forms all proceed. Given the intervallic similarity of the two sets, what emerges is a near palindromic sequence of (by definition) self-inverting harmonies symmetrically disposed around the F that starts each of the row forms on its way, here treated as a pedal so that it sounds in harmony with the chords whose symmetrical structures it completes. The chord progressions that follow, less strictly fashioned than the first but sharing its properties, are derived from the combined retrogrades and inverted retrogrades, and from the combined primes and retrogrades. The more complex chords sustained by flutes, piano, and harp are "bitonal" combinations of verticals derived from the two sets.

EX. 3-13   Igor Stravinsky, *Requiem Canticles*, source array for Lacrimosa

Only by deploying in tandem a pair of sets with a common starting point or "zero pitch" could Stravinsky have generated such an impressive array of self-inverting harmonies — minor seventh chords, augmented triads, whole-tone segments, French sixths, diminished triads and sevenths, plus others without common-practice standing — all motivated by a new syntax to govern their progression. The technique — novel enough, however simple, to elude analytical detection for more than two decades — enabled a new point of contact with a harmonic vocabulary that had provided the stylistic bedrock

EX. 3-14   Igor Stravinsky, *Requiem Canticles*, Libera me

of Stravinsky's early maximalistic ballets, as a comparison with a characteristic passage from *The Firebird* (Ex. 3-17), composed fifty-six years earlier, will confirm.

ACADEMICISM, AMERICAN STYLE

The *Requiem Canticles* had its first performance (the last Stravinsky premiere) under Robert Craft in October 1966, at a concert that took place on the campus of Princeton University. It was a fitting venue, for over the preceding couple of decades Princeton

EX. 3-15   Igor Stravinsky, *Requiem Canticles*, Postlude

EX. 3-16 Igor Stravinsky, *Requiem Canticles*, the two series as deployed in the Postlude

EX. 3-17 Symmetrical harmonies in Igor Stravinsky, *The Firebird*

had become, largely through the efforts of Milton Babbitt, the American stronghold for the theory and practice of serial music. The university administration had actually commissioned the *Requiem Canticles* in 1965, acting on behalf of the family of an alumnus to whose mother's memory the work was dedicated.

Princetonian theory and practice differed critically from that of Darmstadt, with which it was inevitably compared. The difference had to do, certainly, with the personalities involved; but it also reflected differing institutional structures and a difference in the surrounding intellectual, cultural, and economic climate. As we saw in chapter 1, Darmstadt serialism was the fruit of pessimism, reflecting the "zero hour" mentality of war-ravaged Europe. It thrived on the idea of the cleanest possible break with the past. Princetonian serialism reflected American optimism. It rode the crest of scientific prestige and remained committed to the idea of progress, which implied the very opposite attitude toward the past: namely a high sense of heritage and obligation. Where the two coincided was in the conviction that serious artists lived in only history, not in society, and that fulfilling history's mandate meant resisting the temptation of compromise with social pressures and rewards.

Princetonian serialism — or, more generally, American postwar serialism — reflected the remarkable vision of Milton Babbitt (b. 1916), its leading theorist and (at first) its main practitioner. Trained in mathematics and formal logic as well as music, Babbitt quickly saw the possibility of rationalizing the technique of twelve-tone composition, and generalizing its theoretical foundations, on the basis of what mathematicians call "set theory." He formulated his new theoretical approach in a paper, "The Function of Set Structure in the Twelve-Tone System" (1946), which he submitted as a Ph.D. thesis to the Princeton music department. Since there was at that time neither a qualified reader on the music faculty nor an officially instituted Ph.D. program there in music theory or composition, Babbitt was not awarded a doctorate even though he had been hired by the department as a professor, eventually holding an endowed chair in recognition of his achievements. This anomalous and frustrating situation spurred Babbitt to lobby actively for recognition of music composition as a legitimate branch of music research.

Meanwhile, his unaccepted Ph.D. dissertation, circulating widely in typescript, became perhaps the most influential unpublished document in the history of twentieth-century music. (Revised sections were eventually published as articles between 1955 and 193, and Babbitt was finally — somewhat jokingly — awarded his long-deferred degree in 1992, by which time he had retired from active teaching, having received several honorary doctorates including one from Princeton.) The precision of its vocabulary and the logical clarity of its presentation had a revolutionizing effect on academic discourse about music, and not only in America.

Several terms that Babbitt coined in his dissertation, particularly "pitch class" (the class of pitches related by octave transposition and designated with a single letter name), quickly became standard parlance even outside the domain of serial theory, for they named musical universals that had previously required cumbersome phrases to define. Another, already used freely in this book on the assumption that readers will understand it, is "aggregate," meaning the complete set of all twelve pitch-classes. Moreover, Babbitt's appropriation of the mathematical term "combinatorial" made it possible to clarify and rationalize an important concept within serial music that went all the way back to Schoenberg, but had never before been adequately defined or properly understood for lack of a name.

All of these terms originated in set theory, the branch of mathematics, chiefly developed by the German mathematician Georg Cantor (1845–1918), that lies closest to logic. It is basically the study of the relationship between wholes (or aggregates) and parts (or members). A type of music based, like serial music, on the completion of aggregates obviously lends itself to "set-theoretical" description. Every twelve-tone row is an individual ordering of the unchanging aggregate set, so that the most important features of twelve-tone sets are (1) the way in which their particular parts relate to the general whole, and (2) the way in which their parts relate to one another.

Ex. 3-18 is an ingenious analytical table, prepared and first published by George Perle, that summarizes the entire "set complex" on which Babbitt based the first of his *Three Compositions for Piano* (1947), the first work he composed after formulating his set-theoretic approach to twelve-tone composition. The set complex consists of all the row forms employed in the piece, eight in all: two "primes" (original orderings), two retrogrades, two inversions, and two inverted retrogrades. The interval of transposition between similar row forms is always a tritone (six semitones); and the interval between the inverted and noninverted row forms is a perfect fifth (seven semitones), just as it often is in Schoenberg's music.

EX. 3-18   George Perle's analytical table summarizing the "set complex" of Milton Babbitt's *Three Compositions for Piano*, no. 1

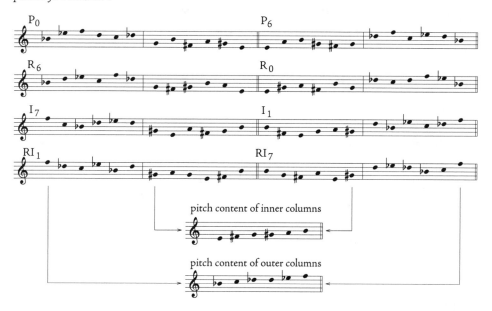

The two shorter staves at the bottom of the diagram show what conditioned Babbitt's choice of row forms. In every case, the pitch content of the two constituent half rows (hexachords) reproduces that of the original statement (P-0). The unordered pitch content of the two complementary hexachords making up a row, then, is a constant for this composition, or (in the language of set theory) an "invariant." The table shows the way in which Babbitt, in keeping with the title of one of the seminal articles spun off from his dissertation, has employed "Twelve-Tone Invariants as Compositional Determinants."[20] The use of such invariants is a way of intensifying the motivic unity of a composition beyond what the mere use of a row guarantees, and that a composing poodle, so to speak, could therefore attain.

Another way of defining the relationship between the row forms is "combinatorial," since their constituent hexachords can combine interchangeably to produce aggregates. Laying out the unordered pitch content of the hexachords in the summary staves at bottom to form ascending six-note scales reveals an interesting characteristic of combinatorial sets — sets, that is, which can be transposed to produce the sort of "hexachordal complementation" we have been observing. The six-note scales (like all complementary twelve-tone hexachords) are intervallically identical, but also palindromic. Whether read from left to right or vice versa, they produce the same sequence of tones and semitones: T-S-S-S-T. (Another way of observing their symmetry is out from the middle, producing three-note S-S-T groups that mirror one another to the left and to the right.)

In his *Three Compositions*, Babbitt plays continually with these constants and symmetries, and with "puns" that arise out of the interplay. The first pair of measures in the first of the set, where (in apparent tribute to the opening of Schoenberg's Suite for piano, op. 25) the left hand has P_0 and the right has P_6, set the tone (see Ex. 3-19a). Each hand completes an aggregate over the length of the pair, but each measure also contains an aggregate formed by the two hands together. The same is also true of mm. 3–4, in which the left hand has RI_1 and the right hand has R_0; mm. 5–6, in which I_7 in the left is pitted against RI_7 in the right; and mm. 7–8, in which the combinatorial pair are R_6

EX. 3-19A   Milton Babbitt, *Three Compositions for Piano*, no. 1, mm. 1–8

EX. 3-19B   Milton Babbitt, *Three Compositions for Piano*, no. 1, last two measures

EX. 3-19C   Milton Babbitt, *Three Compositions for Piano*, no. 1, mm. 9–17

and I_1. In sum, Babbitt has contrived combinatorial pairs of row forms that sum up all the possible relationships between orderings: transposition, inversion, retrograde, and inverted retrograde.

Especially interesting, from the point of view of set theory, is the occasional use of a technique resembling medieval hocket, in which notes played by pianist's two hands alternate in time. The first eight measures, already analyzed for linear and contrapuntal relationships, exemplify this texture as well. When combinatorial sets are in play, the hocketing device allows "secondary sets" (alternative orderings of the aggregate) to emerge like variations on a theme. For example, the notes in the first pair of measures, taken exactly in the order in which they are heard, produce two secondary sets, as follows:

TABLE 3-1

	Secondary set A		Secondary set B		
P₆:	E A B A♭ F♯	G	D♭ F C E♭	D B♭	(:R₆)
	/ \ /		/ \ /		
P₀:	B♭ E♭ F D C	D♭	G B F♯ A	A♭ E	(:R₀)

The use of secondary sets adds another dimension to combinatoriality, since it adds another way in which hexachords with mutually exclusive pitch content may generate aggregates. Throughout the composition, Babbitt uses this principle to guide his choice of successive set forms. The parenthetical indication of the corresponding retrogrades at the end of the table is a reminder that secondary sets may be subjected to the same manipulations as any others; and a glance at the very end of the first piece (Ex. 3-19b) will show how Babbitt used these very retrogrades as if to enclose the entire composition in a palindrome. Like his "post-Webernian" counterparts in Europe, he was fascinated by the symmetries that gave Webern's scores their distinctive profiles; and (again like them) he saw in these patterned interactions between and among multiple set forms the means of creating a truly or "purely" twelve-tone musical syntax. Finally, Babbitt was just as eager as they were to find ways of integrating other "parameters" or measurable variables, such as rhythm and dynamics, into the serial scheme.

AN INTEGRATED MUSICAL TIME/SPACE

But his methods for doing so differed fundamentally from theirs. In works like Boulez's *Structures* or Krenek's *Sestina*, described in chapter 1, the "rhythmic series" were derived from the pitch series by arbitrary numerical association. The note C was associated with the number 1, and so was the thirty-second note; C♯D♭ was associated with 2, as was the sixteenth; D = 3 = dotted sixteenth; D♯E♭ = 4 = eighth; and so on. Rests were arbitrary punctuations. Babbitt saw the arbitrariness of the "Darmstadt" method as a weakness. He drew upon his mathematical training to devise demonstrable analogies between the procedures of twelve-tone permutation as applied to a pitch series and the same procedures as applied to a series of durations. In particular, he found a way of systematically applying the process of inversion to duration.

As long as inversion was conceptualized in terms of traditional musical notation (that is, as a reversal of up-and-down contour on an imagined vertical grid), there could be no meaningful analogy with a strictly linear concept of musical time measured (as it has to be in notation) left-to-right along a horizontal grid, its single direction corresponding to the single irreversible "direction" in which real time elapses. But we do not necessarily think of inversion as a literal reversal of contour. We have no trouble thinking of a sixth as the inversion of a third even if they both ascend or descend. It was thinking about intervals in this way that gave Babbitt his clue to generalizing a theory of inversion that treated pitches not as individual frequencies but as "pitch classes," and that could be applied with equal precision to duration.

Add a perfect fourth to a perfect fifth in the same direction and you get an octave; ditto a major third and a minor sixth, a minor second and a major seventh, two tritones, and so on. Intervals related by inversion always add up to an octave in this way. One of the traditional ways of demonstrating inversion, in fact, is based on this observation: play middle C and the E above and then transpose the C up an octave (or the E down an octave) and the interval between the tones is inverted. To put this in terms of mathematical set functions, one invokes the principle of *complementation*, or completion to a given sum. Any interval complements its inversion to the constant sum of an octave.

This relationship can be easily generalized into a numerical rule if one represents all the intervals as multiples of the smallest interval, namely the semitone. Thus, to recall the first example in the preceding paragraph, a perfect fourth (five semitones) plus a perfect fifth (seven semitones) equals an octave (twelve semitones). Intervallic inversion is thus reducible to a special case of what mathematicians call "complementation to the sum of 12," or in professional jargon, "complementation *modulo* 12" (more colloquially, "complementation mod. 12"). Just as $9 + 3 = 12$ is a universally applicable mathematical fact, so a major sixth (nine semitones) is the inversion of a minor third (three semitones); and so it goes.

And if intervallic inversion is regarded as a special case of arithmetic complementation, then complementation of time durations to a given sum may equally be so regarded, so long as both the sum and the units of measurement are constants. Babbitt sets up just such a scheme in the first of his *Three Compositions for Piano*. The constant unit of value (analogous to the semitone) is the sixteenth note, and the constant sum (analogous to the octave) is six. All that is needed now is a rhythmic "series," or fixed order of quantities, and the analogy with serial pitch organization will be complete.

Let us look once again at the first pair of measures in Ex. 3-19a. The two "hocketing" voices have identical rhythmic groupings. In both, there is an initial group of five sixteenth-notes (or more precisely five sixteenth-note attacks, since the last note is extended to mark the end of the group), followed by a single sixteenth (set off by a following rest), a group of four, and a concluding group of two. That four-element series—5 1 4 2—is chosen cannily to maximize the analogies with pitch ordering. For one thing, the sum of its constituent units is twelve, so that in its complete form it maps neatly onto one complete statement of a pitch row. And for another, it contains two pairs ($5 + 1$, $4 + 2$) that add up to six, so that complementing the series "mod. 6" will not introduce any new elements into it.

The ordering 5-1-4-2, coming first, is the equivalent of a "prime" ordering of a pitch row; and sure enough, it corresponds with prime forms in both voices (= hands). Looking again now at Ex. 3-19b, the end of the piece, which incorporates two retrograde rows, we are not surprised to find that in both hands the rhythmic groupings are likewise reversed: 2 sixteenths + 4 sixteenths + 1 sixteenth + 5 sixteenths. The same rhythmic groupings are found in the right hand in mm. 3–4, in which the pitch succession also embodies a reversed row: 2(EG♯)-4(AF♯BG)-1(C♯)-5(CDFE♭B♭). But the left hand in these measures plays a retrograde inversion, and so here Babbitt employs his complementation technique, subtracting each of the numbers in the reversed rhythmic series from six to produce the corresponding sequence of groupings: 4(FD♭CE♭)-2(B♭D)-5(G♯AGEF♯)-1(B). The remaining ordering, 1-5-2-4, coincides with the first sounding of an unreversed inversion (left hand in mm. 5–6: (F)-(CB♭D♭E♭D)-(A♭E)-(AF♯GB)).

So it goes throughout the piece, with variations. Sometimes Babbitt sounds the pitch series in even sixteenth notes in the space of a single measure, using articulation rather than contrasting note-values to mark off the appropriate rhythmic groupings. At other times he sounds the pitch series not as twelve individual notes but as four trichords (three-note chords), assigning to each a duration corresponding to the appropriate member of the rhythmic series. In the second section of the piece (Ex. 3-19c), marked off from the first by a rest and by a new tempo, he uses these two variants in counterpoint. Each ordering of the pitch series as shown in Ex. 3-18 appears in both guises, as running sixteenths and as trichords.

Successive sections of the composition are distinguished by their textures. The one beginning in m. 18 puts the set forms in a sort of canon, those in the left hand starting on the downbeats, and those in the right starting halfway through the measure. Each half-measure, read vertically, exhibits an aggregate produced by a combinatorial "secondary set." The section beginning at m. 29 presents the linear pitch series in fairly unarticulated form, accompanying them with sharply articulated trichords that express the rhythmic series "pointillistically," marking not successive durations of sound but successive durations of silence between the chordal articulations.

Just as the various permutations of the rhythmic series are associated on a one-to-one basis with the corresponding permutations of the pitch series, so are dynamics coordinated with the other parameters, albeit in less detail. Throughout the composition, prime forms are marked *mezzo piano*, retrogrades *mezzo forte*, inversions *forte*, and retrograde inversions *piano*. In the last section, where the original tempo returns and the first section is replayed in a rough palindrome, the whole dynamic scheme is hushed down by two degrees: primes are now *pp*, retrogrades *p*, inversions *mp*, and retrograde inversions *ppp*.

Anyone who finds beauty in orderliness and control will find it here. Babbitt's achievement was a joyous affirmation of formalism at a time when formalism was beginning its cold war ascendancy in the West, and when artistic merit was defined (according to the "new-critical" classroom shibboleth) as "maximum complexity under maximum control."[21] The whole subsequent course of Babbitt's career as a composer could in this special sense be described as a tireless quest of greater and greater beauty (or "elegance," as mathematicians use the word), for its commitment to an ever increasing, all-encompassing orderly control of an ever more multifarious and detailed complex of relationships is self-evident.

His early compositions could be viewed as a systematic, quasi-scientific program to expand that control and to generalize the twelve-tone system into a unified theory that incorporated all the achievements of its founding generation. In his *Composition for Four Instruments* (1948), Babbitt turned his attention to what he called "derived sets"—his term for twelve-tone rows, like the one in Webern's Concerto, op. 24, that could be broken down into four trichords of identical intervallic content, each of which could be made to represent one of the four basic permutations.

EX. 3-20A   Milton Babbitt, *Composition for Four Instruments*, end

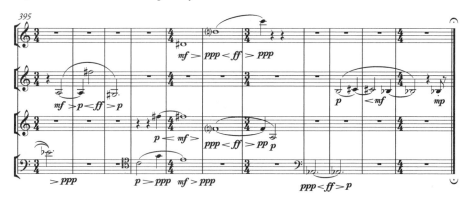

EX. 3-20B   Three forms of the basic set: P_0, P_6, and I_5 in Milton Babbitt, *Composition for Four Instruments*

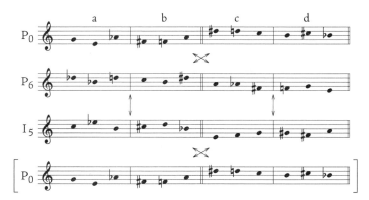

The composition is scored for flute, violin, clarinet, and cello, four instruments of contrasting range and timbre. The basic row from which the entire composition is derived is stated complete—once only—at the very end. That row, consisting of the last three notes played by each of the instruments in turn (Ex. 3-20a), is shown in Ex. 3-20b. The four trichords are laid out roughly in the order in which they are heard: the cello's trichord is labeled *a*, the violin's *b*, the flute's *c*, and the clarinet's *d*. It is very easy to see that when they are laid out in this order the resulting row is combinatorial, since the two hexachords (a + b and c + d) divide the chromatic scale into two mutually exclusive registers. The first hexachord contains all the chromatic pitches between E and A, and the second contains all the rest, from B♭ to E♭. Were the set transposed by a tritone or inverted at the fourth above, the hexachords would exchange pitch content and new aggregates (secondary sets) could be formed by combining the row forms in question contrapuntally.

In the main body of the composition, however, this governing set is replaced by four derived sets, each assigned to one of the four instruments. As shown in Ex. 3-21, the set assigned to the clarinet is derived from trichord *a*, the set assigned to the flute is derived from trichord *b*, the one assigned to the cello is derived from trichord *c*, and the one assigned to the violin is derived from trichord *d*. In each case the "prime" form of the trichord (the one taken directly from Ex. 3-20b) is followed by I, RI, and R. These derived sets maintain the same distribution of pitch content into hexachords as the original set, which means that they have inherited all of its combinatorial properties. Thus, in his "precompositional" work, Babbitt has managed to combine or synthesize the main structural innovations of both Schoenberg (combinatoriality) and Webern (derivation) into a "set of derived sets," which in his later theoretical writings Babbitt would call a trichordal array.

EX. 3-21   The four derived sets in Milton Babbitt, *Composition for Four Instruments*

The composition is laid out in fifteen sections, corresponding to the possible groupings of the constituent instruments (four solos, four trios, six duos, one tutti). Easiest to analyze, of course are the unaccompanied solos, in which each instrument uses only "its" derived set (clarinet at the beginning, cello at m. 139, violin at m. 229, flute at m. 328). These solos are written in a manner reminiscent of Bach's suites and sonatas for unaccompanied violin or cello, in which the division of a single line into distinct registers suggests counterpoint. In Ex. 3-22, the beginning of the fugue from Bach's Fifth Suite for unaccompanied cello (in which differing registers are used to mark off the various subjects and answers) is juxtaposed with the first fifteen measures from the opening clarinet solo in Babbitt's Composition for Four Instruments, with notes occurring in three different registers grouped by enclosing them in boxes.

The analysis in Ex. 3-22 shows Babbitt's clarinet line to consist of a series of "secondary sets" (mm. 1–6, 7–9, 9–12, 12–16), each containing a different shuffling, so to speak, of the four trichords that make up the clarinet's derived row. The trichords are distinguished by register, which permits their notes to be intermixed without loss of identity. The first RI (BE♭C), presented intact at the outset to establish the pattern, sounds next in the upper "voice" in m. 7, in the middle "voice" in mm. 9–11, and again in the upper voice in mm. 14–15. The prime (D♭B♭D) is stretched across mm. 2–6 in the middle voice, reappears in the bottom voice in mm. 7–8, in the upper voice in mm. 11–12, and again in the lower voice in mm. 13–14. The retrograde (A♭EG) is at bottom in mm. 2–5, at the top in mm. 8–9, at bottom again in mm. 10–12, and once again at the top in mm. 13–14. The remaining trichord, the inversion (G♭AF),

EX. 3-22A   J. S. Bach, Fugue from Cello Suite no. 5

EX. 3-22B   Milton Babbitt, *Composition for Four Instruments*, mm. 1–15, with registers delineated

is stretched across the top in mm. 2–6, touches bottom in mm. 8, comes all together in the upper voice at the middle of m. 12, and ends up scraping the bottom again in mm. 15–16.

The clarinet is succeeded in m. 36 by the other three instruments (Ex. 3-23), in a texture contrived so that each individual line is confined to its own derived row, presented trichord by trichord, completing the aggregate with every four. But at the same time the composite of the three lines, taken note by note, completes another series of aggregates (secondary sets). The fifteen sections that make up the piece continually replay this process, the derived sets continuing to complete aggregates in one "dimension" while the secondary sets formed by the composite texture complete them in another. As already hinted, all four instruments come together only in the last section.

The *Composition* is a model, in this regard, of a formalistically conceived work of art. It takes its shape, and has its reason for being, in the exhaustive working out of

EX. 3-23 Milton Babbitt, *Composition for Four Instruments*, mm. 36–59

Accidentals affect only those notes which they immediately precede.

EX. 3-23 *(continued)*

its own material's potential for elaboration. To quote Babbitt's pupil and exegete, the music theorist Andrew Mead, the work is a "watershed of twelve-tone compositional practice" because of its "multidimensional use of purely self-referential structures."[22] Or to paraphrase Adorno, the work is impelled throughout by the "inherent tendency of musical material." (One can apply Adorno's concept to the genesis of an individual work without necessarily endorsing the global application to the history of music that Adorno intended.) But of course the tendency is "inherent" only because the author has made it so (as Mead's term "self-referential" already implies). Even if we prefer to see the rules as coming from the material (or from nature, or from God), it is we who have made them and derive meaning and satisfaction from them—or not.

Babbitt's rules, in the *Composition for Four Instruments*, apply to durations as well as pitch, as indeed they had to. Once he had hit on his method for integrating duration into the serial scheme, it too became part of his music's "inherent" tendency. Put another way, Babbitt regarded composing technique the way most scientists of his generation regarded knowledge: as something that accumulates, a sum total to which each experiment (or composition) adds its mite. Having integrated rhythm into the serial domain, to un-integrate it would be a form of backsliding. Indeed, not to attempt its extension would be irresponsible. Progress imposes obligations.

And so the durational series in Babbitt's *Composition for Four Instruments*—1-4-3-2, to be complemented mod. 5—is applied not only in terms approximating retrogression and inversion, but according to a new technique simulating transposition as well. Going back to the opening clarinet solo (Ex. 3-22b), we may observe the rhythmic series in its "prime" or primitive form at the very outset. The opening B is 1 sixteenth in duration, the following E♭ lasts 4 sixteenths, the C lasts 3 (counting the sixteenth rest that follows the note), and the fourth note, D♭, lasts 2. The fact that rests can be reckoned along with sound within a duration means that, according to Babbitt's rules at this stage of their formulation, a duration is the time that elapses between attacks. What is measured is not the length of sounds, but the distance between what Babbitt would later call "time points." The next four notes (G♭, A♭, E, B♭) are one quarter note, a whole note, a dotted half note, and a half note in duration, respectively. These long values are those of the first four notes multiplied by four. So the first four durations are "really" (that is, conceptually) 1×1, 4×1, 3×1, and 2×1 sixteenths, and the next four are 1×4, 4×4, 3×4, and 2×4. It is easy enough to predict, and then confirm by looking, that the next four durations will be 1×3, 4×3, 3×3, and 2×3; and that the next four after that will be 1×2, 4×2, 3×2, and 2×2. In short, the whole series has been multiplied (or "transposed") by each of its constituent elements in turn.

This process gets us as far as the downbeat of m. 8. At this point the rhythm becomes a composite of all the remaining forms of the rhythmic series — retrograde (2-3-4-1), inversion (4-1-2-3), and retrograde inversion (3-2-1-4) — each multiplied by itself the way the prime form had been. The distribution of set forms (1 vs. 3) mirrors the distribution of instruments (solo clarinet vs. remaining three) in the first two sections of the *Composition*. Ex. 3-24, borrowed from Andrew Mead's analysis, shows how the three superimposed rhythmic series conspire together to produce the rhythms on the musical surface in mm. 8 – 15, while the pitch sequence continues to traverse aggregates both in direct succession (through secondary sets) and as partitioned into registers (derived sets). Thus every note played by the clarinet in these measures participates simultaneously in one or two durational rows and two pitch rows. By the end of the Composition, when the full texture is employed, all four instruments are doing all of this at the same time.

FULL REALIZATION

As its very title promises, Babbitt's next composition, *Composition for Twelve Instruments* (1948, revised 1954), is an attempt to extend the controlling techniques even further,

EX. 3-24   Milton Babbitt, *Composition for Four Instruments*, superimposed rhythmic series integrating durations even more systematically into the serial texture by creating a complete durational analogue to a full chromatic tone row. This is done by assigning to every member of a row two numbers, the first denoting its order within the set, the second its pitch measured in semitones from an arbitrary "zero." If the first pitch in the row is taken as the "zero" pitch, then that pitch will be defined by the numerical pair (0, 0) and the rest will be computed from it. Once assigned to the pitches of P_0, the pitch numbers are treated as constants or absolutes throughout the composition. Applied to the row in the *Composition for Twelve Instruments* (given together with its combinatorially related inversion at the perfect fifth), the assignment of dual designations is shown in Ex. 3-25.

EX. 3-25 P_6 and I_7 from Milton Babbitt's *Composition for Twelve Instruments* (pitched on F), with order and pitch numbers

The rhythmic series conforms to the same dual numerical catalogue. Its twelve order positions carry, as always, the numbers from 0 to 11, and the pitch numbers are converted into duration numbers by substituting sixteenth notes for semitones. Thus the series of pitch numbers in Ex. 3-25 — 0, 1, 4, 9, 5, 8, 3, 10, 2, 11, 6, 7 — would translate into a series of durations as shown in Ex. 3-26. It begins with a dotted half note (= 12 sixteenths) because when doing arithmetic with twelve as the modulus, 12 = 0 (as 13 = 1, 14 = 2, and so on.) The pitches of P_0 are retained in Ex. 3-26 to show how directly a pitch interval translates into a time interval when using this system.

EX. 3-26   Durational series derived from P_0 (Milton Babbitt, *Composition for Twelve Instruments*)

A glance at the exceedingly sparse or pointillistic score, of which the first eighteen measures are given in Ex. 3-27, shows that the first presentation of the row is made, both in terms of pitch and in terms of rhythm, at a transposition of two semitones/sixteenths, evidently because Babbitt did not want to begin with a note lasting a whole measure. So the first note heard, in the harp, is G (F plus two semitones), which means the first time interval between note-attacks will be an eighth note (0 + 2 sixteenths). The whole series of pitch/duration numbers at this transposition (i.e., constant addition to the original set of numbers) will thus be 2, 3, 6, 11, 7, 10, 5, 0 (= 12), 4, 1, 8, 9. These numbers are easily traced in terms of elapsed time between note attacks. For example, the twelfth note sounded is the clarinet D♭ in m. 6; the time interval before the next attack [bassoon G in m. 7] is exactly nine sixteenths, the last number in the durational series; all the intervening durations can be readily verified.

But D♭ is not the last note of P$_2$, the prime pitch series starting on G. Something more complicated is going on in the pitch domain. The first three notes in the score

EX. 3-27   Milton Babbitt, *Composition for Twelve Instruments*, mm. 1–18

EX. 3-27   (continued)

conform both to the pitches and the implied rhythms of P_2, but the fourth note, horn D, is not the expected note. (The expected note, E, does not appear until m. 6, in the flute part.) And that is because Babbitt is starting up another row form from the D, namely RI_9. To complicate matters even further, another prime (P_3) starts with the violin A♭ in m. 1, which is simultaneously the second note of P_2 as traced from the beginning.

EX. 3-27 (continued)

In fact the complications have only begun to be accounted for. It turns out on analysis that every one of the instrumental parts, while participating in the generally unfolding complex of series that we have been describing, simultaneously plays its own unique version of the row. The first twelve notes in the flute part at the top of the score, for example, enunciate yet another simultaneous prime form (P_{11}, starting on E), the first twelve in the oboe part running beneath it make up R_6, the clarinet unfolds I_8, and the bassoon RI_7.

So it goes, all the way down the page, so that a total of twelve individual set forms (three Ps, three Is, three Rs, and three RIs) are simultaneously in play, each one starting on a different note of the chromatic scale so that the first notes in all parts create yet another aggregate (as do the second notes, the third notes and so forth). The completion of the first set of twelve simultaneous series occurs in m. 36. Anyone who wishes to expend the time and effort may verify the facts just enumerated and observe in full detail how every single note in the score fulfills multiple functions, simultaneously participating in the completion of at least three (and sometimes four) pitch aggregates, as well as taking its place in a rhythmic series (and also a series of dynamics that has not been described).

ANOTHER COLD WAR

The reader has perhaps already noticed that Babbitt achieved these impressive feats of logical construction a bit earlier than the monuments of Darmstadt "total serialism" described in chapter 1. They were all on paper before Messiaen wrote his *Mode de valeurs*, to say nothing of Boulez's *Structures* or Stockhausen's *Kreuzspiel*. But with the exception of the *Composition for Four Instruments*, issued in 1949 in manuscript facsimile by *New Music Edition*, a shoestring, composer-staffed periodical (founded by Henry Cowell in 1925 and edited at the time by Elliott Carter), Babbitt's breakthrough compositions languished for years, along with his dissertation, in obscurity. Neither his music nor his theoretical writings became generally available for discussion — and potential influence — until the mid-1950s or later. The *Three Compositions for Piano*, historically the earliest work to serialize durations, did not see the light of day until 1957, a full decade after they were written. Babbitt had to stand by and see himself "scooped" by composers he regarded as his intellectual inferiors — a hard fate for a musician dedicated to modernism in its strongest ideological form, with its perpetual race to the patent office.

It is not surprising, then, that when Babbitt finally gained access to public media, his resentments colored the tone of his discourse, adding greatly to the atmosphere of contention and factionalism that characterized the postwar avant-garde. His public debut, so to speak, came in 1955, when he was invited by the editors of *The Score*, a new British periodical devoted to modern music, to contribute a description of his serial practices. The important article he sent in, modestly titled "Some Aspects of Twelve-Tone Composition" and based on his unpublished dissertation, introduced most of the concepts mentioned thus far to a public readership, notably combinatoriality (illustrated by some passages from Schoenberg's Fourth Quartet) and derivation (illustrated by the row in Webern's Concerto), both "generalized and extended far beyond their immediate functions"[23] by reconceptualizing twelve-tone rows as mathematical sets.

The conceptualization of intervallic inversion as complementation mod. 12 is proposed, along with the application of the same procedure to durations or any other musical parameter that could be specified in terms of a scale of quantities. The article ends with a ringingly optimistic affirmation of new horizons, not only for compositional technique, but for the whole concept of an esthetically autonomous music. "Even this extremely incomplete presentation," Babbitt wrote, "should indicate the possibility of twelve-tone music, organized linearly, harmonically in the small and in the large, rhythmically — indeed, in all dimensions — in terms of the essential assumptions of the system."[24]

The article begins, however, with a fierce blast of righteous indignation at the European avant-garde, whom Babbitt (provoked, no doubt, by their "Schoenberg Is Dead" posturings) despised as feckless enfants terribles. Casting the story in impersonal terms, whether out of modesty or to portray it as more than the one-man show it had in fact been, Babbitt let his European readers know that in the United States "the specific bases for achieving a total twelve-tone work were arrived at by the end of the war." And when,

> a short time later, there were reports of a group of young French, Italian and German composers who apparently shared like aims, their work was eagerly awaited. However, their music and technical writings eventually revealed so very different an attitude toward the means, and even so very different means, that the apparent agreement with regard to ends lost its entire significance. The most striking points of divergence can be summarized in terms of the following apparent attributes of the music and the theory associated with it. Mathematics — or, more correctly, arithmetic — is used, not as a means of characterizing or discovering general systematic pre-compositional relationships, but as a compositional device, resulting in the most literal sort of "program music," whose course is determined by a numerical, rather than by a narrative or descriptive "program." The alleged "total organization" is achieved by applying dissimilar, essentially unrelated criteria of organization to each of the components, criteria often derived from outside the system, so that — for example — the rhythm is independent of and thus separable from the pitch structure; this is described and justified as a "polyphony" of components, though polyphony is customarily understood to involve, among many other things, a principle of organized simultaneity, while here the mere fact of simultaneity is termed "polyphony." The most crucial problems of twelve-tone music are resolved by being defined out of existence; harmonic structure in all dimensions is proclaimed to be irrelevant, unnecessary, and, perhaps, undesirable in any event; so a principle, or non-principle, of harmony by fortuity reigns. Finally, the music of the past — and virtually all of that of the present, as well — is repudiated for what it is not, rather than examined — if not celebrated — for what it is; admittedly, this is a convenient method for evading confrontation by a multitude of challenging possibilities, including — perhaps — a few necessaries.[25]

The Europeans, for their part, were happy to dismiss Babbitt in return. *Il a l'air d'un musicologue*, wrote Cage, reassuringly, to Boulez — "he has the air of a musicologist" — thus casting Babbitt into the outer darkness reserved for academics.[26] But Babbitt reveled in his academicism, portraying himself in this regard as a singularly legitimate heir to Schoenberg, another great composer-teacher with a high awareness of his intellectual responsibilities, and if anything an even more pressing historical conscience. What Babbitt valued in his own art was what academic artists have always valued, namely the demonstration of mastery and technical control. Unlike the European avant-garde, Babbitt sought anything but "automatism," the abject extinction of the self, in extending the purview of serialism. Rather, he sought in his own domain the joyous triumph of technology, and the heady attendant sense of "self-infinitization"[27] (to quote the sociologist Daniel Bell), that contemporary science now promised its practitioners and beneficiaries.

Like Schoenberg before him, Babbitt saw the self-evident merit of the twelve-tone system in its unique capacity to unify a vast complex of objectively defined relationships. By extending the range of the system, he was extending the power of the composer's sovereign control. By loading his compositions with demonstrable relations far past the perceptual saturation point (as he was the first to admit), he demonstrated that limitless power, which he associated not merely with the power of the mind, but with the power of absolute truth, and with the freedom to express it.

LOGICAL POSITIVISM

That was how Babbitt's brand of postwar modernism related to the overarching cold-war debate. Deeply concerned with the restraint that political tyranny can exercise on thought and expression, and aware that even in open societies majority opinion (or commercial interests) can marginalize—or even, without explicitly prohibiting, effectively exclude—unpopular or abstruse thought, Babbitt allied himself and his exceedingly rationalistic musical activities with the philosophy known as logical positivism, the toughest and most skeptical variety of "show-me" empiricism.

The term, which dates back to the 1930s, describes an attitude "classically" expressed in *Der logische Aufbau der Welt* ("The logical structure of the world," 1928), a treatise by the Viennese philosopher Rudolf Carnap (1891–1970), who like Schoenberg had been exiled from his native country by the rise of Nazism. From 1936 to 1952, Carnap taught at the University of Chicago, and had many American disciples including the philosopher Carl Hempel, Babbitt's friend and Princeton colleague (and an important influence on his thinking). Carnap's logical positivism was an attempt to introduce the methods and precision of mathematics and the natural sciences into the field of philosophy, which, he insisted, should stop being a speculative field and become an analytical one, devoted to maintaining rigorous standards of inference and proof. No statement can be regarded as true, for logical positivists, unless it can be shown to derive logically from observed phenomena. Only formal logic and direct observation, then, can ever validly constrain conceptual thought—not tradition, not authority, not political or religious dogma, sentiment, hopes, desires, wishes, or fears, and certainly not threats or reprisals.

Babbitt might have been paraphrasing Carnap when, in a widely discussed lecture called "Past and Present Concepts of the Nature and Limits of Music," he declared that "there is but one kind of language, one kind of method for the verbal formulation of 'concepts' and verbal analysis of such formulations: 'scientific' language and 'scientific' method."[28] In another lecture he quoted Michael Scriven, a historian of science, who had put logical positivism into a memorable nutshell when he observed, "If we want to know why things are as they are . . . , then the only sense in which there are alternatives to the methods of science is the sense in which we can if we wish abandon our interest in correct answers."[29] It is obvious that the targets of Scriven's cautionary remark were religious bigots and political dogmatists. What could possibly be its relevance to the arts, traditionally regarded as the fundamental preserve of subjective judgment or taste?

Zhdanov had given the answer when, acting on behalf of the Soviet Communist Party, he made one man's subjective taste a political dogma. Babbitt sought liberation, not only for himself but also for all artists, from the potential tyranny of taste when he tried, in verbal exhortation but more fundamentally by the example of his work, to make truth rather than beauty the criterion of artistic as well as scientific achievement. The measure of good music, like good science, would be not the pleasure that it gave, or the political tendency that it served, but rather the truth that it contained — objective, scientifically verifiable truth, that is, not truth as a Zhdanov might define it.

The model of truth that logical positivists proposed for science (and, following them, Babbitt for music) was of course that of mathematics. Truth lay in accountability to principles. In math these were axioms and theorems: basic truth assumptions and the proofs that they enabled. In science, these were observed phenomena and logical inferences. Music had its "observables" in acoustic phenomena, and its axiomatic premises in its motivic content or (to use Schoenberg's word) its *Grundgestalten*. The most generalized form motivic content could take was a twelve-tone row. If everything in a composition were accountable to a twelve-tone row, then everything in it was

FIG. 3-5 The artificial earth satellite *Sputnik* ("traveling companion") was launched by the Soviet Union on 4 October 1957; here, scientists view models of it.

verifiably true. And the greater the number of demonstrable relations one managed to embody in the music, the more objective and verifiable truth it contained.

We have already seen how fully Babbitt's own music met these criteria, and his critics were quick to suspect him of a self-serving assertion of privilege. Also troubling was Babbitt's easy assertion of the unique validity of "one kind of language, one kind of method," namely his own, which seemed to contradict the very premise of freedom of expression (or more precisely, freedom from restraint) on which his whole philosophy rested, since it seemed to imply a justification for restraint (should Babbitt have the power to impose it) on anyone who disagreed. But as long as science, in the aftermath of its victory in World War II, retained its unprecedented prestige in America, Babbitt's ideas carried considerable potential weight, at least in academic circles.

As it happened, that prestige and that weight received a powerful boost in 1957, when the Soviet Union successfully launched the first artificial space satellite, called Sputnik ("Traveling Companion"), in an orbit around the earth. Taken by surprise and humiliated, American scientists and politicians made educational reform, particularly in science and technology, a cold-war priority. Government investment in scientific endeavors — "big science" as it was called — gave scientific advancement in peacetime something of the sense of urgency that wartime bomb-development had commanded. Any argument that proceeded from "scientific" premises could now catch something of that urgency.

THE NEW PATRONAGE AND ITS FRUITS

Babbitt seized the moment both to rectify the slight his dissertation had received and to secure for advanced music composition a new sort of academic patronage. On the strength of the "scientific revolution" that had taken place in music thanks to the development by Schoenberg of serial technique and its theoretical extension by Babbitt himself, he now proposed to the Princeton administration that music composition be recognized as a legitimate branch of music research through the awarding of the Ph.D., the highest earned research degree, as the terminal degree in musical composition as well as musicology.

He summarized his arguments and gave them a practice outing in an extemporaneous talk presented to a select audience at the Berkshire Music Center at Tanglewood, the summer festival home of the Boston Symphony Orchestra near Lenox, Massachusetts, where Babbitt had been hired to give a seminar in twelve-tone composition in the summer of 1957. Besides his students and other interested musicians, his audience that afternoon included Roland Gelatt, the new editor of *High Fidelity*, a large-circulation magazine for record collectors and audio enthusiasts, which was published in nearby Great Barrington. Gelatt was trying to give the magazine a new orientation, tipping the balance of its coverage from hi-fi hardware toward more serious music coverage, and asked Babbitt if he could publish the talk. Babbitt at first declined, explaining that he had spoken off the cuff and that there was in fact no written text to publish. A tape had been made, however, and eventually Babbitt agreed to let an edited transcript of the talk appear in the February 1958 issue of the magazine.

He submitted the typescript with "The Composer as Specialist" as its title. A canny editor, Gelatt substituted a far more provocative head for the published text. As "Who Cares if You Listen?", Babbitt's little talk became one of the most widely reprinted and hotly discussed manifestos in the history of twentieth-century music. Although Babbitt's supporters have deplored the title's implications, it purchased for the argument advanced within the article an instant notoriety — and an efficacy — it might never otherwise have earned, and thereby played a significant part in the success of Babbitt's mission.

The article contains passages in which the author does seem to be mocking the musical public (or what he calls "lay listeners"). "Imagine, if you can," one such passage begins, a layman chancing upon a [mathematics] lecture on "Pointwise Periodic Homeo-morphisms." At the conclusion, he announces: "I didn't like it." Social conventions being what they are in such circles, someone might dare inquire: "Why not?" Under duress, our layman discloses precise reasons for his failure to enjoy himself; he found the hall chilly, the lecturer's voice unpleasant, and he was suffering the digestive aftermath of a poor dinner. His interlocutor understandably disqualifies these reasons as irrelevant to the content and value of the lecture, and the devel-opment of mathematics is left undisturbed. If the concert-goer [who has heard the musical equivalent of the math lecture, say a composition by Milton Babbitt] is at all versed in the ways of musical lifemanship, he also will offer reasons for his "I didn't like it" — in the form of assertions that the work in question is "inexpressive," "undramatic," "lacking in poetry," etc. etc., tapping that store of vacuous equivalents hallowed by time for: "I don't like it, and I cannot or will not say why."[30]

Before this passage, however, and using language shrewdly chosen for its "Ein-steinian" resonances, Babbitt had laid out the principles according to which the music that he and other composers of "contemporary serious music"[31] were writing neces-sarily differed from music designed to appeal to "laymen." Its "tonal vocabulary," to begin with, is described as being more "efficient," and less "redundant," meaning that (as we have already observed) each of its "atomic events" participates in a greatly augmented field of functional relationships — or as Babbitt put it, "is located in a five-dimensional musical space determined by pitch-class, register, dynamic, duration, and timbre."

Such music, then, has a greatly increased level of "determinacy" when compared with conventional concert or popular fare, and a greatly increased level of "contextuality" and "autonomy" as well. Any piece so composed will therefore follow unique rules, deducible only from itself, and will therefore be, in a fundamental sense, more "genuinely original" than is otherwise possible. To appreciate its originality, however, listeners must be trained, like their counterparts in physics or mathematics, in contemporary "analytical theory." Without such training, comprehension is impossible. Why then, Babbitt asks rhetorically, "should the layman be other than bored and puzzled by what he is unable to understand, music or anything else?" The difference, however, is that in the sciences, the lay public's inability to understand leads to enhanced prestige, while in music it usually leads in the opposite direction. That is the source of Babbitt's complaint: "It is only the translation of this boredom and puzzlement into resentment and denunciation that seems to me indefensible." What is sought, then, is protection from that resentment and denunciation in the form of patronage. "And so, I dare suggest," rings the culminating sentence, "that the composer would do himself and his music an immediate and eventual service by total, resolute, and voluntary withdrawal from this public world to one of private performance and electronic media, with its very real possibility of complete elimination of the public and social aspects of musical composition."[32] Anyone who knows the history of twentieth-century music will catch the resonance here with the premises of Arnold Schoenberg's Society for Private Musical Performances, advanced some forty years before.

The significant difference — the sign of the times — was the scientific basis of the argument, which pointed in the direction of a different source of patronage. The last three paragraphs of Babbitt's article, the crucial ones, were the paragraphs written, as it were, for the eyes of his university's president:

> Such a private life is what the university provides the scholar and the scientist. It is only proper that the university, which — significantly — has provided so many contemporary composers with their professional training and general education, should provide a home for the "complex," "difficult," and "problematical" in music. Indeed, the process has begun.
>
> I do not wish to appear to obscure the obvious differences between musical composition and scholarly research, although it can be contended that these differences are no more fundamental than the differences among the various fields of study. I do question whether these differences, by their nature, justify the denial to music's development of assistance granted these other fields. Immediate "practical" applicability (which may be said to have its musical analogue in "immediate extensibility of a compositional technique") is certainly not a necessary condition for the support of scientific research. And if it be contended that such research is so supported because in the past it has yielded eventual applications, one can counter with, for example, the music of Anton Webern, which during the composer's lifetime was regarded (to the very limited extent that it was regarded at all) as the ultimate in hermetic, specialized, and idiosyncratic composition; today, some dozen years after the composer's death, his complete works have been recorded by a major record company, primarily — I suspect — as a result of the enormous influence this music has had on the postwar, non-popular, musical world. I doubt that scientific research is any more secure against predictions of ultimate significance than is musical composition. Finally, if it be contended that research, even in its least "practical" phases, contributes to the sum of knowledge in the particular realm, what possibly can contribute more to our knowledge of music than a genuinely original composition?
>
> Granting to music the position accorded other arts and sciences promises the sole substantial means of survival for the music I have been describing. Admittedly, if this music is not supported, the whistling repertory of the man in the street will be little affected, the concert-going activity of the conspicuous consumer of musical culture will be little disturbed. But music will cease to evolve, and, in that important sense, will cease to live.[33]

Babbitt's final sentence, with its familiar tunnel view of musical evolution, "has been often pounced upon,"[34] as one later commentator dryly observed. Its arrogance is indeed palpable, as is the implication — echoing Webern's old battle cry, "All the rest is dilettantism!" — that only one kind of contemporary music was "serious" and "original." But this was the least novel aspect of Babbitt's program. Any reader of this book can easily trace it back to its source in the century-old polemics of the New German School. It was the parallel with math and physics, rather than with romantic notions of organicism, that gave Babbitt's argument its irresistible stamp of timeliness, and Princeton did not resist.

The Ph.D. in musical composition was officially instituted there in 1961, and first awarded, to the British composer Godfrey Winham (1934–75), in 1964. In addition to a musical work, Ph.D. candidates in composition had to submit an essay in theory and analysis. Winham's, called *Composition with Arrays*, was an explication of, and an addition to, Babbitt's latest technical extensions, as were the essays submitted over the next several years by Philip Batstone (*Multiple Order Functions in Twelve-Tone Music*, 1965), Henry Weinberg (*A Method of Transferring the Pitch Organization of a Twelve Tone Set through All Layers of a Composition, a Method of Transforming Rhythmic Content through Operations Analogous to Those of the Pitch Domain*, 1966) and Benjamin Boretz (*Meta-Variations: Studies in the Foundations of Musical Thought*, 1970).

Some of the early recipients of the degree—Mark DeVoto (b. 1940), Michael Kassler (b. 1941), Arthur Komar (1934–94)—did not submit original compositions at all; it was part of the fundamental research concept not to distinguish, at least officially, between music theory and composition, with the perhaps unexpected result that of the dual requirements for the Ph.D. in composition, it was the composition that turned out to be optional.

Kassler's dissertation, *A Trinity of Essays*, was an especially symptomatic contribution: its main component, an essay called "Toward a Theory That Is the Twelve-Note-Class System," was in effect a computer program that could "assert" the operations required to analyze or compose music like Babbitt's (the two processes—analysis and composition—being regarded as a single act performed in two "directions"). Kassler's program was devised not primarily for practical application but as a test of the twelve-tone system as extended by Babbitt and his pupils, the assumption being that, like any scientific theory in the computer age, a musical theory needed to be rationalized and quantified to the point where it could be programmed in order to be validated (that is, shown correct).

The institution of the Ph.D. in composition made the Princeton music department, already a magnet for ambitious young composers thanks to the presence there of Roger Sessions as well as Babbitt, the source of an invincible new credential for career advancement. Other universities were more or less compelled to follow suit. Within a decade, the Ph.D. in composition was common in America, and "Ph.D. music," it was widely if tacitly recognized, meant serial music. That, along with the remarkably cogent "mathematicalization" of twelve-tone theory by Babbitt and his pupils, has been one of the reasons why, firmly rooted in the rich institutional soil of the American university system, twelve-tone music proved such a hardy and tenacious growth in America at a time when the European avant-garde was leaving it behind.

And yet, once "house-broken into the academy" (as Joseph Kerman, an older Princeton alumnus, put it), could serial music retain its avant-garde status? Obviously it could not, nor did it wish to. American postwar serial music has always been a proud, strict academic style, its practitioners more suspicious and derisive than any other contemporary musicians of the whole concept of the avant-garde. What was new (and "scientific") was the equation of academicism with technical innovation, rather than with the conservation and propagation of ancient lore. Thus a term, "academic," that had been used throughout the twentieth century to decry musical conservatism was now actively claimed by a school of composition that called itself new and radical. The implicit paradox, and the attendant crisis of identity, brought a new set of anxieties into play.

ELITES AND THEIR DISCONTENTS

Those anxieties can be sampled in the writings of Edward T. Cone (1917–2004), a Princeton colleague of Sessions and Babbitt, who although a composer by training had a wider impact as a theorist and critic. One of his most interesting and symptomatic writings was a contribution to a symposium on defining a "musical composition," organized in 1967 by the editors of a journal, *Current Musicology*, that had been recently instituted by the graduate students at the Columbia University music department. The symposium was a response to a challenge lately issued by medievalists (most notably Richard L. Crocker of the University of California at Berkeley) to the conventional notion of a stable "piece of music."[35] Most of the contributors to the symposium reacted to the challenge with benevolent interest and good humor.

Not Cone. He pointed immediately to some obvious parallels between the medievalists' challenge and the redefinitions implicit in the work of the "indeterminate" wing of the contemporary avant-garde, and attacked both with phobic fervor. Or rather, counterattacked, for as his conclusion makes clear, he felt that he and his cherished beliefs (beliefs that were reaching a maximal formulation in the work of the Princeton serialists) were themselves under attack. "We may now be entering a definitive post-Renaissance stage of Western culture," he allowed, one that bore some striking features in common with pre-Renaissance culture,

> but I find it misleading to look on what is happening as in any sense a return to older and perhaps more natural modes of perception. Rather, we are confronted by an attack on the whole concept of art. If the attackers win, not only the work of art as we know it but art itself may disappear. Some composers — I use the term only because I do not know what else to call them, except perhaps noncomposers — are loudly proclaiming the Death of Music in a manner that recalls certain stylish theological positions [i.e., the "Death of God" as a metaphor for existentialist philosophy], and they are encouraging their followers to complete its doing-in. Others, more reticent, are nevertheless apparently trying to hasten the process by insisting that whatever one wants to call music *is* music, that what one calls a composition *is* a composition. John Cage's position is more honest. A few years ago, in conversation, he said, "I don't claim that what I am doing is music, or art — or that it has any value. I maintain only that it is an activity, and that it is the one in which I happen to be engaged at present." Such a position is, from a purely personal point of view, unassailable; but if generally accepted by those who call themselves musicians, it means the end of music.
>
> Let us not deceive ourselves. The extreme avant-garde is not trying to offer new definitions of what constitutes a work of art, or to create new forms, or to encourage new modes of perception. The extreme avant-garde has only one attitude toward the arts: it wants to kill them.[36]

That finger-in-the-dike sentiment turned the academy into a sort of fortress, and the mentality of a fortress, however progressive its declared objectives, is reactionary. What motivated such a quick turn toward the right on the part of artists and scholars who regarded themselves (since they favored perpetual progressive change) as constituting the true cultural left? Cone provided a clue in a later essay, "One Hundred Metronomes," published in 1977. The title referred to a recent composition by György Ligeti, the Hungarian refugee who had become an emblem of the Darmstadt avant-garde. It was called *Poème symphonique*. It had no score, just a set of instructions according to which one hundred pendulum-operated metronomes, going at as many different speeds, were to be set in motion and allowed to wind down. The piece ended when the last metronome stopped ticking. An anomaly among Ligeti's works, it is generally written off as a light-hearted spoof of "happenings," although it was performed a few times, and treated by at least some listeners and critics as a legitimate (and even a moving) musical experience.

Cone's essay was not lighthearted. He cast it as a conversation, or a battle of wits, between himself and a (fictitious?) Princeton graduate student in composition who wanted to organize a performance of the piece, and, having been turned down by the rest of the faculty, appealed to Cone in desperation to secure departmental permission to put it on. Cone, too, refused, but at least honored the request with a reasoned rebuttal, based on a quotation from the play *Travesties* by Tom Stoppard: "An artist is someone who is gifted in some way that enables him to do something more or less well which can only be done badly or not at all by someone who is not thus gifted."[37]

The only definition of a work of art that truly matters, then, is not what its effect may be, but what skills its manufacture (or its reception) may require. To make a Babbitt composition required such highly specialized skills that only a few (most of them at Princeton) possessed them, and to receive it in the spirit with which it was put forth required comparable skills on the part of the listener. To produce a Cage or a Nam June Paik composition (or Ligeti's *Poème symphonique*) required only patience, and its reception required only passive endurance. The rarer the skill, it follows further, the "higher" the art. Not surprisingly, such a scale of values put "Ph.D. music" at the top of the esthetic ladder.

It was also quite frankly elitist, in the strongest sense of the word, since by its very nature it selects and maintains a social elite. Both the composition and the performance of such music create elite occasions, which is just what high art had always done in the days of aristocratic or ecclesiastical patronage. The trouble with putting public institutions like universities in the position of the old church or aristocracy as patrons of art is the perceived contradiction between elite esthetics and the political or social egalitarianism on which modern concepts of democracy are based. Elite esthetics are usually defended by distinguishing "elite" from "elitist." One can create, the argument goes, an elite art for its own sake without fostering or assenting to elitist politics, which can serve the cause of social privilege.

The distinction is easier to maintain in theory than in practice, and social elitism is as likely to undergird elite esthetics now as it has ever been. "We receive brilliant, privileged freshmen at Princeton," Babbitt complained to an interviewer about a dozen years after the Ph.D. in composition was up and running, "who in their first year of college are likely to take a philosophy of science course with Carl Hempel, and then return to their dormitories to play the same records that the least literate members of our society embrace as the only relevant music."[38] This comes very close to suggesting that the purpose of "Ph.D. music" is to provide a haven for the brilliant and the privileged comparable to that provided by the rest of an elite education, which trains the members of not only an intellectual but also a social and, above all, an economic elite.

"Under its gloss of prosperity," the sociologist Vance Packard had warned in his book *The Status Seekers* (1959), America was becoming a dangerously divided society, its members constantly seeking "new ways to draw lines that will separate the elect from the non-elect."[39] Classical music, always a social divider in America, was playing its old role, some argued, under a new set of rules. Babbitt's strictures could even be read, by his critics, as an endorsement of the social benefits of pop music. If Princeton freshmen kept in contact after-hours with "demotic" music, a music "of the people" that, shared across class boundaries, tacitly reinforced solidarity between classes, then that music might actually be serving as a valuable social counter-force in a threatened democracy. As we will see in chapter 7, such reasoning drastically elevated the cultural stock of American popular music during the same decade, the 1960s, that witnessed the establishment of "Ph.D. music" as a significant and peculiarly American genre.

Babbitt went on to lament his isolation not only from the average student, but from his "fellow noncomposer faculty members at Princeton and, to a slightly lesser extent only, at Juilliard." In what seems a doubly pessimistic assessment, considering that it was made after the program he had outlined in 1957 had been largely implemented within the university, he concluded that things were worse than ever for "serious music" as he defined it.

> Superficially things might have seemed worse in the 1930s and 1940s. The audience seemed more sophisticated then, but there were not as many opportunities for composers. We do get our music performed now, we do get some recordings, we do occasionally get published. Back then Sessions was getting one or two performances a year in small rooms. That situation has improved, but we have no larger or more knowing an audience. I go to the best of concerts of contemporary music and see the same hundred or so people there week after week. I repeat, because it concerns me so, very few of my colleagues, who grew up on the streets of New York fighting the composer's battle, turn up to hear a young composer's music. As a result many young composers are, I hate to use this word, "alienated" even within their own profession. This is indeed a sad and symptomatic state of affairs, when the very survival of serious musical activity is so seriously threatened, by those within and outside the profession.[40]

Babbitt hated to use the word "alienated" because it was the sort of Marxist jargon that conjured up the shade of Zhdanov. But as Babbitt himself once half-ruefully joked, "everyone wants to compose our music but no one wants to listen to it." Composing it is a fascinating game, as is analyzing it. It is the listening process that has proved durably problematical. Viewed thus, the fate of academic serialism has been predictable. It has fared no differently from any of the other forms of academic music that have arisen over the years, and that might be collectively defined as "music that only a composer could love."

LIFE WITHIN THE ENCLAVE

While far more lasting than its European counterpart, then, postwar serialism in America has owed its survival to patronage in a society that otherwise functions, in music as in other ways, on the basis of commerce. It has been a closed enclave, a hothouse growth, its cultivators standing with backs resolutely turned to their counterparts in other walks of American musical life. Yet despite the misgivings Babbitt voiced in 1976, many experienced their protected life within the hothouse as a golden age for composition.

And, some would argue, for performance as well: as part of the institutionalization of serial music on American campuses, the Schoenbergian ideal of private performance venues for new music was also established on a broad and well-subsidized scale, with specialized student or professional performing organizations cropping up wherever "Ph.D. music" was composed. Music theory also enjoyed an intense growth phase, with faculty positions proliferating along with professional journals concerned with advanced musical composition and its attendant theory. Eventually, in 1966, a lobbying organization, the American Society of University Composers (ASUC), was formed by a group of Princeton faculty, graduate alumni, current Ph.D. candidates, and more loosely affiliated composers, including Weinberg, Boretz, Donald Martino (b. 1931), Peter Westergaard (b. 1931), and Charles Wuorinen (b. 1938).

The first campus "new music" organization was the Group for Contemporary Music, formed in 1962 at Columbia University (as it happens, one of the few universities where the scholars in the music department refused to sanction a Ph.D. for composition, but where a doctoral program was quickly set up, as if in defiance of the department, by the University's School of the Arts; relations were not happy). Its founders were Wuorinen, an expert pianist, and Harvey Sollberger (b. 1938), a flautist, both then graduate students in composition at Columbia, along with the cellist Joel Krosnick, then an undergraduate, who in 1974 joined the Juilliard String Quartet, a sort of forerunner organization that had been founded in 1946 by William Schuman, then president of the Juilliard School, expressly to give exposure to contemporary works in the medium, beginning with those of Bartók and Schoenberg.

Columbia's Group for Contemporary Music was as widely copied as Princeton's Ph.D. program. Both at Columbia and elsewhere (eventually including music conservatories) the performance rosters expanded to include a wide variety of vocalists and instrumentalists; in particular, a new breed of virtuoso percussionist was spawned. The high premium thus placed on new-music virtuosity led to an ever-increasing preoccupation with extended performance techniques — augmented ranges, novel sounds from traditional instruments (especially the piano), novel cross-fingerings to produce chords or "multiphonics" on woodwinds, and so on — on a par with extended formal techniques of composition.

Of the quasi-scientific journals devoted to academic composition and its theory, the semiannual *Perspectives of New Music*, produced at Princeton itself, was uniquely authoritative. Its slightly unidiomatic title was the result of its having been named by its patron, Paul Fromm (1906–87), the German-born Chicago wine merchant who had previously funded the Seminar on Advanced Musical Studies mentioned in chapter 1. The editors were Arthur Berger (1912–2003), then a professor at Brandeis University, and Benjamin Boretz (b. 1934), a former pupil of Berger then writing his Ph.D. dissertation under Babbitt. Many of the articles in the first issue, which appeared in fall 1962, had a sharp polemical or factional edge. Their purpose was to stake out what is known in the academy as "turf," a recognized and respected area of authority.

From this perspective, the most characteristic article in the inaugural issue of *Perspectives* was not by a composer at all, but rather by John Backus, an acoustician on the physics faculty of the University of Southern California, from whom the editors had commissioned a "scientific evaluation" of the four volumes of *Die Reihe* (the Cologne-based organ of the "Darmstadt School" described in chapter 1) that had by then appeared in English translation. The aggressive review Backus produced contrasted the bona fide musical science preached and practiced at Princeton with the fraudulent pseudo-science of the European avant-garde in a fashion that easily matched the derision the American serialists felt toward what Wuorinen called "the 'work' of John Cage and some of his friends."[41]

Backus dismissed the technical language in Stockhausen's writings, for example, as a jargon "designed mostly to impress the reader and to hide the fact that he has only the most meagre knowledge of acoustics."[42] The "pretended display of mathematical erudition" by another, less famous writer is declared to be "pure bluff," through which "the defenseless reader is being thoroughly swindled."[43] Ligeti's analysis of Boulez's *Structures* (discussed in chapter 1) is strategically praised for its clarity, but only the better to expose what it described as "a method that is appalling in its arbitrariness," testifying to "nothing more than a mystical belief in numerology as the fundamental basis for music."[44] The verdict on the composition itself is a little masterpiece of intramural academic invective:

> The possibilities are endless; a computer could be programmed to put down notes according to this prescription and in a very short time could turn out enough music to require years for its performance. By using different numerical rules — using a knight's move, for example, rather than a bishop's move along the diagonals — music for centuries to come could be produced.

On the positive side of the ledger, the same inaugural issue of *Perspectives* also contained a paper by Babbitt laying out his latest extension of twelve-tone technique. Dissatisfied with the incompleteness of his previous operational analogies between pitch and time, Babbitt now proposed a new analogy based on their primary shared property, namely the interval. "Since duration is a measure of distance between time points," he wrote, and

> as interval is a measure of distance between pitch points, we begin by interpreting interval as duration. Then, pitch number is interpretable as the point of initiation of a temporal event, that is, as a time-point number.[45]

Let us imagine a measure of music, in other words, as containing twelve numbered time-points, each corresponding to a successive pitch-point in the chromatic scale. Thus if we take zero to designate both the first pitch-class in a row (say G) and the time point that initiates the measure, 1 would then represent both the pitch-class G♯A♭ and the second time-point in the measure; 2 would denote the pitch class A and the third time-point, and so on. In effect, Babbitt was adopting Messiaen's old concept of the "chromatic scale of time values," but was synchronizing it (as Messiaen had not done) with the chromatic scale of pitches. An ascending chromatic scale would thus be conceptually translated (or to put it mathematically, "mapped") into the twelve elapsing time-points (say sixteenth notes) within a measure in $\frac{3}{4}$ or $\frac{6}{8}$ time.

As Babbitt put it in his article, if the individual "temporal event" or time-point is to retain its identity in the unfolding music,

> it is necessary merely to imbed it in a metrical unit, a measure in the usual musical metrical sense, so that a recurrence of succession of time points is achieved, while the notion of meter is made an essential part of the systematic structure. The equivalence relation is statable as "occurring at the same time point with relation to the measure." The "ascending" ordered "chromatic scale" of twelve time points, then, is a measure divided into twelve equally spaced units of time, with the metrical signature probably determined by the internal structure of the time-point set, and with the measure now corresponding in function to the octave in the pitch-class system. A time-point set, then, is a serial ordering of time points with regard to < [that is, increasing quantity]. At the outset, I do not wish to attempt to avoid the manifest differences between the elements of the pitch system and those of the time-point system, that is, perceptual — not formal — differences. A pitch representative of a pitch-class system is identifiable in isolation; a time-point representative cannot conceivably be, by its purely dispositional character. But an examination of a time-point set will clarify the systematic meanings, and the reasonable musical meanings associated with these new concepts.

Example 3-28 is adapted from the "examination" or demonstration that follows in Babbitt's article. The hypothetical chromatic scale of pitches and time-points is shown in Ex. 3-28a. In Ex. 3-28b, a series of twelve number-pairs is given, in which the first number denotes the order-position within the given series and the second denotes a pitch/time-point position within Ex. 3-28a, the hypothetical chromatic scale. In Ex. 3-28c the second number in each pair is associated with a pitch-class as counted from G (= 0), and in Ex. 3-28d (taken directly from Babbitt's article), the same series is translated into durations by making a similar association of numbers with metrical positions. Numbers that fall within an ascent between 0 and 11 thus find their places within a single measure. Numbers that descend must wait until "the same time point with relation to the measure" comes around again in the next measure. Finally, in Ex. 3-28e, the two interpretations of the number series are combined and distributed into parts for the members of a string quartet.

In mapping the specific time-point series on to a specific pitch-class series, Babbitt created a means of serializing durations that at last fully solved, at any rate to his own satisfaction, the problem of "appalling arbitrariness" to which John Backus had called attention in his condemnation of Boulez's *Structures*. Eventually Babbitt built further on the theory that justified the time-point system, eventually coordinating a twelve-fold gradation of loudness — from *ppppp* to *fffff* — with the pitches and durations so that aggregates could be completed in yet another dimension and yet another level

EX. 3-28   The "time-point system" as expounded in Milton Babbitt's "Twelve-tone Rhythmic Structure and the Electronic Medium" (*Perspectives of New Music*, I:1 [fall 1962])
A. The hypothetical chromatic pitch/duration scale

EX. 3-28B   A pitch/time-point series

$$(0, 0) \; (1, 3) \; (2, 11) \; (3, 4) \; (4, 1) \; (5, 2) \; (6, 8) \; (7, 10) \; (8, 5) \; (9, 9) \; (10, 7) \; (11, 6)$$

EX. 3-28C   A pitch/time-point series translated into actual pitches

EX. 3-28D   A pitch/time-point series translated into actual durations

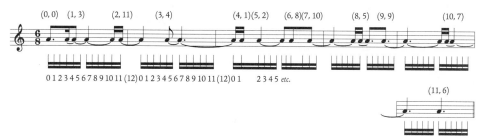

EX. 3-28E   All of the above, combined into a string-quartet texture

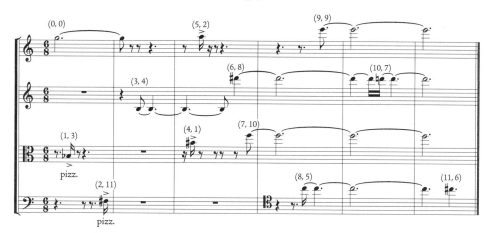

of "relatedness" could be added to the grid within which each and every "atomic event" in Babbitt's music was located.

BUT CAN YOU *HEAR* IT?

Other analysts were quick to note, however, that an irreducibly arbitrary (or "notional") element remained at the heart of Babbitt's procedure, namely the deceptively simple notated meter. Conceived solely as a container for the time points, and never articulated in terms of recurrent rhythmic or accentual patterns, Babbitt's $\frac{3}{4}$ or $\frac{6}{8}$ measure was not in fact "a measure in the usual musical metrical sense," but (like the bars in a transcription of a "medieval" or "Renaissance" motet) just a notational convenience. Rebar the music in $\frac{4}{4}$ or $\frac{7}{8}$, or just shift the bars an eighth note to the right or left, and everything will change for the analyst, although nothing has changed for the listener. What is analyzed, then, are the relationships that are demonstrable in the music as seen on the page, not the music as heard. Is Babbittian (Princetonian? American?) postwar serialism, then, just an enormous flowering of *Augenmusik*? And if it is, does that invalidate its musical quality, or its crucial truth-claims? If it does, then in what way: esthetically? scientifically? Are the two distinguishable? If so, how?

These issues have been debated for decades, both within the serialist school and outside of it. Even those who accept the limitless malleability of human nature and believe that all listening habits are the product of conditioning have questioned the practicability of Babbitt's theorizing, even as they have in many cases adopted it themselves out of admiration for its utopian qualities. Babbitt's Princeton colleague Peter Westergaard (b. 1931), writing three years later in *Perspectives of New Music*, the serialist house organ, registered his qualms in the language of the theory to which he was raising his considered objections. Writing with reference to the *Composition for Twelve Instruments*, in which Babbitt employed twelve-element durational sets for the first time, Westergaard noted that

> we have been at least partially conditioned by pre-Schoenberg pitch structure to hear pitch relationships mod. 12; i.e., we can be expected to hear a family resemblance in the opening interval of any P pitch set be it up a semitone, up thirteen semitones, or down eleven semitones. But have we been even partially conditioned by pre-Babbitt rhythmic structure to hear durational relationships mod. 12; i.e., can we be expected to hear a family resemblance between a dotted quarter note followed by a sixteenth note (the opening "interval" of duration set P_0 [see Ex. 3-26]) and an eighth note followed by a dotted eighth note (the opening "interval" of duration set P_2 [see Ex. 3-27])?
>
> The perceptual problems outlined above are further intensified by problems of performance. It would be difficult enough to differentiate between durations of ten and eleven sixteenth notes defined by pairs of attacks controlled by one player on one instrument. But the attacks which define the durational sets of Composition for Twelve Instruments may come from as many as twelve different players, each playing an instrument with a different response time.[46]

Westergaard added a footnote to the article, possibly at the editors' request, granting that all of these problems "have since been solved by Babbitt in his more recent procedure in which metric position corresponds to pitch number and, hence, duration to interval"[47] — that is, by the time-point system. But few theorists who recognize the "problems" as such have been satisfied that the time-point system has solved them. More frequently they have complained that the solution merely added another purely conceptual, nonperceptual level to the theory, thus removing the music even more decisively from the likelihood of its "auditory construal."[48] That is a phrase coined by George Perle, who went on to dismiss not only the music in question but the analytical literature that has grown up around it, since "it should not need to be stressed that the analysis of a piece of music ought to be relevant to its perception."[49] Needless to say, what Perle took to be a self-evident axiom has proven, since the rise of academic serialism in America, to be as controversial a contention as anyone could possibly adopt.

Perhaps the climax of "theoretical" dissension from within was reached by William Benjamin, a Princeton-trained music theorist, who in 1981 noisily defected from the ranks, charging (in the *Journal of Music Theory*, a rival organ to *Perspectives* published at Yale) that "the music of the post-war avant-garde" was "the first music in history" that "cannot be improvised, precisely imagined, embellished, simplified, or played with in any creative sense," all of which, he felt, justified the assertion that "it is hardly music at all."[50] Strong words. But Benjamin has no greater right to define music than Babbitt. Some analysis of his comments, and Perle's, may help clarify the stakes of the argument — and the historical significance of the musical discourses at the center of the controversy.

ULTIMATE REALIZATION OR REDUCTIO AD ABSURDUM?

The issues at stake go right back to the origins of literate (i.e., notated) music. The "real-time" practices Benjamin invokes — improvisation, embellishment, creative play — are the practices, and reflect the values, of "oral" culture. Their eclipse marks the full ascendancy of literacy — an ascendancy a full millennium in the making. And indeed the values Babbitt's compositional practices maximize — extreme (approaching "total") density, fixity, and consistency of texture, maintained over a long temporal (= "structural") span — are precisely the ones associated with the "spatialization" of music that literacy made possible.

The complete "autonomy" of the postwar serial product, extended to the point where every piece of music is ideally based on unique axiomatic premises, is likewise a conceptual child of literacy, in the sense that works of art within a literate tradition may exist independently of those who make them up and remember them. Musical works that can be remembered or precisely imagined only with difficulty, or that (ideally) cannot be memorized at all, would most completely satisfy this criterion of value — if such a value could be taken as an absolute. Concepts of artistic unity in works of performing art, and, conversely, awareness of the function of the parts within the whole in such works (what we call an analytical awareness), are thus distinctive of literate cultures. A music in which analysis can potentially — and, in extreme instances, even actually — replace the acts of performance or listening could thus be viewed as the highest possible realization of the literate ideal. In historical terms it does indeed represent a pinnacle, an apex, a ne plus ultra, and in the broadest view that may count as its truest historical achievement — or at least its most accurately described historical significance.

The never-to-be-settled question is, at what price? It can never be settled because price stands for values, and equally defensible values can be irreconcilable. What from one perspective may look like a logical culmination or a zenith may look from another like a perversion of values. Those who see and value music only in terms of a historical development will see the triumph of literacy in one way; those who see the primary value of music in the social exchanges it affords will find less to admire. But things and events as such are value-free. Values reside in the observers and their purposes.

The apparent arrogance of the position "classically" exemplified by Babbitt's "Who Cares if You Listen?" is, if you like, the hubris of literacy. But that hubris, however objectionable, cannot be wholly extricated from the good causes it may be seen to serve. It found abundant expression among the great figures of twentieth-century music, especially (of course) in Schoenberg, the greatest apostle of teleological history, who saw the evolution of music as headed inexorably toward the triumph of literate practice (representing "culture" and "autonomy") over every aspect of oral practice (representing atavisms of the "primitive" and the "contingent").

That is what led Schoenberg, and many after him, into what can seem such incorrigibly snobbish attitudes toward performers and listeners, their fellow human beings. His pupil Dika Newlin recalled him announcing that "music need not be performed any more than books need to be read aloud, for its logic is perfectly represented on the printed page; and the performer, for all his intolerable arrogance, is totally unnecessary except as his interpretations make the music understandable to an audience unfortunate enough not to be able to read it in print."[51] As for the listener, "All I know is that he exists, and insofar as he isn't indispensable for acoustic reasons (since music doesn't sound well in an empty hall), he's only a nuisance."[52]

By now we have some awareness of the many social and political (including musico-political) factors that conditioned such remarks. There is no reason to assume that Schoenberg consciously cast himself as the champion of the literate tradition of music as such, nor any reason to assume that the issues of "orality" vs. "literacy" that interest historians today were on his mind. The historical fact nevertheless remains that the politics of the twentieth century drove the discourse of literacy to its extreme, and Babbitt's achievement, both as composer and as theorist of composition, represents what in retrospect seems a historical limit.

To say this is not necessarily to impute to Babbitt any greater consciousness of such a role than Schoenberg possessed, but seeing him as the ultimate protagonist of literacy over orality does help account for the equanimity with which he met the sort of criticism we have been reviewing. In an open letter published in a special double issue of *Perspectives of New Music* commemorating Babbitt's sixtieth birthday in 1976, the composer and music theorist Wallace Berry (1928–91) made bold to advance some questions with regard to the "auditory construal" of the music all the other contributors were celebrating, and the relationship between those well-known difficulties or impossibilities and the, to him, grievous observation that "much music of our time, yours and mine, exists, essentially, in alienation." Maintaining a somewhat detached and stilted diction to offset, perhaps, the emotionally volatile nature of the matters he was broaching, Berry continued:

> It has been the understandable reflex of many of us to assume an attitude of brave defiance in this state of affairs, but I cannot imagine any convincing asseveration of genuine apathy toward it. Nor can we protest that today's music suffers for lack of exposure (and that if it had better exposure it would be understood and welcomed by audiences now so largely repelled by it, if on occasion intrigued at the "primitive" level of the impact of the isolated sonority and the like). And the alienation of which I despair is not merely with regard to our concert halls, which will continue to be governed in large part by crass commercial considerations, but (of course with notable exceptions that prove the point) with respect to our peers, experienced and sophisticated audiences in centers of artistic and cultural adventure and exploration. We can no longer sanctimoniously assail (as repressive, as prejudicially indisposed, as inattentive) those who, *knowing* today's music *and* the historical bases out of which it has evolved, are estranged from that music . . . .
>
> There are episodes in music's history that seem to have proved, finally, while exerting vital and constructive influences upon the course of things both coexistent and to follow, to be fascinating culs-de-sac, important not only in the impact by which, in part, subsequent developments are shaped, but in the intrinsic worth of many individual expressions and in didactic significances. Is it possible that the ultimate developments of serialism have attained, or are reasonably seen as coursing toward, such an end?[53]

In his published response to the essays collected in his honor, Babbitt was courteous enough. Of all the contributors to the volume, he conceded, "Wallace Berry most demands and deserves answers."[54] But he did not rise to the bait, offering instead (quite uncharacteristically) to relegate Berry's questions to the arena of taste, about which, as the saying goes, there can be no dispute. He, too, couched his thoughts in an unnaturally ceremonious idiom, as if to divest them of emotional baggage. But as always, obvious avoidance only succeeds in calling greater attention to the issue being circumvented:

> I do suspect that there may be differences in attitude, normative differences, between us, originating — perhaps — outside of music, and eventuating in our music, or — possibly — proceeding in the retrograde, even retrograde inverted, direction, even if only in that there are those of us who prefer the relative quiet and solace of the dead-end street to the distractions and annoyances of the crowded thoroughfare, although quite a few folks — at one time or another — have found their way to our cul-de-sac, if only because they, mistakenly or misguidedly, took a wrong turn . . . . Just as the philosophy of art has carried its practitioners into the philosophy of mind, our art is ever mindful that whatever one musical mind can create another can come to comprehend, even if it comes — normatively — to decide that it doesn't like it, approve of it, or of the isolation the two of them thereby suffer or enjoy.

But of course Babbitt's careful choice of language allowed the possibility that comprehension come by way of analysis — the contemplation of the musical object as a spatialized whole, by those with special training in the ways of the literate culture — rather than on the more direct perceptual terms Berry had specified. Babbitt saw no reason, then or since, to give an inch of ground to the "oral" culture, which he equated with the "crowded thoroughfare" of commerce. The sacrifice of a listening (rather than a looking) audience was a price he was prepared to pay for purity.

It is worth one more reiteration that the purity Babbitt consciously sought in his theory and practice was not necessarily the purity that is being attributed to it in this account, any more than Copland's or Stravinsky's conscious reasons for embracing serial composition directly reflected or acknowledged the factors invoked in this chapter to explain their actions. Copland, as we have seen, always said that he simply "needed more chords." Stravinsky argued, more categorically, that significant artistic change can only come about through "an irresistible pull within the art" rather than through the sort of "social pressures" that "Marxists," as he put it, preferred to invoke.[55] But even as he said this, his gratuitous, seemingly superstitious sidelong glance at Zhdanov (the Marxist-in-chief where the arts were concerned) told another story. Not only artists, but all who profess to act as conscious or autonomous agents in a complicated world are subject to many influences, including some of which they may perforce be relatively unaware. It is the historian's job to be aware of them and, however fallibly, to describe them.

But even if we allow for its political contingency, Babbitt maintained his position with consistency and integrity, and won for it a virtually universal respect within the academy, even among those convinced, like Wallace Berry, that it represented an historical cul-de-sac. It was only when some of Babbitt's colleagues and former pupils began claiming for academic serialism qualities (such as traditional emotional expressivity) that lay audiences complained of missing, that allegations of bad faith became common.

As one critic put it, it was as if one asked Claire Bloom or some comparably eloquent actor to read "Pointwise Periodic Homeomorphisms," Babbitt's notorious hypothetical math lecture, "with all the expressive resources of voice and gesture she would bring to the role of Ophelia or Desdemona."[56] Such a performance could only seem silly and gratuitous, whether one listened as a "layman" or as a math professor, and made both the textual object and its performance seem inadequate to their respective purposes. Ironically enough, it was only when academic composers seemed ready to retreat a bit from Babbitt's hard line that their position began to lose credibility. It was then that the tide began to turn against the sort of uncompromising "truth" that had been artistically upholdable at the height of the cold war, and that provided academic serialism in America with its philosophical support system.

But we can end this chapter on an even more obviously ironic note. It was when he formulated his time-point system, which implied, and therefore demanded, a precision of rhythmic execution that appeared superhuman even to his supporters, that Babbitt began touting the electronic medium as a necessary practical adjunct of theoretical advance. The already-quoted article in *Perspectives* that first promulgated the time-point system was in fact called "Twelve-Tone Rhythmic Structure and the Electronic Medium," and it contained the prediction that "such pitch and rhythmic extensions of the twelve-tone system" as Babbitt was proposing would inevitably "carry music to the point of purely electronic feasibility," and this because only electronic means could afford the composer a control over his product that would suffice to allow "the necessary characteristics" of his music to be "preserved in the auditory domain, and not merely in the domain of notational specification."[57]

In other words, only electronic media could give music the sort of fixity and exactness in the domain of physical sound that it already possessed in the conceptual domain of notation. It was the triumph of literacy over orality that demanded the final sacrifice of the finite "human" to the infinitely adaptable and obediently automated performance media that would eventually be controlled by computers. Electronic media promised (or, depending on one's perspective, threatened) the ultimate dehumanization of the art, a dehumanization whose status as a logical (inevitable? necessary? desirable?) consequence of literacy now stood revealed.

The irony was, and is, that the same electronic media that enabled composers on the extreme "literate" edge to realize their notated complexities without loss of detail also made it possible to compose without the use of scores at all, and thus inaugurated a new era of improvisational (or "real time") composing. In the end, as we will shortly discover, electronic media would subvert the triumph of literacy and give music a new future.

CHAPTER 4

The Third Revolution

MUSIC AND ELECTRONIC MEDIA; VARÈSE'S CAREER

I BELIEVE THAT THE USE OF NOISE TO MAKE MUSIC WILL CONTINUE AND
INCREASE UNTIL WE REACH A MUSIC PRODUCED THROUGH THE AID OF
ELECTRICAL INSTRUMENTS WHICH WILL MAKE AVAILABLE FOR MUSICAL
PURPOSES ANY AND ALL SOUNDS THAT CAN BE HEARD.[1]

—JOHN CAGE, "THE FUTURE OF MUSIC: CREDO" (1940)

TAPE

When the young John Cage made that boldly capitalized prediction, it seemed like one more fantasy among the many he enunciated in that brash utopian Credo, already sampled in chapter 2. And yet, unbeknownst to him or to his audience, the practical means for implementing it were already at hand. Five years earlier, at a 1935 radio exhibition in Berlin, the German firm AEG (*Allgemeine Elektrizitäts Gesellschaft* or "General Electric Company") demonstrated a new invention called the Magnetophone, a device for converting sound signals into magnetic impulses that could be stored indefinitely on a paper tape coated with a metallic oxide, and then reconverted (or "played back") into sound. Actually, the concept of magnetic sound recording had been described theoretically half a century before that. An ancestor of the magnetophone called the Telegraphone, a Danish invention that recorded sound magnetically on a thin metal wire, was exhibited at the Paris World Exhibition of 1900, and received a prize. (Wire recorders were not definitively supplanted by tape recorders until the middle of the new century.)

Early magnetophones and wire recorders produced a playback of limited frequency range, seriously distorted by background noise, or "hiss." Nobody foresaw any immediate musical applications for such machines. AEG envisioned the magnetophone as an office dictation device, or a means of storing radio programs like news bulletins for rebroadcast. Besides radio stations, early customers included the Gestapo, the Nazi secret police, which used it to record confessions, among other things. But during the war, when German technological advances were hidden from Allied view, the magnetophone was improved to the point where it surpassed the dynamic and frequency response of disc recordings; and the use of a supersonic bias frequency in the recording process dramatically reduced the background noise.

By the early 1940s, German companies were using tape recorders as an intermediate stage in the production of commercial music recordings, rather than recording the sound directly on disc. Not only was the sound quality thereby improved, but also far more could be recorded at a stretch than the amount that could go on a single 78 RPM "side." For the record, so to speak, the earliest continuous tape-recorded opera performance to be commercially released on disc was of *Abu Hassan* (1811), a one-act "Turkish" singspiel by Carl Maria von Weber. It was originally recorded "live" for broadcast on Radio Berlin in 1944, with the young soprano Elisabeth Schwarzkopf, later a great international diva, in the role of Fatime.

Above all, however, tape recordings were easy to handle and manipulate, and made composite editing possible. Good "takes" of different passages could be spliced together. All of a singer's best notes could be included in a single finished product. Performances on records could be made literally flawless, simply by splicing out and replacing all the flaws. The standard joke of the recording studio became the one about the soloist, admiring the playback, being teased by the recording engineer: "Yes, don't you wish you could play like that?"

After the war, the American occupying troops were amazed to find the improved tape recorders in every German radio station. All of AEG's patents having fallen into Allied hands as spoils of war, the machines could be duplicated and marketed in the victorious nations without payment of royalties. The first American tape recorders were produced in 1947 by the Ampex Company, copied from a pair shipped home from Radio Frankfurt by John Mullin, a sound engineer who was serving with the U.S. Army communications corps. One of Ampex's first customers was the crooner Bing Crosby, who began tape-recording his weekly programs at his convenience for later broadcast.

Soon it became apparent to alert musicians that the same advantages in handling and manipulation that served the purposes of commercial recording could also serve the purposes of composition. The cutting and splicing techniques that improved live-recorded performances could also be used to create all kinds of sound collages. In addition, playback speed could be varied, with consequent alterations to the pitch, rapidity, and timbre of recorded sounds. Connecting ("patching") the playback head of one tape recorder to the recording head of another made it possible to store the altered sounds for use in composition.

But that was only the beginning. By reversing the positions of the tape spools on the "deck" of the recording machine, tapes could be played backward, with radical alteration to sound "envelope" or attack-decay properties: a tone played on the piano, for example, became a whooshing, accelerating crescendo to an abrupt cutoff. A length of tape could be spliced into a continuous loop that produced an ostinato effect when played back. Such ostinatos could be montaged into patterns and textures without limit. Additional recording-studio devices like echo chambers, sound filters, and mixers could be patched into the recording circuit for further alterations to sounds stored on tape.

Composers were standing ready to exploit these new possibilities, especially in the ranks of the newly resurgent postwar avant-garde, all warring factions included. Though they may have disagreed about everything else, they were united in greeting the new technological marvel. For "zero hour" types, it offered the most dramatic chance to wipe the slate clean of all existing traditions and techniques. In his 1940 lecture, Cage already hailed the advent of the first genuinely "twentieth-century means for making music."[2] For control freaks, it offered an unprecedented degree of determinacy, since at the splicing block the most complicated or exacting rhythmic relationships (for example) could be worked out in terms of finely measured lengths of tape — the most literal instance imaginable of the "spatialization" of music mooted at the end of chapter 3.

Milton Babbitt, for one, was thrilled by "the notion of having complete control over one's composition, of being complete master of all you survey."[3] At the opposite extreme, that of radical indeterminacy, Cage was also celebrating the possibility "for composers to make music directly, without the assistance of intermediary performers"[4] — more evidence that the perceived polar opposites of advanced music making were united in a common commitment to technological research and development. Cage joyously foresaw the obsolescence of musical notation. For devotees of liberation, whether of sounds or of people, endless prospects loomed.

AN OLD DREAM COME TRUE

All of these approaches to direct "electroacoustic" synthesis of music (to use what later became the standard term) had a considerable prehistory by the middle of the twentieth century. It can be traced back even before the invention of electric current, to music boxes and more elaborate mechanical contrivances such as the Panharmonicon of Johann Nepomuk Maelzel (1772–1838; best known as the inventor of the pendulum metronome), an automated orchestra powered by weights and cylinders, for which Beethoven wrote his "Battle Symphony" (a.k.a. *Wellington's Victory*) in 1813.

The advent of electric power was a spur to many more such inventions, like the Telharmonium (alias Dynamophone), a two-hundred-ton apparatus for producing "scientifically perfect music" in any tuning system, assembled by the inventor Thaddeus Cahill (1867–1934) and exhibited in New York in 1906. An article on this machine in a popular magazine came to the attention of Ferrucio Busoni, the famous pianist-composer and perhaps the most influential teacher of the time, who saw in it the promise of musical emancipation at the dawn of the new century. "Music was born free," Busoni declared in his *Sketch of a New Aesthetic of Music* (1907), paraphrasing Rousseau's *Social Contract*, "and to win freedom is its destiny."[5]

Through the use of machines like Cahill's, music might yet defeat the limitations that less advanced technologies had imposed on it, and at last achieve its true aims, *namely, the imitation of nature and the interpretation of human feelings*[6] (italics original). That would truly be an "absolute music," Busoni rhapsodized. His fantasy of a free music — never achieved but hinted at in "preparatory and intermediary passages (preludes and transitions)"[7] like the introduction before the final fugue in Beethoven's big "Hammerklavier" Sonata, op. 106 — chimes peculiarly with the utopian spirit of the midcentury avant-garde:

> What a vista of fair hopes and dreamlike fancies is thus opened for the ear, and for Art! Who has not dreamt that he could float on air? and firmly believed his dream to be reality? — Let us take thought, how music may be restored to its primitive, natural essence; let us free it from architectonic, acoustic and esthetic dogmas; let

it be pure invention and sentiment, in harmonies, in forms, in tone-colors (for invention and sentiment are not the prerogative of melody alone); let it follow the line of the rainbow and vie with the clouds in breaking sunbeams; let Music be naught else than Nature mirrored by and reflected from the human breast; for it is sounding air and floats above and beyond the air; within Man himself as universally and absolutely as in Creation entire; for it can gather together and disperse without losing in intensity.[8]

That vision of freedom and naturalness inspired many artists and inventors in the early part of the twentieth century to imagine and experiment with all kinds of artificial contrivances. The noisiest, most picturesque faction was the *musicisti futuristi*, a group of Italian artists who sought a musical application of the principles enunciated in the Futurist Manifesto of 1909. This document, by Filippo Marinetti (1876–1944), a poet and novelist, was probably the most radically antitraditionalist proclamation of its day. It called for the erasure of artistic memory — in practical (but not necessarily serious) terms, for the destruction of museums and concert halls — and the consecration of art to the celebration of the highly romanticized dynamics and dangers of twentieth-century life: warfare ("the world's natural hygiene,"[9] according to a Marinetti manifesto of 1910) and conquest on an unprecedented scale, and above all the machines that would provide the means to realize these ferocious ideals. (Not coincidentally, Marinetti was one of the founding members of the Italian Fascist Party.)

Futurismo found direct expression in literature and the visual arts, media in which all it took was imagination and descriptive or illustrative skill to create the appropriate artifacts. Music, however, required equipment; and in the absence of such accouterments, machine music remained at first, for the most part, a utopian fantasy. It gave rise to a little manifesto of its own in 1913 (perhaps significantly, the year of Stravinsky's *The Rite of Spring*), issued in Milan by Luigi Russolo (1885–1947), a painter, and dedicated to Francesco Balilla Pratella (1880–1955), the "grande musicista futurista," who had just composed a raucous choral work called *Inno alla vita* ("Hymn to life"). Russolo's manifesto reached its rhetorical climax in a passage that may have been resounding in Cage's inner ear (its frequent bellowing capitalizations dazzling his mind's eye, too) when he delivered his remarkable prediction in 1940:

> In the nineteenth century, with the invention of machines, Noise was born. Today Noise is triumphant, and reigns supreme over the senses of men. The art of music at first sought and achieved purity and sweetness of sound; later, it blended diverse sounds, but always with the intent to caress the ear with suave harmonies. Today, growing ever more complicated, it seeks those combinations of sounds that fall most dissonantly, strangely, and harshly upon the ear. We thus approach nearer and nearer to the MUSIC OF NOISE. We must break out of this narrow circle of pure musical sounds, and conquer the infinite variety of noise-sounds.[10]

Russolo ended his manifesto with a "scientific" classification of noises into six families, to be produced mechanically by means of some as yet uninvented technology, from which the orchestra of the future would make its music:

1	2	3	4	5	6
Booms	Whistles	Whispers	Screams	Noises	Voices of
Thunderclaps	Hisses	Murmurs	Screeches	obtained by	animals and
Explosions	Snorts	Mutterings	Rustlings	percussion	men: Shouts
Crashes		Bustling	Buzzes	on metals,	Shrieks
Splashes		noises	Cracklings	wood, stone,	Groans
Roars		Gurgles	Sounds	terracotta	Howls
			obtained by		Laughs
			friction		Wheezes
					Sobs

In 1913, Russolo was back with a book, *L'arte dei rumori* ("The art of noises"), which included the first designs for futurist instruments called *intonarumori*, "noise intoners." Together with a percussionist named Ugo Piatti (possibly a pseudonym; the name means "cymbals"), Russolo began constructing them in the form of boxes of varying size, with acoustical horns like the ones on early phonographs attached to their fronts, and with some sound-generating mechanism inside, activated by turning a crank at the rear. They included a *crepitatore* (crackler), a *ululatore* (hooter), a *gracidatore* (croaker), a *gorgogliatore* (gurgler), and a *ronzatore* (buzzer). Between 1914 and 1921 Russolo conducted some *concerti futuristichi* with these instruments in Milan and Paris. A typical composition for them was titled *Il risveglio di una città* ("The awakening of a city"). Except for the several measures reproduced in Fig. 4-1, from an Italian arts magazine of 1914, the scores and parts are lost; the *intonarumori* were speculatively refurbished by Italian musicologists for a recording in 1977.[11] The music was, by all reports, of a loudness sufficient to elicit exciting opposition from the audience; on one occasion irate listeners mounted the stage and attempted a violent intervention, no doubt very much to the composer's taste.

Perhaps inspired by the nightingale episode in Respighi's *Pines of Rome*, Marinetti tried a new tack in 1933: he had some "field recordings" made on 78-RPM discs, including landscape noises, street music, human nonverbal vocal sounds ("the wheh wheh wheh of a baby boy," "surprised Ooooooh of an 11-year-old girl," etc.), rhythmic environmental noises (dripping water, keys turning in locks, electric doorbells), individual tones produced on various musical instruments, "pure silence" (i.e., the sound of the phonograph needle in the groove), and so forth, and assembled the sounds into collages performed by assistants, standing at phonograph turntables, who played the records on cue.

GENERATING SYNTHETIC SOUNDS

Another approach was taken by electrical engineers in several countries, who designed new musical instruments that produced sounds that flaunted the electronic origins that made them sounds specific to the twentieth century. Perhaps the earliest, very likely

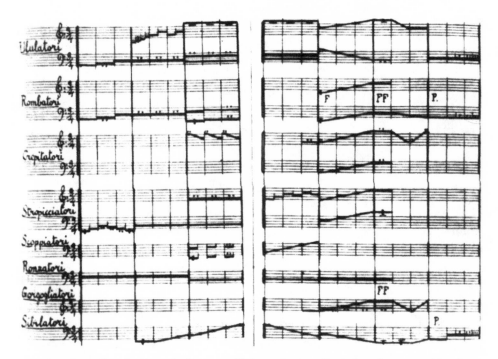

FIG. 4-1   Luigi Russolo, *Il risveglio di una città* ("The awakening of a city," 1914), a composition for an ensemble of futurist *intonarumori* (noise intoners). Reading down the left margin of the score as usual, they are *ululatori* (hooters), *rombatori* (rumblers), *crepitatori* (cracklers), *stropicciatori* (scrapers), *scoppiatori* (exploders), *ronzatori* (buzzers), *gorgogliatori* (gurglers), and *sibilatori* (hissers).

the simplest, and surely the most famous, was invented in 1920 by a Russian physicist named Lev Sergeyevich Termen (1896–1993, also renowned as a television pioneer), who thought he was building a burglar alarm. His device featured a pair of antennas that set up an electromagnetic field, into which the intrusion of any electrical conductor (say a human body) would touch off a signal from a radio oscillator.

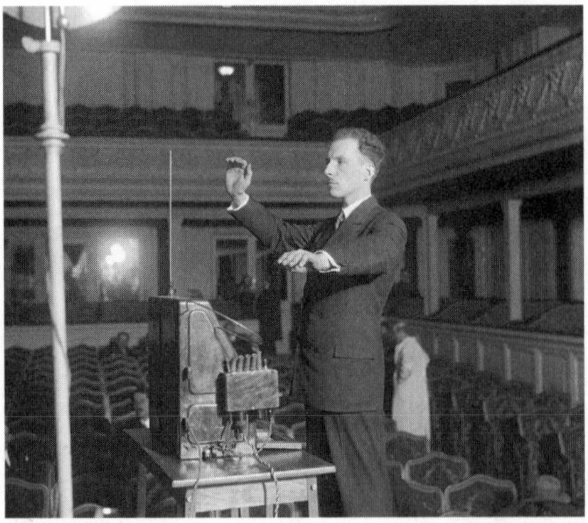

As one approached the vertical antenna at the top of the cabinet, the signal (just a controlled version of the "squeal" one obtained between stations when tuning an early radio) became higher in pitch; as one approached the loop antenna at the side of the instrument, the signal became weaker (and silent if one touched the antenna, making articulations possible). An amateur cellist, Termen amused himself by moving his hands in such a way as to make

FIG. 4-2   Lev Sergeyevich Termen (Leon Théremin) with his *termenvox* (theremin).

the invisible field respond with tunes from his repertory: Massenet's *Elegy*, Saint-Saëns's *The Swan*, and the like. Since he found himself playing his new instrument without touching it, just moving his hands in the air, Termen christened his invention the "etherphone." In March 1922, Termen was summoned to demonstrate his device to Vladimir Lenin, the head of the young Soviet government, in his office at the Moscow Kremlin. Lenin was interested in the machine chiefly as a security device. He wrote to Trotsky, the head of the Red Army, suggesting that they procure some etherphones so that the guard duties of the Kremlin cadets might be reduced. But he also authorized Termen to tour Russia with a free railway pass and show off his invention as a miraculous musical instrument one did not touch, as propaganda for the wonders of electricity (one of Lenin's pet slogans being "Communism is Soviet power plus electrification of the whole country"). In 1924, after Soviet Russia had signed a patent convention with Germany, Termen was sent abroad to set up a facility for the mass production of his instrument, to be marketed as the Termenvox.

In Germany, and later in the United States, where he lived and worked from 1927 to 1938 (both as promoter of his electrical devices and as a Soviet espionage agent), the inventor signed his name Leon Theremin, and his instrument became known, simply, as the theremin. The manner in which it was promoted, and the repertoire that (following the inventor's lead) was normally performed on it, led to its being regarded as something like an electronic violin or cello, rather than a vehicle for a new music. Few composers took an interest in it. John Cage went out of his way, in his lecture on the Future of Music, to deride "Thereministes," who, despite the "genuinely new possibilities" that the device offered in its unbroken frequency continuum, "did their utmost to make the instrument sound like some old instrument, giving it a sickeningly sweet vibrato, and performing upon it, with difficulty, masterpieces from the past." In effect, Cage complained, "Thereministes act as censors, giving the public those sounds they think the public will like." As a vexing result, "we are shielded from new sound experiences."[12] A somewhat more optimistic and imaginative view was taken by Ernst Toch (1887–1964), an Austrian composer who would eventually emigrate to the United States, but who caught the theremin act in Berlin. He realized that the inventor's lack of musical sophistication, and his exclusive interest in marketing his instrument as a medium for conventional performance rather than for composition, made him a poor herald of its possibilities. Reacting precisely the way Busoni might have done, Toch noted that "the concrete material of music has consisted until now of a limited series of exactly fixed pitches and of a limited series of exactly fixed sound colors," and complained that "the closer Theremin in his 'concert' attempts to come to them, to produce them in a deceiving manner, the less interesting his demonstration becomes for the composer." What interested Toch was not the performance of the hackneyed musical selections but rather

> the sound phenomena which, demonstrated before the "concert" and during the lecture as rough raw material, often similar to animal or climatological sounds of nature, appeared during the "concert" as uncalled-for byproducts and hardly noticed waste products. Just in these lies the fertile germ of a true new vista which Theremin lays open to the composer of music, still incalculable in its consequences,

—for in them one heard material that "lies *between* the fixed pitches and *between* the fixed tone colors: rich, tempting, promising and enchanting for the artist."[13]

Most of the music composed for (or performed on) the theremin was of the hackneyed substitute-violin type. The first concerted work for the instrument, *Simfonicheskaya misteriya* ("Symphonic mysterium") by Andrey Pashchenko (1885–1972), composed in 1923 on commission from the Soviet government, incorporated its eerie, otherworldly timbre into a Scriabinesque pastiche for orchestra. The best-known concerto for the instrument, written in 1944 by the Cypriot-American composer Anis Fuleihan (1900–70) for Clara Rockmore (1911–98), a Russian-American violin prodigy who became the world's most accomplished "thereministe," was an exercise in orientalisms. Rockmore's special achievement was to defeat the built-in glissando normally heard between the notes within the theremin's seamless pitch continuum and (with the help of some attachments the inventor designed for her) to actually manage staccato articulations and fast passagework without sacrificing purity of intonation.

It was a marvelous feat, but in light of Toch's comment, it defeated the instrument's potential as a novel resource for composers. The only composer to capitalize fully on the theremin's "defects" was the Australian-American Percy Grainger (1882–1961), best known during his lifetime as a piano virtuoso who, significantly, had studied briefly with Busoni and had been infected with the latter's idealistic notions of musical freedom. The theremin, which had no "natural" tuning system, was completely free of prejudice where intervals were concerned.

Busoni had ended his *Sketch of a New Aesthetic of Music* with ruminations about microtones, but warned that all fixed tuning systems, whether based on equal semitones, quarter tones, or sixth tones, were equally arbitrary artifacts of culture when compared with nature's limitless resources. Tempered keyboard instruments, the great pianist fumed, "have so thoroughly schooled our ears that we are no longer capable of hearing anything else—incapable of hearing except through this impure medium. Yet Nature created an *infinite gradation—infinite!* Who still knows it nowadays?"[14] The theremin, Grainger was quick to realize, offered that infinite gradation to composers. It could turn Busoni's fantasy of a free music into a practical reality.

He had responded immediately to Busoni's *Sketch* with a composition actually titled *Free Music* for string quartet (1907). After hearing Clara Rockmore's debut recital, Grainger arranged the piece for four theremins, and completed a sequel, *Free Music No. 2* for six theremins, in 1936. In a letter to the critic Olin Downes, he echoed Busoni's nature rhapsodies, rejoicing that he had created conditions under which "a melody is as free to roam thru space as a painter is free to draw & paint free lines, free curves, create free shapes."[15] A description he wrote for publication was more reminiscent of *Futurismo*: "It seems to me absurd to live in an age of flying and yet not be able to execute tonal glides and curves."[16] He invented a special notation for his glides and curves, plotting them on graph paper in inks of different colors to represent the different instruments in the ensemble. He never published the scores, however; nor were the Free Musics ever performed. What held Grainger back was the sense, reminiscent of Cage, that music could never be truly free as long as human beings were involved in its performance:

Too long has music been subject to the limitations of the human hand, and subject as well to the interfering interpretations of a middle-man: the performer. A composer wants to speak to his public direct. Machines (if properly constructed and properly written for) are capable of niceties of emotional expression impossible to a human performer.[17]

Grainger was among those who placed their creative ideas on hold, awaiting the advent of a technology that might render them feasible. In 1944, he collaborated with an engineer acquaintance in designing a "Free Music Machine" that would combine the sound-gliding principle of the theremin with a mechanism for performing "complex irregular rhythms accurately, rhythms much too difficult for human beings to execute." They built a working model in 1955, by which time tape technology was available; but Grainger, creatively exhausted, did not take advantage of it.

Meanwhile, as Albert Glinsky, Lev Termen's biographer, put it, "the theremin debate—melodic voice instrument or microtonal sound resource—was easily reconciled among the larger public; it came down to the instrument as simple, quirky entertainment."[18] Until a new wave of interest in the instrument was suddenly inspired in its homeland by the 1991 demise of the Soviet Union, few if any serious compositions for it postdated Fuleihan's concerto. Instead, it became a ubiquitous sound effect in radio dramas (beginning with the *Green Hornet* mystery serial) and science fiction and horror movies, or "psychological thrillers" (beginning with Robert Emmet Dolan's 1944 score for *Lady in the Dark* and continuing the next year with Alfred Hitchcock's classic *Spellbound*, with music by Miklós Rózsa). In the 1950s simple theremin-type devices were marketed in do-it-yourself kits to teenagers, and began turning up in youth-oriented popular music (most famously, in 1966, in the Beach Boys' *Good Vibrations*).

Less notorious than the theremin, and less spectacular, but perhaps more significant in terms of the musical repertory that it stimulated, was a device called *ondes musicales* ("musical waves"), unveiled in 1928 by the French engineer Maurice Martenot (1898–1980) and now called ondes martenot after him. It produces its sound on the same principle as the theremin. At first the performer inserted a finger in a ring and pulled a ribbon from side to side to alter the pitch along a smooth continuum. Later models added a keyboard to make conventional tunings available in addition to glissando effects.

Its greater compatibility with familiar musical styles and playing techniques made the ondes martenot easier than the theremin to assimilate into standard musical practice. Pianists or organists could master it quickly, and it could effectively augment symphony orchestras with extremely low sounds (Arthur Honegger, a member of Les Six, preferring it for this purpose to the contrabassoon) or, alternatively, a high vibrato-laden wail that Olivier Messiaen exploited memorably to evoke the figure of the love goddess in his *Turangalila-symphonie* of 1948. After the war a class in ondes martenot was established at the Paris Conservatory, and Pierre Boulez won his first local fame as an exponent of the instrument.

The trautonium, a third electronic instrument of a type similar to the theremin and the ondes martenot, was invented around 1930 by the German engineer Friedrich

Trautwein (1888–1956), but never had a comparable success. Its playing technique, involving the pressure of a finger against a continuous metal wire on which pitches were marked off, was more easily learned than that of the theremin, but it lacked the ondes's advantage of a keyboard. Hindemith, who made a point of writing concertos or sonatas for every instrument, wrote a *Konzertstück* for trautonium and strings (never published) in 1931. Later a pair of keyboards was added to the design by one of Trautwein's former pupils. In this form the instrument (or at least its sounds) became familiar to moviegoers from the soundtrack score by Bernard Herrmann (1911–75), with Remi Gassman and Oskar Sala, to Alfred Hitchcock's horror thriller *The Birds* (1963).

A MAXIMALIST OUT OF SEASON

Another composer who sought to realize a Busonian vision using electronic instruments as early as he possibly could, but had to wait, was the Franco-American Edgar (or Edgard) Varèse (1883–1965), a remarkable — and remarkably isolated — figure on the avant-garde scene at a time when there was virtually no musical avant-garde to speak of. Like Iannis Xenakis (see chapter 2), Varèse was trained in mathematics and engineering before he studied music seriously. In 1907, after reading Busoni's *Sketch of a New Aesthetic of Music*, he went to Berlin and sought the author out as a mentor. His interest in electric instruments was kindled even before World War I, at first by the "dynaphone," an early sound synthesizer invented by the French engineer René Bertrand.

Varèse moved to New York in 1915 and at first tried to make a career as a conductor. His earliest American opus, on which he worked between 1918 and 1921, was a gigantic orchestral score called *Amériques*. (The title did not refer only to the continents of the New World; in the vocabulary of Europeans, "an America" often meant a magnificent discovery.) It showed the influence of Busoni's "free music" theorizing in the parts it contained for two sirens, acoustical devices consisting of a metal disk pierced with holes arranged equidistantly in a circle and rotated by means of a handle over a jet of compressed air that whistles through the holes at a frequency determined by the speed of rotation. Invented for use as fog signals or as warning devices on fire engines or ambulances, sirens are not normally thought of as musical instruments; but as he put it much later in an essay called "The Liberation of Sound," Varèse "always felt the need of a kind of continuous flowing curve that instruments could not give me"[19] — exactly what Grainger had sought in his *Free Music*. The sirens in *Amériques* are played by two of the eleven percussionists the piece requires.

FIG. 4-3   Edgard Varèse listening to *Poème électronique*, 1958.

And just as Grainger turned from strings to theremins, so Varèse replaced the sirens in *Amériques*, on its French premiere in 1929, with a pair of ondes martenot. For a later piece, a neoprimitivist choral fantasy called *Ecuatorial* to a text from the Mayan scripture *Popul Vuh*, he commissioned from their inventor a pair of theremins of especially high and piercing range, capable of producing near-supersonic frequencies and providing the wailing timbres, soaring glissandos, and endlessly sustained notes that constituted Varèse's imagined pre-Columbian music in all its "elemental rude intensity."[20] The work was first performed in April 1934, under Nicolas Slonimsky, with the specially designed theremins; but when published, the score again specified the more readily available ondes martenot.

That publication did not take place until 1961. Varèse's music of the 1920s and 1930s was out of joint with its time. He was nurturing, or trying to nurture, the complementary spirits of neoprimitivism and futurism far into the age of neoclassic irony, seeking to keep the frantically optimistic Art of Noises alive in a period when the defense of high culture seemed sooner to demand pessimistic retrenchment. The very summit of musical futurism was a trio of rugged compositions by Varèse, composed in New York between 1922 and 1931, that sported titles borrowed from the world of science. *Hyperprism* (1923) and *Intégrales* (1925) were scored for small wind bands with outsize percussion sections. *Ionisation* (1931) was a composition for percussion alone: thirteen players on a total of forty-one instruments.

Varèse's "scientistic" titles are not easily interpreted. Hyperprism refers, presumably, to the intensification of a prismatic (refractive or light-bending) function, hence to the breaking down of a formal whole (e.g., white light) into contrasting components (e.g., spectral colors). That definition has been more or less plausibly related to the episodic nature of Varèse's composition, with its many short sections in contrasting tempos. Integrals, in calculus, are expressions from which a set of functions can be derived; Varèse's title has been interpreted, accordingly, as referring to the subsumption of the many differentiated sections of the composition by that name into a unified whole. In both cases a similar phenomenon — namely, a whole broken down into a contrasting yet interrelated multiplicity — is described from differing perspectives. But so could any sonata or symphony movement. The scientistic titles are evocative rather than explanatory.

Ionisation, the percussion piece, is perhaps easier to describe in terms of an implied program. A far grander, more romantic conception than, say, John Cage's spare, Apollonian *Imaginary Landscapes*, for all its sonic novelty (and despite its seemingly technical title) it makes easily recognized expressive gestures that aim (like the Futurists' Art of Noises, like the work of all maximalists) at a traditionally cathartic emotional effect. Nor is there anything in it of the sarcasm or satire exuded by Shostakovich's percussion entr'acte from *The Nose*, composed a few years earlier. Varèse sought a candid, forthright exaltation of a kind that had been put out of bounds by the canons of fashionable neoclassical taste; but he wanted to achieve it in a manner that truly "suffices to provide musical expression of *our* emotions and *our* conceptions,"[21] as he put it in a roundtable discussion, "La méchanisation de la musique," held in Paris in 1930, while *Ionisation* was in progress.

Beginning darkly and quietly, with siren tones of "curving" pitch and indeterminate "flowing" expanse, *Ionisation* musters increasingly definite rhythms (like the abrupt unison hemiolas at 7), mounting volume (like the entrance of the high and low anvils [*enclumes*] at 9), and a gradually rising tessitura until it reaches a blazing climax that seems to engender fixed musical pitch (piano, tubular chimes, glockenspiel at 13) as if it were the outcome or precipitate of the electrochemical reaction named in the title.

Between them, *Ionisation* and *Ecuatorial* could be said to bring the complementary futurist and neoprimitivist impulses in twentieth-century music to a climax and a temporary conclusion, for after them came a long silence. Between 1934 and 1954, Varèse completed only three works, none of them very substantial: *Densité 21.5*, a sixty-one-measure composition for unaccompanied flute, written in 1936 on commission from the flautist Georges Barrère, who wanted a showpiece to inaugurate his new platinum instrument (21.5 being the specific gravity or density of platinum as it was then measured); *Étude pour Espace* (Study for "Space"), a short chorus accompanied by two pianos and percussion (performed once in 1947 but never published), excerpted from a grandiose choral symphony on which Varèse worked sporadically for decades but never finished; and *Dance for Burgess*, composed at the request of the actor Burgess Meredith, a friend, for a projected Broadway show, but never performed.

During the 1940s Varèse dropped into obscurity. His earlier fame, unsupported by ongoing performances or recordings, lapsed into a reputation for eccentricity. The most characteristic glimpse of him during the silent decade came by way of Henry Miller, an American surrealist writer widely regarded at the time as a pornographer, who included a chapter on Varèse, first published by a London arts magazine, in a collection of travel essays about America, *The Air-Conditioned Nightmare*, that appeared in 1945. It was called "With Edgar Varèse in the Gobi Desert," and it opened with a scenario Varèse had sketched for *Espace*, the never-to-be-finished choral symphony, in 1929. It reads like a high-tech updating of Scriabin's similarly unfinished and unfinishable theosophical *Mysterium*, and provides a fitting epitaph for the spent maximalist impulse:

> The world awake! Humanity on the march. Nothing can stop it. A conscious humanity neither exploitable nor pitiable. Marching! Going! They march! Millions of feet endlessly tramping, treading, pounding, striding. Rhythms change: quick, slow, staccato, dragging, treading, pounding, striding. GO! The final crescendo giving the impression that confidently, pitilessly, the going will never stop . . . projecting itself into space . . .
>
> Voices in the sky, as though magic, invisible hands were turning on and off the knobs of fantastic radios, filling all space, criss-crossing, overlapping, penetrating each other, splitting up, superimposing, repulsing each other, colliding, crashing. Phrases, slogans, utterances, chants, proclamations: China, Russia, Spain, the Fascist states and the opposing Democracies, all breaking their paralyzing crusts.
>
> What should be avoided: tones of propaganda, as well as any journalistic speculation on timely events and doctrines. I want the epic impact of our epoch, stripped of its mannerisms and snobbisms. I suggest using here and there snatches of phrases from American, French, Russian, Chinese, Spanish, German revolutions: shooting stars, also words recurring like pounding hammer blows or throbbing in an underground ostinato, stubborn and ritualistic.

I should like an exultant, even prophetic tone — incantatory, the writing, however, lean and bare, stripped for action, almost like the account of a prizefight, blow for blow, the audience kept keyed-up, tense and unconscious of the style of the announcer. Also some phrases out of folklore — for the sake of their human, near-the-earth quality. I want to encompass everything that is human, from the most primitive to the farthest reaches of science.[22]

"What sort of proclamation can this be?" Miller wrote. "An anarchist running amok? A Sandwich Islander on the war-path? No, my friends, these are the words of Edgar Varèse, a composer."[23] The tone, meant as sympathetic, made it hard to take the described subject very seriously. Even to enthusiasts like Miller, maximalism had reached the point where preemptive caricature was required. "What interests me about Varèse," he went on, "is the fact that he seems unable to get a hearing."[24] But it was not only the indifference of those committed to the "mannerisms and snobbisms" of the neoclassical revival that marginalized Varèse. He was at a technological impasse, imagining a music that could not be realized in actual sound.

"REAL" VS. "PURE"

It was the advent of the tape recorder, the development described at the beginning of this chapter, that rescued Varèse from his creative hiatus and brought about something of a futurist resurgence, coinciding with the emergence of the postwar avant-garde. That made it possible to look upon Varèse's compositions of the 1920s and 1930s not only as quaintly heroic echoes of an exhausted past but, just as plausibly, as harbingers of an abundant future. He found himself cast as a mentor to a new generation of composers, and became the only member of his generation to apply himself to the new technology of "organized sound,"[25] to use the term Varèse offered (in an article published in 1940) as a means of evading "the monotonous question: 'But is it music?'" The question was inevitable, since the new medium of electronic music was able at last to fulfill John Cage's prediction of 1940 and "MAKE AVAILABLE FOR MUSICAL PURPOSES ANY AND ALL SOUNDS THAT CAN BE HEARD," and do it in a way that was entirely practicable. (Cage, too, had offered, "if the word 'music' is sacred," to call the activity he foresaw "organization of sound" and the composer an "organizer of sound.") That meant all at once admitting to the domain of music a wide variety of sounds for which no musical notation existed and to which no existing rules of composition were applicable. But as Varèse somewhat gloomily predicted in "The Liberation of Sound," "I am afraid it will not be long before some musical mortician begins embalming electronic music in rules."[26]

From the beginning, composers of electronic music formed themselves into two main camps, replicating the division that previously existed between the Futurists, who wished to encompass the whole universe of life-sounds into their music, and the Synthesists, as we may call them, who sought sounds specific to the new medium (hence detached, in the manner of abstract art, from the sound repertory of lived reality). The former, who came first chronologically, were the composers of *musique concrète*, a music that advertised itself, and sought its justification, on the basis of its relationship to the sound-world of "concrete" sensory reality.

The term was coined in 1948 by Pierre Schaeffer (1910–95), a sound engineer employed in Paris by the Radiodiffusion française, the French national broadcasting network. The idea went back directly to Filippo Marinetti's prewar *sintesi radiofonici*, and indeed, Schaeffer's first *concrète* compositions were made by montaging sounds preserved on phonograph discs, usually in "locked grooves" that created ostinatos the way tape loops would later do. One of the earliest such pieces, *Concert de bruits* ("Concert of noises"), broadcast over the French radio in 1948, harks back even in its title to the language of Futurism. Its movements included an *Étude aux chemins de fer* ("Railroad study") and an *Étude aux casseroles* ("Saucepan study"). A couple of Schaeffer's early studies, *Étude violette* and *Étude noire*, were based on the sounds of Pierre Boulez's piano playing.

Schaeffer was quick, however, to avail himself of the new possibilities of splicing and of speed and envelope alteration that the new medium of tape editing allowed. Together with Pierre Henry (b. 1927), another sound engineer at the radio studio who had had some formal training in composition, Schaeffer founded the Groupe de Recherche de Musique Concrète (1950), and began issuing fully formed compositions on tape: the first was called *Symphonie pour un homme seul* ("Symphony for one man alone"), and consisted entirely of manipulated body sounds, not limited to those produced by the speech organs. The masterpiece of the original musique concrète studio was Henry's *Orphée*, or "The Veil of Orpheus" (1953), a ritualistic drama, existing only as sounds on tape, that graphically enacts the death of Orpheus, torn limb from limb by the Bacchantes. The

FIG. 4-4   Pierre Schaeffer, pioneer of *musique concrète*.

voyeuristic (or should we call it auditeuristic) preoccupation with violence completes the parallel with Futurism. It provoked a violent counterdemonstration from the audience at Donaueschingen in 1953.

Once tape recorders were installed, many of the prominent postwar avant-gardists, including Messiaen, Boulez, and Stockhausen, paid visits to Schaeffer's studio at Paris Radio. But after a couple of desultory experiments they drifted off again. Only Xenakis stayed, working with musique concrète into the 1960s, and reveling like Henry in a poetry of violence that, in his case, served to sublimate his wartime experiences in works like *Diamorphoses* (1957), which incorporated the sounds of jet engines, earthquakes, and automobile crashes.

The Darmstadt "zero hour" impulse required a different high-tech outlet: that of *elektronische Musik*, which in its original German formulation did not have the general applicability of its English counterpart, "electronic music," but referred to music based exclusively on electronically synthesized sounds—the purer, the better. Synthetic sounds carried no stigma from the world of entertainment, whereas the often amusing or terrifying musique concrète was reminiscent of radio sound effects and the soundtracks of films or animated cartoons. For composers in the Germanic modernist orbit, who set enormous store by the romantic concepts of *ernste Musik* ("serious music," as against "entertainment") and of artistic autonomy, the neutrality of synthesized sound, its freedom from worldly associations, constituted its chief appeal. (They were obviously unaware of the associations that had accrued to the theremin, and later to the trautonium, in Hollywood.)

The German hub of operations for electronic music, as mentioned in chapter 1, was the studio at Radio Cologne that was set up in 1951 with the aid of the American occupying forces, under the direction of Herbert Eimert (1897–1972). Eimert, an early follower of Schoenberg and an authority on twelve-tone music, saw electronic music not as "the great opening up of music to all sounds" that Cage had predicted, but rather as a source of new "parameters" for serial manipulation (overtones, for example, governing timbre), extending the serial reach far beyond what was measurable or controllable on conventionally played instruments. "It is certain that no means of musical control could have been established over electronic material had it not been for the revolutionary thought of Anton Webern," Eimert asserted. "Talk of 'humanized' electronic sound may be left to unimaginative instrument makers,"[27] he added with characteristic intolerance. We know by now whom he had in mind.

The symptomatic early electronic compositions from Cologne were the two serial *Studien* (1953, 1954) by Stockhausen, constructed from the purest sound of all, that of "sine waves," single frequencies without any overtones, obtainable only under laboratory conditions in the studio, never in nature. They are produced by audio generators or oscillators, which can be programmed to emit sounds with prespecified, artificially simple overtone structures, all named from the way their waves look when analyzed by another studio instrument, called the oscilloscope, and displayed on its screen.

The overtoneless signal produces a waveform like a sine curve as plotted by trigonometry students on graph paper. A signal with artificially emphasized even partials produces a waveform with flat peaks, and is therefore called a square wave. One that emphasizes the odd partials looks like the cutting edge of a saw on the screen and is called the sawtooth wave. Another generator produces "white noise," the hissing sound of the full frequency spectrum in simultaneous display. White noise can be processed through a "band-pass filter" to produce sounds of indefinite pitch but identifiable register. Other sound-modifying devices include modulators and reverberators. The first suppresses the fundamentals of two sounds and replaces them with their sums and/or differences; the second enhances sounds by allowing them to echo in an acoustical chamber of variable size.

Stockhausen's *Elektronische Studie II* (1954) was the first electronic composition to be issued not only as a prerecorded tape but also as a published score (Fig. 4-5). The notation resembles conventional musical notation insofar as it is a pair of grids, a vertical grid to represent greater and lesser quantities and a horizontal grid to represent elapsing time. It has three levels. The one on top measures the frequency range of the sine-wave bands in hertz, or cycles-per-second (cps). The one in the middle is a simple centimeter scale to measure duration (at a rate of 76.2 centimeters of unscrolling tape per second). At bottom is a dynamic scale to measure increasing and decreasing sound volume in decibels. The relationship between diagonals and verticals represents the sound "envelope": a vertical line represents a sudden attack or cutoff. Diagonals, depending on their declivities, represent faster or slower crescendos and decrescendos. As already observed in chapter 1, the relationship between the score and the sound in an electronic composition is not the usual one, since there are no performers whose actions need to be prescribed. Conceivably, the score of Stockhausen's study could be used to duplicate the composition in the studio, as an architect's plan can be used to duplicate a building. But there is no practical need for such duplication in the case of electronic music, since a second tape recorder can instantly and automatically record, hence duplicate in playback, the sounds emitted by the original tape.

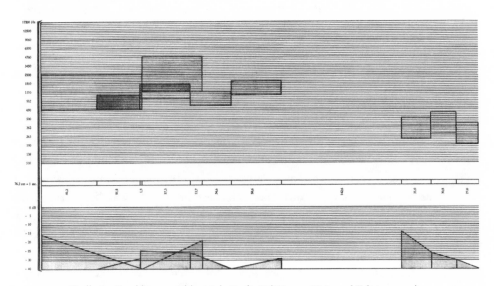

FIG. 4-5   Karlheinz Stockhausen, *Elektronische Studie II* (Vienna: Universal Edition, 1954).

There is even less practical justification for the "Hörpartitur" created ex post facto for *Artikulation*, Ligeti's Cologne exercise of 1958, described and displayed in chapter 60. Its status was rather that of a poster or an art print advertising the work of the studio (and, in cold-war terms, advertising the support "Western" governments were prepared to invest in avant-garde activities for their propaganda value). But that was not the only propaganda context into which the new musical medium was inserted from its very infancy. The rivalry between musique concrète and *elektronische Musik* quickly became the latest bout in the old contest between French *clarté* and *esprit* (clarity and wit) and German *Tiefgründigkeit* (profundity), and between the agreeable naturalness of French art and the labored artifice of German. An official statement issued by the Groupe de Recherche de Musique Concrète and reprinted on the first European commercial recording of tape music (*Panorama de "Musique Concrète,"* issued in 1957 under the auspices of UNESCO), started right off with the warning:

> One of the most common errors with regard to musique concrète is to confuse it with its very different rival, Electronic Music, which originated in Germany and which is entirely concerned with the *artificial*, electronic manufacture of sounds, built up from a basic sinus tone. In truth, so far from eschewing "sound realism" by relying on the electron, musique concrète makes use of real sounds, which are natural, rather than synthetic, in order to rework them with the aid of special instruments such as the tape recorder (*phonogène*) . . . . *Musique concrète* stems more from acoustics, therefore, than from electronics.[28]

This mini cold war was breached somewhat in 1956 with Stockhausen's *Gesang der Jünglinge* ("Song of the youths"), an electronic fantasy inspired by the parable from the biblical Book of Daniel about the survival of the Three Holy Children Shadrach, Meshach, and Abednego in Nebuchadnezzar's burning fiery furnace. The music places the sound of a boy's voice chanting the biblical text together with electronically synthesized signals, but the two layers are kept distinct. Even the recorded voice was manipulated according to serialist principles, as were the "trajectories" by which the sound was circulated among the five groups of playback loudspeakers that were set up for the first performances. (The version of *Gesang der Jünglinge* that was issued on a commercial stereo disc a few years later had to be mixed down to two channels, so that much of the serially structured "directionality" of the original was lost.) The second version of Stockhausen's *Kontakte* (1960) breached another divide: it adds a layer of live performed music (piano and percussion) to a previously completed "pure" electronic score of the same name (1959), thus bridging the gap between music performed in real time, in which notation carries out its usual task, and music definitively fixed on tape without mediation. The piece also marked a veer away from strict serialism toward the collage-like "moment form" that Stockhausen developed as a response to Cage's indeterminacy.

Later still, Stockhausen began applying his collage techniques to concrete sounds, often prerecorded music. His *Hymnen* (1967) is based on the sounds of national anthems from around the world, often set together in a kind of electronic counterpoint that Stockhausen called "intermodulation," whereby the sounds of two or more anthems would be mutually modified by the use of a ring modulator, the studio device that adds and subtracts the frequencies of sounds while suppressing their fundamentals. Stockhausen intended intermodulation as a metaphor for international cooperation, or, more generally, for "the universality of past, present and future, of distant places and spaces."[29] Like Scriabin a half century before him, the composer began to advertise (and perhaps conceive of) his music as a means for actually producing the social and historical changes that it symbolized. Like Cage, Stockhausen began at this point to assume the role of a spiritual guru.

THE NEW TECHNOLOGY SPREADS

Tape music came to America somewhat by accident. Vladimir Ussachevsky (1911–90), then an instructor in music at Columbia University, obtained a grant in 1951 to purchase a pair of Ampex tape recorders on behalf of the department for recording "Composers Forum" concerts on campus for library preservation. The tape recorders and microphones were stored between concerts at Ussachevsky's home or in his office, and he began amusing himself by recording and transforming the sounds of his own piano playing, eventually with the help of an engineer from the university radio station, who created a device for obtaining and controlling "feedback," a type of mechanical reverberation produced by feeding the output of a tape playback into the same tape recorder's recording head.

Ussachevsky presented some of these "experiments," frankly so called, at a Composers Forum of his own on 8 May 1952. Only one, "Underwater Valse" (a demonstration of feedback) was given the dignity of a title. A review by Henry Cowell, in his day also an enthusiastic experimenter with new sounds, welcomed the feedback device less as a technical breakthrough than for the poetic feelings that it evoked. That would be typical of American musique concrète, which generally preferred to work its surrealistic transformations on prerecorded musical sounds rather than on "natural" or environmental ones. Of the feedback, Cowell remarked that

> One would not expect such a series of mechanical repetitions to be related to human experience, yet to nearly everyone the effect seems to suggest some half-forgotten, elusive experience. Several people have testified independently that the sounds correspond to what is heard at one level of consciousness during the process of going under an anesthetic; others recall having heard such automatic sounds in dreams.[30]

Ussachevsky's extension and expansion of instrumental ranges and timbres was also acclaimed. "An A two octaves below the lowest A on the piano was produced by playing a recording of the lowest A at one-fourth speed," Cowell marveled. "The fundamental pitch was inaudible, but its powerful low overtones produced an otherwise unheard-of timbre." Whether experiments or compositions, these early efforts of Ussachevsky's were issued on a commercial recording (*Sounds of New Music*, Folkways, 1958) that gave them permanent status as the earliest "classics" of American electronic music.

One of Ussachevsky's Columbia colleagues, Otto Luening (1900–96), had been a disciple of Busoni's in Switzerland during and immediately after World War I, and was therefore predisposed to take a lively interest in Ussachevsky's tape experiments, seeing in them the promise of finally realizing Busoni's romantic vision of "free music." He invited Ussachevsky to present his experiments that summer at a composers' conference in Bennington, Vermont, and, a former professional flautist, began making experiments alongside him, so that the early sound repertoire of American musique concrète now included the manipulated sonorities of their two instruments, along with sounds of percussion and of conversational speech.

The results of their summer's work were unveiled at a widely publicized and reported concert of "tape music" held on 28 October 1952 at the Museum of Modern Art in New York. Leopold Stokowski, the superstar conductor who had led the premiere performance of Fuleihan's theremin concerto during the war, and of Varèse's *Amériques* before that, was on hand to lend some glamour to the occasion and to make some introductory remarks. They were remarkably to the point: "I am often asked: What is tape music, and how is it made? Tape music is music that is composed directly with sound instead of first being written on paper and later made to sound. Just as the painter paints his picture directly with colors, so the musician composes his music directly with tone."[31] In the audience that evening, entranced, was Luciano Berio, then living in the United States on a fellowship. On his return home, he made contact with Bruno Maderna, the somewhat older Italian avant-gardist who had already taught at Darmstadt and worked both at the Paris musique concrète studio and at the Cologne studio for *elektronische Musik*. Together they established the Studio di Fonologia Musicale at the state-supported radio station in Milan, for which Berio received funding by agreeing to furnish electronic soundtrack music for a series of films to be shown on Italian television.

The Milan studio, thanks to its exceptionally well endowed facilities, its attendant concert series and newsletter, and above all the government grant money it was authorized to dispense, became another magnet, alongside Darmstadt, for international talent. Its first creative emission, a joint composition by the two directors, was *Ritratto di città* ("Portrait of a city"), a collage of city sounds through the course of a working day, assembled in conscious tribute to the pioneering efforts of the *futuristi* for broadcast over the station that supported the studio.

Three of the early classics of the emerging repertoire of tape music were created at the Milan studio. The philosophy that reigned there was intentionally eclectic, in implied criticism of the respective purisms of Paris and Cologne, and the works produced covered the gamut of existing techniques. Berio's *Thema* (1958), subtitled "Omaggio a Joyce," is widely regarded as a masterpiece (perhaps *the* masterpiece) of musique concrète. Its sound source was a reading by the composer's wife, the American singer Cathy Berberian (1925–83), of the first page from the eleventh chapter ("Sirens") of James Joyce's epic novel *Ulysses* (1922):

> Bronze by gold heard the hoofirons, steelyringing.
> Imperthnthn thnthnthn.
> Chips, picking chips off rocky thumbnail, chips.
> Horrid! And gold flushed more.

5   A husky fifenote blew.
Blew. Blue bloom is on the.
Goldpinnacled hair.
A jumping rose on satiny breast of satin, rose of Castile.
Trillin, trilling: Idolores.
10   Peep! Who's in the . . . . peepofgold?
Tink cried to bronze in pity.
And a call, pure, long and throbbing. Longindying call.
Decoy. Soft word. But look: the bright stars fade.
Notes chirruping answer.
15   O rose! Castile. The morn is breaking.
Jingle jingle jaunted jingling.
Coin rang. Clock clacked.
Avowal. *Sonnez.* I could. Rebound of garter. Not leave thee.
Smack. *La cloche!* Thigh smack. Avowal. Warm.
20   Sweetheart, goodbye!
Jingle. Bloo.
Boomed crashing chords. When love absorbs. War! War!
The tympanum.
A sail! A veil awave upon the waves.
25   Lost. Throstle fluted. All is lost now.
Horn. Hawhorn.
When first he saw. Alas!
Full tup. Full throb.
Warbling. Ah, lure! Alluring.
30   Martha! Come!
Clapclap. Clipclap. Clappyclap.
Goodgod henev erheard inall.
Deaf bald Pat brought pad knife took up.
A moonlit nightcall: far, far.
35   I feel so sad. P. S. So lonely blooming.
Listen!
The spiked and winding cold seahorn. Have you the? Each, and for other,
plash and silent roar. Pearls: when she. Liszt's rhapsodies. Hissss.

This prose poem represents music overheard by several of the novel's characters as they walk the streets of Dublin. It is virtual verbal music, reverberating with sounds of hoof beats (*thnthnthn*), coins in pockets (*jingle jingle*), birds at dawn (*notes chirruping answer*), foghorns (*far, far*). It plays with homophones (*Blew. Blue bloom; Ah, lure! Alluring*) and alliterations (*Liszt's rhapsodies. Hissss*) like surrealist song poetry. It names instruments (fife, tympanum, flute, horn), and even alludes to (or parodies) the titles of once-famous songs and arias: "When the Bloom Is on the Rye" (l. 6); "Goodbye, Sweetheart, Goodbye" (l. 20); "Tutto è sciolto" (All Is Lost) from Bellini's opera *La sonnambula* (l. 25); "M'appari" (When First I Saw) from Flotow's opera *Martha* (l. 27); "'Tis the last rose of summer/Left blooming alone" (l. 35). There is even applause

(*Clipclap. Clappyclap*). The whole chapter is often compared with a musical composition replete with thematic development, "tonal" modulation, onomatopoeia, counterpoint, recapitulations and so on, though literary analysts differ as to what form—sonata? fugue?—is being mimicked.

Berio took Joyce's own procedures as his point of departure, "emphasizing and developing," as he put it, "the transition between a perceivable verbal message and musical utterance"[32] that is already present in the original. By filtering the sound of the read text, copying it, cutting and splicing it, altering its speed, reversing it, and setting it in counterpoint (and sometimes in homophony) with itself, the composer converts the words into trills, glissandos, portamentos, and staccatos, turning what was discontinuous in the original into continuous sounds (*Lisztsztszt'shisssssssss*) or breaking what was rhythmically continuous in the original into periodic fragments. Sometimes the process works the other way, proceeding by degrees from musical sound to intelligible speech, blurring even further than Joyce did the line dividing onomatopoeia from semantics. Either way, "I attempted to establish a new relationship between speech and music, in which a discontinuous metamorphosis of one into the other can be developed."[33] As Joel Chadabe, a composer and historian of electronic music, has commented, "Berio said it, but Joyce might have said it as well."[34]

By contrast, *Scambi* (1957), by the Belgian composer Henri Pousseur (b. 1929), eschewed concrete sounds in favor of synthetic ones. The title means "quick changes," or "exchanges," and is based throughout on filtered white noise. The composer compared the process of composing it to sonic sculpture: just as Michelangelo claimed that to make a statue all one had to know was what parts of the marble block to remove, all it took to make electronic music out of white noise was knowing which parts of the sonic spectrum to block when. Inspired by Cage's lectures on indeterminacy, Pousseur cast *Scambi* as an "open form": a set of specifications for filtering, volume settings, and reverberation that could be variously realized in the studio.

The version that was released commercially is the one the composer himself realized at the Milan studio, which (over his protests, so to speak) has become the "canonical" one. Berio, in collaboration with the composer, made another realization to show that it could be done, and so have various composers and studio technicians in Europe and the United States. But traditional notions of authorship have proven hardy. Despite commitment to the superficial freedom of "open form," moreover, *Scambi* represents an effort, characteristic of its time, to maintain traditional reliance on a prescriptive score in a medium that threatened the preeminence of writing and the social hierarchy that writing had always underwritten.

Communicating music from composer to performers (or, as here, to "realizers") through writing elevates the one to the status of commander and lowers the others to the status of slaves. Electronic music promised liberation from this social relation, by turning the composer into a direct and independent maker of an object comparable to those produced by a painter or a poet. Varèse had looked forward to the electronic medium as the composer's savior. "The composer," he complained in the manifesto of 1921, "is the only one of the creators of today who is denied direct contact with the public."[35] The tape medium promised to eliminate the middleman, the performer; but in that case there would be no one to give orders to. That may be one reason why composers of electronic music seem in retrospect to have been so slow to greet it (or even see it) as the harbinger of a postliterate age.

Another early tape composer who relied extensively on scores was Cage, who welcomed the electronic medium as the answer to all his prayers, but who in the 1950s employed it as just another way of filling his chance-predetermined "containers." These precompositional plans or composing scores, on which Cage had been basing his compositions even before discovering chance operations, went on controlling his compositional acts even after the advent of tape recording. Paradoxically, moreover, the use of taped sounds made the process of "indeterminate" composing more arduous than ever.

At Berio's invitation, Cage came to Milan in 1958 to make an electronic realization for *Fontana Mix* (a graphic sound container that he had already prepared and filled with live performance sounds), as an accompaniment to *Aria*, a collage of vocal sounds that he wrote for Cathy Berberian. The principle of tape composition in *Fontana Mix* was similar to the one Cage had previously employed in *Williams Mix* (1952), his first electronic composition. The idea of both pieces went directly back to the epigraph to this chapter, Cage's futuristic fantasy of a universal music that claimed "FOR MUSICAL PURPOSES ANY AND ALL SOUNDS THAT CAN BE HEARD."

Williams Mix was realized with the help of Cage's friends Louis and Bebe Barron, who had set up a little electronic music studio in their apartment where they produced soundtracks for science fiction films, eventually including some famous ones like *Forbidden Planet* (1956). Cage copied from them an encyclopedic library of about six hundred different recorded sounds. He cut them up into countless tape snippets, which he then stored by size in about 175 envelopes inside six big boxes labeled A through F, as follows:

A. City sounds
B. Country sounds
C. Electronic sounds
D. Manually produced sounds, including "normal" music
E. Wind-produced sounds, including voice
F. Small sounds requiring amplification to be heard.

Using the *I Ching* as described in chapter 2, Cage devised the score. Snippets from the six boxes would be spliced into eight tracks for simultaneous playback, each track a mosaic of snippets defined by coin-tossing according to source, duration, pitch, loudness, and manner of cutting. The first task was to compile a gigantic list of coin-determined specifications to guide the splicing of the master tape. As Earle Brown, who volunteered to act as Cage's technical assistant for the project, recalled:

> Anybody could toss the three coins and write down heads, heads, tails, do it again, tails, heads, heads, do it again, oh, three tails . . . . Anybody could do it, so when

anybody would come to visit, John would hand them three coins and tell them how to do it and everybody would be sitting around tossing coins. That was the composing part of it.[36]

The list of coin tosses was translated into a visual representation of each track of tape, drawn actual size. Then came the hard part. Putting the score under a plate of glass on a big table, Cage and Brown cut and spliced tape, laying the fragments end to end right over the score, as if following a dressmaker's pattern. They worked for five months straight, from ten in the morning until five in the afternoon.

> We'd go over and paw through the envelopes until we came to the right one, as called for by the chance process. We'd pick up the envelope, take the piece of tape over, lay the tape on top of the glass under which was the score, and cut and splice exactly as was called for. Then we applied the pieces of recording tape onto splicing tape and then, between pieces of recording tape, we rubbed talcum powder so the splicing tape wouldn't be sticky. After we did this, and we'd gotten a minute or so finished, we used to go over to a studio in New Jersey to make copies on a solid piece of tape. We didn't even have a tape machine. We couldn't hear anything. All we had were razor blades and talcum powder, no tape machine, it's true. If we'd needed to use one, we could have gone to the Barrons' studio. But John was doing it by chance. He didn't need to hear. You only need to hear when you're doing something by taste. It took so long, so bloody long, and it was boring to do all that cutting and splicing. John and I sat at opposite sides of the table and we talked about everything in the world.[37]

Indeed, electronic music in its infancy was probably the most labor-intensive musical medium in all of history. The attraction of the Milan Studio for Cage, when he received the invitation from Berio to produce another "mix," was the presence there of a random number generator to take the place of the coin tossing. The cutting and splicing, however, remained. *Fontana Mix*, which draws on an assortment of sounds provided by the studio and by Radio Italiana, is much shorter than *Williams Mix*. Even so, it took four months to realize. Reacting out of hurt to the usual (but now especially unjust) allegation that writing "chance music" was easy, Cage began making preemptive jokes. He told one reporter, for example, that to write *Fontana Mix* he merely brought a broom into the Milan studio, swept the floor, and spliced together the leavings from everybody else's compositions.

In retrospect, of course, the hard and boring work lent a heroic aspect to the legend of the tape-music pioneers and became a point of pride. Looking back on his "Omaggio a Joyce" in a 1982 interview, Berio made the most of it:

> In order to create certain effects, some sounds had to be copied sixty, seventy, and eighty times, and then spliced together. Then these tapes had to be copied further at different speeds in order to achieve new sound qualities more or less related to Cathy's original delivery of the text.... I didn't surrender to the difficulties. It's surprising now to think that I spent several months of my life cutting tape while today I could achieve many of the same results in much less time by using a computer.[38]

THE BIG SCIENCE PHASE

Additional labor-saving steps were taken in New York, where Luening and Ussachevsky were receiving media exposure, followed by more prestigious performances and, finally, material grants. In December 1952 the pair were invited to appear on the "Today" show, then hosted by the announcer and commentator Dave Garroway. In April 1953, their pieces (including *Incantation*, their first joint composition) were included in a festival of musique concrète presented by Radiodiffusion française in Paris. Next, they received a commission from the Louisville Orchestra, funded by the Rockefeller Foundation, for a concerted piece for tape recorder and orchestra. The result, *Rhapsodic Variations*, was first performed in Louisville on 20 March 1954 and recorded the next year.

Their method of collaboration was simple: they planned the piece together, agreed on which parts each would compose, then went home and did their assignments. In all, Luening and Ussachevsky wrote three compositions that pitted electronic music against the symphony orchestra. *A Poem in Cycles and Bells* (1954) was commissioned and performed by the Los Angeles Philharmonic Orchestra. The New York Philharmonic commissioned *Concerted Piece for Tape Recorder and Orchestra* (1960) for nationwide broadcast on one of Leonard Bernstein's very successful outreach programs for children.

"Lunachevsky" began receiving commissions for theatrical music as well, and this gave the "pure" medium of tape music its widest early exposure. Together they provided incidental "scores" for Orson Welles's 1956 production of *King Lear* at New York's City Center and the 1958 Theater Guild production of Shaw's *Back to Methuselah*. Ussachevsky alone supplied a short electronic sequence to supplement the soundtrack music for Alfred Hitchcock's movie *To Catch a Thief* (1955). Another work of his, *Linear Contrasts* (1958), which included electronically synthesized sounds in addition to transformations of prerecorded musical instruments, was given its premiere at the Baden-Baden Festival in Germany.

Quite unexpectedly, two very conventionally trained musicians had become New York's dynamic duo of the avant-garde, and the very conservative music department where they taught—until then a bastion of neoclassical Americana under the stewardship of the opera specialist Douglas Moore (1893–1969), a pupil and disciple of the ultra-respectable Horatio Parker—found itself on the cutting edge of new music technology. Luening and Ussachevsky began attracting grant money to their institution, which purchased for them more equipment (like the oscillators Ussachevsky began using for the *King Lear* music and the *Piece for Tape Recorder* that derived from it) and in 1955 endowed an on-campus electronic music studio, America's first institutional home for the medium.

The studio moved from a two-story guardhouse that had formerly belonged to an insane asylum to a room behind the campus theater where the Composers Forum concerts were held, to large quarters in a building otherwise devoted to engineering offices. These quarters were made necessary by the purchase, thanks to a $175,000 Rockefeller Foundation grant in 1959, of the RCA Mark II music synthesizer, a gigantic machine that occupied an entire wall. It had about 750 vacuum tubes and a mechanism that activated a multitude of binary switches by scanning punched cards. It could

FIG. 4-6 Otto Luening and Vladimir Ussachevsky in the small teaching studio behind McMillan (now Miller) Theater at Columbia University, ca. 1960.

produce tones of minutely specifiable pitch, duration, and timbre, thus bringing these "parameters" under unprecedentedly minute control. Nevertheless, the romance of difficulty still attached to the process, even though the whole cutting-and-splicing phase was eliminated. Milton Babbitt's reminiscences, speaking from the vantage point of the 1990s (that is, the age of personal computers), recall the many inherent problems and ad hoc solutions with relish:

> The machine was extremely difficult to operate. First of all, it had a paper drive, and getting the paper through the machine and punching the holes was difficult. We were punching in binary. The machine was totally zero, nothing predetermined, and any number we punched could refer to any dimension of the machine. There was an immense number of analog oscillators but the analog sound equipment was constantly causing problems. I couldn't think of anything that you couldn't get, but other composers gave up — it was a matter of patience. Max Mathews [a Bell Laboratories engineer who was then experimenting with the electronic synthesis of speech] once said to me, "You must have the mechanical aptitude of Edison to work with that synthesizer," and I said, "No, I've got the patience of Job." I became irritated with the mechanics of the machine very often. I had to troubleshoot all the time and I was completely dependent upon Peter Mauzey [the lab's technical engineer]. But I learned a lot of tricks, how to cut down on programming time with presets and so on. There were many people who would look at this machine and say, "It's a computer." But it never computed anything. It was basically just a complex switching device to an enormous and complicated analog studio hooked into a tape machine. And yet for me it was so wonderful because I could specify something and hear it instantly.[39]

The nature of the machine changed the nature of the music the lab produced. Under the terms of the grant, negotiated primarily by Ussachevsky on behalf of Columbia University and Babbitt on behalf of Princeton, the new electronic music studio was to be jointly administered by both music departments and called the Columbia-Princeton Electronic Music Center. It became the model for the electronic music studios that soon mushroomed on virtually every American campus where musical composition was taught, especially those that in the 1960s began instituting doctoral programs on the Princeton model described in chapter 3.

In the process, American electronic music was to a significant degree Princetonized. It increasingly took on the characteristics, and served the purposes, described in Milton Babbitt's influential article from the inaugural issue of *Perspectives of New Music* (see chapter 3) in which "time-point" technique was first set forth, and in which the electronic medium was specified as the sole vehicle for achieving the accuracy in time discriminations at unlimited tempos that the system demanded.

But nothing in those days went unaccompanied by polemics. Even before presenting the new technique as such, Babbitt came out swinging at the musique concrète crowd:

> To proceed from an assertion of what music has been to an assertion of what music, therefore, must be, is to commit a familiar fallacy; to proceed from an assertion of the properties of the electronic medium to an assertion of what music produced by this medium therefore must be, is not only to commit the same fallacy (and thus do fallacies make strange bedfellows), but to misconstrue that compositional revolution of which the electronic medium has been the enabling instrument.[40]

That revolution, Babbitt implied, had nothing to do with the much-vaunted expansion of sonic resources or liberation from traditional scales or organizing systems. It had, rather, to do with limits on the application of those organizing systems, both theoretical and actual. "For this revolution," Babbitt asserted,

> has effected, summarily and almost completely, a transfer of the limits of musical composition from the limits of the nonelectronic medium and the human performer, not to the limits of this most extensive and flexible of media but to those more restrictive, more intricate, far less well understood limits: the perceptual and conceptual capacities of the human auditor. Therefore, although every musical composition justifiably may be regarded as an experiment, the embodiment of hypotheses as to certain specific conditions of music coherence, any electronically realized composition which employs resources singularly obtainable by electronic means, in addition, will incorporate certain premises that are either severely circumscribed by the limited confirmed knowledge of the nature of those capacities or by isolated facts of musical perception, themselves obtained mainly with the assistance of electronic media, for incorporation into the premises of the particular work.[41]

As Babbitt less formally expressed it, "the hand is never faster than the ear"[42] (that is, we can always hear more than we can manage physically to perform), but the synthesizer certainly is faster. It can easily be programmed to do what cannot be "heard" — that is, meaningfully parsed — by "the human auditory apparatus." How to keep things within limits? Only by building on the most advanced systems of the past, because "the hypotheses they exemplify already have been widely tested and confirmed," and give some assurance of structural validity. Electronic compositions, this means, cannot be judged otherwise than according to "traditional" musical criteria. And even though Babbitt takes the precaution of always putting the word "traditional" in ironic quotes, he intends no irony at all. So much for all the unprecedented, unlimited sound resources of the new medium! They are written off in advance as musically meaningless:

> At the extreme of "nontraditionalism" is the selection of an uninterpreted formal system, no interpreted instances of which have been musically validated, along with coordinative rules which, likewise, have not been validated independently. In such a case, the probability that such an unrestricted choice from such a large number of possibilities at both stages will yield a significant result is extremely small, or the result itself is likely to be virtually trivial, that is, hardly to admit nonverification.[43]

What is to be sought, then, is not novel sounds or liberation from existing systems but only greater precision in the application of those very systems, allowing their further expansion and elaboration along previously marked-out paths of technical advancement. The electronic medium, in this view, was not the revolutionary transformation that Busoni and Cage had foreseen, and that Varèse awaited, but only a refinement of means toward an academically sanctioned end, that end being Ph.D.-style serialism. Babbitt, it seemed to some, was the "mortician" whose arrival Varèse had glumly anticipated.

For while obviously the most conservative and restrictive view of the new medium, Babbitt's was also the best-funded one, and had the most institutional prestige. That gave it influence. Its "classic" exemplifications were the four compositions that Babbitt himself created on the Mark II synthesizer during the Columbia-Princeton Center's early years. Two of them—*Composition for Synthesizer* (1961) and *Ensembles* (1964)—were composed for tape alone; the other two—*Vision and Prayer* (1961, text by Dylan Thomas) and *Philomel* (1964, text by John Hollander)—combined synthesized sounds with soprano voice, namely that of Bethany Beardslee (b. 1927), an intensely energetic singer gifted with phenomenal accuracy of pitch and rhythm, who had become a fixture of the New York new music scene, and who was married at the time to Babbitt's pupil Godfrey Winham.

At the beginning of *Composition for Synthesizer*, his maiden venture in the electronic medium, Babbitt seemed especially determined to announce that (as he put it in a program note) "the composition is less concerned with 'new sounds and timbres' than with the control and specification of linear and total rhythms, loudness rhythms and relationships, and flexibility of pitch succession."[44] The actual sounds seem to have been contrived with conventional instrumental timbres in mind—piano, pizzicato strings, woodwinds (clarinet or saxophone, bassoon or contrabassoon), unpitched percussion (actually closely spaced aggregates) as punctuation—so as to attract a minimum of attention to what for many composers was the primary attraction, and the primary selling point, of the medium.

Only near the end of the composition does Babbitt exercise his timbral imagination, recapitulating some familiar rhythms and contours with filtered white noise in place of exactly specified pitches. The confidently relaxed and humorous effect would have been difficult, perhaps impossible, to obtain in a real-time performance that taxed the players' concentration the way the compositions of Babbitt described in chapter 62 tended to do. That in itself is a strong argument for the electronic medium, not only as an aid to the composition of highly determined compositions like Babbitt's, but also as an aid to their enjoyment by listeners.

In *Philomel*, the medium is put to effective dramatic use. The title refers to one of the myths embodied in the *Metamorphoses* of Ovid, the classical Latin poet. Philomela is the daughter of the Greek king Pandion and the sister of Procne, wife of the Thracian king Tereus. She is raped by her brother-in-law, who cuts out her tongue so that she can not accuse him. Philomela embroiders her story into a tapestry that she sends Procne, who, enraged, kills her son and serves his flesh to her husband as a meal. Tereus pursues the sisters intending to kill them, but the gods turn them all into birds: Procne becomes a nightingale, Tereus a hoopoe (the bird that fouls its own nest), and the silenced Philomela becomes the songless swallow. Ovid improved on the myth, adding both irony and poetic justice, by making Philomela the nightingale and Procne the swallow, so that the silenced woman becomes the sweetest singer in all the forest.

Hollander's poem is an interior monologue that portrays Philomela's emotional metamorphosis from the agony of rape and pursuit to exultation at her miraculously granted vocal powers. Babbitt pits the live voice against an accompaniment that includes the same singer's taped voice as well as synthesized sound. The beginning (Ex. 4-1) shows Philomel in her silenced state, screaming inarticulately (and inwardly), her voice represented by the taped soprano, sustaining and obsessively returning to the note E, which (as one might easily guess) is the zero pitch of the tone row on which the music is constructed. While it is held, six aggregates are formed around it in whirlwind succession in a process that one analyst has likened to a twelve-voiced canon.[45]

The first aggregate reflects the notes of the twelve-tone row as given across the top of Ex. 4-2, their order transformed into vertical spacing (reading "down"). The whole chord thus arrived at is transposed up a semitone in m. 2 to form the second aggregate, and transposed again, down two semitones, in m. 3. These intervals of transposition invert the intervals of the row itself, and the process continues throughout the excerpt shown, although beginning with the fourth aggregate the row is presented partly verticalized as before and partly as an ordered succession, the more usual way.

The odd rhythmic compressions (four or six even notes in the time of five sixteenths in m. 3, followed by seven in the time of eight sixteenths, four in the time of three, eight in the time of thirteen, eleven in the time of seven) are artifacts of the time-point system described in chapter 3, as the use of the $\frac{3}{4}$ time signature might already suggest. Rhythms like these are obviously more easily programmed on a synthesizer than realized by human beings, whose "auditory apparatus" might have trouble distinguishing one-eleventh of a double-dotted quarter note from one-seventh of a half-tied-to-an-eighth. Using the machine grants the composer freedom from such human limitations; in terms of the "dehumanization of art" that modernists have always longed for, that freedom was indeed a breakthrough.

EX. 4-1 Milton Babbitt, *Philomel*, opening

EX. 4-2   Magic square (prime-inversion matrix) for Milton Babbitt, *Philomel*

	I_0	I_{11}	I_1	I_9	I_4	I_6	I_3	I_2	I_7	I_8	I_5	I_{10}	
P_0	*E*	E♭	F	D♭	A♭	B♭	G	G♭	B	C	A	D	(←R)
P_1	*F*	*E*	G♭	D	A	B	A♭	G	C	D♭	B♭	E♭	
P_{11}	*E♭*	*D*	*E*	C	G	A	G♭	F	B♭	B	A♭	D♭	
P_3	*G*	*G♭*	*A♭*	*E*	B	D♭	B♭	A	D	E♭	C	F	
P_8	*C*	*B*	*D♭*	*A*	*E*	G♭	E♭	D	G	A♭	F	B♭	
P_6	*B♭*	A	B	G	D	E	D♭	C	F	G♭	E♭	A♭	
P_9	D♭	C	D	B♭	F	G	E	E♭	A♭	A	G♭	B	
P_{10}	D	D♭	E♭	B	G♭	A♭	F	E	A	B♭	G	C	
P_5	A	A♭	B♭	G♭	D♭	E♭	C	B	E	F	D	G	
P_4	A♭	G	A	F	C	D	B	B♭	E♭	E	D♭	G♭	
P_7	B	B♭	C	A♭	E♭	F	D	D♭	G♭	G	E	A	
P_2	G♭	F	G	E♭	B♭	C	A	A♭	D♭	D	B	E	
												↑ (IR)	

What sets *Philomel* apart from most of Babbitt's music is its representational dimension, which provides a metaphorical context for interpreting serial procedures that are more often presented as wholly abstract. The poem's dramatic plot, which ends on a note of emotional resolve, gives added resonance to Babbitt's usual habit of ending a composition with the simplest statement of his row material. The last stanzas of the poem describe the transmutation of Philomela's anguish into the nightingale's joyful song:

> Pain in the breast and mind, fused into music! Change
> Bruising hurt silence even further! Now, in this glade,
> Suffering is redeemed in song. Feeling takes wing:
> High, high above, beyond the forests of horror I sing!
>
> I sing in change
> Now my song will range
> Till the morning dew
> Dampens its face:
> Now my song will range
> As once it flew
> Thrashing, through
> The woods of Thrace.

The last quatrain (Ex. 4-3) is finally sung—this once only, and to poignant effect—to the pitches of the aggregate in the basic order, P_0, set forth across the top of the magic square in Ex. 4-2.

EX. 4-3   Milton Babbitt, *Philomel*, end (voice only)

Now my song will range as once it flew thrash - ing through

the woods of Thra - - - - ce.

A HAPPY ENDING

Nevertheless, Babbitt's remarks about taking the limits of the "auditory apparatus" as the limits of compositional technique have to be balanced, as always, against the inevitable slippage between what can be conceptualized in the act of composition (or analysis) and what can be parsed by the mind's ear in the act of listening. For those who consider that to be a problem, the electronic medium offers no solution. Among those who did so consider it was Varèse. Babbitt has recalled Varèse's excitement when he came up to the Columbia-Princeton Electronic Music Center and was given a demonstration of the Mark II synthesizer's capabilities. But Varèse has recorded his dismay at the paltry use to which the machine was being put, as he saw it, by the *pompiers des douze sons*[46] ("bureaucrats of the twelve tones"), as he put it (in a whisper) to Stravinsky, and what he took to be the musically insignificant outcome of all the arduous precompositional planning that went into such administration.

More diplomatically, for publication, Varèse put it this way:

> I am not impressed by most of today's electronic music. It does not seem to make full use of the unique possibilities of the medium, especially in regard to those questions of space and projection that have always concerned me. I am fascinated by the fact that through electronic means one can generate a sound instantaneously. On an instrument played by a human being you have to impose a musical thought through notation, then, usually much later, the player has to prepare himself in various ways to produce what will — one hopes — emerge as that sound. This is all so indirect compared with electronics, where you generate something "live" that can appear or disappear instantly and unpredictably. Consequently, you aren't programming something musical, something to be done, but using it directly, which gives an entirely different dimension to musical space and projection . . . . To me, working with electronic music is composing with living sounds, paradoxical though that may appear. [. . .] I respect the twelve-tone discipline, and those who feel they need such discipline. But it seems much more fruitful to use the total sonic resources available to us . . . . I respect and admire Milton Babbitt, but he certainly represents a completely different view of electronic music from mine. It seems to me that he wants to exercise maximum control over certain materials, as if he were above them. But I want to be *in* the material, part of the acoustical vibration, so to speak. Babbitt composes his material first and then gives it to the synthesizer, while I want to generate something directly by electronic means . . . . I do not want an *a priori* control of all its aspects.[47]

By the time he made these comments (1964), Varèse had managed, despite his advanced years (and his inability to work the electronic equipment without technical assistance), to produce three electronic compositions of his own, which he regarded as the crowning works of his career.

Having received the gift of an Ampex tape recorder, arranged by a painter friend in 1953, Varèse took the machine exactly where a Futurist might have been expected to take it, to iron foundries, sawmills, and other factories in and around Philadelphia. These sounds, augmented by recordings of gongs and other percussion instruments that he kept at home, provided the raw material for three tropes or interpolations of "organized sound" that impinged upon and commented on the music played by a typical Varèsian ensemble of four woodwind players on nine instruments, ten brass (including both bass and contrabass tubas), a piano, and five percussionists manning forty-eight instruments, in *Déserts*, his last big piece. He began writing it in 1949, adopting for the purpose some of the many sketches for *Espace*. When completed in 1954, it was Varèse's first finished ensemble score in more than twenty years.

Could the title have been a nod in response to Henry Miller's lonely encomium that punctuated, and perhaps consoled, Varèse's barren decade? That would be plausible, but Varèse offered an alternative reading of it that resonated with the existentialist mood of the early 1950s. In a program note solicited by Robert Craft to accompany the first recording of the work, Varèse wrote that, for him, the word "deserts" suggests not only "all physical deserts (of sand, sea, snow, of outer space, of empty city streets) but also the deserts in the mind of man; not only those stripped aspects of nature that suggest bareness, aloofness, timelessness, but also that remote *inner* space no telescope can reach, where man is alone, a world of mystery and essential loneliness."[48]

Work proceeded on separate but parallel tracks. First the instrumental parts were composed (and there is a note in the score to the effect that they can be played without interruption in the absence of the taped insertions), but always with the prerecorded sounds in mind. The actual shaping into "organized sound" of the raw sonic material Varèse had recorded and stored came afterward. In January 1954 Pierre Schaeffer invited Varèse to his studio for musique concrète at the Radiodiffusion française in Paris to finish the job. Arriving in October, he recorded some supplementary sounds on oscillators, rapidly twisting the dials to get the radical curves he had always loved, but now extending over a previously unimaginable (or if imaginable, then surely unachievable) frequency range.

Déserts received its first performance in December at the Théâtre des Champs-Elysées (the site, four decades earlier, of the stormy premiere of *The Rite of Spring*). It was conducted by Hermann Scherchen (1891–1966), a new-music specialist of long standing, who like Varèse had been in his youth a disciple of Busoni. Old-fashioned modernists greeted futurism's return with typically sadomasochistic delight. "The work roughs us up, in fact, annihilates us," wrote one. "We have no power over it; it is the work that takes possession of us, crushes us with blows of its terrible fist."[49] The performance was introduced by Pierre Boulez, who paraphrased for the audience a lecture Varèse had given in 1936, in which he had compared his music to opposing planes and volumes in a perpetual dynamic of mutual attraction and repulsion. The advent of electronics, Varèse announced through Boulez, had liberated his music from analogy. Whereas the composer had always striven indirectly to represent movement in space by the use of percussive rhythm, dynamics, and pitch contours, he could now do so directly thanks to the stereophonic deployment of organized sound through speakers.

The instrumental sections of *Déserts* are remarkably like Varèse's ensemble works of the 1920s; it is as if there had never been any break in his creative output, let alone one that had lasted decades. As in his earlier compositions, the instrumental music's shape is determined by the opposition of pitched material, built up into huge, static, often symmetrical "immovable objects" (as in Ex. 4-4) and the "irresistible force" of unpitched percussion. The freely sliding pitch in the taped interpolations exposes the extent to which (just as Busoni had insisted a half century before) the monolithic system of *douze sons* is a prison, and the long, slowly changing sounds that electronics easily produces makes a similar point about time-honored conceptions of rhythm as pulse. It is only in the taped sections that the immovable objects and the irresistible forces can be reconciled and achieve integration. Perhaps that is why audiences found the work—and especially the interpolations of "organized sound"—so moving, and, at a time when the electronic medium was giving renewed impetus to the dehumanization of art, so human.

In 1960–61, at Vladimir Ussachevsky's invitation, Varèse revised the first and third taped interpolations (the latter now including the prerecorded sound of an organ) at

EX. 4-4   Opening up of symmetrical pitch space in Edgard Varèse's *Déserts*

the Columbia-Princeton Electronic Music Center with the assistance of the Turkish composer Bülent Arel (1919–90), who was working there on a Rockefeller grant. By then Varèse had completed a work for tape alone, *Poème électronique*, commissioned by the Philips company to be "delivered," as the architect Marc Treib put it, "from multiple points in space"[50] over an installation of more than four hundred speakers in its famous Le Corbusier–Xenakis pavilion at the Brussels World's Fair in 1958. The effect of these "four hundred acoustical mouths completely surrounding the five hundred visitors"[51] (in Le Corbusier's happy words) was by all accounts a technological marvel, overwhelming even those it offended.

The music was routed through "sound paths" determined by a mixing console that had the capacity to deploy as many as 180 audio and visual signals through telephone relays to the loudspeakers, film projectors, and multicolored light installations. Heard (and seen) by nearly two million visitors over the six-month course of the Fair, and issued more than once thereafter on commercial recordings, Varèse's eight-minute *Poème* is probably still the most widely disseminated all-electronic composition in the short history of the medium. The charge from Philips was to create "effects of sound in space, therefore of movement, of direction, of reverberation and echoes, which until now have never been used in electronic installations." The company was of course primarily interested in showing off its reproductive equipment and was at first dubious about entrusting the task to a composer of the avant-garde; Le Corbusier had to insist with threats. But the idea perfectly suited Varèse's long-standing musical ideas, as did the neoprimitivist visual display that Le Corbusier devised to accompany the organized sound.

FIG. 4-7A Varèse's *Poème électronique* in its original performance space in the Philips pavilion at the Brussels World's Fair, 1958.

Varèse came to the Philips laboratories in Eindhoven, the Netherlands, in the fall of 1957. He brought over some sound materials unused in *Déserts*, and relied further both on the company's own library of recorded sounds (including its extensive commercial line of classical recordings) and on its sound-synthesizing apparatus. The deliberate result was a (for the time) uniquely eclectic conglomeration of ingredients: "Studio recordings were used, machine noises, transposed piano chords and bells, filtered recordings of choruses and soloists," as the composer enumerated them in retrospect. In addition, "oscillators were used to record sinusoidal sounds [i.e., "sine waves"], and literally unheard of sounds were made by mixing and combining all these." In 1959, looking back on the work, which had confused and antagonized the corporate

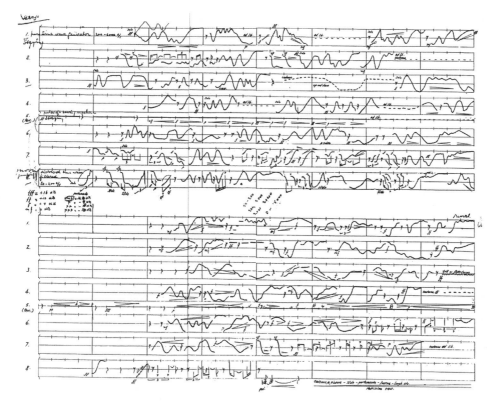

FIG. 4-7B   Varèse's sketch for *Poème électronique*.

executives who had commissioned it, Varèse saw the *Poème électronique* as the high point of his career, the single consummate realization of his musical aims. "For the first time I heard my music literally projected into space,"[52] he recalled. It was to be the last as well. Unfortunately, that spatial projection is the one aspect of the work that, since the scrapping of the pavilion at the end of the Fair, can no longer be experienced except as it finds pale reflection in the two channels of domestic stereo reproduction.

Poème électronique follows a trajectory analogous to that of *Ionisation*, from lesser to greater determinacy. In the earlier piece that trajectory was realized in the transition from nonpitched to pitched percussion sound. In *Poème électronique*, once past the initial bell sounds (a Dutch and Belgian specialty, perhaps a tribute to the locale in which the piece was created and performed), the transition is from abstract "studio" sounds to sounds associated with human agency, whether produced by voice (in solo and in chorus), by hands holding drumsticks, or by fingers at the keyboard. The first vocal apparition — a female voice moaning "Oo-gah!" — is a near quote from the Mayan text of *Ecuatorial*, Varèse's earlier neoprimitivist masterpiece, and brings his career full circle. It accompanied the projected images of African tribal costumes and coiffures, drawn by Le Corbusier from his pictorial anthology *L'art décoratif d'aujourd'hui* ("The decorative art of today," 1925). The up-to-the-minute technology notwithstanding, this was a very old-fashioned modernism for the date. Its "futurism," in an age of actual space-exploration, was retrospective, even nostalgic (Fig. 4-7).

BIG QUESTIONS REOPENED

As will become increasingly clear as this book nears its end and the narrative approaches the present, the truly revolutionary aspect of electronic music was the new relationship it made possible between composers and works. The composer of an electronic composition can produce a "score" exactly the way a painter produces a picture or a sculptor produces a statue: what is produced is a unique original "art object" rather than a set of directions for performance. And therefore, obviously, "score" is the wrong word for it, since a score is something written, and electronic music can dispense with writing. It created the possibility of a postliterate musical culture. It spelled, potentially, the beginning of the end of the culture of which this book is a history.

But then, the literate tradition of music has never entirely supplanted the preliterate tradition, and there is no reason to expect that the postliterate will ever entirely supplant the literate. There will always be a social use for live musical performances of many kinds, and some of these will go on being literate, at least as long as anyone can foresee. The end of the literate tradition will require the end of all its social uses, and of all social relations based on literacy. Such a society is beyond present imagining.

The social question is fundamental, as the history of electronic music itself has demonstrated. One of the medium's prime attractions, for some composers, was its promise of "asociality," the unexpectedly literal realization, in all its logical consequences, of the utopian individualism that was modernism's chief inheritance from romanticism. To put Milton Babbitt's celebration of the absolute control he could now exercise over the electronic medium side by side with his earlier call (in "Who Cares If You Listen?" quoted in chapter 3) for "total, resolute, and voluntary withdrawal from [the] public world" so as to secure "complete elimination of the public and social aspects of musical composition" is to see how fundamentally social the issues involving this (or any) kind of music inevitably remain, no matter how tall the ivory tower, or thick its walls.

That is one paradox. Recalling the point made at the end of chapter 3, that American academic serialism was the most perfectly and exclusively literate of all musical repertories, will uncover an even more fundamental one. The means that Babbitt chose for protecting his purely literate domain from social mediation — namely, the electronic elimination of the performing "middle man" — was precisely the means through which the need for literacy might be transcended. You could not ask for a better illustration of the law of unintended consequences, or of "dialectics," the tendency of extreme positions to engender their opposites or negations.

As Varèse already noted, Babbitt had no intention of giving up scores, since the score was the only place where the integrity of his compositions could be demonstrated. And yet not even Babbitt could bring himself to give up public performance of his compositions, even the electronic ones. Not even he could face the complete elimination of the social aspect of music making when, thanks to electronics, that became a practical possibility, even though he had called for precisely that when it was just a utopian dream. The best evidence of his step back from the brink is the existence of *Vision and Prayer* and *Philomel*, compositions that combined the electronic medium with a live performer, indeed a spectacular virtuoso, a diva.

From the very beginning, in fact, the contradiction between the potentially asocial electronic medium and the eminently social convention of the public concert was perceived as a problem to be solved. Audiences, assembled in a darkened hall, all facing an empty stage, felt imprisoned. Putting a pair of speakers on the stage provided a focus for the audience's gaze, but made them feel silly. And then there was the problem of knowing when to applaud. It could be solved by raising the house lights (analogous to raising the piano lid at the end of Cage's 4′33″), and Luciano Berio experimented (at least once, in a concert the author attended) by having an actor slowly rise from a chair and take off his jacket over the duration of the performance. (The experiment does not seem to have been repeated; the fact that the author cannot recall what piece it accompanied may suggest the reason.) At other concerts, the audience was invited to walk around as if contemplating sculpture. But despite everything, the discomfort audiences felt was acute — and understandable, as long as no real-time musical performance was taking place. You might as well ask them to come to a concert to listen to the same records they could listen to at home, albeit on superior equipment.

From the beginning, then, there was pressure to integrate electronic music into conventional performance media. We have seen some responses to this pressure even earlier than Babbitt's vocal works, in Varèse's *Déserts* and the concerted pieces for tape and orchestra by Luening and Ussachevsky, in which taped sections alternated with instrumentally performed ones. Yet an earlier example was *Musica su due dimensioni* ("Music in two dimensions"), by Bruno Maderna, composed at the Cologne Radio studio in 1952. This solution, while effective enough in a given instance (and, in the case of *Déserts*, conceptually meaningful), was obviously a makeshift. Alternation of media, even if as skillfully dovetailed as Varèse managed in *Déserts* (the unpitched percussion providing a bridge between the media) was not the same as integration; and the longer it was tolerated, the longer it seemed that a true solution was only being postponed.

The first composer to make a specialty of integrating electronic music into live performances was Mario Davidovsky (b. 1934), an Argentine composer who settled permanently in the United States in 1960, originally as a protégé of Babbitt, with whom he had studied at Tanglewood. At Babbitt's invitation, Davidovsky began working (on a Guggenheim fellowship) at the newly founded Columbia-Princeton Electronic Music Center. After an initial effort — *Contrastes* for string orchestra and electronic sound (1960) — in a slightly overlapping alternation mode, he began the series of *Synchronisms* on which his reputation is chiefly based.

As the title suggests, these pieces are counterpoints of electronic sounds and virtuoso performances on a wide variety of instruments or (in one case, no. 4, composed in 1967 on the text of the thirteenth Psalm) voices. The challenge, for composer and performer alike, is to match the virtually unlimited electronic sound spectrum by exploiting the extended playing techniques that new-music performers were then pioneering. The conception proved extremely fruitful; as of 1997 Davidovsky's Synchronisms numbered eleven in all.

One thing that helped make the series so successful was Davidovsky's refreshingly practical and flexible approach to the technical challenges he had accepted, despite what might otherwise seem the purism of his approach to the medium (admitting only synthesized sounds, never *concrète*). The interaction of the taped and live components is not always precisely calculated. As Stravinsky discovered as early as the 1920s, when he attempted a scoring of his ballet *Svadebka* (or *Les Noces*) accompanied by player pianos, it is virtually impossible to synchronize live music with the absolutely fixed speed of mechanical reproductions; human beings, no matter what their intentions or professed attitudes, have great difficulty "feeling" music that way.

Accordingly, Davidovsky attempted exact coordination only in short passages of intricate counterpoint; elsewhere, in more extended passages in which one component clearly accompanied the other, "an element of chance is introduced," he has written, "to allow for the inevitable time discrepancies that develop between live performers and the constant-speed tape recorder."[53] What Davidovsky, no doubt a bit jestingly, called chance was actually just a bit of leeway in the synchronization of parts. Another potential pitfall was the discrepancy between the equal-tempered tuning of the instruments and the unlimited continuous pitch spectrum available to the composer of electronic music, which Davidovsky did not wish to give up. He resorted to subterfuge. "Use is made," as he put it,

> of tonal occurrences of very high density—manifested for example by a very high-speed succession of attacks, possible only in the electronic medium. Thus, in such instances—based on high speed and short duration of separate tones, it is impossible for the ear to perceive the pure pitch value of each separate event; though in reacting, it does trace, so to speak, a statistical curve of the density.[54]

In other words, to recall Babbitt's investigations at the synthesizer, the machine is quicker than the ear. A big barrage of tiny, machine-produced pitched sounds can defeat the best-trained ear's powers of discrimination and counter the sense that the tape is out of tune with the instruments. Davidovsky's machine, however, was not the synthesizer. "Classically" trained in the techniques of the early electronic studio, Davidovsky cut and spliced every one of the sounds in his "statistical curve" (and it is a special pleasure to point this out since, unlike Berio, Cage, or Babbitt, Davidovsky has never complained—that is, bragged—about his heroic investment of *Sitzfleisch*).

Davidovsky's *Synchronisms* are often viewed as the electronic counterpart to Berio's *Sequenzas*, virtuoso studies for solo instruments, of which the first, for flute, was composed, for the Italian new-music star Severino Gazzelloni, in 1958. (This famous series eventually numbered fourteen, the last being for cello.) Davidovsky's *Synchronisms No. 1* (Ex. 4-5), completed in 1963, was also composed for flute. It was written for Harvey Sollberger, one of the founding members of Columbia's Group for Contemporary Music. (Most of the Synchronisms were written for the members of the group as it evolved; in 1971, *Synchronisms No. 6*, composed for Robert Miller, the Group's pianist, received the Pulitzer Prize.)

Synchronisms No. 1 requires two performers, since the tape part must be recued, as is especially evident at the end, when it returns, after a lengthy flute solo, to articulate the final cadence. (See the "start/stop" at the end of Ex. 4-5, the last page of the score.) Different performances can thus have differing lengths: Sollberger's own recorded performance lasts 4′15″, while the one recorded by Samuel Baron, an eminent flautist of an older generation, takes only 3′43″. Even electronic music, it seems, can admit "interpretation," if the composer is willing to allow it.

EX. 4-5   Mario Davidovsky, *Synchronisms No. 1*, end

RECIPROCITY

A less expected form of interaction between live and prerecorded media surfaced around 1960, when a number of composers — many of them, as it happened, of East European nationality — began composing works for conventional instruments that emulated "electronic" sounds. Two aspects of the medium particularly attracted imitators. One was the long, gradually and continuously modified sounds that composers achieved in the studio by using filters and voltage-controlled speed variation, contradicting ordinary assumptions about rhythm and the articulation of musical form.

Since rhythm ordinarily implies the articulation of discrete impulses, music that relied on such endlessly continuous sonorities could seem virtually rhythmless. (A good example is the "King Lear Suite" that Luening and Ussachevsky extracted in 1956 from their incidental music for Orson Welles's production of Shakespeare's play, available on a CRI recording, in which "cold and lonely sounds" that continually change, but without discrete articulations, not only conjure up the wind on the stormy heath, but also "suggest Lear's madness, as he wanders in his fantastic dress of flowers and jingles,"[55] according to the composers' program note.) It offered new answers to that old riddle, how to evoke romantic "timelessness" in a temporal medium.

The other aspect of electronic music that captured the imaginations of composers who were not otherwise drawn to the medium was its use of "frequency bands" of greater or lesser breadth, a phenomenon that occupied a middle ground between the discrete pitches most instruments are constructed to produce and the "unpitched" sounds that some conventional percussion instruments could furnish. Varèse had exploited that middle ground in the taped interpolations in *Déserts*, treating it as a sort of synthesis between the pitched and "unpitched" instrumental sounds of the surrounding sections. He did not try to obtain a similar effect using the instruments themselves.

György Ligeti did try. After *Artikulation* (1958), the electronic piece he synthesized at Stockhausen's studio in Cologne (see chapter 1), he began work on another tape composition, *Atmosphères*, that was to consist entirely of slowly modulating continuous sounds, the meteorological title suggesting that those sounds had a metaphorical resonance for Ligeti similar to the one that it had for Luening and Ussachevsky (whose suite, by the way, was one of the few electronic compositions to have appeared on a commercial recording by the time Ligeti began work on *Atmosphères*).

After spending some time developing the work in the studio, however, Ligeti decided to start over and write *Atmosphères* "for large orchestra without percussion," as the eventual title page announced. The absence of percussion has been interpreted as polemical, so many works of the 1950s avant-garde having followed Varèse's example by greatly expanding the percussion "section" even in chamber works. But percussion instruments chiefly serve articulative purposes, and the whole point of *Atmosphères* was the banishing of articulations from a music of constant timbral and textural flux — "a music," as Ligeti described it, "without beginning or end." (The list of instruments does include a piano, normally a percussion instrument; but it is played by two executants — "they don't have to be pianists", the composer notes in the score — one of whom brushes the strings directly and the other holds down the damper pedal; neither touches the keyboard and so the hammers are never activated.)

Even without percussion, the work is scored for a very large orchestra: eighty-eight players on ninety-three instruments (all the flautists doubling on piccolo; one of the clarinettists playing both C and E♭ instruments), each with a separate part, so that by a very strict definition of terms, the work could be described as a gargantuan piece of chamber music. The very beginning of the piece shows why. The opening chord is scored for the entire string section of fifty-six players, each playing a different note but in the closest possible spacing, so as to produce a single huge cluster that covers all the available tempered pitches from the E♭ below the bass staff to C♯ an augmented octave above the soprano high C, equivalent to depressing two-thirds of the piano keyboard simultaneously. (True, Ligeti sacrifices three pitches in the middle to get this registral spread; anybody willing to waste the time it takes to verify the fact will also see that it makes no perceptual difference.) To this eighteen winds add some additional, smaller clusters (and the contrabassoon supplies the lowest note, a semitone below the lowest double bass, so that the cluster covers a full five octaves).

Attacked *pp* and marked *dolcissimo*, the chord sounds not particularly dissonant, but rather like a dull and distant roar. It is the closest equal-tempered approximation available to the electronic studio's white noise, the simultaneous sounding of the whole frequency spectrum. And Ligeti proceeds to modify the chord precisely the way (the only way) that white noise can be processed in the studio, by filtering it. Section by section the instruments drop out *morendo*, dying away by gradual decrescendo to silence, so as to avoid articulating the narrowing of the "bandwidth" until only the cellos and violas are left.

The whole composition is a series of ingenious variations on this basic filtering move, each marked by a rehearsal letter. At B the whole orchestra trumps the first chord with a cluster that adds an octave on either end. It decays at C into a kind of shimmer, in which all the instruments move from sustained tones to oscillations between two tones; but as the full cluster is maintained at all times, the apparent melodic activity produces no discernable change of pitch content. One is reminded of what chemists call Brownian motion, or of Xenakis's statistical "clouds" (see chapter 2) — perhaps another reason why Ligeti chose to call the piece *Atmosphères*.

The single sharp articulation in the piece takes place at G. Having worked a cluster up by degrees into the stratospheric ceiling range of a quartet of piccolos (a sound that, until digital recording was invented, could not be committed to tape or disc without bloodcurdling "intermodulation distortion" that many took as a sly burlesque of the electronic medium), Ligeti could not resist contrasting it with a cluster in the cellar, growled by eight double basses. That is the only place where he gave in to the principle of contrast rather than slow transformation.

The passage between H and J has become famous as an early example of what Ligeti called *Mikropolyphonie* — "micropolyphony," tiny close-spaced canons that cannot be heard as such because of the pitch saturation, but which guide the composer's hand toward fashioning a typically shimmering texture. At K, the composer contrives a kaleidoscopic array of unison doublings on a single sustained three-note chord encompassing two semitones — what might be termed a "minimal cluster"; then (at L) he gradually broadens the bandwidth by adding semitonal adjacencies on either end.

The return of the full orchestra cluster at N, made even more ethereal by the use of string harmonics, is marked *Tempo primo* — a remark that while perfectly practical (and practicable by the conductor) is nevertheless humorous in the context of a piece that is so wholly without metrical beats, hence devoid of any sense of tempo as the word is normally used. The string harmonics give way to even wispier sonorities at P, as the string players are asked to play with fingers of the left hand only half stopping the strings against the fingerboard so that no focused pitch emerges, just the sound of bow-scrape, and the brass are asked to blow softly without pursing their lips into the usual embouchure, so that only the barely perceptible sound of wind passing through tubes is heard. After a final passage of natural-harmonic glissandos in the strings (an effect pioneered by Rimsky-Korsakov and made famous by Stravinsky), the accumulated sound is allowed to die away in natural piano resonance over a couple of bars of notated "silence" at the end.

RENAISSANCE OR CO-OPTATION?

The laborious exactitude of the notation in *Atmosphères*, and the sheer immensity of the score thus produced, were among its most impressive features. They gave the work the same heroic aura of devoted drudgery — of sacrifice in the name of art — that the tedious "classical" techniques of the tape studio enjoyed. A more direct and radical approach to the project of recreating the sound world of electronic music in live performance was adopted by a group of Polish composers who came to prominence during the "thaw" decade that followed the death of Stalin in the countries of what by then was known as the Soviet Bloc.

That period was marked by considerable social turbulence in the countries that had been "liberated" from fascism by the Red Army, and were now governed by Communist dictatorships underwritten by the threatened return of the Soviet occupying force. The first armed Soviet intervention took place in East Germany in July 1953, to quell a labor uprising in the immediate aftermath of Stalin's demise. A much more serious (because temporarily successful) rising against Communist authority in Hungary was violently put down, as we know, in 1956. During the same year an illegal strike at a metallurgical plant in Poznan, Poland, spread to other cities, and Poland faced the prospect of a similar Soviet invasion. The Communist Party there sought by means of an internal reform and some liberalization of policies to avert that eventuality. In a manner somewhat reminiscent of the measures taken in the Soviet Union itself during World War II, the new leadership (headed by Władysław Gomułka, a Party official who had fallen under suspicion of excessive nationalism in the Stalin years and was briefly imprisoned) sought to recapture the loyalty of the cultural and intellectual élite by relaxing censorship on journalism and the arts.

One of the results was the granting of some administrative autonomy to the Polish Composers Union, including permission to open a window on the West through the so-called Warsaw Autumn Festival, an international showcase for contemporary music. Like most Communist reforms, the Polish liberalization under Gomułka was largely a matter of window-dressing without significant impact on substantive political or social issues. But insofar as the arts were the window, and as long as toleration of modernism was (however cynically) considered a good public-relations investment, Polish composers were allowed some genuine creative freedom.

The way they chose to advertise that freedom, of course, was to emulate the Western avant-garde en masse. In retrospect that may seem merely another sort of conformism, imposed from a different quarter and maintained by a different pattern of incentives and risks. But the subjective experience of many composers was buoyant and optimistic, especially insofar as it vouchsafed contact with counterparts in the West while artists everywhere else in the Soviet Bloc remained isolated. The creative ferment thus engendered, known as the "Polish renaissance," was for a time the wonder of the musical world.

The most forceful impression was made by Krzysztof Penderecki (b. 1933), who announced his presence on the scene in 1959 by winning all three prizes in a competition for young composers sponsored by the Union. The prize money paid for his first trip abroad, where he won the support of Luigi Nono in Italy, Pierre Boulez in Paris, and — most significantly — Heinrich Strobel, the music programmer of the Southwest German Radio in Baden-Baden and director of the Donaueschingen Festival, Germany's oldest and most prestigious new-music scene, which became Penderecki's principal showcase.

For the Donaueschingen Festival of 1960, Penderecki, who was trained as a violinist, wrote *Anaklasis* ("Light refraction") for strings and percussion, in which he exploited many unconventional playing techniques on the border between definite and indefinite pitch. It was one of several early Penderecki scores with titles that pertained to sensory qualities, like *Fluorescences* (1962) for orchestra, *Polymorphia* (1961) for strings, and *De natura sonoris* ("Of the nature of sound," 1966). Full of tone clusters, extreme registers, unusual timbres, they were designated "sonority-pieces" by the composer. Several choral pieces — *Stabat Mater* (1962), *St. Luke Passion* (1963–66) — combined similar "sonorist" techniques with Christian sacred texts, as if to identify one expression of cultural nonconformism, within the context of Communist rule, with another.

Far and away the best known of these compositions, indeed the most famous representative of the whole Warsaw Autumn phenomenon, was the piece for fifty-two solo strings that Penderecki published in 1961 as *Tren ofiarom Hiroszimy* ("Threnody for the victims of Hiroshima"). In conception and effect it is very similar to Ligeti's *Atmosphères*, but its notation is very different. The same long-held, gradually changing tones that Ligeti wrote with conventional note values and very slow metronome settings are notated here simply in terms of their durations in seconds, as measured across the page from left to right. And instead of fixing every pitch in the conventional way, thus building up his clusters by discrete semitones, Penderecki realized (as a string player would) that there was an easier way to obtain indeterminate "frequency bands." The range of a string instrument does not have a precisely determined upper limit.

Therefore, to ask a group of violinists to play "the highest note on the instrument" is to guarantee a cluster.

On the first page of the *Threnody* score (Ex. 4-6), all the instruments are asked to take their "highest notes"; the result is a truly memorable stridency, a veritable scream, fitting indeed for a piece with such a horrific subtext. Other sound material in the piece is generated by rapid alternations of indefinitely high pizzicati with sounds made by bowing below the bridge, bowing right on top of the bridge, even bowing on the tailgut,

EX. 4-6   Krzysztof Penderecki, *Threnody for the Victims of Hiroshima*, beginning

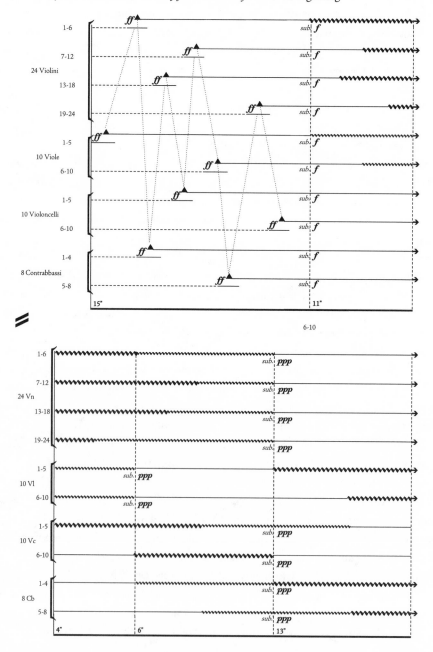

EX. 4-6 (continued)

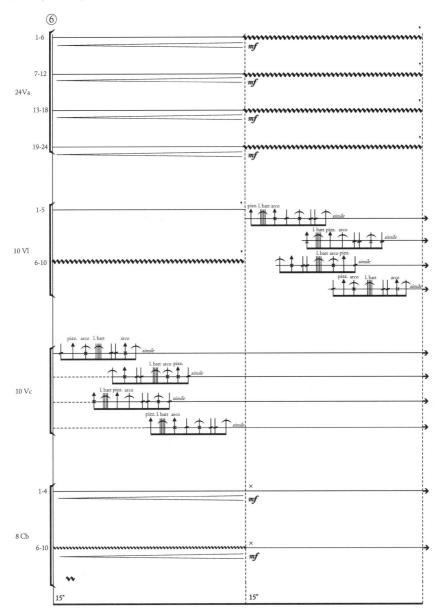

striking the string with the wood of the bow, knocking on the belly of the instrument (as in Xenakis's *Pithoprakta*), as well as the more ordinary gamut of *ponticello, col legno,* and *sul tasto* effects. One English reviewer noted dryly that Penderecki asked his players to "do everything possible on their instruments short of actually playing them."[56]

For each of these stunt effects Penderecki devised a notational symbol, which (before the advent of computer typesetting) had actually to be cast in type by the publisher. Sometimes these symbols succeed one another in groups that are subjected to retrogrades and canons; but again, as in the case of *Atmosphères*, these canons and retrogrades are not really thematic. They are just means of generating complex textures by using an ad hoc algorithm. The effect of widening and narrowing pitch bands is notated graphically for the benefit of the conductor's or analyst's conceptualization of the effect; in the parts, notation by normal chromatic pitch notation (sometimes augmented by special signs for quarter tones) is necessary, since unlike the opening high clusters, these have to be precisely calculated.

Threnody for the Victims of Hiroshima was a very difficult and expensive score to print. The fact that the Polish State Publishing House for Music was willing to make the considerable outlay seems related to the similar expensive promotions accorded avant-garde works by Stockhausen and, especially, Ligeti in Western Europe. In both cases, to showcase the avant-garde was to display a commitment to creative freedom, of propaganda benefit in the cold war. But in Penderecki's case, unlike the others, there was a more overtly political component as well. Calling attention to the United States Army's deadly attack on Japanese civilians, the most destructive single military act in history, was of propagandistic benefit to the Soviet Bloc, the Hiroshima bombing often being cited as a symbol of the American militarism, not to say savagery, that contributed to the breakup of the old wartime alliance against fascism. It made the performance of Penderecki's avant-garde music in Poland a politically correct exercise. That was an adroit feat of cultural politics in itself.

In later years, Penderecki let it be known that the piece published as the *Threnody for the Victims of Hiroshima* was first performed under the decidedly neutral, vaguely Cageian title 8′ 37″, and had been rejected by the publishing house as too expensive a prospect for printing. He gave it (he said) the politically fraught title ex post facto, at the suggestion of the director of the Polish Radio, so as to make it an attractive commodity for promotion by the Communist government — at first in Paris, where it was officially entered in a prize competition under the auspices of UNESCO.[57] The story is plausible, if only because once past the opening "screams" there is nothing in the piece of a comparably pictorial or suggestive character. The screams are screams, it would appear, only because they have been so labeled.

Does this make the composer out to be a cynic? A careerist? Or just someone who knew how to outsmart a formidable and often oppressive state bureaucracy, and thereby score a symbolic victory over authority and oppression (and who might well, like countless others, have sincerely deplored the bombing of Hiroshima)? And was the bureaucracy even outsmarted? Did it not also score a symbolic victory? Co-optation was a game played on both sides of the cold war, in any case; it is a game played on all sides of all fences. Ligeti benefited from it too, in 1968, when Stanley Kubrick exploited *Atmosphères* as, well, atmosphere in the soundtrack for his futuristic fantasy *2001*, and reaped for the composer a gold mine of publicity and name-exposure if not royalty payments from the marketing of record albums (out of which Ligeti has complained of being cheated) such as no avant-gardist had ever dreamt of.

What both of these stories prove, if nothing else, is that not even the avant-garde, which by virtual definition (or by defined purpose) resists commercial or ideological exploitation, has been able to resist it as the twentieth century, that most commercial and ideological of centuries, ran its course.

CHAPTER 5

Standoff (I)

Music in Society: Britten

Art remains outside the line of human conduct, with an end, rules, and values which are not those of the man but of the work to be produced. Hence the despotic and all-absorbing power of art, as also its astonishing power of soothing: it frees from every human care, it establishes the artifex, artist or artisan, in a world apart, cloistered, defined, and absolute, in which to devote all the strength and intelligence of his manhood to the service of the thing which he is making.[1]

—JACQUES MARITAIN, *ART AND SCHOLASTICISM* (1920)

A relationship of opposites had come into being; art had become a critical mirror, showing the irreconcilable nature of the aesthetic and the social worlds.[2]

—JÜRGEN HABERMAS, "MODERNITY — AN INCOMPLETE PROJECT" (1981)

Art is neither a mirror nor a substitute for the world. It is an addition to that universal reality which contains natural man and shows the infinite varieties of ways that man can be.[3]

—GEORGE ROCHBERG, "REFLECTIONS ON THE RENEWAL OF MUSIC" (1972)

Scientists are infatuated with the idea of revolution.[4]

—RICHARD LEWONTIN, *DARWIN'S REVOLUTION* (1983)

HISTORY OR SOCIETY?

Before plunging into the home stretch of the "relative present," the historically undistanced recent past, it is time, in this chapter and the next, for a stocktaking. The essential question of modern art, as it was understood by modern artists during the first two-thirds of the twentieth century, and the essential debate, was whether artists lived in history or in society. Posed literalistically, of course, the question is absurd. Everybody, artists included, obviously lives in both, and society (like everything else human) is a product of history. But as a metaphor for values and loyalties, the question crystallizes the dilemma of a period in which the values and loyalties of artists had become polarized to the point of crisis. In the minds of many, one served one's art or one's society, and loyalty to the one precluded loyalty to the other. One had to choose.

The choice was baldly and memorably crystallized in the art critic Clement Greenberg's article "Avant-Garde and Kitsch," which appeared in 1939 and may well have been the most influential twentieth-century essay on esthetics and the arts. The title stated categorical alternatives. One could be avant-garde, or one could produce kitsch, mere pseudo-art. There was no middle ground, because "a superior consciousness of history" had led those who created "art and literature of a high order" to form a united faction that had "succeeded in 'detaching' itself from society," and, in so doing, had managed "to find a path along which it would be possible to keep culture *moving*."[5]

Important artists, Greenberg contended, "derive their chief inspiration from the medium they work in," from which it followed that "content is to be dissolved so completely into form that the work of art or literature cannot be reduced in whole or in part to anything not itself" and "subject matter or content becomes something to be avoided like a plague."[6] It was inevitable, therefore, that at the late point in history that was the twentieth century, the best artists should be "artists' artists," the best poets "poets' poets,"[7] and that the truly valid art of the period "has estranged a great many of those who were capable formerly of enjoying and appreciating ambitious art and literature, but who are now unwilling or unable to acquire an initiation into their craft secrets." That social estrangement, Greenberg strongly implied, was in itself a criterion of artistic validity.

As we know, these questions were sorely aggravated by mid-twentieth-century politics. The one choice, service to society, had been tainted in one part of the world by the ugly demands of totalitarian dictatorships that dealt harshly with dissidents, and in another by the degrading pressures of capitalist commercialism, at which Greenberg had mainly been railing. The other choice, "disinterested" loyalty to the demands of art and to maintaining the historical evolution of its material, had led to a degree of professional specialization that, even as it offered political consolations, threatened institutional isolation and condemned artists to a social irrelevance that, ironically enough, had no historical precedent.

But of course the split was fraught, as real-life dichotomies always tend to be, with irony. Political authorities who demanded social commitment from artists justified their demands (and certainly their repressions) by appealing to the "mandates of history." Greenberg himself had argued that the "superior consciousness of history" that led the avant-garde into social withdrawal had been in reality "a new kind of criticism of society, an historical criticism."[8] (Putting things this way allowed Greenberg to believe that his esthetics had a Marxist base.) Within the world of music, moreover, the concepts that drove theorizing on the mandates of history and the autonomous development of style were founded on developments that had taken place mainly within the most public (hence socially oriented) musical genres, opera and symphony.

The ideologies that drove the practice of the arts to its unprecedented twentieth-century crisis had historical precedents, and we are familiar with them. Both opposing tendencies can be traced back to the nineteenth century. In music, the antisocial extreme had its origins in the historicism of the New German School, while its opposite originated in the populism and social activism of Romantic opera. We have seen how both sides claimed legitimizing descent from Beethoven—or rather, from aspects of Beethoven's posthumous reception (the "Beethoven myth"). Later, both sides could also claim descent from Wagner, who like Beethoven qualified both as a technical innovator and as a champion of social issues who broadened the social base of artistic appeal.

Since Wagner's time, however, few if any figures seemed able to combine these roles. In the twentieth century they tended, increasingly, to point in opposite directions. Commitment entailed renunciation. If perpetual technical innovation tended to lessen audience appeal, those committed to it could claim to be making a heroic sacrifice. But by the same token, social commitment placed constraints on technical innovation; that too could be regarded as a sacrifice. The only possible exceptions to the great rift were in the realm of opera, with Berg's *Wozzeck*, as ostentatiously innovative in technique as it was gripping in the theater, furnishing the outstanding example. But it was an isolated example, unlikely to be repeated; for since Berg's time, as we have seen, the place of opera, both as popular culture and as a site of high technology, had been usurped by the movies.

The coming polarization of art music into "social" and "elite" categories had already been sensed by many nineteenth-century musicians. Chaikovsky expressed it vividly in letters to his patron, Mme von Meck. As the product of a conservatory education, he had been schooled to regard "absolute music" as the highest form not only of music, but of all art. "Symphonic and chamber varieties of music," he wrote accordingly, "stand much higher than the operatic."[9] And yet he persisted in writing operas notwithstanding, and ultimately came to regard himself primarily as an operatic composer. For, as he put it in a passage that was naturally exploited to the hilt by the Soviet musical establishment, "opera and only opera brings you close to people, allies you with a real public, makes you the property not merely of separate little circles but — with luck — of the whole nation."[10]

"To restrain oneself from writing operas is a form of heroism," Chaikovsky went so far as to assert. And, he continued, "in our time there is such a hero," namely Brahms, a composer Chaikovsky otherwise despised. For this reason, if for no other,

> Brahms is worthy of respect and admiration. Unfortunately, his creative gift is meager and does not measure up to the scope of his aspirations. Nevertheless, he is a hero. I lack that heroism, and the stage, with all its tawdriness, attracts me in spite of everything.[11]

Of course Chaikovsky's tongue was in his cheek when he wrote that; but his irony was effective precisely because it pretended agreement with a widespread opinion even as it gave real assent to the opposite view (just as widely held). These were the positions that became ever more hardened and antagonistic as the twentieth century approached and passed its ideologically fraught middle, to the point where Pierre Boulez could actually call (heroically? terroristically? literally? tongue in cheek?) for the destruction of the world's opera houses, so that the mandates of music history might sooner be fulfilled without the irrelevant competing claims of society.[12]

We can best take the measure of that crux by focusing on two outstanding composers whose careers are often viewed as antithetical. They were, in a sense, stand-ins for Chaikovsky and Brahms, as Chaikovsky framed the split. Both were hailed as heros by their admirers, and perhaps overpraised at times; and both were dismissed as superfluous by their detractors. Each embraced one side of the century's esthetic dichotomy with an extremity that turned them into symbols. Their followings tended to be mutually exclusive, further intensifying the split that defined musical life in the century's "middle third."

But neither was institutionally constrained to espouse the position that he came to symbolize. Both lived in countries whose governments adopted a laissez-faire policy toward the arts, and neither was permanently affiliated with the academy. Thus the commitment of the one to social utility could not be attributed (as, for example, Shostakovich's often was) to totalitarian pressure; and the commitment of the other to the posing and solving of technical problems and to maximum complexity of utterance could not be attributed (as Babbitt's often was) to academic careerism.

Benjamin Britten (1913–76) was a specialist in opera. He was the only major composer who could be called that in the mid-to-late twentieth century, and he knew it; he even described himself to his friend and fellow composer Michael Tippett (1905–98) as "possibly an anachronism"[13] for that reason. (The midcentury avant-garde would have of course agreed.) But he was uniquely successful in his chosen domain — so successful that it was arguably Britten's example that kept the genre viable through the leanest years of its existence, and prevented its lapsing into an exclusively "museum" status.

Just as Chaikovsky in a sense foretold, the accomplishment made Britten the musical darling (as well as the homonym) of his nation, Britain, which had not produced a composer of comparable international standing — and surely none of comparable achievement in opera — since the seventeenth century. He sought and achieved unprecedented social recognition. He was given the honor of a royal commission for an opera to celebrate the coronation of Queen Elizabeth II in 1953, and near the end of his life was elevated beyond knighthood to a "life peerage" or noble title, becoming Lord Britten of Aldeburgh. Britten always explicitly avowed that his commitment to opera stemmed (again echoing Chaikovsky) from a larger view of his calling as public service. He further sought, just as explicitly, to reconcile that calling with a fully modern, if eclectic, musical manner, which (in a sense belying his reputation as a "national" figure) drew extensively on nearly the full range of contemporary European styles, as well as on a number of Asian musics. We shall have a chance, in this chapter, to compare his preaching with his practice on all fronts.

The American composer Elliott Carter (b. 1908), by extreme contrast, spent most of his career as heroically spurning the stage as had Brahms. Only as he neared the age of ninety did he (perhaps emulating the aged Verdi) unexpectedly begin work on an opera, *What's Next?*, a one-act comedy (first performed in 1999) that did not so much involve adapting his musical practice to a new medium as it did contriving a stage action that allegorized (possibly even genially satirizing) that musical practice, famous for its daunting intricacy. It was an anomaly among his works, a jeu d'esprit or witticism, and was frankly presented and received as such.

Carter's chief medium was abstractly titled instrumental music; the string quartet was as central to his output as opera was to Britten's (although Britten did write three quartets). His favored approach was reminiscent of the formal ideals of New Criticism: the expression of an underlying unity through an extreme surface diversity — maximum complexity under maximum control. He strenuously opposed stylistic eclecticism, and deliberately rejected a national (or "Americanist") creative identity in favor of a "universal" (that is, generically Eurocentric) one. As with Britten, we have Carter's own testimony on the social implications of his conscious career choices and his stylistic trajectory, and we will explore them in the next chapter.

SOME FACTS AND FIGURES

Between 1941 and 1973, Britten produced a total of seventeen works for the lyric stage. He established his reputation right after the war with *Peter Grimes* (op. 33), an opera set in Aldeburgh, an English fishing village near the composer's own home. It was first performed on 7 June 1945 by the Sadler's Wells company (now the English National Opera), London's smaller, less prestigious operatic stage, and almost immediately went around the world in a manner reminiscent of the operatic hits of the 1920s. Within three years it had played at London's Royal Opera House at Covent Garden, New York's Metropolitan, Milan's La Scala, and sixteen other locations in France, Belgium, Germany, Italy, Denmark, Sweden, Austria, Switzerland, Hungary, Czechoslovakia, and the United States.

His time freed by *Peter Grimes*'s commercial success, Britten began turning out operas on an almost yearly basis. His next major hit, six years and five operas later, was *Billy Budd* (op. 50), after Herman Melville's shipboard story. In 1953 came *Gloriana* (op. 53), the coronation commission, a historical opera about Elizabeth I, the new queen's namesake. *The Turn of the Screw*, op. 54 (1954), after Henry James's ghost story, was a chamber opera (the "orchestra" consisting of thirteen solo instruments), a genre calculated for the resources, and for the encouragement, of small touring companies. The original touring company that performed it, the English Opera Group, was founded by Britten himself and his lifelong companion, the tenor Peter Pears. It was an outgrowth of his strong commitment to take his art to the people.

Britten's next opera, *A Midsummer Night's Dream* (op. 64) after Shakespeare, came six years later, in 1960. It was first performed at Aldeburgh, a coastal village where Britten and Pears had established a summer festival. In the interim he had written a ballet (*The Prince of the Pagodas*, op. 57) and *Noye's Fludde* (op. 59), a setting of a medieval miracle play for church performance. In the train of the latter came three "parables" or one-act church operas: *Curlew River*, op. 71 (1964), *The Burning Fiery Furnace*, op. 77 (1966), and *The Prodigal Son*, op. 81 (1968). Britten's last two operas were *Owen Wingrave*, op. 85 (1970), composed for television performance, and *Death in Venice*, op. 88 (1973), after the famous novella by Thomas Mann.

None of the later works matched the colossal success of *Peter Grimes*, but at least four — *Billy Budd*, *The Turn of the Screw*, *A Midsummer Night's Dream*, and *Death in Venice* — have joined *Peter Grimes* in the permanent international repertoire. No composer in the postwar period has come close to matching that record. Two other composers have managed to produce international repertory operas: Stravinsky with *The Rake's Progress* (1951) and Poulenc with *Dialogues of the Carmelites* (1956). Virgil Thomson's *The Mother of Us All* (1947), an opera about Susan B. Anthony, has received many performances in America (partly because of its suitability for conservatory and workshop productions) but has never traveled.

Britten's only possible rival as an opera specialist was Gian Carlo Menotti (1911–2007), an Italian-born composer long resident in the United States, who was even more prolific than Britten in the genre, with twenty-five operas to his credit by 1993, most of them written to his own librettos. Menotti's was a strangely lopsided career, however, with amazing early successes followed by near oblivion. His first stage piece, an *opera buffa* called *Amelia al ballo* (1936; most often performed in English translation as *Amelia Goes to the Ball*), was so well received that the Metropolitan Opera accepted it for production in 1938. It brought on a steady stream of commissions, many from broadcast media.

The first of Menotti's truly amazing successes was *The Medium* (1945), a melo-dramatic chamber opera in two acts with a cast of five singers and a mime, and an accompanying orchestra of fourteen pieces. It was first performed in 1946 at Columbia University's Brander Matthews Theater, which a few years earlier had been the site of Britten's first operatic endeavor (an unsuccessful folk opera or operetta called *Paul Bunyan*, to a libretto by the poet W. H. Auden, then like Britten a British immigrant to the United States), and was very likely a precedent or model for Britten's *Turn of the Screw*. Together with a comic curtain raiser called *The Telephone*, *The Medium* was produced on Broadway during the 1947–48 season, and enjoyed a run of 211 performances. Menotti himself directed a Hollywood film adaptation of *The Medium* in 1951, and the United States government sent the double bill on a European tour in 1955.

His next opera, a full-evening "musical drama" in *verismo* style called *The Consul* (1949), was a cold-war saga about the desperate efforts, culminating in suicide, of a would-be emigrant to obtain an exit visa from an unnamed European police state. It, too, had a successful Broadway run, and won both the Drama Critic's Circle Award for the season's best play and the Pulitzer Prize in music in 1950. The next year, Menotti received a commission from NBC television for a Christmas opera, *Amahl and the Night Visitors*, a story of the Three Magi and a miraculous healing. Televised annually for a dozen years and frequently performed by amateur groups and workshops, it may well be the most widely seen opera of all time. Menotti's next opera, *The Saint of Bleecker Street* (1954), about an alleged miracle worker in New York's "Little Italy" district, once again played Broadway, receiving Critics' Circle Awards both as best opera and as best play, and another Pulitzer Prize.

These operas, especially *The Medium* and *The Consul*, are still revived in major houses and can be called repertory items, at least in America. But Menotti would never have another major operatic success, though his career lasted another four decades. His last production on a major world stage was *The Last Savage*, a satire of modern life (including twelve-tone music), which failed miserably at the Metropolitan Opera in 1964. His thirteenth opera, a work for children ("and people who like children") called *Help, Help, the Globolinks!* (1968), about an invasion from outer space (with electronic music to represent the aliens), was the last to be published. His later premieres have been at provincial venues, most frequently the Kennedy Center in Washington, D.C. *The Wedding* (1988) was introduced in Seoul, Korea. In his later years, Menotti was more active as a stage director and impresario (directing the Festival of Two Worlds at Spoleto, Italy, and Charleston, South Carolina) than as a creative figure. His most recent premieres took place under his own auspices.

The reasons for Menotti's apparent failure to stem the ebbing tide for opera while Britten continued to flourish may have had something to do with musical style and invention. Menotti's scores, reminiscent of Puccini both in their melodic and harmonic idiom and in their formal procedures, stopped attracting critical interest while Britten's, continually surprising, commanded the respect of critics otherwise committed to modernism (which Menotti actively resisted and despised). It may be, too, that measuring Menotti's success by the standards of his early Broadway runs is unfair; no other composer of continuously-sung opera ever duplicated that kind of success, either. Critical success and audience success are by no means dependably in alignment.

But the ephemeral success of the one composer and the continually burgeoning success of the other (*Billy Budd*, for example, becoming a repertoire opera only after an initial flop that led to revisions, like some famous works of Verdi and Puccini), suggests that Menotti's works, while explosively effective on first exposure, exhausted their meaning quickly, while Britten's embodied latent meanings that revealed themselves (or that emerged into the light of critical discourse) only over time, engaging performers, audiences, and critics in continual dialogue. That is what makes for a long cultural shelf life, the kind that characterizes and constitutes "classics."

It is that process of emergence that will occupy our attention here, for that is where Britten's historical significance seems to lie. Only in this way can we hope to explain Britten's by now universally recognized stature as a major definer of the contemporary music of his day, and his endurance, despite his refusal to embrace the narrowly stylistic definition of musical contemporaneity that reigned in avant-garde circles at midcentury.

A MODERN HERO

Britten had to overcome considerable odds to realize his potential as a musical dramatist. The breakdown of the opera house as an institution coincided with the onset of the worldwide economic depression of the 1930s, just when Britten was finding his feet as a composer. There was no longer the possibility of an apprenticeship within the institutional structure of the musical theater. Britten, who had resolved to earn his living as a professional composer rather than a teacher, was forced, ironically enough, into the movie industry — the very force that most starkly threatened the continued viability of the lyric stage.

Like Virgil Thomson in America at roughly the same time, Britten earned his living from 1935 to 1937 providing soundtrack scores for government-sponsored documentaries. Work on films like *Coal Face*, on harsh labor conditions in the mining industry (some of the music consisting of recorded collages of simulated industrial sounds anticipating *musique concrète*), or *Peace of Britain*, about the burdens of defense spending on the national economy, increased Britten's sense of solidarity with leftist and pacifist opinion. Both viewpoints were strong in England, as well as America, during the depression decade, which was also the decade of Fascist victories in Germany and Spain that presaged the inevitable coming of World War II.

In 1936 Britten wrote incidental music for *Stay Down Miner*, a play by the Communist writer Montagu Slater (1902–56), produced by the Left Theatre, which took a much more militant line about the labor situation than *Coal Face*. The next year, he composed a *Pacifist March* for an equally militant organization called the Peace Pledge Union. He also wrote music for plays by W. H. Auden and Christopher Isherwood for production by the Group Theatre, yet another of the militant political associations of artists that mushroomed during what Auden later called "the low, dishonest decade"[14] of the thirties.

In 1939, together with Peter Pears, Britten followed Auden and Isherwood in the wave of leftists and pacifists who emigrated from England to North America as war clouds gathered. After a short stay in Canada, Britten and Pears settled for a while in the environs of New York, where they met and befriended Aaron Copland. Having already collaborated with Auden on a number of projects in England, Britten continued the creative association with *Paul Bunyan*, the largest work of his American sojourn. He wrote some important instrumental works in America as well, including a Violin Concerto and a *Sinfonia da Requiem* in memory of his parents.

Auden and Isherwood remained expatriates for the rest of their lives, but Britten and Pears—not without apprehension at the fate that might await them as conscientious objectors—returned to England in 1942, at the height of hostilities. The decision had been made the previous summer. Britten and Pears had gone to southern California for the purpose of reentering the United States from Mexico and thereby qualifying for permanent immigrant status. While there Britten came across an article by the English writer E. M. Forster about George Crabbe (1754–1832), an English poet best known for his grimly realistic depictions of rustic life in the southeastern coastal district of Suffolk, from which he hailed.

FIG. 5-1 Benjamin Britten (at the piano) and Peter Pears; photo by Lotte Jacobi, 1939.

Britten, a Suffolk man himself, was seized with homesickness and conceived the idea that he could only fulfill his musical potential in his aboriginal surroundings, in the bosom of (and in service to) his native society. The conviction was abetted when, pursuing Forster's lead, Pears bought an old edition of Crabbe, where he and Britten found a long narrative poem called *The Borough* (1810), describing life in Aldeburgh, the very town where Britten had purchased a home shortly before emigrating. They immediately began planning the scenario for an opera on its basis.

Early in 1942, while Pears and Britten were awaiting the opportunity (infrequent in wartime) to book boat passage back to England, Serge Koussevitzky, acting on Copland's recommendation, performed the *Sinfonia da Requiem* with the Boston Symphony Orchestra. Impressed with its dramatic qualities, he asked Britten why he had never written an opera. Preferring not to mention *Paul Bunyan*, Britten (as he put it in the Introduction to the vocal score of *Peter Grimes*) "explained that the construction of a scenario, discussions with a librettist, planning the musical architecture, composing preliminary sketches, and writing nearly a thousand pages of orchestral score, demanded a freedom from other work which was an economic impossibility for most young composers."[15]

Later that same year, Koussevitzky's wife Natalie died. She had inherited a tea fortune that had already financed her husband's prewar publishing firm (*Éditions Russes de Musique*). Now, as a memorial to her, the conductor established the Koussevitzky Music Foundation for the commissioning of major works by composers of all nationalities. Britten was informed that he was to be the first recipient of a Koussevitzky Foundation grant of a thousand dollars. (The next was Bartók, for his *Concerto for Orchestra*.) That is how *Peter Grimes* became a reality, and also why Britten's exceptionally prolific career as a composer for the stage only got off the ground in his fourth decade, with his op. 33.

Peter Grimes, the character from *The Borough* that Britten and Pears chose for their protagonist, had already been singled out by Forster, in his article on Crabbe, as an item of special interest: "a savage fisherman who murdered his apprentices and was haunted by their ghosts."[16] When they read his story in full, Britten and his collaborator found that Grimes, sadist though he was, was not an unmitigated villain. Crabbe had used him, in a fashion more typical of realist writers than romantics, to expose social injustice. "No success could please his cruel soul," the poet wrote of his fisherman,

> He wish'd for one to trouble and control;
> He wanted some obedient boy to stand
> And bear the blow of his
> outrageous hand;
> And hoped to find in some
> propitious hour
> A feeling creature subject to his power.

He found the opportunity to indulge his cruelty with impunity thanks to the English workhouse system, which supplied him with indigent orphan boys, utterly without civil rights, whom he could exploit for his own purposes be they legitimate or otherwise. As the Britten scholar Philip Brett has noted, "unlike the typical villain of the Gothic novel, Grimes does not have to resort to kidnapping to place another person under his complete control; he has only to apply to the nearest workhouse."[17] But this implicates society in the crime, as Crabbe makes clear:

> Some few in town observed in Peter's trap
> A boy, with jacket blue and woollen cap;
> But none inquired how Peter used the rope,

> Or what the bruise, that made the stripling stoop;
> None could the ridges on his back behold,
> None sought him shiv'ring in the winter's cold;
> None put the question — "Peter, doest thou give
> "The boy his food? — What, man! the lad must live;
> "Consider, Peter, let the child have bread,
> "He'll serve thee better if he's stroked and fed."
> None reason'd thus — and some, on hearing cries,
> Said calmly, "Grimes is at his exercise."

But after his third apprentice mysteriously dies, the town does ostracize the fisherman, who now must fish alone, and does so where no one else will go:

> There anchoring, Peter chose from man to hide,
> There hang his head, and view the lazy tide
> In its hot, slimy channel slowly glide.

Thus Crabbe exposes a double injustice: Grimes's cruel exploitation of his helpless apprentices, and the townspeople's hypocritical disapproval of behavior in which they have all been complicit. The plight of the criminal fisherman who even so is banished unjustly was a theme of attractive complexity to modern artists like Britten and Pears, who were heirs to an even more relativistic notion of responsibility and blame, an even more exacting sense of social justice, and an even more compelling interest in psychological complexities than the prophetic Crabbe. Grimes was, or could be if suitably fleshed out, a character to set beside the similarly prophetic Büchner's Wozzeck, the delinquent yet pitiable antihero of Berg's famous opera, which had made so strong an impression on Britten that he had once nurtured the hope of studying with Berg (to the dismay of his official teachers at London's Royal College of Music). Indeed, *Wozzeck* would be a model for *Peter Grimes* in ways that went far beyond the general similarity of their protagonists.

SOCIAL THEMES AND LEITMOTIVES

The "social problematic" may have been the initial impetus for Britten and Pears to build their scenario around the figure of Peter Grimes, but the portrait (already emphasized by Forster) of the furtive outcast brooding in the lonely estuary engaged a different level of response in them. It led to the thorough recasting of the title role, and the whole surrounding dramatic plot. "A central feeling for us," Britten later told an interviewer,

> was that of the individual against the crowd, with ironic overtones for our own situation. As conscientious objectors we were out of it. We couldn't say we suffered physically, but naturally we experienced tremendous tension. I think it was partly this feeling which led us to make Grimes a character of vision and conflict, the tortured idealist he is, rather than the villain he was in Crabbe.[18]

Like Shostakovich in *The Lady Macbeth of the Mtsensk District* (another opera that had impressed Britten and that he would emulate), the composer saw his task with

FIG. 5-2   Britten's *Peter Grimes* in its first production, Sadler's Wells Company, London (now the English National Opera), 1945.

respect to his title character as one of exoneration. He and Pears went even further than Shostakovich or Berg had gone in softening the portrait of their hero, making him the innocent (if blundering) victim of prejudice and unjustified persecution. As Pears put it in an article advertising a broadcast performance in 1946, "Grimes is not a hero nor is he an operatic villain." What is he then?

> He is very much of an ordinary weak person who, being at odds with the society in which he finds himself, tries to overcome it and, in doing so, offends against the conventional code, is classed by society as a criminal, and destroyed as such. There are plenty of Grimeses around still, I think![19]

In the opera Grimes is given two apprentices, not three. The Prologue, unpreceded by any overture, portrays an inquest into the death of the first, who had died of thirst aboard Grimes's boat during an ill-advised journey of several days to London. The death is attributed to "accidental circumstances," but Grimes is given a warning not to expect the benefit of the doubt in the future.

To reduce the story, as Britten and Pears recast it, to its barest bones: in act I, Grimes (against the advice of the inquest magistrate) procures another apprentice with the assistance of Ellen Orford, the village schoolteacher (a character transplanted from a different part of Crabbe's *The Borough*), whom he hopes to marry after clearing his name and gaining the town's respect by prospering. In act II, against Ellen's passionate entreaties, Grimes forces the exhausted (and, as Ellen has discovered, roughly treated) new boy out to sea on a Sunday in pursuit of a big shoal of herring. Or so he intends;

goaded to hurry perilously by Grimes (who hears an approaching posse of villagers opposed to his plan), the apprentice loses his footing on a cliff side and falls—again accidentally—to his death. In act III, the apprentice's jersey is discovered on the beach and a manhunt is organized to bring Grimes to justice; he eludes them, but turns up later, dazed and incoherent, and is discovered by Ellen and by Captain Balstrode, a retired skipper (and Peter's only other defender), who now orders him to row out to sea and sink his boat rather than face the implacable if mistaken judgment of the townspeople.

But are they mistaken? Grimes, while no murderer, is indeed responsible for the boy's death. Yet without the fanatical posse of villagers at his heels, he would not have treated the boy so recklessly. The theme of ambiguously shared guilt, already broached by Crabbe, is thus starkly dramatized. The preponderance of guilt is subtly shifted to the townspeople by showing them biased against Grimes from the start, and by showing him to be, as Britten put it, an idealist, full of poetic visions and wholesome aspirations, and therefore morally superior, at least by inclination, to the crowd that condemns him—just as, in the view of the opera's creators, their own status as conscientious objectors was morally superior to that of a society then engaged in bloody warfare, which persecuted pacifists, and yet to which they were now committed to return. (Although Britten and Pears were ultimately dealt with leniently on the strength of their artistic reputations, their fears were not unjustified: the less lucky Michael Tippett was imprisoned for refusing military service in 1943, shortly before Britten embarked on the score).

As soon as the character was reconceived in this way it became possible to assign his part to Pears's tenor range rather than to the traditional villain's baritone, as in the earliest scenario drafts. That may even have been a reason in itself for the transformation of the title role. The most explicit portrayal of Grimes's positive side comes at the end of the first scene in act I, right before a big storm—obviously symbolic but, given the locale, also realistic—blows up. Balstrode exhorts Peter to marry Ellen before taking a new apprentice, so as to quiet gossip and give himself a fresh start. Grimes rejects the idea. "I have my visions, my fiery visions," he insists. "They call me dreamer, they scoff at my dreams and my ambition." But first he'll make himself rich—"These Borough gossips listen to money, only to money"—and then he'll marry Ellen. In this way he will achieve *peace*—a word that, as we can imagine, carried for Britten and Pears a powerful multiple charge. The last words in the scene, sung right before the storm breaks in the orchestra (an entr'acte famous in its own right as a concert piece), is Peter's apostrophe to peace (Ex. 5-1):

> What harbour shelters peace,
> Away from tidal waves, away from storms?
> What harbour can embrace
> terrors and tragedies?
> With her there'll be no quarrels,
> with her the mood will stay.
> Her heart is harbour, too,
> where night is turned to day.

EX. 5-1 Benjamin Britten, *Peter Grimes*, Act I, scene 1, "What Harbour Shelters Peace?"

EX. 5-1 (continued)

The words are by Montagu Slater, Britten's old collaborator in the Left Theatre, who accepted the task of turning the scenario into a full-fledged libretto after Isherwood, Britten's first choice, declined. The music, while conventionally lyrical and voice-dominated, hence "Verdian" rather than "Wagnerian" (to cite the pigeonholes into which twentieth-century operas were customarily slotted), consists nevertheless of a tissue of tiny leitmotives. One is the rising ninth with which Peter's long-breathed

EX. 5-1 (continued)

"peaceful" phrases all begin. It is first heard at the end of the Prologue, at the resolution of an unaccompanied passage (which Britten somewhat ironically called the "love duet") in which Ellen calms the distraught Peter at the end of the inquest (Ex. 5-2). The two singers begin at odds (indeed, in seemingly "remote" keys linked by the shared Ab/G#), and achieve *all'unisono* concord in Ellen's E major.

Another leitmotif, more obvious in the context of Ex. 5-1, is one associated with the gathering storm, to which Grimes sings lines — "away from tidal waves, away from storms," and "terrors and tragedies" — that contrast with the peace for which he longs, as his marcato vocal delivery contrasts with the dominating bel canto luxuriance of his vision.

EX. 5-2   Benjamin Britten, *Peter Grimes*, unaccompanied duet at end of Prologue

EX. 5-2 (continued)

The dramatic crux of the opera, the turning point that seals Peter's tragic fate, comes in the first scene of act II: his stormy quarrel with Ellen over his treatment of the boy, which culminates in his single act of violence on stage when in frustration he strikes out at Ellen and knocks her knitting basket to the ground. The scene is played against a background of Sunday morning congregational singing coming from the church offstage, one of the many "genre" touches that give the opera its naturalistic atmosphere. Like many astute musical dramatists, but especially Verdi, Britten sought every opportunity to integrate the foreground and background through irony. (Another instance came during the previous act, when Grimes, awaiting the arrival of the new apprentice in the town tavern at the height of the storm, tries to join in a round that the townspeople are singing to keep their spirits up, but fails so miserably to keep the tune that he almost wrecks the song for everyone; what could more graphically convey his condition as a social misfit?)

As this calamitous climax approaches, Ellen suggests that the two of them may have been mistaken in thinking that together they might have ended the pattern of cruel behavior that had brought the town's suspicion on Grimes. He flies into a rage (Ex. 5-3a), mocking the comfort he had formerly taken in his vision of domestic tranquillity by singing a contorted parody of the rising-ninth motif ("Wrong to plan! Wrong to try! Wrong to live! Right to die!") that first fails to achieve its goal, stalling at F, a major seventh above the starting note (pushed further, but only as far as an octave), and finally reverses direction, crashing back precipitously from the high A♭ that had been the original goal.

EX. 5-3A   Benjamin Britten, *Peter Grimes*, Act II, scene 1, "Wrong to plan!"

That F is an ominous note for more reasons than its not being A♭. It had been functioning all during the scene as one of the offstage choir's reciting notes (in alternation with B, a sinister tritone away), to which Grimes's tormentors had been singing their unwittingly ironic, hypocritically moralizing commentary to the foreground events. As the crisis nears, the congregation, chanting on F, takes up the Creed. Their note passes to a pair of horns that provides a steady dissonant pedal to underscore the quarrel onstage—dissonant, that is, until Ellen joins their note with the terrible words, "Peter, we've failed!" (Ex. 5-3b).

At this very point, when Peter strikes Ellen and loses all hope of breaking the pattern of his life, the choir of townsfolk is heard again, intoning a "Amen" to their insistent F. And then, most horrible of all, Peter Grimes himself takes up the dread pitch, translating their very word ("So be it!") and resolving the F as a dominant to his highest note, B♭, as he sings "And God have mercy upon me!" and rushes offstage in pursuit of the boy. Recalling the way in which Ellen had musically brought him round at the end of their "love duet," it is hard to escape the appalling perception that, in accepting from the offstage congregation the note (and even the word) to which his persecutors have sung the triumphant conclusion of their Creed, Peter has implicitly accepted their judgment of him. Bereft of his dream of redemption, he is now, in his own

EX. 5-3B Benjamin Britten, *Peter Grimes*, Act II, scene 1, "Peter, we've failed!"

eyes as well as theirs, a criminal to be condemned. And now we have the explanation for his hopeless final acceptance of Captain Balstrode's legally unjustified sentence of death.

The phrase to which Grimes has sung his exit line (and death warrant) now becomes the leitmotif that will dominate the rest of the scene, and more. Immediately repeated by braying brass in a raucous sequence to fix it in the listener's memory, it then becomes the main theme of the choral episode that depicts the gathering of the posse that will eventually intrude on Grimes's hut and bring about the tragic dénouement. But it is not only a theme: it pervades the music, serving now as accompaniment, now as offstage organ voluntary, and sometimes with its contour partially inverted.

EX. 5-4   Benjamin Britten, *Peter Grimes*, Act II, scene 1, "Grimes is at his exercise"

Although it involves real-time action, the episode is constructed in part like an aria with a refrain; and that refrain, sung to the new leitmotif, is the chilling line from Crabbe (one of the few original verses to survive into the libretto) that had established both the town's contempt for Grimes and their indifferent complicity: "Grimes is at his exercise" (Ex. 5-4). The climax comes when the whole town (excepting Ellen and Balstrode) shout the charge of "Murder!" to the strident inversion of the ninth in which Grimes had vested all his hope (Ex. 5-5).

All rush off but for a quartet of women, including Ellen, who remain alone onstage and sing one of the opera's famous set pieces, a pained commentary on the harsh life of the fishing community and the toll it takes on morals — a commentary given added ironic point by being sung, apart from Ellen, by the innkeeper ("Auntie") and her "nieces," the girls she keeps to provide the men of the town with comfort services: three women, in other words, identified by hypocritical convention as immoral, but alone (with Ellen) exhibiting a humanity which the town's more respectable citizens have been exposed as lacking.

Their lyrical quartet is mainly a respite from the mordant leitmotivery of the rest of the scene, but even here a note of irony lurks to complement the irony of Slater's text, with its reference to the "bitter treasure of [the menfolks'] love." A pair of flutes introduces each verse of the quartet with a dissonant ritornello (sometimes compared with the voices of seagulls supplementing the rocking waves of the sea as depicted in the

EX. 5-5   Benjamin Britten, *Peter Grimes*, Act II, scene 1, "Murder!"

accompanying strings) that in its two phrases spans a pair of descending ninths, now irrevocably associated with Grimes's tragedy.

We are not finished with the main leitmotif of that tragedy, however. "God have mercy upon me," also known as "Grimes is at his exercise," now reverberates — at its original pitch, stretched out to a length of eleven beats, and unfolding at the slow tread of a funeral march replete with muffled drumbeats — as the ground bass of the orchestral passacaglia that serves as interlude between the two scenes of act II (Ex. 5-6). Like Berg's *Wozzeck* and Shostakovich's *Lady Macbeth*, Britten's opera relies heavily on interludes, not only as a way of filling the time between scenes, but as a vehicle of manipulative authorial commentary.

The interludes in *Peter Grimes*, it has been observed, alternate in function between scene setting (at the beginning of acts) and meditations on the hero's fate (in the middles), with the Storm in the middle of act I combining both roles. Britten's Passacaglia directly parallels the one that comes midway through the second act of Shostakovich's opera. Like the latter, and like the much shorter entr'acte after the murder in the third act of *Wozzeck*, it forces the audience to reflect obsessively (along with the title character) on a cataclysmic turn of events. In an early draft, Britten had associated the passacaglia with the "boy's suffering," and by using a solo viola in counterpoint against the ground at the outset, turns the interlude into a personal lament (an impression the use of solo strings conventionally conveys; one does not have to know that the viola was the instrument that, after the piano, Britten played best).

ALLEGORY (BUT OF WHAT?)

Britten's and Pears's strong personal identification with the title character has already been cited as a motive not only for composing the opera in the first place, but also

EX. 5-6   Benjamin Britten, *Peter Grimes*, Passacaglia (Interlude IV), beginning

for the hefty alterations that distinguish the musical treatment from the original poem. ("Neglect Crabbe," one critic warned audiences, if they wanted to be able to see the characters "from the composer's standpoint" and really understand the opera.[20]) That identification is most conspicuous in the libretto when Grimes rejects Balstrode's suggestion that he seek employment as a merchant seaman rather than put up with the difficulties of life in the town, saying "I am native, rooted here/by familiar fields,/marsh and sand,/ordinary streets,/prevailing wind." Anyone who knew Britten's own circumstances, driven by homesickness from the safety of voluntary exile to the uncertainties of life within a possibly hostile society at war, could recognize these lines as autobiography; and many did.

To think along these lines is to turn the opera into allegory. How one reads an allegory, of course, depends to a considerable degree on what one has on one's own mind. To the American literary critic Edmund Wilson, who happened to catch the first production on a visit to London, the opera seemed an allegory of the war just past. "This opera could have been written in no other age," he asserted, "and it is one of the very few works of art that have seemed to me, so far, to have spoken for the blind anguish, the hateful rancors and the will to destruction of these horrible years."[21] He saw these dire features embodied in the character of Grimes himself, whose violent nature he read, at first, as symbolizing defeated Germany:

He is always under the impression, poor fellow, that what he really wants for himself is to marry Ellen Orford and to live in a nice little cottage with children and fruit in the garden "and whitened doorstep and a woman's care." Above all, he wants to prove to his neighbors that he is not the scoundrel they think him, that he really means no harm to his apprentices and that he will make a good family man. But he cannot help flying into a fury when the boy does not respond to his will, and when he gets angry, he beats him; and his townsmen become more and more indignant.[22]

Whether Wilson really entertained this curious and limited view of the action, or whether he included it in his essay just to offset his final interpretation, is hard to say; but in the end he comes to see it more the way the opera's creators evidently intended:

> By the time you are done with the opera — or by the time it is done with you — you have decided that Peter Grimes is the whole of bombing, machine-gunning, mining, torpedoing, ambushing humanity, which talks about a guaranteed standard of living yet does nothing but wreck its own works, degrade or pervert its own moral life and reduce itself to starvation. You feel, during the final scenes, that the indignant shouting trampling mob which comes to punish Peter Grimes is just as sadistic as he. And when Balstrode gets to him first and sends him out to sink himself in his boat, you feel that you are in the same boat as Grimes.[23]

Not that the reading of an allegory must conform to the author's precise intentions (or even that it can, since we can never be sure that we know the latter). Britten and Pears very likely read Wilson's critique with a mixture of gratitude and bewilderment: gratitude that he grasped something of the social theme and identified as they did with Grimes, bewilderment that he was able to read his own cynically bleak view of "the whole of humanity" into their work. But whether or not one accepts Wilson's reading, or any particular one, some level of allegorical interpretation seems necessary if the opera is to succeed in its moral, and even its musical, objective. For the music has painted Grimes as an innocent man, and yet he perishes as a guilty one. It does not add up, as the critic J. W. Garbutt forcefully argued in an article that appeared almost two decades after the first performance — and it is already a remarkable testimony to the opera's status as a modern classic that debate about its meaning should have continued even that long. As recently as July 2004, in fact, the London *Guardian* carried an article that refused point-blank either to neglect Crabbe or to consider allegorical readings, condemning the work as "a powerful but an inadvertently immoral opera, that seeks (shades of *Lady Macbeth*) to justify an irredeemable criminal"[24]

Nevertheless "the ending is dramatically memorable,"[25] Garbutt wrote. Few have disagreed. Grimes's mad scene (Ex. 5-7), which follows upon (and effectively silences) the last orchestral interlude, is a nearly incoherent recitative, accompanied by the offstage voices of the posse calling his name and by a single tuba impersonating a distant foghorn. Whatever rudimentary structure it has is provided by a medley of melodic reminiscences that sum up the action Grimes obsessively recalls. Ellen approaches, offering to take him home; he responds with a hopeless reprise of Ex. 5-1, transposed down a semitone. Finally, Balstrode approaches and, *in spoken dialogue*, issues the death sentence. Peter disappears in silence. A reprise of the Interlude that opened Act 1 then shows the Borough awakening to a new day.

Joseph Kerman, in one of the earliest American reviews, marveled at the way in which "music is reduced successively to absolute zero"[26] as the title character is destroyed. Dramatically memorable, indeed. "But is it dramatically just?" asks Garbutt:

Had he some real guilt to atone for, the ending would have been meaningful as well as memorable: the tragic inevitability which Crabbe manages to convey as a force behind his narrative would have lent itself to the opera. But in the absence of established guilt, Peter is accepting death merely because of the Borough's desire for revenge. Balstrode at this moment acts as the Borough's executioner; mentally

EX. 5-7   Benjamin Britten, *Peter Grimes*, Act III, scene 2 (Grimes's mad scene)

EX. 5-7 (*continued*)

weakened, Peter submits. And the Borough celebrates its easy triumph with its routine performances, in the "cold beginning of another day."[27]

Garbutt concludes that the opera succeeds despite the dramatic flaw at its conclusion, owing to the sheer brilliance of Britten's music. "Clearly there is a remarkable musical power in this opera, so dominating our response that we can accept the self-contradictory figure of Peter." And yet his very critique, premised on his refusal to accept that self-contradictory figure, shows his conclusion to be unfounded. More recent critics, notably Philip Brett, have suggested that there is indeed a level at which the contradiction is resolved (or, more precisely, eliminated) through allegory. But the crucial allegory entailed so touchy and ticklish and unresolved a social issue in contemporary life that (as Ellen says when she finds the apprentice's jersey) it became "a clue whose meaning we avoid."

That issue is homosexuality: or more specifically, hidden, "closeted" homosexuality, "the love that dare not speak its name," which was for many, and remains for some, a tormented way of life. Among them were Britten and Pears. That they were "out of it" — social misfits — not only as conscientious objectors but as homosexual lovers was widely known (that is, widely and correctly assumed) at the time of their exile and return. It has been plausibly adduced as one of the reasons for their emigration, along with Auden and Isherwood and many others: "that desire," as Philip Brett describes it, "so common in young gay men, to seek anonymity and freedom by going to the big city, the far-off country — any place, that is, away from the home where they feel at best half-accepted."[28] And it must surely have contributed to the "tremendous tension" that, as Britten put it in a paragraph already quoted, he and Pears "naturally" experienced at the time of their return from America, and led them to transform their Peter Grimes into "a character of vision and conflict."

Their apprehension was justified. Homosexual acts between consenting adults were illegal in Britain and (as the case of Oscar Wilde so dramatically demonstrated) could be vengefully prosecuted, no matter how eminent the offender. Even when unprosecuted, they could brand otherwise respectable figures with a social stigma. This definitely happened to Britten and Pears. Their musical achievements, and the punctilious discretion with which they conducted themselves in public (no longer so pressingly demanded of homosexual couples by today's society), allowed them to become the world famous recipients of official honors (a knighthood for Pears, a peerage for Britten). But they were never at liberty to acknowledge their relationship: the closest Britten ever came was to refer to Pears in a speech as "a congenial partner" with whom "I like giving concerts."[29] And as their fame grew they were also increasingly the butt of cruel jokes intended to diminish them not only as persons but also as artists.

Such jokes were usually uttered in private. But just as fame could shield Britten and Pears from overt harassment, fame protected their most eminent detractor. Sad to say, the most open, public insults ever addressed to them were delivered by none other than Stravinsky, who in his last years dictated several volumes of memoirs and observations to his assistant Robert Craft, and used them to settle scores not only with many figures from his past but also with many contemporaries, including younger composers whom he had reason to envy. Britten, whose extraordinary public success represented something Stravinsky had possessed in youth but had tried in vain to recapture in later life, was a special object of the old man's taunts. He referred to Britten in print, maliciously, as a "bachelor composer,"[30] and even permitted himself a reference to "Aunt Britten and Uncle Pears"[31] in a letter that Craft published after his death.

Britten's and Pears's relationship, officially regarded not only as socially deviant but as diseased by the medical science of the time, was an open secret even when not disparaged. It was always among the subtexts that informed views of the works in which they collaborated. Read as part of an allegory depicting the plight of social misfits, Grimes's implicit acceptance of his "guilt" might be explained even without evoking sexuality. But in light of the stigma attached to his creators' sexual relationship, that acceptance is among the opera's most compelling social themes — one that communicated itself strongly to audiences even without speaking its name. In conjunction with the music, to whose powerful effects Garbutt drew attention, it surely contributed to the opera's lasting hold on the imaginations of listeners. Or as Brett puts it, "the successful realization of so modern a dramatic character is one of the main reasons for the opera's wide general popularity."[32]

Brett continues, "it is the special characteristic of the homosexual stigma (unlike that attached to being black or Jewish) that it is almost always reinforced at home and is thus the more readily 'internalized,' that is, accepted as valid and to a greater or lesser extent incorporated into the values and sense of identity of the person in question."[33] One who has internalized that shame might indeed regard himself as condemned, like Grimes, not for what he has done but for what he is. In addition to introspection (or the exercise of "common sense"), Brett supported his observations by citing the recent literature of "gay and lesbian" or "queer" theory, which has only existed as such since Britten's death. But in offering a convincing interpretation of the opera's most harrowing and problematical issue, namely Grimes's acknowledgment of guilt, Brett is surely justified in his once alarming, now celebrated assertion that "it is to the homosexual condition that *Peter Grimes* is addressed."[34] As such an allegory, he further maintains, the work becomes "all the more poignant and relevant to people today," whatever their sexual preferences or life style; for the social message is all the stronger for its being expressed — nonexplicitly yet unmistakably — in terms of what was in its day a still actively practiced intolerance. The opera thus becomes an indictment of its own contemporary society, not just "the Borough," and Britten's treatment of what was necessarily in its day a tacit social issue can, by anticipating (or even helping to precipitate) changes in public attitudes, appear in retrospect to have been as prescient or "prophetic," in its way, as Crabbe's or Büchner's had been. "One of the things Britten's operas (as well as his other works) seem to achieve is an exploration of various issues surrounding sexuality that the composer could not discuss in any other public form," Brett writes, and he goes on to offer the judgment that Britten's "perseverance in this endeavor is one of the truly remarkable and even noble features of his career."

That the treatment, though veiled in allegory, was conscious and deliberate can be seen clearly enough in retrospect if we reread Pears's characterization of Grimes ("an ordinary weak person, . . . classed by society as a criminal") in the light of his and Britten's "crime." And if any doubt remain, there is a letter from Pears to Britten, written in February or March 1944, about a month after Britten had started sketching the music, but only published in 1991, in which he reassured the composer that "the queerness is unimportant & doesn't really exist in the music (or at any rate obtrude)."[35] For they both knew that the theme of social persecution of homosexuals, however real and pressing, had to remain implicit if the opera was to be received by their contemporaries as bearing a "universal" message about human tolerance.

Armed with these insights, Brett located prefigurings of Grimes's "internalization" of society's condemnation much earlier in the opera than the turning point in the middle of act II. We have already seen what a potent dramatic device Britten made of the musical technique of inversion, turning Grimes's aspiring upward leap of a ninth into a crashing descent to connote the destruction of his aspirations and his doom. The other leitmotif introduced in Ex. 5-1, derived from the music associated with the gathering storm, can also be described, as Brett points out, as an inversion of the "hubbub" motif that accompanies the indignant muttering of the crowd in the opera's opening scene, the inquest Prologue (Ex. 5-8). Nor would it be irrelevant to add in this context, when dealing with a composer as literate and self-conscious as Britten, that the word "inversion" is a frequent code word or euphemism for homosexuality, not only in colloquial speech but also in works of literature (most famously, perhaps, in Proust's monumental novel, *In Search of Lost Time*).

EXOTIC/EROTIC

None of this means that Peter Grimes was actually envisioned or presented by Britten and Pears as homosexual, or that he should be played that way. The plight depicted is not that of sexual "inversion" as such but rather its social consequences, which do not differ in the case of homosexuals from those affecting other persecuted minorities. And yet there are other aspects of the opera that indirectly broach matters associated with, or tangential to, the theme of homosexuality, matters that recur in later works of Britten as well. Unlike Chaikovsky or Copland, or any other previous composer known

EX. 5-8A   Benjamin Britten, *Peter Grimes*, Prologue, "When women gossip. . ."

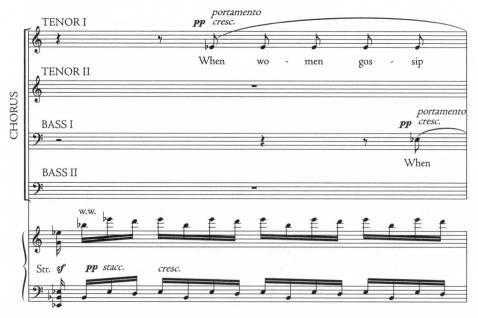

EX. 5-8A   (*continued*)

EX. 5-8B   Benjamin Britten, *Peter Grimes*, Grimes's replique in Act I, scene 1

or thought to be homosexual, Britten did consciously (and perhaps also unconsciously) "thematize" the topic repeatedly. That, too, is an aspect of modernity, and a particularly compelling one that transcends the narrowly stylistic issues to which discussions of musical modernity are often confined.

In *Peter Grimes*, the title character's insistence on having boy apprentices, in conjunction with the evidence of his possible sadism toward them, broaches the issue of pederasty (man-boy love) and the consequent "corruption of innocence" that was long a recognized but unspoken concern in British society, where the education of young boys so often took place in private, single-sex boarding schools. Britten himself attended such a school; his recent biographers have recorded the testimony of friends to whom he allegedly confided that he had been raped by a prep-school master. Incidents like this do not "explain" homosexuality; but they might predispose an artist to thematize man-boy attraction, as Britten did in *Death in Venice*, or violence toward children (as in *The Turn of the Screw*), or vengeful male treatment of overly attractive men (as in *Billy Budd*). Of all modern composers, Britten surely wrote the most for boy singers; and in *A Midsummer Night's Dream* he cast Oberon, the Fairy King, as a male falsettist (or "countertenor")—a boy's voice in a man's body to impersonate a character who schemes for possession of a "changling" (that is, a magically abducted) boy.

The falsetto voice quality is an "exotic" effect, and such effects have always been the bread and butter of opera (defined by Samuel Johnson in the eighteenth century, after all, as "an exotick and irrational Entertainment"[36]). Britten's operatic dramaturgy, and even his musical style, depends to an unusual degree on juxtapositions of exotic and "normal" or "unmarked" elements, perhaps further reflecting his view of himself as a "marked" man. The often startling effects that such juxtapositions produce is another genuinely modernistic aspect of Britten's manner, despite his refusal to accommodate his technique of composition—for "social" as well as musical reasons—to the direction of the midcentury avant-garde. (About serial technique, for example, he wrote, "I can see it taking no part in the music-lover's music-making; its methods make writing *gratefully* for voices or instruments an impossibility, which inhibits amateurs and young children."[37])

Britten's basic manner is well typified by the orchestral music that accompanies the short choral epilogue to the final scene in *Peter Grimes* (Ex. 5-9). It is a reprise of the Interlude at the beginning of act I, which sets the stage for a scene of routine life and work in the Borough, and seems to represent the natural environment in which that life goes on—wind, tide, perhaps skittering eddies, breezes, gulls. The texture is divided into three discrete timbral and tonal layers: a slow melody high in the violins and flute, a cushion of brass consisting of slow chords proceeding from and returning to an A-major triad, and a faster motif in the middle range (clarinet and harp).

In themselves, the various layers are all diatonic and, in themselves, stylistically unremarkable. What is remarkable is their conjunction, which involves both tonal contradiction and an impression of rhythmic discoordination. The middle voice alone is intrinsically somewhat unusual in the way it presents the familiar contents of the "white key" diatonic scale as a tonally ambiguous arpeggio of stacked thirds over two octaves. On two levels, then, Britten contrives idiosyncratic or extraordinary presentations of material that is part of every listener's ordinary musical experience. It is a technique that has been associated with surrealism, and that association seems to serve equally well to characterize Britten's brand of modernism, which is similarly given to "polytonal" effects. It is a technique of identifying the dramatic representation it accompanies or evokes as being at once realistic—*Peter Grimes* is often characterized as a *verismo* opera—and strange.

In Britten's later operas, the juxtapositions take more extreme forms. When (as in *The Turn of the Screw* or *A Midsummer Night's Dream*) they evoke the supernatural, Britten's surrealism often involves playful or sardonic invocations of the "aggregate" or "total chromatic" (the basic stuff of serialism). The very opening curtain music in *A Midsummer Night's Dream*, for example, establishes a magical dream atmosphere with a progression of major triads with roots on all twelve pitch classes (the slow and regular

EX. 5-9   Benjamin Britten, *Peter Grimes*, Act III, scene 2, choral epilogue

string glissandos that connect them evoking the heavy breathing of sleepers), and the "sleep music" in act II is a passacaglia on a progression of four harmonies, each played in a different instrumental color, that exhausts the chromatic scale without any pitch repetitions (Ex. 5-10).

EX. 5-10A   Benjamin Britten, *A Midsummer Night's Dream*, beginning of Act I

EX. 5-10B   Benjamin Britten, *A Midsummer Night's Dream*, the passacaglia ground

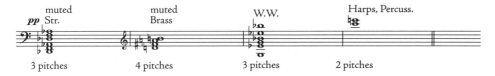

In *The Turn of the Screw*, the spooky two-act chamber opera based on Henry James's novella about the corruption of innocent youth by evil spirits, the whole score is laid out over a twelve-tone harmonic grid (Ex. 5-11a). It consists of a prologue and sixteen scenes in different keys. The outer extremities have A as their tonal center; the middle scenes (last in act I, first in act II) have A♭. The successive centers in the first act can be laid out as an ascending A minor scale (plus the crowning A♭); those in the second act form the inversion of the first: a descending mixolydian scale on A♭ (plus the concluding A). Taken together, the two scales exhaust the pitches of the chromatic scale. Each tiny scene, moreover, is linked with the next by an interlude. The one that follows the Prologue is labeled "Theme" and all the others are Variations on it (see Ex. 5-11b and c).

The Theme, consisting as it does of an ordering of the twelve pitch classes, could be called a tone row; analysts have pointed to it as Britten's accommodation with serialism (roughly contemporaneous with Copland's and Stravinsky's). Like the row in Copland's Piano Quartet (see chapter 3), Britten's theme separates the chromatic scale into two mutually exclusive whole-tone components, comparable to the complementary scales that govern the tonal progressions of the two acts. But unlike Copland's serialism or Stravinsky's, Britten's simple twelve-tone manipulations are unrelated to Schoenberg's

EX. 5-11A   Benjamin Britten, *The Turn of the Screw*, tonal plan (analytical chart by Peter Evans)

techniques and could easily have occurred to a composer who had no knowledge of them. Rather, they are complete rotations or traversals (or "turns") of the chromatic spectrum within a traditional (if not an entirely conventional) key scheme. They illustrate, and were no doubt motivated by, the title concept—a turn that tightens a trap.

In Britten's last opera, *Death in Venice*, he at last hazarded a subject in which pederastic attraction was an explicit theme—and a destructive one, reflecting Britten's own puritanical acceptance (like Peter Grimes's) of society's judgment of his real-life

EX. 5-11B   Benjamin Britten, *The Turn of the Screw*, Theme with pitches numbered

EX. 5-11C   Benjamin Britten, *The Turn of the Screw*, Variation I with pitches numbered

EX. 5-11C   *(continued)*

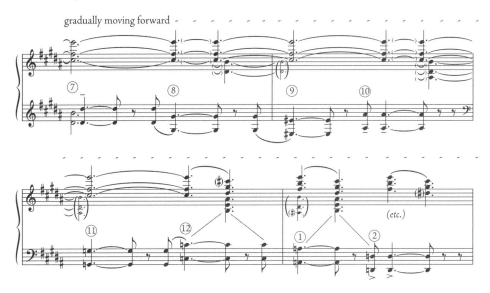

predilections. Mann's novella concerns a great writer, Gustav Aschenbach (thought to have been modeled on Gustav Mahler), who prides himself on the "Apollonian" control he exercises over his work, but who unexpectedly conceives an uncontrollable "Dionysian" passion for Tadzio, a young Polish boy he espies while on vacation in Venice. Aschenbach not only humiliates himself but even destroys himself physically on account of his homoerotic attraction. Unable to bear parting from the object of his forbidden affection, he responds too late to health warnings and perishes in an epidemic.

To convey Tadzio's unselfconscious, dangerous allure, Britten gave a new twist to an old device. He painted the boy (who does not sing) in exotic "oriental" colors, surrounding him with an aureole of Balinese gamelan music. It was not the first time Britten had used these sounds. He first encountered them in the United States, where he met the Canadian composer and ethnomusicologist Colin McPhee (1900–64), who had lived in Bali from 1931 to 1938. McPhee had made arrangements for two pianos of some of his transcriptions of gamelan performances. He and Britten recorded a few of them for the firm of G. Schirmer in 1941.

FIG. 5-3   Britten's *Death in Venice*, act II (Aschenbach observes Tadzio on the Lido beach in Venice). San Francisco Opera, 1997.

The connection with homosexuality was drawn even then: McPhee, like many Euro-American artists, was drawn to Bali not only by its indigenous art, but also by its reputation as a sexual paradise where one could practice "deviant" sex with greater freedom and far less risk of social stigma than one could at home. "Thus," the music historian W. Anthony Sheppard has observed, "Britten's first impressions of Bali and first exposure to gamelan music were filtered through McPhee's unique descriptions, transcriptions, and experiences."[38]

Some scholars have detected echoes of McPhee's transcriptions in the second act of *Peter Grimes*. In 1956 Britten visited Bali and made some transcriptions of his own, mainly of music performed by a boys' gamelan that had actually been organized by McPhee a couple of decades earlier. Thus, even his hands-on experience with gamelan "reinforced an imagined realm of sexual permissiveness that would remain in his Orientalist memory," as Sheppard puts it, establishing a firm "connection between the musical exotic and homosexual opportunity."[39]

Britten almost immediately turned his new gamelan experiences to creative account in a ballet, *The Prince of the Pagodas*, first performed at Covent Garden in 1957. Thus Britten's Tadzio music, for all its idiosyncratic associations, was the work of a genuine gamelan connoisseur. Like McPhee's, Britten's gamelan style employs authentic scales (as closely as Western instruments allow) in the seven-tone *pelog* tuning (Ex. 5-12), scored for an ensemble of mallet percussion instruments including xylophones, marimbas, glockenspiel, and vibraphone.

Like his nineteenth-century French and Russian predecessors, Britten has come in for some criticism on account of his appropriation of exotic music for sensual and sinister effect, a use that tends to encourage the stereotyping of "others." His "orientalism" is more plainly metaphorical than most earlier examples, however; it does not portray an actual oriental subject (as Peter Grimes did not represent an actual homosexual protagonist), but characterizes Aschenbach's way of seeing the object of his desire, and his fantasies. The opera's distinctive musical style arises out of the confrontation of unmarked "Western" music, suggestive of normality and respectability, and the marked music of the East, suggestive of irrepressible and illicit desire. The conjunction presented Britten with new, dramatically charged opportunities for the sort of "surrealistic" layerings and juxtapositions that had always characterized his modernism.

Of course neither side "wins." As in *Peter Grimes*, Britten confronts his audience with an unsolved problem, another mark of a quintessentially modernist sensibility. Interpreted by sympathetic critics like Brett and Sheppard, Britten's operas emerged in the late decades of the twentieth century with renewed force, as (in Sheppard's words) "personal allegories of specific contemporary social issues—whether of homosexual oppression, racial and ethnic intolerance, or of the pacifist's precarious position in a militant, nationalistic society."[40]

TO SERVE BY CHALLENGING

This is an achievement that the adoption of an alienated "avant-garde" stance, and a difficult musical style more typical of midcentury modernists, might well have thwarted.

EX. 5-12   Benjamin Britten, *Death in Venice*, gamelan stylization in Tadzio music

That was the real tension for Britten, in many personally crucial ways genuinely alienated from contemporary society, yet, as he put it, "longing to be used"[41] by that very society, seeing his most useful potential role as that of a faithful and acceptable gadfly who could, by pleasing his audience with satisfying art experiences, lobby for points of view that challenged, and sought to undermine, the complacency of the majority.

The quoted phrase in the foregoing paragraph comes from a speech Britten delivered in 1964, entitled "On Receiving the First Aspen Award." This was a sizable cash prize authorized in 1963 by the Aspen Institute for Humanistic Studies, an organization founded by Walter Paepcke (1896 – 1960), a wealthy Chicago industrialist and philanthropist, whose monetary investment turned Aspen, a former silver-mining boom town in Colorado, into a combined ski resort and summer cultural center. The Aspen Award was instituted to honor "the individual anywhere in the world judged to have made the greatest contribution to the advancement of the humanities."[42] Britten received the award in particular recognition of his *War Requiem*, op. 66, a huge oratorio for three vocal soloists, mixed chorus, boys' chorus, chamber orchestra, symphony orchestra, and organ, commissioned for the dedication of the rebuilt Coventry Cathedral, which had been bombed out during the Second World War, and first performed in the cathedral as part of its consecration ceremony on 30 May 1962. Like so many of Britten's works, the *War Requiem* had ironic juxtaposition at its conceptual core. This time the Latin words of the traditional Requiem Mass, sung by the soprano soloist and the choruses with the large orchestra and organ, were juxtaposed with grim, posthumously published antiwar verses by Wilfred Owen (1893–1918), a pacifist poet killed in action a week before the armistice that ended World War I, sung by the tenor and baritone soloists, personifying soldiers, accompanied by the chamber orchestra.

The inclusion of Dietrich Fischer-Dieskau, a German baritone, in the original performing roster at Britten's express behest turned the occasion into one of symbolic reconciliation between former enemies. It gave enormous added poignancy to the last of Owen's poems, performed in juxtaposition with *Libera me, Domine* ("Deliver me, O Lord"), the final portion of the Requiem liturgy. The poem consists of a meditation on war's waste of life in the form of a dialogue between a killed British soldier and a German whom he had previously killed. In the first performance, and in the recording made the next year under Britten's baton, those roles were taken by Pears and Fischer-Dieskau.

The soprano soloist in the recording was the Soviet singer Galina Vishnevskaya, whose participation balanced that of Fischer-Dieskau as a reminder of the former wartime alliance between the hostile camps of the cold war. The work was received in England, along with the ceremony it accompanied, as a major historical event; it gave Britten, at least for a time, the sort of heroic and official public prominence otherwise enjoyed by modern creative artists only in the Soviet bloc (and only when they behaved). For the moment, it seemed, his formerly suspect pacifism was in harmony with the aspirations of his country, and this concord was reflected in the citation he was given at Aspen, which lauded him as "a brilliant composer, performer, and interpreter through music of human feelings, moods, and thoughts, [who] has truly inspired man to understand, clarify and appreciate more fully his own nature, purpose and destiny."[43]

Britten used this moment of triumph to deliver a sermon at Aspen about the social responsibility of artists, and the responsibilities of society toward its artists. It can be read as a sustained metaphor for the conflict he had always faced between his condition and his aspirations, the risks he felt he had taken in life and in his art, and his satisfaction in having come through. "I want my music to be of use to people, to please them, to 'enhance their lives' (to use [the art critic Bernard] Berenson's phrase),"[44] he said near the end of his address, and followed this up by taking an explicit and very emphatic stand regarding the crux ("History or Society?") that informs this chapter and the next:

> I do not write for posterity—in any case, the outlook for that is somewhat uncertain. I write music, now, in Aldeburgh, for people living there, and further afield, indeed for anyone who cares to play it or listen to it. But my music now has its roots in where I live and work.[45]

This theme was Britten's mantra. Earlier in the talk he had already insisted, repetitiously and seemingly gratuitously, that it was after all "quite a good thing to please people, even if only for today. That is what we should aim at—pleasing people today as seriously as we can, and letting the future look after itself."[46] Earlier still he had indicated why such a seemingly amiable, unobjectionable position had nevertheless to be advanced militantly:

> There are many dangers which hedge round the unfortunate composer: pressure groups which demand true proletarian music, snobs who demand the latest *avant-garde* tricks; critics who are already trying to document today for tomorrow, to be the

first to find the correct pigeon-hole definition. These people are dangerous—not because they are necessarily of any importance in themselves, but because they may make the composer, above all the young composer, self-conscious, and instead of writing his own music, music which springs naturally from his gift and personality, he may be frightened into writing pretentious nonsense or deliberate obscurity.[47]

To those who saw themselves as living only in history, who treated their social peers as a hindrance, and who therefore continued to invest their art with an outdated aristocratic (or "high-culture") aura of inaccessibility, Britten offered a prim pointer on manners: "it is insulting to address anyone in a language which they do not understand."[48] But pieties were balanced with warnings. "Finding one's place in society as a composer is not a straightforward job," he asserted, leaving a great deal unsaid, especially when he hinted that "until such a condition is changed, musicians will continue to feel 'out of step.'"[49] Matters are not helped, he went on, "by the attitude towards the composer in some societies." First he indicted his own, "semi-Socialist Britain, and Conservative Britain before it," which "has for years treated the musician as a curiosity to be barely tolerated." But even greater dangers lurk to the left and right, he told his American audience:

> In totalitarian regimes, we know that great official pressure is used to bring the artist into line and make him conform to the State's ideology. In the richer capitalist countries, money and snobbishness combine to demand the latest, newest manifestations, which I am told go by the name in this country of "Foundation Music."[50]

Britten picked only three composers to praise by name, knowing that the praise would be provocative:

> Recently, we have had the example of Shostakovich, who set out in his "Leningrad" Symphony to present a monument to his fellow citizens, an explicit expression for them of their own endurance and heroism. At a very different level, one finds composers such as Johann Strauss and George Gershwin aiming at providing people—the people—with the best dance music and songs which they were capable of making. And I can find nothing wrong with the objectives—declared or implicit—of these men; nothing wrong with offering to my fellow-men music which may inspire them or comfort them, which may touch them or entertain them, even educate them—directly and with intention. On the contrary, it is the composer's duty, as a member of society, to speak to or for his fellow human beings.[51]

As history, even as social history, not everything (perhaps not much) in this paragraph holds water, and Britten may have known that. But he was engaging in a not-so-covert polemic against the other side of the mid-twentieth-century divide. And he was met with rejoinders in kind.

CHAPTER 6

Standoff (II)

MUSIC IN HISTORY: CARTER

EXPLAIN NOTHING

Perhaps inevitably, the most widely noticed rejoinder to meet Britten's outspoken Aspen address (and the music it defended) came from Stravinsky, who went out of his way to deride the *War Requiem* and its social reception in an essay on recent music, ghostwritten by his assistant Robert Craft, that was first published in 1964 (the year of the lecture) and reissued in book form two years later.

"Behold the critics as they vie in abasement before the wonder of native-born genius,"[1] Stravinsky scoffed. He compared Britten with Hermann Goetz (1840–76), a forgotten German composer who enjoyed a rapturous critical promotion during his lifetime and for a few decades thereafter (George Bernard Shaw placing him "above all other German composers of the last hundred years save only Mozart and Beethoven"[2]—that is, above Wagner and Brahms). The inadequacies of Britten's "cinemascope epic" are sneeringly catalogued: "patterns rather than inventions," "an absence of real counterpoint," "a bounteous presence of literalisms" (like the use of timpani strokes where the text mentions "the drums of time"), and the "sedative" use of the organ. The concluding jab, "nothing fails like success," makes explicit the underlying premise that giving pleasure to one's contemporaries precludes a genuinely "historical" achievement.

Stravinsky's ardent denunciation of the *War Requiem* gains added resonance in counterpoint with another ghostwritten review he had published slightly earlier, in which he had gone just as far out of his way to praise Elliott Carter's Double Concerto for Harpsichord and Piano with Two Chamber Orchestras (1961), a choice example of what Britten had termed "Foundation Music." It had been commissioned, and the many rehearsals that preceded the first performance had been underwritten, by the Fromm Music Foundation, to whose sponsor, Paul Fromm, the work was dedicated. Ex. 6-1 shows a representative page (far from the most complicated) from the Concerto's score, chosen because Stravinsky happened to single it out for praise.

FIG. 6-1   Elliott Carter; photo, 1991.

Surely the first thing that leaps out is how difficult this music must be to perform. The extreme fluidity of both rhythm and tempo are its most conspicuous features, closely followed by the enormous variety of detail, a bit bewildering in music so quiet. The atomistic texture is typical. Absent is anything that looks like a theme; instead there is a montage of rhythmic patterns, the majority of them consisting of strings of

EX. 6-1   Elliott Carter, Double Concerto, p. 101 of the score

notes of equal value (allowing for the ubiquitous group accelerandos and ritardandos). Their interplay is what provides continuity and interest. It would be very difficult to deduce the harmonic principles that guide the counterpoint. Experimental analysis would quickly show that the music, while freely chromatic and fully "emancipated" in terms of dissonance treatment, cannot be referred to a tone row.

To guide listeners through this very unusual composition at the premiere, the composer offered the following program note, which was reprinted as the sleeve note for a recording, also subsidized by the Fromm Foundation, that was issued shortly afterward. (It is quoted in full except for the first sentence, which repeats information given above):

> Completed in August, 1961, it is an antiphonal work for two small orchestras each led by one of the soloists. The harpsichord is associated with an ensemble of flute, horn, trumpet, trombone, viola, contra-bass and percussion (largely metallophones and lignophones [i.e., instruments made of metal and wood]) while the piano is joined by an ensemble of oboe, clarinet, bassoon, horn, violin, cello and percussion (largely membranophones [i.e. drums with skin heads]). In addition to being isolated in space and timbre, the antiphonal groups are partially separated musically by the fact that each emphasizes its own repertory of melodic and harmonic intervals, the harpsichord ensemble: minor seconds, minor thirds, perfect fourths, augmented fourths, minor sixths, minor sevenths and minor ninths; the piano ensemble: major seconds, major thirds, perfect fifths, major sixths, major sevenths and major ninths. Each of these intervals is associated, for the most part, with a certain metronomic speed with the result that the speeds and their inter-relationships are also different for the two groups. Rhythmically the harpsichord is apt to specialize in derivations of the polyrhythm four against seven, while the piano ensemble uses five against three. These fields of specialization of the two groups are not carried out rigorously throughout the work but give way to the more important considerations which come from the fact that the two groups not only have different repertories of musical characters, gestures, logic, expression, and "behavioral" patterns, but that all of these are meant to be combined with each group and from group to group and result in recognizable overall patterns. The motion of the work is from comparative unity with slight character differences to greater and greater diversity of material and character and a return to unity. The form is that of confrontations of diversified action-patterns and a presentation of their mutual interreactions, conflicts, and resolutions, their growth and decay over various stretches of time.
>
> The Concerto, although continuous, falls into seven large interconnected sections. During the Introduction, the two groups in becoming progressively more differentiated state each facet of their material with greater and greater definition. The Cadenza for harpsichord presents in condensed form all the salient characteristics, rhythms and intervals of its ensemble. The *Allegro scherzando* is primarily for the piano ensemble with brief interruptions and comments by the other group. An *Adagio*, largely for the winds of both groups accompanied by accelerating and retarding figurations by the two soloists and the percussion joined occasionally by the strings, follows, and is concluded by an extended duet for the two soloists meeting at a stage in the piano's acceleration and the harpsichord's retardation only to separate as the piano proceeds toward its maximum speed while the harpsichord and its percussion proceed toward their minimum speed simultaneously.
>
> The *Presto* is for harpsichord and all the other instruments except the percussion and the piano, which later constantly interrupts with fragments of the

Adagio. Twice this soloist breaks into a short cadenza based on other elements of its material and its second cadenza leads to an amplification of the questioning inflections of the *Presto* by all the instruments with the percussion dominating. After a brief pause, the work closes with an extended Coda, using the entire ensemble in a series of long-phased oscillations (that include many subsidiary short-phased ones) from one group to the other, during which previous ideas are recalled in new contexts. Reversing the general plan of the Introduction (although not the musical one) these fragments lose their definition bit by bit, become shorter, sometimes more condensed, more dispersed, gradually merging into the slow waves of percussion rolls that move according to the basic polyrhythmic structure of the whole work.[3]

This fairly lengthy note has been quoted in full just to show how uninformative it is. Except for the matter of the relationship between intervals and metronomic speeds, which is left unexplained and arcane, the composer has disclosed nothing that an attentive hearing would not have revealed, perhaps with a peek at the score to corroborate the point about intervallic "repertories." (A glance at the double bass part in Ex. 6-1 will mostly confirm the intervallic repertory of the "harpsichord ensemble;" the wind and cello parts will do the same for the "piano ensemble.") In this it does not differ from the average descriptive sleeve note, often the work of office hacks. Nowhere is there any indication of purpose, whether for the assignment of intervals, or the "behavioral patterns," or the "polyrhythmic structure," or even for the sequence of events, the blow-by-blow narrative to which most of the note's detail is devoted. In other words, the description is entirely "formalist," predicated on Clement Greenberg's assumption, quoted in the previous chapter, that an artwork's form is tantamount to its content, and that (in the case of music) nothing beyond the sounds themselves requires description, let alone explanation.

The only hint at purpose or content comes in the single sentence where "action-patterns" are described in terms of confrontations, interreactions, conflicts, resolutions, growth, and decay, all of these being human actions and life phases. Of course the use of such terms to describe the behavior of musical sounds had a long history by 1961, and it is by no means certain that those who read the note would necessarily think of the literal meaning of the words, or that they were meant to. Nor is any clue given as to what such actions might signify, or (to fasten only on the most obvious musical question) what constitutes a resolution in such a harmonic idiom. The sentence is no more helpful, in other words, than the rest. Take the word "time" out of the sentence, in fact, and it could as easily have been a description of a painting as of a musical composition. Such language might easily have slid unnoticed into an essay or review about abstract expressionist canvases — say an "action" painting by Jackson Pollock — of a kind that by 1961 dominated the museum world and the art market.

The central Adagio, in which rhythm and tempo are at their runniest, is sampled in Ex. 6-2. The ingenious notation, which allows a single conductor to coordinate simultaneously steady, accelerating, and retarding tempi, actually disguises the central fact that the wind instruments (the slowest-moving parts) play at a steady rate. The score, in other words, looks altogether different from how the music is meant to sound—itself a fascinating aspect of the piece, if a somewhat baffling one. But why is all of this happening? Carter does not tell.

Britten would have spoken here of snobbery. Stravinsky, for his part, emphasized the Concerto's "interesting performance problems,"[4] commended Carter's choice of historical model (Berg's Chamber Concerto, he thought), then cheerfully confessed himself unable to understand the all but peerlessly patterned, detail-heavy music except in the broadest "gestural" terms. Giving it a twelve-tone pedigree suggests that Stravinsky was actually mistaken as to its technical premises, probably having made no attempt to parse its syntax. But Stravinsky did not think it ill bred of Carter to address him in a language he did not understand. Indeed, its very inscrutability magnified the Concerto's appeal, giving it an aura to which Stravinsky reacted as if to a religious revelation, declaring, "analysis as little explains a masterpiece or calls it into being as an ontological proof explains or causes the existence of God."[5] Then came the words that have been endlessly repeated in the literature that has grown up around Carter's music: "There, the word is out. A masterpiece, by an American composer." A masterpiece exists as such even (or especially?) when no one understands it, Stravinsky seems to imply. The process through which one recognizes a masterpiece, then, has more to do with pedigree than with cognitive intercommunication—with history, that is, not with society—and it is a matter of faith. Difficulty—especially conspicuous in Carter's music of the 1960s and 1970s, which had the most intricately detailed textures, the most complicated surfaces, and the most abstruse notation of any music of its time—was itself taken as an earnest of masterpiece status, as religious disclosure unveils what the Bible calls a "truth that passeth all understanding." It is remarkable that Stravinsky, who derided British critics for their "abasement" before a false masterpiece, assumed that very same stance to acknowledge what he took to be a true one.

Charles Rosen, the pianist in the first performance of the Double Concerto, offered a secular variation of Stravinsky's piety when he wrote that "it is important for a radically new work to be understood only little by little and too late," because "that is the only tangible proof we have of its revolutionary character."[6] On the face of it both Rosen's and Stravinsky's remarks are examples of a special kind of tautology known as the assumption of a false converse: if masterpieces are inscrutable, then what is inscrutable is a masterpiece; if what is revolutionary is understood too late, then what is not understood now is revolutionary.

Understood within the ideology of romantic historicism and its modernist extensions, the remarks are not difficult to interpret. If artists live only in evolutionary history, then their work has validity only to the extent that it makes a contribution to evolution. The most obvious contributions to evolution are revolutions. They address the future rather than the present. The only proper contemporary audience for a contemporary masterpiece, then, consists of evolutionary historians, whose awareness of historical process allows them to extrapolate from the past to the future. And sure enough, Carter's Double Concerto was given its very successful first performance at a concert held at New York's Metropolitan Museum of Art in conjunction with the Eighth Congress of the International Society for Musicology, at a time when evolutionary historicist views

EX. 6-2 Elliott Carter, Double Concerto, Adagio, mm. 360–374

EX. 6-2 *(continued)*

thoroughly dominated academic music studies. Carter's Concerto, from the moment of its unveiling, was a historic work in the narrowest sense of the word—the sense that, according to the ideology we have been tracing, specifically excluded the social.

FROM POPULISM TO PROBLEM SOLVING: AN AMERICAN CAREER

By the time Stravinsky and Rosen made their remarks, the view they upheld of Carter's music, and of musical value generally, accorded closely with the composer's own. But unlike them, Carter had evolved by slow degrees to the position they assumed as a given. Unlike Britten's, his development as a composer was sluggish and tortuous. The son of a wealthy lace importer, he never had to earn a living from his musical activity and was not particularly ambitious in his youth. His early training exactly paralleled Virgil Thomson's a decade earlier. From Harvard's Francophile music department he went to Paris to study for three years (1932–35) with Nadia Boulanger and came home a confirmed "neoclassicist."

During the following decade, that of the Great Depression and the Second World War, his music conformed to the pastoral and Americanist idioms associated with Copland, whom he praised in a 1939 review for discovering "a kind of beautiful simplicity which bears a definite spiritual relationship to the simple, direct, and honest people of this continent."[7] That same year Carter's ballet *Pocahontas* had its premiere performance by Ballet Caravan on a program that also included Copland's *Billy the Kid*. For his Symphony (1942), he took as a model Roy Harris's Third, in the words of Carter's pupil and biographer David Schiff "the unavoidable Great American Symphony of the day."[8] In one respect, however, Carter's background differed significantly from those of his colleagues in the *Boulangerie*. As a teenager he had met and been befriended by Charles Ives, who was then nearing the end of his active career as a composer. Thus, even before his exposure to Nadia Boulanger he was familiar with, and affected by, the "ultramodern" American music, unknown in Europe, that Ives was bankrolling as the primary sponsor of Henry Cowell's New Music Editions: Ives's own music (particularly the Fourth Symphony, the *Concord* Sonata, and *Three Places in New England*) and the work of Cowell (both his music and his "idea-book" *New Musical Resources*), Carl Ruggles, and Ruth Crawford Seeger.

This was a music of optimistic romantic spirit and enthusiastic experimentalism that retained a strong maximalist thrust in the face of European retrenchment. His formative exposure to it caused psychological problems for Carter during his years of study with Boulanger (one of the retrenchment's guiding spirits) and during his flirtation with the going American populism of the Roosevelt years. Its influence may have hindered his "populist" music from making the easy contact with its intended audience that Copland's enjoyed. In any case, Carter came to see his "social" overtures as unrequited.

At the same time, Boulanger's impressive mastery of traditional craftsmanship and her pedagogical emphasis on professionalism made Carter somewhat squeamish about the provincial American modernism that had nurtured him before his European sojourn. He betrayed his ambivalence in a condescending review of Ives's *Concord Sonata*, faulting it for its conventional (that is, romantic) rhetoric, its lack of formal logic, and an esthetic sensibility that is "often too naive to express serious thoughts, frequently depending on quotation of well-known American tunes, with little comment, possibly charming, but certainly trivial."[9] The review caused a painful and permanent rift in Carter's personal relations with his former mentor; but of course he was writing to and about himself and his own creative impasse, giving advice not to Ives but to himself. It took him a decade to reconcile the contradictions in his own esthetic sensibility; and he only succeeded by resolutely purging it of social aspirations.

Over that decade Carter came back to terms with his "ultramodern" inheritance, in a series of works that on the one hand aspired, or reaspired, to the epic rhetoric of the *Concord* Sonata, which was ultimately traceable to the "transcendent" image of Beethoven that Ives worshiped. This leaning is especially noticeable in Carter's own burly and virtuosic Piano Sonata of 1946. On the other hand, his works of the forties embodied a "problem-solving" attitude toward technique that seemed to put the composer's professional interests front and center, suggesting the research model of modernism already encountered in John Cage and the postwar serialists both in America and in Europe (and anticipated by Cowell's handbook). Carter began to acquire the reputation of a musician's musician—an "original, responsible, serious, adult composer," in the words of his friend and champion Richard Franko Goldman, "whose gifts have not been fully understood or widely appreciated," who "regards each new work as being in some respects a problem peculiar to itself," and who, in consequence, writes "music never lacking in skill but sometimes ingeniously uninteresting."[10]

In the Piano Sonata, piano resonance itself—novel effects obtained by the use of the sostenuto pedal and by silently depressing keys—was the object of technical investigation (not that these effects were unrelated to the Sonata's monumental expressive goals). In smaller works, including *Eight Etudes and a Fantasy* for woodwind quartet and *Six Studies for Four Timpani* (both 1950), the research could seem to be self-motivated, as the use of the term "étude" already attests. "I had become very concerned with the nature of musical ideas," Carter later wrote, "and started writing music that sought to find out what the minimal needs were for the kind of musical communication I felt worthwhile."[11]

Eight Etudes and a Fantasy actually originated in a Columbia University classroom, where Carter was teaching a course in orchestration in the summer of 1949. He sketched ingenious little experiments in woodwind texture on the blackboard to stimulate his pupils' imaginations in writing little pieces of their own to be tried out by a little team of hired players. The objective, clearly, was to make much of little: to construct a coherent musical design out of a minimum of raw material. In the first etude, the material consists of big, crisscrossing intervallic leaps that map out a maximum of textural space in a minimum of time. In the fourth, the material consists entirely of slurred pairs of eighth notes describing a rising semitone, treated like the little tiles that make up a mosaic.

In Etude no. 3 (Ex. 6-3a), the material has been boiled down to a single D-major triad (in the middle range shared by all the instruments), sustained throughout in kaleidoscopically shifting timbres as the players' instruments spell one another by entering and fading out imperceptibly. It is a famous curio, only to be exceeded as a tour de force of economy by no. 7 (Ex. 6-3b), which takes a single sustained pitch, the G above middle C, as a "theme" to be varied by overlapping dynamic shapes and assorted articulations. Carter described it as "draw[ing] out of the fifteen possible tone colors and their combinations and variants due to dynamic and attack differences, a musical discourse entirely dependent on contrasting various types of 'entrances': sharp, incisive attacks as opposed to soft entrances of other instruments."[12] Minimal needs, indeed. And yet the placement of a pair of loud unison attacks at the midpoint gives the seventh etude, despite its measly contents, a vivid shape.

The concluding Fantasy (written later, not at the blackboard) is a fugue on a very long subject combining motives from four of the Etudes. Over its course it "modulates" from the tempo of the first etude to that of the seventh, then the second, and so on, motivic elements of the relevant etude coming to the fore as episodes at each tempo station. At various points the subject is heard in stretto at two tempos simultaneously,

EX. 6-3A   Elliott Carter, *Eight Etudes and a Fantasy*, Etude no. 3

EX. 6-3A   *(continued)*

*"Sneak entrances" throughout this movement.

EX. 6-3B   Elliott Carter, *Eight Etudes and a Fantasy*, Etude no. 7 (beginning)

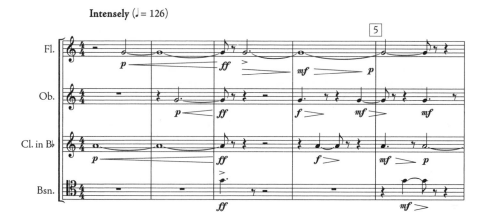

EX. 6-3B (*continued*)

their relationship translated into conventionally notated note-lengths. In the second measure of Ex. 6-4, the bassoon plays the opening of the subject at a metronome rate of [quarter] = 84, the tempo of Etude No. 1, against a statement in the flute that proceeds in even notes of seven sixteenths' duration. The flute is thus playing in a durational ratio of 7:4 vis-à-vis the bassoon. Another way of putting this would be that the flute is playing at a metronomic beat rate of 48, since (7:4) × 12 = 84:48.

The source of this playful superimposition of tempi is, of course, the music of Ives: e.g. the contest of two bands at the middle of "Putnam's Camp" from *Three Places in New England*. Carter has reestablished contact with Ives's example, but only after having extended it to a more arcane ratio (Ives's being a simple 3:2) and abstracting it from its programmatic context. Another, more dynamic sort of superimposition comes at the end of the Fantasy, where the subject is accelerated to the point where it disappears into the blur of a trill while at the same time it is played as a cantus firmus in longer note-values than ever. Each of the instruments participates at various points in both processes.

EX. 6-4 Elliott Carter, *Eight Etudes and a Fantasy*, Fantasy, mm. 108–111

EX. 6-4   (*continued*)

The timpani studies, which were revised and augmented by an additional pair for publication in 1966 (as *Eight Pieces for Four Timpani*), continue the rhythmic explorations of the woodwind Fantasy, with particular emphasis on the technique of proportional, exactly calibrated tempo "modulation." The most sophisticated and thoroughgoing example of it comes in the middle of the seventh piece, called "Canaries" (Ex. 6-5). The title, which may seem surprising in a piece for timpani (and was probably chosen with that surprise in mind), refers not to household warblers but rather to a fast jig-like dance, all leaping and stamping, that was imported to Spain from the Canary Islands in the sixteenth century.

A steady pulse of dotted quarters is established in the third measure of Ex. 6-5. It crosscuts the notated quarter-note pulse, set at the metronome rate of MM96. The relationship between a dotted quarter and a quarter is the hemiola proportion, 3:2. Therefore the metronome speed that would correspond to the dotted-quarter pulse is $\frac{2}{3}$ of 96, or MM64. That shift takes place in m. 6 of the example, and is reinforced by doubling: the timpanist plays the renotated pulse with both hands, using all four drums. The whole passage that follows pits the constant pulse in the timpanist's left hand against a constantly accelerating pulse in the right.

First (m. 8) the right hand reverts to the old quarter note, at 3/2 times the speed of the dotted quarter in the left. In m. 9 the parenthetical accents imply a pulse duration such that two quarters = $\frac{4}{3}$ of the dotted quarter at MM64, or twice the original quarter at MM96, either way implying a pulse of $\frac{1}{2}$ MM96 or MM48. At m. 10 that half-note pulse is filled with three triplet quarters: the right hand has accelerated once again by a hemiola ratio of 3:2. This time the pulse in the right hand is 3 × 48 or MM144, while the left hand is still beating at a rate of MM64. The proportion 144:64 reduces to 9:4, which is why the notation in m. 10 suddenly looks complicated. Notated in terms of the new right-hand pulse, the old left-hand pulse equals 9 sixteenth notes under a triplet bracket. Only the visual appearance of the notation (and the wordy descriptive prose that is now tracking it) are complicated, however; to the ear, two successive hemiola proportions — (3:2) × (3:2) = 9:4 — are easy to follow.

The notation is eased in m. 11, when the triplet brackets are removed, and the new pulse is specified instead by the metronome setting. There is no audible difference between m. 10 and m. 11, except that now the right hand is once again preparing for a hemiola proportion, grouping its quarters by twos. The new implied half-note pulse, as Carter's setting specifies, is MM72. When it is filled by a triplet, as happens in m. 12, the triplet quarter will run at a spiffy MM216. Since 216:64 reduces to 27:8, or (3:2) × (3:2) × (3:2), the old pulse of MM64, still plodding along in the left hand, must now be represented as a duration of twenty-seven thirty-second notes against the right hand's quarter. At m. 17 yet another hemiola proportion is prepared, by grouping the new quarter pulse by two (implying a pulse of MM108) and then dividing the implied half note into a triplet (each quarter now zipping by at MM324!). The new notation of the old pulse now becomes even more finicky, since the notation has followed the right hand through four hemiolas, and the left-hand duration must now be represented as the equivalent of eighty-one sixty-fourth notes, since (324:64) ÷ 4 = 81:16.

At this point the limit of practicable speed has been reached by the timpanist's right hand, and so the pattern of successive hemiolas is broken. The two hands begin alternating in a duple pattern at the rate of the fastest triplets, implying a quarter note pulse that is half of MM324 (= MM162, as notated in m. 24). The notation becomes simple again, but not because the music has become more simple. The complications in

EX. 6-5   Elliott Carter, *Eight Pieces for Four Timpani,* "Canaries," middle section

the notation paradoxically arose in connection with the simplest element in the music: the steady, absolutely fixed and immutable left-hand pulse.

The only way to make the relationships between the constant pulse and the changing pulse metronomically exact was to continually readjust the notation to show the changes, leaving the constant element to adapt. (The weird notation of the Adagio from the Double Concerto in Ex. 6-2 is a more complicated instance of the same principle.) Timpanists performing the piece do not actually have to count durations of twenty-seven thirty-seconds or eighty-one sixty-fourths. All they need to do is keep their left hand swinging at a constant rate and concentrate on the changing patterns in the right. Woodwind and brass players in the Double Concerto's Adagio face a similar problem.

Although the main preoccupation (or compositional "problem") in "Canaries" is obviously rhythmic, the pitches are also organized in a way that reflects preoccupation with "the formation of ideas with minimal material," and that became equally characteristic of Carter's music. From the set of four pitch-classes to which the timpani are tuned (EBC♯F, reading its actual pitches from the bottom up), every interval from the semitone to the tritone can be extracted, which means that every interval there is can be extracted from the given tetrachord, since all other intervals are either inversions or compounds of the basic six (sometimes called "interval classes"). Such "all interval tetrachords," as they are now called in the theoretical literature, are the most economical possible way of expressing (or implying) the full range of intervallic possibilities. There are exactly two such tetrachords. The one Carter used in "Canaries" can be represented in closest spacing as /0 1 4 6/ reading up or down (in this case down from F). The other is /0 1 3 7/. All-interval tetrachords play an increasingly prominent role in Carter's music from this point on, for reasons that will later emerge more fully.

THEORY: THE TIME SCREEN

Tempo modulation, often called "metrical modulation" (a misnomer coined by Goldman in his article of 1951), is Carter's trademark innovation, although (as he has pointed out to more than one interviewer)

> there is nothing new about [it] but the name. To limit brief mention of its derivations to notated Western music: it is implicit in the rhythmic procedures of late fourteenth-century French music, as it is in music of the fifteenth and sixteenth centuries that uses hemiola and other ways of alternating meters, especially duple and triple. From then on, since early sets of variations like those of Byrd and Bull started a tradition of establishing tempo relationships between movements, tempo modulation began to relate movements of one piece together, as can be seen in many works of Beethoven, not only in the variations of Op. 111, but in many places where *doppio movimento* and other terms are used to delineate [exact] tempo relationships. In fact, at that very time, the metronome was invented, which establishes relationships between all tempi. In our time, Stravinsky, following Satie, perhaps, wrote a few works around 1920 whose movements were closely linked by a very narrow range of tempo relationships, and much later Webern did the same.[13]

Carter has also listed various non-Western traditions — Indian, Arabic, Balinese, and West African — as sources of his rhythmic techniques, as well as "jazz of the thirties and forties that combined free improvisation with strict time." The sheer cited range calls for comment, not so much because it flaunts erudition, but because it suggests an important difference between mid-twentieth-century composers and those who lived before the widespread dissemination of sound recordings. Thanks to records, which Carter explicitly acknowledged as the source of his knowledge of African music, but which were probably also a gateway to early Western music (just then being commercially recorded on an unprecedented scale), a composer could live, as Henry Cowell once put it, "in the whole world of music" in a way that could never previously have been imagined.

Like Carter, many composers with this sort of access to such a diversity of musics began to think newly of themselves as universalists or omnibus synthesizers. It gave them a much more immediate contact with exotic musics of all kinds, and a newly immediate sense of themselves as living in history, not only as direct recipients of a particular tradition, but as heirs to the sum total of musical culture. For some, that realization brought with it a vastly magnified consciousness of heritage and obligation. It gave Carter a sense of responsibility toward music and its development, and a new sense of purpose. Or that, at least, is the way he has described his development to Allen Edwards, a sort of Boswell who interviewed him at length and fashioned a widely-read book, *Flawed Words and Stubborn Sounds*, out of Carter's responses. Carter's account of his shift in musical interests has an important bearing on the social and historical issues that this chapter and the previous one jointly address.

Carter has dated the change to the year 1944, which, coincidentally or not, was the year in which his *Holiday Overture*, his most overtly "populist" composition, was rejected for performance by Koussevitzky and the Boston Symphony, despite Copland's enthusiastic sponsorship. In that year, he told his interlocutor,

> I suddenly realized that, at least in my own education, people had always been concerned only with this or that peculiar local rhythmic combination or sound-texture or novel harmony and had forgotten that the really interesting thing about music is the time of it—the way it all goes along. Moreover, it struck me that, despite the newness and variety of the post-tonal musical vocabulary, most modern pieces generally "went along" in an all-too-uniform way on their higher architectonic levels. That is, it seemed to me that, while we had heard every imaginable kind of harmonic and timbral combination, and while there had been a degree of rhythmic innovation on the *local* level in the music of Stravinsky, Bartók, Varèse, and Ives particularly, nonetheless the way all this went together at the next higher and succeeding higher rhythmic levels remained in the orbit of what had begun to seem to me the rather limited rhythmic routine of previous Western music. This fact began to bother me enough so that I tried to think in larger-scale time-continuities of a kind that would be still convincing and yet at the same time *new* in a way commensurate with, and appropriate to, the richness of the modern musical vocabulary.[14]

"What contemporary music needs," he went on,

> is not just raw materials of every kind but a way of relating these—of having them evolve during the course of a work in a sharply meaningful way; that is,

what is needed is never just a string of "interesting passages," but works whose central interest is constituted by the way everything that happens in them happens *as* and *when* it does in relation to everything else. I feel very strongly about this, just because ever since 1944 I have realized that ultimately the matter of musical time is vastly more important than the particulars or the novelty of the musical vocabulary, and that the morphological elements of any music owe their musical effect almost entirely to their specific "placing" in the musical time-continuity.[15]

One could hardly express a fuller commitment to the idea of research and development as the composer's primary task. One's entire responsibility as an artist, as Carter here envisions it, is to maintain the pace of technical innovation set by one's predecessors, to make sure that it applies equally to all musical parameters, and direct its course toward the most productive possible historical evolution. Above all, one must "prioritize" one's goals. Carter is very critical of the work of many if not most of his contemporaries:

It seems to me that many of the works of the Darmstadt school of composers have suffered greatly from the attempt to apply certain mistaken "philosophic conceptions" of time to music itself, though it is clear that the attractiveness of these conceptions about, say, the "interchangeability of musical moments" [a reference to Stockhausen] has its roots in the kind of visually- and spatially-derived mechanistic thinking that originally produced total serialism [a reference to Boulez, and, possibly, to Babbitt as well] and was unconcerned from the outset with the problem of time-continuity and of producing feelings of tension and release and therefore of musical motion in the listener, but dealt rather with unusualness of aural effect, thus reducing music to mere physical sound.[16]

But he shares their commitment to innovation as a primary obligation mandated by history, whatever the consequences may be in terms of the popularity or comprehensibility of the result outside (or even inside) the boundaries of the profession. Carter outlined his own "philosophic conceptions" in an essay called "Music and the Time Screen," which he delivered as a lecture at the University of Texas in 1971 and later published. The discussion recalls somewhat the second lecture in Stravinsky's *Poetics of Music*, with its little dissertation — borrowed from Pierre Souvtchinsky, who had borrowed it from Henri Bergson — on the distinction between ontological (or objective) time, ticked off by a clock, and psychological (or subjective) time, meaning time as we humanly perceive it.

The difference is that where Stravinsky had been content to present the pair as a bald and (for music) value-laden contrast, ontological correlating with "classic" (good) and psychological with "romantic" (bad) musical habits, Carter sees music as deriving its value from its capacity to mediate between the two aspects of time. He adopts as his model a celebrated philosophical discussion of music in Susanne Langer's esthetic treatise *Feeling and Form* (1953). Time is, on the one hand, the experience of passage, and, on the other, the experience of change. Passage is measured by change, which in turn (here Carter quotes Langer; the ellipses are his):

is measured by contrasting two states of an instrument, whether that instrument be the sun in various positions, or the hand on a dial at successive locations, or a parade of monotonous similar events like ticks or clashes, "counted," i.e. differentiated, by being correlated with a series of distinct numbers . . . . "Change" is not itself something represented; it is implicitly given through the contrast of different "states" themselves unchanging.

The time concept which emerges from such mensuration is something far removed from time as we know it in direct experience, which is essentially *passage*, or the sense of transience . . . . But the experience of time is anything but simple. It involves more properties than "length," or interval between selected moments; for its passages have also what I can only call, metaphorically, *volume*. Subjectively, a unit of time may be great or small as well as long or short. It is this voluminousness of the direct experience of passage, that makes it . . . indivisible. But even its volume is not simple; for it is filled with its own characteristic forms, otherwise it could not be observed and appreciated . . . . The primary image of music is the sonorous image of passage, abstracted from actuality to become free and plastic and entirely perceptible.[17]

The deliberate representation of that sonorous image of existence as temporal, Carter asserted, was what the task of all music should be, and what the task of *his* music, uniquely, actually was. By analogy with Langer's "contrasting states," Carter sought ways of combining and contrasting aspects of time—of "passage" or unfolding—within a single texture. For example: the first movement of Carter's Cello Sonata (written last) combines what in his essay he calls "chronometric" time (that is, regular isochrony or equal pulses) in the piano against "chrono-ametric" time (irregular mixtures of values producing a rubato effect) in the cello (Ex. 6-6).

EX. 6-6   Elliott Carter, Cello Sonata, I, opening

EX. 6-6 *(continued)*

To illustrate "metric modulation" in "Music and the Time Screen," Carter selected the passage from "Canaries" for timpani given in Ex. 6-5, and commented that "to the listener, this passage should sound as if the left hand keeps up a steady beat throughout the passage, not participating in the modulations."[18] In this way, he said, he sought to incorporate elements of both kinds of time experience, as Stravinsky had dichotomized them: "pure duration" as against the distortions of our time sense wrought by "expectation, anxiety, sorrow, suffering, fear, contemplation, pleasure, all of which could not be grasped if there were not a primary sensation of 'real' or 'ontological' time."[19] As Carter developed these ideas in his music of the 1950s and 1960s, "the primary questions" he sought to answer in his work as a composer were these: "How are events presented, carried on, and accompanied? What kind of changes can previously presented events undergo while maintaining some element of identity? and, How can all this be used to express compelling aspects of experience to the listener?"[20] His attempts to answer them led him to what he called a special dimension of time, that of "multiple perspective" in which various contrasting characters are presented simultaneously — as was occasionally done in opera, for example, in the ballroom scene from *Don Giovanni*, or in the finale of *Aïda*. Double and sometimes manifold character simultaneities, of course, present, as our human experience often does, certain emotionally charged events as seen in the context of others, producing often a kind of irony, which I am particularly interested in. In doing this so frequently, and by leading into and away from such moments in what seemed to me telling ways, I have, I think, been trying to make moments of music as rich in reference as I could and to do something that can be done only in music and yet that has rarely been achieved except in opera.[21]

Eventually, Carter began to experiment with ways of allowing the components of his multiple perspectives to develop independently rather than present statically contrasting characters. This made for situations — simultaneous accelerandos and ritardandos combined with regular beating, for example, as found in the Double Concerto — that were almost impossible to notate exactly, giving the music the exceedingly forbidding visual appearance that can mislead score-readers even as it conveys essential information to performers. That begins to hint at some of the problems that Carter's music, despite its "minimal" materials and its ingenuous expressive aims, has created not only for listeners but even for professional analysts, and to suggest why his music, like the total serialism he despises, has acquired a reputation for intellectual abstraction and perceptual opacity. The interesting, historically significant point is that such a reputation did nothing to hinder, and much to facilitate, Carter's belated but inexorable progress to eminence, and even preeminence, among the composers of his generation.

PRACTICE: THE FIRST QUARTET

The first composition in which Carter implemented the new musical resources he had developed in the late 1940s at full strength, and over the sustained time span of a "major" work, was his First String Quartet, composed between the fall of 1950 and the spring of 1951 while living on a Guggenheim Fellowship in the lower Sonoran Desert near Tucson, Arizona. That bare biographical fact has done much to encourage Carter's "hermetic" image — deserts, after all, are where hermits live. But Carter himself has knowingly contributed to the mythology surrounding the Quartet. Earlier, he confessed, he had allowed "the desire to remain within the realm of the performable and auditorily distinguishable divisions of time" to restrain his imaginative speculations. But now, "there were so many emotional and expressive experiences that I kept having, and so many notions of processes and continuities, especially musical ones — fragments I could find no ways to use in my compositions — that I decided to leave my usual New York activities to seek the undisturbed quiet to work these out."[22]

Many writers have resorted to undisguised religious imagery when writing about the gestation of the First Quartet: a "monastic" seclusion, a "conversion," following which "a new composer emerged," in David Schiff's frankly hagiographical account, "uncompromising and visionary."[23] But as we know all too well, the word "uncompromising" had social and political as well as religious connotations in the context of the cold war, and Carter corroborated them fully when he told Allen Edwards that the Quartet was his way of "say[ing] to hell with the public and with the performers too."[24] From now on he would identify with the romantic, asocial concept of artistry in its priestliest form, as defined for the twentieth century in the passage from the French theologian Jacques Maritain that stands at the head of the previous chapter. He was now an *artifex*, as unconcerned with edifying the public as he was with shocking it. Henceforth his reference would be to his art alone, and to its history—both the history he had inherited and the history he would make.

The First Quartet is a monumentally engineered construction of multiple perspectives, each of its four movements embodying the idea in a different way. So intent was Carter on the centrality of process over state as the basis of his musical conceptions that he placed the "movement breaks" (or breaks for relaxation) not between the movements but within the second and the fourth movements. All actual progressions between movements are executed without break, by means of "tempo modulation." The Quartet thus displays its four structural divisions in three temporal spans — $[(1 \rightarrow 2) (2 \rightarrow 4) (\rightarrow 4)]$ — already a kind of polyrhythm.

The first movement, "Fantasia," is a study in fixed vs. fluid tempi like Ex. 6-6, but on a vast scale. A number of themes, each associated with a certain tempo (that is an "absolute" or "ontological" clock-measured beat-duration) are put through a series of polyrhythmic (or "polytemporal") montages, each linked with the next by taking one of the tempos as a constant, just as a simple harmonic modulation is a linking of tonalities through a pivot chord, a harmony common to both keys (see Ex. 6-7). The rhapsodic opening solo for the cello is cast in a sort of composed rubato like the beginning of the solo part in Ex. 6-6: diverse note values are mixed together, while accents and long notes are often placed at variance with the notated beat. That rhythmic freedom is contradicted by the regularity of the violin pizzicatos that enter in m. 12, corresponding in its strict sequence of dotted eighths with the regularity of the piano part in Ex. 6-6.

The violin's equal (or isochronous) beats set up the movement's first steady tempo tread. Each note being $\frac{3}{4}$ the value of the notated beat, the violin's implied tempo ($\frac{4}{3}$ of MM72) is MM96. That is the first measured acceleration, or tempo modulation. The next acceleration is led by the cello, which in m. 14 begins breaking up the MM72 beat into quintuplets. Under the quintuplet brace a sixteenth note goes at $5 \times$ MM72, or MM360. At m. 17, the same notes are grouped by threes rather than fives; as the composer notes, the resulting implied dotted-quarter beat is now MM360 $\div$ 3, or MM120. The cello actually begins moving in dotted quarters in m. 20, and two measures later that value is equated with a new quarter-note pulse at MM120. That is the second measured acceleration, once again by an increment of MM24.

At this point (m. 22) the second violin reenters with the same music as in m. 12, transposed up an octave. This time its durations are notated as quarters tied to sixteenths (= five sixteenths, $\frac{5}{4}$ of the notated beat) rather than dotted eighths (= three sixteenths, $\frac{3}{4}$ of the notated beat). But the absolute duration or tempo of the theme is identical on its two appearances, since $\frac{4}{3}$ of MM72 is the same as $\frac{4}{5}$ of MM120: both equal MM96 as in m. 12. The process of successive tempo montages linked by tempo modulations continues throughout the movement.

EX. 6-7   Elliott Carter, String Quartet no. 1, I, mm. 1–29

EX. 6-7 (continued)

The passage beginning at m. 22 is the first in which the entire quartet takes part. Its texture—four separate lines, all radically differentiated in rhythm and, usually, in character—is typical. All the instruments play regular beat-sequences. The cello's regular pulse at MM120 forms the basis of the notation. The viola, entering at m. 25 (past the end of Ex. 6-7), plays three notes to the cello's two; its implied tempo is $\frac{3}{2}$ MM120, or MM180. The second violin, as noted, continues at a rate of MM96. The first violin, although it plays quietly, is sufficiently differentiated from the rest of the texture by its legato articulation to take on the role of soloist, performing a melody that will often recur. Its first four notes are all $3\frac{1}{3}$ $(\frac{10}{3})$ times the length of the notated beat; hence it moves at an implied tempo of $\frac{3}{10}$ MM120, or MM36 (see Ex. 6-8a for a simpler notation), exactly half the speed of the original marked tempo.

The cello, reentering at m. 27, displaces the first violin in the foreground, as Carter marks explicitly. It plays a six-note theme in values notated as halves tied to eighths, or $2\frac{1}{2}$ $(\frac{5}{2})$ times the rate of the notated beat. Its metronome pulse, therefore, is $\frac{2}{5}$ MM120, or MM48. It is given a simpler notation in Ex. 6-8b. Its source is shown in Ex. 6-8c, for it is a quotation of the opening phrase of Ives's First Violin Sonata, a score Ives had sent Carter in manuscript photostat in 1928. Quoting it was an homage to the man whose rhythmic explorations had sparked Carter's own, and perhaps also an act of atonement for the slight delivered in 1939.

EX. 6-8A   Renotations from Elliott Carter, String Quartet no. 1, I, first violin at m. 22

EX. 6-8B   Renotations from Elliott Carter, String Quartet no. 1, I, cello at m. 27

EX. 6-8C   Charles Ives, Violin Sonata no. 1, mm. 1–2 (piano)

Once the cello has begun the Ives quotation, incidentally, none of the instruments is actually playing at the rate of the notated pulse, but all are coordinating their playing with it as a way of keeping together. That is a very common situation in the Quartet. As Carter implied in conversation with Edwards, it is one that is also encountered in a good deal of fourteenth- and fifteenth-century "mensural" music, and very little in between. Carter's rhythmic idiom, beginning with the First Quartet, could thus be termed a modernized and expanded mensural system, with all that the term implies — namely, that notated durations no longer have inherent metrical significance but denote only spans of time that can be freely manipulated and interrelated.

EX. 6-9   Elliott Carter, String Quartet no. 1, I, mm. 197–204

Another spot that resembles the textures of late-medieval music (and that could actually be notated more easily using fifteenth-century notation) is the stretto that begins in the cello and viola at m. 197 (Ex. 6-9). Every instrument as it enters plays at a rate exactly $\frac{3}{2}$ that of the instrument directly beneath it in the score. It is in effect a multiple projection of the successive hemiolas in "Canaries" (Ex. 6-5): the viola plays three dotted quarters against a pair of the cello's nine-sixteenth-note durations, the second violin plays three quarters against a pair of the viola's dotted quarters, and the first violin plays a triplet to each pair of quarters in the second violin. In mm. 201–203, all instruments play even notes in a proportion of 27:18::12:8; the outer numbers reduce to $3^3 : 2^3$, a relationship that would have gladdened the heart of Philippe de Vitry, the venerable theorist of the "Ars Nova"; compare a famous spot (well, famous among musicologists) from Du Fay's *Missa L'Homme Armé*, ca. 1465 (Ex. 6-10).

The passage of successive "prolations" at m. 197 epitomizes the generally accelerating course that leads the first movement into the second, marked *Allegro scorrevole* (fast and flowing), a favorite Carter designation. We can chart the transition by reentering the movement at m. 282, where a sort of recapitulation begins. Themes (though not keys, of which there are no unequivocal examples) begin coming back, starting with a reprise,

EX. 6-10 Guillaume Du Fay, *Missa L'Homme Armé*, Credo, "Genitum non factum est"

EX. 6-10   (*continued*)

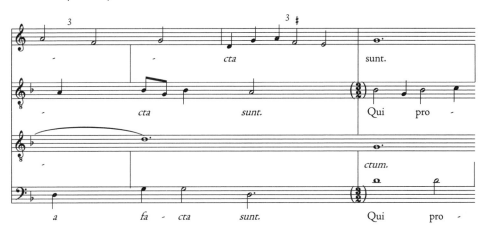

in the viola, of the Ives quotation, embedded this time in a texture that is notated using a quarter-note pulse of MM160.

The viola performs a composed accelerando: the first note of the Ives quotation lasts seventeen eighths, the second fifteen, the third twelve, the fourth just a little under ten. But starting with the F♯ in m. 293, the viola settles into a steady tempo. That note lasts five half notes where the half note is set at MM120. A series of notes that length would move at $\frac{1}{5}$ of MM120, or MM24. But starting in m. 297, the viola begins moving at twice that rate, with notes lasting five eighths under a new metronome setting in which the half-note (=four eighths) is set at MM60. Since $\frac{4}{5}$ MM60 equals MM48, it turns out that the viola has regained the exact original tempo of the "Ives" theme, in preparation for the huge polyrhythmic montage at mm. 312–350, a climactically expanded recapitulation of the original montage in mm. 22–30. Its beginning is shown in Ex. 6-11.

EX. 6-11   Elliott Carter, String Quartet no. 1, I, mm. 312–23

EX. 6-11 (*continued*)

The cello here recapitulates the viola's music at m. 25, and at exactly the same tempo, MM180 (thrice MM60). The first violin recapitulates a theme first heard in the second violin at m. 41, and again at the same tempo, MM300 (5 × MM60). The second violin recapitulates a lyrical melody that was first heard in the viola at m. 70 ff, and again (in simpler notation) in the first violin at m. 112 ff. (The notation at m. 112 is simpler because the metronome pulse (MM135) coincides there with the violin's quarter note.) At m. 312 the relationship between the second violin's tempo and the metronomic pulse is so complicated that Carter supplied an alternative notation to clarify it, but a little computation will show that it is the same tempo as before. Each note now takes four eighths where a group of nine eighths fills the time of a measure at MM60. Each note, therefore, is $\frac{4}{9}$ of a measure, which means that the tune moves at a rate of $\frac{9}{4}$ MM60, or MM135.

The tempi here are so radically differentiated in beat length that—provided the Quartet is well enough performed so that the players are not emphasizing their occasional coincident pulses for the sake of ensemble—one can really sense a texture made up of "multiple perspectives," all coordinated to a single conceptual pulse but perceptually independent of it. It is a heady sensation, likened by Virgil Thomson after the first performance to "four intricately integrated solos all going on at the same time," and well justifying Thomson's unusually enthusiastic description of the Quartet as being "complex of texture, delicious in sound, richly expressive and in every way grand."[25]

One of the things that made the Quartet seem both grand and richly expressive was its deployment of large, dramatic gestures. As the Fantasia's concluding montage proceeds, it also gradually ascends in pitch. By m. 345 all four instruments are sawing away in their highest registers; the breakthrough into the *Allegro scorrevole* — led by the second violin, whose MM135 becomes the uniform fast tempo of the ensemble — can be heard as the inevitable result of applying further pressure to a situation already at the limit of tension. The speed of the second movement is exactly that of the fastest moment in the first (m. 105).

Thematic material for the second movement is drawn entirely from the seven-note motif first heard in violin I in m. 356, and again immediately afterward, inverted and split between the two violins in m. 357 (Ex. 6-12a). As Ex. 6-12b shows, this motif contains both all-interval tetrachords, thus providing a link with the harmonic idiom of the first movement, many of whose themes and local harmonies (like the first four-part chord in the Quartet, m. 5) are similarly constructed. Later in the second movement, when a homophonic or chorale-like texture briefly succeeds the mosaic texture of the outset, the harmonies are again often constructed out of all-interval tetrachords (Ex. 6-12c). The last movement reaches its climax with a passage in which the 0 1 4 6/all-interval tetrachord acts as a universal harmonic regulator to govern the counterpoint (Ex. 6-12d).

EX. 6-12A   Elliott Carter, String Quartet no. 1, violins at mm. 356–7

EX. 6-12B   Elliott Carter, String Quartet no. 1, II, all-interval tetrachords in basic motive

EX. 6-12C   Elliott Carter, String Quartet no. 1, II, all-interval tetrachords as harmonies

EX. 6-12D   Elliott Carter, String Quartet no. 1, IV, all-interval tetrachord as contrapuntal regulator

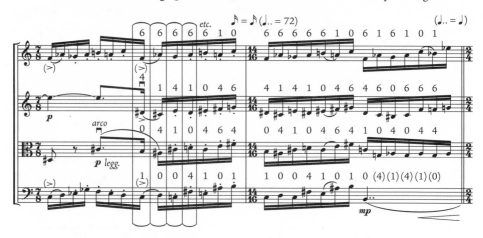

The third movement, Adagio, is another homage to Ives. Like the latter's *The Unanswered Question*, the texture is split between a placid homorhythmic background (the two violins, muted) and an agonized, recitativelike music (viola and cello) in the foreground, all in all a very dramatic rendering of "multiple perspectives." The last movement, titled "Variations," returns to the complicated textures of the first, with even more strongly profiled and differentiated themes (if less complicated polyrhythms in combination), all put through a giddy process of constantly accelerating tempo modulation.

The most dramatic instance is the theme heard in the cello right after the second movement-break, sounding at first like a cantus firmus or passacaglia bass. It is subjected to the sort of motivic development promised by the movement's title, but it also recurs fourteen times in literal form, each time at a faster tempo than the last, until, having accelerated to a tempo twenty-one times that of its initial appearance it reaches the "vanishing point,"[26] as Carter described it, lapsing into a tremolo (Ex. 6-13).

By way of conclusion, the first violin plays a reminiscence of the cello's introductory solo from the beginning of the first movement. Accompanied at one point by the limit-tremolo in the other parts, it has a fraught quality reminiscent of the accompanied violin recitative in the last movement of Beethoven's Quartet in A minor, op. 132. It brings the whole composition full circle, providing a sort of tonal closure when the violin shoots up at the very end to the note E, with which the cello launched its solo at the other end of the Quartet.

But there is another significance to the "cyclic" ending. Carter has told interviewers that he was thinking of Jean Cocteau's surrealist film *The Blood of a Poet* (1933), in which "the entire dream-like action is framed by an interrupted slow-motion shot of a tall brick chimney in an empty lot being dynamited; just as the chimney begins to fall apart, the shot is broken off and the entire movie follows, after which the shot of the chimney is resumed at the point it left off, showing its disintegration in mid-air, and closing the film with its collapse on the ground." The effect establishes a "difference between external time (measured by the falling chimney, or the cadenza) and internal dream

EX. 6-13   Progress of "passacaglia" theme in Elliott Carter, String Quartet no. 1, IV

EX. 6-13 *(continued)*

time (the main body of the work)—the dream time lasting but a moment of external time but from the dreamer's point of view, a long stretch."[27] Multiple perspectives, again, this time on the "global" or structurally unifying level.

RECEPTION

As the excerpts quoted from Virgil Thomson's review have already shown, Carter's quartet enjoyed a remarkable *succès d'estime*, or "reputation success." It taught him a lesson, as he has put it, "about my relationship with performers and audiences." For

> as I wrote, an increasing number of musical difficulties arose for prospective performers and listeners, which the musical conception seemed to demand. I often wondered whether the quartet would ever have any performers or listeners. Yet within a few years of its composition it won an important prize and was played (always with a great deal of rehearsal) more than any work I had written up to that time. It even received praise from admired colleagues.[28]

The paradox not only taught him that he had been wrong to feel it his "professional and social responsibility to write interesting, direct, easily understood music;" it impelled or emboldened him to assert that any composer who followed such a mandate was wrong. On the contrary, he now maintained, "there is every reason to assume that if a composer has been well taught and has had experience (as was true of me in 1950), then his private judgment of comprehensibility and quality is what he must rely on if he is to communicate importantly."

The last word is of course the key, for it is the one that carries implications about value. Carter had indeed communicated importantly. A closer look at the reception his work has enjoyed will shed more light on what it was that made it seem so important just then, and to whom. At first, things went more or less as he expected. He had to wait more than a year before an ensemble — the Walden Quartet of the University of Illinois, to whom the work was eventually dedicated — signaled its willingness to tackle the score. The premiere took place on 26 February 1953 at Columbia University, during a festival of American music sponsored in part by the local public radio station, WNYC. The academic affiliation of the performing group, the academic venue, and the subsidized occasion were all indicative of the kind of marginal public existence an "advanced" composition could count on.

The prize to which Carter refers in the extract above was awarded later in 1953 by the jury of the *Councours international de quatuor* (International quartet-writing competition), held in Liège, Belgium, to which Carter had submitted the work (under the contest pseudonym Chronometros, "time-keeper"). The award guaranteed a performance by the Paris-based Parrenin Quartet, one of Europe's most prestigious ensembles specializing in contemporary music. Their performance, Carter's European debut, took place in Rome, in April 1954, at a music festival presented under the auspices of the Congress for Cultural Freedom. It was greeted with a euphoric review in *Encounter*, the Congress's English-language organ, by the British critic and publisher William Glock, who ran a sort of mini-Darmstadt for British musicians in the village of Dartington, where Carter was a frequent lecturer. (Later, as the powerful controller of music at the BBC, Glock would be one of Carter's most active promoters.) The performance and the review, as David Schiff observes, "immediately established Carter's European reputation."[29]

They did more than that. They plugged Carter's new direction into the politics of the cold war. The Congress for Cultural Freedom was established in West Berlin in 1950, at the instigation of Ernst Reuter, the city's mayor, and with financial backing from the American Military Government (arranged by Melvin Lasky, an American trade unionist serving as a cultural attaché with the Army of Occupation and editor of its German-language monthly *Der Monat*). The organization's Secretary General or director was the composer Nicolas Nabokov (1903–78), a cousin of the more famous writer Vladimir Nabokov, and an old acquaintance of Carter's. (In 1940–41 they had between them made up the music staff at St. John's College, Annapolis.) Similar in origin to the Darmstadt Summer Courses, but with a wider purview and a far more glamorous cast of characters, the Congress was set up to showcase the arts and sciences of the "free world," especially undertakings of a modernist, individualist variety that totalitarian powers rejected and harassed.

Unlike Darmstadt, the Congress had an overt and militant political agenda. Its fundamental purpose, in the words of the American philosopher Sidney Hook, one of its founding members, was to combat "the virus of neutralism that was spiritually disarming the West against Communist aggression."[30] Its first major undertaking was a festival, Masterpieces of the Twentieth Century, a comprehensive exposition of music, painting, sculpture, and literature held in Paris in 1952, with Stravinsky as the guest of honor and nominal spokesman. The main musical tactic was the programming, in an effort to embarrass the Soviets, of several major works of Prokofieff and Shostakovich that were then under a post-Zhdanov ban in their own country. Their promotion as masterpieces, and their reception (by audiences, by some critics, and certainly by Stravinsky), had as much a political as an esthetic motivation.

The Congress was not very successful in its chief mission, that of containing the spread of Communist thinking among European intellectuals in the first decades of the cold war. And it was thoroughly discredited in the mid-1960s when it became known that it had been surreptitiously funded by the Central Intelligence Agency, the notorious bureau of the United States Government for espionage that had been created in 1947 as an instrument of cold-war policy. Sidney Hook complained that Nabokov's arts festivals, the Congress's most conspicuous achievements, were a waste of resources — mere "extravaganzas" and "junkets" without "the slightest perceptible effect in altering the climate of political opinion in Europe, especially in France,"[31] where (as in Italy) the Communist Party was strong in the early 1950s.

The arts, he even went on to assert, can never have such an impact. "Since art has flourished even under political tyrannies," he wrote of the 1952 exposition, "there was nothing the festival presented that could not have been offered to the world under the aegis of an enlightened despotism."[32] The fine arts, in his widely shared opinion, and especially the modern arts with their congenital tinge of elitism, were a poor advertisement for democracy. But if the Congress arts festivals, and their attendant publicity machine, had a negligible effect on cold-war politics as such, they nevertheless did have an important impact on the politics of the art world and on the fortunes of artists.

The Rome festival of 1954, at which Carter's quartet was unveiled to European acclaim, had a slightly different focus from its Paris predecessor. Limited to music, it was (in the words of the English art critic Herbert Read) "not a complacent look at the past, but a confident look into the future."[33] Its purpose was to nominate, through showcase concerts and a series of prize competitions, a corps of standard-bearers for the Congress's highly politicized notion of cultural freedom, which in reality boiled down to sponsorship of the avant-garde, the type of art most obviously uncongenial to totalitarian taste.

That it was also uncongenial to "free world" public taste, and even to the personal taste of the festival organizers, was no object to its promotion. Nabokov, a disciple of the "neoclassical" Stravinsky (which made him a conservative figure in the postwar musical alignment), was nevertheless keenly aware of the propaganda value of promoting atonal and serial music, "which announced itself as doing away with natural hierarchies, as a liberation from previous laws about music's inner logic."[34] Stravinsky, paid $5,000 to attend, was once again the central figure, doubly valuable as a showpiece because of his recent "conversion" to serialism. His presence in Rome "signalled a major moment in the convergence of modernist tributaries in the 'serialist orthodoxy,'" in the words of Frances Stonor Saunders, the Congress for Cultural Freedom's leading chronicler. It was there that Stravinsky and Carter, who had met previously when Carter was a pupil of Nadia Boulanger, renewed their acquaintance, but now as colleagues engaged in a modernist resurgence.

Carter, not a serialist but often taken for one, was a major beneficiary of the pattern of patronage established by the Congress festivals. (At the 1960 Fromm-sponsored Princeton Seminar in Advanced Musical Studies, Carter was coy about his relationship to serialism; when asked whether he used the twelve-tone system he replied, "Some critics have said that I do, but since I have never analyzed my works from this point of view, I cannot say."[35]) That pattern spread to corporate and institutional America through the decade of the 1950s, at first primarily through the Ford and Rockefeller Foundations (both of which had been strong financial backers of the Congress for Cultural Freedom), creating an unprecedented infrastructure of prestige to support and encourage advanced art and its creators.

Institutional, critical, and corporate support made it possible for such artists (especially those blessed like Carter with independent sources of income) to have outstandingly successful public careers in the virtual absence of an audience: a unique and perhaps never to be repeated phenomenon. Indeed in some cases, notably Carter's, the degree of professional and media recognition approached an inverse proportion to the size of the audience; as the latter shrank, performances, recordings, publicity, and prizes mounted. Commissions mounted, too, since a Carter premiere guaranteed wide and auspicious coverage. But it was not just the confluence of money and snobbery (to recall Britten's strictures) that brought this development about. There was a strong component of politics as well — a politics with which few artists in the West were then inclined to differ.

A WHOLLY DISINTERESTED ART?

Carter's next major work after the First Quartet was Variations for Orchestra, composed between 1953 and 1955 on commission from the Louisville Orchestra. It took the quartet's tempo modulation technique a step further, applying it not only to discrete proportional relationships (comparable to gear shifts), but to gradually executed accelerandos and ritardandos as well. This technical refinement, and a great many others, went into the Second Quartet (1959), the style of which was much influenced by Carter's European success and the respect he now enjoyed among the younger composers there (as well as his generational peers, like Luigi Dallapiccola and Goffredo Petrassi, the senior Italian serialists, who heard the First Quartet at its Rome premiere). Carter now had a new peer group with which to compare himself, and a new source of approbation. It led him, in particular, to look for ways of replacing the traditional thematic basis on which his music, even in the Quartet, had always proceeded.

The Second Quartet was commissioned by the Stanley Quartet of the University of Michigan, a counterpart and competitor of the Walden Quartet of the University of Illinois, who were now the proud dedicatees of a famous work. On seeing the score the Stanleys withdrew (though they did negotiate to keep the dedication), and the premiere was actually given by the Juilliard Quartet, the Parrenin Quartet's American counterpart, at a Juilliard School concert.

Where the First Quartet was expansive in structure and highly continuous in its unfolding, the Second Quartet is very concentrated in form and its texture, somewhat like that of the European avant-garde music of the same decade, is extremely fragmented. The work follows a logic of abrupt contrasts rather than methodical transitions. Again following up on an idea of Ives, embodied in the latter's Second Quartet, the instruments are given consistent "characters," and (as Carter put it) the quartet unfolds like a Samuel Beckett play, a colloquy of archetypal personalities who are basically oblivious of one another.

The four characters—"mercurial" first violin, "laconic" second fiddle, "expressive" viola, and "impetuous" cello—are distinguished from one another not only by general style, but also by a rigorous assignment of musical materials. Among them, in keeping with the principles of the First Quartet, are characteristic tempos, of which the second violin's pulse of MM70/140 is the most rigorously maintained (just as the second violin represented the square and stolid "Rollo" of Ives's Second Quartet.) But this time Carter tried to differentiate the members of the quartet in ways having to do with pitch or harmony as well, in reaction to what he evidently perceived as a failing in the First Quartet, in which the organization of pitch is far less rationalized or consistent than that of rhythm. Even sympathetic critics used terms like "a complete morass"[36] to describe the harmony in the First Quartet, and William Glock had ended his review with a caveat: "I do not know whether every aspect of this quartet is satisfying, whether, for example, the harmonies will prove to be right and convincing after many hearings."[37] Having decided that an atonal, or at least a dissonant and chromatic harmonic language was a contemporary necessity, but being skeptical of serialism—especially "total" serialism—as an organizing principle for reasons having to do with the dilemmas of harmonic randomness openly broached for the first time by Ernst Krenek in 1960 (see chapter 1), Carter was faced with the necessity of finding a way, as he put it in an interview, "to regain the sensitivity to individual notes." In other words,

> I felt it became more and more important in a dissonant style to make it seem as though every note counted in some way, or that if something wasn't the right note it would make a great deal of difference. Now, it's very difficult to do that in a very dissonant music, especially in music that moves rather quickly and rather thickly. But I've been very concerned with trying to, so to speak, re-energize the tensions of the notes, the qualities of individual pitches.[38]

In practice, this came down to the qualities of the various intervals. In a memoir of Stefan Wolpe, published shortly after the latter's death in 1972, Carter gracefully gave Wolpe (who took over a class for him at Dartington, William Glock's summer school, in 1956) credit for giving him the idea.

> He started talking about his *Passacaglia* (1938), a piano work built of sections each based on a musical interval—minor second, major second, and so on. At once,

sitting at the piano, he was caught up in a meditation on how wonderful these primary materials, intervals, were; playing each over and over again on the piano, singing, roaring, humming them, loudly, softly, quickly, slowly, short and detached or drawn out and expressive. All of us forgot time passing, when the class was to finish. As he led us from the smallest one, a minor second, to the largest, a major seventh — which took all afternoon — music was reborn, a new light dawned, we all knew we would never again listen to music as we had. Stefan had made each of us experience very directly the living power of these primary elements. From then on indifference was impossible.[39]

Carter's solution to the harmony problem was to combine Wolpe's idea of characterizing intervals with the avant-garde or serialist idea of algorithms. Each of the "characters" in Carter's Second Quartet is assigned a characteristic group of intervals; only major and minor seconds are "unclaimed," to allow for stepwise melodic lines as neutral material. The leaps, from thirds to tenths, are allocated in keeping with the instrumentalists' "personalities" as Carter envisaged them, and allied with expressive styles or playing techniques:

> Violin I: m3, P5, M9, M10 (bravura style)
> Violin II: M3, M6, M7 (strict style; six types of pizzicato)
> Viola: tritone, m7, m9 ("romantic" style; glissando, portamento)
> Cello: P4, m6, m10 (impulsive style; tempo rubato)

The cello's rubati are actually prescribed in the notation, Carter inventing a dotted slur with an arrowhead to indicate spans where the cellist should deliberately rush (or, more rarely, slow down) while the other instruments keep strict time.

In Ex. 6-14, the first score page of Carter's Second Quartet, in which the four characters are introduced, is juxtaposed with the last, in which they take leave of one another after their various attempts at interaction have failed (immediately following the cellist's brief success at seducing or forcing the rest into a dizzy group accelerando and a — literally — shattering climax). An idea of the degree to which Carter has concentrated the form and thematic content of the music, and the deliberateness with which he has done so, may be gained by comparing the cello's opening solo phrase with the expansive cello "cadenza" that opened the First Quartet.

The atomistic texture makes recognition of the characters easy. The instrumental parts do little but display their intervallic and stylistic properties in a perpetual mosaic. Every distinguishing feature identified above can be located in the appropriate

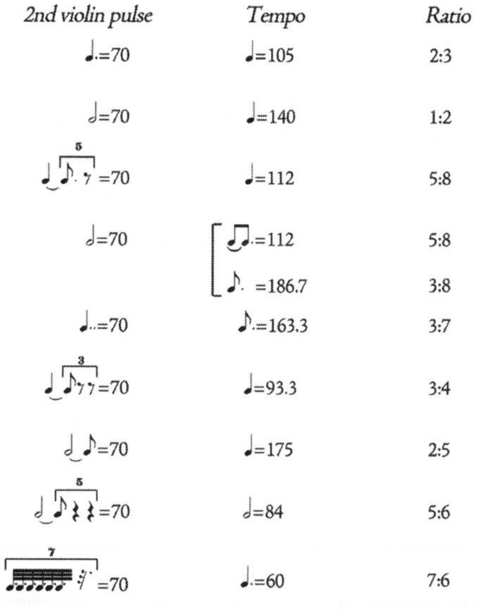

2nd violin pulse	Tempo	Ratio
♩.=70	♩=105	2:3
♩=70	♩=140	1:2
♩♪.=70 (5)	♩=112	5:8
♩=70	♫=112	5:8
	♪.=186.7	3:8
♩.=70	♪.=163.3	3:7
♩♪♪=70 (3)	♩=93.3	3:4
♩ ♪=70	♩=175	2:5
♩♪♪=70 (5)	♩=84	5:6
♬♬♩=70 (7)	♩.=60	7:6

FIG. 6-2 Metronomic plan for Carter's Second Quartet (after David Schiff).

parts. Most characteristic and Carterish of all is of course the rhythmic behavior of the second violin part, which plays even notes that move in a constant hemiola against the notated meter and tempo, so that its implied pulse is $\frac{2}{3}$ MM105, or MM70. David Schiff has published a chart (Fig. 6-2) showing how all the other pulses in the quartet relate to this basic one, always maintained by the second violin, who thus emerges as something more than a Rollo — perhaps the "Chronometros" (that is, Carter) himself.

As to overall harmony, the great problem of the First Quartet, Carter found a solution that was already implicit in the earlier work. Once the various intervals had been assigned to the different instruments, the trusty all-interval tetrachords could be mobilized to provide a suitable nexus between the lines. In the Second Quartet, therefore, Carter tried to put the parts in a counterpoint regulated throughout in the way the passage from the first Quartet in Ex. 6-12d was regulated. The normative character thus invested in the /0 1 4 6/ tetrachord made it (so Carter decided) a suitable melodic close for the entire quartet, executed, as might be expected, by the controlling second violin.

The intricacy of these pitch manipulations, on top of the tempo manipulations "inherited" from the First Quartet, made the process of composition Beethovenishly laborious. The sketches for this sixty-two-page composition, now housed at the Paul Sacher Foundation in Basel, Switzerland, run to some two thousand pages (a fact that was publicized at the time of the premiere). The Second Quartet brought Carter

EX. 6-14A   Elliott Carter, String Quartet no. 2, first score page (all-interval tetrachords circled)

EX. 6-14A   (*continued*)

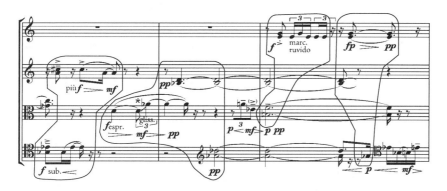

EX. 6-14B   Elliott Carter, String Quartet no. 2, last score page (all-interval tetrachords circled)

recognition in America comparable to what the First had brought him in Europe. It won three major awards, including the Pulitzer Prize. Major performing groups now clamored for the honor of presenting his music, because he now commanded, and his name conferred, as much prestige as theirs. And he continued his efforts to maximalize his style; indeed he was locked into them, for every new work of his was expected to embody some new technical feature that could be touted as a breakthrough. All were eagerly awaited and received as major events.

The Third Quartet (1971), commissioned by the Juilliard School for the Juilliard Quartet to follow up on their success with the Second, maximalized the salient feature of the First Quartet's third movement, which (as we have seen) was in turn a maximalization of the main musicopoetic idea in Ives's *Unanswered Question*. The whole quartet is built around the opposition of two duos — Violin I and Cello vs. Violin II and Viola — that play what amount to two different pieces at the same time. Duo I, which plays in rubato style throughout, plays four movements (Furioso, Leggerissimo, Andante espressivo, Pizzicato giocoso) in the time it takes Duo II, which plays strictly at all times, to play six movements (Maestoso, Grazioso, Scorrevole, Pizzicato giusto, Largo tranquillo, Appassionato). But these movements are not played straightforwardly through by either duo; after their initial appearances in the order given they are crosscut so that they coexist in many different contrapuntal combinations.

Tempo modulations are so frequent, and the resulting polyrhythms so complex, that the publisher prepared a click track to guide the players (wearing earphones) through their individual parts. (The Juilliard Quartet managed to learn the piece well enough to dispense with the click tracks at the premiere; most ensembles use them in performance.) The form is generated, in a manner borrowed from the Double Concerto, by large background polyrhythms (20:21 and 63:64), which determine the placement of the main structural events. Meanwhile, on the audible surface, the individual parts are of concerto difficulty; the textures are "dense and overgrown,"[40] to quote David Schiff, who compares them to a "rain forest" of microscopic detail; and to top things off, each movement played by each duo is characterized by a different dominating interval. Needless to say, this astounding tour de force of calculation and construction won Carter another Pulitzer Prize. It represented a very pinnacle of "maximum complexity under maximum control," to recall the shibboleth of New Criticism.

But, as Schiff went on to observe, "events in the work are sometimes gratuitous acts, seemingly without motivation," although the large gestures form "an unbroken circle, . . . at once a series of sharply contrasted moments and a continuous process."[41] Comments celebrating the complexity of the contrapuntal writing ("traditional species of academic counterpoint never extended to rhythmic proportions as complex as these . . . ") may ring a bit hollow in a world of emancipated dissonance; but Carter had indeed made great efforts to avoid the harmonic fortuity that governed the world of total serialism, even if the listening ear was thwarted by the sheer density of detail from discovering the algorithms that were in operation. Any suspicion that Schiff's use of words like "overgrown" and "gratuitous" bore ironic overtones was carefully countered by the traditional modernist verdict: "although the instruments are never called upon to produce untraditional sounds, the overall sonority is strikingly new."[42] (Actually, the instruments are called upon to produce several new kinds of pizzicato.)

AT THE PINNACLE

Carter had willy-nilly become the chief standard bearer for the traditional modernist view of art and its autonomous history at the very moment when that view began, for reasons that will emerge in the coming chapters, to be embattled (that is, began losing ground). Critics chose precisely the most utopian aspects of Carter's music on which to lavish praise, and began describing his stature, and his achievement, in reckless terms. Reviewing the Third Quartet on its premiere, Andrew Porter (an influential British critic working in New York) dubbed Carter "internationally . . . America's most famous living composer"[43] at a time when Aaron Copland and John Cage, to name only two, were still productive. By 1979, Porter was ready to pronounce Carter "the greatest living composer"[44] without qualification, preferring him to Messiaen (Carter's senior by one day) on the argument that "each new work" of Carter's, unlike Messiaen's, "breaks new ground." A year later, Bayan Northcott, another British critic, launched the article on Carter in the *New Grove Dictionary of Music and Musicians* by observing, quite "factually" as befits a reference work, that "at best his music sustains an energy of invention that is unrivalled in contemporary composition."[45] But a familiar problem gnawed, and a familiar ploy persisted. Porter hailed the Third Quartet as "a major new composition, a piece that is passionate, lyrical, and profoundly exciting," despite the fact that "myriad details passed by uncomprehended." A listener, he warned, "will probably never know exactly how precise any particular performance is," and yet the critic was prepared to affirm that "he will no doubt be more deeply moved by accurate than by loose executions."[46] As we have already seen in the case of Stravinsky's response to the Double Concerto, personal judgment is altogether suspended in favor of "trust in the composer," even when there can be no sensory or rational corroboration. Just as in genuine religious thought, faith is accompanied, indeed generated, by bafflement.

Reviewing Carter's *Symphony for Three Orchestras*, in which the multiple perspectives of the Third Quartet are augmented by a sort of hemiola proportion (three independent sound sources as opposed to two, three disparate "movements" at a time, juxtaposed in various unpredictable and sometimes impenetrable combinations), Porter allowed that "at fourth and fifth hearing, much of the detail still remained elusive"[47] even to one following with the score. As far as he was concerned, the pitch organization was meaningless. Yet even so he did not hesitate to pronounce the ultimate accolade: another masterpiece. The conclusion is inescapable that to Porter, and many other critics, Carter's masterpieces were like the noise made by a tree falling in an empty forest. They existed purely "ontologically," by virtue of their perceived complexity, whether or not anyone actually experienced them. Musical value had received its most purely asocial definition.

Ironically enough, it was just at this time, at the peak of his preeminence as an upholder of "absolute" musical value and protagonist of evolutionary history, that Carter began revealing the poetic (yes, "extramusical") ideas that had motivated some of his most forbiddingly abstract constructions. One of these revelations, perhaps the most important one, concerned the Double Concerto, the work that (thanks in part to Stravinsky's active promotion) had vouchsafed Carter's preeminence. In the sleeve note to the second recording of the work, issued in 1968, Carter reprinted a condensation of the original note, quoted near the beginning of this chapter, but prefaced it as follows:

> The idea of writing this *Double Concerto* was suggested to me by the harpsichordist Ralph Kirkpatrick. As my thoughts took shape, the matter of reconciling instruments with different responses to the finger's touch became a central concern. A concept had to be found that made this instrumental confrontation vital and meaningful. This eventually gave rise to the devising of elaborate percussion parts, the choice of instruments for the two orchestras, and a musical and expressive approach that affected every detail. Various relationships of pitched and non-pitched instruments, with the soloists as mediators, and the fragmentary contributions of the many kinds of tone colors to the progress of the sound events were fundamental. After a time, I began to think of a literary analog to the concerto's expected form—Lucretius's *De Rerum Natura* [On the Nature of Things], which describes the formation of the physical universe by the random swervings of atoms, its flourishing and destruction. Bit by bit, however, a humorous parody of Lucretius in Alexander Pope's *Dunciad* [1728] took over my thoughts, in lines like:

> > All sudden, Gorgons hiss, and Dragons glare,
> > And ten-horn'd Fiends and Giants rush to war;
> > Hell rises, Heav'n descends, and dance on earth;
> > Gods, imps, and monsters, music, rage, and mirth,
> > A fire, a jig, a battle, and a ball,
> > Till one wide conflagration swallows all.

> The beautiful end of Pope's poem seemed to articulate in words the end of the work I had already composed:

> > —the all-composing hour
> > Resistless falls; the Muse obeys the power.
> > She comes! She comes! the sable
> > throne behold
> > Of Night primeval, and of Chaos old!
> > Before her Fancy's gilded clouds decay,
> > And all its varying rainbows die away.
> > Wit shoots in vain its momentary fires,
> > The meteor drops and in a flash expires.

> > * * *

> > Nor public flame, nor private, dares to shine;
> > Nor human spark is left, nor glimpse divine!
> > Lo! thy dread empire, Chaos! is restor'd;
> > Light dies before thy uncreating word:
> > Thy hand, great Anarch! lets the curtain fall;
> > And universal Darkness buries all.[48]

The Double Concerto, it turned out, was a cosmological allegory. David Schiff, Carter's authorized biographer, writing with the composer's approval and active collaboration, elaborated the allegory into a detailed program that took fourteen printed pages to narrate and minutely relate to the musical unfolding, enabling him to claim that behind the sounds of the music lay a "prophetic vision" communicated through "comic irony"[49] — an even more impressive claim, perhaps, than ever. What matters, ultimately, is less whether the poetry directly inspired the music (although Carter did say that he began thinking of Lucretius while the form was only "expected," that is, before the piece was written) than the fact that references to Lucretius and Pope were now being offered to the listener as an explanation of the purpose behind the strange musical discourse and as a guide to its interpretation. At the very least, metaphorical reading made the piece far more accessible to "lay" comprehension. And that was a social gesture.

And a "compromise"? There is no need to ascribe to Carter the ideas, or the motives, of his promoters; but the question nevertheless remains, why was no mention made of the allegory the first time? Was it because of Clement Greenberg's old decree that "subject matter or content" had to be "avoided like a plague" in order to gain the respect of the avant-garde (or even its academic wing)? And why reveal it now?

There may have been some professional mischief in the decision. One of the first audiences to whom Carter revealed the Double Concerto's "extramusical" content was an audience of academic composers at New York University, assembled to hear an interview, or "public conversation," between Carter and Benjamin Boretz, the editor of *Perspectives of New Music*. Boretz kept nudging Carter toward accounting for the impressive "complexity" of the work in terms of total serialism; in particular, he suggested that the heavy use of unpitched percussion might indicate an interest on Carter's part with turning timbre into an independent "structural element," since as he put it (his language unconsciously echoing Greenberg's, some thirty years before), "ultimately there is no way to articulate what a composition is 'about' except by examining the total intersection of its component continuities, textures, and all its other 'media.'"[50] Boretz reacted with discomfort bordering on disbelief when Carter, citing his literary models, said that the work "emerges out of a kind of elementary chaos in the percussion," and "then a great deal happens presenting all its material, and then, in the end, occurs the dissolution of this entire material into chaos, so to speak, with the percussion (as in the beginning)."[51] "I think you might be careful in your use of the word 'chaos,'"[52] Boretz protested, then somewhat frantically tried to get Carter to take it back (or at least discount it) so as to preserve the music, as an abstract product of "structure" and "medium," from the social taint of "content":

> I think it's important to emphasize that the notion is metaphorical because, in fact, when you say that one could regard this unpitched opening and its consequent as a progression from "chaos" to "order," one could equally well invoke any number of other — perhaps seemingly contradictory — images to use as names for exactly this aspect of the relation of the unpitched to the pitched without changing anything in one's understanding or hearing of it in any cognitive sense. In other words, if one were not to use your metaphor, if one were to choose some other metaphor

for what happened, could one not still be describing precisely the same set of musical events, and still in fact arriving at the same unique musical structure? In other words, I don't believe the musical structure is really going to be affected by the particular descriptive label one chooses at *this* level of discourse. And in the same sense, it seems to me that your description of the relation of the instrumental medium to the total composition in the *Double Concerto* would only be a rather general remark about what seems so obviously striking an example of a complex and fundamental relation of medium and structure — that is, a rather deep relation between obviously unique aspects of the medium and obviously unique aspects of the continuity, texture, pitch relations, and sound relations of all kinds. So, could you perhaps reconsider . . .[53]

Carter politely refused Boretz's revision of his answer. By 1968 he could afford to break ranks, slightly, with the Princeton school without soiling his reputation as a serious artist on the most "uncompromising" terms. But there was no question of "populism." His "extramusical" reference was, in the first place, not to the fairly raw experience of life, still less to the sort of social problems Britten addressed in *Peter Grimes*, but to fairly esoteric classical and neoclassical literature. And the "extramusical" content, such as it was, was on a cosmic plane infinitely removed from that of human tribulation and emotion (save that of wonder).

Carter remained for the rest of the century the chief standard bearer of autonomous musical art, and a bulwark against the "postmodernist" tendencies that began to emerge, and threaten the modernist faith, in the 1980s. His reputation gathered ever greater luster after the turn of the century as he continued, astoundingly, to compose with undiminished vigor up to and beyond his own centennial anniversary — an absolutely unprecedented feat of creative longevity that made him, finally, a genuine media sensation. Some evidence of ambivalence can be found, beginning in the eighties, in Carter's writings. He has occasionally argued, apparently against the conventional wisdom, that for all its surface complications and its formidable intellectual rigor, his music has always been at bottom an expression — more properly, a representation — of American ideals. "A preoccupation with giving each member of the performing group its own musical identity characterizes my *String Quartet No. 4*," Carter noted in the preface to that work, published in 1986, "thus mirroring the democratic attitude in which each member of a society maintains his or her own identity while cooperating in a common effort — a concept that dominates all my recent work."

That message, however sincerely meant, has nevertheless been mediated through a discourse of elitism. In Clement Greenberg's terms, Carter has been, preeminently, the late twentieth century's "musicians' musician." His visions of democracy have been of interest primarily to a coterie of professionals: fellow composers, performers, scholars, and academically inclined or affiliated critics, for whom Carter's music has often served as a touchstone of self-congratulation. But the ambiguities of Carter's position were always implicit in the way his music has been promoted, ever since he won his European recognition as a protégé of the Congress for Cultural Freedom, clandestinely funded by the CIA in defiance of the egalitarian (or at least anti-intellectual) biases of the

United States Congress, which would have opposed the use of tax revenues to support élite culture on the European model. Carter thus became one of the protagonists of that "sublime paradox of American strategy in the cultural Cold War," defined by Frances Stonor Saunders, whereby "in order to promote an acceptance of art produced in (and vaunted as the expression of) democracy, the democratic process itself had to be circumvented."[54]

Carter's champions have been particularly vocal in defending asocial theories of music history. Especially prominent among them has been Charles Rosen, already mentioned as the pianist in the first performance of the Double Concerto, and one of Carter's strongest advocates in the concert hall. Since the 1970s, Rosen has been an important writer on music, beginning with *The Classical Style*, a treatise on Haydn, Mozart, and Beethoven, which, having won an important award on publication, has been perhaps the best-selling serious "trade" book (as opposed to textbook) on classical music in the late twentieth century. For forty years, Rosen maintained a substantial literary presence as an essayist and reviewer, largely in the pages of the *New York Review of Books*, one of the most influential of American intellectual journals.

In Carter's success at achieving and maintaining high eminence among contemporary composers despite his lack of audience appeal (an accomplishment in which Rosen himself played a significant role as a performer), Rosen saw evidence that "serious art music will survive as long as there are musicians who want to play it," or, more strongly, that difficult modernist music has triumphed in spite of audience disaffection owing to "the continued presence of an important group of musicians who passionately want to perform it."[55] The history of music, in short, is created, in Rosen's view, by musicians, and only by musicians.

To maintain this even in the case of Carter is to ignore the social factors, above all the prestige machine and its political stimuli, that could counter, and even overbalance the audience (the one social factor that everybody recognizes as such) in influencing the course of history. Rosen saw himself and others like him as playing a heroic resister's role. As the autonomy model continued to lose credence, the claims on its behalf became ever more sweeping and strident; with the end of the cold war in Europe, the model's anachronistic cold-war underpinnings have become ever more blatant. By 2002, another writer, Paul Griffiths, went so far as morally to equate audience reception with Communist oppression, invoking the tribulations of Dmitry Shostakovich as another demonstration, along with Carter's, of resistance to "the limits on artistic freedom that might be imposed by a tradition, a public or a government."[56]

But as the story of Carter's reception makes especially clear, the asocial esthetic is itself a powerful tradition, and governments have at times played a significant role in its propagation. By now it is hard, however passionately one has invested in the autonomy principle, to doubt that Rosen's many meritorious public acts on Carter's behalf were made possible not only by Carter, and Carter's emergence was made possible not only by Rosen. Both have been beneficiaries of the prestige machine in which both were willing participants.

The embattled zeal with which Rosen and comparable writers defend the model of musical autonomy that validates Carter's success has led him, like many academic historians, to devalue and dismiss the role of prestige machines in other periods — notably the aristocratic one that influenced Beethoven toward the writing of the "difficult" late works that altered the course of music history two hundred years ago — and to oppose more recent historians who emphasize social factors alongside "musical" ones. Reviewing the work of one such historian, Tia DeNora, who has documented the role of aristocratic patronage in the formation of Beethoven's musical style, Rosen stubbornly minimized such considerations as "influential forces, but rarely determining ones."[57] The determining forces, in his view, are of course the autonomous activities of composers and performers, people like himself.

But the insistence upon nominating the determining factor instead of evaluating a range of influential ones is a product of the false dichotomy between history and society broached at the beginning of the previous chapter. By the end of this one, it should be clear that the insistence is itself the product of a particular historical juncture, one that is now past. Our task in the concluding chapters of this book will be to assess, and attempt to explain, the situation that has replaced it.

CHAPTER 7

The Sixties

CHANGING PATTERNS OF CONSUMPTION AND THE
CHALLENGE OF POP

WHAT WERE THEY?

As a catchphrase, "the sixties" does not refer precisely to the decade of the 1960s. Coined in nostalgia, in resentment, at any rate in retrospect, the phrase evokes disruption, a period of social division brought on by a confluence of social transformations. First, and in the United States possibly most important, there was a newly militant and newly successful drive for social equality. The movement for the recognition of the civil rights of racial minorities coincided significantly with the phasing out of European colonial rule in Africa and scored an important victory in 1964 with the passage of a comprehensive Civil Rights Act by the United States Congress.

There was also a new impetus toward the assertion of equal rights for women in public life, coinciding with the development of new techniques of contraception (the "birth control pill") that made family planning easier and more subject to women's control. Women now sought greater control over other aspects of their lives, including the right to compete as equals in the workplace, and the right to control childbirth. Betty Friedan (1921–2006) published *The Feminine Mystique*, a broad attack on the notion that women could find fulfillment only in childbearing and homemaking, in 1963. The National Organization for Women (NOW), a powerful pressure group with Friedan as its first president, was founded three years later. Women's rights proved more difficult to secure (on paper, at least) than minority rights. A constitutional amendment guaranteeing them failed repeatedly to win ratification by the states, and the guarantee of legal abortion on demand was only won through the courts in 1973.

Among the other effects of "the pill" was a general loosening of sexual constraints, sometimes called the "sexual revolution," and, as a corollary, a newly public questioning of the social stigma attached to homosexuality, which culminated in 1969 in a riot at the Stonewall Bar in New York, when a group of patrons forcibly resisted arrest, in a routine police raid, in the name of "gay pride." Gay rights has been an issue in legal contention, alongside women's rights and racial or ethnic minority rights, ever since. The challenge to the idea that American society was governed by a "mainstream" consensus (often symbolized by the metaphor of a "melting pot"), or a set of norms to which all its members aspired, was one of the sixties' signal accomplishments. The "mainstream," especially when asserted in the realm of culture, came under increasing fire as a metaphor for an unjust status quo, or a covert locus of authoritarian domination

FIG. 7-1   Civil rights march on Washington, D.C., 28 August 1963.

and oppression. The pluralism thus ushered in (denounced by its opponents as amoral relativism) had a powerful impact on education and the arts.

The Stonewall riot was also an example of a new assertiveness in public protest and civil disobedience that characterized the sixties, aroused in the first instance by widespread opposition to the American government's pursuit of an unpopular war against Communist expansion in Southeast Asia. What the government and the military saw (and defended) as a natural consequence of cold-war policies was increasingly perceived as reckless intervention in the internal affairs of the "Third World," the technologically less advanced nations of Asia, Africa, and Latin America, many of them (like Vietnam, the site of the American war) newly liberated from colonial rule. The Vietnam war was viewed by many as a continuation of colonialist aggression under cover of cold-war politics, as well as an unjustified threat to a generation of American men whose lives were thus put at risk — a threat that, owing to inequities in the draft laws, put a disproportionate and indefensible burden on the same minorities whose rights were a separate (but obviously not unconnected) object of contention and negotiation.

Opposition to the war, which came (especially in the eyes of those whose lives were threatened by the draft) to symbolize the general political and ethical corruption of the powerful countries of "the West," stimulated a new political militancy. Active resistance was mobilized by, and on behalf of, a self-proclaimed "New Left" of radical intellectuals and politicians who questioned the authority of the government to impose its policies on an unwilling population. Others, who became known as "hippies" (from "hip," a slang word meaning aware or up-to-date), indulged in passive resistance, rejecting the social mores of conventional ("bourgeois") society and withdrawing (or "dropping out") from the public sphere into a utopian communitarian "counterculture" devoted to the spontaneous expression of love and to spiritual introspection, the latter often enhanced by the use of narcotics or "psychedelic" (sensation-magnifying or "mind-expanding") drugs like lysergic acid diethylamide (LSD), known medically as psychotomimetic, since they artificially reproduce the symptoms of psychosis, or mental defection from environmental reality.

None of these phenomena originated during the calendar decade of the 1960s, nor did any come to an end with its passing. The active struggle for racial equality went back at least to 1948, when Harry S. Truman made civil rights an important plank in his platform for reelection as president of the United States, and caused a violent split within his party that led to a rival States Rights Democratic (or "Dixiecrat") candidate for president, Strom Thurmond (1902–2003), who campaigned in support of continued racial segregation. In 1954, the United States Supreme Court declared racially segregated schools unconstitutional, and in 1955 the Reverend Martin Luther King Jr. (1929–68) organized a boycott by black residents of Montgomery, Alabama, against the segregated city bus lines. He later attained national prominence by advocating nonviolent but provocative resistance to statutory racial segregation throughout the southern United States.

Opposition to the cold war and to the interventionist policies justified on its behalf also went back to the late 1940s. Popular agitation in support of nuclear disarmament, led by organizations like the Committee for a Sane Nuclear Policy, were a staple of the 1950s, despite the political stigma attached to the "peace" movement by conservative politicians wary (not always groundlessly) of its co-option by Soviet propagandists. Contraceptive devices, including the earliest oral ones, were available before 1960. The movement for women's rights has a history extending back to the nineteenth century. Even the "drug culture" had a pre-sixties history, associated with the "beat generation," a loosely organized group of artists and writers active in the 1950s who rejected the structures and institutions of bourgeois society and sought an intense subjective illumination that became their subject matter.

The identification of all these sociopolitical movements and phenomena with "the sixties" can be attributed in part to the general intensification they all underwent in reaction to the unrest spawned by the Vietnam war, or rather to the gross expansion of the American military presence there, and the attendant casualties, that began under President Lyndon Johnson in 1965. The "counterculture," for example, reached an early peak in the summer of 1967 — known in legend as the "Summer of Love" — when about 75,000 hippies made pilgrimage to the Haight-Ashbury district of San Francisco and turned it into a giant commune awash in psychedelic drugs and procreation-free sex. It is hard not to associate that large figure with another large figure: the 10,000 American soldiers killed in Vietnam that year without any visible progress in the fortunes of an unpopular and increasingly incomprehensible war.

But reference to "the sixties" as a catchphrase in America probably owes the most to a series of violent events that shocked American society and created a watershed in collective memory. The most stunning ones, perhaps, were the three political assassinations that followed one another in short succession: first, that of President John F. Kennedy in Dallas, Texas, on 22 November 1963; second, that of Martin Luther King Jr. in Memphis, Tennessee, on 4 April 1968; and third, a scant two months later, that of Robert F. Kennedy, the late president's younger brother, then campaigning for election as president himself on an antiwar platform, in Los Angeles, California, on 5 June 1968.

In that same spring of 1968, student demonstrators occupied several buildings on the campus of Columbia University, and a week later were forcibly (and, some thought, brutally) ejected by the New York City police, who had been called in by the university administration. Pictures of bloody students filled the newspapers. Then, in August of the same year, prolonged violent confrontations between the Chicago police and antiwar demonstrators outside the Democratic National Convention were broadcast for days on national television. The trial that followed, in which a group of New Left, hippie, and black-activist defendants known as the "Chicago Eight" did their best to mock the proceedings and provoke the judge, was an enormously polarizing event.

So searing were the impressions of the *annus horribilis* 1968, and so dismaying to a society that had prided itself on its capaciousness and tolerance, that the culminating — objectively worse — events that followed in 1970 (like the killing by the Ohio State Militia of four students on the campus of Kent State University; or the lethal explosion of a pipe bomb in New York by a group known as the Weathermen, who had split off from the New Left organization Students for a Democratic Society; or another activist-planted bomb that blew up the mathematics research building at the University of Wisconsin, killing a graduate student who was working late) could not dislodge "the sixties" from their emblematic status.

The meaning or achievement of all that "sixties" unrest, which accomplished no clear objective (not even the ending of the Vietnam war, which sputtered to an ignominious close in 1975), is of course a matter of furious and continuing debate. Some, emphasizing the sexual and psychedelic aspects of the era, look back on the decade as a period of hedonism and irresponsibility that did lasting damage to the social fabric. Others, idealizing its optimism and social activism, look back on it as a period of incipient, unstoppable, irreversible, and eventually positive democratic change. What all must agree on, and what the foregoing description has already tacitly disclosed, is that the era of "the sixties" was driven to an unprecedented degree by young people, chiefly students. The "counterculture" was youth culture, and so was the activism of the period.

Indeed one of the dominant descriptors of the sixties as a historical period is the phrase "generation gap," referring to the massive exacerbation of perennial generational tensions, during that decade and its aftermath, into bitter antagonism. One of the culminating artifacts of the period, dating from 1970, was a movie, *Joe*, that climaxed with the vigilante massacre of a hippie commune by two disgruntled members of the older generation, one a successful advertising man, the other a blue-collar worker, turned improbably (but, in the context of the period, plausibly) into allies by their shared hatred of the young.

Significantly, one of the killers, a family man, was motivated by resentment of the hippie culture that had claimed his daughter; the other, a war veteran, was moved by outrage at student activism and the lack of patriotism it implied. The two manifestations of youth culture, while distinguishable in retrospect (and even at the time), had merged into a single provocation, even as they had been themselves provoked in large measure by a single affront. The movie opened barely two months after the shootings at Kent State, which had sparked the greatest single outpouring of rage on American campuses, with student "strikes" disrupting end-of-year exercises (exams, commencements) all over the country. If nothing else, the spring and summer of 1970 showed what a powerful force youth — or to be more precise, affluent middle-class youth — had become.

THE MUSIC OF YOUTH

The unprecedented freedom of action of the younger generation, amounting in some ways to virtual economic independence, was by the dawn of the 1960s a recognized fact of life not only in American society, but in all the affluent societies of the world. That power was a direct consequence of affluence. Long before it was an independent social or political force, youth was an independent market force. And like any powerful consumer force it was catered to (or, depending on one's attitude, exploited). The two consumer domains that catered most importantly to youth, both of which underwent transformation during the sixties along with "youth culture" itself, were those of clothing fashion and entertainment, chiefly music.

Now that our area of special interest has been named, it must remain our focus. For the first time in this book (and look how late it comes!) we will trace a bit of the history of "popular" music — music disseminated for commercial profit, not primarily through literate media — in its own right, not solely in terms of its appropriation by the literate culture that is our primary subject. The reason we must do this now is that the popular music associated with the youth culture of the sixties became a transforming force affecting all other musics, even as it aspired on its own to usurp their status. Seen in this way, sixties popular music enacted a "revolution" similar to that ascribed to the period's activist culture and "counterculture," for both of which it provided the indispensable soundtrack.

As a preliminary attestation, consider the most momentous countercultural event of all: a free music festival held in August 1969 on a farm near Woodstock, New York — about fifty miles north of New York City — and attended by upwards of half a million hippies and their sympathizers. It was a remarkable, and never duplicated, spectacle of nonviolence to offset the events of 1968, and its memory kept the spirit of the youth movement alive into the 1970s. (And yet every attempt to recapture it — notably the Altamont Festival organized later that year near San Francisco, where members of a motorcycle gang disrupted the proceedings with violent acts that led to at least one highly publicized fatality — was, conversely, symptomatic of the movement's entropy and decline.)

The first music that was aimed expressly at a youth market was that of the "crooners" or male microphone singers of the 1940s, whose up-close, almost whispered style reminiscent of "pillow talk" appealed irresistibly to adolescent girls ("bobby-soxers") in the throes of discovering their sexuality. The most successful of them, Frank Sinatra (1915–98), began his career as a "big-band" jazz singer but reached an early peak of popularity as a soloist singing "ballads," soft, slow, intimate songs in which he modeled his style on that of Bing Crosby (1904–77), who in turn had appropriated some of his signature techniques from the performance practices of African-American blues singers. These included singing on consonants, decorating the tunes with improvised appoggiaturas and slurred melismas, and distending the rhythm, chiefly by delaying stressed syllables.

Sinatra's career as a ballad crooner lasted from around 1940 to 1947, encompassing World War II (when audiences at home were disproportionately female) and the immediate postwar years. After a prolonged slump he made a comeback in the mid-1950s and remained a popular entertainer for the rest of his life, but no longer as a performer appealing primarily to a youth audience. For by then the youth market had been cornered by a style known as rock 'n' roll, "the live wire,"[1] in the nostalgic words of the sociologist Todd Gitlin, one of the main "sixties" historians, "that linked bedazzled teenagers around the nation—and quickly around the world—into the common enterprise of being young." Gitlin's words were well chosen. Far more than any previous popular music, rock 'n' roll made an exclusive appeal to youth. Indeed it is fair to say that it was, at least in part, a style calculated to irritate and antagonize the older generation, and was often marketed expressly as a means of widening the generation gap. Thus, unlike virtually all previous popular music, it was the opposite of family entertainment. It was socially divisive as well as uniting, and in its own way it fostered elitism. It was, in short, a kind of modernism. Gitlin's recollections are droll and to the point:

> Parents who winced, like mine, "How can you stand that noise!" also helped define what it meant to like rock; if there had ever been any doubt, "that noise" now meant, "Something my parents can't stand." To the question, "How can you listen to that stuff?" the teenager answered, in effect: "I've got what it takes, and you, the old, the over-the-hill, don't."[2]

Precisely, in other words, what the devotee of *Wozzeck* implied when coolly confronting the objections of the traditional operagoer, or what total serialism implied in its affront to neoclassicism. As "the sixties" approached, the modernist discourse was beginning to turn generations against one another in more fundamental ways than taste, but taste remained the emblem. In this way, rock 'n' roll was a genuine harbinger of the culture of the sixties.

The terms "rock 'n' roll" and "teenager," as a matter of fact, were nearly coeval. The widespread use of "teenager" or "teen" to mean a person between the ages of thirteen and nineteen was a product of the postwar economic boom. In one of those paradoxes that the sociologist Daniel Bell summed up in the phrase "the cultural contradictions of capitalism,"[3] the independent identity of teenagers, and their economic and cultural freedom, were proclaimed most effectively by the clothing and entertainment markets that most powerfully manipulated and exploited them.

Credit for coining the term "rock 'n' roll" was claimed by Alan Freed (1921–65), a Cleveland disk jockey. His was a new profession that arose when situation comedies and live variety shows deserted radio for the new medium of television, leaving empty air time to fill with nonstop recorded music. Radio stations began pitching their musical offerings to "niche" markets. Freed had the inspired idea of purveying recordings of black performers (known as "race" records when their sales were confined to urban ghettos) to a white youth audience. By the early 1950s such music was being marketed under the less demeaning rubric of "rhythm and blues," or R&B. It was essentially blues and gospel singing enhanced by a driving percussive beat, and had been thought too raw and uncultivated for dissemination on "mainstream" (white) radio.

Freed proved that, given a euphemistic name that further camouflaged its ghetto origins, it was indeed marketable — and then some! — as dance music to white suburban teenagers eager for a badge of identification as members of the "youth culture." The success and dissemination of the new genre were facilitated by technology: cheap, highly portable transistor radios that enabled fans to carry the music around with them everywhere. Freed's claim to have coined its name has been disputed: some historians trace the term "rock 'n' roll" back to rural "Holiness" churches in the deep south as early as the 1920s, when congregations "rocked and reeled" to the antecedents of rhythm and blues, the actual black-American church music that set the words of the gospel to syncopated blues melodies accompanied by guitars, trumpets, and drums. But Freed had the courage — or the commercial savvy — to play R&B recordings by black performers like Ray Charles (1930–2004) and James Brown (1933–2008) while his imitators mainly played "covers" — remakes of R&B songs by white singers who toned down both their insistent rhythm and their often frankly sexual lyrics.

Even the covers, however, retained enough recognizable "race" content to inspire a backlash from white supremacists. That racial provocation, added to a rhythmic insistence that evoked a virtually irresistible kinesthetic (= sexual?) response, made the music controversial whether designated R&B or rock 'n' roll, and whether performed by blacks or by whites. Frank Sinatra, commercially threatened as well as morally affronted by it, told a Congressional investigating committee in 1957, "Rock 'n' roll smells phony and false," and that "it is sung, played, and written for the most part by cretinous goons."[4] But the same provocations also allied the music willy-nilly with the progressive politics of

FIG. 7-2   Elvis Presley, 1957.

the civil rights movement. Never before had a commercial music carried so much heavy cultural and political baggage.

The most successful rock 'n' roll performer by far was the Mississippi-born singer and guitarist Elvis Presley (1935–77), who did more than any other individual to establish the music, in the measured words of the *New Grove Dictionary of American Music*, "as a youth culture and the symbol of teenage rebellion."[5] He made his first records in Memphis, Tennessee, in 1954, the year of the Supreme Court's desegregation decree. He achieved nationwide fame in 1956, when his manager, "Colonel" Tom Parker, negotiated a contract with RCA Victor, a major label with coast-to-coast distribution, and he made the first of his three appearances on the nationally broadcast *Ed Sullivan Show*, the most popular television variety program of the day.

More frankly than any previous white performer, Presley consciously cultivated a "black" style, which, although it played into invidious racial and sexual stereotypes (amplified by suggestive body movements that earned him the nickname "Elvis the Pelvis"), greatly magnified his allure with young white audiences of both sexes, and spurred the movement, alarming to many, toward what Gitlin memorably called "cultural miscegenation."[6] It created a dilemma for liberals who deplored the culturally alien music their children were listening to even as they reacted with indignation to the violent racist backlash the civil-rights movement had spurred. Unconscious (or at least unacknowledged) racial and sexual anxieties were fused, and further widened the generation gap. The third time Elvis the Pelvis appeared on the *Ed Sullivan Show*, the producers made a concession to parental disquiet and showed him only from the waist up. Cutting off his lower body turned him in effect into a castrato, and invested him with all the subversive allure those manufactured uncanny beings had evoked two centuries before.

And yet whatever the rebellious solidarity that teenagers felt for rock 'n' roll in the 1950s, it usually gave way to traditional rites of passage, particularly for white affluent males who could afford higher education. College remained a gateway to "adulthood," in musical taste as in other areas of culture. Surveys by sociologists showed a consistent pattern. Young men who had listened through high school to the "Top Forty" — rock 'n' roll songs plugged on the radio and ranked in popularity according to sales figures for records — renounced them on reaching college in favor of three "adult" musical categories: classical, jazz, and "folk." Colleges and universities actively abetted the change by administering courses, often required, in "music appreciation," which acquainted the leaders of tomorrow with the classical canon and encouraged their identification with it. Jazz history was sometimes offered as an elective, but more commonly jazz was fostered on campuses, along with classical music, through performing organizations and by officially sponsored concerts.

"Folk" music also received sponsorship from campus concert bureaus, but the term is somewhat misleading. In the present context it designates not the work of actual "folk" singers (by definition unpaid amateurs who sang as a by-product of, or an accompaniment to, their daily working lives) but rather that of professional musicians performing popularized arrangements of folk songs (or composed folk-style songs) from around the world. The folk group that commanded the widest following at first was the Weavers, a quartet of singing instrumentalists (on guitar, dulcimer, banjo, recorder, etc.) who came together in 1948. The group's best-known member, Pete Seeger (b. 1919), was the son of Charles Seeger (1886–1979), an eminent musicologist and composer long identified with left-wing politics. Professional folksingers were from the beginning associated with labor and social protest movements.

The Weavers fell victim to the anti-Communist blacklists of the McCarthy era, but not before they had established a successful entertainment model that attracted imitators who kept the "folk" genre alive into the sixties, when several charismatic solo performers began to appear, including Joan Baez (b. 1941), Bob Dylan (originally

FIG. 7-3   Bob Dylan in the 1960s.

named Robert Allen Zimmerman, b. 1941), Judy Collins (b. 1939), and Joni Mitchell (b. 1943). Except for Baez, these singers sang material of their own creation in addition to traditional music, in effect blurring the line between "folk" and "pop."

A taste for "folk" singers or groups remained an indication of political commitment. Although groups like the Kingston Trio (formed in 1957) or Peter, Paul, and Mary (formed in 1961) cultivated a more clean-cut "collegiate" image than the Weavers and steered clearer of overtly controversial material, their songs continued to broach social issues. Peter, Paul, and Mary identified strongly with the antiwar movement, included Pete Seeger songs in their repertoire, and cut a couple of hit records in 1963 that carried messages that were widely interpreted as radical. "Puff, the Magic Dragon" (1963), nominally a children's song, was read (mainly by nervous politicians) as a metaphorical endorsement of the emerging drug counterculture; and "Blowin' in the Wind" (1963) was a Bob Dylan song that warned — or could be read as warning — of the consequences if the civil rights movement were thwarted: "How many years can some people exist before they're allowed to be free?" The line between "folk" and commercial popular music became more and more permeable. Paul Stookey, the "Paul" in Peter, Paul, and Mary, started out as a rock 'n' roll guitarist, and continued to draw on the style of playing in which he was trained. But the absence of percussion, and the eschewal of electric amplification, effectively distinguished the "folk" from the commercial product, and lent it an air of "authenticity" on which folk performers particularly traded. Authenticity, the romantic notion that music is, and must remain, true to itself (that is, to its origins) and aesthetically "disinterested," and that musicians sincerely express their individual personalities, was of course also a major selling point for jazz and classical music, at least as distinguished from commercial pop. But calling it a "selling point" already exposes its illusory (if not downright deceptive) premises.

It was, however, the basis on which that mandatory change of taste that accompanied college enrollment through the 1950s depended. If taste in music was to define one's mature personality, that music had to be regarded as authentically personal in its own right. And along with the issue of personal authenticity went the corollary phenomenon that sociologists observed. No one opted for all three "adult" tastes; at least one had to be rejected, since a sense of personal identity depended on discrimination as well as identification.

THE BRITISH "INVASION"

That rule began to change during the 1960s. As popular music styles continued to develop along with the rest of "sixties" culture, pop began claiming the loyalty of its audience into adulthood irrespective of educational level; and it began claiming the mantle of "authenticity" as well. The watershed, both in terms of musical content and in terms of audience tenacity, was the advent of the Beatles, an English rock 'n' roll group that first performed in America in 1964, soon to be followed by additional British "invaders" like the Rolling Stones, the Who, and many others. They now became the chief model of emulation for American pop performers.

FIG. 7-4   The Beatles returning from America, 1964.

Unlike the earlier generation of rock 'n' roll performers,
the British groups performed
almost exclusively material of
their own creation. Two of
the Beatles, rhythm guitarist
John Lennon (1940–80) and
bass guitarist Paul McCartney (b. 1942), were prolific
songwriters who often collaborated (though never in the
traditional lyricist-tunesmith
fashion; both contributed
both words and music). The
lead guitarist, George Harrison (1943–2001), also wrote
some much-noticed and influential songs for the group,
leaving only the drummer,
Ringo Starr (originally named
Richard Starkey, b. 1940) confined for the most part to the
role of performer.

Their styles were ulti-
mately beholden to the black-

FIG. 7-5   Electric guitar made by Bruce BecVar in 1974.

American R&B antecedents of all rock 'n' roll; and they all conformed to what had
become the standard rock 'n' roll instrumentation (amplified electric guitars and keyboards plus a "trap set" or one-man jazz percussion outfit). But the British groups were
far more eclectic in their stylistic range than their American counterparts had been,
and their creative aims were far more ambitious, emulating those of jazz and classical
musicians, on whom they eventually had an influence that the original "authentic" rock
'n' roll performers never approached.

Mostly comprising middle-class youths with at least a full secondary education,
the British groups had a native inheritance of Anglo-Celtic folk music (partly mediated
through the hymnody of the Anglican church) that gave their melodies a "modal"
character that distinguished it from the American product, lending it a "folk" aura
that conveyed both authenticity and exoticism, heightening its charm for Americans.
The irony was that these were precisely the aspects of their music that seemed most
formulaic and conventional (= commercial) at home, while it was the black-American
component that gave them there the authentic/exotic aura.

Beyond that, Lennon and (especially) McCartney had a nodding acquaintance with
the jazz and classical repertoires, including their most modern varieties, and Harrison
had enough curiosity about non-Western musics to learn to perform creditably on

the Indian sitar. Their record producer, George Martin, was a conservatory graduate who not only was responsible for writing arrangements for the group whenever the performing forces exceeded the original quartet, but also gave them technical and technological pointers that contributed greatly to their distinctive, and ever broadening, sound image. The basic creative work, however, was done by Lennon, McCartney, and Harrison, who like virtually all pop musicians worked exclusively by ear, none of them having been trained to read musical notation with any facility.

Their appeal was phenomenally—to many, incredibly—broad. At first their music was of a lightweight, sweet, and simple if spirited character, and it was to the traditional audience for male pop-singers that they appealed, namely adolescent females (now called teenyboppers). During their second American tour, in the summer of 1965, they filled New York's Shea Stadium (capacity 55,600) with screaming girls and their less excited boyfriends. Some observers were disgruntled by their success, attributing it to dilution. Nat Hentoff (b. 1925), a jazz critic and a left-leaning political commentator, tried to write them off by suggesting that the Beatles "turned millions of American adolescents on to what had been here hurting all the time," but (turning the venom now on the audience) "the young here never did want it raw so they absorbed it through the British filter."[7] But Elvis Presley's raw success had already belied Hentoff's nationalistic grousing; moreover, by then the music of the Beatles was attracting fans from unprecedented walks of musical life, whose enthusiasm, first at home and eventually in America and continental Europe, began influencing the group in unexpected ways. The remarkable synergy thus initiated made the Beatles the truly emblematic musical phenomenon of the sixties, with far-reaching consequences for music history, including the kind of music history this book has been tracing.

DEFECTION

As early as 1963, a very dignified English classical music critic—William Mann (1924–89), the chief reviewer for *The Times* of London, who had seriously studied piano and composition in his youth—surprised his readers by naming Lennon and McCartney the outstanding new composers of the year, and comparing an "Aeolian" chord progression in their song "Not a Second Time" with the heartrending ending of Mahler's *Das Lied von der Erde*, about the loftiest comparison a critic could make in the heyday of the Mahler revival (Ex. 7-1).

EX. 7-1A   Progression from John Lennon/Paul McCartney, "Not a Second Time"

EX. 7-1B Gustav Mahler, *Das Lied von der Erde*, end

("Forever!")

Mann went on to describe "pandiatonic clusters"[8] in another song, and praised the Beatles' modulations to the flat submediant, hallowed as an expressive device since Schubert's day. His article was greeted mainly with chuckles and filed away as an eccentricity (critics, too, sometimes like to "shock the bourgeoisie"). The correspondences Mann found between his favorite classical music and that of the Beatles were not taken seriously as a comment on the Beatles' creative sources or range, but were taken only as an inventory of the critic's own musical tastes and memory. Besides, the net effect of such praise from an established critic was to declare the music "safe" for establishment consumption—perhaps not the greatest endorsement for a pop group in an age of social rebellion.

Their music continued to evolve with the decade, however, in ways that affected both its content and its musical range, and continued to broaden its appeal to various audiences. Beginning with two LP disks, *Revolver* (1966) and *Sgt. Pepper's Lonely Hearts Club Band* (1967), the Beatles produced "concept albums" in which all the songs on an LP record were coordinated, like the individual numbers in a romantic song cycle, to contribute to an overall impression that was unified not only by textual content but by aspects of the musical treatment as well.

Revolver contained songs about social alienation and economic injustice—and not always injustice to underdogs: one song, "Taxman" by Harrison, concerned the perceived injustice of the British tax system on high-income earners such as the Beatles had become. The music was enhanced by whirling electronic effects that seemed to provide a sonic analogue to the visual hallucinations brought on by psychedelic drugs, already reflected in the work of "pop" and "op" artists then straddling the edge between avant-garde and commercial art, and in the graphic designs of Peter Max (b. 1937), the quintessential visual embodiment of the "sixties" spirit.

This taste of the avant-garde was mainly contributed by McCartney, who spent the early months of 1966 (when the other members of the group were away on family vacations and honeymoons) attending concerts of electronic music and listening to recordings of Stockhausen and Berio. The first fruit of this experimental phase was "Tomorrow Never Knows," a song recorded in April 1966 for *Revolver* (Ex. 7-2). Lennon's words ("Turn off your mind, relax and float downstream...") conjured up a "drug trip" while the music unfolded a slow arpeggio over a single C-major triad (inflected at times by neighbor notes in inner voices and a "blue" seventh), accompanied by a drone from Harrison's sitar and further enhanced in the recording studio with reverberation effects, tape loops, and guitar chords recorded and run backward through the tape machine—virtually the whole panoply of musique concrète devices pioneered in the studios of Paris, New York, and Cologne during the previous decade. These devices gave the song a quality that could be captured neither in vocal score (produced,

EX. 7-2   John Lennon/Paul McCartney, "Tomorrow Never Knows," opening

like all popular "sheet music," after the fact), nor even in live performance. In a sense, the Beatles were no longer writing songs. Like some of the avant-garde icons of the day, they were creating collages — finished artworks, artifacts on tape that could not be adequately reproduced in other media. Accordingly, they stopped touring at the end of the year in which their second concept album appeared.

In its songs of social criticism (generally mild but occasionally pungent, as in "Eleanor Rigby," a hopeless portrait of urban loneliness) and its psychedelic electronic colors, *Revolver* struck an authentic "sixties" note, charting territory never previously visited by popular music meant for mass dissemination, partly at the expense of the usual pop subject matter like young love. That new conceptual and musical seriousness was intensified in *Sgt. Pepper's Lonely Hearts Club Band*. The cover showed the newly shaggy, bearded Beatles dressed like the imaginary vaudeville band of the title, standing amid a crowd of cutout portraits of their acknowledged models and mentors. They included all-purpose saints of modernity like Albert Einstein, and all-purpose icons of right thinking like Mahatma Gandhi. And also there, for those who recognized him, was Karlheinz Stockhausen.

Traditional pop entertainment values were by no means abandoned; but, rather daringly, the possibility was skirted. The title song casts the album as an imaginary stage show given by an imaginary concert band. The album ends (or seems to end) with a reprise of the opening number, enclosing not only the concept but the musical contents in a structure transcending the individual songs. But the album turns out not to end with that musical recapitulation. There is a harrowing coda of commentary in the form of "A Day in the Life," the final song, which (in the words of the critic Ian MacDonald) seemed to anticipate "the shift from 1967, the year of peace and love, to 1968, the 'year of the barricades.' "[9] Its ending is shown in Ex. 7-3.

This unusually long song (5′33″, too long for a 45 RPM single, or for conventional disk-jockey treatment) was inspired by the violent death of a friend, Tara Browne, a rich dilettante who savored the countercultural scene and who (possibly under the influence of LSD) had crashed his sports car into a parked van. The lyrics consist in part of a surrealistic collage of glumly dispassionate newspaper reports — of Browne's death, of a story on potholes in a Lancastershire town, of a military victory (surely an oblique reference to Vietnam) — followed by an invitation to a drugged escape ("I'd love to turn you on . . . ").

The real message of the song, ambiguous and disquieting, is delivered between the verses, by a sound effect borrowed directly from the avant-garde's bag of tricks. Forty London orchestral musicians (twelve violinists, four violists, four cellists, two double-bassists, a harpist, an oboist, two clarinettists, two bassoonists, two flutists, two French hornists, three trumpeters, three trombonists, a tubist, and a timpanist) were recruited for the recording sessions, which took place in January and February 1967. They were each given a chart consisting of a low note and a high note, and were instructed to play gradually from the one to the other over a span of twenty-four bars, choosing the exact pitches ad libitum, making no attempt at rhythmic coordination with the other musicians, and getting louder all the while. As McCartney knew, it was the kind of thing one expected in a score by John Cage (or perhaps by Krzysztof Penderecki); and George Martin, who helped plan it, was delighted that the hired musicians reacted to the idea with the same bewilderment otherwise reserved for the likes of Cage and Penderecki.

The powerful chaotic crescendo thus produced appears twice in the recording; once in the middle and again at the end, where it is followed by a big E-major triad banged

EX. 7-3   John Lennon/Paul McCartney, "A Day in the Life," end

EX. 7-3 (continued)

out by three pianos (dampers raised) and a harmonium. As the chord faded away, the recording engineer "rode gain," compensating for its decay by boosting the volume, so that the sound hung uncannily in the air for almost a minute, more than a fifth of the song's total running time. To conclude, a bit of "empty air" from the studio sessions was spliced on, which was not really empty but contained some low, incomprehensible background muttering and laughter from the members of the group. On the LP album as originally issued, this final component was recorded on the continuous inside groove, so that (as the critic Allan Kozinn put it) "the Beatles could be heard chortling continuously until the listener lifted the stylus from the disc."[10] What did all this mean? What *could* all this mean? The latter, of course, was the operative question, for a large part of the album's reception took the form of endless speculation, exegesis, and debate—unequivocally an "art" (as opposed to "entertainment") reception.

William Mann saw vindication in this, and came back with a more elaborate essay in the *Times*, "The Beatles Revive Hopes of Progress in Pop Music," published on 1 June 1967 in the immediate aftermath of *Sgt. Pepper*. The very title carried a freight of "classical" discourse, for it was only in the "historicist" realm of the classics that stylistic progress had become a byword. Pop traditionally trafficked in (indeed, was often defined by) quick—even planned—obsolescence. (The nice thing about popular music, the snobbish quip used to go, is that it is not popular for very long.)

Now, Mann observed, the Beatles were producing a music that did not fade so quickly, in part because they were growing up with their audience, and in part (reciprocally) because their audience was staying loyal to them in a fashion that defied pop precedent. Their secret, he suggested, lay in their ever-expanding eclecticism:

> The young teenagers of 1963 who fell like hungry travellers upon the Merseyside Beat [i.e. the music emanating from Liverpool, the Beatles' hometown, on the Mersey River] are now much older and more sophisticated, and more experienced in adult ways. Pop music still has to cater for them and for the distinctive characteristics they have by now assumed. Mod, rocker [i.e., followers of London "sixties" fashions in dress and music respectively], intellectual, rebel, permissive, careerist, all get comfort of inspiration from different music, and The Beatles have held their supremacy because they can dip into all these inkwells with equally eloquent results.[11]

Mann pointed to the powerful lyrics of songs like "Eleanor Rigby" and rightly sensed the influence of Bob Dylan in stimulating the new social consciousness of pop. He welcomed the "oriental" sitar into the stylistic mix, along with the "more or less disciplined whorls of electronically manipulated clusters of sound"[12] (for which, he primly noted, "the vogue word" was "psychedelic music"). He cited the "hurricane glissandi" and "whoosh noises" of "A Day in the Life" as the reason for the song's notoriously misguided temporary ban on the BBC, although (as he pointed out) the lyrics of several other songs also contained "ambivalent references to drug-taking."

Mann ended his piece with a combination of taunt and prayer, noting that the banned song "is more genuinely creative than anything currently to be heard on pop radio stations, but in relationship to what other groups have been doing lately *Sgt. Pepper* is chiefly significant as constructive criticism, a sort of pop music master class examining trends and correcting or tidying up inconsistencies and undisciplined work, here and there suggesting a line worth following."[13] This was "art" talk. It envisioned improvement as its own reward, implying art for its own sake.

Others were prepared to go further. Ned Rorem (b. 1923), an American composer with the reputation of a specialist in art songs, faithful to the prewar American "pastoralist" idiom and therefore suffering a loss of prestige in the heyday of academic serialism, contributed an essay, "The Music of The Beatles," to the *New York Review of Books*, a highbrow literary weekly, early in 1968. It

FIG. 7-6   Ned Rorem in 1968.

opened with a calculated shock—"I never go to classical concerts anymore, and I don't know anyone who does"[14]—and went on from there to settle a bunch of old scores.

For Rorem, the Beatles were a resurgence of genuine musical creativity after the long drought inflicted by the postwar avant-garde. Significantly, given the ethos of the sixties, "it is not through the suave innovations of our sophisticated composers that music is regaining health, but from the old-fashioned lung exercise of gangs of kids."[15] Rorem dismissed Nat Hentoff's complaint: "That the best of these gangs should have come from England is unimportant; they could have come from Arkansas." The important thing was the very opposite of what Hentoff (and most rock 'n' roll enthusiasts) thought it was. "Our need for them," Rorem insisted, "is neither sociological nor new, but artistic and old, specifically a *renewal*, a renewal of pleasure." Referring to the "new sensibility" proclaimed in literature by critics like Susan Sontag (1933–2004), who had recently published a book of essays, *Against Interpretation* (1966), calling for "an erotics of art"[16] to replace the intellectualism of the avant-garde, Rorem accused contemporary music of lagging the way music had always lagged: "All other arts in the past decade have to an extent felt this renewal; but music was not only the last of man's 'useless' expressions to develop historically, it is also the last to evolve within any given generation—even when, as today, a generation endures a maximum of five years (that brief span wherein 'the new sensibility' was caught)."[17] The secret of the Beatles, according to Rorem, was the secret of all good music: good tunes, leavened with what Rorem pretentiously dubbed "the Distortion of Genius." Like many others, Rorem pointed to the unexpected harmonies that spiced the music, attributed by some to the influence of folk music, by others to the Beatles' unschooled amateurism. But his prime example was "A Day in the Life," in which "crushing poetry" is "intoned to the blandest of tunes." Rorem compared this with the ironic strategies of modern dance, citing the choreography of Martha Graham ("she gyrates hysterically to utter silence, or stands motionless while all hell breaks loose in the pit"[18]). But "because The Beatles pervert with naturalness they usually build solid structures, whereas their rivals pervert with affectation, aping the gargoyles but not the cathedral."

Where William Mann had allowed himself a specific reference to Mahler and an implicit one to Schubert, Rorem went overboard with comparisons, calling upon Monteverdi, Ives, Poulenc, Ravel, Stravinsky, Bartók, Hindemith, and finally, inevitably, Mozart:

> The Beatles's superiority, of course, is finally as elusive as Mozart's to [Muzio] Clementi [1752–1832, a once-famous English composer and pianist of Italian birth, probably chosen because readers of the *New York Review* were likely to have played his much-assigned sonatinas as children]: they spoke skilfully the same tonal language, but only Mozart spoke it with the added magic of genius. Who will define such magic?[19]

And this was his conclusion, tinged at once with nostalgia and with cold-war anxiety:

> If (and here's a big if) music at its most healthy is the creative reaction of, and stimulation for, the body, and at its most decadent is the creative reaction of and stimulation of the intellect — if, indeed, health is a desirable feature of art, and if, as I believe, The Beatles exemplify this feature, then we have reached (strange though it may seem as coincidence with our planet's final years) a new and golden renaissance of song.[20]

It is easy enough to see what Rorem was trying to accomplish in this hyperbolic essay. It was an obvious "co-option," an attempt to use the Beatles as a weapon in his own battle of revenge with the academic avant-garde. The most direct sally came in a parenthesis, an attempt to preempt and neutralize the predictable defenses of his highbrow readers against the incursion of popular culture into their domain:

> There *are* still people who exclaim: "What's a nice musician like you putting us on about The Beatles for?" They are the same who at this late date take theater more seriously than movies and go to symphony concerts because pop insults their intelligence, unaware that the situation is now precisely reversed.[21]

In effect, Rorem was issuing an invitation to the concertgoing public to defect. And the invitation was heeded, very likely well beyond Rorem's expectation or wish. The late 1960s were precisely the time when sociological surveys stopped showing university students switching their taste allegiances as a matter of course, as a normal part of the "maturing" process. Henceforth, that rite of passage would no longer be required. From this point on, popular music was seen increasingly as part of an "alternative culture" to which not just hippies but educated people of all stripes, even "intellectuals," could adhere.

ROCK 'N' ROLL BECOMES ROCK

That alternative culture was located at first in "alternative media," shoestring newspapers and magazines that began proliferating in the mid-sixties to serve the counterculture and the protest movement as the two began drawing closer together, and to provide an alternative source of information and opinion, uncorrupted by commercial or "official" constraint. The first — *The Los Angeles Free Press* (1964) and the *Berkeley Barb*

(1965) — appeared in California. *The East Village Other*, the paradigm alternative journal, started publication in New York in October 1965, and then came a deluge: *Rolling Stone* (1967), *Rat* (1968), and many others. All of these publications featured music criticism — serious criticism, of a kind formerly reserved only for classical music and, less often, jazz — evaluating and explicating the music deemed relevant to their clientele: the loosely defined genre of pop that around 1966 took the name "rock."

Rock was not merely an abbreviation of rock 'n' roll, although that was obviously its derivation. Rather, it designated music consciously composed and performed as part of that combined counterculture/protest movement that the alternative press addressed. That music now traced its lineage only indirectly to the rural or working-class African-American sources that nourished rock 'n' roll. The counterculture was not listening to Elvis. The direct ancestor was the British wave, and the immediate model was *Sgt. Pepper*. This meant that rock was a music created and performed by white musicians, largely for an audience that was white and bourgeois (however antibourgeois its posture). Although it celebrated the voluntary poverty of the counterculture and the high idealism of protest, it was the product and expression of a moneyed and materialistic segment of society, as betokened above all by the emphasis it placed on high technology.

On this basis, the British sociologist Arthur Marwick has described the rock scene between 1966 and 1975 as an expression of financial elitism that justified itself by paying lip service to themes of social amelioration while enjoying the benefits of affluence in the form of expensive drugs and the even more expensive sound systems it now took to get the full effect of rock records.[22] The bands that arose in emulation of the post–*Sgt. Pepper* Beatles were also bound to make large financial outlays. As the investment in electronics technology became more critical, the more attenuated became the connection between rock and the original sources of rock 'n' roll, and the more pop aspired to the prestige of art. Thus the alternative culture became a meeting ground of art and entertainment categories formerly pigeonholed categorically as high and low. This was the first symptom, in the sphere of art and entertainment, of what is now called postmodernity.

On the pop side of the ledger, the kind of upward "sociostylistic" mobility associated with Gershwin's "symphonic jazz" resurfaced. In his 1967 review of *Sgt. Pepper*, William Mann noted with approval the attempt to unify the whole album around a recurrent theme that involved musical reprises. The unity, he allowed, was loose and "slightly specious," but eminently "worth pursuing."[23] He confidently predicted that "sooner or later some group will take the next logical step and produce an LP which is a popsong-cycle, a Tin Pan Alley *Dichterliebe*." Although his terminology was excruciatingly out of date, Mann was on the mark. To strive for larger statements than a pop single could allow became a prime characteristic of British and American rock. In 1969, the Who exactly fulfilled Mann's prediction with an album, *Tommy*, in which the constituent songs — all composed by lead guitarist Pete Townshend (b. 1945) — were linked in a continuous sequence describing the life of a "deaf dumb and blind boy" with a genius for playing pinball machines, whose success makes him a role model for underdogs everywhere. Although it was in fact a narrative song cycle, *Tommy* was promoted as "the first rock opera." Eventually it was adapted for stage production, and even (very gaudily) for the movies. It became a milestone in the development of "progressive rock." That term was borrowed from the "progressive jazz" of the 1950s, an esoteric and artistically ambitious outgrowth of bebop associated with the Beat poets. Progressive rock bands like Velvet Underground (from 1965) or Blood, Sweat, and Tears (from 1968) often included members with jazz and classical training. The trio Emerson, Lake, and Palmer (Keith Emerson [b. 1944] on keyboards, Greg Lake [b. 1948] on electric bass, Carl Palmer [b. 1951] on drums), widely regarded as the quintessential progressive rock band, specialized in arrangements of popular items from the classical repertoire like Musorgsky's *Pictures at an Exhibition* (album released 1972) and Copland's *Fanfare for the Common Man* (single released 1972).

By the 1970s, there were even more "advanced" pop strains known as "art rock" and "avant-garde rock," associated with individuals such as Frank Zappa (1940–93), Robert Fripp (b. 1946), and Brian Eno (b. 1948), and with groups like Queen (from 1971) and Talking Heads (from 1976). These musicians sought to subvert the "low" associations of rock 'n' roll with even more explicit appropriations from what the musicologist and rock historian Michael Long (borrowing the term from medieval rhetoric) calls "high expressive registers."[24]

Queen's single "Bohemian Rhapsody" (1975) announces (and ironically joshes) these sociostylistic aspirations in its very title, as did the name of the album, *A Night at the Opera* (borrowed from a Marx Brothers film comedy), in which it was rereleased the next year. Mainly composed by the group's lead singer Freddie Mercury (1946–1991), it is a sort of seven-minute rock cantata (or "megasong") in three distinct movements, the product of upwards of 100 hours of studio work — a figure touted in promotion much the way Elliott Carter's 2,000 pages of sketches for his String Quartet no. 2 were touted. *A Night at the Opera* was advertised as "the most expensive album ever made," recalling the way in which the RCA Mark II synthesizer had been touted when it was purchased for the Columbia-Princeton Electronic Music Center about a decade before, and it contains long strings of esoteric allusions like the one in Ex. 7-4. The song was never performed live. For promotional purposes a prerecorded videotape was prepared, in which the members of the band "lip-synched" the lyrics to accompany the original single on the soundtrack.

These overtures met with a strong response from some "classical" musicians, perhaps strongest among certain "unaffiliated" or nonacademic sectors of the avant-garde. Luciano Berio, whose music had previously been a stimulus for Paul McCartney (as Berio may or may not have been aware), welcomed the developments that had transformed rock 'n' roll into rock as early as the summer of 1967 in an essay ("Commenti al Rock") that appeared in the *Nuova Rivista Musicale Italiana*, then Italy's most prestigious musicological journal. Berio's article effectively — imperialistically? — reclaimed rock for the European tradition. "It is remarkable," he started off by observing, "that the phenomenon of rock (whose origins can be found in American popular music) needed

EX. 7-4   Freddie Mercury, *Bohemian Rhapsody*, A-major section

an English group, The Beatles, in order to burst into full flower." The next paragraph explained just what "full flower" entailed:

Rock as it is at present in the USA (above all in California) and in England (above all in The Beatles' records) represents an escape from the restrictions of its stylistic origins, a tribute to the liberating forces of eclecticism. The musical eclecticism which characterizes its present physiognomy is not a fragmentary and imitative impulse and it has nothing in common with the spent residue of abused and stereotyped forms—which are still identifiable as rock and roll. Rather, it is dictated by an impulse to accept and include and—using rather rudimentary musical means—to integrate the (simplified) idea of a multiplicity of traditions. With the exception of the beat, loud and often unvaried, all its musical characteristics seem sufficiently open to allow for every possible influence and event to be absorbed.[25]

There is always a whiff of patronization when a sophisticate like Berio admires "freshness," "naturalness," or "spontaneity," the rock virtues he singled out for praise, and more than a whiff when he remarks that "one of the most seductive aspects of rock vocal style is, in fact, that there is no style."[26] A very old-fashioned neoprimitivism shows through when Berio detects in rock the "Utopia of a return to origins," or when he celebrates the "purity" of its instrumentation. When a rock band imports "foreign" sounds, he marvels, it always purifies them. In rock, "the sound of the trumpet, for example, is always simple and spare, without mutes or special effects, as in a painting by Grandma Moses: its sound is either baroque or Salvation Army." The essay concludes with the wry observation that "the 'decadent' sound of trumpets played with mutes would be the signal that the moment for Rock at the Philharmonic has arrived; I sincerely hope that this moment will never come."[27] Concern for the authenticity of the other is a traditional imperialist (or "ghettoizing") concern. Some might detect a parallel if somewhat contradictory implication of racism (though surely not consciously intended) in a white European's celebration of rock's "escape" from its origins in African-American culture.

But it is clear, withal, that Berio was genuinely impressed by rock's absorption of high technology, even envious of it. It put rock "ahead" of contemporary developments in classical music, and that was the highest criterion of value that a classical avant-gardist knew. "Microphones, amplifiers and loudspeakers," he wrote, "become not only extensions of the voices and instruments but become instruments themselves, overwhelming at times the original acoustic qualities of the sound source."[28] Rock held the promise of a true integration of the electronic and acoustic in a performed music — a problem that (as we saw in chapter 4) the avant-garde (including Berio) had had some trouble solving.

The beginnings of academic respectability attached to rock at around the same time, and this was perhaps the ultimate portent of change. It can be read clearly, if only in retrospect, in "On the Music of the Beatles," an essay by Joshua Rifkin (b. 1944), an eminent American musicologist and early-music conductor. It was written in 1968, when Rifkin was enrolled as a graduate student at Princeton University studying musicology with Arthur Mendel and composition with Milton Babbitt. (Earlier he had studied at Darmstadt with Stockhausen.) But it was not published until 1987 (in a retrospective anthology, *The Lennon Companion*), by which time Rifkin himself, in a trenchant preface, was able to put his own essay in a historical perspective.

The article lavished praise on the music of the Beatles for its "remarkable economy of means and organization," and on the Beatles themselves for their "tight integrative control over detail," the "tensile propulsive force" of their rhythm, their "complex textures," their "unprecedented richness and structural depth."[29] Theirs was "the first popular music that not only sustains detailed analysis but even demands it."[30] And Rifkin supplied in abundance what he thought the music demanded, backing up his assertions with musical examples and analytical charts of a kind habitually employed in classroom dissection of canonical texts (and by their very nature unintelligible to the artists whose products they sought to elucidate). The culminating argument was adapted from "Who Cares If You Listen," Milton Babbitt's credo of the ivory tower, an unlikely source of praise for anything popular, perhaps, but a high authority in the eyes of the readers to whom Rifkin was addressing his arguments.

> Writing in the late 1950s, Milton Babbitt stated that a popular song "would appear to retain its germane characteristics under considerable alterations of register, rhythmic texture, dynamics, harmonic structure, timbre and other qualities." Perhaps the most significant innovation of The Beatles—and one that has not yet received adequate attention—is that they have created a popular music that resembles "formal" or "serious" music in the relevance of every detail to the identity of the composition.[31]

If this was an argument that sought to insulate the music of the Beatles from the strictures of the academic elite, representing it as exceptional among popular musics rather than as an indication of what popular music had (or might) become, that is because, as Rifkin candidly and very perceptively pointed out in 1987, his article was "an attempt at justifying the Beatles in terms of a particular ideology and, in so doing, to encompass them safely within its boundaries."[32] That was the ideology of academic modernism, "the heady blend of Schenker, Schoenberg and logical positivism once so prevalent in certain academic corners of the American musical landscape." It did not allow Rorem's appeal to dumb "pleasure," and so a more circuitous route to appreciation was necessary.

The article, in short, was an attempt to exorcise a threat that could not be openly acknowledged at the time, and that presaged a crisis. For, as Rifkin noted in hindsight, "anyone aware of such things" from the vantage point of 1987,

> will also know how much the grip of that ideology has now slackened on even some of its most enthusiastic adherents. Ironically, for me, as for not a few of my friends and colleagues, The Beatles themselves played no little role in that slackening process. The very passion that we conceived for them provoked troubling questions: how could these musically unlettered kids, operating more or less collectively, produce something that we could see as somehow coterminous with the products of those fearsomely learned individuals who alone, we imagined, could create "serious art"? Faced with such contradictions, we could either abandon the passion, try to reconcile it with the aesthetic and other paradigms to which we knowingly and unknowingly subscribed, or start to wonder about the paradigms themselves. We couldn't do the first; for a while, as my article attests, some of us tried the second; but ultimately, and perhaps inevitably, most of us wound up with the third.[33]

Rifkin implied at the time that his was the first serious critical article on the Beatles, or on rock, since it was the first to use the methods of formal academic analysis. "Most criticism of pop music," he alleged, "contents itself with breathless accounts of the writer's responses to the pop scene; critics who have attempted to deal with actual music usually betray a comprehension so severely limited as to obscure rather than clarify the subject at hand."[34] But as he later attested, his recourse to analysis was a dodge. Rifkin, a skilled composer and arranger, paid a more direct sort of tribute to the Beatles with *The Baroque Beatles Book* (1965), a record of clever arrangements of Beatles' tunes in the form of fugues, keyboard variations, trio sonatas, and suite movements scored for a typical early-eighteenth-century "Bach" or "baroque" orchestra replete with continuo. It had a big sale among record collectors who, like Rifkin, were primarily committed to the classical canon but found the Beatles irresistible.

But as Rifkin surely knew, by the time he wrote his ultra-academic tribute to the Beatles a new breed of pop critic had emerged in the alternative press, and was even then beginning to infiltrate the mainstream media and the academy. These writers, while they often avoided "textualizing" the performances about which they wrote (thus remaining true to the "oral" processes of pop creation and dissemination, in which notation comes last, and serves only commercial purposes), nevertheless wrote as "serious" and even erudite critics, with a high awareness of history—both of the medium itself (in terms of styles and influences) and of its social and cultural environment—and an often superior grasp of sociology and cultural theory to ground their judgments.

Although they came to their profession during the heyday of rock's claim to intellectual status, their detailed knowledge and critical purview encompassed the earlier history of rock 'n' roll and its sources in folk music and blues. They were able to draw previously unchronicled connections between those genres and between rock 'n' roll and earlier genres of American popular music both white and black, not only uncovering the true (and academically disreputable) historical sources of the styles that had begun to impress white educated audiences, but also establishing a popular-music canon (yes, pop "classics") that furthered the arrival of popular music studies as a legitimate branch of both musicology and cultural history.

The pioneer publication was *Crawdaddy!*, a mimeographed sheet with a press run of 500, founded in 1966 by Paul Williams, then a seventeen-year-old student at Swarthmore College. (By the end of 1968, when Williams sold it, it was a professionally printed magazine with a circulation of 25,000.) At first it consisted entirely of the editor-publisher's own musings. One such, a much-reprinted article called "How Rock Communicates," gave the flavor of the new pop criticism. It opened with a group of epigraphs that included one from Pete Townshend of the Who, and one from *Feeling and Form*, Susanne K. Langer's weighty treatise on aesthetics (quoted as an inspiration by Elliott Carter in chapter 6).

Another widely anthologized early essay from *Crawdaddy!*, later expanded into a book, was "The Aesthetics of Rock" by Richard Meltzer (then a philosophy student at the State University of New York at Stony Brook; among his teachers there was Allan Kaprow, the avant-garde artist associated in the late 1950s with "happenings"—see chapter 2). Meltzer's range of reference went from James Joyce to Hegel's *Phenomenology of Spirit* to Lennon and McCartney to the pop artist Andy Warhol to Bob Dylan and on to the analytical philosopher W. V. Quine. There is no whiff of neoprimitivism here. What these students were doing, clearly, was putting their response to popular music in touch with their other intellectual pursuits, something that would never have occurred to earlier generations of British or American students. It was at once an illustration of and a stimulus to the change in the patterns of consumption that so transformed popular music, and then all music, in the sixties.

Among the more professional breed of rock critic who fostered (and were fostered by) this change were Robert Christgau (b. 1942) and Greil Marcus (b. 1945). Christgau gained wide exposure as a columnist (1967–1969) for *Esquire*, a popular men's magazine, and then went to the *Village Voice*, a somewhat older, respectable counterpart to the alternative press of the sixties, where he eventually became a senior editor and reared a new generation of critics. Marcus became recordings editor of *Rolling Stone* in 1969, while pursuing a graduate degree in American studies at the University of California at Berkeley. He is the author of several scholarly books on American popular music, including *Mystery Train: Images of America in Rock 'n' Roll Music* (1975), which laid the foundation for the serious historical study of the genre.

A breakthrough was reached in 1970, when the *Los Angeles Times* hired Robert Hilburn (b. 1939) as a permanent staff critic after publishing occasional pieces of freelance rock criticism (by Hilburn and others) for four years. During Hilburn's tenure the paper developed the widest coverage of popular music of any American newspaper, where previously only the classical concert scene had been regularly reported in the daily press, reflecting the economic status and cultural interests of its presumed readership. The *New York Times* followed suit in 1974, when it hired John Rockwell (b. 1940), a Berkeley Ph.D. in German cultural history who was already covering classical music for the paper, as a permanent rock critic. (Later Rockwell served a term as general editor of the paper's Sunday Arts and Leisure section.) The incorporation of rock criticism on newspaper "culture" pages, all but universal by the end of the 1970s, was perhaps the most decisive symptom of the revolution the sixties had wrought in the patterns of musical consumption.

Rockwell's *All American Music: Composition in the Late Twentieth Century* (1983) was another symptom. It was the first "synchronic" survey to treat the whole spectrum of musical activity within a nation at a certain moment in its history in what became known as "multicultural" terms, implying a studied avoidance of hierarchy and an equally studied eschewal of norms. Rockwell's twenty chapters covered everything from "The Northeastern Academic Establishment" (with Milton Babbitt the focus) to Broadway musicals to art-rock, black "soul" music, and "Latino" pop, not just in an effort to paint a musical portrait of American society, but also to identify and communicate the value of each musical manifestation, however controversial.

FUSION

This fusion of purviews in a single critical patchwork was inspired by rock, or rather by rock's success in overthrowing social hierarchies as expressed in music. Rock as a democratizing force had strong repercussions within all other fields of musical production, influencing all of the genres (folk, jazz, classical) that had formerly been considered alien or antithetical (in a word, superior) to the commercial pop scene. The influence of rock as a democratizing or leveling force on these other genres produced furious controversies. In particular, it inspired backlashes from those interested in insulating or protecting the "authenticity" of the non-pop genres from commercial contamination.

The infiltration of "folk" began with covers. In 1965, a band called the Byrds recorded Bob Dylan's "Mr. Tambourine Man," the anthem of the drug counterculture, with amplified instruments and a heavy dance beat, and sold a million copies, many times more than Dylan's original recording. Three years later they began giving songs by Dylan, Pete Seeger, and even Woody Guthrie (1912–67), the left-leaning patriarch of the folk scene and Dylan's mentor, the full high-tech electronic studio treatment. That much was legitimate business.

But when Dylan himself took up the use of electrically amplified instruments, many of his fans regarded it as an act of betrayal. He was heckled at the Newport Folk Festival in the summer of 1965 and actually booed the following year while touring in England. A serious motorcycle accident later in 1966 caused a lengthy withdrawal from live performance, during which time he forswore the rock influence and went back to acoustic instruments. (The songs he recorded during this period — the "basement tapes" as they are called — have become cult classics.) But as many sensed at Newport, including Pete Seeger and the folk song collector Alan Lomax, who, according to a durable legend, together tried backstage to sever Dylan's power cables with an ax, Dylan's defection doomed pure "folk" as a genre with a mass following.

"Within a year," Greil Marcus has written, "Dylan's performance would have changed all the rules of folk music — or, rather, what had been understood as folk music would as a cultural force have all but ceased to exist."[35] All the "folk" singers who grew up along with Dylan — Joni Mitchell; Peter, Paul, and Mary — had to convert to a rock style or face effective extinction. Resistance and resentment, at first, were as much social as musical. To the folk elite, as Mike Bloomfield, Dylan's lead guitarist at Newport, testified in retrospect, "rock was greasers, heads, dancers, people who got drunk and boogied"[36] — that is, people who didn't know how to dress or behave at concerts, and who used illicit substances.

FIG. 7-7   Miles Davis, 1960s.

Even greater controversy (because it entailed race among its social issues) surrounded the jazz-rock fusions that began to take place at the end of the 1960s. Again, it was the perceived "defection" of a universally acknowledged "great" that brought matters to a head. Miles Davis (1926–91) was one of the leaders, in the late 1940s, in the rise of bebop, jazz's most esoteric and individualist (that is, modernist) phase. As such, he was conspicuous within the jazz faction most self-consciously concerned with the identity of their music as an art form, as distinct from entertainment. Davis acted the role of artist, "disinterestedly" concerned with beauty rather than interested in fame or fortune, with special vehemence, even going so far as to play at times with his back to the audience and leave the stage without acknowledging applause. But he was also, in the words of the critic Barry Kernfeld (writing in the *New Grove Dictionary of American Music*), "the most consistently innovative musician in jazz from the late 1940s through the 1960s,"[37] which also reflected his voraciously modernist bent.

It created a dilemma for his admirers, therefore, when Davis's questing spirit led him, beginning in 1968, to collaborate with "sidemen" or accompanying artists who played electric keyboards and guitars, and drummers who backed his improvisations with a heavy rock beat, an alla breve beat that seemed like jazz at half speed, subdivided (to compound the transgression) equally rather than into the swinging "jazz eighths" rhythm that for many was the indispensable hallmark of true jazz. Two Miles Davis albums, *In a Silent Way* and *Bitches Brew*, lit a fire of debate that even two decades later had not died down. As late as 1990, the African-American jazz critic Stanley Crouch pronounced a ringing anathema on them in *The New Republic*, a journal of opinion mainly read by the white liberal establishment:

> And then came the fall. *In a Silent Way*, in 1969, long, maudlin, boasting, Davis's sound mostly lost among electronic instruments, was no more than droning wallpaper music. A year later, with *Bitches Brew*, Davis was firmly on the path of the sellout. It sold more than any other Davis album, and fully launched jazz rock with its multiple keyboards, electronic guitars, static beats, and clutter. Davis's music became progressively trendy and dismal. His albums of recent years prove beyond any doubt that he has lost all interest in music of quality.[38]

There is no need to make a musical test of these claims, because it is clear that the complaint is not musical but social. It is the very presence of rock (embodied in its "electronic" instrumentarium) that is decried, in a strangely inverted replay of the original fear of transgression or "cultural miscegenation," now manifested from the black perspective. Despite its roots in R&B, rock was since the British invasion irrevocably identified as a white genre, and its infestation of jazz was regarded, in the words of the playwright and black nationalist Amiri Baraka (originaly named LeRoi Jones, b. 1934), as a "desouling process."[39] When, finally, a white jazz critic, John Litweiler, seconded the rhetoric, and made it even more pointed (comparing the new Davis sound to "the enduring, debilitated stimulation of a three-day drunk on white port wine"[40]), the cult of authenticity took on a familiar colonialist tinge. Jazz-rock fusion, it was argued, appealed mainly to the rock audience, namely middle-class, educated whites, and was therefore inauthentic. (But by then, "pure" jazz was also playing chiefly to a white audience, ironically enough, even if it was performed by blacks.) The main difference, and it was a big difference, was in the size of the audience, not its racial complexion. The underlying issue, as usual, was commercial appeal, and the mixed scorn and envy that it inspired.

INTEGRATION WITHOUT PREJUDICE?

Unlike "folk," which never recovered its pure identity after the infusion of rock, jazz (or rather, some eminent jazz musicians) recoiled from "fusion" into a purism comparable to that of academic modernism. This recoil mirrored a larger one within American society. The "melting pot" ideal that saw America as a land offering equal opportunity to all who were willing to shed their ethnic particularities and assimilate (or "integrate") into the general culture was now widely questioned by minorities and vocally rejected by some of their spokesmen. In its place, many now embraced the principle of multiculturalism (or, in its more strident variants, cultural nationalism), a far less sanguine view that expressed the disillusion of those who, during the turbulent decade of civil-rights violence, concluded that the melting-pot or integrationist ideal was a smokescreen concealing and protecting the interests of the existing white (and Christian, and male) power structure.

The movement toward integration had received its biggest boost in 1954, when the United States Supreme Court, in deciding a case called *Brown v. Board of Education*, ruled unanimously that racially segregated schools were unconstitutional because separate facilities, excluding minorities from the majority "mainstream," stigmatized the excluded and were therefore inherently incompatible with the constitution's guarantees of legal equality for all citizens. That moment had its musical reflections. One, it could be argued, was the success of Elvis Presley, a white performer who frankly emulated a black style (but without the degrading camouflage of blackface makeup). Another was the so-called Third Stream.

The term, and to a large extent the music to which it referred, was the brainchild of Gunther Schuller (b. 1925), a remarkably versatile musician who began his career as a French horn virtuoso (occupying the solo horn chair in the Metropolitan Opera Orchestra from 1945 to 1959), who composed prolifically (chiefly in a serial idiom), and who maintained an enthusiastic interest in jazz that led him to become one of the major historians of the genre. Schuller coined the phrase in 1957 to denote (in his words) "a type of music which, through improvisation or written composition or both, synthesizes the essential characteristics and techniques of contemporary Western art music and various ethnic or vernacular musics."[41]

It is a slightly misleading (and slightly patronizing) definition, since jazz was by 1957 far from a purely ethnic or vernacular music (nor, beyond its being written, could anyone have actually defined the "essence" of contemporary Western art music except contentiously). But the broadness of the definition reflected Schuller's ecumenical conviction, characteristic of its optimistic time, that "any music stands to profit from a confrontation with another." The Third Stream was envisioned as the confluence of two "mainstreams." "Western art music," in Schuller's view, "can learn a great deal from the rhythmic vitality and 'swing' of jazz, while jazz can find new avenues of development in the large-scale forms and complex tonal systems of classical music." In practice, the Third Stream was the fruit of a collaboration between Schuller and John Lewis (1920–2001), a jazz pianist and arranger who had studied theory and composition at the Manhattan School of Music and who was already interested in reconciling jazz techniques both with the larger forms of literate composition and with modernist structural ideals. Even his improvisations, in the words of one critic, had "a degree of motivic unity that is rare in jazz."[42] In 1951, Lewis teamed up with the vibraphonist

Milt Jackson (1923–99) in the Milt Jackson Quartet (the remaining players being a bassist and a drummer), which the next year was renamed the Modern Jazz Quartet (MJQ) under Lewis's direction. The MJQ quickly gained a reputation as a "progressive" ensemble, whose refined and somewhat cerebral signature sound (sometimes identified as "cool jazz") was a florid counterpoint between Jackson's solos and Lewis's unusually melodic accompaniments.

It was on the basis of this already somewhat "classically" oriented, hence de-vernacularized (and despite all the members' being African-American, de-ethnicized) jazz approach that Schuller, who as a twelve-tone composer employed a similarly devernacularized idiom, developed the Third Stream idea. He promoted it in terms that unabashedly proclaimed the values, and even the slogans, associated with the liberal integrationist moment in American social policy:

> Third Stream is a way of composing, improvising, and performing that brings musics together rather than segregating them. It is a way of making music which holds that *all musics are created equal*, coexisting in a beautiful brotherhood/sisterhood of musics that complement and fructify each other. It is a global concept which allows the world's musics—written, improvised, handed-down, traditional, experimental—to come together, to learn from one another, to reflect human diversity and pluralism. It is the music of rapprochement, of *entente*—not of competition and confrontation. And it is the logical outcome of the American melting pot: *E pluribus unum.*[43]

For an idea of Third Stream music in practice we can compare a composition by Schuller with one by Lewis. Schuller's *Transformation* (1957) is composed for a jazz combo precisely matching the instrumentation of the MJQ, plus an ensemble of orchestral instruments (winds and harp). This is Schuller's program note:

> In *Transformation* a variety of musical concepts converge: twelve-tone technique, *Klangfarbenmelodie* (tone-color-melody), jazz improvisation, and metric breaking up of the jazz beat. In regard to the latter, rhythmic asymmetry has been a staple of classical composers' techniques since the early part of the twentieth century (particularly in the music of Stravinsky and Varèse), but in jazz in the 1950s it was still an extremely rare occurrence. As the title suggests, the work begins as a straight twelve-tone piece, with the melody parceled out among an interlocking chain of tone colors, and is gradually transformed into a jazz piece by the subtle introduction of jazz-rhythmic elements. Jazz and improvisation take over, only to succumb to the reverse process: they are gradually swallowed up by a growing riff which then breaks up into smaller fragments, juxtaposing in constant alternation classical and jazz rhythms. Thus, the intention in this piece was never to fuse jazz and classical elements into a totally new alloy, but rather to present them initially in succession—in peaceful coexistence—and later, in close, more competitive juxtaposition.[44]

Ex. 7-5 shows the "reverse process" Schuller describes, in which the fully notated music of the "classical" instruments gradually swamps the partially notated music of the improvising combo. Lewis's *Sketch* (1959) pits the MJQ against a string quartet. The two groups share a fund of motivic elements (notably a short scale figure descending a minor third); but again, as in Schuller's piece, they alternate rather than collaborate, the

EX. 7-5   Gunther Schuller, *Transformation*, fig. [J] to fig. [L]

*) From here on until K
2nd, 4th beat gradually
more & more pronounced

"composed" music acting sometimes as a frame, sometimes as a harmonic background, for the improvised. Ex. 7-6 shows the end of the piece, the only moment that attempts the "integration" of all the performers in a single texture. Neither Schuller's piece nor Lewis's actually attempts, let alone achieves, the kind of integration or fusion that theoretical descriptions of Third Stream seem to promise. The idea of two indigenous musical currents meeting on absolute terms of equality was attractive to Americans. But in actual musical practice, Third Stream compositions left the crucial questions — were the currents truly indigenous? could they really meet as equals? — unanswered, and the trend had effectively died out by the 1980s. Even in its brief heyday the idea met with considerable skepticism, especially after Schuller characterized Third Stream as "the Europeanization of jazz."[45] This ill-starred term reactivated notions of upward social mobility, and not just for jazz.

EX. 7-5 (*continued*)

EX. 7-5 (continued)

Yet Third Stream never aroused the antagonism that jazz-rock fusion inspired; and that must be because the musics it sought to fuse — conservatory-style composition (in Schuller's case twelve-tone) and "progressive jazz" — were both of them considered elite musics at the time. The offspring born of their wedlock could be comfortably accommodated, in the context of the late 1950s and early 1960s, to the idea of "maturation of taste" as a rite of passage. Neither jazz nor classical listeners needed to fear that their elite status would be compromised by a taste for Third Stream.

Jazz-rock fusion, on the other hand, was seen as part of a general encroachment of commercialism on art that practitioners and devotees of elite genres all saw at first as a mortal threat. Indeed, rock did seem to be swallowing up everybody's audience, and appeared to traditionalists of all stripes as the common enemy, even as it was claiming the allegiance of many who would previously have "graduated" to one of the traditional elite genres. By the end of the 1960s popular music accounted for more than 70 percent of all record sales, leaving jazz, folk, and classical to compete for the remainder. Since then the disparity has only grown. In the 1990s, classical music and jazz each commanded a measly 3 percent of record sales. They had become "niche" products. For classical music in particular, which had always claimed a universal "human" appeal (and founded its sense of superiority to other genres precisely on its vaunted universality), it seemed a

EX. 7-6   John Lewis, *Sketch*, end

EX. 7-6 (*continued*)

death sentence. The history of classical music in the last three decades of the twentieth century was basically a history of coping with the threat put in motion by the sixties.

RADICAL CHIC

One of the ways one copes, of course, is to adapt. Since this book is a history of music in the literate or art tradition, "classical" adaptations and fusions with the popular will be the subject of a closer look in a separate chapter. They mainly originated in the English-speaking countries, the original breeding grounds of rock. But we can end this chapter with a look at a couple of continental European responses to the sixties and to its popular music. These took the form not of technical adaptation or stylistic appropriation, but of attitudinal conversion, the vaunted "revolution in the head." One noteworthy response was Hans Werner Henze's. We last encountered Henze, in chapter 1, as a somewhat uneasy but obedient participant in the Darmstadt avant-garde. In despair over Germany's wartime descent into barbarism, and what he saw as the country's refusal to come to terms with the horrors of its past, Henze had emigrated in 1953 to Italy. There, without giving up commitment to his Schoenbergian technique (adopted as much in a spirit of political protest as of esthetic conviction), Henze strove for what his biographer Robert Henderson called "a fusion of the German and the Italian spirit, a projection of the north-German polyphonic temperament into the arioso south, with Bellini, Donizetti, Rossini and Verdi appearing as important influences."[46] Not surprisingly, he became something of an opera specialist during this phase of his career, turning out six operas during his early Italian period.

The last of the six, *The Bassarids* (1965), was a long one-acter à la *Salome* or *Elektra*, set to a libretto by W. H. Auden and Chester Kallman, the same team that had furnished the words for Stravinsky's *The Rake's Progress* a decade and a half before. It is a retelling of Euripides's *Bacchae*, in which the calm domain of the abstemious and reasonable Pentheus, the King of Thebes, is invaded and destroyed by the wild followers of Dionysus, the god of wine. Despite the subject matter, Henze's opera is a rather cerebral work, its four big scenes cast (in a manner somewhat reminiscent of *Wozzeck*) as the four movements of a symphony.

As might be expected from someone who had made it his mission as an artist to warn against the return of Nazi irrationality—that "silly and self-regarding emotionalism, behind which it is impossible not to detect...something militantly nationalistic, something disagreeably heterosexual and Aryan"[47]—Henze portrayed the Dionysian revels harshly, as a brutal and wholly destructive force. "The occasional late Romantic exuberance that is found in my works is not intended to be exuberance as such but its anachronistic opposite,"[48] Henze wrote about *The Bassarids*. It is a perfect summary of the despairing irony that world war followed by cold war had produced.

The Bassarids, brilliantly staged, had a magnificent reception when it was unveiled at the Salzburg Festival, Europe's swankiest summer music venue; but after finishing the score, as he recounts in his autobiography, Henze felt a persistent malaise that rendered him emotionally numb through the whole autumn of 1965, preventing him from enjoying performances of his own music by others, or his own performances of his favorite music:

> I remember conducting Mahler's First Symphony with the Berlin Philharmonic and can still recall my inner emptiness, a kind of apathy that constantly plagued me, so that everything I touched or attempted to touch went wrong. It was a feeling that I was unable to shake off, not only on this pointless, dispiriting evening at the Philharmonic but also in my private dealings with my fellow human beings. Everything felt joyless and uninspired.[49]

And then he heard the Rolling Stones. The occasion was the band's Rome debut, on New Year's Eve, 31 December 1965, at the Piper's Club, a big barn of a building that had been outfitted and equipped for rock concerts. In a memoir, Henze describes his encounter with the Stones as an epiphany:

> They made an enormous impression on me, and for weeks I tried to reproduce this impression in my own music, but without success. The technique is entirely different. For the time being we must accept this fact, but whether it will be so forever is another question. To me it seems important and desirable that Pop Music should be brought into contact with "our kind," which is so much older and more difficult: the contact could be of value to both sides. One day the difference will be entirely done away with.[50]

In an essay written some time later Henze elaborated the point:

> In the course of the development of music I can even see, or rather sense, possibilities that complex orchestral or symphonic music will move in a direction where it will all of a sudden come upon pop music. It could come about one day that the difference will disappear between *musique savante* and the music that young people enjoy so much.[51]

It is especially noteworthy that this sentence, so subversive of every modernist assumption, appeared in an article called "Musik ist nolens volens politisch"—Music Is Willy-Nilly Political (that is, political whether or not it wants to be). The initial reaction of pleasure, not far in spirit from Ned Rorem's eulogy to the Beatles, had metamorphosed with Henze into a discourse of radical egalitarian politics, paralleling the coming together of the counterculture and political activism. Henze was soon caught up in the leftist politics of the German student movement.

The overtly (and angrily) political music that he wrote during his period of friendship, beginning in 1967, with violent "new leftists" like Rudi Dutschke, the leader of the German Student Socialist League (a counterpart to the American organization Students for a Democratic Society), quickly regained the alienated and alienating—grating and ugly—edge associated with the modernist avant-garde. A truer memento of Henze's initial encounter with rock was a work called *Musen Siziliens* ("The muses of Sicily"), a "Concerto for chorus, two pianos, wind instruments and timpani on fragments from the Eclogues of Vergil," composed in the early months of 1966 under the direct impact of the Rolling Stones.

Henze had received a commission for a work suitable for amateur choruses to sing. He connected that requirement with the new aims that rock had inspired in him. He went quite out on a limb for an elite modernist, "employing utterly simple formulas, with the music circling around single notes and tonal centers, so that it would be enjoyable to sing, even for amateur choirs, and the playing of the two solo piano parts should be fun both for pianists and audience."[52] Putting that simple gratification together with texts from classical poetry sounds like a prescription for just the sort of neoprimitivist music—Carl Orff's, for example—that had been shamelessly exploited by the Nazis, and that the postwar avant-garde had denounced for (it seemed) the best of reasons.

But somehow the Rolling Stones erased that sinister parallel, at least temporarily, from Henze's consciousness. The rock group had, ironically enough, the very same effect on him that the Bacchantes had on poor King Pentheus, according to the cautionary tale that Henze had just retold in *The Bassarids*. He did not go all the way to Orff for a model, but he did come up with a music reminiscent of some of Stravinsky's later neoclassical works, in particular a couple of lively pastoral pieces called Eclogues (one in the 1932 *Duo concertante* for violin and piano, the other the middle movement of his 1943 *Ode* for orchestra) that also evoked Virgilian poetry. These must have been among Henze's conscious models (along with Satie, whom, Henze wrote, "in making myself over into a beginner again I happened on as if on an old acquaintance"[53]).

The third movement of *Musen Siziliens* is called Silenus, after the leader of the satyrs, and sets a text from Vergil that depicts an antique version of the scene that Henze had witnessed, and been so thrilled by, on the night of 31 December 1965. "Then he began to sing," the text begins:

> and no more was said. And now a miracle — you might have seen the
> Fauns and the wild creatures dance lightly to the tune and stubborn
> oak-trees wave their heads.
> Rocky Parnassus is not so deeply moved by the music of Apollo;
> Ismarus and Rhodope have never known such ecstasy when
> Orpheus sang.

EX. 7-7   Hans Werner Henze, *Musen Siziliens*, III (Silenus), mm. 108–11

The music certainly lives up to Henze's description, reaching climaxes on C-major arpeggios (Ex. 7-7) and a blazing C-major conclusion that might have made Orff blush. This was modernist high treason, and Henze was excoriated for it in the modernist press. Hans Heinz Stuckenschmidt (1901–88), Schoenberg's first biographer, who was now a professor of music history at the Technical University of Berlin and the most authoritative critic in the city, muttered that the piece contained several passages "that could no longer be described as modern" in a review that carried the headline, "Henze Turns the Clock Back."[54] Thirty years later, Henze made this retort in his autobiography:

> Did people really think me capable of such a strong-man act, I wondered? Which clock did Stuckenschmidt mean? And how late was it anyway? In the hearts of so many people at this time there still existed this *esprit de corps* that demanded that every deviation from the officially prescribed rules and regulations that were dictated by curiously structuralist progressive thinking and that were applied to both life and art with equal rigor had to be denounced and punished without a moment's delay. But who was in charge of this organization? Who set the standards? Pierre [Boulez]? Or the frightful Heinrich Strobel [the new-music impresario; see chapter 4]? A kangaroo court? A central committee, a shady academy somewhere, in Darmstadt perhaps? No, that really was inconceivable. But why, in heaven's name, did people not slowly get used to seeing and accepting

artistic objects for what they are, namely, as independent creatures with lives of their own? That would at least have been a beginning.[55]

Ultimately, then, the encounter with rock had nudged Henze away from the view that placed artists and artworks in a determined historical sequence. He would henceforth see himself, and would try to get others to see themselves, as not just living in history. A passage from "Musik ist nolens volens politisch," meanwhile, went the rest of the way and asserted that artworks and artists exist first, and most essentially, in a social network. Looking forward to "the liberation of art from its commercialization," Henze made some Utopian predictions:

> I visualize the disappearance of the musical elite and of globetrotting virtuosi; the overcoming of all this ideology of stardom in music, which I regard as a relic from the previous century and as a *maladie de notre temps*. It would mean that the composer is no longer a star, as today, but an *uomo sociale* [a social being], someone who learns and teaches. He would be someone who shows other people how to compose; I could envisage composing becoming something that all people can do, simply by taking away their inhibitions. I think there is no such thing as an unmusical person.[56]

These are the somewhat utopian ideas that in the 1970s and 1980s were often pigeonholed as "postmodernist," and that received their most conspicuous summary in a tract by the French cultural theorist Jacques Attali called *Bruits* (1977; translated into English as *Noise: The Political Economy of Music*). Henze's was a remarkably early formulation, brought on by an unexpectedly overwhelming encounter with British rock in the mid-sixties. The final irony is that by the 1990s, when he wrote his autobiography, Henze suppressed (or repressed) that aspect of his esthetic odyssey; neither rock nor the Rolling Stones are mentioned in that book in connection with *Musen Siziliens*. (The quotations given above come from Henze's program note to the first recording, made when the piece was new). But these vagaries will be something to trace in the final chapters of this book.

Perhaps the emblematic response to the sixties on the part of what was by now becoming the senior generation of the European avant-garde was *Sinfonia*, a sprawling composition for eight amplified solo voices and orchestra in four movements (later expanded to five), composed in 1968, the "year of the barricades," by Luciano Berio, whose bemused, somewhat patronizing tribute to rock and to "the liberating forces of eclecticism" that the new popular music had unleashed is already familiar to us. *Sinfonia* (to be pronounced, Berio has said, with the accent on the second syllable, rather than the third as in ordinary Italian) was one of a group of commissions issued by the New York Philharmonic in connection with its 125th anniversary in 1967; this explains why English is the dominating language of the texts.

The idea of "fusion" was embedded at *Sinfonia*'s core. The virtuoso voice parts were composed for the Swingle Singers, a vocal octet founded by the American conductor Ward Swingle (b. 1927) to perform a "crossover" repertoire that encompassed everything from Renaissance madrigals to arrangements of current pop songs. Their most successful recording, "Bach's Greatest Hits," was a lively and impressively pitch-perfect recital of Bach keyboard pieces sung to the accompaniment of a jazz rhythm section (bass and traps) in the "scat" style popularized by jazz singers who vied with instrumentalists by improvising to meaningless syllables (or "vocables"). Especially in the fifth and last movement of the revised *Sinfonia*, Berio exploited their near-incredible agility and accuracy.

The texts enunciated in the previous movements already constituted a wildly eclectic collage. Much of the time the singers vocalized on vowels or other phonemes, in the fashion of much avant-garde music that explored the soft edge dividing (or connecting) music and language. Against this background of primal lingual soup the first movement pits readings from *The Raw and the Cooked* (1964), a treatise by the "structural anthropologist" Claude Lévi-Strauss (b. 1908), whose subversively "relativistic" theories on the correspondences between modern thought, including scientific and historical thought, and ancient or prehistoric myth had made him a hero of the sixties New Left. The readings Berio selected were from creation myths, and the mysterious opening thus stands in a Romantic line beginning with Haydn's oratorio *The Creation*, and extending through Beethoven's Ninth (quoted explicitly in Berio's third movement) and Wagner's *Ring*, on to the great twentieth-century torsos like Scriabin's *Mysterium* and Schoenberg's *Jakobsleiter* that had achieved mythic stature in the historiography of "Western music."

That is ambitious company, and Berio intended a new commentary on the eternal question of the relation between the present and the past. The most explicit discussion comes in the third movement, the most famous one, in which the corresponding movement of Mahler's Second Symphony (which already contained semihidden, ironic allusions to works by Beethoven, Schumann, and Bruckner) unwinds virtually in its entirety as a background to a frantic projection of "graffiti," some in the form of spoken words (many drawn from Samuel Beckett's novel *The Unnamable*, the bible of postwar existentialism from which the epigraph to chapter 1 in this book is also drawn), others in the form of whispered solmization syllables, still others in the form of allusions in the orchestra to a panoply of repertoire items from Bach, Beethoven, and Brahms to Debussy, Ravel, Schoenberg, and Stravinsky (not omitting Berio himself and other Darmstadt alumni). The orchestra also adds some startling dissonant clusters, perhaps in the spirit of revolutionary slogans scrawled on the walls of public buildings.

What was later widely identified as "postmodernist" commentary on the simultaneity of the past and the present thanks to media and memory, and the impossibility of innovation except through unexpected juxtaposition and collage, is foreshadowed here. But that is not all. The word *graffiti* (writing on walls) is especially apposite for this movement, since among the words muttered or shouted by the singers are slogans ("Forward!" "We shall overcome!") that Berio took down from the walls of Paris during the 1968 student riots at the Sorbonne, which he had witnessed at first hand.

Among all the other things it can be construed as being, then, Berio's collage was a panorama of the moment of historical disruption and unrest that was "the sixties." The idea of an overload of experience was conveyed in a manner somewhat reminiscent of the manner of a medieval motet: the texts are often fragmented by hockets and voice exchanges, and often compete simultaneously for the listener's attention, so that the overall effect, as Berio put it in a program note, was one of "not quite hearing"—an experience that was, he said, "essential to the nature of the musical process," just as it was part of the experience of living through a turbulent time. Even the appropriation of Mahler as the soundtrack for Berio's sonic newsreel was a comment on the decade, since the sixties, which began with Mahler's birth centennial year, were the decade of Mahler's triumphant return (or rather his long-deferred admission) to the active symphonic repertoire, in which performances conducted by Leonard Bernstein, the Philharmonic's conductor and *Sinfonia*'s dedicatee, had played a crucial role.

Also straddling the archaically ritualized and the ultratopical is the second movement of *Sinfonia*, "O King." Its structure is like a modernized isorhythmic motet, with an abstractly conceived pitch ostinato interacting and overlapping with an abstractly conceived rhythmic ostinato. Interacting, meanwhile, with both of these is a series of vowel sounds enunciated by the singers, derived according to a similarly abstract plan from a structural typology of vowels developed before the war by the British linguist Daniel Jones. (Readers interested in the full details of these pitch, duration, and vowel "rows," and in tracking their deployment, can find a detailed analysis in David Osmond-Smith's handbook, *Playing on Words: A Guide to Luciano Berio's "Sinfonia"* [London, 1985]; it requires seventeen pages to lay out all the ingenious details.)

Toward the end of the movement, these stately and impersonally interacting cycles give way to a more obviously manipulated passage that leads to a climax (Ex. 7-8) in which the vowels are permuted into a different order and equipped with consonants to articulate them, revealing for all to hear (or perhaps "not quite hear") that they are the constituent vowels of the phrase "O Martin Luther King." The movement is in fact a memorial to the slain civil-rights leader, and forms a kind of delta into which several other of *Sinfonia*'s symbolic streams flow. The relationship of such a memorial to a panorama of the sixties is self-evident. Less obvious, perhaps, is the relationship to the Lévi-Strauss readings in the first movement, which had coalesced toward the end on the mythical idea of the *héros tué*, the "slain hero." Berio had written "O King" in 1967 as a tribute, and decided, after King's martyrdom, to adapt the piece (originally scored for a single singer and a chamber ensemble) for the large forces of *Sinfonia* to serve as a commemoration, and (as he has told interviewers) as a rebuke to the Americans for their slow progress toward racial justice. To incorporate such sentiments into so ostentatious a technical tour de force, or to filter their expression through so arcane a medium of representation, raises some serious ancillary questions, however—questions that threaten to reopen some old misgivings about the relationship of elite art and civil society.

These questions were reformulated in the aftermath of the 1960s, by the journalist and social critic Tom Wolfe (b. 1931), under the rubric of "radical chic." Wolfe coined the phrase in the title of a much discussed and debated magazine article that described a party given by Leonard Bernstein and his wife in their Park Avenue duplex penthouse apartment, in January 1970 (on the eve of Martin Luther King Jr.'s birthday), to raise money for the legal defense of the Black Panthers, one of the most

EX. 7-8   Luciano Berio, *Sinfonia*, II ("O King")

radical activist organizations of the day on behalf of minority rights, and one of the most controversial owing to their recourse to confrontational and occasionally violent tactics — tactics (including openly anti-Semitic rhetoric) that were contributing to the sundering of the bonds of solidarity between blacks and white liberals that King had sought to strengthen, and undermining, perhaps permanently, the integrationist "melting-pot" ideal.

An invited guest, Wolfe subjected the occasion to a scathing satire born of his impression that the sentiments motivating the Bernsteins' espousal of the Panthers' controversial cause were less altruistic than narcissistic. The climax, of both outrage and hilarity, came when Wolfe quoted Bernstein as expressing his solidarity with the Black Panthers by citing his own "problem about being unwanted"[57] as an artist in America, putting his own self-pity front and center. The implicit accusation was that pampered elites, whether social or intellectual or artistic, were incapable of any other response to social problems than a self-centered or frivolously self-regarding one, and that their acts of apparent (even subjectively sincere) social conscience amounted to nothing more than a means of self-congratulation.

It was a blunt and maliciously overstated attack, but many acknowledged its grain of truth. The taint of glamour was at odds with the claim of sincerity; solidarity was compromised by condescension. The same contradiction has dogged the reception of high artistic tributes to the causes of social underdogs and to the iconic embodiments of such causes, like Martin Luther King Jr. Who is the true hero of an ostentatious tour de force like Berio's "O King"? Is it the righteous man to whom it was dedicated, or is it the clever man who devised it? The former would in all likelihood not have recognized the tribute. Indeed, it is questionable whether anyone could get the point of the piece, or even notice the emergence of King's name, without consulting a program note or an analysis. It was another case, to recall Benjamin Britten's Aspen lecture (quoted in chapter 5), of being addressed (discourteously, Britten would have insisted) in a language one did not understand.

Why was such a language deemed necessary or appropriate for such a purpose? Could there be a sincere or effective tribute to the civil-rights movement on terms so esoteric? Or had the voice of reverent conscience become, in the gloomy words of the cultural historian A. N. Wilson, "inaudible against the din of machines and the atonal banshee of the emerging egomania called The Modern"[58]? Answers to these questions are not self-evident. But the questions persisted and nagged, and contributed to the erosion of faith in the sanctity of high art that found its watershed in the "postmodern" decades that followed the sixties.

CHAPTER 8

A Harmonious
Avant-Garde?

MINIMALISM: YOUNG, RILEY, REICH, GLASS; THEIR
EUROPEAN EMULATORS

Removal of context was an important point in the magic of music.[1]

—BRIAN ENO (1981)

Believe it or not, I have no real interest in music from Haydn to Wagner.[2]

—STEVE REICH (1987)

NEW SITES OF INNOVATION

The first identifiable group of composers in the literate tradition whose music not only exemplified but throve on the blurring of sociostylistic categories discussed in the previous chapter were the ones associated with a nebulous stylistic or esthetic category known as minimalism. The term, as usual, was applied to the music ex post facto, and its relevance to the object it purports to describe is debatable. Of the alternatives that have been proposed over the years, "pattern and process music" might be the most neutrally descriptive. But as one of its protagonists, Steve Reich (b. 1936), has observed, "Debussy resented 'Impressionism.' Schoenberg preferred 'pantonal' to 'atonal' or 'twelve-tone' or 'Expressionist.' Too bad for them."[3]

As will become all too clear in what follows, there is no single technical or stylistic feature that unites the music of all the composers to whom the term "minimalist" has been applied, nor is there any technical or stylistic feature that is unique to their music. In some ways, the name is an obvious misnomer, since one of the most conspicuous features of "minimalist" music is extravagant length—length one might be tempted to call "Feldmanian," except that Morton Feldman (see chapter 2), despite his trademark wispiness, is not normally classified as a minimalist. Minimalist music definitely comes out of what is often (if oxymoronically) called the "avant-garde tradition," but much of it has been commercially successful beyond the dreams of most classical composers, and beyond the dreams of "traditional" avant-gardists by virtual definition.

That commercial success is one of the factors that have made the music controversial within the world of "classical modernism." That contradiction is among the factors that have led to the coinage of a new term, "postmodernism," to describe the most innovative art (not only music) of the last quarter of the twentieth century. The validity of the term, and its possible range of meanings, will be more thoroughly considered in the next chapter; but it should at least be mentioned at this point that among the defining characteristics of postmodernism, as normally understood, is precisely the blurring of sociostylistic categories that gave rise — or at least gave currency — to minimalism.

Minimalism can neither be strictly delimited to the "classical" sphere nor divorced from it. Its practitioners are as often listed and discussed in encyclopedias and dictionaries of popular music as in surveys of "modern music." Its existence and success have thus been among the strongest challenges to the demarcation between "high" and "popular" culture on which most twentieth-century esthetic theorizing and artistic practice have depended. One of the involuntary spokesmen from whom the epigraphs above were lifted, Brian Eno, is normally classified as a rock musician (albeit a somewhat atypical one), while the other, Steve Reich, is normally classified as a classical composer (albeit a somewhat atypical one).

It would be hard to justify the classification purely on the basis of musical style. The distinction seems rather to be based on the kinds of training they received. Eno had an art-school education and is relatively untutored in traditional music theory, while Reich had a university education and a more formal initiation into the literate tradition of music. But both create music for ensembles of amplified instruments. Both draw eclectically on many musical traditions (literate as well as nonliterate, "Western" as well as "non-Western") formerly thought to be entirely separate if not incompatible. And both participate as sound-makers in the real-time performance of their own work, though neither is a performing virtuoso or a conductor.

The first and last of these traits, at least, had previously been far more characteristic of pop artists than of classical composers. But if one had to name the single crucial feature that unites all musicians in the minimalist movement and underlies all their attitudes, it would have to do with their relationship to the recording and communications technologies that set the twentieth century apart from all previous centuries. They are the first generation of musicians who grew up taking those technologies and all their implications for granted. They received their formative musical experiences from records and broadcasts, and they founded their idea of the musical world on the full range of experience to which those technologies gave access.

One could fairly say, on these grounds, that the minimalists constitute the first truly and authentically and fundamentally and exclusively *twentieth-century* generation of musicians. To say this may seem eccentric or even faintly ridiculous, since they arrived on the scene most of the way toward the twenty-first century. But that lag represents the time it took for twentieth-century technology to make its full impact on twentieth-century art. What it also represents, of course, is the fundamental irrelevance of arithmetical fictions like centuries to the march of events, and their capacity for clouding the minds of historians.

But everything that has been said so far about minimalism — the length of its products, its expanded range of cultural reference, its technological advancement — might seem to suggest that "maximalism" would have been a better name for it. Was there really nothing about the movement to justify its actual label? There was something, of course; but to see it one needs to place the origins of minimalism in a historical context. That context can be supplied by recalling the sneering question (already quoted anonymously in chapter 2) with which Charles Wuorinen, the most prominent academic serialist of his generation, tried, in the early sixties, to dismiss the work of the nonacademic avant-garde: "How can you make a revolution when the revolution before last has already said that anything goes?" That was indeed a quandary for those committed to the idea of perpetual innovation, and it reminds us how easily that idea can lead (as seen in chapter 2) to the debasement of the currency of modern art. It is no wonder then that, in implicit answer to Wuorinen's question (which, minus its implied hostility, was their question, too), a new musical avant-garde arose by decade's end, proclaiming the value of "that which is created with a minimum of means,"[4] and resolving "to concentrate on and delimit the work to be a single event or object."[5] The obvious answer to "Anything goes!" was "No it doesn't!" The new maxim was "Reduce!"

Calls for radical reduction had been heard before. Mies van der Rohe's "functionalist" battle cry ("Less is more!") had long since resounded through the halls of architecture; streamlining had long been the established modernist ideal. Neoclassicism had long ago been heralded by its French proponents as the *style dépouillé*, the "stripped-down style." But the new strip-down far exceeded the limits of the old. It became, perversely, yet another form of maximalism: a virtual contest, staged throughout the third quarter of the century — first in the visual arts, somewhat later in music — to see who could strip away the most, on the assumption that the barest, most elemental expression was by that very token the most authentic.

As early as 1948 the abstract expressionist Barnett Newman (1905–70) exhibited an oil painting, *Onement 1*, that consisted of a single field of uniform red-brown color with a single stripe of red-orange, about an inch wide, running down the middle. Newman's best-known work, *Stations of the Cross* (1958–66), is a series of seven canvases divided vertically at intervals by black or white bands of various uniform widths. Mark Rothko (1903–70) won his greatest fame for enormous canvases divided into two or three floating rectangles of luminous color. Such pictures, with their insistence on stasis, were widely regarded as a reaction or an antithesis — or at least an alternative — to the wild, flamboyantly turbulent "action paintings" of Jackson Pollock, which had dominated the New York art scene in the decade preceding Pollock's violent death in an automobile crash. In place of Pollock's emotional turmoil, Newman and Rothko offered refuge in impersonal (Newman called it heroic) sublimity.

Younger artists went further. In 1951, John Cage's friend Robert Rauschenberg produced a series of paintings consisting of nothing but panels of white house-paint on unprimed canvas. A few years later, Ad (Adolph) Reinhardt (1913–67) did it in black. By 1965, "Minimal Art," or "Minimalism," had been officially christened by the philosopher and critic Richard Wollheim in an influential magazine article, and entered the standard parlance of the art world.[6] Like "Impressionism," the term was coined with hostile intent; the critic was protesting what he saw as minimal (that is, insufficient) artistic content in the work of some recently exhibited painters. But like the older term, it was apt enough to fill a gap in terminology, and eventually lost its sting. It became a neutral term of reference and was even adopted by some artists as the name of a self-conscious esthetic program.

It spawned theorists. Ad Reinhardt "maximized" Mies van der Rohe's old functionalist dictum into a minimalist credo: "Less in art is not less. More in art is not more. Too little in art is not too little. Too much in art is too much."[7] And he issued a set of "Rules for a New Academy" that began with "The Six General Canons or Six Noes" (yes, there are really seven) —

- No realism or existentialism
- No impressionism
- No expressionism or surrealism
- No fauvism, primitivism, or brute art
- No constructivism, sculpture, plasticism, or graphic arts
- No collage, paste, paper, sand, or string
- No "*trompe-l'oeil*," interior decoration, or architecture

— and ended with "Twelve Technical Rules" (yes, there are really sixteen):

- No texture
- No brushwork or calligraphy
- No sketching or drawing
- No forms
- No design
- No colors
- No light
- No space
- No time
- No size or scale
- No movement
- No object, no subject, no matter
- No symbols, images, or signs
- Neither pleasure nor paint
- No mindless working or mindless non-working
- No chess-playing[8]

The last rule was a waggish allusion to Marcel Duchamp, the venerable Dadaist, who had given up painting for chess. And surely Reinhardt's spoofy list, like Duchamp's "ready-mades" or Cage's "silent" pieces, was in part a Dada-inspired test of the limits of the "art" concept. Just as surely, though, it was a sign of the times as well — times that again called for irony, coolness, and detachment in the face of the public turbulence described in the preceding chapter. Minimalism in art was related to the counterculture, if not exactly (or directly) its product. It was a way of "tuning in and dropping out." Under close scrutiny, Rauschenberg's white paintings or Reinhardt's black ones revealed tiny variations in hue and brushwork. To pay such anomalously pure artistic values such anomalously close attention was a way of ostentatiously not paying attention to what was so loudly claiming attention in the world outside.

The term "minimal" entered the vocabulary of music criticism in 1968, in an article by the English composer and critic Michael Nyman (b. 1944) about Cornelius Cardew. We met Cardew in chapter 2 as the quintessential "anything goes" man, so obviously the term has undergone some change in its musical applications since Nyman first used it. What struck Nyman as minimal about Cardew was the process of composition rather than the result. The same goes even more emphatically for Cage's 4'33", sometimes called the ne plus ultra of minimal (if not "minimalist") music, since the composer contributes so little to what happens during its specified duration. But again, the content, being unspecified, might as well be maximal as minimal. In any case, neither Cardew's *Scratch Music* nor Cage's 4'33", nor any piece of indeterminate or purely conceptual art, can fulfill the terms of musical minimalism, for such works are not "created with a minimum of means," nor do they "concentrate on and delimit the work to be a single event or object."

But chapter 2, the same chapter that described the work of Cardew, also included a description (and even the complete "score") of a work that did conform to those specifications. That work was La Monte Young's *Composition 1960 #7* (see Fig. 2-8a), consisting in its entirety of a notated perfect fifth (B-F♯) and the direction "hold for a long time." And La Monte Young was the author of the two defining phrases requoted in the foregoing paragraph. The early date of both *Composition* and the definitions entitles Young to recognition, at least in books like this, as the conceptual founder of the American "minimalist school," even if he contributed relatively little to the eventual path it took.

LEGENDARY BEGINNINGS

The status of founder always commands an aura. Young's is the name that shimmers in accounts of minimalism, despite (or rather, because of) the infrequency with which his music has ever been performed. In chapter 2 we encountered him in connection with Fluxus, the loose association of artists and musicians on the fringe of the New York art scene who promoted "happenings" — acts of "performance art" or dreams of conceptual art that might or might not include music. As mentioned in that discussion, *Composition 1960 #7* was the only one of Young's compositions of that period that used musical notation, the others specifying actions other than sound-producing ones, even if they did use musical equipment. The one most often cited by connoisseurs of eccentricity is his *Piano Piece for David Tudor #1*: "Bring a bale of hay and a bucket of water onto the stage for the piano to eat and drink. The performer may then feed the piano or leave it to eat by itself. If the former, the piece is over after the piano has been fed. If the latter, it is over after the piano eats or decides not to."

Young's association with Fluxus was brief and uncharacteristic. His fascination with sounds "held for a long time," however, was of long standing and wielded a strong and highly ramified influence. His early career, albeit hopelessly encrusted by now in mythology of his own and others' making, illustrates the division within the music world that his later career transcended. Born in rural Idaho, Young grew up listening to popular music on the radio and playing jazz saxophone. (After making his avant-garde reputation, he preferred to say that his real musical education consisted of listening to the endless hum of high-tension wires and the sublime squalling of thunderstorms.) As soon as he got to UCLA, he was put on the same Schoenbergian compositional regimen as everyone else. (The teacher who encouraged him in his earliest composing was Leonard Stein, Schoenberg's old California assistant.) On his own he discovered Webern, whose sparseness spurred him to emulation.

The product of an urge to surpass, even if only a paradoxical sort of surpassing in restriction, limitation, and reduction, Young's early efforts demonstrate yet again the strange kinship between the new minimalism and the old maximalism. During the summer of 1958, between his UCLA commencement and his enrollment in the graduate composition program at UC Berkeley, Young composed a String Trio, ostensibly modeled on Webern's op. 20. Its first 159 measures are shown in Ex. 8-1. It may well be the most notorious composition ever produced in class by a first-year graduate student.

The music in Ex. 8-1 consists of the unfolding of a single chromatic aggregate — what in Webern would be called a single twelve-tone row. The first three pitches introduced are, moreover, typically Webernian in the way the cello's D fills the pitch-class space between the viola's C♯ and the violin's E♭, completing a symmetrically disposed unit. Among the classics of early atonality are a couple of Webern pieces in which the unfolding of a couple of chromatic aggregates furnished the entire musical content. In one of his *Three Little Pieces for Cello and Piano*, op. 11 (1914), Webern managed to pare the contents down to a single aggregate, like the one in Ex. 8-1. That might already be considered a kind of minimalism.

But Webern's pieces take seconds to perform, whereas Young's opening aggregate (about a quarter of the entire piece), in which the three instruments together produce only eleven discrete sounds (single notes or double stops), takes eleven minutes to unfold, of which the first five are occupied by the first three notes. The extreme slowness of the unfolding, also describable as the extreme length of time the process occupies, magnifies the impression of "minimal" musical content far beyond anything even remotely suggested by Webern.

Also magnified far beyond anything actually found in Schoenberg or Webern is their notorious idealism. Critics have often called attention to aspects of notation in their work (like the "hairpin" crescendos on single piano notes in Schoenberg's op. 23) that relate to the "idea" rather than the sound of the music. Young's Trio abounds in notational features unrelated to the sonic realization. The many tempo changes that take place on rests (or in the middle of sustained tones) are instances, as are the many "syncopated" entries made without any accentuation or surrounding pulse against which syncopations may be measured, or even perceived, by the ear.

The willingness (or compulsion, or capacity) to take things to unaccountable extremes immediately marked Young's work as "avant-garde" in the classical meaning of the word. There is no doubt, then, about the esthetic from which minimalism emerged.

EX. 8-1   La Monte Young, String Trio, mm. 1–159

EX. 8-1 *(continued)*

It was, at first, an art of alienation and social disaffection in the late, late romantic tradition. Young's uncompromising commitment to the ideology of modernism is further reflected in his widely quoted remark: "Often I hear somebody say that the most important thing about a work of art is not that it be new but that it be good, but I am not interested in good; I am interested in new — even if this includes the possibility of its being evil."[9]

The Trio has lived in legend as an emblem of that stance. Its legend has several distinct phases, beginning with the legend of its angry rejection by the composer's professors at Berkeley, continuing with the legend of high praise from Stockhausen (allegedly overheard, and later reported, by Cardew) at Darmstadt in the summer of 1959, and cemented by an almost complete absence of performances, so that its reputation is sustained almost entirely by history books and hearsay, and by Young's avowal, borne out (if only indirectly) by subsequent events, that his purpose in writing the Trio was to "influence the history of music."[10] Never published—it is on deposit along with the rest of Young's graduate-school submissions at the Berkeley music library and otherwise available only from the composer—the hour-long Trio has had only a handful of documented public airings (some of them in arrangements for other ensembles of strings). The first was a reading arranged by Seymour Shifrin (1926–79), Young's composition teacher, in an effort to persuade him that the outlandish time-scale was a miscalculation. The tiny audience consisted of the rest of the seminar. Perhaps the most recent performance, by three members of the Arditti Quartet (a well-known ensemble specializing in contemporary music) took place at a London music festival in 1989.

Much primed by the legend, the work was received this time in a manner reminiscent of the way Morton Feldman's music is now usually interpreted: as a spiritual exercise. The cello's consonant perfect fifth at the end of the row, unusual in twelve-tone music (although it returns at various transpositions in other instrumental parts when the row is subjected to standard serial permutations), was singled out as prophetic by those who interpreted the Trio in the context of the transformations "minimalist" writing had undergone in three decades of subsequent development. Edward Strickland, an early historian of minimalism, shrewdly observed that "the extended fifth," unexpected and therefore striking in its serial context, "was soon to recur in Young's work in a totally different context—i.e., no context, as the entire content of *Composition 1960 #7*."[11]

MUSIC AS SPIRITUAL DISCIPLINE

But the "spiritualizing" interpretation carried conviction. By 1989 Young had made a decisive turn toward a religious lifestyle, having in 1970 become a disciple of Pran Nath, an Indian musician and spiritual guru. In the early 1960s, after moving to New York, he and his wife, the painter and performance artist Marian Zazeela, had founded the Theatre of Eternal Music, an ensemble dedicated to the devout daily rehearsal and very occasional performance of his work, which consisted of several enormous, ongoing, and unfinishable compositions, reminiscent in concept of the famous torsos (Scriabin's *Mysterium*, Ives's *Universe*) of early-twentieth-century music. They achieved their huge dimensions through the application of improvisatory and ritualistically repetitive techniques to tiny preplanned and notated musical ideas or "modules," following a set of verbal instructions that Young (possibly recalling his serial training) calls "algorithms." These utopian compositions, such as *The Four Dreams of China*, realizable only in small snatches, have been "eternally" in progress since the early 1960s. Perhaps needless to say, they no longer employ twelve-tone procedures, Young having come to see a contradiction between the all-encompassing, undifferentiated twelve-tone approach to pitch and his ideal of concentration, delimitation, and singleness. Pitch has

FIG. 8-1   La Monte Young with Pran Nath and Marian Zazeela, 1971.

been the area, in fact, to which he has applied the most rigorous restrictions, arriving finally at an approach based on natural acoustical resonance (invested, in his thinking, with purity and holiness) that virtually excludes conventional chromaticism of any kind. Since the mid-1970s, much of Young's composing and performing energy has been devoted to *The Well-Tuned Piano*, a body of music to be played on a piano tuned in a system of just (or Pythagorean) intonation.

However restricted the material, all of Young's compositions are predicated on the idea of infinite extension in time, achieved with the aid of electronic drones, or (in *The Well-Tuned Piano*) of a technique of synchronizing the musical rhythm with the acoustical beats arising out of the justly tuned intervals to set up a continuous resonant aura in the performing space and thus defeat the piano's quick sonic decay. By the time he set up the Theatre of Eternal Music, Young began associating his principle of "sustenance," or long-sustained sounds, with the long-tone exercises that characterize the monastic practices of many religions, including Hinduism and Buddhism. Long tones sung or played on wind instruments are invested with the spiritual significance of controlled breathing, a prelude to meditation in which the body is pervaded with the divine spirit.

Young's brand of musical minimalism thus became (for him) a form of esoteric religious practice, a discipline to be carried out by and in the presence of initiates rather than performed before the general public. Accordingly, as his career continued, Young deliberately withdrew from the public eye, or whatever corner of it he had access to, giving few concerts and issuing or authorizing recordings only at rare intervals. The latter have tended to become cult objects, like the so-called "Black LP" produced in

Germany in 1970: a long-playing record encased in a black plastic sleeve with program notes on the back reproduced from the composer's own calligraphy in faint gray ink, à la Rauschenberg. (The front of the sleeve is decorated with a mandala-like design by Zazeela in the same barely discernible color.)

Side I contains, in the composer's words, "a section of the longer work *Map of 49's Dream The Two Systems of Eleven Sets of Galactic Intervals Ornamental Lightyears Tracery*, begun in 1966 as a subsection of the even larger work *The Tortoise, His Dreams and Journeys* which was begun in 1964 with my group The Theatre of Eternal Music." Its title is *31 VII 69 10:26–10:49 pm*, and it consists of exactly twenty-three minutes of wordless chanting by Young and Zazeela, recorded at a Munich art gallery on 31 July 1969 at the time specified by the title, to the accompaniment of a sine-wave generator that gives out a continuous G below middle C. Zazeela's part is confined to doubling the drone, while Young's voice slides among tones that harmonize with the drone at perfect Pythagorean intervals: unison, octave, octave plus minor seventh, fourth, and major second (the progressions from the fourth below to the octave below or the second above supplying perfect fifths as well; see Ex. 8-2). Near the end, Zazeela moves briefly from the drone to the second and then resumes the drone.

EX. 8-2   La Monte Young, *31 VII 69 10:26–10:49 pm*, transcribed from "Black LP"

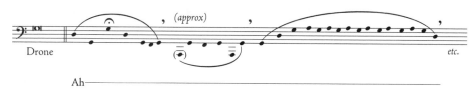

The second side of the record contains even less apparent variety. It is called *23 VIII 64 2:50:45–3:11 am the Volga Delta* and consists of 20'15" of uninterrupted sound produced by Young and Zazeela by drawing double bass bows along the sides of a gong. It is intended as a demonstration of harmonic complexity, requiring for this purpose the same kind of unusually close and concentrated attention to small variations as Ad Reinhardt's black paintings (a concentration best achieved, by the composer's open avowal, with the assistance of cannabis or some other consciousness-expanding drug). It may be played either at the standard $33\frac{1}{3}$ RPM turntable speed or at half speed (available in the early sixties on some specially adapted phonographs used for office dictation) to bring some of the higher overtones down into the range of human audibility. A jacket note explains, "One may listen to the pieces at soft levels, but ideally the sound should fill the room if the playback equipment can do so without distorting." The desired volume challenges not only the capabilities of the equipment but also the listener's endurance. This is obviously not music meant for casual or recreational listening, or for the average (or even specialized) music audience.

Young's role in the propagation of minimalism as a secular fine-art practice, then, has been played largely behind the scenes. He has neither participated in nor benefited from its burgeoning public and commercial success but has affected its progress indirectly through the musicians with whom he has associated. Characteristically, this group crosscuts the old boundary between popular and serious music, diffusing Young's influence into a wide variety of avant-garde musics on both sides of the Atlantic.

One of Young's most regular early associates, the Welsh-born John Cale (b. 1942), who performed on amplified viola in the Theatre of Eternal Music between the end of 1963 and late 1965, went on to join the singer and songwriter Lou Reed (b. 1943) in forming the "alternative rock" band the Velvet Underground, and later collaborated with Brian Eno. Another alumnus of the Theatre, the percussionist Angus MacLise (1938–79), participated along with Cale in a short-lived predecessor to the Velvet Underground called the Primitives. Tony Conrad (b. 1940), an avant-garde filmmaker with formal training in mathematics, played amplified violin and bowed electric guitar in the Theatre. It was he who introduced Young to the mathematical principles of just intonation.

A CONTRADICTION IN TERMS?

Young's most conspicuous early disciple was Terry Riley (b. 1935), the composer through whom minimalism first impinged on the consciousness of "mainstream" performers and critics and found a wide audience. A fellow graduate student at Berkeley, Riley also chafed against the forced regimen of serial composition then administered at the school. Unlike Young, he managed to complete an M.A. in 1961, but only by writing a twelve-tone composition, immediately disavowed, to satisfy the degree requirement. (Coincidentally or not, it was another string trio.)

What really interested Riley at the time was the composing he was doing to accompany a local modern dance ensemble. Like many others, he experimented with tape loops. He also made use of a device called an echoplex (developed by Ramon Sender, a San Francisco sound engineer) that was similar to the feedback generator Vladimir Ussachevsky had played with a decade earlier in New York (see chapter 4). It fed the signal emitted by a tape recorder's playback head back into the recording head, thus producing a sort of ever-accumulating canon.

Shortly after receiving his Berkeley degree, Riley took some of the tape loop pieces he had composed for the dance group and, subjecting their already repetitive sounds to echoplex treatment, came up with a relatively lengthy composition based almost entirely on reiterations of sometimes recognizable, more often unrecognizable fragments of previously used material. He called it *Mescalin Mix* after the name of a psychedelic

FIG. 8-2 Terry Riley, Munich, 1992.

drug produced from cactus plants, a forerunner of LSD, that was popular among the San Francisco Beat poets and their successors, the hippies. By drawing this association, Riley made explicit the connection between the new avant-garde and the same counterculture out of which progressive rock was about to emerge.

Replacing Young's "sustenance" with "looping" as the carrier of minimalism's infinite expanse proved a decisive move, especially when Riley followed up with a piece that transferred the looping technique to the domain of "live" music, music performed by humans in real time. This was not the first instance of live music imitating electronic; the recent "sonorist" compositions of the Eastern European avant-garde—Ligeti's *Atmosphères*, Penderecki's *Threnody*—had that distinction. But by combining the looping principle with Young's "algorithmic" method, Riley set the stage for the next, and possibly the last, true "revolution" in the history with which this book is concerned. From it emerged what Riley himself called "music that could be avant-garde and get an audience too."[12] From the traditional modernist perspective, the idea of a "popular avant-garde" was simply a contradiction in terms. But then, so was the idea of "traditional modernism." Both apparent oxymorons were products of the changes the sixties had wrought in patterns of musical consumption, something never foreseen by the modernists of the earlier twentieth century or their theoretical spokespersons. The work that provided the decisive practical refutation of earlier modernist (or historicist) theory was a composition, written in the spring of 1964, to which Riley gave the frankly provocative title *In C*.

Ex. 8-3 is the complete "full" score of *In C*. One is not likely to guess by looking at it that the composition of which it is the notation lasts anywhere between half an hour and three full hours, to cite the range of its documented performances. It is best known from a Columbia recording issued in 1968, which preserves a studio performance by the composer with members of the Center of the Creative and Performing Arts in the State University of New York at Buffalo. That performance lasts exactly forty-four minutes.

Each of the fifty-three numbered "modules," which can be played by "any number of any kind of instruments" (including vocalizing singers) either at the notated pitch or at any octave transposition (and using either the notated time values or any arithmetic augmentation or diminution thereof), is to be "looped"—that is, repeated ad libitum before moving on to the next. The piece is over when all performers (in practice usually somewhere between a dozen and thirty) have reached the last module. Dynamics and articulations are ad libitum as well, and players are free to omit modules unsuitable to their playing technique, and to pause between or even within modules.

Percussion may be added, too, so long as it keeps strict time. The only constraints are for the sake of homogeneity of result: players are discouraged from using instruments that uniquely represent a given range or octave transposition, or from running too far ahead of the rest of the ensemble (or staying too far behind), and all players should be regulated by the same eighth-note pulse (given out audibly by a timekeeper who plays the top octave of Cs on a piano or a high tuned percussion instrument like a xylophone or glockenspiel).

Thus the players, while given far more freedom of spontaneous choice than in conventional notated music, remain disciplined participants in a collective undertaking comparable to the Indonesian gamelan, to whose music Riley was attracted. *In C* is in no sense an "aleatoric" composition or a free-for-all, but rather an "algorithmic" one, controlled by a set of firm if loosely specified rules. Its unfolding is highly structured. Sustained and moving parts are balanced to produce interesting textures; and when, as Riley has said he intended, no more than four modules are in play at any given time, the

EX. 8-3   Terry Riley, *In C*, full score

music falls into clear sectional divisions marked by the introduction of new pitches and the disappearance of old ones.

Thus introduction of F♯ at the fourteenth module (seemingly a segment from the Indonesian *pelog* scale) marks an important sectional divide. (Modules 11 to 13 can also be construed as typical gamelan figures in *pelog* tuning.) Confinement to the scale segment E–B (with F♯) from module 22 to 28 marks another. Modules 29–30 might seem to mark a return to the opening "title" tonality, but any impression that *In C* is actually—that is, functionally—in C in ordinary tonal terms is contradicted by the end. The note C is avoided from module 45 on, and the last five modules introduce the note B♭. The most one could say is that the piece passes through a modular tonal scheme in accordance with its overall modular construction.

The extraordinary reception Riley's piece enjoyed on its premiere performances, at the San Francisco Tape Music Center on 4 and 6 November 1964, surprised everyone. Alfred Frankenstein (1906–81), the venerable (and unusually tolerant) critic of the *San Francisco Chronicle*, then in his thirtieth and last year on the paper, was bowled over. "At times," he wrote, "you feel you have never done anything all your life long but listen to this music and as if that is all there is or ever will be, but it is altogether absorbing, exciting, and moving, too."[13] He was the first of many to compare its slowed-down time scale, its gradual evolutionary unfolding, and its "climaxes of great sonority [that] appear and are dissolved in the endlessness" to the sublime effect of a Bruckner symphony.

But just as obviously, *In C* was a model of a very different kind of social behavior from that of a symphony orchestra. Riley is on record as rejecting the "symphony" model:

> I distrust the organization of the orchestra, which is like the army. You've got this general sitting in his chair, then the lieutenants, and so on down to the privates in the back rows. There's a lot of that kind of politics in the orchestra, which I find pretty disagreeable as a way to make music together. Not all orchestras are guilty of this kind of hierarchy, but it exists to a degree in most. So it just didn't seem like a very healthy climate.[14]

Instead, *In C* represented a model of cooperative behavior of a kind that was at the heart of the sixties counterculture, with its hippie communes and ashrams, and the explicit parallel between the symphony orchestra, emblem that it was of the musical establishment, and the worst aspects of military life was a pointed reminder of what the counterculture was countering at the time of America's most unpopular military engagement. Also evident at a glance, and equally crucial to its immediate appeal, was *In C*'s relative ease of performance. It does not require highly trained professional musicians, although nothing precludes their participation. It lends itself equally well to all kinds of nonstandard ensembles, and it encourages mixtures of players from different walks of musical life. It received many performances by rock bands and early-music groups, and among the instruments in its first performance were jazz saxophones, rock guitars, and recorders.

The piece could be seen, from all of these perspectives, as proposing a more democratic, less hierarchical organization of society that might have appeared utopian in "real life," but that could be actualized directly in music. It offered a working experience of countercultural paradise, or (as it was described in *Glamour* magazine) "the global village's first ritual symphonic piece."[15] Yet even the amount of specification that the notation of the piece and its loose performance algorithm retained eventually came to seem politically undesirable to the composer, who virtually abandoned notation for the next twenty years, devoting himself to solo and group improvisation with the algorithms and modules propounded through direct interaction—a virtual reversion (or, as some preferred to see it, a regression) to an oral culture. Riley became known for all-night improvisation concerts for small, devoted countercultural audiences. His main communication with the outer world was in the form of recordings that preserved "multitrack" improvisations, put together by a process of "overdubbing" one improvised part on others that had already been recorded. Riley's best-known multitrack improvisations were issued on another Columbia LP disk in 1969.

The force behind Riley's perhaps unexpected access to a major commercial "classical" label was David Behrman (b. 1937), a Harvard-trained composer and sound engineer who had been converted to experimental music, and who worked from 1965 to 1970 as a producer for Columbia Masterworks. There he was given the go-ahead by the label's president Goddard Lieberson (1911–77), an Eastman-trained composer, to sample the counterculture, whose work was after all cheap to produce on records, in an effort "to capture the imagination of the young audience."[16] Side I of Riley's new disk contained a nineteen-minute, largely pentatonic, ostinato-based improvisation called *A Rainbow in Curved Air*, in which the multiply recorded composer played electric organ, amplified harpsichord, "rocksichord" (electronic keyboard), dumbec (a small Persian drum), and tambourine. The other side had twenty-two minutes of less structured improvisations on soprano saxophone (an instrument Riley briefly took up following La Monte Young's example) and electric organ, called *Poppy Nogood and the Phantom Band*. The liner note consisted entirely of a utopian environmental fantasy, recalling the turbulent war-protest conditions that provided the counterculture with its impetus:

> And then all wars ended/Arms of every kind were outlawed and the masses gladly contributed them to giant foundries in which they were melted down and the metal poured back into the earth/The Pentagon was turned on its side and painted purple, yellow & green/All boundaries were dissolved/The slaughter of animals was forbidden/The whole of lower Manhattan became a meadow in which unfortunates from the Bowery were allowed to live out their fantasies in the sunshine and were cured/People swam in the sparkling rivers under blue skies streaked only with incense pouring from the new factories/The energy from dismantled nuclear weapons provided free heat and light/World health was restored/An abundance of organic vegetables, fruits and grains was growing wild along the discarded highways/National flags were sewn together into brightly colored circus tents under which politicians were allowed to perform harmless theatrical games/The concept of work was forgotten[17]

The fundamental question these pieces raised could be paraphrased: Could an avant-garde of harmonious simplicity really be an avant-garde? There is no doubt that if avant-garde means marginalization, then Riley was avant-garde. His music was never to be found in establishment venues, whether concert halls or commercial radio.

If avant-garde means technical innovation, then Riley was avant-garde. His music, especially the improvisation disks, made use of cutting-edge technology. Even *In C* was structured in a way that could not be entirely accounted for by citing precedents, whether "classical," "pop" or "world-music."

But if avant-garde means alienation, then Riley was anything but avant-garde (except in relation to the academic establishment from which he was a renegade, and which his music accordingly enraged). In sharp contrast to Young's, Riley's music bent over backward — too far, some thought — to be inclusive and audience-friendly, and cast an implicit negative judgment on elite art. Its most obviously "retrograde" tendency was its reembracement of consonance. But such a move was retrograde only from the historicist perspective, which required that all art build directly on the achievements of the immediate past, and toward a goal that those earlier achievements implied. That was never the aim of the avant-garde.

The very fact that Riley's music located the site of innovation elsewhere than in the domain of "pitch organization" implied a rejection of yesterday's modernism, as did all truly avant-garde art. It was precisely the same gesture, in relation to academic serialism, as the one that postwar serialists had made in relation to neoclassicism. It expressly denied the main premise of its elite academic predecessor, as peremptorily summed up by Milton Babbitt when he observed that, since pitch is the most precisely quantifiable of all musical parameters, it was therefore inconceivable that "under any reasonable application of the world 'important,' it could be suggested that pitch is not the most important of the musical dimensions, since its susceptibility to musical structuring includes and exceeds that of any other dimension."[18] Riley's music suggested, on the contrary, that there are other measures of musical importance besides the abstract structuring of pitch, and other available sites of significant innovation.

Of course it is also true that Riley's music of the 1960s bore conspicuous traits in common with the most crassly commercial musics of the 1970s. One was "disco," a style developed in "discothèques," nightclubs where people danced to recorded music, and where pop music was "remixed" by disc jockeys into all-night marathons of relentlessly repetitive, electronically realized "sequences" of commonplace riffs. Another was "New Age" music, a commercial offshoot of the counterculture, which consisted of sweet and soothingly repetitive "mood music" for piano or electric keyboards (or harp or acoustic guitar), meant to accompany the meditative practices of tired businesspeople, many of them former hippies, in search of surcease from the stresses of success. Like any other once-new music, Riley's was often assimilated in the minds of its critics to the routine practices it had helped set in motion, and it suffered in retrospect the negative judgments the routines inspired.

But Riley himself had no part of those routines, or at least no part of their commercial success. More than any other "minimalist," Riley lived the actual life of the counterculture. Just when he could have capitalized on the success of his Columbia albums he "dropped out" into a virtually nomadic existence, gave up formal composition and public exposure, and disappeared from sight until he was rediscovered as a "classic" in the 1980s. So if avant-garde implies the disinterested service of art in implied protest against its commercial exploitation, then once again the composer qualifies, even if his works are finally judged not to.

"CLASSICAL" MINIMALISM

For many listeners, the most characteristic and style-defining aspect of *In C* is the constant audible eighth-note pulse that underlies and coordinates all of the looping, and that seems, because it provides a constant pedal of Cs, to be fundamentally bound up with the work's concept. Like much modernist practice since at least Stravinsky, it puts the rhythmic spotlight on the "subtactile" level, accommodating and facilitating the free metamorphosis of the felt beat — for example, from quarters to dotted quarters at the twenty-second module of *In C* — and allows their multiple presence to be felt as levels within a complex texture. It may be surprising, therefore, to learn that the constant C-pulse was an afterthought, adopted in rehearsal for what seemed at the time a purely utilitarian purpose (simply to keep the group together in lieu of a conductor), and that it was not even Riley's idea. It was Reich's.

Steve Reich came from a background very different from Young's and Riley's. Where they had a rural, working-class upbringing on the West Coast, Reich was born into a wealthy, professional-class family in cosmopolitan New York. Like most children of his economic class, Reich had traditional piano lessons and plenty of exposure to what in later years he mildly derided as the "bourgeois classics." He had an elite education culminating in a Cornell baccalaureate with a major in philosophy. Then came a year of intense private instruction in composition with Hall Overton (1920–72), a composer who combined classical and jazz idioms in a manner comparable to Gunther Schuller's Third Stream (see chapter 7).

Next, Reich put in three years of graduate study in the Juilliard School's rigorous and traditional (though nonserial) composition program, studying with prominent pedagogues like Vincent Persichetti (1915–87), who had been Overton's teacher, and William Bergsma (1921–94). Finally, lured by the presence of Luciano Berio on the faculty, Reich enrolled at Mills College for a master's degree, which he received in 1963. It was the sort of training that usually led to a career as an elite modernist rather than an avant-gardist.

In interviews, Reich has stated that the impressions that led him to his own personal musical predilections, and eventually to his decision to attempt a career as a composer, date from his fifteenth year, when friends introduced him, in close succession, to recordings of Stravinsky's *Rite of Spring*, Bach's Fifth Brandenburg Concerto, and bebop, then the most modern form of jazz. The obvious common denominator of what might otherwise seem the three unrelated styles that aroused his enthusiasm is, of course, the presence of a strongly articulated subtactile pulse, the very thing that Reich (who participated in the first performances) contributed to *In C*. Baroque music has it, a lot of twentieth-century music (including both Stravinsky's "Russian" style and jazz) has it, but the repertoire of "bourgeois classics" — the music "from Haydn to Wagner," as in this chapter's epigraph — generally lacks it. Rejecting the traditional classical repertoire as a source of inspiration was Reich's first youthful "avant-garde" gesture.

Having discovered that subtactile "rhythmic profile" (as he called it), Reich switched from piano lessons to lessons in drumming. Significantly, though, his first percussion teacher was a "classical" one—who later became the principal timpanist of the New York Philharmonic, no less. It was only at Mills College that he discovered, again through recordings, the "non-Western" styles of percussion playing—West African drumming and Balinese gamelan—that effectively liberated his creative thinking from the assumptions of his traditional training. Eventually, he sought out native teachers in these traditions (drumming in Accra, Ghana, in 1970; gamelan in Seattle and Berkeley in 1973–1974) to gain hands-on experience. But the decisive, appetite-inducing exposure came through records. The global or "world music" orientation that Reich's music (like most minimalist music) exemplifies and serves is thus among the most palpable indications of the way recording technology redefined musical transmission in the twentieth century.

Late-twentieth-century transmission, in a word, was "horizontal." All musics past and present, nearby and far away, were, thanks to recording and communications technology, simultaneously and equally accessible to any musician in the world. The way in which this horizontal transmission supplanted the "vertical" transmission of styles in chronological single file (the assumption on which all historicist thinking depends) was the genuine musical revolution of the late twentieth century, the full implications of which will be realized only in the twenty-first and beyond. Its immediate effect on Reich, and the many composers his work has stimulated, was to convince him—to quote one of those composers, John Adams (b. 1947)—that a truly valid twentieth-century music would be "a music that is essentially percussive and pulse-generated rather than melodic and phrase-generated."[19]

After finishing the master's course at Mills, Reich stayed in the San Francisco Bay Area for a while and was associated, like many avant-gardists there, with the San Francisco Tape Music Center. (That was where he met and befriended Riley.) The earliest pieces of his to achieve wide notice were a pair of tape-loop compositions inspired directly by *In C*. The first, *It's Gonna Rain* (1965; originally titled "It's Gonna Rain; or, Meet Brother Walter in Union Square after Listening to Terry Riley"), was based on just the three titular words, spliced out of a recording of a gospel sermon delivered by Brother Walter, a San Francisco street preacher, in November 1964. The sermon was about Noah and the Flood. The implied warning of the title phrase, in the context of the scariest phases of the cold war like the still recent Cuban missile crisis, was timely and topical.

The other tape-loop piece, *Come Out* (1966), had a political subtext related to the civil-rights struggles of the sixties. It became Reich's breakthrough to recognition, thanks to its inclusion in one of David Behrman's Columbia records (*New Sounds in Electronic Music*, 1967). The composer's original program note described both the occasion that inspired the piece and the distinctive technical process that made it a milestone in the emergence of minimalism:

> *Come Out* was composed as part of a benefit, presented at [New York's] Town Hall in April, 1966, for the re-trial, with lawyers of their own choosing, of the six

boys arrested for murder during the Harlem riots of 1964. The [recorded] voice is that of Danniel Hamm, then nineteen, describing a beating he took in the Harlem 28th precinct. The police were about to take the boys out to be "cleaned up" and were only taking those that were visibly bleeding. Since Hamm had no actual open bleeding, he proceeded to squeeze open a bruise on his leg so that he would be taken to the hospital — "I had to, like, open the bruise up and let some of the bruise blood come out to show them."

The phrase "come out to show them" was recorded in both channels, first in unison and then with channel 2 slowly beginning to move ahead. As the phase begins to shift, a gradually increasing reverberation is heard which slowly passes into a sort of canon or round. Eventually the two voices divide into four and then into eight.

By restricting oneself to a small amount of material organized by a single uninterrupted process, one's attention can become focused on details that usually slip by. A single repeated and gradually changing figure may well be heard as a composite of several figures. Finally, at any given moment, it is open to the listener as to which pattern within the pattern he hears.[20]

After becoming a famous and much-interviewed figure, Reich tended to romanticize as serendipity, a happy accident, the discovery of the "phasing" process, through which identical tape loops feeding into two speakers or headphones go in and out of phase with one another (or more precisely, out and back into phase). According to one version of this much-repeated account, he intended the two channels through which he played *It's Gonna Rain* to remain synchronized, but on the cheap equipment he was using, one unexpectedly began to gain on the other. "The sensation I had in my head," as they played into the composer's earphones, "was that the sound moved over to my left ear, moved down to my left shoulder, down my left arm, down my leg, out across the floor to the left, and finally began to reverberate and shake" before it eventually "came back together in the center of my head."[21]

The point of the story as told and retold in retrospect is that the composer, in defiance of his modernist upbringing, was willing to decide that the phase phenomenon itself was more interesting than anything he might do with it, so he simply allowed it to play itself out. In its provocative modesty it was a genuinely avant-garde, shock-the-bourgeois gesture, and it was amply repaid with abuse from the relevant bourgeoisie, the academic modernists from whose ranks Reich had defected. They represented the status quo, he a force for change — hence a true avant-garde movement, neither conservative nor nostalgic, even though it renounced complexity and social alienation.

The controversies that swirled around minimalism when it began to have an impact confirmed the basic truth of the situation Reich's parable symbolized, but the parable as such was just a story. In fact, *It's Gonna Rain* and *Come Out* were planned from the start to exploit the "phasing" process, which Terry Riley had already discovered in a couple of tape pieces from 1964–65 that used another feedback device (somewhat more sophisticated than the echoplex), which Riley had christened the "time-lag accumulator." Reich employed a more rudimentary technology: he merely applied his thumb to the supply reel feeding the second channel to slow it slightly and allow the first to gain time. Then he rerecorded the mix of the two channels and repeated the process to produce a four-part phase texture, and then doubled it again so that eventually the sound texture consisted of eight parts in a very complex ratio of speeds. That was no serendipity: it took a great deal of premeditated labor.

Reich's phase compositions did differ considerably from Riley's, however. As Keith Potter, a historian of minimalism, emphasizes, "while Riley always allowed his patterns to accumulate into a psychedelic wash of sound, Reich generally stressed the audibility of his gradually shifting phase relations."[22] It was the process—inexorable and systematic—that mattered to him, because it gave the music a sense of purpose, or what Kant (as a former philosophy major like Reich would surely have remembered) called *Zweckmässigkeit*, the likeness of a purpose. For Kant that was the essence of art, and so it was for Reich.

Anything that goes back to Kant goes back to the very dawn of esthetics. But Reich's stripped-down purposiveness differed to such a degree from the conventional expressive or formal purposes of art (to say nothing of the crasser purposes of pop) as to seem new in kind. He expounded his philosophy in a forbiddingly grim (and rather prim) essay of 1968 called "Music as a Gradual Process." "I do not mean the process of composition, but rather pieces of music that are, literally, processes," the manifesto began, and then continued in short explosive paragraphs like planks in a political platform. Here are a few:

> The distinctive thing about musical processes is that they determine all the note-to-note (sound-to-sound) details and the overall form simultaneously.
>
> I am interested in perceptible processes. I want to be able to hear the process happening throughout the sounding music.
>
> To facilitate closely detailed listening, a musical process should happen extremely gradually. Performing and listening to a gradual musical process resembles:
>
> pulling back a swing, releasing it, and observing it gradually come to rest; turning over an hourglass and watching the sand slowly run through to the bottom; placing your feet in the sand by the ocean's edge and watching, feeling, and listening to the waves gradually bury them.
>
> Though I may have the pleasure of discovering musical processes and composing the musical material to run through them, once the process is set up and loaded, it runs by itself.
>
> What I'm interested in is a compositional process and a sounding music that are one and the same thing. While performing and listening to gradual musical processes, one can participate in a particular liberating and impersonal kind of ritual. Focusing in on the musical process makes possible that shift of attention away from *he* and *she* and *you* and *me* outward toward *it*.[23]

The italicized *it* and the implied overcoming of self described in the last paragraph have a Zen Buddhist ring, which brings John Cage to mind. But although he acknowledged the influence of Cage on his thinking, Reich nevertheless rejected Cage's music, because "the processes he used were compositional ones that could not be heard when the piece was performed; the process of using the *I Ching* or imperfections in a sheet of paper to determine musical parameters can't be heard when listening to music composed that way."[24] In other words, Cageian indeterminacy had the same fatal flaw as academic serialism: "the compositional processes and the sounding music have no audible connection," and therefore, for Reich, are devoid of listening (as opposed to analytical or historical) interest.

More explicitly than most musicians at the time, Reich made a political point of this. Citing the complaint of another composer that in the kind of musical process he envisioned "the composer isn't privy to anything,"[25] Reich insisted that that is just the way things ought to be. The next sentence was Reich's most outspoken challenge to the reigning modernist aesthetic: "I don't know any secrets of structure that you can't hear."[26] The composer's implicit ascendancy over the listener was overthrown. Reich deliberately cast himself, like Schoenberg before him, as a Great Emancipator. But whereas Schoenberg (like Cage) purported to liberate sounds, Reich (like a sixties agitator) was out to liberate people.

SECRETS OF STRUCTURE

Like Cage (and like the Dadaists before him), Reich proposed a limit case to test his theory to a logical extreme: a composition called *Pendulum Music*, composed (or more precisely, conceived of) in 1968, the same year as the manifesto. It was first performed at the university of Colorado–Boulder and repeated at the first all-Reich concert, which took place at the Whitney Museum of American Art in New York on 27 May 1969. Scored for "three or more microphones, amplifiers and loudspeakers," it is as close a musical analogue to the three ordinary process-experiences described in the manifesto (watching the swing, watching the hourglass, burying one's feet) as he could devise.

According to the "score" (actually just a verbal instruction or "algorithm"), the microphones are "suspended from the ceiling or from microphone boom stands by their cables so that they all hang the same distance from the floor and are all free to swing with a pendular motion." Loudspeakers are positioned under the microphones face upward, so that they will produce feedback noise when the microphones are directly above them. Then the microphones are pulled back and released. As they swing like pendulums over the loudspeakers, they produce a series of feedback pulses that will inevitably go out of phase as the pendulums, gradually coming to rest, slow down. Having released the

F I G. 8-3   New York premiere of Steve Reich's *Pendulum Music*, 27 May 1969.

mike-pendulums, the score specifies, "the performers then sit down to watch and listen to this process along with the rest of the audience." What makes the music, then, is not the composer, not the performer, but *it* (call it the force of gravity).

In concept, Reich's *Pendulum Music* is virtually a duplicate of György Ligeti's notorious *Poème symphonique* for 100 metronomes of 1962 (see chapter 3). The difference is that the earlier piece was at least partly meant as a spoof, while Reich's was meant in deadly earnest—and also, taking far less time to unfold, makes a reasonable rather than comically preposterous demand on the listener's attention. *Pendulum Music* is the conceptual paradigm or limit-case to which all of Reich's early works for conventional performing forces can be meaningfully related.

But it does not require musicians for its performance. It often provided background music at exhibitions of "minimal" art, with the artists, or museum staff, doing the "performing." As "furniture music," it hardly fulfilled the composer's intention of providing a focus of close attention. That role was accomplished much more significantly, and with far greater impact, by Reich's "phase" compositions for pianos, violins, and log drums, composed between 1967 and 1969. Virtuoso pieces in their way, they were responses to the same impulse that motivated Riley's *In C*: the need to apply techniques first discovered in the realm of tape music to standard vocal and instrumental media.

But where Riley deliberately kept things easy, Reich's phase pieces can be arduous to execute with the required precision. It seems that he considered not only the back-transfer from tape to live music making itself but also the effort and the arduousness to be necessary if the product was to be effectively "humanized" and rendered communicative. The difficulty of his music, requiring skilled professionals for its performance and thereby satisfying a traditional elite modernist criterion, has made Reich, of all the composers who inhabit this chapter, the most academically acceptable. He has enjoyed far greater respect than the others among "uptown" musicians and "mainstream" critics.

Piano Phase (1967) is a three-part composition for two pianos, with each major section consisting of a one-measure diatonic or pentatonic module (or "basic unit" in Reich's terminology) that is subjected to the same phase process that Reich first achieved by retarding the turning of a tape reel. The first basic unit is shown in Ex. 8-4. It is an elusively complex rhythmic construction in its own right, a melody that emerges as a composite of two rhythmic figures in a hemiola relationship: the right hand plays three repetitions of the two-note group F♯-C♯ while the left plays two repetitions of the three-note group E-B-D. The interaction of patterns between the two hands is subtly complicated (or contradicted) by the differently patterned interaction of two distinct registers, E-F♯ and B-C♯-D, conjunct scale segments separated by a skip of a fourth.

EX. 8-4   Steve Reich, *Piano Phase*, first "basic unit"

The two pianos begin by playing the figure in unison, the way the two tape recorders had begun in *Come Out*. While one pianist holds the tempo steady, the other very gradually gains on it, producing at first an enhanced resonance as the parts go slightly out of phase; then a kind of hocket, with the second piano playing on the "off thirty-seconds." Finally, after another resonant blur, the second piano will be one sixteenth-note ahead of the first; here the two pianists are instructed to lock into the same tempo again, producing a sort of canon at the sixteenth-note which establishes a new point of departure for the next phasing process. After twelve such processes, the original unison is regained.

What is curious, and somewhat ironic given the premises of the "Gradual Process" manifesto, is the ambiguity of the overall structure. Listeners are normally aware only of the steady progress toward the goal of regained unison. According to the terms of the manifesto, that is exactly what the composer intended. But the manifesto contained an interesting escape clause: "Even when all the cards are on the table and everyone hears what is gradually happening in a musical process, there are still enough mysteries to satisfy all."[27] And indeed, there is a mysterious corollary to this or any other strict phase process: as a moment's reflection will confirm, its second half is (and must be) automatically the retrograde of the first half, with the relationship between the two players reversed. So, is the process a single linear gesture or a double, out-and-back trajectory like so much Western classical music?

This ambiguity was first pointed out by Paul Epstein, a music theorist on the faculty of Temple University, in an article of 1986, more than two decades after the piece was written.[28] It turned out that, in seeming contradiction of Reich's manifesto, there was after all a "secret of structure" in *Piano Phase* that listeners did not know. But if, as seems likely, the composer himself was unaware of (or did not envision) the retrograde, which was irrelevant to his purpose in composing the piece, then his famous maxim — "I don't know any secrets of structure that you can't hear" — remains literally true. (Of course, the last three words of the maxim are another escape clause, since — exactly as Milton Babbitt has always argued — once anything has been pointed out and conceptualized, it *can* be heard.) Nothing, it turns out, not even a minimalist structure, is ever devoid of ambiguity.

Reich's last strict, if somewhat simplified, phase composition took the minimalist ideal to another sort of limit. *Clapping Music* (1972) is instrumental music without instruments, or rather, percussion music made with the body alone. Two performers begin in unison, clapping a simple riff that one of them will maintain unchanged throughout the piece. As in *Piano Phase*, the riff contains twelve subtactile pulses. The other player, skipping the gradual speedup, jumps to the second "phase," in which the pattern is rendered as a canon at an interval of one pulse. After a while, a similar jump extends the canon to an interval of two pulses, then three, and so on until unison is regained. All the notation that is needed to perform this or any other algorithmic composition is the basic unit, plus instructions for permuting it. Nevertheless, Ex. 8-5 shows all the permutations so as to make all the resulting hockets and syncopations scannable at a glance.

EX. 8-5   Steve Reich, *Clapping Music*

Comparing the unison rests in the thirteen modules will bring the palindrome effect easily into view. Nos. 1 and 13, of course, are identical. Nos. 2, 7 (the midpoint), and 12 are also identical: they are the ones without any unison rests. Nos. 3 and 11 each have one unison rest. If you scan no. 3 beginning at the rest from left to right, and no. 11 beginning at the rest from right to left, they will match. Nos. 4 and 10 have two unison rests. Scan no. 4 from left to right beginning at its first unison rest, and no. 10 from right to left beginning at its second unison rest, and they will match. Nos. 5 and 9, with one unison rest, will match if scanned the way 3 and 11 were scanned. Nos. 6 and 8 have two unison rests. Scan them the way nos. 4 and 10 were scanned, and they too will match. None of this will be obvious to a casual listener; this piece, too, has its "secret structure."

Clapping Music was written for the road, when the ensemble known as Steve Reich and Musicians began touring. ("Hands," Reich drily explained, "are easy to transport.") It was used as an introductory piece, to give the audience an instant grasp of what "gradual process" meant. By then, however, having laid his conceptual foundation with a manifesto ("Music as Gradual Process"), a limit piece (*Pendulum Music*), and various strict phase exercises for tape and live performers, Reich had somewhat relaxed the rigor of his procedures. On the model of the African and Indonesian musics he was learning, he began experimenting with patterned processes that were less predictable than the "pure" phase pieces with which he had found his voice. But even if less predictable, they remained just as inexorable.

The work that really showed the possibilities of Reichian minimalism was *Four Organs* (1970). The small and relatively inexpensive electric organs for which the piece is scored, called Farfisas, were a staple of rock bands. The very necessary accompaniment was provided by a pair of maracas, which provide a constant subtactile pulse against which the gradually unfolding structural process could be precisely measured. That new process was the gradual filling of the available sound-space within the basic unit. Ex. 8-6 shows the beginning of the process, and the end.

EX. 8-6   Steve Reich, *Four Organs*, beginning (figs. 1–8) and end (last two figures)

EX. 8-6 (continued)

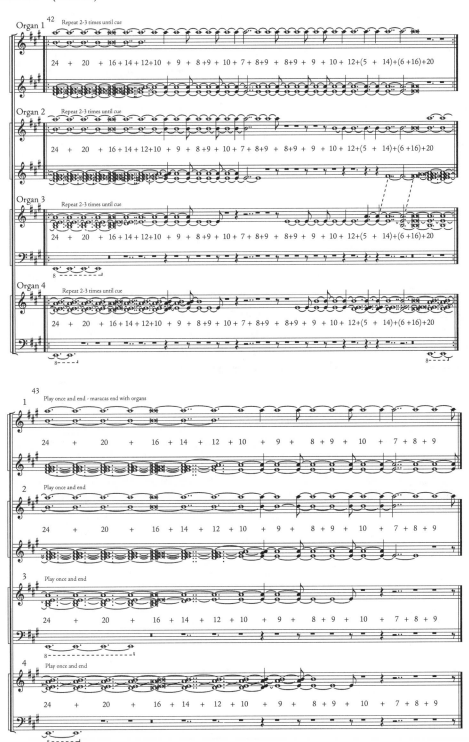

At the outset, the available space is measured out by the maracas with eleven pulses. For minimalist purposes that is a magic number, because it is a prime number. Divisible neither by two nor by three, it remains always subtactile; it cannot be grouped mentally into a regular *tactus* or felt beat. In practice, the eleven is subdivided into 3 + 8, as established by the basic unit, which consists simply of two identical chords that fall on the first and fourth pulse of each measure. The process that governs the entire piece, while unrelated to "phasing," was similarly systematic and rigorous. It consists of a single "rhythmic construction" (Reich's term) that gradually replaces the rests in the basic unit with notes, as shown in Ex. 8-6.

Once the basic unit has been filled—or as Keith Potter nicely puts it, once "the original pairs of irregularly pulsing chords have silted up into a continuous sound"[29]—the unit begins to lengthen, eventually expanding to a gargantuan 265 measures of held-out but internally fluctuating harmony that reminds many listeners (including Reich, who claimed to have been inspired by it) of Perotin's late twelfth-century *organa quadrupla* for the Cathedral of Notre Dame—another remote yet direct influence, this one collapsing more than seven centuries of historical time, made possible by recordings. The held-out chord is one often described by jazz musicians as a "dominant eleventh," in which an extra pair of thirds is stacked on top of a dominant seventh built on E, thus: E-G♯-B-D-F♯-A. In practice, since the top A is sounded during the early stages of the piece only on the first and fourth eighths, it seems to resolve like an appoggiatura to the held-over G♯, the first alteration to the basic unit.

That impression of resolution is confirmed by the way in which *Four Organs* comes to an end. Unlike Reich's phase pieces, it neither comes full circle nor reaches a saturation point. Instead, the low E and its doublings are filtered out of the last sustained chord, followed very slowly by the remaining notes one by one, until the piece finally comes to an end, somewhat surprisingly, on the two highest pitches, the fourth E-A. The fact that this ending takes listeners by surprise belies Reich's semifacetious contention that all that *Four Organs* comes down to, finally, is a single, enormously slowed and sustained V–I cadence in A major. The experience of listening to it should be enough to convince anyone that functional harmony is as much a function of rhythm as it is of pitch relations; distend the former enough and you dissolve the latter. But *Four Organs* does signal a new (or revived) interest in harmonic progression and voice leading, and does return pitch to a position of significance, if not primacy, in the articulation of musical shape.

"ALL MUSIC IS FOLK MUSIC"

Four Organs marks a divide in Reich's output between the rigorously experimental works of the sixties and what proved to be the more immediately appealing works that followed. The piece is still sufficiently uncompromising in its minimalist approach to serve as a litmus test dividing "mainstream" listeners from the coterie of its devotees. The latter notice, and become fascinated by, the gradual processes; the former mainly notice, and become irritated by, the repetitions. This became clear in January 1973 when the young conductor Michael Tilson Thomas (b. 1944) offered the piece to a Boston

Symphony subscription audience in New York's Carnegie Hall, and elicited perhaps the last memorable twentieth-century succès de scandale. (Among the uncorroborated details that went from mouth to mouth was a woman shouting, "All right, I'll confess!") For the next decade, Reich's primary venues would remain the art museums and downtown halls where various "alternative" musics rubbed shoulders, and his principal means of disseminating his work remained his own touring group. Further exposure to concert audiences would wait. But in the meantime, Reich's style underwent a change.

His output in the 1970s was dominated by two hour-long works. *Drumming* (1971), which can last up to eighty-six minutes depending on how many times the basic units are repeated, is scored for a nine-piece percussion band plus a piccolo player and two women vocalists singing "vocables" (nonmeaningful syllables). Both the rhythmic patterning of the piece and the integration of voices into the ensemble were influenced directly by the African music Reich had studied on location in 1970. The rhythmic unit is expanded from the eleven pulses of *Four Organs* to twelve. The addition of that extra eighth-note makes a huge difference, of course, because it allows the exploitation of hemiola effects by grouping the subtactile eighths, variously and/or simultaneously, into tactile pulses — "felt" beats — of varying length: two (six to a bar), three (four to a bar) and four (three to a bar).

The unfolding process is complex, combining the older phase technique with the "rhythmic construction" (or gradual fill-in) of *Four Organs*, now balanced against its opposite, "rhythmic reduction" (the gradual replacement of notes with rests). The piece achieves its grandiose length through contrasts of tone color. The first of its four large sections is scored for tuned bongo drums; the second, for marimbas and voices; the third, moving into an unsingably high register, uses glockenspiels, with whistling and piccolo piping replacing the voices; the fourth combines all forces. As a result of all of these interacting factors, *Drumming* was a technical tour de force, creating (in John Adams's words) "an interesting large-scale musical structure without recourse to harmony."[30] It served for several years as the staple of Reich's touring group, greatly increasing the size of his coterie of devotees to the point where he began filling large halls (mainly on college campuses) and attracting imitators.

Perhaps more noteworthy than its structural principles, of interest primarily to other composers, was the effect that *Drumming* had on audiences. Its complexity notwithstanding, the euphoria it produced in receptive listeners (so much more typical of pop than of contemporary classical composition) made it newsworthy and, of course, controversial, not only because it challenged the basic definition of avant-garde art, but also because listeners were obviously responding to more than just the beguiling sound patterns. There was also the unstated but strongly implied (or metaphorical) social meaning that arose directly from its African antecedents. When witnessed live, Adams noted,

> performances of *Drumming* have the flavor of a ceremony, with the performers uniformly clad in white cotton shirts and dark pants, moving gradually during the course of the work from the bongos, to the marimbas, to the glockenspiels, and finally to all the instruments for the finale. The sense of ritualistic precision and

unity is furthered by performers playing from memory and by their performing face-to-face, two on a single instrument.[31]

To put it another way, the work presented a model of harmonious social interaction that bore interesting comparison with theories just then being advanced about the primary value of music. In an influential book ambitiously titled *How Musical Is Man?* (1973), based on lectures delivered in 1969–1970 at the University of Washington, the English ethnomusicologist John Blacking (1928–90), then occupying the chair of social anthropology at Queen's University, Belfast, presented a thesis that argued that "humanly organized sound" was a necessary precondition to "soundly organized humanity," from which it followed that music could — should? — be valued according to the degree to which it reflected that reciprocity and furthered the implied objective of social harmony.

Blacking in effect renewed (or modernized) a position that went all the way back to Plato (at least), and that had Count Leo Tolstoy as its most prominent recent exponent in Europe. Though venerable, it had been much weakened in the West by cold-war suspicion of the social as a criterion of artistic value. It was indeed obvious that social criteria of artistic value had been tyrannically abused under totalitarian regimes. But Blacking, who in addition to being an anthropologist was a trained classical pianist, argued that the opposite tendency — toward individualism and the competitive display of skill and originality — had reached a similar, no less deplorable condition of abuse in the highly developed technological societies of postwar Western Europe and America.

FIG. 8-4   Steve Reich and Musicians performing *Drumming*.

Basing his thesis on observations made during two years of fieldwork among the Venda, a South African tribe, Blacking noted that among his informants, and in most sub-Saharan African societies, all members are considered to be "musical" in that they are "able to perform and listen intelligently to their own indigenous music,"[32] while in his own British society only a few specially gifted people are credited with "musicality." "Must a majority be made 'unmusical,'" he asked, "so that a few may become more 'musical'?" Did that heightened and exclusive conception of musicality lead to the creation of a better or more valuable music than is available in societies where everyone is considered musical? Or did the concept of musicality with which he was brought up reflect a more general abuse of technology to further the social hierarchies and exclusions on which the British class system depended?

Those technologies began with notation, by means of which "music could be handed down by a hereditary elite without any need for listeners." They included complex machines, like the piano, which relatively few could afford, and to operate which required years of training. By the modern period they entailed advanced and esoteric techniques for encoding sound, the products of which were indecipherable except to those trained in producing them. The difficulties of such procedures, and the special qualifications they called for, were habitually taken in advanced societies as evidence of their value. But what did such values say about such societies?

Ethnomusicology, Blacking asserted, was the discipline best suited—indeed, created—to answer such questions. It was a new discipline, named (by the Dutch music scholar Jaap Kunst) as recently as 1950. It was often thought of by "Westerners" as the study of "non-Western" musics, or "oral" musics, or "folk" or "traditional" musics, and when defined in this way it could be seen as the continuation of an older tradition in musicology, sometimes called "comparative musicology" or "musical ethnology," that took as its subject matter anything that was not "urban European art music"[33] (to quote the definition of ethnomusicology given in *The New Grove Dictionary of Music and Musicians*). That was the view of the field from within academic musicology, as laid out by the German founders of the discipline in the 1880s.

Blacking, following an alternative model proposed by anthropologists like Alan Merriam (1923–80), granted ethnomusicology a much wider purview. Merriam called it "the study of music in culture,"[34] and Blacking went so far as to declare it to be the only truly universal musicological method. The first chapter of *How Musical Is Man?* ends with a ringing manifesto:

> Functional analyses of musical structure cannot be detached from structural analyses of its social function: the function of tones in relation to each other cannot be explained adequately as part of a closed system without reference to the structures of the sociocultural system of which the musical system is a part, and to the biological system to which all music makers belong. Ethnomusicology is not only an area study concerned with exotic music, nor a musicology of the ethnic—it is a discipline that holds out hope for a deeper understanding of all music. If some music can be analyzed and understood as tonal expressions of human experience in the context of different kinds of social and cultural organization, I see no reason why all music should not be analyzed in the same way.[35]

It is not difficult to discern the political subtext that undergirded these opposing views of ethnomusicology, the one arising out of musicology and the other out of anthropology. The first kept "urban European art music"—a genre traditionally studied through its outstanding individual practitioners, the great composers—front and center. The methods it employed were analysis and style criticism, the first showing how "the music works" as an autonomous structure and the second "how the composer worked" as an autonomous individual.

That approach was often justified by calling on a distinction that anthropologically inclined ethnomusicologists themselves had coined: *etic* versus *emic*. "Etic" was short for phonetic, a kind of linguistic (or, by extension, musical) transcription that sought to record everything heard by the transcriber, without any consideration of its significance. "Emic," short for phonemic, was a transcription that sought to reflect what was of significance to the informants (that is, the speakers whose language was being transcribed). A phonetic transcription, for example, would include every tiny variant in vowel sounds made by the utterer of a sentence, and every tiny variation in pitch produced by the singer of a melody. A phonemic transcription would exclude chance variations (slurred speech, singing out of tune) that did not affect meaning as perceived by the informants. Since only an insider to a language or a musical system (whether native or "acculturated") can apply the latter criterion, *etic* and *emic* are anthropologists' shorthand for "outsider's perspective" and "insider's perspective."

It is natural, according to the older view of both musicology and ethnomusicology, that Western musicians will study the music of "their own tradition" (that is, the music to which they are insiders) differently, both as to approach and as to method, from music of traditions to which they are outsiders. The one is central to their experience and interests, the other peripheral. Ethnomusicology, in this view, is by definition an etic discipline, suitable only for "other" music, or else, exceptionally, to music within the Western tradition about which "little or no historical information is available and no body of music theory exists"[36] (to quote again from the *New Grove Dictionary*), and where, therefore, scholars must proceed entirely by inference (that is, "etically").

The newer, more inclusive view of ethnomusicology, as expressed most militantly by Blacking, refuses to recognize the special position of urban European art music or its special relationship to the musicologists who study it. Those special privileges maintain an unjustifiable status quo in support of a socially destructive value system. Rather, by stripping the products of European art music of its privileges and studying it "etically" alongside the other musics of the world, one can bring to light that overly individualistic and socially exploitative value system, and possibly find within scholarship the means toward social betterment. To say, with Blacking, that "all music is folk music,"[37] enabled one to expose and counter the ways in which the seemingly innocent study of music, by endorsing a hierarchy that places the great composers (all white, male, and of European stock) at the incontestable top, has lent support to imperialism and racism and sexism. Adopting an openly and actively political stance, the new ethnomusicology (and the "new musicology" that emerged in response to it) refused to allow that there is any nonpolitical alternative; there are only covertly political ones.

As the next chapter will make plainer, these principles are among the ways of late-twentieth-century thinking that have been collectively labeled "postmodernist." The way in which they oppose some of the basic tenets of modernism should already be plain. The way in which Blacking's ethnomusicological position and its social implications parallel the development of Steve Reich's compositional practice (and *its* social implications) should also be clear, even though there is no evidence that Reich studied Blacking (or even heard of him) despite the fact that they often echo one another's words. Reich, equally unbeknownst to Blacking, had written in 1968 that "all music turns out to be ethnic music."[38] Both Reich and Blacking were part of a growing wave of "sixties" skepticism that had ample repercussions, beginning in the 1970s, both in scholarship and in the arts.

Reich has often said that he is interested not in imitating the sounds of African or Asian musics (mere "chinoiserie," as he calls such imitations) but rather in adapting their structural principles in order to achieve similar effects. "The pleasure I get from playing," he wrote, regardless of whether the music played is Balinese, African, or his own, "is not the pleasure of expressing myself but of subjugating myself to the music and experiencing the ecstasy that comes from being a part of it."[39] His aim in composing—that is, setting up musical processes—was to provide himself and his audience with something to which they could subjugate themselves together.

Now compare Blacking:

> Performances by combinations of two or three players of rhythms that can in fact be played by one are not musical gimmicks: they express concepts of individuality in community, and of social, temporal, and spatial balance, which are found in other features of Venda culture and other types of Venda music. Rhythms such as these cannot be performed correctly unless the players are their own conductors and yet at the same time submit to the rhythm of an invisible conductor. This is the kind of shared experience which the Venda seek and express in their music making.[40]

Blacking was describing the way in which Venda musicians perform intricate complexes of hemiola patterns that together cooperate to produce a series of equal subtactile pulses at the heard surface. He could just as well have been describing Reich's *Drumming*. The crucial difference, however, was that Reich sought not to express concepts found in other features of his own culture, or other types of "urban European art music" (especially the types written by his established contemporaries), but to propose an alternative to them that implied both a musical contrast and a social critique. That critical perspective, hostile to existing institutions and established social relations and even threatening them, makes it not only possible but essential to regard *Drumming* as being, within its own context (and despite its mounting popularity), an avant-garde composition. It produced historical change.

A POSTMODERNIST MASTERWORK?

Reich's other large work of the 1970s, *Music for 18 Musicians* (composed between 1974 and 1976), has acquired emblematic status. Far less immediately evocative than

Drumming of exotic musics, it represents a synthesis of all the techniques Reich had developed over the preceding decade; and in its use of electronically amplified solo strings, winds, and voices in counterpoint with the ever-present Reichian percussion and keyboards it proposed an alternative, increasingly normative orchestral sound for the late twentieth century. Perhaps the most influential fully notated composition of the decade, it is often described as the first postmodernist masterwork. Although calling it that may be yet another contradiction in terms, the phrase does call attention to the important role it played in renovating the terms on which music was composed and evaluated.

Basically an expansive synthesis of the harmonic structure of *Four Organs* with the rhythmic design of *Drumming*, Reich's *Music for 18 Musicians* unfolds a kaleidoscope of evolving and interacting melodic patterns, all controlled by a common measure of twelve quick-moving subtactile pulses, over a majestically slow-moving chord progression that pulses through the ensemble at the outset at a rate of fifteen to thirty seconds per chord, and is then repeated at the rate of four to six minutes per chord, with the string instruments playing long sustained tones. Each of these long spans provides the background for a "small piece," as Reich calls his closed rhythmic constructions, mostly cast in simple, easily perceived ABA forms. The composition in its totality is a chain of eleven of these small pieces, which, because it recapitulates a previously heard harmonic progression, achieves a preordained closure of its own, reinforced by a final, relatively rapid cruise through the eleven chords at the end.

The most significant resemblance between *Music for 18 Musicians* and *Drumming* is in the manner of its performance. It, too, embodies a highly ritualized set of prescribed actions, in which players (including the composer, when the piece is performed—as it almost always is—by his own ensemble) move from place to place on the stage, their physical movements and resulting sound-output regulated not by a conductor but by the vibraphone player, whose prescribed actions signal the end of each "small piece" and cue the next with a special recurrent tune reserved for the instrument's distinctive timbre. The vibraphone thus impersonally embodies the role of the master drummer in an African ensemble, the "invisible conductor" to which all the players, the composer included, impersonally submit, sacrificing their individual freedom not to a specially empowered individual who alone is free, but to a collective and transcendent ideal of ecstasy-producing accuracy.

The whole hour-long piece, although it has a meticulously notated score and parts, can be followed from the harmonic skeleton given in Ex. 8-7, which shows the eleven-chord progression whose triple cursus provides the composition with its structure. While entirely diatonic, requiring not a single accidental, it is obviously no functional progression. Roots are often equivocal (as is especially obvious in the first chord); the spacing, with wide gaps between the bass dyad and the rest, is eccentric; there is no strong cadence or even any pure consonant triad. Most of the harmonies are of the kind jazz musicians call "added-note chords." One cannot even confidently assign the progression to the A-major or the F♯-minor reading of the key signature. The most one can say, perhaps, is that by choosing a strictly diatonic but weakly articulated pitch field and (relatively) consonant harmonies the composer has made the pitch domain relatively unobtrusive, the better to focus listeners' attention on the rhythmic processes. The change of harmony every five minutes or so amounts to a cleansing of the palate rather than a dramatic event.

EX. 8-7   Steve Reich, *Music for 18 Musicians*, "cycle of chords"

The "opening chorale," or rapid harmonic traversal, unfolds through "hairpin" (crescendo-decrescendo) dynamics corresponding to the length of a wind-player's breath. The bass and treble instruments come separately to the fore, thus further attenuating any sense of harmonic function or progression. During the slow-motion progression that makes up the body of the work, most of the interacting rhythmic/melodic cells are based on the $\frac{12}{8}$ pattern already familiar from *Clapping Music*. These cells occasionally introduce pitches foreign to the sustained harmony, and even the bass occasionally uses foreign and even chromatic pitches as embellishments (yet further lessening its structural role). All of this may be observed in the first "small piece," based on the first chord, as sampled in Ex. 8-8. Despite these liberties, or even because of them, there is always a very firm distinction between what is structural (i.e., related to the basic progression) and what is decorative. It is the stringently limited and static nature of the structural material that maintains the tie between this very elaborate and colorful composition and the reductive minimalist ideal. Gone, however, is the ascetic atmosphere of early minimalism. Compared with the monochromatic schemes of Reich's previous music, the variegated timbres of *Music for 18 Musicians* are extravagant, even voluptuous.

Reich acknowledged the change in a 1977 interview with Michael Nyman. The all-important process, he now allowed, was more his business than his audience's:

> I'm not as concerned that one hears how the music is made as I was in the past. If some people hear exactly what's going on, good for them, and if other people don't but they still like the piece, then that's OK too. . . . There was a didactic quality to the early pieces, and looking back I'd say that, when you discover a new idea, it's very important to present that idea in a very forceful and clear and pared-down way. . . . But once you've done that, what do you do? What I was really concerned with in *Music for 18 Musicians* was making beautiful music above everything else.[41]

These are no longer the words of an avant-gardist, but those of an artist who feels his battle has been won. That may account for the sense of celebration that fills *Music for 18 Musicians*. Over its course distinctive features of Reich's previous work pass in review: the glockenspiels from *Drumming*, the maracas from *Four Organs*, the pentatonic patterns from the early phase pieces. By the time the ninth "small piece" is reached, the texture—combining the expanding "rhythmic construction" idea of *Drumming* with the progressive canons of *Clapping Music*—has become very laden and intricate, but also euphoric.

Even within the minimalist purview, it now appeared, it was possible to achieve "maximum complexity under maximum control," and beginning with *Music for 18 Musicians* Reich began to command the full respect of some influential mainstream or academic critics. But at the same time Reich's music broadened its appeal to what

EX. 8-8   Steve Reich, *Music for 18 Musicians*, mm. 99–105

EX. 8-8   (continued)

became known as the "crossover" audience. Reich's ensemble gave the premiere of *Music for 18 Musicians* at New York's Town Hall, a classical venue, in April 1976. Two years later, his recording of the piece for ECM, a small German label that specialized in avant-garde jazz, sold 100,000 copies — obviously not just to the avant-garde audience — and the ensemble performed the piece before a sell-out audience at the Bottom Line, one of New York's most famous rock clubs. Add another two years and Steve Reich and Musicians would be filling Carnegie Hall.

Reich began to receive commissions from major orchestras (New York Phil-harmonic, San Francisco Symphony), which led him for a time to modify his style considerably. That was "rather fortunate," said Brian Eno, "because that meant I could carry on with it,"[42] meaning the earlier, more ascetic and rigorous minimalist manner that now went over quite decisively into art-rock. There was no longer any point even in attempting to draw the line, formerly so sharp and well patrolled, between the high and low genres of music, at least where the impact of minimalism was concerned; nor was there any way of telling where the movement's impact had been greater. Minimalism turned out to be for music a great leveler, for which reason traditional modernists regarded it as the direst of threats. And that made it the most easily cited, if not necessarily the most representative or significant, embodiment of "postmodernism."

"CROSSOVER": WHO'S ON TOP?

Yet not even *Music for 18 Musicians* marked the crest of the minimalist wave. That decisive moment came on Sunday, 21 November 1976, seven months after the premiere of *18*, when *Einstein on the Beach*, a four-act opera by Philip Glass (b. 1937), composed in collaboration with the avant-garde theater director and stage designer Robert Wilson (b. 1941), played to a packed Metropolitan Opera House in New York. The wildly enthusiastic audience, perhaps needless to say, did not consist of Met subscribers. Instead, it was as if the "downtown" New York arts scene — painters, conceptual artists, experimental theater hands, art-rockers and their fans, along with a scattering of curious "classical" musicians who felt distinctly like onlookers — had migrated northward and invaded the precincts of high art for a night. "Who are these people?"[43] one of the opera house administrators supposedly asked Glass. "I've never seen them here before." As Glass tells the story, "I remember replying very candidly, 'Well, you'd better find out

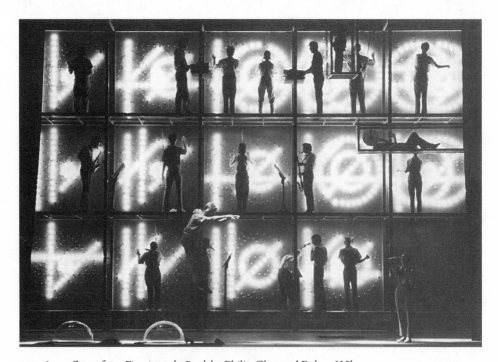

FIG. 8-5   Scene from *Einstein on the Beach* by Philip Glass and Robert Wilson.

who they are, because if this place expects to be running in twenty-five years, that's your audience out there.'"

It has not turned out that way. As of the year 2000, the Metropolitan Opera was still running on its traditional repertoire, leavened by only the occasional premiere, and was still supported by its traditional, if noticeably aging, audience. If anything, the crossover phenomenon has worked the other way over the long haul; the one Glass opera to play the Met since *Einstein on the Beach* (*The Voyage*, an actual Metropolitan Opera commission performed in 1992 to commemorate the five-hundredth anniversary of Columbus's voyage to the New World) is decidedly tamer, more "mainstream" than his works of the seventies. Like Reich, and like many musical radicals, Glass has been mellowed by success. But the *Einstein* performance was nonetheless a watershed.

Glass's development paralleled Reich's in many ways, though with some significant variations. His early training in his native Baltimore was entirely conventional, as were his fledgling years as a composer. Unlike Reich, Glass majored in music at the University of Chicago, where he matriculated at the precocious age of fifteen. He then went on to Juilliard and studied with the same teachers, Bergsma and Persichetti, as Reich. They were initially more successful in instilling in Glass the neoclassical and public-spirited values of the preserial American academy. On his graduation with a master's degree in 1961, Glass received a Ford Foundation grant to become composer-in-residence to the Pittsburgh public schools, for which he turned out a quantity of simple functional music, some of it (including choral settings of poetry by Walt Whitman and Carl Sandburg) in a somewhat "Americanist" idiom. Glass's music of this early period, almost all of it subsequently withdrawn by the composer, has been compared to the work of Hindemith and Copland.

In 1963, Glass applied for a Fulbright Fellowship to follow in Copland's footsteps as a pupil of Nadia Boulanger, then still teaching at the American Academy at Fontainebleau near Paris. He spent two years in France, and this is where he had his musical epiphany. It did not come from Boulanger; like Reich, Glass found his voice as a result of an unforeseen brush with non-European music. He took a job with the famous Indian musician Ravi Shankar (b. 1920), notating from recordings the music Shankar had composed at his sitar to accompany a documentary film. From this task Glass learned, as he put it, "how music may be structured by rhythmic patterning rather than by harmonic progression." From Paris he went to India to study at its source the music by which he now wanted to be influenced.

FIG. 8-6 Ravi Shankar performing on the sitar.

Like Reich, who had learned similar lessons from African and Indonesian musics, Glass quickly realized that he would have to make his own performance opportunities. He thus joined in what, in retrospect at least, seems the signal "convergence" in the mid-to-late 1960s between rock performers who, unusually, wrote their own material and classically trained composers who, unusually, performed their own material. Like Reich, Glass adopted the amplified instruments of rock, putting the electric organ at the center of his sound world, and in 1968 he formed the Philip Glass Ensemble to perform the works he was composing in a style he initially referred to as "music with repetitive structures."[44] For a while Reich and Glass, who had known each other slightly at Juilliard, were eager collaborators. Glass reencountered his old acquaintance shortly after his return from India, at a gallery concert in March 1967 at which Reich's *Piano Phase* was performed in a luxurious four-piano arrangement, and was immediately moved to emulate it by stripping down his style even further. He rigorously excreted the last trappings of dissonance and chromaticism from his music, these being the badges of Western harmonically driven modernism, and rid his textures of all reference to conservatory-style counterpoint or part-writing. Like Reich, he explored subtactile pulses at fast tempos and steady loud volumes. For two years each performed in the other's ensemble, and each egged the other on toward ever more rigorous systematization of the single musical dimension — rhythm and duration — they now thought worthy of development. For a while their creative exchange resembled the one a few years earlier between Riley and Reich on the opposite coast. They even collaborated for a while on a subsistence occupation: Chelsea Light Moving, consisting of two composers with strong backs and a van.

But their partnership quickly became a purist rivalry, as each tried to outstrip the other's commitment to rigor and system, showing that the competitive modernist spirit, though under challenge, was still alive and well. To match Reich's achievement yet maintain his creative individuality, Glass came up with a processual method, distinct from Reich's "phase" procedure, that reflected his involvement with Indian classical music. In place of Reich's progressive canons, which introduced a form of "Western" contrapuntal complexity into the texture, Glass concentrated on what he called "additive structure" (shrewdly rechristened "additive and subtractive"[45] by the critic K. Robert Schwarz), which could be applied to single musical lines played by solo instruments or by ensembles employing unison doubling or rudimentary homorhythmic textures in parallel or similar motion, something prohibited by the conservatory rulebook and therefore that much more radical in concept.

As usual, the first embodiment of the process, *Strung Out* (1967) for solo amplified violin, was the most rigorous and radical. A twenty-minute barrage of relentless eighth-notes employing only five pitches, it consisted of a pentatonic module that was subjected to variations by increasing or decreasing its length by one note at a time. Each modification became a repetitive module in turn, so that the overall impression was one of constantly expanding and contracting phrases, a rigorously maintained undifferentiated (isochronous) rhythm that was continually and subtly reinterpreted metrically. Even further reduced was *1 + 1* (1968), in which the sound was produced not by a standard instrument, but by tapping a tabletop — an anticipation of Reich's *Clapping Music*.

Two Pages for Steve Reich (1968) was the first piece composed for the Philip Glass Ensemble. It applies the additive-subtractive technique at its purest and most radical to a variable unison ensemble of electric keyboards and amplified wind instruments. Its 107 modules are each repeated an indefinite number of times, so that the piece is of variable duration. The rigorous process that relates each module to its predecessor and successor is self-evident to anyone glancing at the score. Like Reich, Glass did not keep any secrets of structure. On the contrary, he delighted in calling attention to the process, equating it with the musical content. Long stretches of vocal music in *Einstein on the Beach* have no other text than the counting of the notes in the modules.

In 1969, the title of *Two Pages for Steve Reich* became *Two Pages*. The rivalry had turned unfriendly, and remained so. Reich has attributed the falling-out to Glass's unwillingness to acknowledge his creative debts, but the younger composer's attraction to the theater and his greater affinity for the rock scene were bound to separate them eventually, leading Glass out of Reich's immediate orbit and ultimately toward the operas that made him famous. Those operas, in turn, had a strong and openly acknowledged influence on the art-rock of the 1970s and 1980s.

Less openly acknowledged, indeed often finessed or even deliberately clouded, is the question of rock's influence on the development of Glass's music. That Glass, of all the pioneering minimalists, had the strongest ties to Anglo-American pop music has always been clear. His music, while it avoids the most obvious rock instruments (electric guitars and trap-set percussion), is often amplified to the earsplitting level typical of rock bands. It is far more often played in rock clubs than Reich's. Beginning in 1977, recordings of Glass's music were issued by rock labels, and he began writing pieces that conformed in length and shape to the specifications of a rock single. By the 1980s he was collaborating as closely with rock musicians like David Byrne (of the Talking Heads) and Paul Simon as he ever had collaborated with Reich. He even served for a while as producer for a rock band. And beginning in 1970, one of the regular members of his ensemble, along with the actual singers and players, has been a "sound designer" (audio engineer and mixer) named Kurt Munkacsi, who had started his career as an electric bass player in a rock band and had previously worked alongside George Martin for the Beatles, and whose key role in producing (or "cranking up") the Philip Glass sound was standard in pop but unprecedented in classical music. By the 1990s, Glass was repaying the compliment rock musicians had paid him with works like his *Low Symphony* (1992), based on thematic material derived from a rock album, *Low* (1977), by Brian Eno and David Bowie — "symphonic rock" to recall or parallel the "symphonic jazz" of the 1920s.

But was there a rock input in Glass's style, beyond mere "sonic" or technological matters like instrumentation and amplification, to counterbalance the later influence and homage? Glass himself has been coy when asked. In an interview with the rock and jazz critic Robert Palmer (1945–97) following the spectacular Met performance of *Einstein on the Beach*, Glass responded to a question about "crossover" in a way that surprised his interlocutor. Though willing to be described as a standard-bearer for "the era of the serious composer as performing musician and pop hero,"[46] Glass insisted that there was still "one important distinction between pop and concert music," adding, "I think it's the only important distinction." Asked to elaborate, he continued:

> When you talk about concert musicians, you're talking about people who actually invent language. They create values, a value being a unit of meaning that is new and different. Pop musicians package language. I don't think there's anything *wrong* with packaging language; some of that can be very good music. I realized long ago that people were going to make money off my ideas in a way that I'm not capable of or interested in doing. It doesn't bother me; the two kinds of music are just different. One thing these English and German groups *have* done, though, they've taken the language of our music and made it much more accessible. It's been helpful. If people had heard only Fleetwood Mac [i.e., an "ordinary" American rock group] this music would sound like music from outer space.[47]

These are precisely the "late, late romantic" distinctions — between creator and disseminator, innovator and imitator, art and commerce (or "culture industry") — that had stood previously in the way of "crossover" by denying its possibility, or at least its legitimacy. Glass had effectively reinstated the old hierarchy of high and low. Within such a model influence can flow only one way (since if it flowed the other way it would be not influence but debasement). The only concession Glass is willing to make beyond what Schoenberg or Adorno would have allowed is that "packaged language" is not intrinsically corrupt or dehumanizing. But the squeamishness is palpable; to admit to an influence from popular culture beyond the borrowing of its hardware would have compromised Glass's status as a serious artist — in his own eyes.

DISCO AT THE MET

Rock critics have understandably been quicker to call attention to the stylistic affinities between Glass's music (or minimalism generally) and pop, although few have put the matter bluntly in terms of influence. Michael Walsh, writing in *Time* magazine, was content to observe that "rock and minimalism share obvious characteristics, including a steady beat, limited harmonies and hypnotic repetition."[48] Robert Coe, in the *New York Times* magazine, credited the Philip Glass Ensemble with providing the means "to place new experimental music on a continuum ranging from academic modernism to progressive rock and jazz,"[49] and noted particularly Glass's apparent influence on disco, the 1970s commercial genre with which Terry Riley had also been associated. But the chronology of Glass's relationship with rock does not necessarily support the one-way model; and one young critic, Gregory Bloch, has dared suggest that disco, that most commercial (and therefore disdained) of rock genres, may have been among the elements that conjoined to produce Glass's "operatic" style.[50]

As noted above, the word "disco" is short for *discothèque*, a nightclub where people danced to recorded music. The disc jockeys who played the records were skilled artists who sequenced and remixed a multitude of short individual tracks into all-night marathons, a technique already reminiscent of Glass's "module" procedure, which was about to take its own quantum leap into marathon length just as disco was becoming fashionable. By the middle of the decade, disco had become not just a performance practice but a compositional genre that produced single "tracks" of previously unheard-of length, in which the vocal lines, to quote the rock historian Joe Stuessy, were "more like repeating patterns than melodies in the traditional sense."[51]

The first disco "classic," Donna Summer's *Love to Love You Baby* (1975), blew a single song up to seventeen minutes' duration (requiring an entire 12″ LP side) by a succession of swirling riffs performed on electric keyboards and synthesizers, supported by a percussion track that divides an insistent four-beat-to-a-bar pulsation into subtactile eighths and sixteenths. Compare *Einstein on the Beach*, also composed in 1975, which though cast in four acts (each containing two or three scenes about the length of *Love to Love You Baby*, connected by musical joints that Robert Wilson called "knee plays"), was performed in a single five-and-one-half-hour bout, without intermission. The program displayed a note, "the audience is invited to leave and reenter the auditorium quietly, as necessary,"[52] just as the dancers at a discothèque left and reentered the dance floor as the spirit moved them.

While suggestive, these parallels are inconclusive as historical evidence. But Glass's rock appeal, his success in drawing on the huge rock audience, and the status of his music as a meeting ground for fans of many kinds of music (hence an auspicious or ominous breaker-down of categories), are established facts. John Rockwell's review of *Einstein on the Beach* in *Rolling Stone*, by then the principal American rock magazine, emphasized the last point, hailing Glass's work as "genuine fusion music that can appeal effortlessly to fans of progressive rock, jazz, and even disco."[53] And with that appeal came a financial success that undermined one of the chief distinctions Glass had previously drawn between his activity and that of the "packagers."

Whatever its relationship to disco, Glass was also led to his operatic conception and its majestic sense of scale by his collaborator. *Einstein on the Beach* was far from Robert Wilson's longest theatrical marathon. *The Life and Times of Joseph Stalin* (1973) lasted twelve uninterrupted hours. A series of static tableaux with a stage-filling cast of nonprofessional extras, it was already called an opera even though there was no musical score. For Wilson, opera was a sort of visual term connoting monumental pageantry. His attraction to larger-than-life, fetishized historical figures or "icons" as nominal subject matter (Freud and Queen Victoria as well as Stalin and Einstein) was the consequence of this massive, virtually immobilized theatrical conception, which, as Robert Palmer writes, "one ends up wandering within rather than watching."[54] Glass's music with its endless modules seemed its predestined sonic clothing.

The scenario and music of *Einstein on the Beach* were planned on the basis of a set of drawings by Wilson, and revolve around three recurrent images: a train, a courtroom scene (that includes a bed), and a spaceship. (The relevance of the second image to Einstein is never explained.) The title character occasionally wanders onstage as an onlooker, playing the violin. (At the Met and on the original recording Einstein was played by Paul Zukofsky, a well-known new-music specialist.) There is no summarizable plot, nor is there a libretto. Actors engage in mumbled monologues and the singers either count their eighth notes or sing solfège syllables (according to the French conservatory or "fixed-doh" method that Glass learned in his student years).

"When numbers are used," Glass has written, "they represent the rhythmic structure of the music. When solfège is used, the syllables represent the pitch structure of the music. In either case, the text is not secondary or supplementary, but is a description of the music itself."[55] What lends coherence to the whole is the patterned coordination of what Glass calls "visual themes and musical themes." At the opera's slowed-down time-scale, the images became mandalas or focal points for meditation, and the musical modules resembled mantras, the endlessly repeated passivity-inducing vocables of tantric Buddhism. Many viewers compared their experience of the opera to a dream.

All of this recalls surrealism. Most early viewers with a modernist frame of reference compared *Einstein on the Beach* to the Gertrude Stein–Virgil Thomson *Four Saints in Three Acts* of forty years before—another nonlinear, nonnarrative theatrical presentation in which the verbal component posed deliberate enigmas that listeners were invited to invest with mystical significance. The difference was that Thomson's ingratiating music, with its obvious references to folk and vernacular styles, made a far less overtly avant-garde impression than Glass's resolutely abstract modules in their raw, rocklike timbres. The fact that Glass's music was consonant and intermittently "tonal" did nothing to lessen that impression of aggressive stylistic novelty.

The extreme musical unity of the work is suggested in Ex. 8-9, which shows the basic musical stuff of two whole scenes. Act II, sc. 2 accompanies the recurrent train imagery (here titled "Night Train"); the concluding act IV, sc. 3 (plus Knee Play 5) accompanies the final apparition of the spaceship. The module on which the "Night Train" episode is based consists of a pentatonic hemiola idea (Ex. 8-9a), whereas the concluding scene is based on a harmonic module (Ex. 8-9b) that provides thematic material for several other scenes and "knee plays" as well. Glass describes it as "a progression of five chords," and represents it as follows—

$$
\begin{array}{l}
\text{key of f} \\
\text{f}\underline{\quad}\text{D♭}\underline{\quad}\text{B♭♭} \\
\text{(i) (VI) (IV♭)} \\
\qquad\quad \downarrow \\
\qquad\quad \text{A}\underline{\quad}\text{B}\underline{\quad}\text{E} \\
\qquad\quad \text{(IV) (V) (I)} \\
\qquad\quad \text{key of E}
\end{array}
$$

—commenting that it "combines both a familiar cadence and a modulation in one formula."[56] He analyzes the half-step descent between the roots of the first and last chords as motion to the leading tone, demanding resolution. "As it is a formula which invites repetition," he notes, "it is particularly suited to my kind of musical thinking."[57] It crops up throughout *Einstein on the Beach* in many figurations and voicings, many if not most of them "incorrect" according to textbook rules of voice-leading.

The rigor with which the minimal material shown in Ex. 8-9 was expanded to form the respective scenes impressed all listeners, both those who regarded Glass's technique as impressively single-minded and those who thought it woefully simpleminded. What was most extraordinary was the visceral response that the music elicited, especially the Spaceship finale — extraordinary, at any rate, to the "classical" musicians in attendance, who associated the visceral with the popular, and therefore distrusted it. The response was calculated. As Glass told an interviewer:

> I decided that I would try to write a piece that left the audience standing, and I've almost never played that music without seeing everyone leave his seat; it's the strangest thing, almost biological. In fact, sometimes I've done concerts where I've played the Spaceship, and then as an encore played the last part of the Spaceship, and the same thing happens again.[58]

The effect was polarizing, to say the least. At the enthusiastic extreme was the response of Ransom Wilson (b. 1951), a flutist and conductor who attended the Metropolitan Opera performance. He was completely won over to the cause of minimalist music and has since become one of its leading exponents. "There were no intermissions," he marveled:

> The work continued relentlessly in its grip on all of us in that packed house. Suddenly, at a point some four [actually five] hours into the opera there occurred a completely unexpected harmonic and rhythmic modulation, coupled with a huge jump in the decibel level. People in the audience began to scream with delight and I remember well that my entire body was covered with goose bumps.[59]

"So much," a less enthusiastic critic observed, "one may elicit from a pithed frog."[60] And indeed, there were many who worried at the music's brute "biological" manipulativeness, even as they acknowledged the rarity of gooseflesh at a new music event. There were mutterings about behavior-modification therapy and authoritarian control. Elliott Carter, who did not attend the performance but read about it, sounded an alarm worthy of Cassandra (or at least Adorno). Minimalists, he warned, "are not aware of the larger dimensions of life. One also hears constant repetition in the speeches of Hitler, and in advertising. It has its dangerous aspects."[61]

EX. 8-9A   Philip Glass, *Einstein on the Beach*, "Night Train" module ("first theme" in Glass's analysis)

EX. 8-9B   Philip Glass, *Einstein on the Beach*, "Spaceship" module ("third theme")

Minus the animus and alarm, some music historians have tended to agree. One historian, Robert Fink, has associated the rise of minimalism with "Madison Avenue" (i.e., the advertising industry) and claimed that the key text for understanding its appeal is *The Hidden Persuaders* (1957), a best-seller by the American social critic Vance Packard (1914–1996), who popularized — and thus helped reinforce — the perception that American society consisted of a mass of consumers constantly subjected to manipulation by corporate schemers who created in them previously unsuspected (and to that extent "unreal") desire.[62] Such an observation about music was not in itself anything new. Manipulation of desire had been the business of music (some would say the chief business) since at least the time of Wagner's *Tristan und Isolde*. What was new in advertising (according to Packard) and in music (according to Fink) was the insidious, "subliminal" nature of the pitch.

AMERICANIZATION

Whether or not the means employed by minimalist composers were insidious, they were surely the (inevitable?) product of the society in which all of the composers considered in this chapter had grown up. Reich has not only recognized but celebrated this fact, justifying his rejection of European modernist styles by remarking that whereas "Stockhausen, Berio and Boulez were portraying in very honest terms what it was like to pick up the pieces of a bombed-out continent after World War II," the American experience had been different, and demanded a different medium of expression. "For some Americans in 1948 or 1958 or 1968 — in the real context of tail-fins, [the rock 'n' roll singer] Chuck Berry and millions of burgers sold — to pretend that instead we're really going to have the dark-brown angst of Vienna is a lie, a musical lie."[63]

In its seemingly indiscriminate, insatiable, world-devouring eclecticism, its live adaptation of musical techniques originating in the hardware-driven tape studio, and its tendency toward a kind of factory standardization ("mass-production" of repeated modules, equal pulses, terraced dynamics with sometimes only one terrace), minimalism exemplified — and was the (only?) honest product of — the commodification, objectification, and exteriorization of the affluent postwar American consumer society, hailed by many as the economic salvation of the world and decried by just as many as the ultimate dehumanization of humanity.

And as the values of American society spread, so did its musical embodiment. Minimalism has unquestionably been the most influential, worldwide, of any musical movement born since the Second World War. It is the first (and so far the only) literate musical style born in the New World to have exerted a decisive influence on the Old. It is the musical incarnation of "the American century." No wonder it has been controversial. The seemingly paradoxical fact, moreover, that many who have succumbed to its influence have been consciously opposed to "Americanization" (whether defined as materialism, as "economic imperialism," or as "globalization") can be interpreted either as another proof that musical technique as such is politically and culturally neutral, or as another proof that practice reveals a truth that theory denies in vain — a fancy way of saying that actions speak louder than words.

Consider the Dutch composer Louis Andriessen (b. 1939). Like most of his contemporaries, he went through a serial period at school, and then a "sixties" phase in which he took inspiration from Cage. His New Left sympathies eventually caused him to mistrust the elitism of the avant-garde, but to regard the Soviet model of musical populism as equally tainted. What was left was minimalism, a style that has been embraced as "democratic" by many Europeans — and particularly, it seems, in the Low Countries, where in 1980 the Belgian composer Wim Mertens published the first book anywhere on the subject (*Amerikaanse repetitieve muziek*, issued three years later in English translation), and where in the same year Philip Glass's second opera, *Satyagraha*, commissioned by the city of Rotterdam, had its world premiere. (The opera, far more conventional in conception and in musical style than *Einstein on the Beach*, concerned the life and influence of Mahatma Gandhi; the title is Sanskrit for "truth-force.") Like Reich and Glass, Andriessen founded his own performing ensemble, De Volharding (Perseverance), composed mainly of musicians with jazz backgrounds. The reasons he gave for doing so were more overtly political than those offered by his predecessors. Where Reich and Glass spoke of making their own performance opportunities rather than waiting for mainstream recognition that might never come, Andriessen declared that "orchestras are only important for the capitalists and the record companies," while the people demanded a music that "brought highbrow and lowbrow together."[64] The first model for such a music was Riley's *In C*, which Andriessen first heard in 1971. Quickly, however, his attention turned to Reich, whose music he admired above all for its inclusivity: "The music was open to many different kinds of influences from all over the world," he told an interviewer, "and I recognized very many open doors for the future"[65] at a time when modernism seemed to be at an academic dead end.

For De Volharding and its more rock-oriented successor band, Hoketus, Andriessen wrote a series of cantatas in which the pulsing minimalist style was applied to texts purporting to espouse political activism. One of them, *De Staat* ("The State"), composed between 1972 and 1976, is a raucously repetitive score, quite Glassian at times in its additive processes. It employs women's voices, violas, oboes, horns, trumpets, and trombones, all in groups of four, plus a pair of electric guitars, a bass guitar, two pianos, and two harps to accompany — or rather, confront — the famous passages from Plato's *Republic* that deal with musical ethos, the power of music to influence character and affect behavior, and the necessity for political censorship and prescription. The exuberant music and the repressive text seem to be at odds until one looks more closely at the words and realizes that Andriessen's bellicose sonorities do in fact conform to Plato's prescription for a music that will inspire warriors. Is he for censorship, then, or against it? The composer makes the most of the ambiguity, as if to dramatize his own ambivalence toward the place of music in contemporary society. On the one hand, he has written, "everybody sees the absurdity of Plato's statement that the Mixolydian mode should be banned because of its damaging effect on the development of character, . . . something similar to the 'demoralizing nature' of the Rolling Stones' concerts." But on the other, "perhaps I regret the fact that Plato was wrong: if only it were true that musical innovation represented a danger to the State!"[66]

Andriessen described his cantata frankly as "a contribution to the discussion about the place of music in politics." In notes accompanying its first recording, he outlined a theory of musical sociology:

> To keep the issues straight it is necessary to differentiate between three aspects of the social phenomenon called music: 1. its conception (devising and planning by the composer), 2. its production (performance) and 3. its consumption. Production and consumption are by definition if not political then at least social. The situation is more intricate when it comes to the actual composing. Many composers feel that the act of composing is "suprasocial." I don't agree. How you arrange your musical material, what you do with it, the techniques you use, the instruments you score for, all of this is determined to a large extent by your own social circumstances, your education, environment and listening experience, and the availability — or non-availability — of symphony orchestras and government grants. The only point on which I agree with the liberal idealists is that abstract musical material — pitch, duration and rhythm — is suprasocial: it is part of nature. There is no such thing as a fascist dominant seventh. The moment the musical material is ordered, however, it becomes culture and, as such, a given social fact.[67]

It was presumably this last factor, the political implications of musical ordering (i.e., style), that impelled Andriessen to fashion his minimalist structures out of harmonies so much more dissonant than those used by his American counterparts. (See Ex. 8-10, which shows the end of the repressive Platonic dialogue and the orgy of orchestral self-congratulation that follows it.) According to the age-old European modernist conceit, it is dissonance that creates a political edge — an edge of resistance. The same dissonance, however, has always most dependably alienated the very audience which politically activist or populist composers claim to address. And, following another well-established catch-22, Andriessen's efforts to maintain a maverick position have been frustrated by official recognition.

He has occupied a prominent teaching post at the government-supported Hague Conservatory since even before *De Staat*. The supposedly subversive cantata was awarded two prestigious prizes in 1977, including one from the Dutch government; and its first recording was issued by the Composers' Voice label, a noncommercial enterprise underwritten by the same government that has awarded the composer prizes and pays his salary. The indulgent treatment Andriessen has received (and accepted) from the state his music ostensibly challenges has cast his musicopolitical agenda in an equivocal light: is it genuine activism, or is it just another show of radical chic?

It is a dilemma from which escape is virtually impossible. In a later cantata, *De Stijl* (1985), scored for an ensemble of amplified winds, electric keyboards and guitars, and crashing "heavy metal" percussion (what Andriessen, echoing Reich, calls "the terrifying twenty-first-century orchestra"[68]), the composer paid far more explicit tribute to the "countercultural" sources of his inspiration in an effort to obliterate once and for all the social barriers between styles. "I think it's very good to do that," he says:

> I would again use the word democratic, the desire to break down those borders. I think it's almost a duty, and not only for composers. I hope that the future will bring us a better world in which the difference between high and low, and rich and poor, is smaller than it is now.[69]

Andriessen has also made a point of preferring African-American to Anglo-American pop as a stylistic model, and he has wholeheartedly embraced disco in defiance of its low critical standing. And yet *De Stijl*, which has since been incorporated into a huge four-act opera directed by Robert Wilson (*De Materie* or "Matter," 1989), calls for resources that put it out of reach to all but the most elite performance venues. It has so far been performed only for "high" (that is, according to the composer's equation, rich as well as white) audiences, and appreciated mainly by professionals.

Andriessen's greatest contribution, perhaps, has been as a teacher. Alone among the major minimalists, he occupies a distinguished academic chair, and he has been a magnet to composers from many countries, including England and the United States, where the musico-social boundaries have been more fluid than on the European continent, but where minimalism has yet to make comparable academic inroads. His American disciples have gone on to form groups of their own. Their names—Bang on a Can

EX. 8-10   Louis Andriessen, *De Staat*, mm. 719–734

EX. 8-10 (*continued*)

and Common Sense Composers Collective, to mention two — are political statements in themselves, showing a determination to keep the elusive dream of "sociostylistic" integration on minimalist principles alive into the twenty-first century.

CLOSING THE SPIRITUAL CIRCLE

The ethical sensibility that informs Andriessen's intentions (as, to a more or less declared extent, it does the music of all the minimalists) is the link between his openly declared political activism and its seeming antithesis, exemplified by a group of composers who use minimalist techniques to evoke or induce a state of passive spiritual contemplation. The pioneer figure here is the Estonian-born Arvo Pärt (b. 1935), whose turn toward spirituality was especially self-conscious, since it took place in a country that, as a consequence of the 1939 Hitler-Stalin pact, had been incorporated into the militantly atheistic Soviet Union. (Estonia regained its independence in 1991, but by then Pärt had been living abroad for more than a decade.)

Educated to compose first in a neo-Romantic, then a neoclassic manner, Pärt (like a number of other young Soviet composers) rebelled against Socialist Realism in the 1960s by embracing serialism, its cold-war antithesis. Not finding in serialism a congenial alternative, he experienced a prolonged creative block which he managed to overcome thanks in part to his discovery of medieval and Renaissance music, to which he was exposed as a result of the belated spread into the Soviet Union of the "early music" movement, long established in the concert life of Western Europe and America.

Early music performers revived ancient repertoires, and also experimented with "period" performance of the more standard eighteenth- and nineteenth-century repertoire. Many impulses fed the movement. Besides the historicist emphasis on "authenticity" that the movement advertised and actively propagated, there was always a seemingly contradictory tendency to look for novelty—as well as refuge—in the more or less distant past. For Soviet musicians of the 1960s, early music offered a back door to religious experience, since so many ancient musical repertoires were associated with ancient rituals and liturgies. One could treat religious themes in code (or, to use the Russian term, in "Aesopian" language) by making stylistic reference to those repertoires.

Pärt's Symphony no. 3 (1971), the only composition he finished between 1968 and 1976, is full of echoes of the medieval music he was discovering together with his friend Andres Mustonen, who the next year founded Hortus Musicus, Estonia's first professional early-music ensemble. Ex. 8-11 shows a couple of themes from that work. The first embodies a fourteenth-century double-leading-tone cadence decorated with a "Landini sixth." The other is a plainchant-derived melody treated as a cantus firmus against a pure diatonic "discant."

By 1976, Pärt had managed to excrete obvious archaisms like these from his style while retaining the pure diatonic idiom of Ex. 8-11b. Thus he had found an independent

EX. 8-11 Two themes from Arvo Pärt, Symphony no. 3: "Doubled leading-tone" cadence, and chantlike cantus firmus

route to the austerely reduced tonal vocabulary then being adopted, unbeknownst to him, by Reich and Glass. His next step, paradoxically, was one that could have occurred only to a composer brought up with the creative precepts of socialist realism and its principle of *obraznost'* or "imagery," which encouraged composers to convey specific ideas in music by imitating and adapting the sounds (including the music) of surrounding reality. Applying this highly materialistic stylistic principle to the task of conveying impressions of spirituality and sublimity, Pärt fastened on the sound of bells — a sonic component of religious rituals in many traditions, but particularly in that of the Russian Orthodox Church. The evocation of bell sounds became for Pärt the sonic equivalent of an icon: a holy image that embodied mystical belief in material form.

Pärt's bell-imagery ranged from obvious onomatopoeia — bell imitations, often achieved by using a prepared piano (already freighted with "countercultural" associations courtesy of John Cage) — to a unique harmonic idiom that Pärt worked out during the early 1970s and that he called his "tintinnabular" style. A pitch produced by a tuned bell is an exceptionally rich composite of overtones, in which the fundamental can be all but overwhelmed by dissonant partials. To achieve a comparable sonic aura, Pärt accompanied the notes of a diatonic melody with "overtones" produced by the notes of an arpeggiated tonic triad in some fixed relationship to the melody notes. The English early-music singer and choral director Paul Hillier, who has become Pärt's most devoted exponent both in performance and in print, has attempted a theoretical elucidation, based in part on extensive interviews with the composer, of Pärt's tintinnabular style.[70] The analytical examples that follow are his.

In each of them, an ascending A-minor scale is harmonized according to a particular application of the method. In Ex. 8-12a, the scale or melody-voice (M-voice) is harmonized by a "tintinnabuli"-voice (T-voice) that consists of the next higher pitch in the A-minor triad. Hillier calls this "1st position, superior." Ex. 8-12b shows the "1st position, inferior," in which the notes of the M-voice are accompanied by the next lower pitch of the triad. Exx. 8-12c and 8-12d show the "2nd position," in which the T-voice pitch is the next but one in the triad. In Ex. 8-12e, the T-voice from Ex. 8-12b is transposed up an octave, so that all the intervals are inverted: fourths become fifths, thirds become sixths, seconds become sevenths. Such transpositions can be applied to any of the other positions. Finally, Ex. 8-12f shows the M-voice accompanied by an "alternating" T-voice in which the 1st position superior alternates with the 1st position inferior. This technique, too, can be applied to any position.

The product is a sort of oblique organum, comparable (but far from identical) to the kinds of chant-harmonizations that were practiced as early as the ninth century. When two or more M-voices are treated in counterpoint, each will carry a T-voice (or, alternatively, a single T-voice can be shadowed both above and below by M-voices

EX. 8-12A   Arvo Pärt, "tintinnabulation," 1st position, superior

1st position, superior

EX. 8-12B   Arvo Pärt, "tintinnabulation," 1st position, inferior

1st position, inferior

EX. 8-12C   Arvo Pärt, "tintinnabulation," 2nd position, superior

2nd position, superior

EX. 8-12D   Arvo Pärt, "tintinnabulation," 2nd position, inferior

2nd position, inferior

EX. 8-12E   Arvo Pärt, "tintinnabulation," T-voice from Ex. 67-12b transposed up an octave

EX. 8-12F   Arvo Pärt, "tintinnabulation," M-voice accompanied by "alternating" T-voice

alternating

moving in parallel). The point is that an M-voice plus a T-voice is conceived as an indissoluble unit. In compound textures, the result is a modern harmonic idiom, not by any means free of dissonance (unless the second and seventh are conceived, as Pärt's quasi-Pythagorean usage suggests, as consonances). Its relationship to medieval harmonic idioms is demonstrable, but it is not in itself a historical pastiche.

Since 1982, Pärt has employed the tintinnabular style almost exclusively in vocal works with Latin sacred texts. They are concert works rather than works meant for actual liturgical use; but their purpose, as the composer envisions it, is sacred. The tintinnabular style is frankly meant, by virtue of the constant presence (thanks to the T-voice) of the major or minor triad, as a manifestation of the eternal presence of God. "Such a sacralizing view of music," Hillier comments, "is neither unique nor eccentric; it has correspondences thoughout music history, and is found in abundance in non-Western musics—moreover, without the self-consciousness forced upon it by a secular and materialistic society."[71] A good practical example is the conclusion of Pärt's setting of the St. John Passion (1982), composed shortly after the composer's emigration from the Soviet Union. Each four-note chord sung by the chorus consists

EX. 8-13   Arvo Pärt, St. John Passion, *Conclusio*

of two M-voices (alto and bass) moving in parallel sixths, accompanied by T-voices in 1st position, superior (Ex. 8-13).

Pärt's best-known works are a trio of instrumental compositions written in Estonia in 1977. *Fratres* ("Brethren"), a sort of wordless chorale in irregular meter accompanied by a steady drone fifth and interspersed with a rhythmic percussion, exists in numerous arrangements: for violin and piano, for string quartet, for twelve cellos, for large chamber ensemble, and so on. *Cantus in memoriam Benjamin Britten*, for string orchestra and bell, is strikingly "minimal" in conception. It consists of a repetitively descending A-minor scale that gradually unfolds by the progressive addition of a note to each repetition (A, A-G, A-G-F, A-G-F-E, A-G-F-E-D, etc.). The scale is treated as a mensuration canon for five composite voices (each an M plus a T) entering one by one, each in a lower octave than the last, and moving at a rate twice as slow. When the process has played itself out, the last and slowest voice completing the scale, the piece ends.

The most extended work of Pärt's early tintinnabular period, and perhaps the most representative, is a two-movement concerto grosso for two violins, string orchestra, and prepared piano, emblematically titled *Tabula rasa* ("clean slate") to celebrate the composer's fresh start. The first movement, called *Ludus* ("game," or "play") is marked "con moto," and consists of progressively lengthening and loudening bouts of fiddling activity. The second movement is called *Silentium* ("silence") and is marked "Senza moto." Its beats, at M.M. =60, conform to the ticking seconds on the clock. Its musical substance consists of a three-part lengthening mensuration canon for the cellos playing halves and quarters, the tutti first violins playing wholes and halves, and the solo violin playing breves and wholes. Ex. 8-14a shows the beginning.

The other string instruments, except the basses, are occupied with shadowing the canonic voices with tintinnabuli derived from the D-minor triad. The violas accompany the cellos at the second position above; the second violins of the tutti accompany the first at the second position below; and the second soloist surrounds the notes played by the first soloist with quarter-notes in alternating first position, the rests on each first-violin attack ensuring that each note of the solo line is accompanied by a tintinnabulation that reverses the order of the preceding one (first low-high, then high-low). Whenever the first soloist returns to the starting D, the prepared piano and the pizzicato basses reinforce it with an evocation of a tolling bell.

The main canonic theme describes a series of widening gyres, making the soloist's returns to the tonic pitch increasingly infrequent (hence increasingly significant in effect). The final arc goes out of the cello range, and the double basses join in to complete the last phrase (Ex. 8-14b). They stop one note short of completion, as they must (E being their lowest note). But that failure to complete dramatically

EX. 8-14A   Arvo Pärt, *Tabula rasa*, II (*Silentium*), mm. 1–8

EX. 8-14A (continued)

EX. 62-14B Arvo Pärt, *Tabula rasa*, II (*Silentium*), end

emphasizes the ensuing silence, to which the whole movement is cast retrospectively as an elaborate prelude. Wholly without chromaticism, infused with a steady pulse and a single omnipresent harmony, and played at a single subdued dynamic, the movement is a startlingly successful evocation of stillness, very easily (some would say all too easily) read as religious quietism.

The relationship between radical reduction of means and wholeness of spirit is an ancient religious truth (the basis, to begin with, of monasticism), and also the basis of twentieth-century neoprimitivism. Pärt has knowingly drawn on both of these traditions in conversation with Hillier, describing his gradual arrival at tintinnabular music as a spiritual quest:

> In my dark hours, I have the certain feeling that everything outside this one thing has no meaning. The complex and many-faceted only confuses me, and I must search for unity. What is it, this one thing, and how do I find my way to it? Traces of this perfect thing appear in many guises — and everything that is unimportant falls away. Tintinnabulation is like this . . . . I work with very few elements — with one voice, with two voices. I build with the most primitive materials — with the triad, with one specific tonality.[72]

It is noteworthy that every one of the composers associated with radically reductive styles in the 1960s and 1970s (save only Andriessen, who has committed himself to another sort of faith) has found his way to religious belief, and has regarded his musical and spiritual quests as dual manifestations of a single impulse. Young, Riley, and Glass have all embraced some version of Asian religion: Young and Riley practice Yogic meditation and Glass has been a devotee of Tibetan Buddhism since the mid-sixties. Reich, brought up in an agnostic household, found his way back to orthodox Judaism in the 1970s.

In addition to Pärt, several other European composers have associated reductive musical styles with resurgent Christianity in the 1970s. Henryk Gorecki (b. 1933), who first achieved recognition as a member of the Polish "sonorist" avant-garde alongside Penderecki, reembraced the Roman Catholic faith (partly, as with Pärt, as an act of political resistance) and also reembraced a simple, consonant style of writing that might otherwise have been taken as evidence of cooperation with the Soviet-dominated cultural politics of his homeland — where he was in fact, as director of the Conservatory in the industrial city of Katowice, a musical politician; he resigned the post in 1979, after composing a number of Latin choral pieces in honor of the newly elected Polish pope, John Paul II.

One of the early fruits of his new style, the Third Symphony (1976), consists of three movements, each a slow threnody, or song of lamentation, for soprano soloist and orchestra. The second movement, a setting of a prayer scrawled on the wall of a cell at one of the Gestapo's detention headquarters in Nazi-occupied Poland, and the third, a setting of a folk song, were the kind of composition expected of a Polish adherent of socialist realism. The first movement, however, longer than the other two combined, was a setting of the Lament of the Holy Cross, a fifteenth-century Polish prayer.

Strictly diatonic and highly repetitive, Gorecki's setting was indeed akin to the music then being composed by Pärt and the western minimalists. The composer did not know their work at the time, nor did anyone seem to draw the connection in the years that followed. But in 1991, fifteen years after its first performance in Katowice, a New York record executive heard a Polish recording of the work and realized its potential for capitalizing on the popularity that Pärt's "holy minimalism" was generating, partly on the coattails of the "New Age" style of soothing popular music, marketed to people experimenting with relaxation techniques like the "transcendental meditation" popularized by the Maharishi Mahesh Yogi, who had become famous as the Beatles' guru in the late 1960s.

The new recording, issued in 1992 and heavily plugged on radio stations normally devoted to pop music, sold over a million copies within three years' time, making it one of the best-selling classical albums ever, and Gorecki was assimilated retroactively to the ranks of the "holy" or "mystical" minimalists — a marketing term eagerly appropriated in derision by modernist skeptics, wary as ever of the affinities between minimalism and pop, and eager to write the new phenomenon off as a fad manipulated by the record industry.

But it has continued to make inroads among serious professionals as well as consumers. The English composer John Tavener (b. 1944) is one. He had a conventional academic education in music, which left him a fluent serialist with expert electronic studio skills. *The Whale*, a dramatic cantata on the biblical story of Jonah, scored such a sensational success after its premiere in 1968 that it was noticed by John Lennon and his wife Yoko Ono and recorded in 1970 by Apple Records, the company formed by the Beatles to issue their own work. For a while, Tavener was the poster boy for the much-touted convergence of the classical and pop avant-gardes.

Another work issued on the Apple label, *Nomine Jesu* (1970), was the first of Tavener's to show a minimalist tendency. The name of Jesus is chorally intoned throughout on a single harmony (a half-diminished seventh, a.k.a. the "Tristan chord") as a background for a collage of singing and speaking solo voices and atonal passages for a pair of alto flutes, harpsichord, and organ. An increasingly reductive tendency in his musical style accompanied an increasing preoccupation with mystical subject matter until, having previously inclined from the Presbyterian church of his upbringing toward Roman Catholicism, Tavener formally converted in 1977 to the Russian Orthodox faith — an unusual choice for an Englishman, but already associated, through Pärt, with austerely religious minimalism. (Tavener was actually introduced to Eastern Orthodox Christianity by his first wife, a Greek ballerina.)

Tavener has echoed Pärt's devotion to the concept of a musical artifact that can function as a "sounding icon." That meant ridding his work of any sense of development: "Any idea that is worked out in a human way does not exist,"[73] he tells interviewers. Above all, there must be no sense of structural dualism or opposition (hence no "functional harmony"). Instead there should be a sense of "habitation," a listening environment evoked by sounds, particularly drones, that do not change over the course of the work, as in performances of Byzantine chant, which is always accompanied by a steady bass drone on the final of the mode known as the *ison*. Like Pärt, Tavener uses bells (in his case English handbells) to evoke an appropriately iconic atmosphere, and composes in a manner inspired by Byzantine hymnody, which uses a system of eight modes, distinguished from one another not by scales or finals but by a repertoire of characteristic melodic turns.

Tavener's *Ikon of Light* (1983), a setting of a tenth-century Greek hymn for chorus and string trio, can furnish a useful test of the composer's unusually explicit claim (one that is more or less implicit in the work of other minimalists as well) that his work is founded on a rejection of the "Western tradition" in which he was brought up, and which in the name of humanism had driven the spiritual out of art. "The whole western idea of man-made techniques, like sonata form, fugue, canon," he insists, has been rendered "useless" by the catastrophic history of the twentieth century: "I don't see what purpose it has in the world today."[74] Instead, his hymn celebrates what is eternal and indestructible.

The opening section, the text of which consists entirely of repetitions of the single word *phos* (light), projects a "sonic icon" in a manner quite similar to Pärt's. It pits the chorus, which sings a single unchanging chord, against the strings, which play a series of six dyads (thirds and tritones) that together exhaust the twelve pitch-classes of the chromatic scale (Ex. 8-15). The juxtaposition of constancy and flux is a fairly transparent metaphor for the opposition of the human and divine, while the eventually (and intentionally) predictable sequence of events turns the musical unfolding into a ritual game (*ludus*).

EX. 8-15   John Tavener, *Ikon of Light*, opening section in analytical reduction

Constructing a four-minute span of music out of twelve chords, six of them identical, takes reduction to a La Monte Youngian extreme, an impression made all the more vivid by the coincidental use of a string trio drawing its sonorities out to extraordinary lengths (to represent, as Tavener puts it, "the soul yearning for God"). The rest of the setting proceeds as a palindrome. Its seven sections are disposed symmetrically around the fourth and longest one, at the center. This central section is itself a palindrome in which the last part is a rough retrograde inversion of the first (thus reversed in two dimensions). Palindromes achieve completion by returning to their starting point: here to here, rather than here to there. For "Western" teleology they substitute a circular temporality, and have been a metaphor of timelessness in music at least since the fourteenth century, as Tavener has recognized by titling a choral work of 1972, *Ma fin est mon commencement* ("My end is my beginning"), after the famous palindromic rondeau by Guillaume de Machaut.

But of course Machaut, palindromes and all, is just as much a part of the "Western" tradition as sonata form, fugue, and canon. Tavener's acceptance (and exploitation)

of the tempered chromatic scale for purposes of metaphor and imagery also puts him within, rather than outside, the body of "man-made techniques" that he regards with suspicion. Perhaps, then, the minimalist impulse, despite its compelling affinity for everything remote in time and place, and despite its angry negation of some conspicuous features of the immediate musical past, is (like so many other avant-gardes) an outgrowth of tendencies inherent within the capacious tradition it has claimed, one-sidedly, to reject.

CHAPTER 9

After Everything

POSTMODERNISM: ROCHBERG, CRUMB, LERDAHL, SCHNITTKE

The Modern Age, which sounds as if it would last forever, is fast becoming a thing of the past.[1]
—CHARLES JENCKS, *WHAT IS POST-MODERNISM?* (1986)

. . . we realize that only the present is really real . . . because it is all we have . . . but in the end it, too, is shadow and dream . . . and disappears . . . into what?[2]
—GEORGE ROCHBERG, EPIGRAPH TO ACT 3 OF *MUSIC FOR THE MAGIC THEATER* (1965)

Where does all this lead us? Quite appropriately, nowhere.[3]
—LEONARD B. MEYER, "FUTURE TENSE: MUSIC, IDEOLOGY, AND CULTURE" (1994)

What it does do, I think, is threaten the mind-set of modernists who believe that the artist is a high priest who breaks laws and creates new ones that advance civilization.[4]
—FRED LERDAHL, "COMPOSING AND LISTENING: A REPLY TO NATTIEZ" (1994)

POSTMODERNISM?

Because it was often relatively consonant in harmony and employed ordinary diatonic scales, minimalist music was frequently attacked as "conservative" by academic modernists, for whom the term was the deadliest of slurs. But the charge was unconvincing. The contexts in which familiar sounds appeared in minimalist music, and the uses to which they were put, were too obviously novel, and the effect the music produced was too obviously of the present. Besides, "progressive" music, against which minimalism was being implicitly measured in such a comparison, was following a technical and expressive agenda that had been set at least a quarter of a century, even half a century, before. It no longer seemed quite immune to the epithet it habitually hurled.

It was this very confusion (at least in rhetoric) between what was progressive and what was conservative, and an attendant loss of interest in making the distinction, that seemed to signal a fundamental ideological change in the last quarter of the twentieth century. Even if it could not be dismissed as conservative, the music of the minimalists did affront and threaten progressive musicians of the older generation in some fundamental way. And that way had to do with another, older, less overtly politicized sense of the word "progressive."

Describing the intended effect of his pattern-and-process compositions, and the sort of listening approach that it required, Philip Glass warned that he aimed for a musical experience that "neither memory nor anticipation," those most basic cognitive tools, "has a place in sustaining."[5] Here was the threat: as Leonard Meyer pointed out in the article from which this chapter's third epigraph was drawn, "if musical experience does not involve development or remembrance, expectancy or anticipation, then many of the ideas and values that until recently informed the aesthetics of music become either untenable or irrelevant."[6]

Meyer called these threatened values "Romantic." But since (as Meyer himself liked to say) what we usually call modernism is really "late, late Romanticism,"[7] it was modernist values that were under threat of being supplanted. What do you call the ism that supplants modernism? Why, postmodernism, obviously (if you're in a hurry); and so a term was coined that gained considerable currency in the mid-to-late 1970s, and that by the middle of the 1980s had become a cliché. Like many terms coined in periods of uncertainty, it was a notorious catchall. Defining it is a notorious fool's errand. But it is an errand we have to at least try running.

The field in which the term was first applied, or in which it first cropped up, was architecture. That might have been expected, since architecture was the field in which the "modern" had (or seemed to have) the most stable definition, and it was also a field from which utilitarian concerns could never be entirely eliminated. Modern architecture was associated with abstraction, functionalism, streamlining, and economy. It sought to embody the universal values of an industrial age, and express them in the "pure," nonrepresentational terms of its media—glass, reinforced concrete, steel.

Postmodern architecture made a somewhat ironic peace with ornament, with representation, with pluralities of taste and, above all, with convention. Its motivation, frankly asserted by Charles Jencks, both a practitioner and a historian of the trend, was "the social failure of Modern architecture," its inadequacy to "communicate effectively with its ultimate users."[8] It did not make people feel at home. Used extensively in public housing projects, it amounted, in the eventual view of many disillusioned architects and disgusted urban planners, to an insult delivered by well-fed snobs who could afford comfort on their own terms to people forced to inhabit inhospitable buildings that gratified the builders' romantically "disinterested," purely "esthetic"—that is, dehumanized—tastes and their infatuation with science and technology, epitomized by Le Corbusier's definition of a house as a "machine for living."[9] But postmodern architecture, Jencks pointed out, was no simple rejection of the modern style. Rather than mere "revivalism" or "traditionalism," it was a compromise solution that tried to balance ideals and social realities by means of what Jencks called "double coding,"[10] a strategy of communicating on various levels at once. To put it oxymoronically (hence postmodernly), postmodern architecture was "essentially hybrid." The only exclusive "ism" postmodernism upheld, Jencks insisted with a twinkle, was pluralism.

Jencks's discussion raised familiar issues. We have encountered a similarly unhappy split between aesthetic and social values in modernist music, and have heard grumbling about its elitism and inhospitality. But the social issues can never be as acutely drawn in music as they can in architecture, since nobody is forced to live in a musical composition. A building can be, both literally and figuratively, a prison; and that is why architecture became the bellwether of the reaction against the oppressive effects of modernism and the oppressive values they were seen to embody. But while (to risk a pun) the musical situation was less concrete, there is ample evidence that musical postmodernism (or, more cautiously, the music associated by commentators with postmodernism) arose in comparable reaction against a perceived aesthetic oppression, and that the move led to a comparable outcome. A condition formerly considered necessary was eventually judged to be both unnecessary and undesirable, and was accordingly overthrown.

Among the Romantic (modernist) values Meyer saw threatened by the attitude that Philip Glass expressed was that of organicism, the belief that "all relationships in a work of art should be the result of a gradual growth," a "process of development . . . governed by an inner necessity and an economy of means such that nothing in the work is either accidental or superfluous."[11] This ascetic ideal, reminiscent of the strict functionalism of much modern architecture, was what caused so many to reject the repetitiveness of minimalist music (and notice nothing else about it). It violated what Meyer calls the "almost religious reverence for the values of necessity, economy and unity."[12]

Whatever unity repetition conferred on a minimalist composition was more than outweighed by its sinful superfluity. And because minimalist repetitions, unlike Wagnerian sequences, did not quicken desire in anticipation of a goal, they lacked "inner necessity"—or, in the more damning variant hurled abusively by offended modernists, they lacked "inner life." In a word, although they were obviously processual, minimalist repetitions were not "progressive" in that older meaning of the word. They did not progress to a determinate end.

That lack of "progressiveness" or goal-oriented purposiveness implied an even greater threat to the values modernism had inherited from Romanticism. For, ever since the middle of the nineteenth century, the ideal of goal-oriented purposiveness provided Romantics and their modernist progeny with their theory of history as well, and all its attendant obligations. Historicism was an even more fundamental modernist drive than organicism. It was historicism—belief in what the postmodernist theorist Jean-François Lyotard called the "master narrative"[13] that defined values and imposed obligations—that convinced so many artists that the austerities of modernism were necessary whether one liked them or not.

But in the shadow of nuclear holocaust and threatened environmental disaster, even natural scientists—the very ones who first infected Romantic artists with ideas about organicism and historical determinism, the very ones whose values had been so aggressively appropriated by academic modernists—were abandoning their previously unquestioned faith in the desirability of continuing growth and innovation. The march of knowledge and technology was not a value in itself, some scientists began to argue, and the purportedly "objective" or value-free ideology that underwrote scientific advances (and, for modernists, artistic ones as well) was not blameless when it produced harmful or inhumane effects. Progress, it was increasingly recognized, came at a price. It did not lead inevitably to utopia; it could just as well lead to disaster. In any case, it could no longer proceed without a moral reckoning.

Taking these "dystopian" rumblings into account as early as 1961, the political scientist Robert Heilbroner wrote presciently about the loss of what he called "historic optimism—that is, a belief in the imminence and immanence of change for the better in man's estate, the advent of which can be left to the quiet work of history."[14] By 1994 it was easy enough for Leonard Meyer to connect the dots and conclude in retrospect that "the end of historic optimism marks the beginning of postmodernism."[15] This suggests a connection between postmodernism and the "Green" movements that emerged in the politics of Europe and America in the 1970s in opposition to continued industrial expansion—economic modernism—in the name of "timeless" human and environmental values. And that is perhaps as close to a general definition of postmodernism as we are likely to get.

The "postmodernism" that became a subject of angry academic—and to a limited extent, political—debate in the 1980s and 1990s was the extension of this loss of faith to nihilistic extremes like radical skepticism or radical relativism. The first was the refusal to regard any proposition as inherently true or definitively proven; the second was the refusal to accept any hierarchy of values at all. One could regard these extensions as abuses—intellectual or moral aberrations all too easily exploited by cynics like "Holocaust deniers"—without necessarily opposing the original postmodernist impulse.

ITS BEGINNINGS FOR MUSIC

The most direct evidence of a postmodernist turn in music came right alongside the Green challenge to the idea of progress. The big story of the 1950s, we may recall, had been the "conversion" to serialism of figures like Copland and Stravinsky—a story that paid the highest tribute to, and considerably strengthened, the master narrative. Two decades later, the big story and the most convincing evidence that the master narrative was losing its grip were the almost equally conspicuous conversions that took place in the opposite direction.

That story begins (or we can begin effectively to tell it) with the first performance, on 15 May 1972, of the String Quartet no. 3 by George Rochberg (1918–2005). Until then, Rochberg had seemed an untroubled academic modernist—and a distinguished one whose works had been honored with many coveted awards. He was not only a prominent exponent of serial composition, but a noted theorist of serialism as well. In 1955 he published a small book called *The Hexachord and Its Relation to the Twelve-Tone Row*. Based on a thorough study of some of the late works of Schoenberg, it was a pioneering investigation of the technique that Milton Babbitt would later christen "combinatoriality". Like Babbitt, Rochberg applied his theoretical inquiries directly to his compositions, for example in a much-played and much-studied *Duo concertante* for violin and cello (1953), a work whose performance medium was particularly well suited (and probably chosen) to display the contrapuntal possibilities of hexachordal combinatoriality. The composer of such a work was obviously, and fruitfully, committed to the ideal of perpetual technical advance. That commitment found reflection in Rochberg's appointment in 1960 as the chairman of a major American music department, at the University of Pennsylvania.

Rochberg's String Quartet no. 2 (1961) attracted wide attention precisely on account of its advanced technique. Like Schoenberg's Quartet no. 2, which evidently inspired it, Rochberg's quartet incorporated a part for a soprano soloist in addition to the four strings. She sings (in English translation) the opening and closing stanzas of one of the "Duino Elegies" by the German poet Rainer Maria Rilke (1875–1926). The poem is a meditation on the passage of time and the transience of life, in response to which Rochberg devised a complex scheme of superimposed tempos to call attention, as the poem is sung, to the temporal matters it treats. Rochberg named Ives as the progenitor of his technique of "tempo simultaneity"; but of course the most conspicuous recent embodiment of the idea had been Elliott Carter's String Quartet no. 1 (which, as it happens, had been issued on a recording in 1958, the year before Rochberg started work on his Quartet no. 2). It is hard not to see Rochberg's Quartet as vying with Carter's, applying the most advanced contemporary rhythmic style to an equally advanced hexachordal-combinatorial organization of pitch.

In any case, Rochberg identified himself through this work as a composer interested in exploring and extending the latest techniques of his craft, thinking that to be the best way of achieving a truly contemporary intensity of expression. In a program note he wrote to accompany the first recording of the Quartet no. 2, Rochberg justified his rather detailed description of his innovative technique with the comment that "it is impossible to separate the 'what' of a work from its 'how.' "[16] That could stand as a singularly concise précis of modernist principles.

In the decade that followed the Second Quartet, possibly again inspired by Ives, Rochberg experimented with collage techniques. In *Contra mortem et tempus* (1965) — a quartet for violin, flute, clarinet, and piano, whose title (Against Death and Time) again evokes Rilke — he wove a densely expressionistic contrapuntal fabric out of lines extracted from various atonal or twelve-tone works by Ives, Alban Berg, Edgard Varèse, Pierre Boulez, Luciano Berio, and himself. In keeping with so much modernist music, the collage was a "secret structure." The works on which it drew were unlikely to be recognized by most listeners, especially as the reweaving emphasized (to quote a critique by the musicologist Alexander Ringer, a friend of the composer) "the fundamental sameness of so many pitch successions in panchromatic music."[17] Rochberg's next collage piece, *Music for the Magic Theater* (also composed in 1965), took a somewhat more daring step, juxtaposing source material distinguished not by "fundamental sameness" but by extravagant dissimilarity: a divertimento by Mozart; a symphony by Mahler; the "Cavatina" from Beethoven's Quartet in B♭, op. 130; the famous beginning of Webern's *Concerto*, op. 24; Stockhausen's *Zeitmässe* for wind quintet (itself a famous study in rhythmic and textural complexity); Varèse's *Déserts*; "Stella by Starlight" (a transcribed Miles Davis recording); and several works by Rochberg himself, including the String Quartet no. 2. What all of these source-works had in common was a descending chromatic motif that gave the work a hidden unity — another "secret structure."

The title of the composition is a reference to the final section of Hermann Hesse's novel *Steppenwolf* (1927), one of many modern novels to explore the theme, derived from Nietzsche by way of Freud, of contradiction between the demands of social harmony and the untamed beast of man's inner spirit. In the Magic Theater (i.e., the mirror of the mind), the title character — outwardly an ordinary middle-class citizen named Harry Haller, but on the inside a raging wolf of the steppes — comes face to face with Mozart, the paragon of benign detachment and spiritual wholeness: in other words, everything that modern man lacks.

Mozart, at first unrecognizable in modern dress and wigless, leads Haller to a primitive "wireless receiver" (radio), which is playing a Concerto Grosso by Handel. The music comes through the static woefully distorted. Haller protests, but Mozart cautions that it does not matter. Here is an excerpt from his sermon:

> You hear not only a Handel who, disfigured by wireless, is, all the same, in this most ghastly of disguises still divine; you hear as well and you observe, most worthy sir, a most admirable symbol of all life. When you listen to wireless you are a witness of the everlasting war between idea and appearance, between time and eternity, between the human and the divine. Exactly, my dear sir, as the wireless for ten minutes together projects the most lovely music without regard into the most impossible places, into snug drawing-rooms and attics and into the midst of chattering, guzzling, yawning and sleeping listeners, and exactly as it strips this music of its sensuous beauty, spoils and scratches and beslimes it and yet cannot altogether destroy its spirit, just so does life, the so-called reality, deal with the sublime picture-play of the world and make a hurley-burley of it. It makes its unappetizing tone-slime of the most magic orchestral music. Everywhere it obtrudes its mechanism, its activity, its dreary exigencies and vanity between the ideal and the real, between orchestra and ear. All life is so, my child, and we must let it be so; and, if we are not asses, laugh at it. It little becomes people like you to be critics of wireless or of life either. Better learn to listen first! Learn what is to be taken seriously and laugh at the rest.[18]

Just so, the middle section (act II) of Rochberg's *Music for the Magic Theater* subjects the "sublime, divine" Adagio movement from Mozart's Divertimento, K. 287, to the hurly-burly of modernity. At first, Mozart's music is merely rescored from the original string quartet to an ensemble of fifteen players (roughly the "orchestra" of Schoenberg's Chamber Symphony, op. 9). The piano, in a concertante role, sometimes takes over the original inner parts, at other times adds "graffiti" of its own in a Mozartean style. The first violin part is transposed up an octave, where it acquires an ethereal tone color that sounds (according to the composer's program note) "as though it were coming from a great distance."

At the close, Mozart indicates a cadenza by placing a fermata over the last $^6_4$ chord. At this point, all sorts of music composed since Mozart's time come piling on, "besliming" its sensuous beauty according to Hesse's prescription (Ex. 9-1). The $^6_4$ chord is never resolved. But the last movement (act III) enacts the acceptance of modernity that Hesse's Mozart recommends: as the work continues, Mozart's music becomes less a contrasting ground, but is instead drawn into dialogue and eventual harmony with the modern "graffiti" until the interrupted cadence from the previous movement is resumed and completed. As Ringer puts it, the jarring interjections eventually "manage to make music with Mozart."[19]

There is always a strict demarcation in *Music for the Magic Theater* between "then" and "now." The chasm between past and present is not really bridged, since "tonality" is still marked as meaning "the past," which (according to an epigraph in the score) "haunts us with its nostalgic beauty." Ultimately, then, Rochberg's quotation of "tonal" music alongside "atonal" in *Music for the Magic Theater* does not (yet) imply rejection of modernism. Symbolically acknowledging the distance between past and present affirms our sense of living in a contemporary world that is marked off by a barrier from what has gone before, thus affirming the essential "truth" of modernism.

A PARENTHESIS ON COLLAGE

In any case, the use of collage to represent the hurly-burly of the modern age was hardly unprecedented in 1965 (even if its most widely played example, Berio's *Sinfonia*,

EX. 9-1A   George Rochberg, *Music for the Magic Theater*, II, end

EX. 9-1A   *(continued)*

still lay three years in the future). Not to mention Ives, or even the French surrealist music of the 1920s, at least two prominent composers had by then made collage their main expressive vehicle. One was Bernd Alois Zimmermann (1918–70), a German composer whose opera *Die Soldaten* ("The soldiers"), composed over a six-year period from 1958 to 1964, is a multidimensional collage in which split-level dramaturgy allows as many as seven scenes to play simultaneously, sometimes further augmented by the use of film and slide projections. Each scene, while coordinated with the rest, has a distinctive musical profile that often features quotations from the music of the past (Bach chorales, the *Dies Irae*, etc.) alongside Zimmermann's own serial constructions.

EX. 9-IA *(continued)*

Some of Zimmermann's scores, like the riotous *Musique pour les soupers du Roi Ubu* ("Music for King Ubu's repasts," 1962–66), consist of nothing but a tissue of promiscuous quotation. Zimmermann's collages expressed his conviction that the modern concept of time necessarily embodied a simultaneous awareness of past, present, and future, and that music, being "an experience which occurs both in time while also embodying time within itself," should consist of symbolic "orderings of progressions of time"[20] in the fullness of its modern conception.

His reliance on preexisting materials made Zimmermann suspect in the eyes of some of his contemporaries, who insisted on traditional modernist values of novelty, originality, and, above all, autonomy. Stockhausen insulted him with the dread term *Gebrauchsmusiker* (maker of music that is not for its own sake), associated with the discredited Hindemith. But by 1966 Stockhausen was making collages himself: first *Telemusik*, an ecumenical "world music" mix that celebrated technology's potential for bringing people and cultures together, then *Hymnen* (1967), a collage of national anthems distorted as if by a short-wave radio tuner. The influence of the despised Zimmermann is noticeable not only in the genre to which these pieces belonged, but also in their obvious "message-mongering."

By 1969, a year before his death by suicide, Zimmermann was prepared (in his *Requiem for a Young Poet*, an elegy for three poet friends who had killed themselves) to pile Beatles songs on top of Beethoven's Ninth, while simultaneously piping in the recorded voices of Churchill, Stalin, Joseph Goebbels (Hitler's propaganda minister)

EX. 9-1B   George Rochberg, *Music for the Magic Theater*, III, resumption and completion of the cadence

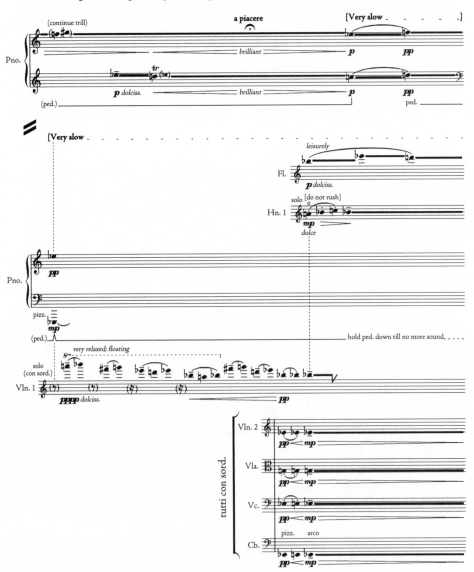

and Joachim von Ribbentrop (Hitler's foreign minister), plus the noise of a political demonstration, all to be cut off abruptly by the sound of a lone poet's voice (one of the dedicatees) begging for peace.

The other master *collageur* was the Canadian-born Henry Brant (1913–2008), who had concluded as early as 1950 that "single-style music, no matter how experimental or full of variety, could no longer evoke the new stresses, layered insanities and multi-directional assaults of contemporary life on the spirit."[21] He developed a modus operandi that added spatial separation to the recipe, specifying his new technique in the form of four "rules": compositions must comprise a multiplicity of "distinct ensemble groups, each of which keeps to its own style, highly contrasted to the styles of the other groups"; they must be as widely dispersed as possible "throughout the hall (not merely upon the stage)"; they should be independent in rhythm and tempo; and they ought to contain a degree of "controlled improvisation or what I call 'instant composing,'" to ensure "spontaneous caprice and individual complexity of material quickly available," and the "instant playability of technically difficult passages."

Brant loved to point out that his first composition written to this prescription — *Antiphony I* (1953), for five separated and independent orchestral groups — predated Stockhausen's celebrated *Gruppen* for four orchestras by three years. But while the groups in *Gruppen* all pass around the same serially-constructed material, the groups in *Antiphony I*, each requiring its own conductor, all play in highly contrasting styles. A hearty maximalist, Brant traced his own development in terms of ever-expanding media and ever-increasing density of information:

> *Millennium 2* (1954) surrounds the audience on three sides with an unbroken wall of brass and percussion, and introduces cumulative 20-voice jazz linear heterophony pitted against a controlled 6-voice polyphony. In *Grand Universal Circus* (1956), contrasted dramatic situations, each based on a different creation myth with its own independent musical setting, are simultaneously enacted in widely separated locations in the theater. In *Concerto with Lights* (1961), a small (audible) orchestra occupies the stage while another ensemble of musicians, working light switches from musical notation, project visual images on the ceiling in exact but silent rhythms contrasted to those sounding from the stage. In *Voyage Four* (1963), the entire wall space of the hall is occupied by banks of instruments, as is the area under the orchestra floor, producing at times an almost total directional immersion of the hearer in sound.[22]

Brant's *Kingdom Come* (1970) pits a full symphony orchestra on stage against a circus band in the balcony. The former "plays at a strident forte throughout, in its highest-tension registers, and expresses its anxieties in long, frenzied phrases, celebrating life in the human pressure cooker."[23] The latter plays music suggesting "the bashed-up ruins of rusty calliopes still screeching; at other times a kind of computerized purgatory, all wires crossed, circuits blown to Kingdom Come, still grinding out the answers to its mispunched programs." It includes a soprano "who impersonates a psychotic Valkyrie." The two orchestras "engage in head-on collisions . . . culminating in a final array of smash-ups which leaves the contradictory premises of the piece unreconciled." By the next decade Brant was ready to trump this dystopic vision with a more optimistic image of harmonized human diversity: *Meteor Farm* (1982), the grandest spatial piece of all, combines a symphony orchestra with a jazz band, an Indonesian gamelan ensemble, African drummers, and classical Indian soloists, all ranged around and above the audience.

A Brantian assemblage is a collage of characteristic media rather than of quotations from preexisting music à la Zimmermann or Rochberg, but it aims similarly to evoke modern life in its irreducible heterogeneity. Although these composers were all of them certifiably of the avant-garde, the collage style began in the 1960s to seep into the work of "mainstream" artists as well. We have already observed the way media and style collages helped express the ironies and pathos of Britten's *War Requiem* (chapter 5). Even Shostakovich, in his last symphony, the Fifteenth (1971), made recourse to enigmatically emblematic quotations. The first movement incorporates an unmissable phrase from Rossini's *William Tell* Overture, and the finale opens with (and returns to) the "Fate" leitmotif from Wagner's *Die Walküre*. The nature of Shostakovich's sources (solid "bourgeois classics" as Steve Reich would say) and the obviously portentous function of the quotes serve to domesticate the technique, draining it (freeing it?) of its avant-garde associations.

But, as all of these examples have shown, as an expressive resource collage remained well within the accepted boundaries of modernist practice, in no way contradicting or threatening its premises. Brant's progressively more ambitious collages subscribe fully to the modernist "onward and upward" project — ever grander, ever bigger, ever more omnivorous. Like other modernist devices that became conventional, collage was easily absorbed, in moderate doses, into the mainstream concert repertoire. There is no reason to apply a term like "postmodernism" to it.

COLLAGE AS THEATER

Two *collageurs* of the 1960s did begin to prefigure postmodernist ideas and values, however. One was George Crumb (b. 1929), a colleague of Rochberg's (from 1965) at the University of Pennsylvania, who between 1963 and 1970 composed eight works to texts by the Spanish surrealist poet Federico García Lorca (1898–1936): *Night Music* (1963); four books of madrigals (actually settings for solo soprano and chamber ensemble, composed between 1965 and 1969); *Songs, Drones, and Refrains of Death* (1968); *Night of the Four Moons* (1969, inspired by the Apollo 11 moon landing that year); and *Ancient Voices of Children* (1970).

Like almost all American composers of his generation, Crumb was trained in the academic modernist styles of the

FIG. 9-1   George Crumb in his garden, 1987.

time. One of his early works, *Variazioni per orchestra* (1959), contains an homage-quotation from Berg's *Lyric Suite* (as the *Lyric Suite* had contained one from *Tristan und Isolde*), and his Sonata for solo cello (1955), one of his most widely performed compositions, is much indebted to Bartók. Dealing with Lorca's shocking imagery, full of nightmare visions and wild contrasts, aroused in Crumb "an urge to fuse various unrelated stylistic elements" so as to achieve similarly incongruous juxtapositions in his music.

Quotation of existing music was only one of the means Crumb employed to gain this breadth of reference. Strains of Bach and Chopin, particularly, waft through some of these pieces. Often, like Rochberg's quotations, they are etherealized: in *Ancient Voices of Children* the pianist plays an excerpt from Bach's "Notebook for Anna Magdalena" on a toy piano, and at the very end the oboist wanders slowly offstage while playing the "Farewell" motif from Mahler's *Song of the Earth*. But a more frequent source of disorienting imagery comes from the use of incongruously mixed timbres, often altered after the fashion of Cage's prepared piano.

A native of West Virginia, Crumb drew on youthful memories for some of these effects: banjo in *Night of the Four Moons*; electric guitar played "bottle-neck style" by sliding a glass rod over the frets hillbilly-fashion in *Songs, Drones, and Refrains of Death*; mandolin, harmonica, and "musical saw" (a carpenter's saw set in vibration by a violin bow while being bent against the player's knee) in *Ancient Voices of Children*. These sounds of the American countryside are regularly combined with those of recognizably Asian percussion instruments like Tibetan tuned "prayer stones," or Japanese "temple bells." Altered timbres are obtained by sliding a chisel on piano strings, threading paper between the strings of a harp, fingering a violin or cello tremolo while wearing thimbles, tuning the unison strings on a mandolin a quarter tone apart, blowing into a flute while also singing, dipping a gong into a tub of water. Instrumentalists are required to sing, singers to play instruments.

Crumb's eclecticism was far more extreme than Rochberg's or Zimmermann's; but the difference was not just quantitative. It was different in quality as well, because its heterogeneous sources were not implicitly arranged in a time continuum. The ingredients in Crumb's collages were chosen not as representatives of styles but as expressive symbols of "timeless" content. Quoting Bach and Mahler in the context of Lorca was not an exercise in incongruity, but an affirmation of the relevance of all to all. There is no need for the sort of harmonizing or reconciling gestures Rochberg employed in *Music for the Magic Theater*, because the quotations were not jarring intrusions to begin with.

Nor were the heterogeneous timbres necessarily evocative of their specific origins. Nor were they mere atmospheric colors. Crumb was one of the first composers (in the 1980s their number would multiply) to make timbre his primary creative preoccupation, varying and nuancing it with great subtlety and resourcefulness while reducing the music's formal structure to simple repetitive or strophic designs and stripping its sound surface down to bare monodic or heterophonic textures. Critics marveled at the way in which timbre, often thought a decorative "nonessential," could successfully replace the more "substantial" elements of music — the elements out of which most of the standard techniques in the modernist arsenal were assembled. Where the music of Rochberg, Zimmermann, and Brant seemed as much burdened by a sense of history as that of any modernist, Crumb's seemed virtually amnesiac, drawing on the music of all times and places as if it were all part of one undifferentiated "now" (as, thanks to recording technology, it had in fact become).

On top of this, Crumb joined with other composers of the 1960s and 1970s in introducing elements of theater or ritualized movement not only into vocal but even into instrumental compositions. As a result, his music became something of a fad with choreographers, whose efforts popularized it far beyond the usual reach of avant-garde music. *Ancient Voices of Children* joined the repertoires of four ballet companies — three in America, one in Lisbon — during the first two years of its existence. By 1985, Crumb's works had received more than fifty choreographic treatments.

Black Angels (1970) for amplified string quartet, in which the players wear masks and are asked to chant meaningless syllables and numbers in various languages and lend a hand as percussionists on maracas, tam-tam, and tuned water goblets, was the most celebrated instance of Crumb's instrumental theatrics and became perhaps the most imitated composition of its decade. It was composed at the height of the Vietnam war and its rituals — including a snatch of Schubert's "Death and the Maiden" Quartet played with a bizarre technique (bowing above the left hand with reversed fingering) that produces a weirdly strangled timbre — enact a kind of surrealistic funeral to protest the killing.

"Dance of the Sacred Life-Cycle," the third movement of *Ancient Voices of Children* (Fig. 9-2), embodies most of Crumb's distinctive gestures. The music is scored for a soprano or mezzo-soprano, an offstage boy soprano, an oboist, a harpist, an amplified pianist, a mandolinist, and three percussionists. It unfolds in two notated systems. The first consists entirely of an introduction for the woman singer, vocalizing into the piano to produce an eerie resonance. Her cry, "Mi niño!" sets the Dance, entirely notated on the second system, in motion.

The percussionists, notated across the bottom of the page, now enter, performing an ostinato pattern borrowed from Ravel's 1928 ballet, *Boléro*. Their crescendo-decrescendo pattern lends to the music whatever overall shape it possesses. Meanwhile, the setting of the poem, a question-and-answer dialogue between a mother and her unborn child, is notated in a literally circular form to symbolize the "life cycle" which birth initiates. The basic dialogue of mother and child, represented by the letter A, is performed by the two singers using Schoenberg's "sprechstimme" technique. The chief dance melody, for oboe, is represented by the letter B. The mother's refrain, "Let the branches ruffle in the sun and the fountains leap all around," sung in a wild melisma by the soprano accompanied by a jangle of papered harp and quarter-toned mandolin, is represented by the letter C. Letter D denotes the two longest speeches in the poem, one for the child and one for the mother, unset by the composer, but to be performed with the same kind of exaggerated contour as the *Sprechstimme*; and E is a closing phrase for the electric piano.

The parts so designated overlap in a threefold cursus, A^1-B^1-C^1-D^1-E^1||A^2-B^2-C^2-D^2-E^2||A^3-B^3-C^3, followed by a "cadence" (notated at the lower right), consisting of a shriek (or the instrumental equivalent) for all participants.

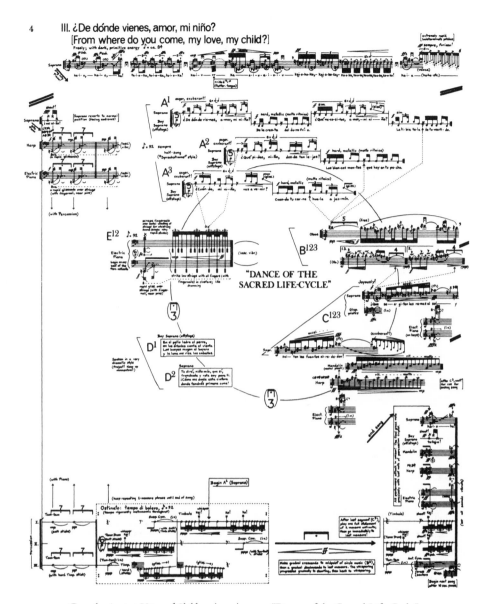

FIG. 9-2   Crumb, *Ancient Voices of Children* (1970): no. 3, "Dance of the Sacred Life-Cycle."

Unusual layouts and graphics, like the circular notation of the Dance, were another of Crumb's signature devices. Some works of his are notated on circular staves, others on spirals, still others in the shape of crosses. But the intention, as Crumb has explained it, is not only symbolic (as in the *Augenmusik* or "eye music" of old). Circular staves can represent all kinds of mystical notions, it is true, but they are also the most efficient way of notating a *moto perpetuo* (and were used for that purpose since the early fifteenth century). The look of the page in Fig. 9-2, reminiscent of the old choir-book format, visually reinforces the idea of collage—an assemblage rather than an organic unity. Layouts that avoid the usual alignment of parts have the further advantage of freeing performers from their habits: "I suppose I could have written it out straight," Crumb told an interviewer, "but I wanted to get the performers away from thinking vertically — I didn't want them too conscious of the vertical relationship of the parts,"[24] which would have led (he feared) to a too-literal coordination with the incessant metrical pulse.

The striking thing about Crumb's collages is their uncomplicated form and spare texture — utterly unlike Brant's or Zimmermann's saturated glut and clutter — and the loving way in which they gather up so much that had been expressly targeted for modernist exclusion. There is considerable sentimentality and nostalgia in the music: not so much a nostalgia for familiar or comforting music as a longing for a lost directness of expression. That directness could be disconcerting. Reviewing *Ancient Voices of Children*, Andrew Porter (Carter's advocate) admitted good-naturedly that "any tough, suspicious old critic thinks that he is being got at, and worked over emotionally by a battery of tearjerking devices such as Puccini himself might envy."[25] But Puccini-loving audiences responded to it without distrust, placing Crumb's output in the same paradoxical category as the minimalists': certifiably avant-garde-sounding music that (for a while, anyway) attracted a genuine popular following. During a rough decade from the mid-1970s to the mid-1980s, Crumb was the most frequently and widely performed of living American composers.

But possibly because Crumb's gestures and sound-shapes were closer than the minimalists' to the going avant-garde styles of the time, his music has not worn as well as theirs. Some of his onetime promoters have looked back on the Crumb-boom with a certain squeamishness. "The rituals were always a little silly — earnest academics wearing party masks and parading about solemnly while whacking percussion,"[26] John Rockwell wrote in perhaps not altogether candid retrospect. "The drama was a little shallow; the succession of spooky motives led to a patchy continuity, the chanting of numbers and foreign words was meaninglessly portentous, and much of the interest relied on timbres whose novelty did not last long,"[27] wrote Kyle Gann from an end-of-century vantage point. That Crumb retained a modernist addiction to novelty may have exacted another sort of price as well. In the mid-1980s he fell silent, unable to keep the new timbres coming.

Quite a different trajectory was set in motion by *Eight Songs for a Mad King* (1969), a piece of angry chamber music – theater by the English composer Peter Maxwell Davies (b. 1934) that had a lot outwardly in common with the gentler work Crumb was doing at about the same time. It was composed for a group called the Pierrot Players, which had been cofounded in 1967 by Davies and his friend Harrison Birtwistle (b. 1934). The two had been fellow students at the University of Manchester; Davies had gone on from there to Princeton, where from 1962 to 1965 he received a thorough grounding in academic modernism, American style. The Pierrot Players, as the name advertised, was founded in tribute to Schoenberg's *Pierrot lunaire*. The membership consisted of virtuoso performers on the instruments required by the Schoenberg composition, plus a percussionist. Their concerts featured performances of *Pierrot lunaire* that sought to re-create its original character as a piece of outlandish music theater, with a singer costumed as a commedia dell'arte character and the instrumentalists concealed behind a screen, followed by similarly theatrical chamber works by the group's founders.

Eight Songs for a Mad King was the fourth of five resolutely shocking Davies compositions first performed by the Pierrot Players that sought to revive the effects, and to an extent the techniques, of German expressionism. In the first, *Revelation and Fall*, a nun in a blood-red habit shouted obscenities through a public-address system. In the second, *L'homme armé* (based on Davies's completion of an anonymous fragmentary fifteenth-century Mass), a female singer dressed as a Catholic priest enthusiastically orates in Latin St. Luke's account of Judas's betrayal of Christ. The third, *Vesalii icones* (named after the anatomical drawings of the sixteenth-century physician Andreas Vesalius), featured a naked dancer who sits at an out-of-tune piano and plays a staid Victorian anthem before gyrating lewdly about a cellist clad in a choirboy robe.

Composed to a text by the Australian poet Randolph Stow based on contemporary memoirs of King George III of England, *Eight Songs for a Mad King* draws on the old convention of the "mad scene," an operatic mainstay since the seventeenth century, to depict the mental agonies of the unfortunate monarch who in the years following the ruinous American Revolution succumbed to raving fits. The dramatic premise was supplied by an old anecdote according to which the mad old king spent endless days seated at a little mechanical organ teaching his pet bullfinches to sing. Four members of the Pierrot Players — the flutist, clarinetist, violinist, and cellist — performed inside big plastic "birdcages," while the singer-actor playing the king ran amok in their midst. Since depicting madness can "rationalize" any irrationality, it served here to justify bizarre parodies of old music. In the seventh song, "Country Dance (Scotch Bonnett)," the ironic object of the farce is "Comfort Ye, My People," the opening tenor recitative in Handel's *Messiah* (Ex. 9-2).

EX. 9-2   Peter Maxwell Davies, *Eight Songs for a Mad King*, VII ("Country Dance")

EX. 9-2 (continued)

Defacing old music venerated by tradition with incongruous performance styles (here, "smoochy" ragtime and Victorian hymnody) and "extended" vocal technique was nothing new, but in this case the avant-garde elements seem to be as much the butt of the unfriendly humor as the hallowed original. One critic, David Paul, has suggested that in the context of the 1960s, the figure of the mad king, a once-powerful figure rendered impotent, might stand not only (a bit wishfully, perhaps) for the period's social upheavals, but might also be a metaphor for the dogmatic inelasticity of modernism, rendered impotent and irrelevant in the face of the egalitarian plurality of styles that was ineluctably emerging in the wake of the sixties.[28]

Whether or not that was Maxwell Davies's intention, he received a lesson in the impotence of modernism when the piece was performed, and its final gesture—the smashing of the violinist's instrument by the singer-actor portraying the deranged king — failed to shock the royally entertained audience, long inured to whatever jolts a modernist might try to administer. In any case, *Eight Songs* and *Vesalii icones* were a turning point for the composer, who turned his back on avant-gardism, embraced an increasingly non- or pre- if not postmodernist approach, and embarked on a career path increasingly reminiscent of Benjamin Britten's: residence in the country (in Maxwell Davies's case, the Orkney Islands), engagement with the surrounding community, composition of "useful" music including operas and concertos for young performers, unironic rapprochement with traditional genres and conventional styles.

Nobody could have foreseen in 1969 that between 1975 and 1996 this composer, of all people, would write six proper symphonies cast deliberately in a line with those of Sibelius, long a favorite with British audiences. The only shocking aspect of Maxwell Davies's later career was his defection from the company of shockers (and his severing of ties to his former modernist comrades, including the unreformed Birtwistle).

APOSTASY

It was still possible to shock, however, and Rochberg proved it. Nothing in the work of previous *collageurs*, including Rochberg himself, prepared audiences or critics for his Third Quartet, even though its continuity with his previous works is obvious in retrospect. Its first movement, marked *Allegro fantastico; violente; furioso*, raised no eyebrows. Fantastic violence and fury were the modernist stock in trade, and the music was based on harmonies that, while suitably dissonant, were altogether familiar: every chord in Ex. 9-3a is a composite "atonal triad" plus inversion, a harmony of stacked fourths and tritones that had been in widespread use since the early years of the century, and the melodic motive is an arpeggiation of the same harmony, equalizing the "vertical" and "horizontal" dimensions in a manner long associated with Schoenberg and Bartók. This was a time-tested, everyday — hence conservative — "new music" gambit.

The shock of the new came in the third movement, a set of variations marked *Adagio sereno, molto espressivo e tranquillo; pure* (Ex. 9-3b). Its three-sharp key signature means what it says: this is a work in a fully functional A major, confined to a style

EX. 9-3A   George Rochberg, Quartet no. 3, I, beginning

EX. 9-3B   George Rochberg, Quartet no. 3, III, mm. 1–32

that (according to one baffled critic) "César Franck would have deemed harmonically unadventurous."[29] So he would; for the style (not only as regards harmony but as regards the treatment of the instruments) is identifiably that of Beethoven's late quartets, and in affect the movement alludes specifically to the Cavatina from op. 130 and the "Heilige Dankgesang" ("Hymn of Thanksgiving") from op. 132.

Coming as it does after two movements in unspectacular (and anonymous) but nevertheless solidly identifiable twentieth-century style, the stylistic contrast is obviously related to the collage techniques Rochberg had been employing for nearly a decade. But for its duration, the Adagio was not a collage but a pastiche — something that had no modernist credentials at all. (Later, Rochberg extracted it from its original context and reissued it in an arrangement for string orchestra called "Transcendental Variations," in which ingenuous pastiche completely supplants ironic collage.) It actually sounded like Beethoven, and — as the author of this book can attest — the 1973 Nonesuch recording by the Concord Quartet (the group that had commissioned the piece) quickly became a favorite item for "guess the composer" games.

A composition like this broke all the rules. There was little or no "distancing." The impression was one not of sophisticated irony, but (as with Crumb) of disconcerting sincerity. Unlike the neoclassicism of the 1920s, in which aspects of the morphology and phonology of obsolete styles were revived amid a syntax that was wholly contemporary, Rochberg's Adagio revived the syntax as well, treating Beethoven's style as if it were not obsolete at all. To write in an obsolete style as if it were not obsolete was to challenge the whole idea of stylistic obsolescence. And to challenge that idea was to put in question the "necessity" of the twentieth century's stylistic revolutions — the most sacred of all modernist dogmas.

Of course there were many composers, especially in America, who had come of age in Stravinsky's "neoclassical" (or Copland's "Americanist") orbit, and who wrote in more or less conventional "tonal" idioms all through the period of stylistic revolution. They included celebrities like the charismatic, photogenic Leonard Bernstein, one of the most prominent conductors of the period, who led the New York Philharmonic from 1957 to 1969 (and was thereafter "conductor laureate" for life). Television had made him by the 1960s probably the most famous classical musician in the world. Nearly a decade before Rochberg made headlines with his Third Quartet, Bernstein wrote *Chichester Psalms* (1965), a eupho-nious choral composition in B♭ major that rode the coattails of his personal fame to a popular-ity that, it is safe to say, no other classical composition of the decade ever approached. But it was not perceived as making (or challenging) history; quite the contrary.

Ned Rorem, another Ame-rican traditionalist, familiar to us for his showy tribute to the Beatles (chapter 7), wryly observed of the stir that Roch-berg's Quartet was making that

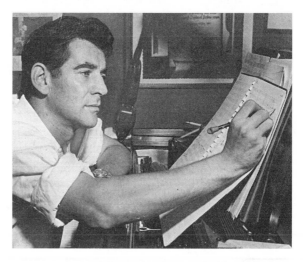

FIG. 9-3   Leonard Bernstein, photographed by Al Ravenna in 1955.

people who quit smoking gain a sort of praise that people who never smoked at all never get, even though the latter are the more virtuous. And while it was not exactly praise that Rochberg was getting (although traditional antimodernists and other lapsed or lapsing modernists did greet the Third Quartet with some enthusiasm), the point hit home. Within the view of history that supported modernism, "tonal" composers in the twentieth century, no matter how famous or successful, were historically insignificant — and the relative lack of attention that they are paid in narrative histories, even this one, shows how influential the modernist "master narrative" has been on historical writing.

But nobody could write Rochberg off that way. "Once one of the foremost serial composers"[30] (in the words of a younger colleague), he had done the unthinkable: he had been at the vanguard and quit. His significance as an academic modernist had been universally acknowledged, so he could not now be ignored. Regarded as an apostate, he was hailed and reviled in equal measure for the act he had committed rather than the music he produced. In similar fashion, when three years later a "neotonal" piece (Sonata for Solo Violin by Hans Jürgen von Bose) was finally performed at Darmstadt, the audience erupted in protests and catcalls reminiscent of the *Rite of Spring* premiere sixty years before. Unlike the latter, however, the performance was literally drowned out and the performer was forced to stop. Because it took place in Germany, where artists had been regularly shouted down by politicians within living memory, the protest begot more protests.

Whether in New York or Darmstadt, the initial reaction was provoked entirely by the style of the music rather than its specific content or expressive effect, which only corroborated the pattern of reception that had always attended twentieth-century music, *The Rite* and all. But rather than glorying in a succès de scandale, which would have confirmed him (however perversely) as a modernist, Rochberg decried the pattern and set out to demolish it. No other century had been as style-conscious as the twentieth, he complained. In no other century did each and every composer feel such a compulsion to "view his situation in terms of where he's been, where he is now, and where he must go."[31] These were the bedrock tenets of modernism, so deeply ingrained that most composers were not even aware of alternatives.

In part Rochberg himself was responsible for the polarized way in which his quartet was received, for he did everything he could to provoke it. In a program note that accompanied the 1973 recording, he preempted the debate he knew was coming with a searching discussion that must count among the earliest self-conscious proclamations of a postmodern sensibility in — and for — music. (It was the first of many increasingly acid musicopolitical polemics that he would write over the next two decades.) The quotation in the preceding paragraph about twentieth-century composers' need to, so to speak, take their historical temperature comes from this essay. Rochberg strongly implied that this compulsion, in which he had shared as much as anyone, amounted to a neurosis, and that the place to attack the disease and cure it — its root cause, so to speak — was the modern Western unidirectional concept of time itself. "Current biological research," he declared,

> corroborates Darwin: we bear the past in us. We do not, cannot begin all over again in each generation, because the past is indelibly printed on our central nervous

systems. Each of us is part of a vast physical-mental-spiritual web of previous lives, existences, modes of thought, behavior, and perception; of actions and feelings reaching much further back than what we call "history." We are filaments of a universal mind, we dream each others' dreams and those of our ancestors. Time, thus, is not linear, but radial.[32]

The scientific "evidence" the composer adduced may be written off as puffing; but the belief it supported was real, and there for all to hear in the music. It was born, Rochberg said, of an honest reappraisal of the old paradox that bedeviled all composers in the twentieth century: "the music of the 'old masters' was a living presence; its spiritual values had not been displaced or destroyed by the new music."[33] There was an inherent and unhealthy contradiction in a philosophy of history that compelled one to reject earlier styles, when the persistence of those same styles was a fact of every musician's daily life. Rochberg began to suspect that he, like every other committed modernist composer, had cut himself off from the expressive possibilities that enabled the older music to survive. That renunciation, he feared, probably doomed his music and that of his contemporaries to oblivion.

Rejecting the modernist imperative, Rochberg wrote, was something he could not do "without great discomfort and difficulty, because I had acquired it, along with a number of similar notions, as a seemingly inevitable condition of the twentieth-century culture in which I had grown up."[34] Virtually every aspect of his unconscious heritage had to be brought to consciousness and jettisoned (a process that sounds very much like Freud's description of psychoanalysis) if he was to compose a movement like the Third Quartet's Adagio and mean it:

> I have had to abandon the notion of "originality," in which the personal style of the artist and his ego are the supreme values; the pursuit of the one-idea, uni-dimensional work and gesture which seems to have dominated the esthetics of art in the 20th century; and the received idea that it is necessary to divorce oneself from the past, to eschew the taint of association with those great masters who not only preceded us but (let it not be forgotten) created the art of music itself. In these ways I am turning away from what I consider the cultural pathology of my own time toward what can only be called a *possibility*: that music can be renewed by regaining contact with the tradition and means of the past, to re-emerge as a spiritual force with reactivated powers of melodic thought, rhythmic pulse, and large-scale structure.[35]

It was the last of these considerations, large-scale structure, that made the return to tonality necessary in Rochberg's view, because only tonality (with its power of forecasting and delaying cadences) gave music the dynamic momentum that made possible the genuinely coherent and expressively meaningful articulation of long temporal spans. What Rochberg's essay did not explain, however, was why it was desirable or even necessary to evoke the styles of *particular* "old masters." (In the finale of the Third Quartet, Mahler is just as recognizably evoked as Beethoven had been in the Adagio; and toward the middle of the Adagio, the fast cross-string arpeggios are reminiscent — surely deliberately — of the luminous ending of Schoenberg's *Verklärte Nacht*, an emblem of consolation.) That was the hardest aspect of Rochberg's changed manner for colleagues and critics to accept. Another question worth asking is why Rochberg should have come to his impasse, and then his turning point, exactly when he did. The essay does not really explain that, either.

Only later did Rochberg divulge the answer to the second question. It turned out that his postmodernist revolt did not happen as spontaneously as he had formerly implied, nor were the reasons for it as theoretical as his discussion of them had been. His last serial work was a trio for piano, violin, and cello, completed in 1963. The next year the composer experienced a personal tragedy, when his twenty-year-old son Paul, a poet, succumbed to cancer. He found he had no vocabulary with which to mourn his loss or seek solace from it. "It became crystal clear to me that I could not continue writing so-called 'serial' music," the composer told an interviewer. "It was finished, hollow, meaningless."[36] Having made this admission, Rochberg went on to confess that his objective in reverting to "tonality" was less to debate theories of history than simply to recapture a lost expressive range. "The over-intense manner of serialism and its tendency to inhibit physical pulse and rhythm led me to question a style which made it virtually impossible to express serenity, tranquillity, grace, wit, energy."[37]

ESTHETICS OF PASTICHE

But the first question remains: why evoke the styles of particular "masters" rather than use the language of tonality in a more generic way that might ultimately become one's own? Rochberg never answered this question, and some were therefore led to the conclusion that his motives were shallow. Pastiche composition (as opposed to actual quotation) had never before been used for any other purpose than instruction, or the formal demonstration of skill. To use it as a method for sincere expression of personal emotion seemed a contradiction in terms. But one of Rochberg's major contentions, in his essay on the Third Quartet, was that one's personal emotions are never only that, but are also part of the "physical-mental-spiritual web" that connects people.

Yet if true, that point would apply equally to the old masters, the composers Rochberg adopted as his models, who after all did manage to create the personal idioms that he was content to imitate. (And it would also apply, say, to Poulenc and Prokofieff, who wrote, and to Britten and Shostakovich, who were still writing, in personal tonal idioms even in the twentieth century.) To understand Rochberg's conviction that he had to speak in the recognizable voices of the past one needs to take a further step into specifically postmodernist terrain.

In the "Postscript" to his novel *The Name of the Rose* (1983), the Italian writer Umberto Eco described the dilemma of "belatedness," the sense of coming after everything that mattered. Many artists and critics have identified that despairing sentiment as the distinguishing esthetic frame of the late-twentieth-century mind. Some have associated it with modernism, with its heavy sense of history's burden. But the typical modernist solution to the dilemma was to try to evade the burden through voracious innovation. Dubbed the "anxiety of influence" in 1973 by the literary critic Harold Bloom (often invoked by music historians in connection with Brahms, the first of the burdened moderns), that compulsion to allude to but also to distort and "misread" the past was interpreted, in Bloom's briefly influential theory, as the main engine driving the breakneck history of the arts. When that anxiety subsides into detached acquiescence, Eco argued, postmodernism begins. "I think of the postmodern attitude," he wrote,

> as that of a man who loves a very cultivated woman and knows he cannot say to her, "I love you madly," because he knows that she knows (and that she knows that he knows) that these words have already been written by Barbara Cartland [1901–2000, a famous romance novelist]. Still, there is a solution. He can say, "As Barbara Cartland would put it, I love you madly." At this point, having avoided false innocence, having said clearly that it is no longer possible to speak innocently, he will nevertheless have said what he wanted to say to the woman: that he loves her, but he loves her in an age of lost innocence. If the woman goes along with this, she will have received a declaration of love all the same. Neither of the two speakers will feel innocent, both will have accepted the challenge of the past, of the already said, which cannot be eliminated, both will consciously and with pleasure play the game of irony. But both will have succeeded, once again, in speaking of love.[38]

Eco (as if practicing the detachment that he preached) wrote lightheartedly about what many artists have experienced as a tragic state of affairs. The sincerity that so surprised and disconcerted critics and colleagues in Rochberg's resumption of a premodernist style, according to Eco's account of postmodernism, was bought at the price of a greater "global" irony. Rochberg expresses his own heartfelt emotion "as Beethoven (Mahler, Schoenberg) would put it," for according to Eco, there is no other way of doing so at the fallen end of the twentieth century. Using an innocent language innocently—using tonality "in one's own way"—is no longer even an option. The choice is bleak: either renounce expression altogether or borrow a voice.

The implication is indeed depressing: just as we can communicate artistically only through the studied simulacra of styles that were once spontaneous, so our emotions themselves have become simulacra. Rochberg's quest to regain the full range of sincere emotional expression that had been available to artists (and other humans) before the horrors of the twentieth century is thus doomed to failure; but the failure is noble, because it faces the unhappy truth of contemporary life rather than retreating, as modernism had done, into a self-satisfied, self-induced (and socially isolating) delusion of freedom. "Postmodernism," in this view, means resignation to (or making the best of) a state of diminished capacity.

Whether read at face value, as a brave and potentially fruitful undertaking to turn back the clock at the last minute, or in Eco's wry interpretation as a forlorn but necessary (and therefore still brave) coping with a hopeless reality, Rochberg's postmodernism was taken by many if not most of his fellow professionals as intolerable backsliding. It inspired a backlash; and as always, the backlash accomplished more than the original initiative had done toward publicizing and validating "new romanticism" as a timely creative option. As earlier, in the case of architecture, the fulminations did not do what they were supposed to do but instead helped turn postmodernism, or at least Rochberg's variety of it, into a media event. Within a few years, the New York Philharmonic commissioned its composer-in-residence, Jacob Druckman (1928–96), to organize a festival of recent music called "Horizons '83: Since 1968, A New Romanticism?"

The loudest protests came from the most committed modernists. Among critics that meant Andrew Porter, who scoffed at the festival as a "swing to the right"[39] comparable to Ronald Reagan's election to the presidency, which in music as much in politics meant "the repudiation of newly enlightened ways, the reinforcement of old prejudices, the championship of easy mediocrity, and self-indulgent nostalgia." Porter saw his task, correctly, as first of all to defend the modernist view of history. "In theory," he allowed of Rochberg's about-face, "there is no reason a modern composer shouldn't write a Monteverdian madrigal as good as any Monteverdi wrote (or an artist paint in Vermeer's manner a Christ at Emmaus as moving as if it had been painted by Vermeer himself)."[40] But the allowance — especially the calculated reference to Vermeer — was in fact derogatory. Mentioning Vermeer brought to mind Hans van Meegeren, the artful forger whose "Vermeers" had made him rich. It was van Meegeren to whom Rochberg should be compared, Porter implied, because, he insisted, it doesn't ever happen in practice that a simulacrum is as good as an original.

But, comes the postmodernist retort, that is only because we know it is a simulacrum and judge it by irrelevant standards of authenticity. And it is only prejudice, such an answer might continue, that allows Porter to assert a priori that when Rochberg writes in the manner of Beethoven or Mahler, "it becomes apparent not only that he is not their peer but also that he has donned fancy dress." But authenticity was not the only point to be raised in objection to the new postmodernist turn. When Rochberg came forward with an opera, *The Confidence Man* (after Melville), entirely composed in "pastiche" idioms, the critic was ready to make his political allegations explicit. "The effect of this music," Porter warned,

> can perhaps be pernicious. It was disturbing to hear one of our abler young violinists remark at a symposium that he would rather play good Amy Beach than bad Elliott Carter. (Is there any bad Elliott Carter?) Rochberg writes reactionary stuff — music whose appeal is to closed, unadventurous minds. I know nothing of his extramusical beliefs, but his works could become cultural fodder for the New Right: Down with progressive thought! Down with progressive music![41]

That kind of critical hysteria is good press for any composer. And even though he distorted it with a dubious political analogy, Porter was correct to identify progress as the issue dividing modernists and postmodernists. Sometimes Rochberg's defenders have tried to justify him on the old grounds, by claiming (to quote his younger colleague Jay Reise) that his recontextualizations of "tonal" styles "have led to a highly progressive music,"[42] since one hears common-practice tonality differently when it is presented neither as the unquestioned norm nor as an inert relic of the past, but as one among equally valid alternatives for composers of the present. "That George Rochberg's music directly involves the past — for the sake of reopening the entire question of what is expressively valid in a transhistorical sense — is what spurs the erroneous conclusion that his music is reactionary," Reise concluded. "A careful and sensitive listening to Rochberg's recent music will clearly reveal, however, his exceptional role in the progress of music in our time."[43]

By casting Rochberg's eclecticism as novel rather than nostalgic, Reise emphasized its kinship with what Charles Jencks called "double coding" in architecture. Juxtaposing historical references without respect for their chronology does alter one's apprehension of them. The objective in both cases is for styles formerly thought of as part of an inexorable historical progression ("decorative" to "functional" in architecture, "tonal" to "atonal" in music) to be regarded as expressive rather than historical categories, all equally available to artists of the present, whose "transhistorical" reach is for that reason richer in possibilities than that of any previous generation of artists. But that viewpoint is possible only if one renounces the idea of historical progress in the arts. To call it progress (or progressive) in its own right only creates a needless paradox.

Beginning with his Quartet no. 7 (1979), Rochberg's music settled into a distinctive idiom reminiscent of what in historical terms used to be viewed as a "transitional" style poised on the cusp of atonality — a style bridging or synthesizing late Mahler, say, and early Schoenberg. To use such a style as an entirely stable idiom, not "pregnant with the seeds of the future" or leading inexorably to something else — using it, that is, in a manner altogether foreign to the way confirmed historicists like Mahler or Schoenberg themselves regarded it — is another way of liberating music from the tyranny of history. In a "transhistorical" view there is no such thing as a transitional style. To achieve that perspective is the essential postmodernist project.

ACCESSIBILITY

Partly following Rochberg's example, partly in response to a general turn away from utopian thinking that mounted through the 1980s toward a dramatic climax in the fall of the Berlin Wall and the end of the cold war in Europe, several other prominent and successful serialists (and a few avant-gardists of a different stripe) defected to "tonal" idioms that the master narrative had long since declared dead. The loosening of cold-war thinking allowed the reopening of many old and ostensibly settled questions, including the question whether commitment to historical progress was worth the sacrifice of the audience. No longer shadowed by the specter of totalitarianism, "accessibility" regained a measure of respectability. Where Rochberg described his acts and motives strictly in "poietic" (maker's) terms — his own need for freedom of choice and expressive scope — younger converts to tonality put things "esthesically," in terms of the audience and *its* needs.

Two of the most prominent central European avant-gardists, György Ligeti and Krzysztof Penderecki, made spectacular neoromantic swerves in the 1970s. Penderecki's may have been stimulated by the *Solidarność* (Solidarity) movement in Poland, an independent workers' initiative that led ultimately to the fall of Communism there. Seeing social solidarity rather than social alienation as the most progressive political and social force is fatal to modernism. In any case, Penderecki began writing in a style that reminded Poles of the work of Mieczyslaw Karlowicz (1876–1909), a younger Polish contemporary of Mahler and Richard Strauss. Audiences abroad, unfamiliar with Karlowicz, tended to hear the music in terms of the latter's models in the New German School: one critic likened Penderecki's Second Symphony, composed for the New York Philharmonic in 1980 and reverently incorporating the familiar carol "Silent Night" as thematic material, to "Christmas at Wotan's."[44] Later, after the fall of Communism, Penderecki's style mutated again to a middle position resembling the later work of Shostakovich.

Ligeti's turnaround was stimulated by a lengthy stay in California in 1972, as composer-in-residence at Stanford University. There he heard the early minimalist works of Riley and Reich, and imitated them in *Clocks and Clouds* (1973) for women's chorus and orchestra. The second of his Three Pieces for Two Pianos (1976) is titled "Self-Portrait with Reich and Riley (and Chopin in the Background)." The opera *Le grand macabre* (1978) continued following the trend toward eclectic collage, now admitting rock. Finally, in his Trio for Violin, Horn, and Piano, written in 1982 as a companion piece to Brahms's trio for the same combination of instruments, Ligeti put himself into a picture with Brahms himself, along with Bartók, by then regarded (especially in Hungary) not as a "modern" but as a "classic." He frankly described the work as his regretful acknowledgment that the avant-garde had run out of steam, and that continued adherence to its ideals was a far more retrogressive stance than the "retro" styles that were taking its place.

The most prominent American defector after Rochberg was David Del Tredici (b. 1937), another alumnus (along with La Monte Young and Terry Riley) of Seymour Shifrin's composition seminar at the University of California at Berkeley. Unlike the others, Del Tredici went from Berkeley to Princeton and at first seemed destined for the career that such a move implied. His early works, beginning in 1958, were serial compositions that fastened, like Rochberg's, on the unifying possibilities of hexachordal combinatoriality, and also displayed a virtuosic flair for crafty counterpoint.

Syzygy (1966), his best-known work from this period, is one of several based on

FIG. 9-4   David Del Tredici.

texts by James Joyce. A twenty-five-minute setting of two Joyce poems ("Ecce Puer" and "Nightpiece" from *Pomes Penyeach*) for a virtuoso soprano and chamber orchestra with French horn as co-soloist, it has a first movement, based entirely on palindromic motives, that plays its pitches back from the midpoint in transposed retrograde and with string and wind parts reversed (see Ex. 9-4a), and a second movement that contains a cadenza for the two soloists in which the soprano sings a canon by inversion with herself by splitting her line into two registers, each independently setting the same line of text (Ex. 9-4b).

EX. 9-4A   David Del Tredici, *Syzygy*, The midpoint of the palindrome in I

EX. 9-4A (continued)

EX. 9-4B David Del Tredici, *Syzygy*, The canon by inversion in II

In both movements, the contrapuntal texture makes spectacular use of polyrhythms. Like Rochberg in his Second Quartet, Del Tredici was definitely keeping up with the Joneses (that is, with Elliott Carter). The title, an astronomical term meaning an alignment of heavenly bodies, refers to the arcane relationships — the palindromes and inversions — that so infest the composition. The composer remarked that he was always fascinated with the word and its queer spelling, which suggested that it was some other, nonexistent, word spelled backward.

Like many pieces by Princeton alumni, *Syzygy* was made for analysis, and received the full treatment in *Perspectives of New Music*, but it acquired a cult following not only among connoisseurs of serialism but also among connoisseurs of musical eccentricity as an adorably esoteric in-joke by a composer "with a fondness for strict procedures but with the rarer ability" — in the words of Oliver Knussen (b. 1952), a bright young English composer and conductor — "to see their bizarre side."[45] One *bizarrerie* that would not escape even the most casual observer is the use of a huge $2\frac{1}{2}$-octave carillon of tubular chimes requiring two players, which made performance of the piece, for all intents and purposes, fiscally prohibitive.

At this stage of his career, then, Del Tredici aimed at, and received, high professional esteem for exceedingly clever works composed in an esthetic vacuum. As far as the general public was concerned he did not exist; nor did it for him. No one would have predicted in 1966 that within ten years he would have forsaken serialism altogether, or that he would exercise his ingenuity in ways designed to tickle the fancy of subscription audiences in major concert halls. The catalyst was Lewis Carroll, whose poems (mainly drawn from *Alice in Wonderland*) would become for him a greater obsession, and a more fertile source of bizarre compositional scheming, than James Joyce had ever been.

Del Tredici's devotion to Carroll was even more consuming than Crumb's to Lorca. He has since acknowledged the programmatic (or even political) role that his identification with Carroll's "sexual secrets" played in channeling his composing activities, even though his own secrets (homosexual) were of a different order from Carroll's (pedophiliac). Between 1968 and 1996, he composed some dozen works on texts from Carroll's masterpiece ("some dozen" because various items were rescored, reused, reshuffled, and grouped into composites, and a definitive enumeration is impossible). Almost all of them are scored for a solo soprano voice amplified to compete with huge Straussian orchestras, plus in most cases a concertante "folk group" containing saxophones, banjo, mandolin, accordion, and (sometimes) electric guitars.

The first of them, called *Pop-Pourri*, was a typical "sixties" amalgamation of "high" and "vernacular" styles; when he composed it, Del Tredici thought of it as an isolated response to a transient historical moment. But then came a five-movement *Alice Symphony* (1969), followed by *Adventures Underground* (1971) and *Vintage Alice* (1972). By then, thinking enough was enough, he took his leave of Carroll with a sixty-five-minute epitome, pointedly titled *Final Alice* (1975), written in response to a commission from six major orchestras plus the National Endowment for the Arts in honor of the United

States' bicentennial. It is based on the final episode of *Alice's Adventures in Wonderland*, in which Alice observes, and finally upsets, the trial of the Knave of Hearts. The soloist must both narrate the tale and sing four interpolated arias.

Final Alice still contained a few twelve-tone passages to accompany magical transformations like Alice's fantastic growth. In context, the atonal music was an illustrative foil, in which the tone rows have the same distorting and disorienting effect as the accompanying glissandos for an amplified and reverberated theremin. They have become a sort of sound effect. The main musical matter, the four dazzling arias, are a virtuoso test both for the singer and for the composer, since they all amount to a huge set of variations on a single homely "Victorian"-sounding tune (Ex. 9-5a). The music appealed greatly to the kind of audience that relished, say, Strauss's *Don Quixote* (1897), another set of stunningly orchestrated, programmatic variations. The 1976 recording of *Final Alice* by its original performers (the soprano Barbara Hendricks and the Chicago Symphony under Sir Georg Solti, to whom the work is dedicated) was a classical "chart-topper" in the weeks following its release — a first for a contemporary composition.

But *Final Alice* was not the end. Its success brought in more commissions, and in 1980–1981 there followed the gargantuan *Child Alice*, another Alice Symphony — or better, perhaps, a composite cantata — that has hardly ever been performed in toto. The first of its four parts, *In Memory of a Summer Day* (commissioned by the St. Louis Symphony Orchestra and first performed in 1980), itself an hour long, has three movements — "Simple Alice," "Triumphant Alice," and "Ecstatic Alice" — framed by an Introduction and a Postlude. The whole composition, like *Final Alice*, is a set of variations on another simple "Victorian" tune (Ex. 9-5b).

EX. 9-5A   David Del Tredici, *Final Alice*, main tune

EX. 9-5B   David Del Tredici, *In Memory of a Summer Day*, main tune

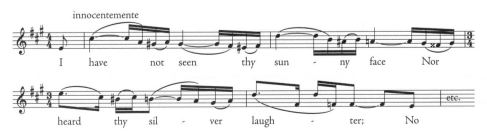

The palpable discrepancy between these homely materials and the prodigious structures to which they give rise, replete with *Götterdämmerung*-like culminations (marked "highpoint" and even, where necessary, "climax of climaxes" in the scores) and fantastically detailed, rhythmically intricate orchestral textures is in some sense the point of these pieces. In *Final Alice* the ironic incongruity between simple contents and inconceivably artful presentation seems quite explicit, as in Aria 3 ("Parody Variations"). But sometimes the artful textures and orchestration seem deliberately to recede from the forefront of the listener's attention, and at such moments the irony becomes precarious. It is when the composer seems to mean it that his music can become troubling. The fourth movement of *Child Alice*, called *All in the Golden Afternoon*, commissioned by the Philadelphia Orchestra and premiered in 1981, lasts almost another hour and consists of

- a lush A♭-major setting ("Aria") of the seven-stanza "Preface Poem" to *Alice's Adventures in Wonderland*
- an orchestral "Fantasia" in A major
- a "Lullaby" set to the last two stanzas of the same poem
- a "Cadenza" (five minutes' worth of melismas on the single word "Alice")
- yet another setting ("against all reason"[46] as the composer confesses or brags in a program note) of the last stanza of the title poem,
- a coda, back in A♭ major, titled "In Conclusion (Sunset)," in which (quoting again from the program note) "steadily pulsing strings support a glowing texture, over which the soprano, as if from a great distance, floats, again and again, the poem's opening line—'All in the golden afternoon.'" Again and again—and again and again

Del Tredici's *Alice* pieces are only nominally about Alice. What they are really all about is excess—glut, overindulgence, binging on voluptuous sonority and honeyed harmony. Their reception has belied the easy charge of pandering, since for every listener who has reveled along with the composer there was at least one who reacted as one might to a seven-course meal of cotton candy; and for every critic who hailed the composer's phenomenal mastery of variation technique and orchestration there were at least two who decried his "elephantine wallowing"[47] (Porter) in Carroll's delicate whimsy or attributed the way in which the composer was squandering his ingenuity to some sort of morbid pathology (their dismissals occasionally couched in thinly veiled homophobic terms).

Child Alice, the most transgressively extravagant piece of all, was also the first of Del Tredici's Carroll-inspired orgies to dispense altogether with "distancing" atonalisms. Nor has there been any subsequent backsliding on his part into modernism. Any suspicion that the composer's intention was anything but provocative is dispelled by the title of the 1985 orchestral fantasy, *March to Tonality*, which touts the recovery of conventional harmony as, yes, progress. It is a paradox that Del Tredici loves to milk, telling an interviewer, for example, that "for me, tonality was actually a daring discovery. I grew up in a climate in which, for a composer, only dissonance and atonality were acceptable. Right now, tonality is exciting for me. I think I invented it. In a sense, I have."[48]

But flouting (and in puncturing, exposing) the puritanism of the modernist "high church" is only part of the story. There is also the nostalgia for a happy childhood that Del Tredici habitually asserts in defense of his sincerity, to prove (curiously echoing the modernist line) that his turn toward tonality was conditioned by an inner necessity. In the same interview, he wittingly or unwittingly echoed (in a sort of retrograde inversion) Schoenberg's famous account of the irresistible forces that drew him kicking and screaming into atonality:

> About halfway through *Final Alice*, I thought, "Oh my God, if I just leave it like this, my colleagues will think I'm crazy." But then I thought, "What else can I do? If nothing else occurs to me, I can't go against my instincts." But I was *terrified* my colleagues would think I was an idiot. People think now that I wanted to be tonal and have a big audience. But that was just not true. I *didn't* want to be tonal. My world was my colleagues — my composing friends. The success of *Final Alice* was very defining as to who my real friends were. I think many composers regard success as a threat. It's really better, they think, if *nobody* has any success, to be all in one boat.[49]

But immediately after this squeamish protest against suspicion of pandering came affirmation:

> Composers now are beginning to realize that if a piece excites an audience, *that doesn't mean it's terrible*. For my generation, it is considered vulgar to have an audience really, *really* like a piece on a first hearing. But why are we writing music except to move people and to be expressive? To have what has moved us move somebody else? Everything is reversed today. If a piece appeals immediately, sensuously, if an audience likes it: all those are "bad things." It is really very *Alice in Wonderland*.

Later, Del Tredici was able to tell a sympathetic younger composer that "I used to play the complete first draft of *Final Alice* just one time each day and then would consider my response: where was it dull, illogical, too much, too little? My *immediate* response was all I valued. I wanted to hear the piece as, eventually, the audience would — once through, without preparation."[50]

COGNITIVE CONSTRAINTS?

Del Tredici's defiantly friendly identification or solidarity with the audience is reflected in the tougher, more "scientific" (or at any rate, more academic) stance adopted by Fred Lerdahl (b. 1943), a composer who has been impelled by postmodernist qualms to study structural linguistics and cognitive psychology in an effort to understand and possibly define the limits within which music must be composed if it is to be intelligible to listeners. This project is the most controversial of all, precisely because of its theoretical nature. It is not merely a description of one person's composing practice, but seeks general truths on which prescriptions can be based. Lerdahl has been accused of promoting his own music by "universalizing" it as a norm for listening. "No," he has objected, "I do not tell people how to listen; I try to find out how they listen."[51] Not everybody wants to know this, and there are good reasons why.

Like all utopian ideas, modernism is basically optimistic. The notion that composers are free to organize their music in unprecedented ways, and that it is up to audiences to adapt to them, is based on a "behaviorist" psychological model. Such a model assumes that the mind is a tabula rasa, a clean slate on which experience is inscribed and reinforced by practice. The mind's activities are conceived as responses to external stimuli, and forms of behavior can be learned, according to this theory, through positive or negative reinforcements (a.k.a. rewards and punishments). Serial music, or any other kind of highly structured music, however novel, is no less intelligible than tonal music, on this model; it is just that listeners have less practice with it. This is the model of mental behavior associated with B. F. Skinner (1904–90), one of the most influential psychologists of the twentieth century, whose theories had a profound impact on modern educational methods — an impact that coincided, as it happened, with the heyday of academic serialism.

Skinnerism received a strong challenge in the 1960s from the work of the linguist Noam Chomsky (b. 1928), who sought to explain how people can learn to form original utterances — sentences they have never heard spoken — on the sole basis of imitating languages that they hear, without any formal instruction in rules. In the case of one's native language, after all, one always "learns the rules" after one has already learned the language. To a large extent, therefore, the rules governing language must be axiomatic assumptions of which we are not conscious. They must be instinctual.

Or, to put it the way Chomsky did, all natural language possesses a "deep structure" that conforms to the innate structure of the mind — a concept that behaviorists had long since rejected. It is a pessimistic concept, since if there is such a thing as an innate mental structure, then it has limits that can in principle be discovered. In the Chomskian view, the mind is not "perfectible." Rather, it is decisively biased. There are some things we humans can learn and some things that we cannot, some ways of processing information that we can practice, some that we cannot. And if that is so, it follows that the mind is no tabula rasa. It is equipped to process only certain kinds of information.

In 1983, together with a linguist named Ray Jackendoff, Lerdahl published a novel study of tonal harmony that sought, on the Chomskian model, not to build up a theory of harmonic practice on the basis of its materials (chords and progressions), but rather to uncover or infer the psychological processes ("transformations") to which musicians and other listeners intuitively subject the chords and progressions of tonal music in order to perceive (and produce) "meaningful" utterances. Borrowing directly from Chomsky's vocabulary, Lerdahl and Jackendoff called their book *A Generative Theory of Tonal Music*.

A generative theory of language, they write, models the "unconscious knowledge" that users of a language innately possess as "a formal system of principles or rules called a *grammar*, which describes (or 'generates') the possible sentences of the language." The objective is to infer the mental rules that make linguistic (or musical) structures coherent and intelligible to listeners, and the rules that make coherent and intelligible linguistic (or musical) structures "creatable" by speakers or composers. Ideally, if the theory is correct, the rules in both cases are the same. Language and music must communicate on the basis of assumptions and processes that composers and listeners innately share. The question a generative theory answers is, "How?"

That tonal music (like natural language) is hierarchically structured is obvious to all competent listeners. The essential task that all theories of tonal music perform is that of describing its hierarchies. The novelty of Lerdahl and Jackendoff's generative theory is its Chomskian assumption that listeners perceive hierarchies when listening to a piece of tonal music intuitively, without having to be taught to make such discriminations. They propose four main intuitive processes that all listeners bring to bear on tonal music:

(1) grouping structure
(2) metrical structure
(3) time-span reduction
(4) prolongational reduction

The first "expresses a hierarchical segmentation of the piece into motives, phrases, and sections." The second "expresses the intuition that the events of the piece are related to a regular alternation of strong and weak beats at a number of hierarchical levels." The third "assigns to the pitches of the piece a hierarchy of 'structural importance' with respect to their position in grouping and metrical structure." And the fourth "assigns to the pitches a hierarchy that expresses harmonic and melodic tension and relaxation, continuity and progression." In addition, the authors posit what they call *well-formedness rules*, which "specify the possible structural descriptions." That is, they act as gatekeepers between meaningful utterances and "noise," and (for example) tell us when we have heard a mistake in execution. And they posit *preference rules*, which "designate out of the possible structural descriptions those that correspond to experienced listeners' hearings of any particular piece."[52] That is, they mediate possible contradictions or ambiguities among the simultaneously processed hierarchies. It is at this last level that really creative composing and listening take place.

None of this is news. As a theory of tonal music Lerdahl and Jackendoff's "generative grammar" is uncontroversial except insofar as it describes musical perception as intuitive, the product of an innate mental predisposition, rather than a wholly learned behavior. (In other words, it is controversial in exactly the same way, and to exactly the same extent, that Chomsky's theories are controversial within linguistics.) Within the relatively settled world of tonal music, the distinction between calling perception intuitive and calling it learned did not make enough of a practical difference to warrant much dispute.

The book contained one hugely contentious passage, however: the last section of the next-to-last chapter, titled "Remarks on Contemporary Music," in which the authors took up what must have been a pressing concern for most readers who had worked through the text to that point. The whole basis and justification of nontonal or "post-tonal" music, as everybody knew, had been the assumption that musical perceptions were wholly learned, and therefore infinitely malleable. Could that assumption be reconciled with Lerdahl and Jackendoff's assumption that musical perceptions were in part intuitive—that is, ingrained and "natural"?

Obviously, it could not. Where there is no pitch hierarchy, and where (as a result of "a tendency to avoid repetition,"[53] long since asserted by Schoenberg as a sort of ethical imperative) there is no metrical hierarchy, listeners cannot perform the intuitive tasks on which a generative grammar depends. They cannot group the music into meaningful segments; they cannot identify strong and weak beats; they cannot assign individual pitches any structural importance on which the experience of tension or relaxation depends. Prevented from applying well-formedness rules, the listener cannot distinguish a significant musical utterance from "noise." The conclusion must be that, as far as unaided listeners are concerned (as opposed to formal analysts, eyeing the score), all atonal music is cognitive noise.

We have seen that some modernist composers (most notably Krenek and Cage) had accepted that characterization of their music, arguing that the question of "understanding" is esthetically irrelevant. (Others, notably Babbitt, have claimed that their atonal music is the cognitive equal of tonal music, a claim that depends utterly on the Skinner model.) Lerdahl and Jackendoff, unwilling to be sidetracked, assert that their judgments about atonal music are not concerned with compositional practice. "We do not wish to address the cultural or aesthetic reasons for this tendency, nor do we want to make value judgements,"[54] they insist. Their concern is not with the composer but with the listener.

But it is hard to shake free of value judgments, and it is questionable whether, for example, the following passage from Lerdahl and Jackendoff's notorious "section 11.6" can really be read as esthetically neutral:

> To the degree that the applicability of these various aspects of musical grammar is attenuated, the listener will infer less hierarchical structure from the musical surface. As a result, nonhierarchical aspects of musical perception (such as timbre and dynamics) tend to play a greater, compensatory role in musical organization. But this is not compensation in kind; the relative absence of hierarchical dimensions tends to result in a kind of music perceived very locally, often as a sequence of gestures and associations.[55]

The touted complexity of serial music (or of Carter's celebrated polyrhythmic structures) is thus challenged on its own terms. Music structured nonhierarchically is implicitly reduced to a kind of nonlinguistic or prelinguistic communication—grunts, sign language, or otherwise rudimentary conveyance of primitive needs and moods, if that. Whatever the complexity of its structural organization (discoverable from the score), its level of aural communication is drastically coarsened and blunted. The impression of a value judgment despite disclaimers is confirmed by a nearly explicit assertion toward the end of the discussion, where the "total serialism" of the Darmstadt and Princeton schools is the object of scrutiny. To the extent that nonpitch elements are serialized, they only enlarge the domains

> that do not directly engage the listener's ability to organize a musical surface. In each of these cases, the gulf between compositional and perceptual principles is

wide and deep: insofar as the listener's abilities are not engaged, he cannot infer a rich organization no matter how a piece has been composed or how densely packed its musical surface is. It is in this sense that an apparently simple Mozart sonata is more complex than many twentieth-century pieces that at first seem highly intricate.[56]

In the end, although the authors contend that their theory "says nothing about the relative value of compositional techniques," and allow that "whatever helps a composer compose his music is of value to him," their parting shot (with its deliberate allusion to the notorious title — "Who Cares If You Listen?" — under which Babbitt's most widely read statement of Skinnerian principles was published in 1958) was read the only way it could be, as a gauntlet:

> We believe, nonetheless, that our theory is relevant to compositional problems, in that it focuses detailed attention on the facts of hearing. To the extent that a composer cares about his listeners, this is a vital issue.[57]

These tough words were widely remarked, and lots of umbrage was taken. But they could be dismissed on the grounds that Lerdahl and Jackendoff's proposals were backed up by nothing more than a hypothesis, and also because they had only negative implications. The authors' gloomy diagnosis of the state of contemporary composition was not accompanied by any suggestions for improvement. Without a positive program, it was just one antimodernist tirade among many. (Nor was it even the first to claim a "scientific" basis: Paul Hindemith, in his composition textbook of 1937, had tried to demonstrate the "unnaturalness" of atonal music by referring to the natural harmonic series; but as everybody knew that the practice of tonal harmony did not entirely conform to natural acoustical phenomena anyway, the demonstration fell flat.)

WHERE TO GO FROM HERE?

As with Chomsky's theories, the success or failure of Lerdahl and Jackendoff's arguments will have to depend on something other than direct empirical confirmation. That is because, as the authors admit, if the mind has a "hard-wired" structure that enables it to process only some kinds of information, then any inquiry into its nature is itself constrained by the limits that a preset structure implies. If the theory is true, the innate knowledge (or "unconscious theory") that enables a human being to acquire and use a language without direct instruction is by its very nature "unavailable to conscious introspection."[58] All one can do is adduce the otherwise unexplained (if not inexplicable) phenomena that led to the suspicion that such mental predispositions exist. This scattered indirect evidence is of three types: (1) clinical, (2) anthropological, and (3) historical.

1. The clinical evidence[59] comes from the negative results of experiments in which subjects are asked, for example, to complete twelve-tone aggregates, or to observe the boundaries between aggregates. The fact that trained musicians cannot do these things under laboratory conditions suggests that the completion of aggregates (on which the

"composing grammar" of twelve-tone music is based) does not constitute a cognitively significant "closure," and that the technical premises of serial composition are therefore not available to cognition.

2. The positive evidence for mental predispositions comes from anthropological (or within music, the ethnomusicological or "comparative") observation and testing of universals, a process that was greatly complicated in the late twentieth century by its being politicized. Hypothesized universals are mainly tested by looking for counterexamples. Since much human oppression is justified on the basis of assumed biological imperatives (e.g., that women, since they are the ones who bear children, are "natural" caregivers and nurturers and therefore should be confined to the home), there has been a strong political incentive to find evidence that such imperatives do not exist — or rather, that our assumptions about human nature are based not on nature but on politically-motivated social consensus. Hence the strong political interest, for example, in the work of Berkeley anthropologist Nancy Scheper-Hughes, whose 1992 book *Death without Weeping: The Violence of Everyday Life in Brazil* asserted (or was read as asserting) a counterexample to the assumed universality of the "maternal instinct."

Because belief in the existence of cultural universals is so easily turned to regressive (or repressive) political applications, an interest in establishing universals has sometimes been assumed to be in essence politically reactionary. That charge is certainly overstated and unfair; but even if not reactionary or ill-intentioned, belief in cultural universals is undoubtedly pessimistic and antiutopian. Behind cultural universals, if they are truly universal, must necessarily stand biological limitations that are transhistorical ("timeless") as well as ubiquitous, and that must ultimately come into conflict with faith in unlimited or unlimitable progress.

These transhistorical constraints do not constrain music, which can assume any form composers can imagine for it (that is, conceptualize). But they do constrain listeners (including composers when they listen), and limit their ability to make perceptual sense out of musical concepts. The whole tragicomedy of twentieth-century music, for a believer in cognitive constraints, subsists in the lack of congruence between "composing grammars," on which there are no limits, and "listening grammars," on which there are inescapable limits.

Or as Leonard B. Meyer (already identified in this chapter as a precociously postmodernist music theorist) has put it:

> It is a mistake — albeit a common one — to conceptualize the problem as a search for "musical" universals. *There are none.* There are only the acoustical universals of the physical world and the bio-psychological universals of the human world. Acoustical stimuli affect the perception, cognition, and hence practice of music only through the constraining action of bio-psychological ones.[60]

Among these possible bio-psychological universals, Meyer has identified the threshold of pitch discrimination, which has militated against the development of microtonal music; the so-called "Seven, Plus or Minus Two" rule about the number of elements that can be comprehensibly related (which might help explain the prevalence of pentatonic and diatonic modes); the need for functional differentiation of elements if utterances are to be memorable or even intelligible (obviously related to Lerdahl and Jackendoff's "time-span reduction" principle); and an inverse correlation between motor activity and cognitive tension (which may explain some of music's affective properties, or "why a plaintive adagio seems more 'emotional' than a persistent presto"[61]).

Meyer also proposes that we need to classify our sense impressions in order for them to communicate information, and that these classifications are perceived as "syntactic [i.e., structural] hierarchies."[62] Borrowing from information theory, he posits that redundancy is necessary for comprehension. For all these reasons, Meyer was prepared to conclude as early as 1967 (in a book called *Music, the Arts, and Ideas*) that serial music was, if not altogether cognitively opaque, certainly more difficult to comprehend than anyone's degree of exposure was likely to offset.

3. As for historical evidence, it goes back to the very dawn of recorded musical histroy — indeed, to a new dawn that broke when a new starting point was identified in what was billed as " the world's oldest melody," a "Hurrian" (or Sumerian) hymn dating from somewhere around 1200 BCE, and it was observed that the most remarkable thing about the song was how unremarkable it seemed. Already it used our familiar "diatonic pitch set" and accompanied it with harmonic intervals that we still classify as consonances.

The ancient song, excavated piecemeal between 1950 and 1955, was successfully transcribed in 1974, exactly when the controversy on cognitive constraints and their implications for musical practice was heating up. It may have been for that reason that Professor Richard Crocker, who performed the song before a scholarly audience, became perhaps the only musicologist ever to have his picture published on the front page of the *New York Times* as a direct result of his professional activity (Fig. 9-5).

Lerdahl attempted to address the problem of negativity, and proposed practical remedies for the malaise to which he and Jackendoff had called theoretical attention, in an article of 1988 called "Cognitive Constraints on Compositional Systems." To dramatize the problem of incongruity between composing and listening grammars, he cited a classic of cold-war modernism and its subsequent reception.

Boulez's *Le Marteau sans Maître* (1954) was widely hailed as a masterpiece of post-war serialism. Yet nobody could figure out, much less hear, how the piece was serial. From hints in [a 1963 article by the composer], Lev Koblyakov at last determined [in a 1977 article] that it was indeed serial, though in an idiosyncratic way. In the interim listeners made what sense they could of the piece in ways unrelated to its construction. Nor has Koblyakov's decipherment subsequently changed how the piece is heard. Meanwhile most composers have discarded serialism, with the result that Koblyakov's contribution has caused barely a ripple of professional interest. The serial organization of *Le Marteau* would appear, 30 years later, to be irrelevant. The story is, or should be, disturbing.[63]

World's Oldest Song Reported Deciphered

Near-East Origin

By LACEY FOSBURGH
Special to The New York Times

BERKELEY, Calif., March 5—The soft sounds of what is now believed to be the oldest song in the world were played here today at the University of California.

"This has revolutionized the whole concept of the origin of Western music," Richard L. Crocker, professor of music history at Berkeley, said today.

The discovery proves that Western music is about 1,400 years older than previously known and dates back to the ancient Near-Eastern civilization of at least the second millenium B.C.

Scholars have always believed that Western music originated in Greece, but this indicates it came from the Near East.

"We always knew there was music in the earlier Assyro-Babylonian civilization, but until this, we did not know," Professor Crocker said, "that it had the same heptatonic diatonic scale that is characteristic of contemporary Western music and Greek music of the first millenium B.C."

The song, which sounds to contemporary Western ears like a lullaby, a hymn or a gentle folk song, was last heard, scholars said, about

Continued on Page 18, Column 1

The New York Times/Teresa Zabala
Richard L. Crocker playing reproduction of a lyre

Out of Prehistory

By HAROLD C. SCHONBERG

The startling discovery of the Hurrian cuneiform tablet containing a cult love song pushes back the frontier of notated music well over a thousand years.

An Appraisal

Up to now, the oldest piece of music in notated form has been a fragment of Greek papyrus containing a song in the "Orestes" of Euripides. That dates from the fourth century B.C. The new discovery is put at about 1800 B.C.

Listening to this music (heard in a two-minute excerpt on the telephone) puts a listener back into musical prehistory. The sound of the lyre, constructed by Prof. Robert R. Brown from 4,600-year-old instructions, has the primitive quality associated with crude plucked instruments. The music, proceding in double notes and short rhythmic phrases, usually in semitonal up-and-down shifts, sounds equally primitive as far as its actual texture goes.

But there is one surprise. Professor Brown, Prof. Anne D. Kilmer, who worked on the text, and Prof. Richard L. Crocker of the music department of the University of California in Berkeley, are confident that the piece of

Continued on Page 18, Column 3

FIG. 9-5   The musicologist Richard L. Crocker on the front page of the *New York Times* (6 March 1974), playing the world's oldest song on a reproduction of a Babylonian harp.

Whether readers were disturbed depended largely on their age. *Le Marteau* exemplified the lack of concern on the part of modernist composers for the comprehensibility of their music. In 1954, when composers were focused entirely on esthetics and ideology, few regarded that as a problem. By 1988, when composers were beginning to focus on psychology and to address their social isolation, many did. Indeed, many young composers were resentful. As a consequence of having been taught to divorce their conscious methods from the unconscious intuitions that they share with listeners, they found themselves painted into a cold corner. They were faced, as Lerdahl put it, "with the unpleasant alternative of working with private codes or with no compositional grammar at all."[64]

What could be done about it? For those unwilling to employ "historical" styles—or rather, for those unable to regard traditional tonality as anything other than "historical" — Lerdahl tried to imagine what a novel composing grammar might be that took listening grammar into account. In this sense he was trying, ostensibly, to find a realistic (and more or less optimistic) middle ground between despairing postmodernists like Rochberg who were condemned to "a parasitic relationship with the past"[65] and unreconstructed utopians like Babbitt or Carter or Boulez, who still found it possible to believe that "one's own new system was the wave of the future."[66]

The bulk of the article consists of stipulating conditions or "constraints" (seventeen in all), derived from the earlier *Generative Theory* but not limited to tonal music, that would ensure that compositional grammars maintained contact with listening grammars. The objective was to enable listeners to utilize the unconscious strategies described in the earlier book to infer musical structure. Thus in order to enable grouping, a musical surface must present the listener with a sequence of discrete events; in order to enable time-span reduction, it must present a discernable functional hierarchy; in order to enable the perception of metrical structure, there must be "a degree of regularity in the placement of phenomenal [i.e., perceived] accents"; and in order to enable prolongational reduction, it must specify "stability conditions" (in effect, it must "de-emancipate" dissonance).

As Lerdahl's list proceeds it becomes more and more specific, shading from minimum necessary conditions into the ideal conditions that will satisfy the author's "aesthetic claims": first, that "the best music utilizes the full potential of our cognitive resources," and second, that "the best music arises from an alliance of a compositional grammar with the listening grammar."[67] Since the second esthetic claim merely restated the aim that furnished the argument's starting point, its placement as the argument's conclusion was obviously circular. Nor was that the only difficulty: by the end of the article, the author confessed a little sheepishly that, having pursued his theoretical insights into the realm of practical application, he found that "the constraints are tighter than I had bargained for." Like Rochberg, he discovered by rejecting it a resistant utopian streak within himself: "Like the old avant-gardists, I dream of the breath of other planets. Yet my argument has led from pitch hierarchies to an approximation of pure intervals, to diatonic scales and the circle of fifths, and to a pitch space that prominently includes triads."[68]

Yet, unwilling to admit that his proposed constraints "prescribe outworn styles," he resolved to regard the constellation of traditional elements that have somehow forced themselves back into the picture not as an imperative but as "a reference point for other kinds of pitch organizations, not because of its cultural ubiquity but because it incorporates all of the constraints." The article ends with a postmodernist "historical implication" similar to Rochberg's, but differently grounded:

> The avant-gardists from Wagner to Boulez thought of music in terms of a "progressivist" philosophy of history: a new work achieved value by its supposed role *en route* to a better (or at least more sophisticated) future. My second aesthetic claim in effect rejects this attitude in favor of the older view that music making should be based on "nature." For the ancients, nature may have resided in the music of the spheres, but for us it lies in the musical mind. I think the music of the

future will emerge less from twentieth-century progressivist aesthetics than from newly acquired knowledge of the structure of musical perception and cognition.[69]

Lerdahl's conclusion was pounced upon at least as much as the conclusion of Babbitt's "Who Cares If You Listen?" Modernists going back as far as Schoenberg, after all, saw their mission as one of emancipation above all, and here was a call to de-emancipate not only dissonances, but composers as well. The theory's descriptive and prescriptive components were conflated by those who found intolerable the suggestion that humans are subject to innate limitations, and the word "constraint" was widely, perhaps deliberately, misread. A lecturer at Darmstadt accused Lerdahl of being "bent on enslaving the listener, who is expected to listen 'correctly,' by conforming to grammar-dictated conventions."[70] Despite his disclaimers, he was portrayed along with Rochberg as a purveyor of nostalgia.

But however controversial or unverifiable its claims, Lerdahl was expressing a view that over the course of the century's last decades, and hardly owing to his influence alone, gradually assumed dominance. Just as Charles Jencks could contend in 1986 that, although the critical consensus still favored modern architecture, "in any international competition now more than half the entries will be Post-Modern,"[71] so by the late 1980s most young composers were persuaded, like Lerdahl, of the necessity for congruity between composing grammars and listening grammars.

Especially in America, virtually all the emerging talents in the last two decades of the century were "neotonalists" (or "neoromantics," as they tended to be called by their critics), by upbringing or conversion. A short alphabetical list of them, confined only to Americans, would include *John Adams (b. 1947), *Stephen Albert (1941–1992), *William Bolcom (b. 1938), *John Corigliano (b. 1938), Richard Danielpour (b. 1956), *John Harbison (b. 1938), *Aaron Jay Kernis (b. 1960), Libby Larsen (b. 1950), Stephen Paulus (b. 1949), Tobias Picker (b. 1954), *Christopher Rouse (b. 1949), David Schiff (b. 1945), *Joseph Schwantner (b. 1943), Michael Torke (b. 1961), *Joan Tower (b. 1938), and *Ellen Taaffe Zwilich (b. 1939). (The asterisks denote winners of Grawemeyer and Pulitzer prizes, the most prestigious forms of recognition available to "classical" composers; in 1999 the Grawemeyer Award went to the English composer Thomas Adès, born in 1971, who fits a similar stylistic profile.) It is worth noting, moreover, that composers born in the 1940s tended to be less equivocal about their embrace of a "tonal" composing grammar than those born in the 1930s, and those born in the 1950s and 1960s or later, who never went through a serial period, are the most straightforwardly "tonal" of all. Critics whose tastes and allegiances were formed earlier have been unpleasantly amazed to find that "the younger Romantics," in the words of Jonathan W. Bernard, "are an even more conservative group, by and large, than their senior colleagues."[72] Bernard ascribes this "unnatural" situation to American provincialism and voices the

> hope that, in all respects that matter, the expression "return to tonality" is a misnomer, that composers, audiences, performers, and critics will eventually tire of the dwelling on the past and other retrogressive aspects of this movement, and that the progressive elements that shine forth in some of its better products will win out in the twenty-first century.[73]

Robert P. Morgan, the author of *Twentieth-Century Music* (1991), probably the last survey of its kind to be written from an uncorrupted modernist perspective, ended it with a complaint that "the openness and eclecticism of current musical life has been bought at the expense of a system of shared beliefs and values and a community of artistic concerns."[74] The easiest dismissals come from those who invoke the traditional modernist taboo against popularity, accusing composers who have broken faith with the hermetic styles mandated by history of cynical pandering—"courting" fickle and recalcitrant audiences who have no real interest in the authentic tasks and purposes serious composers are required to face. "Composers anxious to make that career breakthrough see immediate public response as more important than approval by peers, conductors and music critics," huffed one music critic (in the *San Francisco Chronicle*) after a concert season that had included premieres of new works by Adams and Tower. "Given the audiences and the commercialization of art," he went on,

> it's not surprising that many ambitious composers will try to tap that market any way they can. Simplified styles, borrowing on the tried and true, romantic and mystical cover stories, the parody and quotation of older music, and slick scoring are hallmarks of the new and chic "postmodernism." With remarkable ease, the glib practitioners of the 1980s win grants, awards, commissions and residencies. The panels and juries that give these awards do not seem guided by criteria of quality.[75]

To grumblings such as these postmodernists retort that the progressive/retrogressive dichotomy on which Bernard's classification depends is a relic of an outmoded and rightly discredited philosophy of history. "Modernist ideology, while still dominant in an institutional sense, has become old-fashioned," Lerdahl has written. "For a younger generation it embodies attitudes about human nature and history that are no longer credible."[76] It is those who hold on to their habitual views in the face of a changing set of sociological and epistemological conditions (or what scientists call a "paradigm") who should be described as conservatives. As to Morgan's complaint, postmodernists contend that the "community" to which modernists nostalgically refer was more nearly a "hegemony," a system of institutional domination rather than a consensus. Meanwhile, the San Francisco critic's impugning of postmodernist motives in defense of an undefined "quality," like all *ad hominem* (or *ad feminam*) rhetoric, simply evades the issues. Modernists and their supporters were also, in their day, routinely accused of conspiracies.

ONE PROPOSAL

The issues can be clarified somewhat by examining Fred Lerdahl's actual composing style, to see how it compares with his unusually explicit and outspoken theorizing. It turns out to be not quite as beholden to "outworn styles" as his theories caused him to worry, or the accusations of his critics might seem to suggest. It is based, rather, on a compromise between, on the one hand, a reinstated ("de-emancipated") use of consonance and dissonance to effect tension and release, and, on the other, the kind of symmetricalized chromatic pitch relations that had a long history in twentieth-century practice (particularly in Bartók and Berg), but that had only lately achieved comprehensive theoretical formulation in an influential treatise, *Twelve-Tone Tonality*, by the veteran American composer George Perle (b. 1915), the first edition of which was published in 1977.

In that same year Lerdahl wrote a string quartet in which he first began to apply to contemporary problems of composition the principles that he and Jackendoff were developing for their "listening grammar" of tonal music. It is a "programmatic" work, like many works by theorists in the throes of formulation, in the sense that it sets forth its theoretical orientation as part of the actual musical argument. To put it bluntly, in addition to being a work of art, the quartet provides both an illustration and a practical test of the theory.

The de-emancipation of dissonance is evident from the very start (Ex. 9-6). The consonant dyad G-D is stated in the first measure, repeated in the second, and, in the fourth, established through a cadence as a stable reference point (not to say a tonic). Even though no triads have yet been heard, it is clear that the piece is "tonal," and that functional (if not necessarily conventional) harmonic closures will play a part in articulating its form. As Lerdahl has put it, "tonality is a psychological condition, not a stylistic one."[77] To put the functional premises of his quartet in terms of a cognitive grammar, one could say that a series of harmonic events unfolds in such a way that the listener is able to group them into discrete (and lengthening) time-spans characterized by fluctuations of harmonic tension. The listener, in short, is enabled (and encouraged) to apply intuitively the four processes held by the generative theory to translate aural stimuli into musical sense.

The fifth chord is distinguished from the others not only statistically, by merely being different, but also qualitatively by being dissonant. Its relationship to the tonic dyad, moreover, is easily specified in terms of function, since every one of its four notes can be interpreted as a leading tone (two converging on G, two on D). Thus measures 3–4 constitute a "departure and return," the basic form-defining gesture in traditional tonal music, even if the sonorities are not exactly those of traditional tonal music.

Notice now that mm. 3–4 are enclosed within double bars and labeled "III." They form a unit that takes its place in a series of such units that unfolds over the course of the piece and defines its form. Each begins and ends with the normative consonance, and (once other harmonies are introduced in the third unit) each performs a departure-and-return. Each is also longer than its predecessor. Group I lasts three beats, group II lasts four, III lasts five, IV lasts 7, V lasts 14, VI lasts 19, and so on. The later and longer groups expand in a rough 3:2 proportion, leading the ear to organize ever-greater time spans through prolongational reductions.

The complex of upper and lower leading tones operating in tandem in group III already suggests that harmonic motion is proceeding according to a pair of symmetrical ("equal sum") interval matrices like the ones deduced by Perle, among others, when investigating Bartók's composing methods. (The difference, of course, is that Bartók's matrices never converged on perfect fifths to produce the kind of consonant reference sonority or functional tonic on which Lerdahl's system here depends.) The impressionis

EX. 9-6   Fred Lerdahl, String Quartet no. 1, sections I–XIV

confirmed in group IV, when another chord is interpolated between the initial tonic dyad and the leading-tone complex, and it, too, relates to its companions by mirror-inversion: the first violin's intervallic succession in m. 6, a descending tone and semitone, is mirrored by the second violin's ascent by the same intervals to converge on G (allowing for an octave displacement at the end), while the viola and cello reproduce the same pattern implying convergence on D (allowing for the cello's substitution of the more resonant "root" G at the end).

We have made enough observations to warrant a hypothesis, as set forth in Ex. 9-7a, where complete symmetrical matrices that converge on G and D are superimposed. Every chord in the quartet through m. 12 consists of a superimposed pair of dyads in the same position within their respective matrices. The first chord with more than four pitches in it, in m. 13, adds a dyad from the symmetrical matrix in which the G-D tonic is embedded as a unit (Ex. 9-7b). Having added the third matrix, we can now account for every harmony until the second measure of group VIII (not shown in Ex. 9-6), where the dyad E♭-B♭ (followed eleven beats later by its tritone complement, A-E) invokes the matrix given in Ex. 9-7c.

And so it goes. Successive Roman-numeral groups expand both in terms of the time-span they enclose and in terms of the pitch field on which they draw; in each case we are led from the normative consonance to a progressively further-out point and back again. The process provides for considerable variety (sometimes very dramatically expressed, like a sudden "modulation to E" near the middle of the piece) within a tightly organized and unified pitch system.

EX. 9-7A   Fred Lerdahl, String Quartet no. 1, analytical sketches, inversional matrices on D and G superimposed

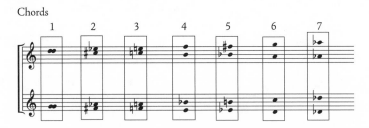

EX. 9-7B   Fred Lerdahl, String Quartet no. 1, analytical sketches, inversional matrix that includes reference dyad G-D

In the later, lengthier sections, Lerdahl sometimes underscores both the expanding durational plan and the there-and-back trajectory by inserting literal palindromes that open out gradually from motion in eighths to dotted halves and contract back to eighths as the pitches run in reverse (e.g., Ex. 9-8). These help the listener infer

EX. 9-7C   Fred Lerdahl, String Quartet no. 1, analytical sketches, matrix that includes E-flat–B-flat and A-E

the compositional strategy from the musical surface. The consciously constructed compositional grammar is "transparent," as Lerdahl would say, to the unconscious listening grammar. Or as Steve Reich would put it, the composer knows no secrets of structure that his listener cannot discover.

Although he describes his music as part of what he calls the "postmodern resurgence" of tonality (or more exactly, of hierarchical pitch and metric organization), it is clear that Lerdahl's postmodernism is of a very different character from Rochberg's or Del Tredici's. It entails no consciously formulated expressive or representational purpose, nor any impulse to revive past styles; and, while it certainly takes listeners into account as arbiters of intelligibility, the intended audience seems to be basically the same academic audience that modernist composers address.

EX. 9-8   Fred Lerdahl, String Quartet no. 1, section (C_4)

Lerdahl's reputation is far more academically circumscribed than Rochberg's or Del Tredici's, and he writes mainly for campus new-music ensembles. He has even stated, in response to the usual attacks, that "serious composers, myself included, pay more attention to the work than to the audience,"[78] and his sole stated theoretical preoccupation has been with devising and validating new techniques of composition. It is possible, ultimately, to regard his work as "progressive" in the "reformist" sense, correcting defects or errors that have deflected the evolution of music from the path of true progress. (The main error, as he puts it, was that of putting "complicatedness"[79] — a musical surface densely cluttered with unprocessable information — in place of "complexity," a depth or richness of structural relations that a listener is able to infer from that surface.) Nevertheless, his is an equally significant manifestation of the postmodernist impulse, precisely because it has taken place within the ivory tower, and within the traditional academic discourses of formalism and even science. Lerdahl's project remains one of research and development, but it is no longer wholly "disinterested." Innovation can no longer be validated solely on the basis of the old "master narrative." Innovation must now pass a listener test, and that implies an "esthetic" — that is, a criterion of artistic quality — with a necessary social component. Cold-war purity, "Western"-style, has been breached, perhaps irrevocably.

THE END OF SOVIET MUSIC

What, then, about cold-war purity, "Eastern"-style? The complementary orthodoxy, adhered to (and sometimes enforced) within what during the cold war was called the Soviet bloc, demanded above all the "accessibility" and "transparency" of style that (when embraced by Rochberg or Lerdahl) the Western critical establishment deemed heretical, and frowned upon the idea of stylistic progress that had led the music of "bourgeois decadence" into social isolation. One might expect that as the frigidity of the cold war eased, so might doctrinal rigidity on both sides. And indeed, as social criteria crept back into (and undermined) Western modernist commitments, formalist ideas played a similar role among composers in Eastern Europe — at first among a subversive minority, later more openly and commonly. The principal effect in the East, as in the West, was a growing and finally dominant eclecticism.

Besides the general liberalizing trend that followed the death of Stalin, known as the "Thaw" after the title of a 1954 novella by the Soviet writer Ilya Ehrenburg (1891–1967), a number of specific circumstances brought young Soviet musicians into previously risky or forbidden contact with the music of the European avant-garde. Official visitors from abroad, especially the Italian composer Luigi Nono, who occupied a singular position as a member of both the Western avant-garde and of the Communist Party, brought with them scores by "Darmstadt" composers and made gifts of them both to libraries and to individuals. The Canadian pianist Glenn Gould (1932–82) made a Soviet tour in 1957, during which he gave an informal recital for students and teachers at the Moscow Conservatory, playing works by Berg, Webern, and Krenek and lecturing through a translator about the technique of serial music. The most spectacular such occasion was an eightieth-birthday-year (1962) visit by Igor Stravinsky, who performed his music, met with students (and with the Soviet prime minister Nikita Khrushchev), and was accepted thereafter in his homeland as a "Russian classic." The nascent impact of Western avant-garde music on Soviet musical life was furthered by the presence in Moscow of two immigrants who, although little known to the public, enjoyed considerable professional prestige. The older of the two was Filip Gershkovich (1906–89), a Romanian-born composer and music theorist who had studied with Berg and Webern, composed his first twelve-tone score in 1928, and fled from Nazi persecution to the Soviet Union in 1940. His music being unperformable in Russia at the time, Gershkovich worked as a music editor and an orchestrator of soundtrack music for films. He began attracting private theory pupils in the 1950s.

One of them was Andrey Volkonsky (1933–2008), a young Moscow composer who belonged to a celebrated princely lineage (immortalized by Tolstoy in *War and Peace*) and was born in Geneva while his family was in exile from the Soviet Union. From 1945 to 1947 Volkonsky lived in Paris, where he studied piano with the Romanian-born virtuoso Dinu Lipatti. He was long reputed to have been one of Nadia Boulanger's many pupils in composition, but it seems he made the claim only to pad his résumé when applying to the Moscow Conservatory after his family's repatriation in 1947. At the Conservatory he became the pupil of the senior Soviet composer Yuri Shaporin (1887–1966). His early compositions met with success, particularly a *Concerto for Orchestra*, written under Shaporin's direction, which was performed in 1953, the last Stalinist year. That same year, however, a fellow student denounced Volkonsky for having scores by Schoenberg and Stravinsky in his possession, and he was expelled from the Conservatory on the pretext that he had missed the beginning of classes owing to the birth of his first child.

Enjoying the protection of Shaporin (and, it was widely assumed, of Shostakovich), Volkonsky retained his membership in the Union of Soviet Composers; his exclusion from the Conservatory only confirmed his unorthodox stance. In 1956, having connected with Gershkovich, Volkonsky produced *Musica stricta*, the first twelve-tone composition by a Soviet citizen. The irony of such a title for a work that became emblematic of creative freedom was only a facet of a more general cold-war irony: musical behavior that in the West would have been regarded as the height of conformity meant just the opposite within the Soviet sphere of influence. At a time when Soviet writers and visual artists on the cutting edge were beginning to explore social and political themes that had been taboo as subjects for treatment while Stalin was alive, their musical counterparts were withdrawing as far as possible from social commitment. Formalism was for musicians the most effective way of displaying nonconformism.

A piano suite in four movements, *Musica stricta* is cast in an idiosyncratic twelve-tone idiom that is actually not at all strict. It is by no means confined in its pitch materials to twelve-tone rows, and when twelve-tone rows are used, they are varied in ways that are unrelated to Schoenbergian or Webernian procedures. "I didn't really understand the techniques very well," the composer admitted to an interviewer in 1999, "but I understood the principle."

I did some things incorrectly, but it's good that I didn't do everything correctly. There are octaves, which Schoenberg forbade, and also triads, which Schoenberg also forbade. But I simply didn't know about that. I thought I had written a twelve-tone composition, and it's true that those techniques can be found in places. And because of that I named the piece *Musica Stricta*, because of the strict techniques, although I unwittingly used them entirely according to my own manner.[80]

In effect Volkonsky had responded as a listener to the sound of early twelve-tone music (or even earlier Viennese atonal music), rather than as an analyst to its technique. The writing is full of the stacked fourths and tritones ("atonal triads") that abound in much early-twentieth-century music. The second movement, the easiest one to analyze in terms of row technique, is actually a sort of fugue or ricercar in which four rows seem to compete for dominance of the contrapuntal texture (Ex. 9-9). Volkonsky, who was then the Soviet Union's only professional harpsichordist as well as its only twelve-tone composer, evidently fell back on the formal procedures of the Baroque repertoire, with which he was exceptionally familiar, as a frame to accommodate what was for him, as much as for any Soviet musician, a highly unfamiliar method of composing.

EX. 9-9   Andrey Volkonsky, *Musica stricta*, II, mm. 1–9

By the time he composed *The Lamentations of Shchaza* (*Zhaloba Shchazï*, 1961), for soprano and instrumental quintet (English horn, percussion, harpsichord, violin, and viola), Volkonsky had had access to some of the representative scores of the "Darmstadt" school, obviously including Boulez's *Le Marteau sans maître*, which the work diligently imitates in its sound and gestures (although not in its strictly technical procedures, which, as Fred Lerdahl pointed out, were then quite arcane). Boulez returned the complement by performing Volkonsky's work in London and Berlin in the late 1960s, thus bringing the existence of a Soviet "underground" avant-garde to the attention of musicians in the West.

By then Volkonsky had several companions. Edison Denisov (1929–96), a protégé of Shostakovich, was especially energetic in promoting advanced Western techniques and esthetic principles among his contemporaries. His apartment, like Volkonsky's, became a lending library for scores that he had procured, beginning in the late 1950s, from Nono, Boulez, Stockhausen, Bruno Maderna, and other Darmstadters. He also agitated for performances of work by the advanced Soviet composers of the 1920s, hoping to forge a connection that would circumscribe the era of socialist-realist conformity. After analytical studies with Gershkovich and several trips to the Warsaw autumn festival, Denisov made his debut as an avant-gardist with a twelve-tone cantata, *The Sun of the Incas* (1964), composed to a text by the Chilean poet Gabriela Mistral (1889–1957) and dedicated to Boulez.

A second center of Soviet avant-garde activity arose in Kiev (now the capital of Ukraine), the closest large Soviet city to Warsaw. Three Kiev composers—Leonid Hrabovsky (b. 1935), Valentin Silvestrov (b. 1937), and Volodymyr Zahortsev (b. 1944)—became known in the West when Joel Spiegelman (b. 1933), a composer and harpsichordist on the faculty of Sarah Lawrence College, brought their twelve-tone compositions back with him from a trip to the Soviet Union and had them performed, together with works of Volkonsky and Denisov, in New York. A benchmark for the recognition of Soviet twelve-tone music was reached in 1968, when Silvestrov's Third Symphony, subtitled "Eschatophony," became the first composition by a Soviet composer to be performed (under Maderna's baton) at Darmstadt.

The next year, an orchestral work by another Soviet avant-gardist—*Pianissimo* by Alfred Schnittke (1934–98)—was performed at the Donaueschingen Festival, the other major West German contemporary-music showcase, which had in fact commissioned it. The composer, who had already had pieces performed in East Germany and Poland, was at the time earning his living in Moscow by writing soundtrack music for animated cartoons. He was not allowed to attend the festival. The restrictions placed on his employment and travel were heavily publicized, as was the program that the work was supposed to illustrate, a torture scene from Franz Kafka's story "The Penal Colony," in which an inmate is pricked by a multitude of tiny needles that inscribe a slogan on his body.

The music, consisting of a tone cluster that expands à la Ligeti until it becomes a sonic cloud, must have sounded fairly old-hat at Donaueschingen but for the fact that it was the work of a Soviet composer. That was enough to tinge its Darmstadt conformism with iconoclasm — a typical cold-war inversion. But there was also a somewhat subtler sense in which Schnittke's composition could be taken as un- or anti-Soviet, and that was the sense suggested by its title. Soviet composers were expected to make affirmative public statements, *fortissimo*. To speak in atonal whispers was genuinely countercultural (more for the whispers than for the atonality), and invested the oddly un-Slavic name of this shadowy Soviet son of a German-Jewish father and a Russian-born but ethnically German mother, whose first language was that of his parents and who divided his time between writing utilitarian film scores for a livelihood and unperformable masterworks "for the drawer," with a romantic aura of martyrdom that continued to dominate reportage about him for the rest of his life.

POLYSTYLISTICS

Over the next decade, then, Schnittke emerged, together with Denisov and the Soviet Tatar composer Sofia Gubaidulina (b. 1931), as one of the so-called "Big Troika" of late-Soviet nonconforming composers regarded throughout Europe and America as major figures in contemporary music. Of the three, Schnittke was of particular interest for the way his career trajectory seemed to complement those of the Western postmodernists, taking his music out of the Darmstadt or Donaueschingen orbit and into the major or "mainstream" concert venues. This further stimulated press interest in him during his lifetime, and vouchsafed his posthumous reputation as a defining force in the music of the twentieth century's final quarter.

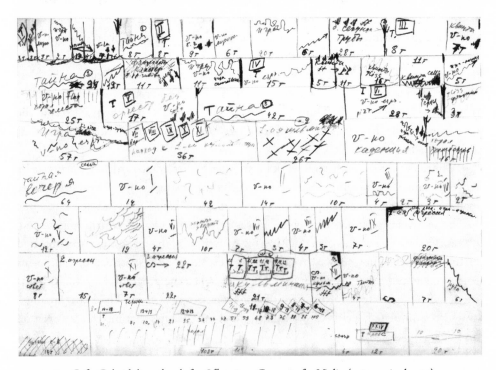

FIG. 9-6   Sofia Gubaidulina, sketch for *Offertorium*, Concerto for Violin (1980, revised 1986).

Like so many composers in the 1970s (but unlike Denisov, who remained faithful to the ideals of the 1950s, and to an orthodoxly "Boulezian" conception of the avant-garde), Schnittke abandoned serial technique out of a conviction that no single or "pure" manner was adequate to reflect contemporary reality, and that stylistic eclecticism — he called it "polystylistics" — had become mandatory. The watershed was Schnittke's First Symphony (1972), the collage to end all collages, a grim riot of allusion and outright quotation, much of it self-quotation, in which Beethoven jostles Handel jostles Haydn jostles Mahler jostles Chaikovsky jostles Johann Strauss, and on into ragtime and rock, with parts for improvising jazz soloists. Here, too, the distinctive Schnittke orchestra first announced itself, an omnivorous combine to which the harpsichord is as essential as the electric bass guitar. All styles and genres are potentially and indiscriminately available to it. It is the musical equivalent of the chemist's nightmare, a universal solvent.

Like Mahler or Ives, Schnittke envisioned his symphony as a musical universe, enfolding all that is or could be within its octopus embrace. But it was not a loving embrace. Schnittke's Tower of Babel proclaimed not acceptance of all things, but — as the work's "dramaturgy" betokens — more nearly the opposite, an attitude of alienation in which nothing could claim allegiance. At its beginning only three musicians are onstage. The rest of the orchestra enters gradually, improvising chaotically until the conductor, who enters last, calls a halt. At the end, the players make random exits until (improving on Haydn's "Farewell" Symphony), only a single violinist is left on stage, playing a childishly banal solo. But then everybody suddenly returns and seems ready to begin the piece all over again with the same unstructured freak-out as before. Again the conductor gives a signal, but instead of silence the orchestra gives out a sudden unison C — simplicity itself — on which note the symphony finally reaches an end.

Simplicity so unearned and perfunctory can suggest no resolution, just dismissal. The world of Schnittke's First Symphony recalls Dostoyevsky's nihilistic world without God, where everything is possible — and so nothing matters. Within the oppressively administered world of Soviet totalitarianism, where nothing was possible and everything mattered, the sarcastic suggestion that all or nothing was the only available choice came as a dismally disaffected message. It was clearly the work of a resentful, marginalized artist. To that extent, at least, it remained securely modernist in attitude.

And yet its very indiscriminateness contradicted modernist assumptions. Rather than postmodernism, the First Symphony signified mere "post-ism," after-everythingism, it's-all-overism. The work was so despairing — so subversive of socialist realism's obligatory optimism — that it was allowed only a single performance in 1974, in Gorky (now Nizhniy Novgorod), a "closed city," off-limits to foreigners, later notorious as the site of the dissident physicist Andrey Sakharov's exile, before it was consigned to the index of prohibited works that lasted until Mikhail Gorbachev, the last Soviet leader, proclaimed the age of *glasnost'* ("openness") in the late 1980s.

It took the addition of gallows humor to suggest a postmodern way out. Concerto Grosso No. 1 (1977), the first Schnittke composition to gain a big reputation in the West, deploys three distinct stylistic strata: the highly disciplined, intensely fiddled neobaroque passagework the title promised; an amorphous atonal sonic lava-flow; and syrupy Soviet pop music at its stalest, banged out on a prepared piano sounding like a cross between Radio Moscow's signature chimes and the beating of ash cans. (No points for guessing which one wins out in the end.) The Concerto Grosso established the pattern that would distinguish Schnittke's version of postmodernist collage. No longer despairingly helter-skelter like the First Symphony, Schnittke's polystylism now took shape through bald, easily read contrasts. Plush romantic lyricism, chants and chorales and hymns (real or made-up), actual or invented "historical" flotsam (neoclassic, neobaroque, even neomedieval, as one finds in Pärt, a close friend of the composer), every make and model of jazz and pop—all of this and more are the ingredients. As they are stirred together, the pot frequently boils over in violent extremes of dissonance: tone clusters (a Schnittke specialty), dense polytonal counterpoint (often in the form of exceedingly close canons), "verticalized" melodies whereby the individual notes of a tune are sustained by accompanying instruments until they are all sounding together as a chord.

Yet however harsh, aggressive, or even harrowing, the music never bewilders because it is never abstract. Discord, heard always as the opposite or absence of concord, functions as a sign, and so do all the myriad stylistic references. They do not merely stand for themselves, but point. It is this "semiotic" or signaling aspect, a traditional characteristic of Russian music (and especially of Shostakovich, Schnittke's obvious model), that makes Schnittke's later music so easily "read"—or rather, so easily paraphrased on whatever terms (ethical, spiritual, autobiographical, political) the listener may prefer. Nor did Schnittke neglect more traditional signaling devices like leitmotifs or symbolically recurring chords and sonorities.

The result, as one critic observed, was "socialist realism minus socialism."[81] For some, it was hard to see any real difference between Schnittke's postmodernism and old-fashioned Soviet "unmodernism." But there was a difference, and it was a crucial one, because nothing was off-limits any longer. Both socialist realism and Western avant-gardism had harbored taboos. While a student, conforming to the former, Schnittke knew that there were things he and his fellows could not do. But while dabbling in Darmstadt serialism, there were also things he and his fellow nonconformists could not do. For full inclusiveness, the rigid dichotomy that reflected and supported the divided postwar world had to be rejected. It was a solution that, as we have seen by now, transgressed equally on both sides of the cold-war boundary.

With an unlimited stylistic range at one's disposal, one could construct contrasts of a previously inconceivable extremity. Out of them one could achieve a more vivid instrumental "dramaturgy" than anything previously attempted in Soviet music. Maximalism could stage a comeback. Schnittke's postmodernism reengaged with the grandest, most urgent, most timeless—hence (potentially) most banal—questions of existence, framed the simplest way possible, as primitive oppositions. With a bluntness and an immodesty practically unknown since the First World War, Schnittke's music tackled life-against-death, love-against-hate, good-against-evil, freedom-against-tyranny, and (especially in concertos) I-against-the-world.

As Alexander Ivashkin, his friend and biographer, put it, no one since Mahler had so unashamedly "undressed in public"[82] as did Schnittke. In doing so, Schnittke recaptured the heroic subjectivity with which bourgeois audiences love to identify. The concerto, which has both a built-in exhibitionism and a built-in "oppositionism," was the ideal medium for such a project, and so it is not surprising that Schnittke produced more concertos than any other major composer of his generation—twenty-two in all, including seven for violin (if one counts as concertos the orchestral arrangements of his two violin sonatas), three for piano (including one for piano four-hands), two for cello, two for viola, and seven concerti grossi for multiple soloists (counting among them a piece called *Konzert zu 3* for violin, viola, cello, piano, and strings).

This unique body of work was composed almost as if in collusion with an outstanding generation of late-Soviet soloists, particularly string virtuosos. Schnittke's concentration on the traditionally humanoid, voice-aping strings, so often shunned for just that reason by old-fashioned modernists like Stravinsky, was another token of his spiritual kinship with the "neoromantics" in the West. But his music resembled theirs only slightly. Increasingly, the polystylistics were attached to an urgent moral program; and in this, perhaps, Schnittke showed himself a composer in the time-honored Russian, not just Soviet, tradition after all.

"Good," in Schnittke's moral universe, was associated with a naive diatonicism exemplified by the finale of the first cello concerto (1986), a "Thanksgiving Hymn" à la Beethoven, composed shortly after the composer's recovery from the first of a series of strokes that eventually took his life. "Evil" came in two forms. Absolute evil is represented by references to raucous popular music: its apotheosis comes in the third movement of the Third Symphony (commissioned and first performed in 1981 by the Leipzig Gewandhaus Orchestra), where a platoon of anarchic rock guitars spewing feedback distortion attacks a panorama of German classics—a tribute to the Leipzig performers and their distinguished tradition.

Schnittke's most interesting music, perhaps, was that associated with "relative evil" or moral realism, consisting of "good" music distorted by avant-garde techniques. Consequently, for many listeners the most affecting Schnittke compositions are not the resolute, quasi-religious ones in which good triumphs, or the tragic ones in which evil is given unequivocal victory (like the Viola Concerto, with its pathetic, brutally quashed attempts at a harmonious cadence). In these, as the post-Soviet musicologist Levon Hakobian points out, the "moral of the story," playing "an all-too-conspicuous role,"[83] often reduces the musical content to a sort of accompaniment. But the works whose arguments vacillate at some fraught point between triumph and tragedy are often fascinating. A particularly compact and effective work of this kind is the Concerto for Piano and Strings (1979), written for the composer's wife but first performed by the Soviet pianist Vladimir Krainev. The main theme, given many long preparations and a couple of climactic statements, is a stout chorale in C major that bears a small but probably not coincidental resemblance to the harmonized Orthodox chant, *Gospodi, spasi ny* ("Save us, O Lord") that opens Chaikovsky's famous *1812* Overture (Ex. 9-10). But on its every appearance, it has to fight its way through a barrage of "noise" in the form of disfiguring chromatics, or heterophony, or polytonality, or clusters, or microtones, or glissandi, or . . .

EX. 9-10A   Alfred Schnittke, Concerto for Piano and Strings, fig. 6

EX. 9-10B   Pyotr Ilyich Chaikovsky, *1812* Overture, beginning

A macabre waltz section, reminiscent of many similar passages in Shostakovich but vastly exceeding them in harshness, reaches a point of maximum tension ("evil"), after which the piano, in a cadenza, tries in vain to shake off the malign influence. The ensuing reprise of the chorale (Ex. 9-11) shows the crazed soloist and the accompanying group at their point of greatest mutual disaffection. The soloist finally manages to derange the chorale, and a typically Schnittkean disintegration or entropy sets in. In the coda, the piano and orchestra seem to be back in sync, but the pianist's last melody is a twelve-tone row, and the orchestra, having picked up each tone and sustained it, is left holding a gigantic "aggregate harmony" at the end. To the metaphysical maximalists of the early twentieth century — Scriabin, Schoenberg, Ives — who emancipated dissonance, the aggregate could mean wholeness. Within the context of Schnittke's "de-emancipated" idiom, it seems more like the ultimate in disorientation.

But while sharply dichotomized, extremes of consonance and dissonance (or tonality and atonality) do not register as incongruous within a style like Schnittke's. They no longer stand for separate stages in a historical development. They are equally available, located not on a historical but on an expressive continuum. As in all the postmodernist music we have surveyed, dissonance is once again heard in relation to consonance, which resumes its status as the tacitly asserted (if easily destabilized) norm. The ease with which the normal is destabilized is perhaps the essential Schnittkean metaphor for our fallen moral state. There is no escaping the preachiness of that message.

The tendency to sermonize, more than anything else, has made Schnittke a controversial figure. Moral commitment had long fallen victim to irony in modernist art, whether East or West; nor is black-and-white much of a moral color scheme. Upholders of "eternal moral categories"[84] (as one admiring post-Soviet critic has described Schnittke) are exactly the sort that disillusioned sophisticates, especially in countries where artists risk nothing more than public indifference or the withholding of a grant, are apt to denounce as the sheep's clothing of complacency or worse.

But Schnittke's Soviet background weighed in his favor. In the 1970s, following the expulsion of the dissident writer Alexander Solzhenitsyn from the USSR, it became fashionable in the West to look for signs of resistance in all late-Soviet art, and this

EX. 9-11   Alfred Schnittke, Concerto for Piano and Strings, reprise of chorale

EX. 9-11 (continued)

gained for Soviet artists a measure of Western interest and respect that had formerly been denied them on the cold-war assumption that Soviet art was created under conditions of coercion and served the interests of the totalitarian state. (The notion that the better Soviet artists were dissident in direct proportion to their perceived artistic standing was of course just another way of stating the same cold-war prejudice.)

The tendency to look for messages-in-a-bottle in Soviet art was given a powerful boost in 1979, when a book called *Testimony* appeared, its subtitle proclaiming it to be "The Memoirs of Dmitry Shostakovich as Related to and Edited by Solomon Volkov." The portrait the book painted of Shostakovich as a disaffected liberal, inserting anti-Communist messages between the lines of his compositions to encourage those of his countrymen "with ears to hear," came at the right time. Its authenticity has been convincingly questioned (and zealously defended), but that debate has been a sideshow, hardly impinging on the book's powerful appeal to many readers' imaginations. Coinciding with the emergence of postmodernist styles in the West, and the weakening of the modernist grip on musical attitudes, the Shostakovich of *Testimony* became an interpretive touchstone against which a great deal of other music could be measured.

Schnittke, more than any other composer, reaped the benefit of this development and began to command Shostakovich's immense and growing following. Long oppressed by the same ideological dictatorship that had oppressed Shostakovich, Schnittke (unlike Shostakovich) survived it, and survived the nihilism to which his First Symphony had once attested. The appeal of his music, like Shostakovich's, lay for many listeners less in its actual sound patterns than in their sense of the composer's moral and political plight (and the fragility of his life, as his many debilitating illnesses became known). That empathy, born of historical awareness, lent an extra concreteness, an extra force to his musical plots and arguments — that is, to the way in which audiences construed and valued his paraphrase-inviting stylistic antitheses and juxtapositions.

The Shostakovich debates, and Schnittke's special status among his contemporaries, were perhaps the last musical symptoms of the cold war. By the time the cold war ended in Europe (with the fall of the Berlin Wall in 1989, followed by the dissolution of the Soviet Union in 1991), not only Schnittke, but practically his whole generation of Soviet composers — Volkonsky, Gubaidulina, Pärt, Hrabovsky, and many others — were living abroad (mainly in Germany and the United States), the result of a mass emigration or "brain drain" that paralleled the one that attended the beginning of Soviet power in 1917. Denisov, though he never emigrated, spent at least part of every year, beginning in the 1980s, in Paris, as a guest of IRCAM (Institut de Recherche et Coordination Acoustique/Musique), Boulez's new-music research foundation. Post-Soviet Russian music dissolved into the general European modernist and postmodernist currents, of which it forms a newly vital, if no longer always stylistically distinctive, constituent.

* * * * * * * *

The term "postmodernism" is obviously unsatisfactory and temporary, a stopgap. Rochberg rejects it because it is semantically dependent on the modernism he opposes. Other writers, like Jonathan Kramer (1942 – 2004), a composer and critic who wrote one of many retorts[85] to Rochberg's undeniably shrill polemics, suggest that postmodernism is merely the next stage in the history of modernism (which might seem to confirm Rochberg's discomfort with the term). Leonard B. Meyer, who astutely predicted some of its attributes in theory when hardly any artist was putting it consciously into practice, used terms like "fluctuating stasis" or "stable pluralism" or "ahistorical and acultural taste" to describe the era that would necessarily follow the progress-driven ideology of modernism, whose eventual doom was inscribed in its very premises.

Looking back on his predictions in 1992, Meyer noted with some satisfaction that the triumph of communications technology had irrevocably replaced that kind of linearity with a cultural "Brownian motion," which he proceeded to define by recalling the physicist James Clerk Maxwell's analogy to "a swarm of bees, where every individual bee is flying furiously, first in one direction and then in another, while the swarm as a whole is either at rest or sails slowly through the air."[86] There are signs, however, that technology may have brought about yet another revolution, the effects of which are only slowly looming into view, but which will decisively change the nature of music in the twenty-first century and beyond. It remains, in one last chapter, to explore some of these possibilities.

CHAPTER 10

Millennium's End

THE ADVENT OF POSTLITERACY: PARTCH, MONK, ANDERSON, ZORN; NEW PATTERNS OF PATRONAGE

There are so many composers these days, you cannot perform all the worthy music that is being written.[1]
— WILLIAM SCHUMAN, A "CONVERSATION" (1984)

If the amorphous "new spirit" of contemporary music has any coherence at all, it lies in its spontaneity, immediacy, its fondness for subconscious decision-making . . . associated in part with the demise of the composer-scribe.[2]
— NIGEL OSBORNE, INTRODUCTION ("EDITORIAL") TO *MUSICAL THOUGHT AT IRCAM* (1984)

Radios, records, and tapes allow the listener to enter and exit a composition at will. An overriding progression from beginning to end may or may not be in the music, but the listener is not captive to that completeness. We all spin the dial . . .[3]
— JONATHAN KRAMER, *THE TIME OF MUSIC* (1988)

I like to say that I'm really rootless. I think that the music that my generation is doing is really rootless in a lot of ways, because we listened to a lot of different kinds of music from an early age, . . . and as a result we don't really have a single home.[4]
— JOHN ZORN, IN CONVERSATION WITH COLE GAGNE (1991)

[We're] simplifying the pitch landscape to allow you to pay attention to something else.[5]
— PAUL LANSKY, IN CONVERSATION WITH KYLE GANN (1997)

I remember Cage writing about [the painter] Jasper Johns, and how if Johns sees anything on his canvas that remotely resembles anything someone else has done, he destroys it. It took me a while to realize that there's just the opposite way to be an artist: to be a kind of omnivorous personality. I think Stravinsky was one, and certainly Mahler was, and Bach as well—somebody who just reached out and grabbed everything, took it all in and through his musical technique and his spiritual vision turned it into something really great.[6]
— JOHN ADAMS, IN CONVERSATION WITH DAVID GATES (1999)

GRAND OLD MEN

To say that modernism "collapsed" in the last quarter of the twentieth century would be as one-sided and misleading (and perhaps as wishful) as the old claim that tonality had collapsed in the same century's first quarter. It is worth one last reminder that all "style periods" are plural, and that the dominance of trends is never as absolute or obvious as historical accounts inevitably make them seem. At century's end, just to pick the most conspicuous examples, Milton Babbitt (aged eighty-four) and

FIG. 10-1 Fifty-two New York composers photographed by Bruce Davidson at the United States Customs House on 29 September 1999. Milton Babbitt and Elliott Carter are the two figures closest to the camera, with George Perle at left in the second row and Paul Lansky behind Perle.

Elliott Carter (aged ninety-two) were both still impressively productive as composers (Fig. 10-1).

Karlheinz Stockhausen was still keeping up appearances as an avant-garde icon: in 1995, he made some headlines with a string quartet in which the players "phoned in" their parts from separate helicopters in which they were airborne. (The Salzburg Festival, which commissioned it, was prevented from producing it by local environmentalists.) Six years later, aged seventy-two, the composer was awarded a large prize for the work by the Deutscher Musikverleger-Verband (the German Music Publishers' Association). Still an enfant terrible at heart, Stockhausen made much bigger headlines later in 2001 with the remark that the terror attack that destroyed New York's World Trade Center was "the greatest work of art there has ever been."[7] Though shocking at the time, the sentiment (or fantasy) was familiar: Hans Werner Henze, in an essay of 1964, recalled Stockhausen "at the beginning of the 1950s," looking down on Vienna through the window of an automobile and gloating, "In a few years' time I will have progressed so far that, with single electronic bang, I'll be able to blow the whole city sky-high!"[8]

In the year 2000 another old firebrand, Pierre Boulez, was honored at the age of seventy-five with the Grawemeyer Award, the most lucrative of all classical music "purses" (which the year before had gone to the twenty-eight-year-old Thomas Adès, a model postmodernist from England), for *Sur incises*, an exemplary serial composition scored for three pianos, three harps, and three "mallet" percussionists. Like most Boulez compositions by that time, it was based on an earlier work; the prize was generally regarded as a well-earned "lifetime achievement" award.

These composers, all highly distinguished and quite loftily unaffected by recent trends, remained the object of the sort of critical adulation that always attends grand old men. But their ages were significant. Their styles remained modern, but they were the opposite of new. Whether serial (like Babbitt's and Boulez's) or not (like Stockhausen's and Carter's), their music identified them as senior composers, working in idioms that even their most respectful juniors had to regard as outmoded. Despite their honors, they knew that they had been marginalized, and took it hard. Carter expressed his resentment at the success of the "New Simplicity" indirectly, in titles like *A Celebration of Some 100 × 150 Notes* (a short orchestral piece first performed in 1987), and by—like Stravinsky—employing spokespersons, notably his pupil and biographer David Schiff, to vent his spleen at "the tyranny of the audience."⁹ Babbitt, invited to comment on recent developments in the program book for the 1984 sequel to the "New Romanticism" festival described in the previous chapter, delivered himself of a self-pitying tirade, "The More Than Sounds of Music," in which he came close to casting himself and his colleagues as victims of an esthetic mugging by unnamed (but plainly enough identified) totalitarian forces. It would be an interesting exercise to ferret out all the code words in its concluding paragraphs:

> It is certain to be observed that the "music" being buried, at least in the archives, will be mourned by few, since it was loved by so few. If "good" or "worthy" is to be determined by the counting of ears (at least that is an explication of that supervenient), then let it be noted that there is a musical arena where the true cultural heroes of this people's cultural democracy hold forth, where a mere seventy-five million copies of a single record album are purchased. And if this be adjudged a rude category error, where should the category boundaries be drawn, and by whom? By those who will not or cannot offer reasons, and so only can be called unreasonable? By such a mighty computermite as condemns Brahms for his elitist, inconsiderate "just another modulation" (the very language of the condemnation reveals the sophistication of the analysis)? By those who dismiss a work by the invocation of *a prioris* as to what music (allegedly) has been, or never was, and therefore should be?
>
> Perhaps music today does present a confusing, even confused picture; for all that it is a truism to remark that the world of music never before has been so pluralistic, so fragmented, with a fragmentation which has produced severe factionalization, it is nonetheless true. But not even those composers who dare to presume to attempt to make music as much as it can be rather than the minimum with which one obviously can get away with music's being under the current egalitarian dispensation would wish to have contemporary compositional variety (however skeined, stained, or—even—strained) diminished by fiat, mob rule, or verbal terrorism.¹⁰

But the rejection, this time, had been performed not by "the people," or by journalists or concert managers or recording executives, but by the writers of tomorrow's music.

TERMINAL COMPLEXITY

The youngest composers working in styles and media comparable to those of the grand old men were around forty by the time Babbitt wrote his fulminations. Two of them, Brian Ferneyhough (b. 1943) and Michael Finnissy (b. 1946), were English composers associated with the Darmstadt Summer Courses, where Ferneyhough coordinated the composition program between 1984 and 1994. They formed the nucleus of a group identified with "the New Complexity," a term coined by the Australian music theorist Richard Toop in direct and embattled reaction against the advancing tide.

Their manifestos, many of them unprintable in a book like this, were worthy successors to the original Darmstadt blasts surveyed in chapter 1. And their music was, at least in appearance, even more complicated. To speak of the appearance of the music is in this case not trivial, because composers associated with the New Complexity put much of their effort into finding notations for virtually impalpable microtones, ever-changing rhythmic divisions and tiny gradations of timbre and loudness in an effort to realize their ideal of infinite musical evolution under infinitely fine control and presented with infinite precision, with absolutely no concession to "cognitive constraints." As a result, to quote Christopher Fox (another British composer who has worked at Darmstadt), their scores "pushed the prescriptive capacity of traditional staff notation to its limits, with a hitherto unprecedented detailing of articulation." [11]

The claim displays a familiar sort of bravado, but it is probably true: see Fig. 10-2, from Ferneyhough's String Quartet no. 2 (1980). It is not an unusually complicated page for Ferneyhough, but it shows clearly his device of "nested rhythms" (tiny sextolets in the time of five sixteenths within medium triplets inside of big quintolets, etc.) that motivated the notational extremities, plus the individual editorial attention given every single note (each with its own articulation mark and, usually, its own dynamic) and the "extended" playing techniques (trilled artificial harmonics, microtonal glissandos, etc.) that reflect the composer's determination to diversify at all costs. "It is imperative," the composer wrote, "that the ideology of the holistic gesture be dethroned in favor of a type of patterning which takes greater account of the transformatory and energetic potential of the sub-components of which the gesture is composed." [12] Nothing is too small to be individuated, or given a distinctive written shape. The "late, late Romantic" implications are familiar enough: the notes are rugged individuals whose rights must be respected.

But despite the evident progress it fostered in notational technology the movement was too obviously a rear-guard action to inspire much interest. Nobody took the "new" in New Complexity seriously, not even its coiner. "Still complex" is what he really meant, wrote Toop, "but who uses labels like that?: they don't sell well!" [13] Even its sympathizers kidded it: Barry Truax (b. 1947), a Canadian composer and acoustician, good-naturedly undermined Ferneyhough's ideology of endless differentiation with the remark that, after all, the New Complexity was "a lotta notes." [14] That could be a selling point: Michael Finnissy proudly billed his 5½-hour *History of Photography in Sound* as being (in pointed comparison with the minimalists) "the longest *non-repetitive* piano piece to be performed." [15] But Eric Ulman, a former pupil of Ferneyhough, aired some tough objections of a kind that had always dogged modernist art, but now seemed especially relevant. "Sometimes," he warned,

> the "complex" score becomes an intimidation mechanism, staving off critical scrutiny by cultivating incomprehension, substituting colorful notational and verbal detail for musical detail, and depending on an inevitable inaccuracy of interpretation for either a genuinely improvisatory performative power or a final excuse for the failure of the material to present itself audibly. [16]

The notational detail was significant, even if the music was not; for its intricacy set a benchmark that is never likely to be equaled, let alone surpassed. The primary concern of this final chapter will be to show why this is so.

"BIG SCIENCE" ECLIPSED

Although he remained a commanding presence on the musical scene, Boulez lost his hold on young composers even as he created opportunities for them. One reason

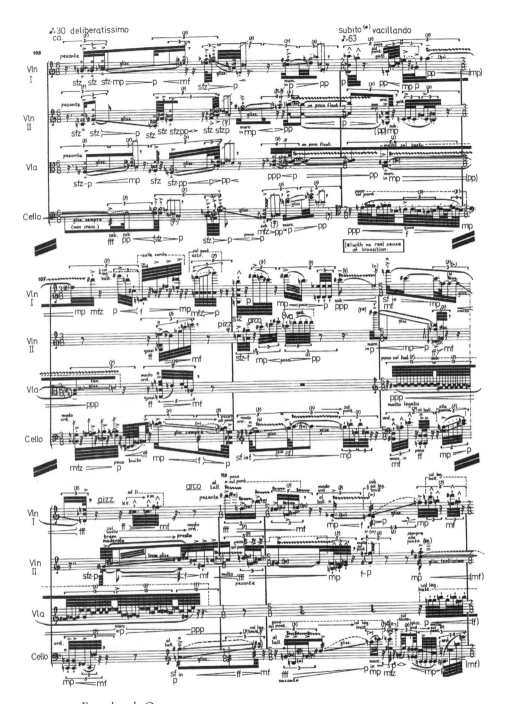

FIG. 10-2 Ferneyhough, Quartet no. 2.

was the steady decline in his productivity over the 1970s, caused in part by his engagement between 1971 and 1977 as music director of the New York Philharmonic, and by his simultaneous conducting commitments elsewhere and everywhere. Even after leaving the Philharmonic post, Boulez has been active mainly as a conductor with a heavy international schedule, in incessant demand for commercial recording of early-twentieth-century repertoire with major orchestras, and as leader of a handpicked new music group, the Ensemble InterContemporain.

Composition went on the back burner. Four years after giving up full-time employment as a conductor, Boulez produced *Répons* (1981), a twenty-minute composition for chamber orchestra, six solo instruments (two pianos, harp, vibraphone, glockenspiel, and cimbalom) and live electronics. An extended, thirty-three-minute version of the piece was performed the next year, and in 1984 a full-hour, "full evening" variant was unveiled and taken on an international tour. The longer versions contained no actual new material but were developments, in the traditional motivic sense, of the original piece. That mode of meticulous elaboration has become Boulez's primary compositional method. *Répons* was further cannibalized in two chamber works, both titled *Dérive* (I, 1984; II in two versions, 1990, 1993). Since then Boulez has produced only one short piano piece (*Incises*, 1994) that is not a reworking of earlier pieces, some going back to the 1940s; and (as we know) *Incises* itself was cannibalized in the Grawemeyer Award-winning composition of 1998.

This strangely symptomatic way of living, compositionally, in the past seems related to the circumstances of Boulez's late career. *Répons* was composed at IRCAM, the electro-acoustical research institute the French government (under President Georges Pompidou) set up for Boulez as an inducement to lure him back from America. Fully operational from 1977, when Boulez took up the reins, it was touted as a "meeting place for scientists and musicians,"[17] but in practical terms it amounted to a sort of laboratory, well stocked with electronic and computer equipment and well staffed with technicians, to which composers from all over the world (as well as some musicologists and music theorists) were invited for residencies and fellowships. Boulez retained the directorship of the center until 1992 and devoted much of his energy to its administration. But creatively he was from the start a somewhat isolated figure even there. Even there, a basic esthetic and generational divide loomed up.

In 1984, when Boulez finished the final version of *Répons*, he was fifty-nine years old, between one and two decades older than any of the support staff. Most of the technicians came from (or at least had significant exposure to and knowledge of) the world of commercial pop music, where as much or more progress was being made in audio technologies than in the world of the cloistered avant-garde. And while nobody thought that IRCAM was going to be hospitable to pop music, the differences in background and viewpoint nevertheless showed up in attitudes toward technology, its applications, and its benefits.

As the stately beneficiary of unprecedented government largesse, and no doubt remembering the wall-covering, $175,000 Mark II synthesizer bestowed on Babbitt by corporate patrons at the Columbia-Princeton electronic music lab, Boulez was fervently committed to the conspicuous consumption of technology. He had his own custom-built "machine" at IRCAM, the 4X computer developed by the Italian engineer Giuseppe di Giugno to Boulez's specifications. The 4X was an enlarged and more sophisticated version of a "live electronic music" device called a Halaphone, which could modify the timbres of instruments as they were being played, and disperse their outputs, by means of a computer program, among the speakers of an electro-acoustical installation. The engineer who processed these transformations and moved the sounds around during the performance was in effect a member of the performing ensemble. (Boulez had first employed a Halaphone in an instrumental septet called *Explosante-fixe*, composed in 1971.)

The 4X, an exceptionally rapid computer for its day, greatly enhanced the capacity and versatility of real-time digital sound processing. It was (to borrow a phrase from Dominique Jameux, a musicological disciple of Boulez) "the technological 'trophy' of IRCAM,"[18] and conferred status on the few who were qualified and privileged to use it. Or as Boulez's personal technician put it, the 4X was "the Rolls Royce of computer music."[19] Its size, costliness, and complexity, and the difficulty of running it (which required a special expertise that few if any composers possessed), made it an indispensable emblem of progress, and a tangible justification for the whole IRCAM enterprise, which relied heavily on public funds. The Institute's commitment to spectacular big-system development — "Big Science," as it was called in America — thus had a nationalistic significance for the French in addition to an artistic one.

But there was a paradoxical or ambivalent side to high-tech modernism, since one of the principal tenets of the modern movement had always been the composer's autonomy or freedom from external factors. So technology, whatever prestige or possibilities it may deliver, is inherently suspect. It must be kept in its place; it must never seem to dominate or determine the artist's conception. As Jameux put it (speaking for Boulez), there must be no compromise of "the necessary priority of compositional thought over the empiricism of dealing with a machine."[20] Hence *Répons* is a completely composed composition (to put it as redundantly as the situation demands), with a fully specified score that includes a part for an engineer or "sound designer" who performs it exactly the same way every time.

Thus, even as the maximum technological potential is demanded, its application is held in check. Jameux comments that the work "derives its armature from the perenniality of a completely notated score, which could almost be played and suffice in itself,"[21] that is, without the electro-acoustical transformations. So, paradoxically, the legitimacy of the computer technology is established by limiting it almost to the point where it becomes superfluous. "Whatever the degree of success of the processes of transformation, and of the electro-acoustic equipment in general, the 'machine' treatment seems subordinated to a relatively traditional musical text," she writes. "We do not have the impression (although this is a purely personal opinion) that the available technology *gave rise* to the composition, but rather that an abstract idea — enshrined in the title — led to a score written in the light of what technology could offer *in addition*." It is safe to say that this squeamishness was not only the commentator's, but the composer's as well.

IRCAM's support staff, meanwhile, was more and more intrigued with the burgeoning "digital revolution," the commercial development of personal computers and software that miniaturized, standardized, and democratized technology. A rift opened up between Boulez, whose aristocratic disdain for small machines reflected his high modernist commitments, and David Wessel (b. 1942), an American psycho-acoustician and composer with a jazz background, who was serving as IRCAM's director of pedagogy, over the introduction of mass-produced Apple Macintosh computers and Yamaha synthesizers. An impasse was reached in 1984, when Boulez forbade the move and Wessel (who had negotiated independently with the American and Japanese companies) ordered them anyway.

There was even a political component to the struggle: production of the 4X machine had been contracted through the French government to a company (Dassault/Sogitec) that was mainly engaged in the design and manufacture of high-tech aircraft and munitions equipment for the military. IRCAM was thus implicated in what Americans call the "military-industrial complex." Those advocating the downsizing of technology made it a "Green" issue; those committed to Big Science invoked traditional avant-garde hostility to commercialism.

Georgina Born, an English anthropologist and cultural critic with a musical background who in 1984 had received a grant to conduct an "ethnography" of IRCAM as a thesis project, built her narrative (published in 1995 as *Rationalizing Culture: IRCAM, Boulez, and the Institutionalization of the Musical Avant-Garde*) around this controversy, which she luckily happened to be on the scene to witness, casting it as a paradigmatic modernist-postmodernist confrontation. She made a compelling case for its significance, especially in the light of the outcome. Despite Boulez's opposition, the "dissident" faction led by Wessel triumphed, even if Wessel himself was disaffected in the process and departed for the University of California at Berkeley, where he became head of a Center for New Music and Technology. The downsizing of technology, while a personal defeat for Boulez, nevertheless transformed IRCAM in accordance with changes that were sweeping the whole world of information processing, keeping the Paris institution relevant and, in effect, saving it.

The essential irony of late-twentieth-century art — the transformation of the *avant-garde* (vanguard) into an *arrière-garde* (rear-guard) precisely because of its commitment to an old concept of the new — was thus dramatically encapsulated. The change of course at IRCAM reflected in microcosm the transformations in the wider world that led the American composer Kyle Gann to suggest that "centuries from now, the years 1980 to 1985 may well appear one of the most significant watersheds in the history of music."[22] It is of course far too soon to gauge the accuracy of such a prediction, but the world that many musicians inhabit at the time this text is being written did come into being then. And to describe it is a fitting way to conclude a book devoted to tracing the history of the fine art of music in the West. For the defining feature of that history, as emphasized from page one, has been its reliance on written transmission; and what the digital revolution of the 1980s presaged above all was liberation from the literate tradition to which Boulez remained so unbendingly attached, and its probable eventual demise.

TWENTIETH-CENTURY "ORALITY"

Yet at the same time another point emphasized throughout the present multivolume narrative has been the persistence of the oral tradition. It has never been fully supplanted in Western classical music or anywhere else. To learn any instrument one needs a live teacher who instructs as much by example as by verbal precept. We all know songs—including "composed" songs like "Happy Birthday" or "Take Me Out to the Ball Game"—that we learned by ear. No musical repertoire, not even the Beethoven symphonies, is wholly fixed and transmitted by its text; there are always unwritten performing conventions that must be learned by listening and reproduced (and that, like spoken languages, change over time).

The point has already been made, moreover, that the one musical medium that originated in the twentieth century—namely, the electronic—is the one that depends least on writing. It achieves what written texts achieve—namely, the fixing of the unique artwork—even better than written texts can do, and it does so without the use of texts. Or rather, "text" and "work" can fuse under electronic conditions so as to produce a definitive work-object (phonograph record, tape reel, cassette, CD, MP3 file) in a way that the intervention of human performers inevitably precludes.

So there have been two ways of doing without writing since the mid-twentieth century: the novel "autographic" or performerless way, in which the composer creates a unique object (as a painter produces a canvas) that can be mechanically reproduced but requires no reenactment in order to go on existing; and the age-old, traditionally "oral" way, in which there are only live performances, not objects (only acts, not texts). But an orally transmitted performance can also be recorded. And so twentieth-century technology has provided a bridge between the two methods of nonliterate art-production; or rather, it has enabled the two methods to surround and attack the literate tradition like pincers. The paradoxical fact is that recording and electro-acoustical technologies have not only produced their own media, but also spurred the professional revival in the late twentieth century of age-old oral practices normally associated with folklore, giving rise to the genre that is known, for want of a better term, as performance art. So before resuming our account of the digital revolution of the 1980s, we need to fill in a bit of "oral" background.

HOBO ORIGINS

The great precursor here was Harry Partch (1901–74), as close to a total maverick or "alternative" figure as the history of music can provide. He not only talked the talk of a maverick; he lived the life as well. His was a nomadic existence that included a period in 1935 (at the depths of the Great Depression) as a "hobo" or vagrant, a homeless wanderer living in various transient shelters along the West Coast of the United States. A diary he kept during this period, published posthumously under the title *Bitter Music*, shows him translating his social alienation into an artistic program. There are many Musorgsky- or Janáček-like notations of overheard "speech-melodies" (Ex. 10-1), followed by attempts at harmonizing them, and even a few sketches that shape them into dramatic scenes, including some that eventually found their way into his "music-dance drama" *King Oedipus*.

His hobo experiences became the subject matter for several of his works. Four of them, gathered up into a suite or cycle called *The Wayward*, constitute a unique

FIG. 10-3   Harry Partch.

panorama of depression life. *Barstow: Eight Hitchhiker Inscriptions from a Highway Railing at Barstow, California* (1941, revised 1968) was the first. The others were *US Highball: A Musical Account of a Transcontinental Hobo Trip* (1943, revised 1955), *San Francisco: A Setting of the Cries of Two Newsboys on a Foggy Night in the Twenties* (1943, revised 1955), and *The Letter: A Depression Message from a Hobo Friend* (1943, revised 1972). Inspired by his resentments, and by ancient and exotic models of ritual theater, Partch, though trained in it, turned his back on the entire tradition of Western music — its tuning systems, its instruments, its conventional notations, its social practices, its customary venues — and sought to create a better alternative: a didactic and communal *Gesamtkunstwerk* (he called it "integrated corporeal theater"[23]) founded on a musical system that harnessed the fabled powers of just intonation, speech-song, and choric dancing to exert spiritual influence and effect social change.

"I am first and last a composer," Partch wrote in 1942. "I have been provoked into becoming a musical theorist, an instrument builder, a musical apostate, and a musical idealist, simply because I have been a demanding composer."[24] His inability to compromise (or to work with collaborators as equals, as the choreographer Alwin Nikolais found out in 1957[25]) was at once the source of the considerable fascination his work exerted during his lifetime — and even more powerfully after his death, when he became a legendary "pioneer" — and the source of its incommunicability except through the person of the composer.

Partch wrote a large book, *Genesis of a Music* (1949, revised 1974), to expound his theories. It contains an irately skewed history of music ("Corporeal versus Abstract Music") to legitimize his ideas and make them seem like the answer to all the big questions; a detailed and mathematically sophisticated treatise on his tuning system; and a description, replete with photographs, of the numerous imaginatively designed and skillfully built instruments he had had to make in order to provide the forty-three unequally tempered tones to the octave that his modal theories demanded.

The Partch instrumentarium comprised plucked and bowed string instruments, "adapted" with extra-long fingerboards on which intonation points were marked, as on medieval monochords; "chromelodeons," or modified reed organs; "kitharas," harps or lyres played with plectra; "harmonic canons," or psalteries played with plectra; adapted kotos; many tuned percussion instruments, including marimbas and mbiras in many sizes; and "cloud chamber bowls," tops and bottoms of twelve-gallon Pyrex bottles sawed off to precise measurements (so called because the original ones came from a radiation laboratory at the University of California at Berkeley). These instruments, visually beautiful, were always visible in performance, on stage along with the singers and dancers in Partch's theatrical works, like the pianos in Stravinsky's *Les noces.*

Partch did invent tablature notations for his instruments; Ex. 10-2 shows the beginning of *Barstow* both in Partch's tablature and as transcribed by the musicologist Richard Kassel to show (approximately) the actual pitches. But like ancient neumes, Partch's tablatures best served performers who had already rehearsed "hands-on" with the composer, or with someone to whom the composer had transmitted the work orally. Thus, to perform his music adequately, Partch's charismatic presence was always required. As his reputation grew, he was invited to residencies and research fellowships at educational institutions (among them the Universities of Wisconsin and Illinois and Mills College in Oakland, California). There he would gather around him groups of interested students and musicians, whom he taught by example, and put on recitals and, later, dramatic spectacles.

Once performed, however, they could be adequately preserved only in record-ings—a bitter irony, given Partch's extreme commitment to the physicality of live performance. "I believe in musicians who are total constituents of the moment, irre-placeable," he wrote, "who may sing, shout, whistle, stamp their feet; in costume always or perhaps half naked, and I do not care which half."[26] But he was the truly irreplaceable

EX. 10-1   Harry Partch, *Bitter Music,* speech melodies

component. A Columbia LP disk, issued in 1968 and containing three works including *Barstow*, was the only stereophonic recording of fully professional quality he ever made.

On his death his instruments went to Montclair State University in New Jersey, and from there to the Smithsonian Institution. A few of his disciples, notably Danlee Mitchell, a percussionist and conductor who was Partch's companion from 1956 to his

EX. 10-2A   Beginning of Harry Partch's *Barstow*, Partch's tablature

EX. 10-2A (*continued*)

death, have continued to perform on them or on replicas. In the 1980s, Mitchell brought Partch's work to Europe for the first time. But the likelihood of Partch performances diminishes every year, even as historical interest in his work has mounted and its influence has spread. A ruinous limit on dissemination was the price Partch paid for his idealism.

Two of his music theater pieces, preserved in fairly primitive recordings on Partch's own "Gate 5" label, were actual adaptations of ancient Greek plays, putting Partch in a noble line going right back to the Florentine Camerata at the wellsprings of opera. *King Oedipus* (1951), based on W. B. Yeats's translation of Sophocles, was produced at Mills College in 1952 and, because the Yeats estate withheld permission to use the text, it was revised for recording (at the Sausalito Arts Fair) in 1954. It is probably the purest and most effective extant example of Partchian *Gesamtkunstwerk*. The most famous Partch composition, *Revelation in the Courthouse Park*, after Euripides's *Bacchae*, is less representative. It was staged in 1962 at the University of Illinois, where one of Partch's admirers, the microtonal composer Ben Johnston (b. 1926), was on the faculty. It was intended as an overt and timely political statement, and as such it caused some modification of the composer's usual style.

Revelation was inspired by Partch's perception of a parallel between the orgiastic rites of Dionysus as portrayed by Euripides and "two phenomena of present-day America."[27] One was the Pentecostal revival meeting ("religious ritual with a strong sexual element"), and the other was the reception that pop singers like Frank Sinatra and Elvis Presley enjoyed among their fans. "I assume," Partch wrote drily, "that the mobbing of young male singers by semihysterical women is recognizable as a sex ritual for a godhead."[28] It stood in his mind for the triumph of "mediocrity and conformity" in postwar America and their threat to the founding values of the American republic, namely the rights and the integrity of the individual.

Scenes from Euripides are juxtaposed with contemporary counterparts depicting a small town's reaction to a visit by an updated Dionysus, a hybrid faith-healer and rock 'n' roll star named Dion, something like an Oral Roberts (or a Billy Graham) and an Elvis Presley rolled into one. King Pentheus and his mother Agave, the chief victims of the Dionysian frenzy in Euripides, become "Sonny" and "Mom." Under the wild influence of Dion, the crazed Mom murders the skeptical Sonny. The audience is invited to contemplate, and to "consider" (in the words of W. Anthony Sheppard, a historian

EX. 10-2B   Beginning of Harry Partch's *Barstow*, as transcribed by musicologist Richard Kassel

*All grace notes are played on the beat and are followed immediately by the main note.

of twentieth-century music theater), "the menace of mindless group behavior."[29] The score, uniquely for Partch, combines his singular neoantique idiom with American vernacular styles, in keeping with the alternation of scenes. It is no "crossover," however. The use of popular styles in illustrating the degradation of the townspeople renders a fiercely negative (as well as misogynistic) judgment on them.

The tragedy of *Revelation in the Courthouse Park* unwittingly exposes Partch's own fatal ambivalences. His life experiences at the margins of society imbued him with an implacable individualism to which the drama gave overt approval. "I was not going to be straitjacketed by anyone," he snarled defiantly at an interviewer in the year of his death, "I was going to be completely free." He saw himself, like Sonny, threatened by the herd instincts at the core of American life. But his manner of functioning as an artist inevitably made him a charismatic leader like Dion, requiring what Ben Johnston called "cultlike devotion"[30] from his performers. And Dion was nothing if not a "corporealist," from whom Partch could not withhold a grudging (homoerotic) admiration. He saw his own staged embodiment of evil as "an exotic altar priest whose revolving ass is not a lustful and transitory whim, but a divine right."[31] His inability to resolve these conflicts ensured that his work, imprisoned in its idiosyncrasies and dependent on his own function as an altar priest, would effectively die with him.

So his posthumous influence, while potent, has been almost entirely in the realm of ideas and social practice rather than in actual musical practices or styles. "Among his disciples may be counted all American composers who employ just intonation and most of those who use microtones,"[32] claimed one of them, Andrew Stiller, who went on to ascribe to Partch's influence all kinds of later developments from percussion music to multimedia music theater to minimalism to "sound-sculpture" installations. A more realistic assessment would cast Partch as a spiritual forerunner to musicians of a "Green" persuasion, who responded, as the times caught up with him, less to Partch's actual music than to the example of his easily romanticized existence. He has been elected posthumously to the "bum aristocracy"[33] that (as we may read in *Bitter Music*) he despised in life.

That is why, despite Partch's musical purism, his denigration of popular culture, and his classical training, he became, according to the pop critic Damon Krukowski, "one of a handful of composers who seem to interest rock musicians."[34] Musically he had little in common with them, but he worked the way they do. His style was a function of his medium (or vice versa); he composed viscerally, at his instruments; he rehearsed his musicians by rote and performed from memory. And that has made him an inspiration not just to rock musicians but to the increasing number of composers who have relied, in the quarter of the twentieth century that Partch missed, on various sorts of oral transmission to disseminate their work.

IMAGINARY FOLKLORE

In this sense, Partch's most direct conceptual descendant is Meredith Monk (b. 1942), a composer whose career was only beginning at the time of his death, and who has never mentioned him among her influences. Like Partch, she began as a lonely outsider, creating an eccentric music "corporeally," by training her own voice to do things no one (at least within the traditions of her schooling) had thought of doing before. At a time when no one could duplicate (or was interested in duplicating) her effects, she became her own performance medium. She told an interviewer, who asked whether her pieces were autobiographical, that her relationship to her work went deeper than that. "I was using," she said,

> myself as material. I was very objective about it, though, so it wasn't really autobiographical. It was more that my hair was material, and my singing with a guitar was material. It was personal in a way that I let myself use myself—anything that I had—as material. But then it was made into a piece of poetry, because it was extremely objectified.[35]

Partch could have said that. Monk's music was, like his, produced at the outset from within her own body. But where Partch (like the ancient Greeks) did everything for the sake of words and their expressive projection, Monk tried to dispense with words without dispensing with the expressive projection. Most of her early compositions are solo songs, with simple piano accompaniments (usually ostinatos and grounds) for herself to play while producing an astonishing variety of nonverbal vocal sounds: sometimes invented syllables sung conventionally, sometimes more elemental sonorities—unusual wobbles and vibratos, nasal timbres, extreme registers, guttural breathing, vocalized inhaling—that Monk, preempting a common reaction from listeners, called "folk music from another planet."[36] Looking back on her early work in 1979, she summed it up as "working with the solo voice as an instrument."

> After classical voice training and experience as a folk and rock singer, I realized that I wanted to create vocal music that had the personal style and abstract (as well as emotional) qualities that come into play in the creation of a painting or a dance. My method began as one of trial and error: translating certain concepts, feelings, images and energies to my voice, seeing how they felt, how they sounded, and then refining them into a musical form. Over the years I have developed a vocabulary and a style designed to utilize as wide a range of vocal sound as possible.[37]

At the time she was recalling, a person with Monk's training inevitably assumed that painting and dance were nonrepresentational media that channeled subjective feeling into objective form in the manner of abstract expressionism. Monk's ideal was a kind of musical (or vocal) abstract expressionism, and that required the dethroning of words. "The voice itself is a very eloquent language," she told an interviewer, "and I've always felt that singing English on top of it is like singing two languages at the same time."[38] To another interviewer, she elaborated:

> Usually, if I do use text, it will be very simple, and it will be there as much for the sound of it as for the meaning. I also think that music, itself, is such an evocative medium. It's very openhearted. And I don't like the idea that people have to work through the screen of language . . . . Language, in a way, is a screen in front of the emotion and the action. I like the idea of a direct communication that bypasses that step . . . [39]

And again like Partch, at a certain point Monk made "an inevitable decision"

> to teach some of my techniques to other voices in an attempt to expand my writing—to see if these principles could be translated (transferred) to other singers and made into group forms. My main concerns in the group music have been to work with the unique quality of each voice and to play with the ensemble possibilities of unison, texture, counterpoint, weaving, etc.[40]

Monk's "classical" training shows through in her use of the word "writing" as an interchangeable equivalent for "composing." But just as her early solo work, while fully composed (never improvised), had been unwritten, since there was no need to communicate the music to any other performer, so the ensemble music remained unwritten, the product (like rock) of intensive daily rehearsal and rote memorization. The avoidance of notation was partly due the fact that there were no conventional symbols for the vocal effects Monk had been evolving. But only partly. "I don't know how you would notate some of the vocal work," she said when asked,

> and I don't know if I want to or not. I'm struggling with that right now because I do want to pass my work on. It's not that I don't want to have other people do it, but I think that the way it's made comes from a primal, oral tradition that is much more about music for the ears. In Western culture, paper has sometimes taken over the function of what music always was.[41]

Whether by accident—ontogeny recapitulating phylogeny, as a biologist might say—or by design (on the basis, perhaps, of her music history classes at Sarah Lawrence College), many of the textures and structures Monk has employed in her ensemble music recall the textures and structures of medieval genres—organum, hocket, rondellus—that found their way into written sources only after considerable development as oral practices.

The first work Monk created after forming her own performing ensemble was the wordless *Dolmen Music* (1978), for six singers, a cello (played by one of the singers), and percussion (played by another). The title, derived from an old Breton word that refers to prehistoric cult monuments like Stonehenge (upright stones supporting a horizontal stone), evokes an imagined antiquity. The various movements—"Overture and Men's Conclave," "Wa-ohs," "Rain," "Pine Tree Lullaby," "Calls," "Conclusion"—seem to suggest the primordial rituals and practices out of which music emerged. "In all cultures there are what I would call archetypal songs—the lullaby form, work song, love song, march, funeral song."[42] Just as by avoiding words she sought a universal vocal language, so "it's interesting to hook into these song categories that exist all over," forms that speak wordlessly of life's functions and their ubiquitous, eternal round.

At the very end of *Dolmen Music* all of the voices coalesce into a "composite" parallel organum (multiple fourths, fifths, and octaves) of the kind described in ninth-century Frankish treatises. Twentieth-century musicians of the avant-garde making contact with their ninth-century forebears dramatizes the idea of "cyclic time," a notion that many in the late twentieth century have found irresistibly attractive, and have used as a weapon for dismantling the idea of linear historical progress.

Monk has occasionally made this agenda explicit. Asked by an interviewer how she felt she related to the "Western musical tradition," she snapped, "I know there are people very concerned about where they fit into music history; but I would say that's a very male point of view."[43] As with many marginal figures who are eventually discovered by the mainstream, Monk has had to make an accommodation with convention. In the late 1970s she began (like Steve Reich) to record her music for the German ECM label, and she embarked on a series of concert tours that by the mid-1980s amounted to as much as four months a year. Finally, in 1986, a consortium that included the Houston Grand Opera and the American Music Theater Festival commissioned from her a full-length opera, *Atlas*, based loosely on the discoveries of Alexandra David-Néel (renamed Alexandra Daniels in the opera), the first European woman to travel in Tibet. It was first performed in Houston in February 1991.

Unlike Monk's earlier theater compositions (some of which she had rather loosely called operas), *Atlas*, which requires a cast of eighteen singers and a ten-piece pit band, actually looked like an opera: a sequence of scenes with action and costumes and a semblance of plot. It remained almost entirely wordless, however, using the "language of the voice" to tell the story of Alexandra's quest — through desert heat and Arctic cold, rain forests and agricultural communities, finally back home — in a way that sought to translate the explorer's discoveries into universal emotional experience. And it kept faith as far as possible with Monk's "oral" ideal. The instrumental music, mainly the sort of accompanying ostinatos and grounds Monk had formerly extemporized at the keyboard, had to be written down so as to be playable at sight (see Ex. 10-3), but the vocal music was, much of it, worked out in rehearsal and committed to memory as before.

FIG. 10-4   Meredith Monk as Alexandra Daniels in *Atlas* (Houston Grand Opera, 1991).

EX. 10-3   Meredith Monk, *Atlas*, ostinato from "Travel Dream Song"

♩ = 144

Another concession Monk had to make in *Atlas* was to electronic technology, something she had hitherto resisted. Her pit band included electronic keyboards and "samplers" (to be further discussed below) to increase the range of sounds available to a small ensemble. But she used electronics the way she used notation, as sparingly as possible. It was a principled renunciation. Some of her earliest pieces (like some of Steve Reich's) were created by layering tape loops. In Monk's case all the layers contained recordings of her voice, and the composite was then used as an accompaniment to a dance performance or film. But once she had an ensemble she rejected the process of "overdubbing" in performance (although she retained it as a creative tool). She told one of her many interviewers that she often worked pieces out by layering voice tracks, but then taught the various tracks to different singers, since the object of composing was to enable a performance (an act in real time, a social process), not just produce an object (a score or CD).

"I don't think anything can really replace people making music together,"[44] she said, leaving little doubt that "can" really meant, "should." Technology, with its inevitable tendency to "reify" and "commodify" (i.e., turn whatever it touches into things for sale) endangered the social and disinterested aspects of performance. Like Partch, she had a finger in the dike but could not stop the flood. The ironic fact is that her music (like Partch's, like everyone's) is now known primarily through commercial recordings.

Her increasing fame finally landed Monk a contract, announced early in 2001, with Boosey and Hawkes, the most distinguished and commercially potent classical music publisher in a shrinking industry, to disseminate her works in written form. This meant not only taking them down from recordings (a task performed by the publisher's staff, subject to the composer's approval), but also codifying and verbally explicating her vocal techniques for the first time, and distributing compact discs of Monk's performances along with the scores "as an aid to performance practice and interpretation."[45] A publisher, in other words, is trying belatedly, and for commercial gain, to reclaim Monk's quintessentially oral art for the literate tradition. Contradictions abound.

A FEMININE REDOUBT

But the literate tradition is undeniably weakening under pressure from visual media and audio technologies, and performance art like Monk's is one of the symptoms. Most other performance artists have fewer scruples than she about accepting technological innovation, are less resistant than she to reification, and are consequently less likely prospects (or targets) for reclamation by those who trade commercially in notation.

Is it a coincidence that most of them are women? How could it be one, given that performance art is the only creative musical scene that women have ever dominated? Unsurprisingly, male and female explanations for the phenomenon vary in perspective. Kyle Gann, unable to come up with more than two names of men who "use their own voices and bodies as material for their music" but having easily listed a dozen women who did so and claimed to know dozens more, suggested that such an activity "involves a vulnerability, a publicly emotive expressiveness, that men in our society are perhaps too inhibited to indulge."[46] Susan McClary, the feminist musicologist, puts it somewhat differently. "Women's bodies in Western culture," she writes, "have almost always been viewed as objects of display."[47] It is the traditional role of women in the performing arts to be a "body set in motion for the pleasure of the masculine gaze." And she quotes Laurie Anderson (b. 1947), one of the most successful performing artists of the 1980s and 1990s, as corroboration: "Women have rarely been composers. But we do have one advantage. We're used to performing. I mean like we used to tap dance for the boys."[48]

The difference, of course, is that performance artists write their own scripts. "Women have rarely been permitted agency in art," McClary writes, "but instead have been restricted to enacting—upon and through their bodies—the theatrical, musical, cinematic, and dance scenarios concocted by male artists."[49] One can observe those prejudices and restrictions against women's creative agency over the whole range of musical histroy. Performance art is one way in which women have been able to wrest creative agency from its traditional custodians while maintaining, as Anderson whimsically suggests, their traditional "advantage," and without becoming authoritarian figures themselves. Performance art, as a site of female self-representation, thus found itself a natural ally of the feminist movement.

Some performance artists espoused an aggressive feminism. One, Karen Finley (b. 1956), who performed acts of sexual degradation upon herself such as smearing her nude body with chocolate, became the object of a fierce controversy in 1990 when the National Endowment for the Arts withdrew a grant to her at the behest of several enraged congressmen. Others, like Anderson, taking a less confrontational but still politically engaged approach, sought to beguile rather than harangue. Anderson cultivated an androgynous persona in her "punk" hairstyle and unisex (often leather) attire, deliberately downplaying her sexuality, which, as McClary remarks, "given the terms of the tradition [of feminine performance], always threatens to become the whole show."[50]

Yet in another way she does actively contest rather than evade gender stereotypes,

FIG. 10-5   Laurie Anderson, 1985.

and that is in her enthusiastic embrace of technology, the very domain that Meredith Monk has tended to shun. As McClary comments, by mastering high tech "she displaces the male subject who usually enacts that heroic feat." Also heroic is the sheer Wagnerian scale on which Anderson operates, with one-woman shows (or "solo operas,"[51] to use John Rockwell's term) that combine visual images, words, and music, and that last four and five hours, sometimes split over two evenings (though her popularity is mainly based on excerpts that have been disseminated—all right, marketed—as recorded "singles" and music videos).

Yet she does it all with a wink. An Anderson performance rarely goes by without recourse to a wide array of digital hardware. The hardware includes samplers and sequencers that enable instantaneous manipulation (including "looping") of sounds recorded on the spot; "drum machines" that synthesize percussion tracks; and voice-distorting machines like the vocoder (which blends the voice with keyboard-controlled harmonies so that one can "sing" whole chords) or the harmonizer, which radically transforms pitch and timbre, giving a user of either sex a potential range from the squeakiest soprano to the boomingest basso (or what Anderson calls her "Voice of Authority"). Trained as a violinist, she has even rigged up an amplified fiddle with tape playback heads so that a bow strung with audiotape can play (and distort) intelligible words on it. The Anderson that performs (particularly when heard in recordings) is in effect a synthesized instrument, capable of simultaneously shamming and mocking superhuman vocal (and instrumental) feats.

Self-parody is an essential part of the performance (but so is seriousness); that is one reason why so many critics have called Anderson the postmodern artist par excellence. Her breakthrough piece, "O Superman" (1980; an excerpt from the seven-hour multimedia presentation *United States* first performed complete in 1983), is a particularly teasing example of that interplay. Subtitled "For Massenet," on one level it is a straight parody of the aria, "O souverain, ô juge, ô père" (O King, O Judge, O Father) from Massenet's grand opera *Le Cid* (1885), in which the title character prays for victory on the eve of battle. Anderson's translation of the opening line, "O Superman, O Judge, O Mom and Dad," takes it down many pegs, even as she identifies herself with a heroic operatic tenor. (Who's making fun of whom—or what?) On another level it is a sincere tribute to Charles Holland (1909–87), an African-American opera singer whose career, thwarted by racism at home, had perforce to be carried on in Europe. (Anderson heard him sing the Massenet aria in a farewell recital in 1978.)

The audience does not necessarily have access to this background information, of course. (*Le Cid* is a pretty well forgotten opera; "O souverain" is known today only to retired performers, voice teachers, recital buffs, record collectors, and maybe a few stray scholars.) But the ironic interplays certainly inform what the audience does hear. The song begins with Anderson's voice, looped by the sampler into an unhurried Ha-ha-ha-ha-ha that lasts the length of the performance. When it comes to the words, Anderson's voice is expanded by the vocoder into two alternating chords (C major and E minor) with two tones in common including the pedal pitch, differing by only a hypnotically reiterated semitone. The whole song rocks gently back and forth between them like a babe in arms while the weird synthesizer-voice, joined gradually by Farfisa organ and a couple of winds, croons a dozy meditation, warm and comforting and matter-of-fact yet also somehow sinister, on . . . what?

> O Superman. O Judge. O Mom and Dad.
> Hi. I'm not home right now.
> But if you want to leave a message, just start talking at the sound of the tone.
> Hello? This is your mother. Are you there? Are you coming home? Hello? Is anybody home?
> Well you don't know me but I know you. And I've got a message to give to you. Here come the planes.
> So you better get ready, ready to go. You can come as you are, but pay as you go. Pay as you go.
> And I said: OK! Who is this really? And the voice said:
> This is the hand, the hand that takes. This is the hand. The hand that takes. Here come the planes.
> They're American planes, made in America. Smoking or nonsmoking?
> And the voice said:
> Neither snow nor rain nor gloom of night Shall stay these couriers from the Swift completion of their appointed rounds.
> 'Cause when love is gone, there's always justice, and when justice is gone, there's always force,
> and when force is gone, there's always Mom. Hi Mom!
> So hold me, Mom, in your long arms. So hold me, Mom, in your long arms, In your automatic arms, In your electronic arms.
> So hold me, Mom, in your long arms, Your petrochemical arms,
> Your military arms,
> In your electronic arms . . .

A lullaby of annihilation? Of robotization? Of self-imprisonment? An Orwellian nightmare of sweetly instilled thought-control? Or (more topically) a demurrer at the lullingly soft-spoken yet military-minded Ronald Reagan's election as president? The song seems to be about the potential horrors of technology, yet its medium is very high tech. (Who is laughing—ha-ha-ha—at what?)

Whether despite or because of its ironies and ambiguities, something in *O Superman* touched a nerve. Semiprivately pressed at the instigation of Anderson's promoter as a 45 RPM single (with another affably nightmarish Anderson song—*Walking the Dog*, about a domestic relationship going up in flames—as the flip side) in a tiny edition of 1,000, the song was played on the air in Great Britain and shot briefly to the top of the pop charts. To fill the orders, Anderson signed a contract with Warner Brothers Records, a major pop label. Sales of *O Superman* grossed over a million dollars. It lifted Anderson out of the avant-garde and into the popular culture.

That freakish, never duplicated success is why Anderson's CDs are usually marketed as rock recordings, while those of Meredith Monk are found in classical bins. The arbitrariness of the classification is symptomatic of the nature of performance art, just as performance art is symptomatic of postmodernism. Their superficial differences—Anderson highly verbal, openly political, and urbane; Monk pre- or postverbal, only implicitly political, and "artless"—are outweighed by their similarities, the most striking of which is the irreducibly oral/aural nature of their products. Translate their work into notes on a page and everything that counts is lost.

MUSIC AND COMPUTERS

But the medium least dependent on notation had always been electronic music, which can bypass the performance process as well as the pencil-and-paper process. And no medium was more thoroughly transformed during the 1980s than electronic music, thanks to the advent of personal computers, the very thing that Pierre Boulez was so determined to stave off. From the perspective of midcentury modernism he was right to fear it. Personal computers revolutionized every aspect of music making from composition (including nonelectronic composition) to performance to distribution to consumption. And at every level their effect has been to simplify and democratize the art. But in the process they may have dealt the literate tradition a slow-acting death blow.

THE ELITE PHASE

The beginning of "computer music" can be specified with greater precision than perhaps any comparable event in the history of music. It took place in Summit, New Jersey, in 1957, when Max V. Mathews (b. 1926), an engineer at Bell Telephone Laboratories, produced computer-generated musical sounds with his "transducer," an instrument he invented that could convert audio signals into digital information that could be stored or manipulated by a computer and then reconverted into audio signals. (Its initial purpose was to simulate and recognize speech so that some of the tasks that telephone operators performed could be automated.)

At first, what attracted the interest of engineers and, eventually, composers to the new medium was the classically modernist prospect of overcoming all limitations on creative sovereignty. "With the development of this equipment carried out at the Bell Telephone Laboratories, the composer will have the benefits of a notational system so precise that future generations will know exactly how the composer intended his music to sound," Mathews wrote. "He will have at his command an 'instrument' which is itself directly involved in the creative process." And even more grandly:

> Man's music has always been acoustically limited by the instruments on which he plays. These are mechanisms which have physical restrictions. We have made sound and music directly from numbers, surmounting conventional limitations of instruments. Thus, the musical universe is now circumscribed only by man's perceptions and creativity.[52]

The new freedom came at a high price. The composing process for computer-assisted music was at first almost unbelievably cumbersome, and would remain so for a long time. Here is how Mathews, its inventor, described it in prospect:

> Any sound can be described mathematically by a sequence of numbers. Our composer thus begins by determining what numbers specify the particular sounds in which he is interested. These numbers are then punched on IBM cards; the

cards are fed into the computer and the digits recorded in the memory of the machine. The computer is thus able to generate limitless sounds, depending on the instructions given it by the composer. The latter, instead of writing the score in notes, programs his music by punching a second set of IBM cards, which when fed into the computer cause it to register on tape certain sounds from its vast storehouse.[53]

But here is how Kyle Gann, a composer, described it in retrospect:

> From these early days to the late 1970s, computer music was made by punching Hollerith computer cards in stacks of maybe 3,000 for a few seconds' worth of music, sending those cards out to a mainframe computer for processing, then having the resulting number-coded tape run through a digital-to-analogue converter to get actual sound. This generally meant punching your cards and waiting two weeks for them to come back — often only to find that some number error or miscalculation had torpedoed the desired results.[54]

The composers willing to pay the price, naturally, were the composers to whom the prospect of infinite control was most attractive. This chiefly meant Princeton and Columbia composers at the outset, and only partly because their universities were located within forty miles of Bell Labs. "Using a computer," wrote Charles Dodge (b. 1942), who studied at both universities, "it is realistically possible for a composer to structure all elements of his composition (e.g., tempo, timbre, rate and shape of attack and decay, register, etc.) to the same degree as pitch and rhythm."[55] To "structure," in those days and in those places, of course meant to serialize.

The earliest fruits of the Bell transducer program, presented on a commercial LP record called *Music from Mathematics*, consisted in the main of little experimental pieces by engineers in which the purpose was working the kinks out of the program. (The quotations given above from Mathews come from the sleeve notes to this recording.) Since the best way of testing the accuracy of one's results was to measure it against a known prototype, one of the bands on the record contained a sixteenth-century fantasia for three computer-simulated recorders, and another was the voice-synthesized rendition of "A Bicycle Built for Two" ("Daisy, Daisy") that became famous when Stanley Kubrick put it to dramatic use in his futuristic movie *2001: A Space Odyssey*.

But the record also contained two twelve-tone studies by David Lewin (1933–2003), later an eminent theorist and music analyst, who had graduated from Harvard in mathematics and from Princeton in composition, and whose computer pieces were attempts at serializing multiple "parameters" like duration and register. (But also featured was an unnotatable *Noise Study* by James Tenney (1934–2006), a disciple of Cage, in which complex sounds were allowed to modify one another in a manner that proved more indicative of things to come.) The first course in computer music technology was offered at Princeton in 1966 by Godfrey Winham as part of the university's newly approved Ph.D. program in composition. Among the earliest composers to use the computer regularly as a creative instrument was J. K. Randall (b. 1929), a Princeton professor whose earliest computer compositions, like Lewin's, sought serial control over every measurable aspect of the musical result.

Soon afterward a computer music-synthesis program was established at Columbia, Princeton's electronic music partner; it, too, was affiliated (through Vladimir Ussachevsky) with Bell Labs. Dodge, a widely noted young serialist then completing a doctorate in composition, was its star. At first, in keeping with his enthusiastic comment quoted above, he was attracted to the computer as a sort of performer — an instrument capable of coping (in the words of Kurt Stone, a celebrated music editor of the period) "with superhuman structural and interpretative complexities so typical of much of today's music."[56]

Changes (1969–70), Dodge's first computer composition, resembled his earlier pieces for conventional instruments (like *Folia*, a very complicated chamber nonet commissioned by the Fromm Foundation and performed at Tanglewood in 1965), and used the new medium very much the way Milton Babbitt had used the big RCA synthesizer. The machine was programmed to store digitally and convert into an analog recording a fully written-out twelve-tone composition that live performers might also perform (provided they could be programmed with equal precision).

Dodge's next computer piece, though, was a turning point. He received a commission from Nonesuch Records (an adventurous company that had already had great success with *Silver Apples of the Moon*, a composition produced by Morton Subotnick directly on tape using an electronic synthesizer) to create a piece of computer music that could be marketed on disk. The work he produced, *The Earth's Magnetic Field*, was based on numbers derived from measurements that geophysicists at Columbia's Goddard Institute for Space Studies had taken of fluctuations in the earth's magnetism caused by the sun's radiation (the so-called "solar wind") over the course of the year 1961. The measurements are averaged every three hours (for a yearly total of 2,920 readings) according to a scale known as the Kp index, which has twenty-eight values or degrees of magnitude (Fig. 10-7).

On the second side of the record, Dodge arbitrarily assigned the twenty-eight values to the tones of an equal-tempered chromatic scale covering two octaves plus a major third (twenty-eight semitones), and from other aspects of the geophysical data he derived some equally arbitrary but consistent rules for varying tempo, dynamics, and timbre. The result was an atonal and dissonant texture, not organized according to twelve-tone principles but similar to twelve-tone music in harmonic effect. That is, it was harmonically undifferentiated and undirected, and was therefore typical of the academic music of Dodge's generation. Nothing newsworthy about that.

On the first side of the disk, however, Dodge accepted a correlation between Kp measurements and musical pitches that had been previously worked out by one of the astrophysicists at Goddard, a musical amateur who mapped the measurements

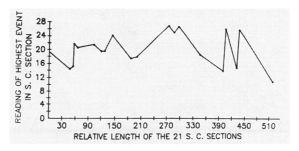

FIG. 10-6   Graph of sunspot activity used to control aspects of the composition in Charles Dodge's *Earth's Magnetic Field*.

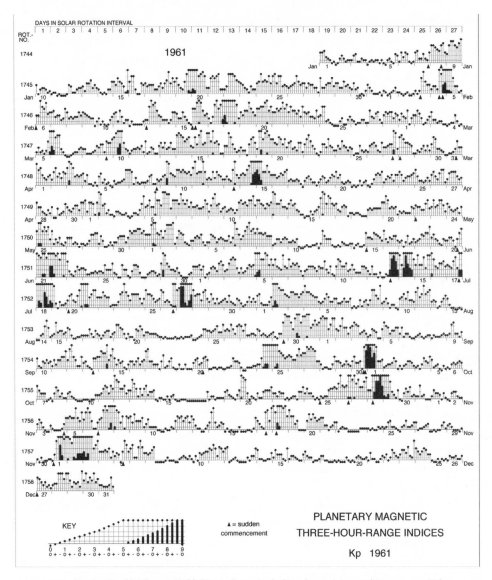

FIG. 10-7 Dodge, *Earth's Magnetic Field*, Kp readings, including the time interval January 1 to February 6, 1961.

onto a diatonic scale that covered four octaves and a second. The result was a series of quirky, catchy tunes that listeners (perhaps with the kind of chemical assistance that prevailed among lovers of "alternative musics" in 1970) could imagine the sun "playing" on the terrestrial atmosphere. The record sold like hotcakes.

Dodge never returned to serial music. Instead, he became particularly interested in speech synthesis (the original Bell project) and its musical applications. A set of exercises called *Speech Songs* (1972), in which Dodge read a set of little poems by his friend Mark Strand several times into Mathews's transducer and then electronically resynthesized, modified, and mixed the sounds of his own readings, became a cult classic. "Laughter at new music concerts, especially in New York these days, is a rare thing," the composer wrote in 1976, "and it has been a source of great pleasure to me to hear audiences respond with laughter to places in all four of the *Speech Songs*."[57] The second in the series plays on the cusp between the obviously synthesized and the possibly "real" sound of a voice.

In 1980 Dodge produced a hilarious sequel: *Any Resemblance Is Purely Coincidental*, in which the raw material was the recorded voice of the great operatic tenor Enrico Caruso. Against expectations, work with the computer had nudged him away from the serious but hermetic project that originally attracted him, and also away from musical idioms that could exist in notation apart from the new medium. At the same time, high technology conferred sufficient prestige to license (or excuse) an "accessible," even humorous musical result that might again court the "lay" audience academic musicians had, it seemed, permanently forsworn. Computers, of all things, seemed to promise relaxation of the quixotic standards of difficulty by which composers in the academy had sought to justify their existence. Improbably enough, the most advanced technology was leading some of its elite practitioners toward a postmodernist posture.

SPECTRALISM

Jean-Claude Risset (b. 1938), a French composer and mathematician, received his training under Mathews at Bell Labs between 1964 and 1969 and went on to become the first computer *chef* at Boulez's IRCAM (1975–79). His research specialty was the matching and manipulation of recorded instrumental and natural sounds as a way of bridging the gap between the two mutually antagonistic worlds of early electronic music as described in chapter 4: the world of musique concrète, which made collages of "real" sounds, and that of the "tape studio," where only electronically produced sounds were used. The computer offered a way of combining the rich sonic resources of the one and the precise composerly control of the other.

A Risset composition of 1968, "Fall," from *Music for Little Boy* (a suite from an incidental score to a play about the aftermath of the bombing of Hiroshima), gave an impressive inkling of that potential. Having made a thorough study of the overtone structures of instrumental timbres and their relationship to perceived pitch, Risset was able to create in sounds the analogue to a nightmare in which a character imagines that he is the bomb itself, falling through space until the dreamer awakens. "This fall," Mathews wrote in a note accompanying a recording of the piece, "is psychological and never reaches any bottom."[58] By changing the relative strength of the overtones in the complex timbre of a descending glissando, the computer interferes with the listener's perception of register. When a "subjective" octave is reached, the original pitch is actually restored so that an uncanny illusion of endlessly descending pitch is produced.

Experiments like these were musically rudimentary but vastly suggestive. In fact a whole "school" of French composers arose in the mid-1970s in response to music produced, like Risset's, on the basis of computer analyses and transformations of timbre. What is particularly interesting about these composers — most prominently Gérard Grisey (1946–98) and Tristan Murail (b. 1947) — is that their *musique spectrale* ("spectral" or "spectralist" music) is not "computer music." It is neither (necessarily) composed nor performed with the aid of a computer and does not (necessarily) use electronic media. It is, rather, an approach to musical form, and particularly to orchestration, that not only was inspired by the precedent of computer music but would have been inconceivable without that precedent — a preliminary inkling of how pervasive the influence of computers has been on music since the 1970s.

In spectral music "the material derives from the natural growth of sonority," Grisey told an audience at Darmstadt in 1978. "In other words there is no *Grundgestalt* (no melodic cell, no complex of notes or note-values)."[59] Rather than an arbitrary basis in the composer's imagination, spectral music finds a natural grounding in the physical qualities of sound, its "spectrum" of overtones as objectively analyzed by an unprejudiced machine. Grisey's *Les espaces acoustiques* ("Acoustic spaces"), a cycle of five pieces ranging in size from solo viola with an optional "electro-acoustical environment" (*Prologue*, 1976) to full orchestra (*Epilogue*, 1985), derives its material from a sonogram, or computer analysis, of the relative amplitude or prominence of sixty-six overtones arising from a low E (41.2 cycles per second), produced as a trombone "pedal" or as the fourth string of a double bass when played in various ways (arco, pizzicato, sul ponticello, etc.).

Chord progressions are produced by variously sampling the upper partials. Bass lines are often the product of combination or difference tones. "Dissonance" is introduced by transposing some of the upper partials so that they become "inharmonic" (i.e., they no longer resonate as integral multiples of the fundamental frequency). In *Partiels* (1975), for eighteen players, the third item in *Les espaces acoustiques*, the overall trajectory is from harmonicity through inharmonicity to disintegration, ending in silences, rustling percussion and isolated bass clarinet moans. In the fourth piece, *Modulations* (1977), the formal progression is from harmonicity to inharmonicity and back again to the pure spectrum of E, but the overtone series is inverted (the large intervals now coming at the top and proceeding downward in ever decreasing increments), and the harmonies reflect the spectra produced on a trombone timbre by the use of various mutes, which act as filters. Four such spectra are set in counterpoint by an orchestration that separates the ensemble into four antiphonal groups.

Inharmonicity is emphasized in the scoring by increasing the "roughness" of sound with nonpitched percussion, string ponticello, wind overblowing, and the like, and returning to smoother sounds when inharmonicity "resolves" to harmonicity. Since the natural overtone series has no "tempering," spectral harmony is an unusual idiom in which tempered "inharmonic" intervals actually resolve to microtonal but acoustically pure "harmonic" ones. But since spectral music is played not by overtone-free sine-wave generators (as it might be in the computer lab) but by instruments that have their own harmonic spectra, the objective of spectral music is not to reconstitute or reproduce the timbre of the sonority analyzed in the sonogram, but rather to orchestrate unique timbre complexes — and "beautiful" ones at that, orchestration being the area in which the composer exercises subjective choice in manipulating the raw sonogram material.

Thus there is in spectralism, as in any composed music, an arbitrarily shaped component that reflects the composer's tastes and preferences. But that component inhabits the realm of timbre rather than the more traditional realm of rhythmicized pitches and intervals. In this, some have seen a continuing French (or "impressionist") predilection. In any case, it was not surprising that after a period of teaching at the University of California at Berkeley, Grisey should have been hired by the Paris Conservatory as a professor of orchestration, only later being given a composition class.

Spectral music resembles earlier electronically influenced instrumental music, like Penderecki's "sonorist" scores or especially Ligeti's *Atmosphères*, with which it shares a predilection for long, slowly-changing sounds. Like all "high-tech" music of its period, it depended on privileged access to rare and expensive equipment housed in elite research institutions like industrial labs, universities, and state-subsidized endowments such as IRCAM. Paul Lansky (b. 1944), a veteran of Winham's Princeton seminar, estimated that "by 1979 you could probably get a good computer-music studio for $250,000, if you could raise it."[60] After twenty years, in other words, it was still something only institutions could afford, and therefore a place to which entry was limited both by available time and by social barriers like mandatory professional affiliation.

"THEN ALONG CAME MIDI!"[61]

The exclamation is Lansky's, in recognition of the "great and revolutionary accomplishment" that, as we have seen, some writers have greeted as the dawn of a new musical era. Like the earlier elite phase of computer music, but this time by design rather than fortuitously, the new musical era was the by-product of industrial innovation in pursuit of profits. It was literally — and directly — created by capitalism, and can stand therefore as a musical monument to the global triumph of the free market and the worldwide conversion to an "information-based" economy. Since the latter is the standard economists' criterion of postmodernity, the "MIDI revolution" is perhaps the most intrinsically entitled of all late twentieth-century musical developments to the status of "postmodernist" standard-bearer.

The word MIDI is an acronym for "Musical Instrument Digital Interface." It was a protocol — a set of specifications — agreed upon by representatives of computer and synthesizer manufacturers between 1981 and 1983 to standardize their products so that they could all interact (and so that everybody's sales might stimulate everybody else's). This development took place virtually simultaneously with the beginning of mass-produced and affordable minicomputers of the kind that have since become ubiquitous household items.

All of a sudden, this nexus vastly miniaturized and domesticated the hardware required for computer synthesis of music. "I don't think anyone can really appreciate the meaning of this unless they have spent six months getting a [mainframe computer] to go 'beep,'" Lansky wrote. His description of the change, written in 1989 when it was still a recent thing, is the most vivid testimony on record:

> This really created a democratization of computer music in which it was no longer solely the domain of wealthy institutions and professors who could devote years to mastering its intricacies. . . .. Those of us who had sweated with software realized quite quickly that to get ninety-six oscillators singing in real time at a 50-kiloHertz sampling rate, and for less than two thousand dollars, was no trivial

accomplishment. And the Macintosh [the personal computer manufactured by Apple] really blew us away. One could only admire this cute little machine that you could lift with one hand and take with you anywhere, that could give you intimate control over those ninety-six oscillators. . . . I still marvel when I am able to open a factory-sealed box and get sound out within twenty minutes.[62]

The new accessibility and ease of sound synthesis using home computers connected via MIDI to synthesizers was accompanied by the development and marketing of a pair of inventions that similarly revolutionized the process of patterning and manipulating sound materials — that is, composition itself. One was the sampler, a device that stores and instantly retrieves recorded sounds of any kind; can subject them to instantaneous ("real-time") modifications like transposition, compression, elongation, "looping," or reversal; and can even engineer the gradual transformation of any recorded sound into any other by a process similar to video "morphing." The other was the sequencer, a device that puts digitally stored sounds into a programmed order that can encompass thousands of individual units.

Samplers work on the same principle as digital recording itself. Whereas earlier forms of recording (now called "analog") actually simulated continuous sound waves in the form of grooves in shellac or plastic disks (phonograph records) or by magnetizing iron filings (tape), digital recording samples waveforms in tiny slices (up to 50,000 per second) and stores the slices as numerical information that when reconverted and played back gives the illusion of continuous sound as a moving picture produces the illusion of continuous motion out of a rapid sequence of still photographs. A sampler does not just store microscopic bits like these but can accommodate and transform recorded units of up to three minutes' duration. As Gann writes, a composer using a sampler equipped with a keyboard "can record a cicada, a train whistle, a car crash, and play cicada melodies, train whistle melodies, car crash melodies." The "old promise of electronic music — that any noise could become available for musical use"[63] — became a practical reality in a way that the pioneering composers of musique concrète could never have imagined.

Between 1980 and 1984, the price of a sampler capable of all the operations just described fell from about $25,000 to about $1,300, putting it within range of mass marketability. At the same time, the operations performed by a sequencer were made available in the form of software programs that could be installed in personal computers. As a result, by the mid-1980s (to quote Gann once again), "it was possible for middle-class teenagers to have, in their bedrooms, music-producing equipment that put to shame the great electronic studios of a mere 10 years before."[64] The "classics" of electronic music have aged — become quaint — in a way that no other music of its time has done, since even if music does not "progress," technology certainly does. Speaking from two generations of classroom experience on both sides of the lectern, Gann writes that Varèse's *Poème électronique* (see chapter 63) "sounded like music from Mars when I first heard the old Columbia recording in 1972, but students today giggle when they hear it. Its spooky 'ooooo gaaah' voice samples seem camp in comparison with the sampling experiments of any ambitious high school computer jockey."[65]

FIRST FRUITS

The sample-based composition best known to audiences at century's end—the first "classic" of the new technology—was *Different Trains* (1988), a late or "post-minimalist" composition by Steve Reich. It was commissioned by and dedicated to Kronos Quartet, a San Francisco-based ensemble with a self-avowed postmodern repertoire (mixing avant-garde compositions and twentieth-century "classics" with transcriptions of early music, "world music," jazz, and rock) and over 400 hundred premieres to its credit. In keeping with the group's adventurous spirit, Reich, who had already been planning to use a sampling keyboard for his next composition, wrote a piece that pitted the live quartet against two prerecorded quartet tracks and a track of sampled voices that compared the composer's experience as a child in the early 1940s, shuttling back and forth across the continent between the New York and Los Angeles residences of his divorced parents, and the simultaneous experiences of Jewish children in Europe, who were being transported by train from the ghettos of Eastern Europe to the Nazi extermination camp at Auschwitz.

The live and recorded quartets play in a typically "minimalist" style, only this time their chugging subtactile pulses symbolize the actual chug and clack of moving trains, evoked also by periodic train whistles that in the piece's midsection are transformed into air-raid sirens as Reich's own childhood memories give way to the imagined nightmare of the Holocaust. The sampled voices in the first section are those of the composer's childhood governess, interviewed in later life, and a train historian. In the middle section, the voices are those of Holocaust survivors, collected from oral history archives. In the final section, samples from the two sources are mixed.

The samples, resolved into musical phrases approximating their pitch and contour, dictate the music's tempos and tonal modulations. (It was because the live quartet needed to be coordinated with the shifting tempos of the samples that the recorded quartet tracks, which set the tempos and provide the live quartet with cues, were necessary.) The understated climax comes in the third section, when the train historian's voice is heard matter-of-factly remarking, "Today, they're all gone." Remembering his voice from the first section, one knows that he was talking about the American transcontinental trains of the 1930s and 1940s. But remembering the second section, one cannot help relating his comment to the Jewish children, too. Both a synthesis of the subject matter and an effective musical close, the moment is haunting. (The coda adds another ironic and quintessentially postmodernist stab: one of the survivors recalls the Germans' sincere love of music, preventing today's music-loving listeners from deriving any complacent sense of moral superiority from their esthetic sensibilities.)

Different Trains is almost unique among artistic memorials to the Holocaust in its successful avoidance of pomposity and false comfort. There are no villains and no heroes, just the perception that while this happened here, that happened there (or, as Reich told an interviewer, "There but for the grace of God . . ."), and a stony invitation to reflect. Since then, Reich has used the voice-sampling technique in a series of multimedia compositions (or "documentary video operas") that he has produced in collaboration with his wife, the video artist Beryl Korot. Like *Different Trains*, they all use collage techniques to address contemporary social and moral concerns.

One, *The Cave* (1993), is a meditation on the conflict between Israelis and Palestinians viewed against its historical background as symbolized by the cave of Machpelah, believed to be the burial site of the patriarch Abraham. Another, *Three Tales* (2000), juxtaposes accounts of the destruction of the German airship Hindenburg in 1937; the atomic and hydrogen bomb tests at Bikini Atoll between 1946 and 1958; and Dolly the sheep, the first successful cloning of a mammal, in 1997. A warning against blind faith in technological progress, the work adopts a typically ironic postmodern stance insofar as it is itself an example of art that relies on — or, even, arises out of — the application of advanced technology.

Reich's applications of the new technology remain conservative, however, as one might perhaps expect from a composer of his generation. For more thoroughgoing applications one must turn to composers born in the 1950s or later, for whom it was a "given" rather than a challenge to be mastered. At the radical extreme is John Oswald (b. 1953), a Canadian composer who fashions compositions entirely out of samples of existing music, and who flaunts his postmodern challenge to the whole idea of "original composition" by defining his method of musicmaking as "plunderphonics." A CD by that name, issued in 1989, was a collage of humorously altered and intermixed rerecorded sound bites from every source in sight, juxtaposing the standard classical repertoire (Beethoven, Stravinsky), rhythm-and-blues (James Brown), standard pop (Beatles, Michael Jackson), hardcore rock (Metallica), and country-and-western (Dolly Parton). Knowing that his "electroquoting" violated copyrights, he distributed the disc free of charge, with the additional (unenforceable) proviso that copies could not be resold. Nevertheless, "prudes in the Recording Industry"[66] (as Oswald has referred to the lawyers who threatened him) filed suit and succeeded in having the disc suppressed the next year, their pretext being a cover illustration that illustrated the album concept (which included the "aural-sex transformation" of Dolly Parton's voice into a male register) with a copyrighted photo of Michael Jackson's head atop a nude female torso.

Of course the stir thus created was good for business; soon afterward Oswald received not only permission but an actual commission from Elektra/Nonesuch to create a plunderphonics compact disc from its own extensive catalog that the firm could market as a sort of advertisement. (It was called *Elektrax*.) Other sampler composers, like Carl Stone (b. 1953), perform their work "live," sitting onstage with a laptop computer and tapping its keys to summon forth prerecorded performances, looped and "morphed" into configurations the original artists would not have recognized.

MODERNISTS IN POSTMODERNIST CLOTHING?

Even composers who do not actually (or always) use the new machines write in a manner that vividly reflects their influence. John Zorn (b. 1953) has been touted by the *New Grove Dictionary* as "an archetypal example of the composer in the media age."[67] Putting it more bluntly, he writes that "I've got an incredibly short attention span," and that his music is meant for listeners who, like him, grew up with television.

In some sense, it is true that my music is ideal for people who are impatient, because it is jam-packed with information that is changing very fast. . . . You've got to realize that speed is taking over the world. Look at the kids growing up with computers and video games—which are ten times faster than the pinball machines we used to play. There's an essential something that young musicians have, something you can lose touch with as you get older. . . . It's a whole new way of thinking, of living. And we've got to keep up with it. I'll probably die trying.[68]

Maybe it is not quite that new; Zorn's pronouncements are not that different from the ones that filled Futurist manifestos nearly a hundred years ago. If they had our technology, the Futurists would surely have lived as fast as we do. But the point is that we do have the technology and can realize some old dreams. Zorn's perfervid paragraph comes from the notes that accompany *Spillane* (1986), a much-discussed collage balanced on the cusp between improvisation and composition, live performance and sample patchwork, that seemed determined to take eclecticism to its limit.

Zorn first made his name as the leader of an improvising band that dazzled audiences with its ability to shift styles in midstream (or midphrase), and a range of reference that recognized no boundaries, incorporating Josquin des Prez, TV jingles, Indian ragas, and every type of American pop. His self-proclaimed models were the soundtracks that accompanied the animated cartoons (Bugs Bunny, Road Runner) that children his age imbibed in great quantities on TV. These cartoon scores were composed of studio-recorded snippets that were spliced and intercut to follow the breakneck antics on the screen. Another source of inspiration was commercial novelty bands like the one led by Spike Jones (1911–65), who began by incorporating unusual percussion instruments into his arrangements of pop standards and proceeded from there into a boundless world of wacky sound effects. The first big hit scored by Spike Jones and His City Slickers—*Der Fuehrer's Face* (1942), in which the familiar Nazi salute ("Heil!") was accompanied throughout by a Bronx cheer (or "raspberry")—originally accompanied a Walt Disney war-propaganda cartoon. Zorn's band became proficient in the use of raucous sound effects—screams, whistles, gunshots, explosions—that punctuated the music and served as signals to the players for sudden changes of tempo and texture.

While no short-range "structural" coherence could be detected in a Zorn composition—that was in a way the whole point—his performances made sense as accompaniments to a vividly implied scenario. Just as Spike Jones affectionately spoofed tender love ballads, the twenty-five-minute *Spillane* (named after Mickey Spillane, whose Mike Hammer detective novels were the basis for many popular Hollywood low-budget or "B" movies) parodies the soundtrack of a manically condensed "gumshoe" mystery, mixing screams, police dogs and sirens, jazz combos, "fade" and "dissolve" effects using synthesizers, muttering voices adding atmosphere to instrumental solos, and so on. The CD version subjects the music to further "cinematic" manipulation, treating the live performance sounds like raw material for sampling and intercutting, just as studio sound editors treat the music of an actual soundtrack.

Such an ambitious work could no longer be achieved with the required precision through actual on-the-spot improvisation, so Zorn began organizing his work with the use of file cards containing directions for the performers. "I give the musicians the music for the section that we'll be working on," he told an interviewer:

> We'd rehearse it, get it perfect, and then record it onto tape. Then I'd give them the music for the second section of the piece. Bit by bit we'd build it up. An additive process, with the musicians concentrating on the details of one section at a time, but relatively blind, as far as where the piece is going. Like a director in film, only I would have the overall perspective. We'd roll the tape back, listen to the previous section recorded, and then just where they're supposed to come in, I'd cue them and they'd begin performing. It's like a series of short live performances put directly onto tape. No splices, no splices ever. Everything just put right into place on tape using A-B sets of tracks so that you never actually cut into the previous performance. Sections literally overlapped, with the reverb of the previous section dying behind the beginning of the following one.[69]

When his recordings began attracting the attention of "legitimate" performing groups (including the inevitable commission from Kronos Quartet), he made as little compromise as possible with traditional notation and the kinds of forms it enabled (or imposed). *Cat o' Nine Tails* (1988), the Kronos score, consisted of sixty "moments" (borrowing a term from Stockhausen) on file cards that covered a typical Zorn "mishmash" (his word), ranging from allusions to the standard repertoire to cartoon noises to "random" effects. Some were fully notated. At other times, the musicians are told something like "between this written piece and that written piece, you have six seconds to fool around with *col legno* [drawing the wood of the bow across the strings]."[70] But even when unwritten, this was composed rather than improvised music; the initiative belonged at all times to the composer, who planned each "random" effect in advance.

The music remained a sort of soundtrack; but its resolute nonlinearity reminded many critics of the cutting techniques employed on "Music Television" (MTV), where (reversing the traditional procedure) visual accompaniments were added to music tracks to allow for their exposure on TV. These supersophisticated treatments suggested to many artists that the much-decried short attention span of the TV or video-game generation was not a dulling of wits but more probably the opposite. The ever-faster pace of media impressions had greatly speeded the process of comprehension. Concepts of linear logic and "organic" wholeness that had previously dominated musical esthetics were called into question. Indeed, as the epigraph from Jonathan Kramer at the top of this chapter confirms, listening (or, more generally, perceptual) habits fostered by the age of remote-controlled tuners and car radios eventually, and inevitably, affected the way in which music was composed. Zorn's is perhaps the most consummate manifestation, but it is far from an isolated or negligible one.

And as his music became more ambitious and widely recognized, the composer began, despite his protestations and affectations, to be treated as an adult. No longer regarded as a throwback to the irresponsible naïveté of a Spike Jones, he was held more accountable for the contents of his product. It was in some ways a painful compliment. In the early 1990s, appearances by Zorn's band were picketed in Los Angeles by Asian-American women offended by his stereotypical depiction of a Japanese love slave in "Forbidden Fruit" (1987) and the cover art on some of his more recent CDs, especially *Torture Garden* (1990), which showed Asian women being subjected to sexual abuse.

These protests came at a time when several avant-garde artists were under intemperate attack by members of the United States Congress who disapproved of the disbursement of tax revenues, through the National Endowment for the Arts, to recipients whose art embodied controversial or (to them) offensive messages. The situation was complicated by the widespread perception that these attacks were directed more at the Endowment itself than at the artists, who were being used, in effect, as scapegoats to justify an otherwise indefensible political posture. Zorn at first defended himself as if he were under a comparable attack, asserting his right to free expression and portraying his critics as censors. "You're really not able to step back and analyze what you're doing," he told an interviewer in 1992:

> I really try to just follow my instincts, whether it pisses off people who are trying to be politically correct, or who are concerned with a certain musical tradition. That cannot concern me; I can't think about trying to censor my work. I've got to follow through wherever my crazy mind takes me. Artists stand on the outside of society. I think that's an important point: I see the artist as someone who stands on the outside; they create their own rules in a lot of ways and shouldn't try to be socially responsible; being irresponsible is the very point of their existence. That's what makes that person able to comment on what's going on around them, because they aren't restricted by the censors or the powers that be — or in the case of what's happening in the arena today, the Big Brother that used to be watching in the '60s is now your next-door neighbor. . . .
>
> I'm figuring a lot of shit out, drawing my moral line, and saying, "Fuck you. I don't need this. I've got to follow my artistic vision, whether you think that it's repulsive or anti-women or anti-Asian or whatever. I have to follow it through.[71]

Despite the postmodernity of his media, Zorn was expressing a typically modernist bravado. Yet eventually, at the urging of the Nonesuch record firm (with which he later broke), he agreed at least to repackage the offending CDs and issued a somewhat grudging apology: "As an artist you can't please everyone. If I took all their criticism to heart I'd never create anything. I don't want to make it harder for Asians in this country; I'm on their side. But frankly, I don't think my records are doing that."[72] Under commercial pressure, an intransigent artist was forced or shamed into a compromise with public decency. From the modernist perspective, that had to count as a defeat.

But Susan McClary, writing as a postmodernist, gave the outcome of the collision between Zorn, his label, and his public an interestingly optimistic interpretation, seeing public indignation as distinctly preferable to the public indifference that had, in the century following Baudelaire, typically greeted modern "art" music, at least in the democratic West. "If art music has been spared such scrutiny for several decades," she comments, "it is in large part because so little was at stake for either composer or audience."[73] She argues further that the far greater public scrutiny, and occasional outcry, that contemporary popular culture attracts — even though its "level of transgression" is often far tamer than Zorn's open embrace of sadism — is evidence of popular culture's greater creative vitality, or at least its greater pertinence to issues that truly matter to most people.

To maintain this position may be to underestimate how much the issue of creative freedom truly matters to artists. The geopolitical polarization engendered by the cold war made that freedom — or, more precisely, that perception of freedom — an issue worth the sacrifice of public relevance to many artists in the West, who saw totalitarian regimentation as, if not the only alternative, then at least the one that needed to be most vigilantly resisted, whatever the social cost. That was indeed a heavy stake for composers, if not for audiences.

But if that is true, then McClary's optimism is not misplaced. If anything, it is even more cheering to note the coincidence of postmodern esthetics, which embrace exchange and communication between artist and public and all the attendant risks, and the end of the cold war with its hardening influence on cultural attitudes. The year 1989, which saw the fall of Communist regimes in Eastern Europe and the opening of the Berlin Wall, may in the end have been as great a watershed for Euro-American art as it has been for Euro-American politics. Polarizing attitudes that once held artists on both sides of the Iron Curtain captive have been deconstructed, perhaps permanently, by the march of events on the eve of the twenty-first century.

In the West, it may no longer be quite so necessary for artists to maintain belief in "the irreconcilable nature of the esthetic and the social worlds," to quote the German cultural critic Jürgen Habermas, voicing a creed that goes back long before the cold war, to the wellsprings of Romanticism. Yet John Zorn, who practically paraphrased Habermas in some of the vulgar remarks quoted above, turned right around and told an interviewer that "I'm at the point now where maybe I can make somebody cry with music; that's been a dream all my life."[74] The contradiction, the seesaw between social alienation and social communion, was as old as Romanticism itself. Postmodernism seems to have encouraged communion to reassert its rights.

A GLIMPSE OF THE FUTURE?

Even composers who do not use samplers use sequencing programs, and this has affected virtually everyone's musical style. Very common since the 1980s have been "layered" textures of polymetrically superimposed instrumental ostinatos, something that can be produced effortlessly by a computer with a MIDI connection to a bunch of synthesizers. Laying down track upon track is curiously reminiscent of the techniques of "successive" composition associated with the medieval motet. As in the case of Meredith Monk's vocal compositions, the late-twentieth-century avant-garde links up with musical practices prevalent in an age when literacy had not yet gotten very far in supplanting oral composition and transmission. Computer-assisted "real-time" electronic composition — used sometimes in performance, sometimes as a basis for written elaboration — is another aspect of the same resurgence of "orality."

Computer interface has affected performance as well. Digital "controllers" that record and store information that tracks the physical actions of players can be hooked up via MIDI to virtually any instrument to reproduce, edit, and modify a real-time performance: a player-piano, for example, that can reproduce a pianist's rendition at any tempo, at any transposition that the keyboard will accommodate, with changed dynamics, even with octave doublings (not to mention corrected errors). Other machines (e.g., "electronic gloves") can complement the sounds of a live performance with computer-controlled modifications instigated by the players' movements. Dancers can create their own musical accompaniments in the act with movement sensors that activate synthesizers.

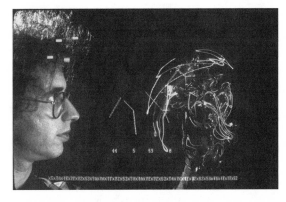

FIG. 10-8   Tod Machover (b. 1953), director of computer music applications at the Massachusetts Institute of Technology, modeling his "electronic glove," officially named Exos Dexterous Hand Master.

Nor have basic changes been exclusively technological. As always, technological breakthroughs have had unpredicted reverberations and will go on having unpredictable ones. Gann notes a basic "philosophic" or attitudinal change in composers since the advent of samplers: rather than the individual note, he has declared, the musical "atom" or minimal manipulable unit has become any sound complex that can be recorded and stored. To use his actual words, sampling has "led music away from atomism toward a more holistic approach."[75] If one regards serialism, which manipulates individual notes with singular assiduousness, as the most "atomistic" style, then Gann's remark offers a possible explanation for the paradoxical effect that working with computers has had on so many composers who originally approached the medium as a means of securing easier control over an ever greater range of serial algorithms, but who instead found themselves seduced into rejecting their motivating premises.

But the implications do not end even there. Observing that it is notation that creates the "note" (as opposed to the "tone"), Gann suggests that "the sampler frees composers from the habits inculcated by Western notation." And indeed, it is now not only possible, but increasingly common, to create, "perform," and preserve music that is recognizably within the traditions of classical music without ever using notation. Music, without any necessary loss of conceptual complexity or novelty, can now take leave of the eye. The lineaments of a postliterate age are clearly discernable.

"Composed" (that is, fixed rather than improvised) music will surely go on being not only possible but common in a postliterate age, just as it had been possible and common in preliterate ages, and as it remains in nonliterate societies. In preliterate cultures compositions can be fixed in memory and reproduced orally or (with rehearsal) by ensembles of performers; in the postliterate future pieces will go right on being fixed and reproduced in those time-honored ways, but it will also be possible to fix them digitally and reproduce them via synthesizer or via MIDI. Indeed, it is already possible to do these things, even if only a minority of composers now work that way.

When a majority of composers work that way, the postliterate age will have arrived. That will happen when — or if — reading music becomes a rare specialized skill, of practical value only for reproducing "early music" (meaning all composed music performed live). There has already been much movement in this direction. Very few, especially in America, now learn musical notation as part of their general education. The lowered cultural prestige of literate musical genres has accompanied the marginalization of musical literacy and abetted it; the availability of technologies that can circumvent notation in the production of complex composed music may eventually render musical literacy, like knowledge of ancient scripts, superfluous to all but scholars.

Related to the general loss of musical literacy in the wider culture has been the decline of the music-publishing industry. Amateur and school performance of literate repertoires having become far less prevalent than in the past, the demand for "sheet music" shows signs of eventually drying up. New music being at once the most expensive of all types to publish (because it must be freshly set up and edited and because the composer must be paid) and the least promising of a financial return, it is no wonder that, as Gann puts it, "music publishers have quit publishing all but a tiny amount of the most conservative new music." Interestingly, though, Gann does not see this entirely as a loss. Like many adventurous composers at the end of the twentieth century, he looks forward to the benefits as well as the costs of the coming postliterate musical culture:

> It is nearly impossible for a composer to get his or her scores distributed through commercial channels in the 1990s. On the other hand, compact discs have become relatively cheap to produce, and distribution channels have multiplied. Therefore, whereas the mid-twentieth-century composer distributed his music through scores and had a difficult time getting recorded, those possibilities are reversed for today's young composer. To at least some extent this reversal has been healthy, for midcentury composers showed a tendency to consider the score the actual music, with a corresponding loss of concern for how the music sounded; today, more and more music can be judged only for how it sounds, for the score may either not exist or be practically unavailable.[76]

And yet, although in the long run it cannot help affecting style along with every other aspect of musical life, it is by no means clear that the advent of postliterate composition will necessarily produce any immediate change in musical style. After all, the advent of notation did not have any immediate effect on the style of the music it was invented to preserve. It coexisted with oral methods for at least a couple of centuries without gaining the upper hand; nor have oral methods been wholly supplanted. There is every reason to expect a similar period of coexistence at the other end of the history of music as a literate tradition, one that will last far longer than this book will go on being read.

And yet eventually the advent of literacy did have a profound impact on musical style. Twelfth-century plainchant (for example, the Kyrie *Cum jubilo*, discussed and analyzed in the first volume of the Oxford History of Western Music), composed after notation had been in wide monastic use for at least 200 years, and after a body of "theory" or analytical work had grown up around the written-down and musically (or "modally") classified Gregorian chant, was written in an elegantly integrated and interwoven form that bore all the earmarks of analytical thinking — the kind of thinking that relates parts to wholes. That is the kind of thinking that notation facilitates (or, indeed, enables).

Now compare John Zorn's description of his music, quoted above, as being shaped by an "additive process, with the musicians concentrating on the details of one section at a time, but relatively blind, as far as where the piece is going." That is nonanalytical, indeed antianalytical thinking. Still an exceptional (and therefore noteworthy) way of thinking about composed music at the end of the twentieth century, it may be a harbinger of the postliterate future, when such thinking about music will be considered normal and undeserving of comment.

To a considerable extent postliterate media have already accustomed us to non-analytical or additive thought processes: think of broadcast news with its "sound bites," or MTV with its brusque nonlinear cutting techniques that have influenced all movie editors. Additive thought processes are no less intrinsically "intelligent" than analytical ones, but they require different skills: quick processing of impressions rather than "deep" reflection, the drawing of inferences from surface juxtapositions (contrasts) rather than underlying connections (similarities). That is the way one has to listen to Zorn's music, and that of many if not most of his contemporaries, to say nothing of his juniors. Postliterate listening as well as postliterate composition is already upon us.

But we are not unprepared. As the epigraph atop this chapter from the theorist Jonathan Kramer reminds us, "we all spin the dial." Even when we listen to the traditional repertoire of classical music at the start of the twenty-first century, we often if not usually listen to it out of context and out of sequence. If we turn on the car radio en route to the shopping mall, we may briefly visit the development section from the first movement of a favorite symphony, and encounter the finale on our way home. Our clock radio usually greets us in the morning with the middle of a highly structured piece, but we experience no serious disorientation even if the piece is unfamiliar, as long as it conforms (as "radio music" is sure to do) to one or more of the many prototypes we have stored in our memories. The same process of comparison with prototypes makes collage compositions intelligible and (sometimes) interesting.

BACK TO NATURE?

Our ease with fragmentary listening may be an artifact of (or an adaptation to) modern living. But it might also be "natural," as at least one recent theory of music, itself possibly an artifact of the burgeoning postliterate age, contends. That theory, called "concatenationism," received its most extensive exposition in a 1997 book called *Music in the Moment*. The title reflects an abiding interest of many theorists of avant-garde music (like Jonathan Kramer), who have responded to Karlheinz Stockhausen's notion of *Momentform*, the idea that contemporary composition is (or may be, or should be) based on a series of unique irreducible impressions or *Gestalts*, a concept that obviously points toward the "musical atom" theories of high-tech theorists of the 1990s like Kyle Gann.

Music in the Moment, however, was the work of a philosopher, Jerrold Levinson, rather than a composer or a music theorist, and the theory it propounded was instantly controversial. Levinson maintained that the idea of "moment form" actually described all actual musical listening (no matter who was doing it), and that holistic (or integrated, or unified, or "organic") theories of musical form, as well as holistic or unifying systems of formal analysis (up to and including the vaunted Schenkerian method, taught by the 1990s in many European and virtually all American conservatories and universities, which reduced complex compositions to a single underlying or overarching basic progression called the "Ursatz"), were based not on listening to music but on looking at it — or rather, at its notation.

Musical coherence as actually perceived by listeners, Levinson argued, was based on moment-to-moment connections, grasped and processed "additively" as the music actually unfolded in time, not on the far-ranging "global" relationships analysts analyzed (and which composers trained to analyze that way might try to conceptualize in composing). Such relationships, Levinson argued, being atemporal, were essentially amusical. Inquiring into "the degree to which musical understanding requires reflective or intellectual awareness of musical architecture or large-scale musical structuring," the philosopher concluded that "that degree is approximately zero." Instead, he maintained, "all that basic understanding requires is, as it were, listening in the moment."[77]

The position was surely overstated for effect. Everybody knows from experience that memory and prediction play a significant part in musical understanding, just as they do in understanding any temporal unfolding: all speech (not only narratives), as well as drama, cinema, and dance. Experience, moreover, hones everybody's memory and prediction skills, and our understanding of any utterance is laden both with unconscious theory and with awareness of context. Nobody literally listens only in the moment. But as Levinson forcefully argued, nobody literally listens to musical wholes either. He stated the "concatenationist" position in the form of four postulates:

1. *Musical understanding* centrally involves neither aural grasp of a large span of music as a whole, nor intellectual grasp of large-scale connections between parts; understanding music is centrally a matter of apprehending individual bits of music and immediate progressions from bit to bit.

2. *Musical enjoyment* is had only in the successive parts of a piece of music, and not in the whole as such, or in relationships of parts widely separated in time.

3. *Musical form* is centrally a matter of cogency of succession, moment to moment and part to part.

4. *Musical value* rests wholly on the impressiveness of individual parts and the cogency of successions between them, and not on features of large-scale form per se; the worthwhileness of experience of music relates directly only to the former.[78]

This argument, which has been confirmed in some of its aspects by empirical psychological testing, was widely welcomed as being at the very least a healthy corrective to its opposite extreme; and its welcome was enhanced by its timing. It joined the other forces and tendencies toward postliteracy that this chapter has been describing.

It had always been one of the main virtues of musical notation that it enabled music to become visual as well as aural, and to occupy space as well as time. In this way music could be stored and stockpiled, easily taken from place to place, learned otherwise than by rote, and conceptualized in new ways, some of them indispensable to the art of composition as it evolved over a thousand years of development. But it also always fostered the vices of its virtues, at least potentially, since it always offered lettered or "learned" musicians the temptation of concentrating on the virtual reality of music-as-seen — "spatialized representations"[79] of music, as Levinson called them — in preference to the physical reality of music-as-heard.

As related in chapter 3, that trend reached a disquieting peak, in some of the music composed in the mid-twentieth century, especially in the academy, the seat of learning. And at the same time another peak began to be decried, namely the bland literalism that had become the norm in academically influenced performances of classical music, which strove above all to reproduce the music as it looked on the page, sometimes in active contemptuous rejection of the traditions of performer-to-performer dissemination that persisted as an oral component of modern musical culture. Both kinds of hyperliteracy were significantly reined in during the last quarter of the twentieth century.

In its more radical formulations Levinson's theory was obviously a reaction (and probably an overreaction) to these unhappy peaks. But more significant was the seriousness with which it was taken to heart by many turn-of-the-century musicians, including repentant analysts and composers, despite Levinson's specific disclaimer that he was addressing not learned musicians but musical amateurs like himself, whose habits of listening and appreciating music he had set out to defend against academic snobbery. "No doubt some people," he conceded,

> having acquired analytical dispositions and descriptive technical resources in the course of their musical education, found their fundamental listening transformed to a truly significant degree. But I am not one of them, and I suspect that such listeners are not the norm among those who can rightly claim both to know and to love the bulk of what constitutes the broad repertoire of classical music. It is an implicit aim of this book to defend such listeners — ones who, though untutored, are experienced, attentive, and passionate.[80]

But he had touched a nerve among the tutored as well, many of whom had to agree with Levinson, in spite of themselves, that much of the theory that supported twentieth-century composition (and performance) was based on a "tendency to misapply the results of musical analysis,"[81] and ultimately, therefore, on a misapplication of musical literacy. The swerve toward postliteracy, instigated by "Green" mavericks like Partch and Monk and powerfully abetted by new technologies, had received a theoretical reinforcement within the very bastion of the literate tradition. It is less relevant to our present purposes to try and decide how valid Levinson's theory is than to see it (and, more particularly, its reception) as a symptom of a general tendency that had many other symptoms as well. Suffice it to say that such a theory would never have gained a serious hearing in the musical academy had it appeared a quarter of a century earlier than it did.

One final augury of an emergent postliterate culture, and a particularly vivid one, was the rise at the very end of the twentieth century of "interactive sound [or sound-and-image] installations" — computer software programs that allow users to call forth very complex sound patterns, sometimes allied with visual patterns as well, merely by moving through a space equipped with sensors and deploying an electronic glove or handheld signaling device. The creators of such programs—Luke DuBois, Mark McNamara, Timothy Polashek, Jason Freeman, David Birchfield, and others whose installations were displayed at a spectacular and widely reported exhibit mounted at Columbia University in connection with an electronic music festival in July 2000—call themselves "sound designers" rather than composers. (Recall Beethoven's insistence, near the end of his life, on calling himself a "sound poet" or *Tondichter* rather than a composer.) And rightly so, for their work eliminates distinctions between composers, performers, and listeners. The user of an interactive installation is all three at once—or none of the above.

Anthony Tommasini, a reviewer for the *New York Times*, found the exhibit "seductive and unsettling," not least (he thought) because once listeners become empowered to create music instantly to their individual taste, there will be no need for critics, either. But he managed to console himself with an interesting thought:

> For those of us who persist in thinking of a musical composition as a creative statement of a trained and artistic individual, there was one reassuring thing: though the users of these interactive installations worked alone, having witnesses watching and listening on extra earphones seemed a large part of the enjoyment. So composers as we have known them may disappear someday. Yet perhaps the concert, or at least a new kind of collective listening experience, will continue.[82]

PAYING THE PIPER, CALLING THE TUNE

That, at any rate, is one possible future that may be projected at the dawn of the third millennium on the basis of trends observable at present. Whether it is a probable future (let alone "the" future) will depend on as yet unforeseeable factors and variables of a kind that always conspires to make monkeys out of "futurologists." As always, among the most potent and volatile factors will be patterns of patronage. So let us end this chapter, and this book, with one last look at how that factor—of all factors the one most susceptible to "external" stimuli (demographic, sociopolitical, economic)—has been functioning.

Ever since the watershed of the sixties, predictions of the imminent demise of "classical music" have been rife. Its audience, undermined by the decline in public music education and decimated by defections to pop, was assumed to be aging, indeed dying off. Whether as a symptom of this process or as one of its causes, media coverage for classical music steadily and drastically diminished over the 1970s and 1980s (coinciding with the rise in "serious" pop coverage), as did the number of radio stations that purveyed it.

In the 1970s, classical music accounted for 20 percent of record sales in Japan, its most avid market, 10 percent in Western Europe, and 5 percent in North America. As the medium of commercial recording switched in the mid-1980s from LP to CD, and the American market share for classical record sales stabilized at approximately 3 percent (about the same as jazz, increasingly regarded and described as "America's classical music"), its status was relegated to that of a "niche product," serving a tiny, closed-off clientele whose needs could be met with reissues rather than costly new recordings of the standard repertoire. Major symphony orchestras, especially in the United States, found themselves without recording contracts, with serious consequences for the incomes of their personnel. Major labels began concentrating on "crossover" projects, in which the most popular classical performers collaborated with artists from other walks of musical life in an effort to achieve sales that might transcend the limits of the classical "niche." The huge fees such artists commanded virtually squeezed others out of the recording budget altogether. Classical music seemed destined to become the culture industry's "basket case."

The implications for composers seemed particularly grave, since this period of attrition had no effect on the numbers trained within the protected walls of the academy, which as always offered temporary insulation from the vagaries of the market. The result was a vast overpopulation of composers, whose numbers swelled even as their outlets contracted. Their activity, as already implied above, came ironically to resemble the sort of self-publication and self-promotion that was known in the declining Soviet Union (where it was a response to political rather than economic pressure) as *samizdat*. Their work met no measurable consumer demand and found little source of subsidy. Its main purpose became the securing of academic employment and promotion—another sort of niche—that enabled its creators to train the next generation of socially unsupported and unwanted composers, and so on in possibly meaningless perpetuity.

In the late 1980s and 1990s, however, that pattern began unexpectedly to change, permitting the emergence of a composing elite—tiny, perhaps, but larger than ever before—whose work was suddenly in demand, sought out by traditional performance organizations for performance at major venues, and who could in some cases live off their commissions and performance royalties without seeking academic employment. New York's Metropolitan Opera, for example, which had not presented a premiere since the 1960s, commissioned four operas during the this period, of which three achieved production: *The Ghosts of Versailles* (1987; produced 1991), an opera by John Corigliano based on *La mère coupable* ("The guilty mother"), the one remaining member of Beaumarchais's *Figaro* trilogy that had not already been turned into an operatic classic by Mozart (*The Marriage of Figaro*) or Rossini (*The Barber of Seville*); *The Voyage* (first performed on Columbus Day, 1992) by Philip Glass, commemorating the 500th anniversary of Columbus's arrival in the New World; and *The Great Gatsby* (first performed on New Year's Day, 2000) by John Harbison, based on the novel of the same name by F. Scott Fitzgerald.

The Harbison work had been jointly commissioned by the Met and the Chicago Lyric Opera; this ensured that it would have a life beyond its premiere production (and also allowed the composer the chance to revise the opera on the basis of its reception, as was traditional in opera's heyday, but discouraged in the later twentieth century both by economic conditions and by the ideology of modernism). The Met and the Chicago Lyric also issued a tandem commission to William Bolcom for an opera based on Arthur Miller's play *A View from the Bridge*, premiered in Chicago in 1999 and significantly revised for its New York performances in 2001.

FIG. 10-9   Scene from act I of Philip Glass's opera *The Voyage*.

Nor were these houses alone: the San Francisco opera commissioned several works in the 1990s, including *A Streetcar Named Desire*, after Tennessee Williams's play, by André Previn (b. 1929), and *Dead Man Walking* by Jake Heggie (b. 1961), based on a memoir of death row prisoners by Sister Helen Prejean that had already been turned into a major Hollywood movie. Just how "bankable" a commodity the Met thought new opera now might be is indicated by the generous terms of the commissions — especially the one to Glass, who received $325,000. (Expenditures on the production approached $2 million.)

In part this seeming rebirth was a result of the changes wrought by "postmodernism" in the relative prestige of composing styles. Harbison had been trained as a serialist, and of course Glass was one of the founders, in the 1960s, of "hard-core" minimalism. Both had abandoned their earlier avant-garde positions and were now meeting in the vast moderate middle ground labeled "neoromanticism." And yet there had always been relatively "accessible" composers available for commissioning, including some specialists in vocal or theatrical genres like Ned Rorem or Hugo Weisgall (1912–97), who had gone untapped by the major houses all during the 1970s and 1980s. It seemed that the new interest in opera had to do with new sources of money to support it. It was tied, that is, to the interests of new patrons.

A NEW TOPICALITY

The new interest in supporting classical composition in traditional "audience" genres affected the concert hall as well as the opera house. The most spectacular case, perhaps, was that of John Corigliano's First Symphony (1989), first performed in 1990 by the Chicago Symphony Orchestra, and later, internationally, by almost 100 others. Along with its lavish orchestration (including parts for virtuoso piano and cello soloists), its rhetorical intensity, and its at times poignant use of collage, the symphony's topicality contributed to its success. A memorial to victims of the AIDS epidemic, it had four movements each dedicated to the memory of a deceased friend, and gave public expression to the composer's "feelings of loss, anger, and frustration," in alternation with "the bittersweet nostalgia of remembering."

So if the composer John Adams's "impression," voiced to an interviewer in November 2000, was a true one—namely, "that in terms of commissions there's never been a more bullish period in American history"[83] than the 1990s—it is testimony

FIG. 10-10   John Adams, 1991.

to a new consensus among composers and their patrons that contemporary classical music can and should have the sort of topical relevance more usually found in popular culture, and that works relevant to the topical concerns of the contemporary cultural elite are the ones that will be (and should be) rewarded. John Adams was in a good position to know, having been among the most conspicuous beneficiaries of this dispensation. One of the moments that defined its emergence, in fact, took place in 1990, when the San Francisco opera rescinded a commission it had given to Hugo Weisgall for on opera on the "timeless" biblical story of Esther in favor of a topical opera by John Adams called *The Death of Klinghoffer*, based on the killing by Palestinian terrorists of an American Jew on board an Italian cruise ship in 1985.

Klinghoffer was the second opera Adams had composed in collaboration with the poet Alice Goodman (b. 1959) and the director Peter Sellars (b. 1957). The first, *Nixon in China* (1987), was the work that originally stimulated the new wave of commissions. Largely on the strength of Sellars's reputation as an operatic enfant terrible (known for radical "updatings" of familiar operas, such as a *Don Giovanni* set in the New York slums and a *Marriage of Figaro* set in a luxury apartment building often assumed to be Trump Tower), and on the assumption that it would satirize one of America's most controversial political figures, the opera had been jointly commissioned by four houses: the Houston Grand Opera, the Brooklyn Academy of Music, the John F. Kennedy Center for the Performing Arts in Washington, D.C., and the Netherlands Opera. Its four premieres took place between October 1987 and June 1988.

The work confounded expectations by being cast not as a farce but as a heroic opera that turned the title character, as well as the Chinese leaders Mao Tse-tung

FIG. 10-11   Scene from act I of the opera *Nixon in China* (Houston Grand Opera, 1987).

and Chou En-lai, into mythical representatives of their countries — naively idealistic young America and ancient, visionary China. Adams's music, like that of Glass's *Voyage*, was set in what could be called a "postminimalist" style, in which the freely grouped and regrouped subtactile pulses and arpeggios of minimalism, and interesting textures obtained by pitting pulses at differing rates of speed in counterpoint, were reconciled with a fairly conventional harmonic idiom, naturalistic vocal declamation, a neat "numbers" format replete with entertaining choral and dance sequences, and frequent references to various styles of popular music. A fairly standard orchestra was given a late-twentieth-century, somewhat Steve-Reichian sonic edge by replacing the bassoons with a quartet of saxophones, and by adding a pair of pianos and a keyboard sampler to the percussion section.

Adams's harmonies move around circles of major and minor thirds as consistently as traditional harmony moves through circles of fifths, thus making the early-twentieth-century "Franco-Russian" idiom the foundation of his late-century style, and making the same sort of end run around the twentieth century's German and German-influenced music that the midcentury "neoclassicists" (especially the French-trained Americans of the "Boulangerie") had made in their day around the Germanic music of the nineteenth century. But in Adams's work that idiom is "demaximalized," domesticated, made comfortable. Chords that Stravinsky might have mixed into dissonant "polyharmonies" succeed one another in gleamingly consonant progressions.

To take one example, one of the score's most characteristic progressions puts in alternation the two triads that together had made up Stravinsky's so-called *Petrushka-chord* as early as 1911. (In Ex. 10-4a it is quoted from Chou En-lai's toast to the Nixon party near the end of act 1.) Later, as the toasting scene reaches its climax, Adams astutely allows the subtactile pulse to drop out, so that an irregular succession of halves and dotted halves, formerly controlled by a steady stream of quarters, can ring out as if spontaneously, achieving a true emotional climax. The harmonies here form a module, a chain of triads with roots related by thirds (cast, Philip Glass–like, in a textbook-defying voice leading that grants full rights of citizenship to the $^6_4$ chord), which picks up extensions and interpolations as it repeats (Ex. 10-4b):

$$[C (+m3) E\flat (-M3) B (+m3) D (-M3) B\flat]$$
$$[C (+m3) E\flat (-M3) B (+m3) D (-M3) B\flat]$$
$$[C (+M3) E (-M3)]$$
$$[C (+m3) E\flat (-M3) B (+m3) D (-M3) B\flat]$$
$$[C (+M3) E (+M3) A\flat (+M3) C]$$

Nixon in China differed from most twentieth-century operas by reinvoking music's power of enchantment, surrounding historical characters with a "transcendent" aura that turned them into "timeless," godlike figures. In particular, this characteristic set the opera off from the topical operas or *Zeitopern* ("now-operas") of the 1920s and 1930s. Where in the disillusioned aftermath of World War I audiences enjoyed an operatic genre that debunked the myth of "timeless" art, in the super-affluent, triumphant

EX. 10-4A   John Adams, *Nixon in China*, Act I, Chou En-lai's toast

EX. 10-4A (continued)

post–cold war decade audiences sought through art the monumentalization of their own historical experience.

The operatic mythologizing of Richard M. Nixon's most impressive diplomatic coup displeased a minority who objected to the way it helped turn memory away from the domestic scandal that ended his presidency. It disturbed others who objected to the

EX. 10-4B John Adams, *Nixon in China*, Act I, choral response

EX. 10-4B (*continued*)

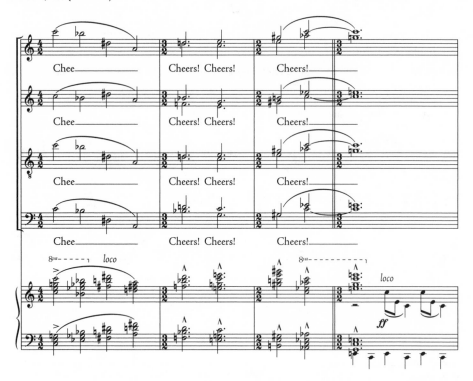

callow way it cast the bloody Chinese Communist dictatorship, fresh from the excesses of the Cultural Revolution, in an uncritical, heroic light. But the critical consensus that formed over the remaining years of the twentieth century seemed to favor the aesthetic eclipse of "mere" history or politics. The critic Alex Ross went so far as to predict that "a century from now audiences will still be fascinated by this opera, and that some listeners will have to double-check the plot summary in order to remember who Richard Nixon was."[84] Its value, like that of all great art, the critic implied, was independent of its relationship to external reality, and that value was its capacity to create spiritual archetypes.

And yet that very evaluation, that very assignment of values, was the product of an external reality; and another external reality, that of Arab-Israeli conflict, prevented *The Death of Klinghoffer* from having a comparable success. The work was commissioned, on the coattails of *Nixon*'s success, by another international consortium that included the Brooklyn Academy of Music, the Théâtre Royale de la Monnaie (Brussels, Belgium), the Opéra de Lyon (France), the San Francisco Opera, the Glyndebourne Festival (Scotland), and the Los Angeles Festival of the Arts (or rather, by their various corporate sponsors).

Adams modeled the work to a degree on the Bach Passions, with choral commentaries from mythologized communities of Jewish and Palestinian exiles (cast as the biblical offspring of Jacob and Ishmael) set in dramatic counterpoint against the bloody events of November 1985. As with *Nixon in China*, the subject matter sufficed to make the work controversial, and attracted attention (and audiences) to it. It was to many, moreover, a hopeful sign that "high" art was participating in an ongoing political and moral debate, and might therefore seem less marginal to contemporary society and culture. But this time, the stance of transcendence was widely read as an arrogant, or at least a complacent, evasion of moral judgment.

One critic, echoing the claims of the work's creators, wrote that "as the authors' approach to this sensitive subject is classical, no 'sides' are taken,"[85] a comment which elicited from another critic this perhaps overwrought rejoinder:

> Bach, the ostensible model, who knew not "classical," took sides, all right. Or should we prefer a "classical" Passion, in which Christ and his betrayers are treated "evenhandedly"? If such moral indifference is an accurate measure of what the "classical" has now become, then the "classical" deserves its fate. Its death may ultimately be judged a suicide.[86]

He went on to complain at the way "the forms of old sacred genres (in this instance, the Bach passions) are appropriated to cloak moral blankness and opportunism in a simulated religiosity," and in so doing, may unwittingly have put a finger on the "external reality" that undergirded the seemingly sudden new viability of classical music. At a time of gross materialism and commercialism widely compared in America to the "Gilded Age" at the end of the previous century, classical music (Wagner then; Adams now) was being marketed for its powers of "uplift" to a guiltily affluent audience ("robber barons" then; "venture capitalists" now) eager to depict itself as humane.

Peter Sellars, the mastermind behind both Adams-Goodman operas, made the claim quite forthrightly. "I think in this age of television and Hollywood film, if classical music is going to stick around, there'd better be a very good reason," he told an interviewer. Then, shifting oxymoronically into the language of commerce, he added, "We have to offer something that is not available otherwise. I think it is spiritual content, which is what's missing from the commercial culture that surrounds us." This time, the subject under discussion was not an opera but a new collaboration by Sellars and Adams, and a more overtly religious one: a topically slanted nativity oratorio called *El Niño*, commissioned by another international consortium — Théâtre du Chatelet (Paris), the San Francisco Symphony, Lincoln Center for the Performing Arts (New York), the Barbican Centre (London), and the British Broadcasting Corporation — and performed according to the terms of the commission in Paris, San Francisco, Berlin, New York, and London between December 2000 and December 2001. It will make an apt final exhibit for this book.

A NEW SPIRITUALITY

El Niño was one of a number of works of flamboyant "spiritual content" commissioned and performed under prestigious auspices to solemnize the new millennium. Another, Philip Glass's Fifth Symphony (1999), was (like several of Mahler's symphonies, or the finale of Beethoven's Ninth) an oratorio in all but name, scored for five vocal soloists, mixed chorus, children's choir, and orchestra. Its subtitle, "Requiem, Bardo,

Nirmanakaya," pits the Latin title of the service for the dead (representing the world's past) against the Tibetan word for "in between" (as in the Tibetan Book of the Dead—*Bardo Thodol*—which describes the soul's journey after death) and the Sanskrit Mahayana Buddhist term for rebirth or bodily transformation (representing mankind's hoped-for future). The text draws on "a broad spectrum of many of the world's great 'wisdom' traditions,"[87] as the composer put it in a program note, translated from Greek, Hebrew, Arabic, Persian, Sanskrit, Bengali, Chinese, Japanese, Tibetan, Hawaiian, Zuñi, Mayan, Bantu, and Bulu scriptures. The symphony was commissioned by the ASCII Corporation, a computer software company, for performance at the Salzburger Festspiele, Europe's most exclusive summer music festival.

Another example was the cycle of four Passions—Matthew, Mark, Luke, and John—that the German choral conductor Helmut Rilling, with the support of the city of Stuttgart and the publisher Hänssler Musikverlag, commissioned from a quartet of composers, one a German and three with conspicuously "multicultural" backgrounds, for premiere performances in Rilling's home city to be followed by world tours. Luke went to Wolfgang Rihm (b. 1952), a neo-Expressionist representing the Germanic "mainstream." Mark went to Osvaldo Golijov (b. 1960), an Argentinian-born Jew residing in the United States (where he studied with George Crumb), who composed a lavish collage of Latin American, Afro-Cuban, and Jewish cantorial idioms and stole the show.

Matthew was assigned to Tan Dun (b. 1957), a Chinese composer trained at the Beijing Conservatory and Columbia University, who had demonstrated his suitability for the Passions project with a work entitled *Symphony 1997 (Heaven Earth Mankind)* for orchestra, children's chorus, an ensemble of Chinese temple bells, and a solo cello part written for Yo-Yo Ma, a Paris-born American cellist of Chinese descent who had been making a specialty of "crossover" undertakings involving repertoires as diverse as jazz, Brazilian pop, Appalachian folklore, and the classical music of Central Asia.

John, finally, went to Sofia Gubaidulina, the post-Soviet composer of actual Central Asian ("Tatar" or Mongolian) descent then living in Germany, whose predilection for religious subject matter had been considered a mark of political dissidence in the waning years of Soviet authority. Yet the fact that two of the composers chosen for the Passion project were not Christian—Golijov, for one, cheerfully admitting that it was only after receiving the commission that he looked into the New Testament for the first time—suggests that the impulse behind it was something other than religious in the customary or doctrinal sense of the word.

The Adams-Sellars oratorio was also of distinctly "multicultural" content. Its texts were drawn from the New Testament, the Aprocrypha, the old English Wakefield Mystery Plays, and a Latin Hymn by Hildegarde von Bingen (the twelfth-century German abbess whose own music had achieved an improbable popularity in the late twentieth century via recordings, supplemented by modern poems by several Latin Americans, including Sister Juana Inés de la Cruz (1651–95), Rubén Dario (1867–1916), Gabriela Mistral (1899–1957), and, most prominently, Rosario Castellanos (1925–74), who combined an artistic career with a diplomatic one, serving at the end of her life as the Mexican ambassador to Israel.

One of the oratorio's most striking moments was the juxtaposition, near the end, of the terse biblical account of the Slaughter of the Innocents (Herod's massacre of all the male children younger than two years of age in Bethlehem to ensure that the infant Jesus would not survive) with *Memorial de Tlatelolco* ("Memorandum on Tlatelolco"), a long poem by Castellanos sung by the soprano soloist with choral support, that furiously protests the violent police repression of a student demonstration that took place on 2 October 1968 at Tlatelolco Square in Mexico City, which more than 400 years earlier had been the site of the last bloody confrontation between the Aztecs and the Spanish conquistadors led by Hernando Cortez (13 August 1521).

The poem bears witness to a crime that went unreported at the time by the government-controlled Mexican press. Its inclusion in the oratorio text draws explicit parallels between religious observance, acts of political conscience or resistance, and the role of artists as keepers of public memory and conscience. Adams's setting reaches, within the limits of the composer's openly avowed commitment to an ingratiating idiom, a pitch of intensity reminiscent of Expressionism in its use of wide intervals to distort the lyric line.

The oratorio's final number balances the vehemence of the *Memorial de Tlatelolco* by juxtaposing an Apocryphal account of the infant Jesus's first miracle, in which he commanded a palm tree to bend down so that his mother could gather its dates, with a consoling poem by Castellanos that pays respects to an Israeli palm tree for inspiring a moment of peaceful reflection amid the turbulence of the contemporary Middle East. Here Adams underscores the message of solace and chastened optimism by, as it were, resurrecting the Innocents in a children's chorus that gets to sing the oratorio's last word — "Poesia" (poetry) — accompanied by a pair of Spanish guitars.

There is something satisfyingly symmetrical, perhaps, in drawing on a work with a religious (and specifically Christian) subject to end a historical narrative that begins with the liturgical music of the Roman Catholic Church. But that symmetry is illusory, as is any hint of closure. There is a world of difference between actual service music and an entertainment that alludes to sacred tales, and that difference reflects the fundamental trajectory of art — "high" art, at any rate — within Western culture over the past millennium.

The symmetry is fortuitous as well. The narrative begins with sacred music only because it was the first music to be written down — a distinction that came about only partly because it was sacred. And it is ending with a sacred entertainment only because at the moment of writing that sort of work seems to be the most marketable and profitable music the literate tradition can boast at a time when its end has become foreseeable.

The sacred as marketable, as profitable: it seems a paradoxical notion, even a blasphemous one. But it is not unprecedented. Nearly 300 years ago, Handel's oratorios made similarly opportunistic — and similarly successful — use of sacred subject matter to exploit the market. And just as we now resolve the paradox in Handel's case by reading through the sacred metaphor to what we take to be the Handelian oratorio's "real" (i.e., nationalistic) appeal, it may not be too early to attempt a similar reading of the "multicultural" religiosity that found such impressively widespread musical expression at the end of the twentieth century.

Historians agree that Handel's oratorios achieved their amazing success not only by dint of their musical caliber, but also by flattering their elite English audience — a mixture of nobility and high bourgeoisie (comprising "the first Quality of the Nation," to quote a noteworthy review that greeted Handel's *Israel in Egypt* in 1739) — with comparisons to the biblical Hebrews, God's chosen people. The audience that patronizes the work of the successful sliver at the top of today's seething heap of struggling classical composers is a new social elite. It has been identified by the social critic David Brooks, the author of *Bobos in Paradise*, an amusing but penetrating study published in 2000, as "bourgeois Bohemians" (Bobos) — the highly educated nouveaux riches of the Information Age, who live comfortably and fashionably but retain a sentimental attachment to the "sixties" concerns of their youth, and who are most effectively flattered by art that reflects their ethical self-image. "The people who thrive in this period are the ones who can turn ideas and emotions into products," writes Brooks. And that, among other things, is what composers do.

The cherished Bobo self-image is one of personal authenticity, constructed not in terms of a wholly original worldview but in terms of eclecticism — an individual selection from among the unlimited choices on the global cultural and spiritual menu. The greatest challenge the new establishment faces, according to Brooks, is "how to navigate the shoals between their affluence and their self-respect; how to reconcile their success with their spirituality, their elite status with their egalitarian ideals."[88] Their task, in constructing their identity, is to reconcile values that had been traditionally at odds: bourgeois values of ambition, social stability, and material comfort on the one hand, and on the other, bohemian values that identified with the victims of the bourgeois order: the poor, the criminal, the ethnic and racial outcast. The essential dilemma is that of reconciling the need for spirituality with the even more pressing need for personal autonomy and unlimited choice, since "real" religion imposes obligations and demands sacrifices.

It is not too difficult to see how the spiritualized classical music of the turn-of-millennium catered to these needs and predicaments. Audiences looking for purifying experiences are easily beguiled by symbols of innocence, hence the ubiquitous children's choirs in the works described above. (But that is nothing new: children's voices have long been exploited as an insurance policy by traders in romantic nostalgia: Mahler's Second, Third, and Fourth Symphonies all feature real or metaphorical child-performers, as did the work of Soviet composers at times of particularly intense political pressure.) The success of "Holy Minimalists" like Pärt, Gorecki, and Tavener in the 1980s was more specifically related to the coming Bobo phenomenon. It already bespoke the desire for a way to return "aesthetically" or "appreciatively" to a world of "spiritual wholeness" without assuming the burdens of an actual religious commitment.

The added attraction of "multiculturalism" — eclecticism writ large — in the works of the 1990s completes the parallel with the Bobo mentality, which places the highest premium on "personal" pastiche. A Princeton University study of contemporary religious practices, cited by David Brooks, turned up an extreme but characteristic example: a twenty-six-year-old disabilities counselor, the daughter of a Methodist minister, who described herself to her interviewer as a "Methodist Taoist Native American Quaker Russian Orthodox Buddhist Jew."[89] Philip Glass's post-minimalist Fifth Symphony was made for her, indeed *of* her.

The Adams-Sellars *El Niño* tapped into another time-honored trope of innocent authenticity, especially as it was performed during its initial run, with dancers interpreting the content of the words alongside the singers, and with a simultaneous film by Sellars adding yet another level of commentary. The film paralleled the unfolding story of the Nativity with footage showing the unaffected lives of anonymous members of Los Angeles's Hispanic community: a Chicano couple stood in for Joseph and Mary, their baby for Jesus, some rookie policemen for the shepherds, some local fortune-tellers for the Magi, and so on. Audience members and critics alike exclaimed at the beauty of the film, of the nameless actors, and of their emotional lives.

One of the most scathing passages in Brooks's study is devoted to precisely this sort of updating of the old myth of neoprimitivism. The immediate subject is travel:

> The Bobo, as always, is looking for stillness, for a place where people set down roots and repeat the simple rituals. In other words, Bobo travelers are generally looking to get away from their affluent, ascending selves into a spiritually superior world, a world that hasn't been influenced much by the global meritocracy.... Therefore, Bobos are suckers for darkly garbed peasants, aged farmers, hardy fishermen, remote craftsmen, weather-beaten pensioners, heavyset regional cooks—anybody who is likely to have never possessed or heard of frequent flier miles. So the Bobos flock to or read about the various folk locales where such "simple" people live in abundance—the hills of Provence, Tuscany, Greece, or the hamlets of the Andes or Nepal. These are places where the natives don't have credit card debts and relatively few people wear Michael Jordan T-shirts. Lives therefore seem connected to ancient patterns and age-old wisdom. Next to us, these natives seem serene. They are poorer people whose lives seem richer than our own.[90]

But as Adams and Sellars showed, you don't have to travel so far to ogle "indigenous peoples" or "noble savages." Any urban ghetto can supply them in quantity. Nor is it clear that displaying an estheticized, romanticized fantasy image of the poor for the edification or titillation of the affluent really furthers egalitarian ideals. Will imagining the poor as leading lives richer than one's own inspire social action on their behalf? Or will such a notion foster complacency? Will it inspire a true reconciliation between material comfort and social conscience? Or will it allow the comfortable to congratulate themselves on their benevolence and silence the nagging voice within?

Is the new spirituality, then, just another screen behind which high art engages in its traditional business of reinforcing social division by creating elite occasions? The old questions that bedeviled modernism have not gone away with the advent of postmodernity—which is another reason, perhaps, to doubt whether postmodernism is anything more than the latest modernist phase. Or are such moralizing concerns of dubious benefit to art or to artists, whose task of creating beauty is a constant imperative, transcending the politics (or the "political correctness") of the moment? The debate goes on.

And so we must take our leave of it without resolution. We have observed at least three coexisting if not contending strands of literate musical composition at the end of the twentieth century. There is a thinning faction of traditional modernists, mostly aging but not without younger recruits, who maintain the literate tradition at its most essentially and exigently literate. There is a vastly overpopulated stratum of composers, as yet virtually without a nonprofessional audience, who avail themselves of new technologies that presage the dilution and eventual demise of the literate tradition. And there is a small elite of commercially successful caterers to the needs of a newly ascendant class of patrons who currently control the fortunes of the mainstream performance and dissemination media, insofar as these remain open to elite art. All three are energetically active, productive, endowed with genuine talent. Which will prevail in the long run?

In the long run, it has been wisely observed, we are all dead.[91] That long a run is of no concern to the historian. At present, things remain in motion. That is all we can ask for. The future is anybody's guess. Our story ends, as it must, in the middle of things.

Notes

CHAPTER 1: STARTING FROM SCRATCH

1 Cyrus Durgin, *Boston Daily Globe*, 19 October 1946, quoted in Howard Pollack, *Aaron Copland*, p. 417.

2 *Time* magazine, 28 October 1946; quoted in Aaron Copland and Vivian Perlis, *Copland since 1943* (New York: St. Martin's Press, 1989), p. 68.

3 *New York Herald Tribune*, 24 November 1946; this is one of the few Thomson reviews that was never collected for publication in book form.

4 Leonard Bernstein to Aaron Copland, 27 May 1947; reproduced in facsimile in *Copland since 1943*, p. 70.

5 Arthur Berger, "The Third Symphony of Aaron Copland," *Tempo*, no. 9 (Autumn 1948): 25.

6 Bernstein to Copland, 8 November 1948; quoted in *Copland since 1943*, p. 71.

7 *Copland since 1943*, p. 71.

8 George F. Kennan, "The Sources of Soviet Conduct," *Foreign Affairs*, July 1947 (originally signed "X," this memo is now widely known as "The 'X' Article").

9 "Formalizm," in *Muzïkal'naya èntsiklopediya*, ed. Yuriy M. Keldïsh, Vol. V (Moscow: Sovetskaya Entsiklopediya, 1981), col. 907.

10 Quoted in Alexander Werth, *Musical Uproar in Moscow* (London: Turnstile Press, 1949), pp. 53–54.

11 *Musical Uproar in Moscow*, p. 86.

12 Victor Aronovich Belïy, quoted in *Musical Uproar in Moscow*, p. 72.

13 Quoted in Nicolas Slonimsky, *Music since 1900* (4th ed.; New York: Scribners, 1971), p. 1374.

14 "Declaration of the Second International Congress of Composers and Musicologists in Prague, 29 May 1948," quoted in Slonimsky, *Music since 1900*, p. 1378.

15 Quoted in Nicolas Nabokov, "1949: Christmas with Stravinsky," in *Stravinsky: A Merle Armitage Book*, ed. Edwin Corle (New York: Duell, Sloan and Pierce, 1949), p. 143.

16 René Leibowitz, *Schoenberg and His School*, trans. Dika Newlin (New York: Philosophical Library, 1949), p. x.

17 *New York Times Book Review*, 27 November 1949; quoted in Anne C. Shreffler, "Who Killed Neo-Classicism: The Paradigm Shift after 1945," paper read at the Sixty-second Annual Meeting of the American Musicological Society, Baltimore, 8 November 1996.

18 Theodor W. Adorno, *Philosophy of Modern Music*, trans. Anne G. Mitchell and Wesley V. Blomster (New York: Seabury Press, 1973), pp. 41–46.

19 *Philosophy of Modern Music*, pp. 32–37.

20 Leibowitz, *Schoenberg and His School*, pp. 210–25.

21 *Ibid.*, p. 211.

22 "German Music in the 1940s and 1950s," in Hans Werner Henze, *Music and Politics: Collected Writings 1953–81*, trans. Peter Labanyi (Ithaca: Cornell University Press, 1982), p. 40.

23 *Ibid.*, p. 36.

24 Pierre Boulez, "Eventuellement. . . ," in *Stock-takings from an Apprenticeship*, trans. (as "Possibly. . .") by Stephen Walsh (Oxford: Clarendon Press, 1991), p. 113.

25 René Leibowitz, "Béla Bartók ou la possibilité de compromis dans la musique contemporaine," *Temps modernes* III (1947–48): 705–34; trans. Michael Dixon, as "Béla Bartók, or the Possibility of Compromise in Twentieth-Century Music," *Transitions 1948* (Paris) no. 3 (1948): 92–122.

26 Leibowitz, "Bartók," *Transitions 1948*, no. 3, p. 120.

27 Boulez, "Schoenberg Is Dead," in *Stocktakings from an Apprenticeship*, p. 211.

28 *Ibid.*, p. 213

29 Adorno, "Das Altern der neuen Musik" (1954), trans. Susan H. Gillespie (as "The Aging of the New Music"), in T. W. Adorno, ed., *Essays on Music*, Richard H. Leppert (Berkeley and Los Angeles: University of California Press, 2002), pp. 197–98.

30 "Schoenberg Is Dead," p. 214.

31 Henze, "German Music in the 1940s and 1950s," p. 43.

32 Paul Griffiths, *Olivier Messiaen and the Music of Time* (Ithaca: Cornell University Press, 1985), p. 151.

33 Peter Hill, "Piano Music II," in *The Messiaen Companion*, ed. P. Hill (Portland, Ore.: Amadeus Press, 1995), p. 319.

34 Boulez in conversation with Celestin Deliège, quoted in Dominique Jameux, *Pierre Boulez*, trans. Susan Bradshaw (London: Faber and Faber, 1991), p. 52.

35 Boulez, "Possibly. . . ," in *Stocktakings*, p. 133.

36 Quoted in Edward Rothstein, "Ernst Krenek, 91, a Composer Prolific in Many Modern Styles" (obituary), *New York Times*, 24 December 1991.

37 Ernst Krenek, "Extents and Limits of Serial Techniques," in *Problems of Modern Music: The Princeton Seminar in Advanced Musical Studies*, ed. Paul Henry Lang (New York: Norton, 1962), p. 83.

38 *Ibid.*, p. 90.

39 *Ibid.*, pp. 90–91.

40 Stanley Cavell, "Music Discomposed," in *Must We Mean What We Say?: A Book of Essays* (Cambridge: Cambridge University Press, 1976), p. 195.

41 *Ibid.*, p. 187.

42 *Ibid.*, pp. 194–95.

43 *Ibid.*, p. 196.

44 *Ibid.*, p. 196.

45 *Ibid.*

46 *Ibid.*, p. 202.

47 *Ibid.*, p. 198.

48 *Ibid.*, p. 201.

49 *Ibid.*, p. 206.

50 György Ligeti, "Pierre Boulez: Entscheidung und Automatik in der Structure Ia," *Die Reihe* IV (1958): 60.

51 Quoted in Boulez, "Stravinsky Remains," in *Stocktakings from an Apprenticeship*, p. 109.

52 *Stocktakings*, p. 109.

53 *Scolica enchiriadis* (ca. 850 CE), trans. Lawrence Rosenwald, in P. Weiss and R. Taruskin, *Music in the Western World: A History in Documents* (2nd ed., Belmont, CA: Thomson/Schirmer, 2007), p. 34.

54 Michael Kurtz, *Stockhausen: A Biography*, trans. Richard Toop (London: Faber and Faber, 1992), p. 24.

55 *Ibid.*, p. 36.

56 Harold Rosenberg, *The Tradition of the New* (Chicago: University of Chicago Press, 1982), p. 9.

57 Quoted in Paul Griffiths, *György Ligeti* (London: Robson Books, 1983), p. 11.

58 *Ibid.*, p. 14.

59 Ligeti, "Pierre Boulez: Entscheidung und Automatik in der Structure Ia," p. 63.

60 Quoted in Griffiths, *György Ligeti*, p. 22.

61 Ernő Lendvai, *Bevezetés a Bartók-müvek elemzésébe* (Introduction to the analysis of Bartók's works); *Bartók stílusa* (Bartók's style) (both Budapest: Zenemukiadö, 1955).

62 See Richard Toop, *György Ligeti* (London: Phaidon, 1999), p. 57.

63 Quoted in Adrian Thomas, "Panufnik, Sir Andrzej," in *New Grove Dictionary of Music and Musicians*, Vol. XIX (2nd ed.; New York: Grove, 2001), p. 46.

Chapter 2: Indeterminacy

1 On Cage's claim to have studied composition with Schoenberg, see Michael Hicks, "John Cage's Studies with Schoenberg," *American Music* VIII (1990): 125–40.

2 Alan Gillmor, "Interview with John Cage (1973)," quoted in David Revill, *The Roaring Silence. John Cage: A Life* (New York: Arcade Publishing, 1992), p. 30.

3 John Cage, "The Future of Music: Credo," in *Silence: Lectures and Writings by John Cage* (Cambridge: The M.I.T. Press, 1966), p. 4.

4 *Ibid.*, p. 5.

5 "List of Percussion Instruments Owned by John Cage" (2 July 1940), now at the John Cage Archive, Northwestern University Music Library; handout accompanying Tamara Levitz, "The Africanist Presence in John Cage's *Bacchanale*," University of California at Berkeley musicology colloquium, 24 March 2000.

6 See Revill, *The Roaring Silence*, p. 84.

7 *Ibid.*, p. 88.

8 *Ibid.*, p. 89.

9 *Ibid.*, p. 90.

10 Gillmor, "Interview with John Cage (1973)," quoted in Richard Kostelanetz, *Conversing with Cage* (New York: Limelight Editions, 1988), p. 43.

11 Cole Gagne and Tracy Caras, *Soundpieces: Interviews with American Composers* (Metuchen, N.J.: Scarecrow Press, 1982); quoted in Kostelanetz, *Conversing with Cage*, p. 91.

12 Quoted in Revill, *The Roaring Silence*, p. 99.

13 John Cage to Pierre Boulez, summer 1952; Jean-Jacques Nattiez, ed., *The Boulez-Cage Correspondence*, trans. Robert Samuels (Cambridge: Cambridge University Press, 1993), p. 133.

14 Paul Hersh, "John Cage," *Santa Cruz Express*, 19 August 1982; quoted in Kostelanetz, *Conversing with Cage*, p. 79.

15 John Cage, "45′ for a Speaker," in *Silence*, p. 155.

16 John Cage, "History of Experimental Music in the United States," in *Silence*, p. 73.

17 John Hollander, "*Silence* by John Cage," *Perspectives of New Music* I, no. 2 (spring 1963): 138.

18 Friedrich von Schiller, *Naïve and Sentimental Poetry; and, On the Sublime: Two Essays*, trans. Julius A. Elias (New York: Frederick Ungar Publishing, 1966), p. 129.

19 Thomas Wufflin, "An Interview with John Cage," *New York Berlin* I, no. 1 (1985); quoted in Kostelanetz, *Conversing with Cage*, p. 115.

20 John Cage, "45′ for a Speaker," in *Silence*, p. 155.

21 See Immanuel Kant, *Critique of Judgment*, Vol. I, §17: "*Beauty* is the form of the *purposiveness* of an object, so far as this is perceived in it *without any representation of a purpose.*"

22 Interview with Arlynne Nellhaus, *Denver Post*, 5 July 1968; Kostelanetz, *Conversing with Cage*, p. 106.

23 Roman Ingarden, *The Work of Music and the Problem of Its Identity*, trans. Adam Czerniawski, ed. Jean G. Harrell (Berkeley and Los Angeles: University of California Press, 1986), pp. 2–6.

24 Revill, *The Roaring Silence*, p. 196.

25 *Ibid.*, pp. 166–67.

26 Lydia Goehr, *The Imaginary Museum of Musical Works: An Essay in the Philosophy of Music* (Oxford: Clarendon Press, 1992), p. 264.

27 John Cage, *Empty Words: Writings '73 to '78* (Middletown, Conn.: Wesleyan University Press, 1979), pp. 7–9.

28 Letter to the editor, *Los Angeles Times*, 30 January 1977; quoted in Revill, *The Roaring Silence*, p. 207.

29 Quoted in Revill, *The Roaring Silence*, p. 208.

30 Quoted in Kathan Brown, "The Uncertainty Principle," *The Guardian* (London), 3 August 2002.

31 Quoted in Revill, *The Roaring Silence*, p. 190.

32 Charles Hamm, "Cage, John (Milton, Jr.)," in *New Grove Dictionary of American Music*, Vol. I (London: Macmillan, 1986), p. 334.

33 Leo Castelli, in "John Cage: I Have Nothing to Say and I Am Saying It," American Masters documentary directed and coproduced by Allan Miller, written and produced by Vivian Perlis; PBS broadcast 16 December 1990.

34 Robert Rauschenberg, *Ibid.*

35 Morton Feldman, "Liner Notes," in *Give My Regards to Eighth Street: Collected Writings of Morton Feldman* (Cambridge, Mass.: Exact Change, 2000), p. 5.

36 Iannis Xenakis, "La musique stochastique: Éléments sur les procédés probabilistes de composition musicale," *Revue d'esthétique* no.14 (1961).

37 Bálint András Varga, *Conversations with Iannis Xenakis* (London: Faber and Faber, 1996), p. 78.

38 *Ibid.*, p. 55–56.

39 See Harold Bloom, *The Anxiety of Influence* (New York: Oxford University Press, 1973), and *A Map of Misreading* (New York: Oxford University Press, 1975).

40 William Bland and David Patterson, "Wolff, Christian," in *New Grove Dictionary of Music and Musicians*, Vol. XXVII (2nd ed.; New York: Grove, 2001), p. 504.

41 Cage, *Silence*, p. 93.

42 Cornelius Cardew, "Introduction," in *Scratch Music*, ed. Cornelius Cardew (Cambridge: The M.I.T. Press, 1974), p. 9.

43 *Ibid.*, p. 12.

44 *Ibid.*, p. 9.

45 "A Scratch Orchestra: Draft constitution," in *Scratch Music*, p. 10.

46 *Scratch Music*, p. 62.

47 *Scratch Music*, p. 61.

48 "Introduction," in *Scratch Music*, p. 12.

49 Charles Wuorinen, interviewed by Barney Childs (1962), in *Contemporary Composers on Contemporary Music*, eds. Elliott Schwartz and Barney Childs (New York: Holt Rinehart Winston, 1967), p. 371.

50 Cornelius Cardew, "John Cage: Ghost or Monster?" in Cardew, *Stockhausen Serves Imperialism and Other Articles* (London: Latimer New Dimensions Limited, 1974), p. 35.

51 *Ibid.*, p. 36.

52 *Ibid.*, p. 39.

53 Cardew, "Stockhausen Serves Imperialism," in *Stockhausen Serves Imperialism and Other Essays*, p. 48.

54 *Ibid.*, p. 49.

55 Quoted in Michael Nyman, *Experimental Music: Cage and Beyond* (New York: Schirmer, 1974), p. 61.

56 Quoted in Nyman, *Experimental Music*, p. 64.

57 Nyman, *Experimental Music*, p. 66.

58 Reproduced in Nyman, *Experimental Music*, p. 67.

59 Quoted in Nyman, *Experimental Music*, p. 13.

60 Reproduced in Nyman, *Experimental Music*, p. 70.

61 Quoted in Nyman, *Experimental Music*, p. 74.

62 Quoted *Ibid.*

63 "Relations: Friends and Allies Across the Divide; Merce Cunningham and Nam June Paik," *New York Times Magazine*, 16 July 2000, p. 11.

64 Quoted in Nyman, *Experimental Music*, p. 74.

65 *Ibid.*

66 *Baker's Biographical Dictionary of Musicians* (6th ed.; New York: Schirmer, 1978), p. 1279.

67 "Relations: Friends and Allies Across the Divide: Merce Cunningham and Nam June Paik"

68 *Baker's Biographical Dictionary of Musicians* (6th ed.; New York, Schirmer, 1978), p. 1118.

69 John Cage, "Preface," *Notations* (New York: Something Else Press, 1969), n.p.

70 Feldman, "Liner Notes," p. 6.

71 Quoted in Nyman, *Experimental Music*, p. 45.

72 Feldman, "Liner Notes," p. 6.

73 Quoted in Nyman, *Experimental Music*, p. 45.

74 Morton Feldman, "Give My Regards to Eighth Street," in *Give My Regards to Eighth Street*, p. 101.

75 Paul Griffiths, "A Marathon for 3 Players and the Ears," *New York Times*, 6 April 2000, Section E, p. 10.

76 See Walter Benjamin, "The Work of Art in the Age of Mechanical Reproduction" (1936), in Benjamin, *Illuminations* (New York: Harcourt Brace Jovanovich, 1968), pp. 217–53.

77 Griffiths, "A Marathon."

CHAPTER 3: THE APEX

1 Paul Hindemith, *The Craft of Musical Composition*, trans. Arthur Mendel (New York: Associated Music Publishers, 1942), p. 154.

2 Robert E. Stripling, quoted in Nicolas Slonimsky, *Music since 1900* (4th ed.; New York: Scribners, 1971), p. 1396.

3 Hans Eisler, in *Evening Moscow* (*Vechernyaya Moskva*), 27 June 1936, read into the Congressional Record by Robert Stripling on 24 September 1947; Slonimsky, *Music since 1900*, p. 1399.

4 Quoted in Aaron Copland and Vivian Perlis, *Copland since 1943* (New York: St. Martin's Press, 1989), p. 185.

5 Paul Hume, "Music Censorship Reveals New Peril," *Washington Post*, 25 January 1953; *Copland since 1943*, p. 186.

6 Quoted in *Copland since 1943*, p. 193.

7 Copland, interviewed by Mildred Norton in the *Los Angeles Daily News*, 5 April 1948; quoted in Howard Pollack, *Aaron Copland: The Life and Work of an Uncommon Man* (New York: Henry Holt and Co., 1999), p. 283.

8 Quoted in Pollack, *Aaron Copland*, p. 284.

9 Aaron Copland, "Fantasy for Piano," *New York Times*, 20 October 1957; quoted in Pollack, *Aaron Copland*, p. 446.

10 *Copland since 1943*, p. 339.

11 Leonard Bernstein, "Aaron Copland: An Intimate Sketch," *High Fidelity*, November 1970; quoted in Pollack, *Aaron Copland*, p. 448.

12 Paul Henry Lang, quoted in Pollack, *Aaron Copland*, p. 501.

13 Aaron Copland, *Music and the Imagination: The Charles Eliot Norton Lectures 1951–1952* (Cambridge: Harvard University Press, 1952), p. 75.

14 "Rencontre avec Stravinsky," *Preuves* II, no. 16 (1952): 37.

15 Robert Craft to Sylvia Marlowe, 4 October 1949 (by courtesy of Kenneth Cooper).

16 As reprinted in Eric Walter White, *Stravinsky: The Composer and His Works* (Berkeley and Los Angeles: University of California Press, 1966), p. 431.

17 Ernst Krenek, "Extents and Limits of Serial Technique," in *Problems of Modern Music*, ed. Lang (New York: Norton), p. 75.

18 Reproduced in Robert Craft, *A Stravinsky Scrapbook, 1940–1971* (London: Thames and Hudson, 1983), p. 120.

19 Igor Stravinsky and Robert Craft, *Memories and Commentaries* (Garden City, N.Y.: Doubleday, 1960), p. 100.

20 The article appears in Lang, *Problems of Modern Music*, pp. 108–21.

21 David Littlejohn, *The Ultimate Art: Essays Around and About Opera* (Berkeley and Los Angeles: University of California Press, 1992), p. 40.

22 Andrew Mead, *An Introduction to the Music of Milton Babbitt* (Princeton: Princeton University Press, 1994), p. 55.

23 Milton Babbitt, "Some Aspects of Twelve-Tone Composition," *The Score*, no. 12 (June 1955): 56.

24 *Ibid.*, p. 61.

25 *Ibid.*, p. 53–54.

26 John Cage to Pierre Boulez, 17 January 1950; Nattiez, ed., *The Boulez-Cage Correspondence*, p. 48.

27 Daniel Bell, *The Cultural Contradictions of Capitalism* (1976), in Patrick Murray, ed., *Reflections on Commercial Life: An Anthology of Classic Texts from Plato to the Present* (New York: Routledge, 1997), p. 435.

28 Milton Babbitt, "Past and Present Concepts of the Nature and Limits of Music," in *International Musicological Society: Report of the Eighth Congress, New York 1961*, Vol. I (Kassel: Bärenreiter Verlag, 1961), p. 398.

29 Quoted in Milton Babbitt, "Contemporary Music Composition and Contemporary Music Theory as Contemporary Intellectual History," in *Perspectives in Musicology*, eds. Barry S. Brook, Edward O. Downes, and Sherman van Solkema (New York: Norton, 1972), p. 180.

30 Milton Babbitt, "Who Cares if You Listen?," *High Fidelity*, February 1958; reprinted in P. Weiss and R. Taruskin, *Music in the Western World: A History in Documents* (2nd ed., Belmont, CA: Thomson/Schirmer, 2007), p. 483.

31 *Ibid.*, p. 481.

32 *Ibid.*, p. 484.

33 *Ibid.*

34 Joseph Kerman, *Contemplating Music: Challenges to Musicology* (Cambridge: Harvard University Press, 1985), p. 104.

35 Some of the arguments and speculations that Crocker and his collegues put forth to challenge the assumptions of modern musicians are reflected in the section headed "What is Art?" in R. Taruskin, *Music from the Earliest Notations to the sixteenth Century*(Oxford, 2009), pp.00–00

36 Edward T. Cone, "What Is a Composition?" (contribution to a symposium, "Musicology and the Musical Composition"), *Current Musicology*, no. 5 (1967): 107.

37 Quoted in Edward T. Cone, "One Hundred Metronomes," *The American Scholar* XLVI (1977): 444.

38 Milton Babbitt, interviewed in Deena Rosenberg and Bernard Rosenberg, *The Music Makers* (New York: Columbia University Press, 1979), p. 57.

39 Quoted in Richard Severo, "Vance Packard, 82, Challenger of Consumerism, Dies" (obituary), *New York Times*, 13 December 1996, p. A24.

40 *The Music Makers*, pp. 58–59.

41 *Contemporary Composers on Contemporary Music*, p. 370.

42 John Backus, "*Die Reihe*: A Scientific Evaluation," *Perspectives of New Music* I, no. 1 (Fall 1962): 169.

43 *Ibid.*, p. 170.

44 *Ibid.*

45 Milton Babbitt, "Twelve-Tone Rhythmic Structure and the Electronic Medium," *Perspectives of New Music* I, no. 1 (Fall 1962): 63.

46 Peter Westergaard, "Some Problems Raised by the Rhythmic Procedures in Milton Babbitt's Composition for Twelve Instruments," *Perspectives of New Music* IV, no. 1 (Fall–Winter 1965): 113.

47 *Ibid.*, p. 113n.

48 George Perle, *The Listening Composer* (Berkeley and Los Angeles: University of California Press, 1990), p. 115 (quoting Joseph Dubiel).

49 *Ibid.*, p. 121.

50 William Benjamin, "Schenker's Theory and the Future of Music," *Journal of Music Theory* XXV (1981): 170.

51 Dika Newlin, *Schoenberg Remembered: Diaries and Recollections 1938–1976* (New York: Pendragon Press, 1980), p. 164 (recorded 10 January 1940).

52 Schoenberg to Alexander von Zemlinsky, 20 March 1918; in Arnold Schoenberg, *Letters*, ed. Erwin Stein, trans. Eithne Wilkins and Ernst Kaiser (Berkeley and Los Angeles: University of California Press, 1964), p. 54.

53 Wallace Berry, "Apostrophe: A Letter from Ann Arbor," *Perspectives of New Music* XIV/2–XV/1 (double issue, "Sounds and Words: Milton Babbitt at 60"): 195, 197–98.

54 Milton Babbitt, "Responses: A First Approximation," *Ibid.*, pp. 22–23.

55 Igor Stravinsky and Robert Craft, *Conversations with Igor Stravinsky* (Garden City: Doubleday, 1959), p. 127.

56 R. Taruskin, "How Talented Composers Become Useless," *New York Times*, Arts and Leisure, 10 March 1996, p. 31; rpt. in R. Taruskin, The Danger of Music and Other Anti-Utopian Essays (Berkeley and Los Angeles: University of California Press, 2009), p.87

57 Milton Babbitt, "Twelve-Tone Rhythmic Structure and the Electronic Medium," pp. 77–78.

CHAPTER 4: THE THIRD REVOLUTION

1 John Cage, *Silence: Lectures and Writings by John Cage* (Cambridge: The M.I.T. Press, 1966), pp. 3–4.

2 *Ibid.*, p. 6.

3 Milton Babbitt, in Joel Chadabe, *Electric Sound: The Past and Promise of Electronic Music* (Upper Saddle River, N.J.: Prentice Hall, 1997), p. 18.

4 Cage, *Silence*, p. 4.

5 Ferruccio Busoni, *Sketch of a New Esthetic of Music*, trans. Theodore Baker, in *Three Classics in the Aesthetic of Music* (New York: Dover Publications, 1962), p. 77.

6 *Ibid.*, p. 76.

7 *Ibid.*, p. 79.

8 *Ibid.*, p. 95.

9 Filippo Tommaso Marinetti, *Le Roi Bombance* (1910).

10 Luigi Russolo, "The Art of Noises: Futurist Manifesto," trans. Stephen Somervell, in Nicolas Slonimsky, *Music since 1900* (4th ed.; New York: Scribners, 1971), p. 1298.

11 *Musica futurista*, Fonit Cetra FDM 0007 (2 LP).

12 Cage, *Silence*, p. 4.

13 Ernst Toch, "Theremin und Komponist," *Neue Badische Landes-Zeitung* (6 December 1927), trans. Richard and Edith Kobler, in Albert Glinsky, *Theremin: Ether Music and Espionage* (Urbana: University of Illinois Press, 2000), p. 67.

14 *Three Classics in the Aesthetic of Music*, p. 89.

15 Quoted in Glinsky, *Theremin*, p. 252.

16 *Ibid.*

17 *Ibid.*

18 Glinsky, *Theremin*, p. 252.

19 Edgard Varèse, "The Liberation of Sound," in *Perspectives on American Composers*, eds. Benjamin Boretz and Edward T. Cone (New York: Norton, 1971), p. 32.

20 Edgard Varèse, *Ecuatorial* (New York: Ricordi, 1934), prefatory note.

21 Quoted in Fernand Ouellette, *Edgard Varese*, trans. Derek Coltman (New York: Orion Press, 1968), p. 104.

22 Henry Miller, *The Air-Conditioned Nightmare* (New York: New Directions, 1945), pp. 163–64.

23 *Ibid.*, p. 164.

24 *Ibid.*, p. 165.

25 *Perspectives on American Composers*, p. 32.

26 *Ibid.*

27 Herbert Eimert, "What Is Electronic Music?" *Die Reihe* (English-language edition, trans. Leo Black) I (1959): 6, 9.

28 *Panorama of Musique Concrète* (London/Ducretet-Thomson DTL 93090).

29 Karlheinz Stockhausen, liner notes to *Hymnen für elektronische und konkrete Klänge*, Elektronische Realisation WDR Köln (Deutsche Grammophon Gesellschaft 139421/22 Stereo).

30 Henry Cowell, "Current Chronicle: New York," *Musical Quarterly* XXXVIII (1952): 600.

31 Quoted in liner notes to *Tape Music: An Historic Concert* (Desto Records, DC 6466).

32 "Interview with Luciano Berio," in Barry Shrader, *Introduction to Electro-Acoustic Music* (Englewood Cliffs, N.J.: Prentice Hall, 1982); quoted in Chadabe, *Electric Sound*, p. 49.

33 Berio, "Poesia e Musica—un' esperienza," *Incontri Musicali* III (1958); quoted in Chadabe, *Electric Sound*, p. 50.

34 *Electric Sound*, p. 50.

35 Quoted in Ouellette, *Edgard Varèse*, p. 66.

36 Quoted in Chadabe, *Electric Sound*, p. 56.

37 *Ibid.*, pp. 56–57.

38 "Interview with Luciano Berio," quoted in Chadabe, *Electric Sound*, p. 50.

39 Quoted in Chadabe, *Electric Sound*, pp. 16–17.

40 Milton Babbitt, "Twelve-Tone Rhythmic Structure and the Electronic Medium," *Perspectives of New Music* I, no. 1 (Fall 1962): 49.

41 *Ibid.*

42 Milton Babbitt, *Words about Music*, eds. Stephen Dembski and Joseph N. Straus (Madison: University of Wisconsin Press, 1987), p. 173.

43 "Twelve-Tone Rhythmic Structure," p. 50.

44 Liner note to "Columbia-Princeton Electronic Music Center" (Columbia Records MS 6566, 1964).

45 Richard Swift, "Some Aspects of Aggregate Composition," *Perspectives of New Music* XIV/2–XV/1 (1976): 241.

46 Igor Stravinsky and Robert Craft, *Dialogues* (Berkeley and Los Angeles: University of California Press, 1982), p. 109.

47 Gunther Schuller, "Conversation with Varèse," *Perspectives on American Composers*, pp. 38–39.

48 Edgar Varèse, liner note to *The Music of Edgar Varèse, Vol. 2* (Columbia Masterworks ML 5762, 1960).

49 Jean Roy, *Musique française* (1962); quoted in Ouellette, *Edgard Varèse*, pp. 188–89.

50 Marc Treib and Richard Felciano, *Space Calculated in Seconds: The Philips Pavilion, Le Corbusier, Edgard Varèse* (Princeton: Princeton University Press, 1996), p. 11.

51 Jean Petit, *Le Poème électronique Le Corbusier* (Paris: Éditions de Minuit, 1958), p. 25.

52 Quoted in Ouellette, *Varèse*, p. 200.

53 Notes to Composers Recordings CRI SD-204 (1965).

54 *Ibid.*

55 Notes to Composers Recordings CRI — 112.

56 Frank Howes, *The Times*; quoted in Bernard Jacobson, *A Polish Renaissance* (London: Phaidon, 1960), p. 147.

57 Ludwik Erhardt, *Spotkania z Krzysztofem Pendereckim*(Warsaw: Polskie Wydawnistwo Muzyczne, 1975), Wolfram Schwinger, *Penderecki: Begegnungen, Lebensdaten, Werkkommentäre*(Stuttgart: Deutsche Verlags-Anstadt, 1979). My thanks to Tim Rutherford-Johnson for the references.

CHAPTER 5: STANDOFF (I)

1 Jacques Maritain, *Art and Scholasticism* (1920), trans. J. F. Scanlan (New York: Scribners, 1930), Chap. III ("Making and Doing").

2 Jürgen Habermas, "Modernity: An Incomplete Project," in *The Anti-Aesthetic: Essays on Postmodern Culture*, ed. Hal Foster (Port Townsend, Wash.: Bay Press, 1983), p. 10.

3 George Rochberg, "Reflections on the Renewal of Music" (1972), in Rochberg, *The Aesthetics of Survival: A Composer's View of Twentieth-Century Music* (Ann Arbor: University of Michigan Press, 1984), p. 235.

4 Richard Lewontin, "Darwin's Revolution," *New York Review of Books* XXX, no. 10 (16 June 1983).

5 Clement Greenberg, "Avant-Garde and Kitsch" (1939), in Greenberg, *The Collected Essays and Criticism*, Vol. I (Chicago: University of Chicago Press, 1988), pp. 7–8.

6 *Ibid.*, pp. 8–9.

7 *Ibid.*, p. 10.

8 *Ibid.*, p. 7.

9 P. I. Chaikovsky to N. F. von Meck (1879); A. A. Orlova, ed., *Chaikovskiy o muzïke, o zhizni, o sebe* (Leningrad: Muzïka, 1976), p. 117.

10 Chaikovsky to von Meck, 27 September 1885; Chaikovsky, *Polnoye sobraniye sochineniy: Literaturnïye proizvedeniya i perepiska*, Vol. XIII (Moscow: Muzïka, 1971), p. 159.

11 Chaikovsky to von Meck, 11 October 1885; *ibid.*, p. 171.

12 Jan Buzga, "Interview mit Pierre Boulez in Prag," *Melos* XXXIV (1967): 162.

13 Humphrey Carpenter, *Benjamin Britten: A Biography* (New York: Scribners, 1992), p. 193.

14 W. H. Auden, "September 1, 1939."

15 Quoted in Philip Brett, *Peter Grimes* (Cambridge Opera Handbooks; Cambridge: Cambridge University Press, 1983), p. 148.

16 E. M. Forster, "George Crabbe: The Poet and the Man" (1941); Brett, *Peter Grimes*, p. 4.

17 Brett, *Peter Grimes*, p. 2.

18 Murray Schafer, *British Composers in Interview* (1963); quoted in Brett, *Peter Grimes*, p. 190.

19 Pete Pears, "Neither a Hero Nor a Villain" (1946); Brett, *Peter Grimes*, p. 152.

20 Desmond Shawe-Taylor, review of first performance, *New Statesman*, 9 and 16 June 1945; Brett, *Peter Grimes*, p. 158.

21 Edmund Wilson, *Europe without Baedeker* (2nd ed.; New York: Noonday Press, 1966); rpt. in Piero Weiss, *Opera: A History in Documents* (New York: Oxford University Press, 2002), p. 308.

22 *Ibid.*, p. 309.

23 *Ibid.*

24 James Fenton, "How Grimes Became Grim," *The Guardian* (London), 3 July 2004.

25 J. W. Garbutt, "Music and Motive in *Peter Grimes*" (1963); Brett, *Peter Grimes*, p. 170.

26 Joseph Kerman, "Grimes and Lucretia," *The Hudson Review* II (1949): 279.

27 J. W. Garbutt, in Brett, *Peter Grimes*, p. 170.

28 Brett, *Peter Grimes*, p.187.

29 Benjamin Britten, *On Receiving the First Aspen Award* (London: Faber and Faber, 1964), p. 21.

30 Igor Stravinsky and Robert Craft, *Themes and Episodes* (New York: Knopf, 1966), p. 101.

31 Stravinsky to Nicolas Nabokov, 15 December 1949; Robert Craft, ed., *Stravinsky: Selected Correspondence*, Vol. I (New York: Knopf, 1982), p. 369n93.

32 Brett, *Peter Grimes*, pp. 194–95.

33 *Ibid.*, p. 191.

34 *Ibid.*, p. 187.

35 Peter Pears to Benjamin Britten, 1 March [?] 1944; Donald Mitchell and Philip Reed, eds., *Letters from a Life: Selected Letters and Diaries of Benjamin Britten* (Berkeley and Los Angeles: University of California Press, 1991), p. 1189.

36 Samuel Johnson, *Lives of the English Poets* (1779).

37 Schafer, *British Composers in Interview*; quoted in Carpenter, *Benjamin Britten*, p. 336.

38 W. Anthony Sheppard VI, *Revealing Masks: Exotic Influences and Ritualized Performance in Modernist Music Theater* (Berkeley and Los Angeles: University of California Press, 2001), p. 143.

39 *Ibid.*

40 *Ibid.*

41 Britten, *On Receiving the First Aspen Award*, p. 21.

42 *Ibid.*, p. 7.

43 *Ibid.*

44 *Ibid.*, pp. 21–22.

45 *Ibid.*, p. 22.

46 *Ibid.*, p. 17.

47 *Ibid.*, p. 14.

48 *Ibid.*, p. 12.

49 *Ibid.*, p. 14.

50 *Ibid.*, p. 15.

51 *Ibid.*, p. 12.

Chapter 6: Standoff (II)

1 Igor Stravinsky and Robert Craft, *Themes and Episodes* (New York: Knopf, 1966), p. 13–14.

2 *The World*, 22 November 1893; in Bernard Shaw, *Music in London 1890–94*, Vol. III (New York: Vienna House, 1973), p. 100.

3 Elliott Carter, liner note to Epic Records BC 1157 (1962).

4 Igor Stravinsky and Robert Craft, *Dialogues and a Diary* (Garden City, N.Y.: Doubleday, 1963), p. 48.

5 *Ibid.*, p. 49.

6 Charles Rosen, "One Easy Piece," *New York Review of Books*, February 1973; in Rosen, *Critical Entertainments* (Cambridge: Harvard University Press, 2000), pp. 283–84.

7 Elliott Carter, "Once Again Swing; Also 'American Music,'" *Modern Music*, January 1939; in Else Stone and Kurt Stone, *The Writings of Elliott Carter* (Bloomington: Indiana University Press, 1977), p. 46.

8 David Schiff, *The Music of Elliott Carter* (London: Eulenburg Books, 1983), p. 115.

9 Elliott Carter, "The Case of Mr. Ives," *Modern Music*, March 1939; *The Writings of Elliott Carter*, p. 51.

10 Richard Franko Goldman, "Current Chronicle," *Musical Quarterly* XXXVII (1951): 83–84.

11 Elliott Carter, "Music and the Time Screen," in *Current Thought in Musicology*, ed. John W. Grubbs (Austin: University of Texas Press, 1976), p. 67.

12 *Ibid.*

13 Allen Edwards, *Flawed Words and Stubborn Sounds: A Conversation with Elliott Carter* (New York: Norton, 1971), pp. 91–92n.

14 *Ibid.*, pp. 90–91.

15 *Ibid.*, p. 92.

16 *Ibid.*, pp. 93–94.

17 Susanne Langer, *Feeling and Form* (1953); quoted in Carter, "Music and the Time Screen," p. 66.

18 Carter, "Music and the Time Screen," p. 70.

19 *Ibid.*, p. 68.

20 *Ibid.*, pp. 73–74.

21 *Ibid.*, p. 77.

22 Liner note to Nonesuch Records H-71249 (1970).

23 David Schiff, *The Music of Elliott Carter* (2nd ed.; Ithaca: Cornell University Press, 1998), p. 55.

24 Edwards, *Flawed Words*, p. 35.

25 Virgil Thomson, "A Powerful Work," *New York Herald Tribune*, 5 May 1953; Thomson, *Music Reviewed 1940–1954* (New York: Vintage Books, 1967), p. 370.

26 Elliott Carter, liner note to Columbia Records ML 5104 (1956).

27 Nonesuch Records liner note (1970).

28 *Ibid.*

29 Schiff, *The Music of Elliott Carter* (1983), p. 152.

30 Sidney Hook, *Out of Step* (New York: Carroll and Graf, 1988), p. 440.

31 *Ibid.*, p. 445.

32 *Ibid.*, p. 446.

33 Quoted in Frances Stonor Saunders, *The Cultural Cold War: The CIA and the World of Arts and Letters* (New York: The New Press, 2000), p. 221.

34 Saunders, *The Cultural Cold War*, p. 223.

35 Elliott Carter, "Shop Talk by an American Composer," in *Problems of Modern Music*, ed. P. H. Lang (New York: Norton, 1962), p. 58.

36 Joseph Kerman, "American Music: The Columbia Series," *The Hudson Review* XI, no. 3 (Autumn 1958): 422.

37 William Glock, "Music Festival in Rome," *Encounter* II, no. 6 (June 1954): 63.

38 Benjamin Boretz, "Conversation with Elliott Carter," *Contemporary Music Newsletter* II, nos. 7–8 (November–December 1968): 3.

39 Elliott Carter, untitled memoir, in "In Memoriam: Stefan Wolpe (1902–1972)," *Perspectives of New Music* XI, no. 1 (Fall–Winter, 1972): 3.

40 Schiff, *The Music of Elliott Carter* (1983), p. 260.

41 *Ibid.*, pp. 260–61.

42 *Ibid.*, p. 260.

43 Andrew Porter, "Mutual Ordering," *The New Yorker*, 3 February 1973; rpt. in Porter, *A Musical Season: A Critic from Abroad in America* (New York: Viking Press, 1974), p. 140.

44 Porter, "Famous Orpheus," *The New Yorker*, 9 January 1979; Porter, *Music of Three More Seasons* (New York: Knopf, 1981), p. 281.

45 Bayan Northcott, "Carter, Elliott (Cook, Jr.)," in *New Grove Dictionary of Music and Musicians*, Vol. III (London: Macmillan, 1980), p. 831.

46 Porter, *A Musical Season*, pp. 145–46.

47 Andrew Porter, "Great Bridge, Our Myth," *The New Yorker*, 7 March 1977; Porter, *Music of Three Seasons* (New York: Farrar Straus Giroux, 1978), p. 529.

48 Elliott Carter, liner note to Columbia Records MS 7191 (1968).

49 Schiff, *The Music of Elliott Carter* (1983), p. 210.

50 Benjamin Boretz, "A Conversation with Elliott Carter," p. 3.

51 *Ibid.*

52 *Ibid.*

53 *Ibid.*, pp. 3–4.

54 Saunders, *The Cultural Cold War*, p. 257.

55 Charles Rosen, *Critical Entertainments*, p. 317.

56 Paul Griffiths, "Play That Old Piece if You Must, but Not for Old Time's Sake," *New York Times*, Arts and Leisure, 2 June 2002.

57 Charles Rosen, "Did Beethoven Have All the Luck?" *New York Review of Books*, 14 November 1996; Rosen, *Critical Entertainments*, p. 115.

CHAPTER 7: THE SIXTIES

1   Todd Gitlin, *The Sixties: Years of Hope, Days of Rage* (New York: Bantam Books, 1987), p. 37.

2   *Ibid.*, p. 42.

3   Cf. Daniel Bell, *The Cultural Contradictions of Capitalism* (New York: Basic Books, 1976).

4   Quoted in Linda Martin and Kerry Segrave, *Anti-Rock: The Opposition to Rock'n'Roll* (New York: Da Capo Press, 1993), p. 46.

5   Ken Tucker, "Presley, Elvis (Aaron)," in *New Grove Dictionary of American Music*, Vol. III (London: Macmillan, 1986), p. 624.

6   Gitlin, *The Sixties*, p. 39.

7   Quoted in Ned Rorem, "The Music of the Beatles," *New York Review of Books*, 18 January 1968; in Elizabeth Thomson and David Gutman, *The Lennon Companion* (New York: Schirmer, 1987), p. 100.

8   Quoted in Allan Kozinn, *The Beatles* (London: Phaidon, 1995), p. 74.

9   Ian MacDonald, *Revolution in the Head: The Beatles' Records and the Sixties* (New York: Henry Holt, 1994), p. 15.

10 Kozinn, *The Beatles*, p. 159.

11 William Mann, "The Beatles Revive Hopes of Progress in Pop Music," *The Times*, 29 May 1967; *The Lennon Companion*, p. 89.

12 *Ibid.*, pp. 91–92.

13 *Ibid.*, p. 93.

14 Ned Rorem, "The Music of the Beatles," in *The Lennon Companion*, p. 99.

15 *Ibid.*, p. 104.

16 Susan Sontag, "Against *Interpretation*" (1964), in *Against Interpretation and Other Essays* (New York: Delta Books, 1967), p. 14.

17 Rorem, "The Music of the Beatles," in *The Lennon Companion*, p. 104.

18 *Ibid.*, p. 105.

19 *Ibid.*, p. 106.

20 *Ibid.*, p. 109.

21 *Ibid.*, p. 100.

22 See Arthur Marwick, *British Society since 1945* (London: Pelican Books, 1982), p. 128.

23 Mann, "The Beatles Revive Hopes," in *The Lennon Companion*, p. 93.

24 Michael P. Long, "Is This the Real Life? Rock Classics and Other Inversions," University of California at Berkeley musicology colloquium, 1998.

25 Luciano Berio, "Comments on Rock," *Nuova Rivista Musicale Italiana*, May/June 1967; *The Lennon Companion*, p. 97.

26 *Ibid.*, p. 98.

27 *Ibid.*, p. 99.

28 *Ibid.*, pp. 97–98.

29 Joshua Rifkin, "On the Music of the Beatles," in *The Lennon Companion*, p. 116ff.

30 *Ibid.*, p. 126.

31 Ibid., p. 124.

32 The Lennon Companion, p. 113.

33 Ibid., pp. 113–14.

34 Rifkin, "On the Music of the Beatles," in The Lennon Companion, p. 115.

35 Greil Marcus, Invisible Republic: Bob Dylan's Basement Tapes (New York: Henry Holt, 1997), p. 13.

36 Quoted in Marcus, Invisible Republic, p. 14.

37 Barry Kernfeld, "Davis, Miles (Dewey, III)," in New Grove Dictionary of American Music, Vol. I (London: Macmillan, 1986), p. 585.

38 Stanley Crouch, "Play the Right Thing," The New Republic, 12 February 1990, p. 35.

39 Quoted in Gary Tomlinson, "Cultural Dialogics and Jazz: A White Historian Signifies," in Disciplining Music: Musicology and Its Canons, eds. Katherine Bergeron and Philip V. Bohlman (Chicago: University of Chicago Press, 1992), p. 83.

40 Ibid., p. 79.

41 Gunther Schuller, "Third Stream," in New Grove Dictionary of American Music, Vol. IV, p. 377.

42 Thomas Owens, "Lewis, John (Aaron)," in New Grove Dictionary of American Music, Vol. III, p. 41.

43 "Third Stream Revisited," in Musings: The Musical Worlds of Gunther Schuller (New York: Oxford University Press, 1986), p. 119.

44 Musings, pp. 131–32.

45 "The Avant-Garde and Third Stream," Musings, p. 121.

46 Robert Henderson, "Henze, Hans Werner," in New Grove Dictionary of Music and Musicians, Vol. VIII (1980 ed.), p. 492.

47 Hans Werner Henze, Bohemian Fifths: An Autobiography, trans. Steward Spencer (Princeton: Princeton University Press, 1999), p. 207.

48 Ibid., p. 208.

49 Ibid., p. 209.

50 Hans Werner Henze, liner note to Deutsche Grammophon Gesellschaft 139 374 Stereo (ca. 1970).

51 "Does Music Have to Be Political?" in Hans Werner Henze, Music and Politics: Collected Writings 1953–81, trans. Peter Laban (Ithaca: Cornell University Press, 1982), pp. 169–70.

52 Henze, Deutsche Grammophon liner notes.

53 Ibid.

54 Henze, Bohemian Fifths, p. 212.

55 Ibid., p. 194.

56 Henze, Music and Politics, p. 171.

57 Tom Wolfe, Radical Chic and Mau-mauing the Flak Catchers (New York: Farrar Straus Giroux, 1970), p. 71.

58 A. N. Wilson, God's Funeral: The Decline of Faith in Western Civilization (New York: Norton, 1999), p. 12.

Chapter 8: A Harmonious Avant-Garde?

1 Jim Aiken, "Brian Eno," *Keyboard* 7 (July 1981); quoted in Eric Tamm, *Brian Eno: His Music and the Vertical Color of Sound* (New York: Da Capo Press, 1995), p. 17.

2 Edward Strickland, *American Composers: Dialogues on Contemporary Music* (Bloomington: Indiana University Press, 1991), p. 47.

3 *Ibid.*, p. 45.

4 La Monte Young, quoted in K. Robert Schwarz, *Minimalists* (London: Phaidon, 1996), p. 9.

5 La Monte Young, quoted in Keith Potter, *Four Musical Minimalists* (Cambridge: Cambridge University Press, 2000), p. 48.

6 Richard Wollheim, "Minimal Art," *Arts Magazine*, January 1965, pp. 26–32.

7 Lucy Lippard, *Ad Reinhardt: Paintings* (New York: Jewish Museum, 1966), p. 23.

8 Quoted in Edward Strickland, *Minimalism: Origins* (Bloomington: Indiana University Press, 1993), pp. 44–45.

9 La Monte Young, "Lecture 1960," in Potter, *Four Musical Minimalists*, p. 48.

10 Potter, *Four Musical Minimalists*, p. 34.

11 Strickland, *Minimalism: Origins*, p. 121.

12 Quoted in Potter, *Four Musical Minimalists*, p. 148.

13 Alfred Frankenstein, "Music Like None Other On Earth," *San Francisco Chronicle*, 8 November 1964; quoted in Schwarz, *Minimalists*, p. 43.

14 Terry Riley, quoted in Geoff Smith and Nicola Walker Smith, *New Voices: American Composers Talk about Their Music* (Portland, Ore.: Amadeus Press, 1995), p. 234.

15 Quoted in Samuel Lipman, "From Avant-Garde to Pop," *Commentary* LXVIII, no. 1 (July 1979): 59.

16 Quoted in Potter, *Four Musical Minimalists*, p. 133.

17 Liner note to Columbia Records MS 7315 (1969).

18 Milton Babbitt, "Contemporary Music Composition and Contemporary Music Theory as Contemporary Intellectual History," in *Perspectives in Musicology*, eds. Barry S. Brook, Edward O. Downes, and Sherman van Solkema (New York: Norton, 1972), p. 165.

19 John Adams, "Reich, Steve [Stephen] (Michael)," in *New Grove Dictionary of American Music*, Vol. IV (London: Macmillan, 1986), p. 23.

20 Liner note to Odyssey Stereo 32 16 0160 (1967).

21 Jonathan Cott, "Interview with Steve Reich," in *Steve Reich: Works 1965–1995*, booklet accompanying Nonesuch Records 79451-2 (set of 10 compact discs), p. 28.

22 Potter, *Four Musical Minimalists*, p. 165.

23 "Music as a Gradual Process" (1968), in Steve Reich, *Writings on Music 1965–2000* (New York: Oxford University Press, 2002), pp. 34–36, condensed.

24 *Ibid.*, p. 35.

25 James Tenney, quoted in Reich, "Music as a Gradual Process," *Writing on Music*, p. 35.

26 "Music as a Gradual Process," *Writings on Music*, p. 35.

27 *Ibid.*

28 Paul Epstein, "Pattern Structure and Process in Steve Reich's *Piano Phase*," *Musical Quarterly* LXXII (1986): 146–77.

29 Potter, *Four Musical Minimalists*, p. 201.

30 Adams, "Reich," in *New Grove Dictionary of American Music*, Vol. IV, p. 25.

31 *Ibid.*

32 John Blacking, *How Musical Is Man?* (Seattle: University of Washington Press, 1973), p. 4.

33 Barbara Krader, "Ethnomusicology," in *New Grove Dictionary of Music and Musicians*, Vol. VI (London: Macmillan, 1980), p. 275.

34 Alan P. Merriam, "Definitions of 'Comparative Musicology' and 'Ethnomusicology': An Historical-Theoretical Perspective" (quoting Merriam, *The Anthropology of Music* [1964]), *Ethnomusicology* XXI (1977): 202.

35 Blacking, *How Musical Is Man?*, pp. 30–31.

36 Vincent Duckles, "Musicology," in *New Grove Dictionary of Music and Musicians* (1980 ed.), Vol. XII, p. 836.

37 Blacking, *How Musical Is Man?*, p. x.

38 Reich, "Music as a Gradual Process," in *Writings on Music*, p. 35.

39 Steve Reich, *Writings about Music* (Halifax: Nova Scotia College of Art and Design, 1974), p. 44.

40 Blacking, *How Musical Is Man?* p. 30.

41 Steve Reich, interviewed by Michael Nyman, *Studio International*, November/December 1976; quoted in Schwarz, *Minimalists*, p. 80.

42 Quoted in Tamm, *Brian Eno*, p. 24.

43 Philip Glass, *Music by Philip Glass*, ed. Robert T. Jones (New York: Harper and Row, 1987), p. 53.

44 Quoted in Schwarz, *Minimalists*, p. 107.

45 Schwarz, *Minimalists*, p. 120.

46 Robert Palmer, liner note to Glass, *Einstein on the Beach* (Tomato Records TOM-4-2901 [1976]), p. 5.

47 Philip Glass, quoted in *Ibid.*

48 Michael Walsh, "The Heart Is Back in the Game," *Time*, 20 September 1982; quoted in Gregory Bloch, "Philip Glass and Popular Music: Influence and Representation," University of California at Berkeley seminar paper, spring 2000.

49 Robert Coe, "Philip Glass Breaks Through," *New York Times Magazine*, 25 October 1981, p. 72.

50 Bloch, "Philip Glass and Popular Music."

51 Joe Stuessy, *Rock and Roll: Its History and Stylistic Development* (Englewood Cliffs, N.J.: Prentice Hall, 1994), p. 349.

52 Metropolitan Opera House program, 21 November 1976; reproduced in booklet accompanying Tomato Records, TOM-4-2901 (1977), p. 6.

53 John Rockwell, "Steve Reich and Philip Glass Find a New Way," *Rolling Stone*, 19 April 1979; quoted in Bloch, "Philip Glass and Popular Music."

54 Palmer, liner note to *Einstein on the Beach*, p. 7.

55 Philip Glass, "Notes on *Einstein on the Beach*," booklet accompanying Tomato Records, TOM-4-2901 (1977), p. 10.

56 Philip Glass, "Notes on *Einstein on the Beach*," p. 11.

57 Quoted in Potter, *Four Musical Minimalists*, p. 330.

58 Cole Gagne and Tracy Caras, *Soundpieces: Interviews with American Composers* (Metuchen, N.J.: Scarecrow Press, 1987), p. 216.

59 Ransom Wilson, liner note to EMI Angel Records DS-37340 (1982).

60 R. Taruskin, "Et in Arcadia Ego; or, I Had No Idea I Was Such a Pessimist until I Wrote This Thing," lecture delivered to the Seminar on the Future of the Arts (Chicago Seminars on the Future, forum on Aesthetics), 13 April 1989; rpt. in R. Taruskin, The Danger of Music and Other Anti-Utopian Essays (Berkeley and Los Angeles: University of California Press, 2009), p. 14.

61 Quoted in Walsh, "The Heart Is Back in the Game," *Time*, 20 September 1982, p. 60, col. 3.

62 Robert Fink, *Repeating Ourselves* (Berkeley and Los Angeles: University of California Press, 2005).

63 Edward Strickland, *American Composers: Dialogues on Contemporary Music* (Bloomington: Indiana University Press, 1991), p. 46.

64 Quoted in Schwarz, *Minimalists*, p. 205.

65 *Ibid.*, p. 206.

66 Liner note to Composers' Voice CV 7702/c (Amsterdam: Donemus, 1978).

67 *Ibid.*

68 Quoted in Schwarz, *Minimalists*, p. 207.

69 *Ibid.*, p. 208

70 Paul Hillier, *Arvo Pärt* (Oxford: Oxford University Press, 1997).

71 Hillier, *Arvo Pärt*, p. 92.

72 Liner note to ECM Records New Series 1275 (1984).

73 "John Tavener and Paul Goodwin talk to Martin Anderson," *Fanfare* XXII, no. 4 (March/April 1999): 28.

74 *Ibid.*

CHAPTER 9: AFTER EVERYTHING

1 Charles Jencks, *What Is Post-Modernism?* (London: Academy Editions, 1986), p. 7.

2 George Rochberg, epigraph to Act 3 of *Music for the Magic Theater* (Bryn Mawr, Pa.: Theodore Presser, 1965).

3 Leonard B. Meyer, "Future Tense: Music, Ideology and Culture," postlude to *Music, The Arts, and Ideas* (2nd ed.; Chicago: University of Chicago Press, 1994), p. 349.

4 Fred Lerdahl, "Composing and Listening: A Reply to Nattiez," in I. Deliège and J. Sloboda, *Perception and Cognition of Music* (Hove, East Sussex: Psychology Press, 1997); quoted from prepublication typescript (1994), p. 4.

5 Philip Glass, quoted in Wem Mertens, *American Minimal Music*, trans. J. Hautekiet (New York: Alexander Broude, 1983), p. 79.

6 Meyer, "Future Tense," p. 327.

7 Leonard B. Meyer, "A Pride of Prejudices; or, Delight in Diversity," *Music Theory Spectrum* XIII (1991): 241.

8 Jencks, *What Is Post-Modernism?*, p. 14.

9 Cf. Le Corbusier, *Vers une Architecture* (1923): "A house is a machine for living in. Baths, sun, hot-water, cold-water, warmth at will, conservation of food, hygiene, beauty in a sense of good proportion. An armchair is a machine for sitting in and so on."

10 Jencks, *What Is Post-Modernism?*, p. 14 (Jencks dates his coinage to the year 1978).

11 Meyer, "Future Tense," p. 327.

12 *Ibid.*

13 Jean-François Lyotard, *La condition postmoderne: Rapport sur le savoir* (Paris: Éditions de minuit, 1979), p. 2. The English term "master narrative" was coined by Frederic Jameson in his foreword to the English translation of the book (Jean-François Lyotard, *The Postmodern Condition: A Report on Knowledge*, trans. Geoff Bennington and Brian Massumi [Minneapolis: University of Minnesota Press, 1984], p. xii) as a rendering of Lyotard's term *grand récit*, of which, according to Lyotard, there are two basic strains: the master narrative of emancipation, which governed modernist theories of history, and that of speculation, which underlay modernist theories of science.

14 Robert L. Heilbroner, *The Future as History* (New York: Grove Press, 1961), pp. 47–48.

15 Meyer, "Future Tense," p. 331.

16 Liner note to Composers Recordings CRI 164 (1964).

17 Alexander Ringer, "The Music of George Rochberg," *Musical Quarterly* LII (1966): 424.

18 Hermann Hesse, *Steppenwolf*, trans. Basil Creighton (New York: Frederick Ungar, 1957), pp. 301–2.

19 Ringer, "The Music of George Rochberg," p. 426.

20 Andres D. McCredie (with Marion Rothärmel), "Zimmermann, Bernd Alois," in *New Grove Dictionary of Music and Musicians* (2nd ed.), Vol. XXVII, p. 837.

21 Liner note to Desto Records, DC-7108 (Henry Brant: Music 1970 [*Kingdom Come* and *Machinations*]).

22 *Ibid.*

23 *Ibid.*

24 Donal Henahan, "Crumb, the Tone Poet," *New York Times Magazine*, 11 May 1975, p. 50.

25 Andrew Porter, *A Musical Season* (New York: The Viking Press, 1974), p. 125.

26 John Rockwell, *All American Music: Composition in the Late Twentieth Century* (New York: Knopf, 1983), p. 78.

27 Kyle Gann, *American Music in the Twentieth Century* (New York: Schirmer, 1997), p. 226.

28 David Paul, "Three Critics and a Mad King," University of California at Berkeley seminar paper, December 2000.

29 Andrew Porter, "Questions," *The New Yorker*, 12 February 1979; rpt. in A. Porter, *Music of Three More Seasons* (New York: Knopf, 1981), p. 305.

30 Jay Reise, "Rochberg the Progressive," *Perspectives of New Music* XIX (1980/81): 396.

31 Liner note to Nonesuch Records H-71283 (1973).

32 *Ibid.*

33 *Ibid.*

34 "On the Third String Quartet," in Rochberg, *The Aesthetics of Survival* (Ann Arbor: University of Michigan Press), p. 240.

35 Liner note to Nonesuch H-71283.

36 Cole Gagne and Tracy Caras, *Soundpieces: Interviews with American Composers.* (Metuchen, N.J.: Scarecrow Press, 1982), p. 340.

37 Liner note to Nonesuch H-71283.

38 Umberto Eco, *Postscript to The Name of the Rose* (New York: Harcourt Brace Jovanovich, 1984), pp. 67–68.

39 Andrew Porter, "Tumult of Mighty Harmonies," *The New Yorker*, 20 June 1983; rpt. Porter, *Musical Events: A Chronicle, 1980–1983* (New York: Summit Books, 1987), p. 466.

40 Andrew Porter, "Questions," p. 306.

41 Andrew Porter, "A Frail Bark," *The New Yorker*, 16 August 1982; *Musical Events*, p. 292.

42 Reise, "Rochberg the Progressive," p. 395.

43 *Ibid.*, p. 406.

44 R. Taruskin, "Et in Arcadia Ego."

45 Oliver Knussen, "David Del Tredici and 'Syzygy,'" *Tempo* no. 118 (1976): 15.

46 Stagebill, New York Philharmonic, 2 June 1983, p. 20d.

47 Andrew Porter, *Musical Events*, p. 468.

48 Rockwell, *All American Music*, p. 77.

49 *Ibid.*, pp. 82–83.

50 Paul Moravec, "An Interview with David Del Tredici," *Contemporary Music Review* VI, part 2 (1992): 21.

51 Fred Lerdahl, "Tonality and Paranoia: A Reply to Boros," *Perspectives of New Music* XXXIV, no. 1 (winter 1996): 246.

52 Fred Lerdahl and Ray Jackendoff, *A Generative Theory of Tonal Music* (Cambridge: M.I.T. Press, 1983), pp. 8–9.

53 *Ibid.*, p. 297.

54 *Ibid.*

55 *Ibid.*, p. 298.

56 *Ibid.*, p. 300.

57 *Ibid.*, p. 301.

58 *Ibid.*, p. 5.

59 For a listing of some relevant articles, see Lerdahl, "Tonality and Paranoia," p. 249n5.

60 Leonard B. Meyer, "A Universe of Universals," *Journal of Musicology* XVI (1998): 6.

61 *Ibid.*, p. 9.

62 *Ibid.*, p. 12.

63 Fred Lerdahl, "Cognitive Constraints on Compositional Systems," in *Generative Processes in Music*, ed. John Sloboda (New York: Oxford University Press, 1988), p. 231.

64 *Ibid.*, p. 235.

65 *Ibid.*, p. 236.

66 *Ibid.*, p. 235.

67 *Ibid.*, pp. 255–56.

68 *Ibid.*, p. 256.

69 *Ibid.*, pp. 256–57.

70 James Boros, "A New Totality?" *Perspectives of New Music* XXXIII (1995): 546.

71 Jencks, *What Is Post-Modernism?*, p. 13.

72 Jonathan W. Bernard, "Tonal Traditions in Art Music Since 1960," in *The Cambridge History of American Music*, ed. David Nicholls (Cambridge: Cambridge University Press, 1998), p. 562.

73 *Ibid.*, p. 566.

74 Robert P. Morgan, *Twentieth-Century Music* (New York: Norton, 1991), p. 489.

75 Robert Commanday, "Composers Blow Their Own Horns," *San Francisco Chronicle*, 30 October 1988 (Datebook, p. 17).

76 Fred Lerdahl, "Composing and Listening: A Reply to Nattiez," prepublication typescript, p. 5.

77 Fred Lerdahl, musicology colloquium, University of California at Berkeley, February 2001.

78 Lerdahl, "Composing and Listening," p. 6.

79 Lerdahl, "Cognitive Constraints," p. 255.

80 Quoted in Peter J. Schmelz, *Listening, Memory, and the Thaw: Unofficial Music and Society in the Soviet Union, 1956–1974.* (Ph.D. diss., University of California at Berkeley, 2002), pp. 93–94.

81 R. Taruskin, *Defining Russia Musically* (Princeton: Princeton University Press, 1997), p. 101.

82 Alexander Ivashkin in conversation with the author, Glasgow, October 2000.

83 Levon Hakobian, *Music of the Soviet Age 1917–1987* (Stockholm: Melos, 1998), p. 284.

84 L. Ivanova, "Ot obryada k èposu," in *Zhanrovo-stilisticheskiye tendentsii klassicheskoy i sovremennoy muzïki* (Leningrad: Leningradiskiy Gosudarstvennïy Institut Teatrï, Muzïki i Kino, 1980), p. 174.

85 Jonathan Kramer, "Can Modernism Survive George Rochberg?" (response to Rochberg's "Can the Arts Survive Modernism?"), *Critical Inquiry* XI, no. 2 (1984): 341–54.

86 James Clerk Maxwell, "Science and the Nonscientist" (1965); quoted in Leonard B. Meyer, "Future Tense," p. 349.

CHAPTER 10: MILLENNIUM'S END

1 Robert S. Hines, "William Schuman Interview," *College Music Symposium* XXXV (1995): 138.

2 Nigel Osborne, Introduction ("Editorial") to *Musical Thought at IRCAM, Contemporary Music Review* I, part 1 (1984): i.

3 Jonathan Kramer, *The Time of Music* (New York: Schirmer, 1988), p. 45.

4 Cole Gagne, *Soundpieces 2: Interviews with American Composers* (Metuchen, N.J.: Scarecrow Press, 1993), p. 516.

5 Kyle Gann, *American Music in the Twentieth Century* (New York: Schirmer, 1997), p. 274.

6 David Gates, "Up From Minimalism," *Newsweek*, 1 November 1999, p. 84.

7 Remark made at a press conference at the Hotel Atlantic, Hamburg, on 16 September 2001 (original German as reported in the Hamburg newpaper *Die Zeit* on 18 September: "das größte Kunstwerk, das es je gegeben hat").

8 Hans Werner Henze, *Music and Politics: Collected Writings 1953–81*, trans. Peter Labanyi (Ithaca: Cornell University Press, 1982), p. 39.

9 David Schiff, *The Music of Elliott Carter* (1st ed.; London: Eulenburg Books), 1983.

10 Milton Babbitt, "The More Than the Sounds of Music," in *Horizons '84: The New Romanticism—A Broader View* (New York Philharmonic souvenir program, June 1984), pp. 11–12.

11 Christopher Fox, "New Complexity," in *New Grove Dictionary of Music and Musicians*, Vol. XVII (2nd ed., New York: Grove, 2000), p. 802.

12 Brian Ferneyhough, "Form—Figure—Style: An Intermediate Assessment," *Perspectives of New Music* XXXI, no. 1 (winter 1993): 37.

13 Richard Toop, "On Complexity," *Perspectives of New Music* XXXI, no. 1 (winter 1993): 54.

14 Barry Truax, "The Inner and Outer Complexity of Music," *Perspectives of New Music* XXXII, no. 1 (winter 1994): 176.

15 Ian Pace website (www.ianpace.com/text/history2.htm).

16 Eric Ulman, "Some Thoughts on the New Complexity," *Perspectives of New Music* XXXII, no. 1 (winter 1994): 204–5.

17 Tod Machover, "A View of Music at IRCAM," *Contemporary Music Review* I, part 1 (1984): 1.

18 Dominique Jameux, "Boulez and the 'Machine,'" *Contemporary Music Review* I, part 1 (1984): 19.

19 Georgina Born, *Rationalizing Culture: IRCAM, Boulez, and the Institutionalization of the Musical Avant-Garde* (Berkeley and Los Angeles: University of California Press, 1995), p. 285.

20 Jameux, "Boulez and the 'Machine,'" p. 18.

21 *Ibid.*, p. 20.

22 Kyle Gann, "Electronic Music, Always Current," *New York Times*, 9 July 2000, Arts and Leisure, p. 24.

23 W. Anthony Sheppard VI, *Revealing Masks: Exotic Influences and Ritualized Performance in Modernist Music Theater* (Berkeley and Los Angeles: University of California Press, 2001), p. 180.

24 Harry Partch, *Bitter Music: Collected Journals, Essays, Introductions, and Librettos*, ed. Thomas McGeary (Urbana: University of Illinois Press, 1991), p. ix.

25 See Bob Gilmore, "'A Soul Tormented': Alwin Nikolais and Harry Partch's *The Bewitched*," *Musical Quarterly* LXXIX (1995): 80–107.

26 Quoted in Andrew Stiller, "Partch, Harry," in *New Grove Dictionary of Opera*, Vol. III (London: Macmillan, 1992), p. 895.

27 Partch, "Revelation in the Courthouse Park" (1969); *Bitter Music*, p. 245.

28 *Ibid.*

29 Sheppard, *Revealing Masks*, p. 212.

30 Quoted in Sheppard, *Revealing Masks*, p. 223.

31 Partch, *Revelation in the Courthouse Park*, libretto; *Bitter Music*, p. 353.

32 *New Grove Dictionary of Opera*, Vol. III, p. 896.

33 *Bitter Music*, p. 69.

34 Damon Krukowski, "Vox populi," *Bookforum*, winter 2000, p. 18.

35 William Duckworth, *Talking Music: Conversations with John Cage, Philip Glass, Laurie Anderson, and Five Generations of American Experimental Composers* (New York: Da Capo, 1999), pp. 352–53.

36 *Ibid.*, p. 359.

37 Liner note to Meredith Monk, *Dolmen Music*, ECM Records 1–1197 (1981).

38 Geoff Smith and Nicola Walker Smith, *New Voices: American Composers Talk about Their Music* (Portland, Ore.: Amadeus Press, 1995), p. 189.

39 Duckworth, *Talking Music*, p. 359.

40 Liner note to ECM 1–1197.

41 Smith, *New Voices*, p. 189.

42 Smith, *New Voices*, p. 191.

43 Smith, *New Voices*, p. 192.

44 "A Conversation with the Composer" (interview with David Gere), booklet accompanying Meredith Monk, *Volcano Songs*, ECM New Series 1589 (1997).

45 *Boosey & Hawkes Newsletter*, October 2000, p. 8.

46 Gann, *American Music in the Twentieth Century*, p. 208.

47 Susan McClary, *Feminine Endings: Music, Gender, and Sexuality* (Minneapolis: University of Minnesota Press, 1991), p. 138.

48 Quoted in *Ibid.*, p. 139.

49 *Ibid.*, p. 138.

50 *Ibid.*

51 Rockwell, *All American Music*, p. 125.

52 Max V. Mathews and Ben Deutschman, liner note to *Music from Mathematics*, Decca Records DL 79103 (ca. 1962).

53 *Ibid.*

54 Gann, *American Music in the Twentieth Century*, p. 266.

55 Charles Dodge, liner note to *Computer Music*, Nonesuch Records H-71245 (ca. 1970).

56 Kurt Stone, "Current Chronicle: Lenox, Mass.," *Musical Quarterly* LI (1965): 690.

57 Liner note to *Synthesized Speech Music by Charles Dodge*, Composers Recordings CRI SD 348 (1976).

58 M. V. Mathews, liner note to *Voice of the Computer*, Decca Records DL 710180 (1977).

59 Gérard Grisey (trans. A. Laude), liner note to G. Grisey, *Partiels*, *Dérives*, Erato Stereo STU 71157 (1981).

60 Paul Lansky, "It's about Time: Some Next Perspectives (Part One)," *Perspectives of New Music* XXVII, no. 2 (summer 1989): 271.

61 *Ibid.*, p. 272.

62 *Ibid.*, pp. 272–73.

63 Gann, *American Music in the Twentieth Century*, p. 270.

64 Gann, "Electronic Music, Always Current," p. 24.

65 *Ibid.*, p. 21.

66 "Composer to Composer with John Oswald," http://redcat.org/season/music/johnoswald2.html.

67 Peter Niklas Wilson, "Zorn, John," in *New Grove Dictionary of Music and Musicians*, Vol. XXVII (2nd ed.), p. 869.

68 John Zorn, liner note to *Spillane* (1987); quoted in Susan McClary, *Conventional Wisdom: The Content of Musical Form* (Berkeley and Los Angeles: University of California Press, 2000), p. 146.

69 Gagne, *Soundpieces 2*, pp. 519–20.

70 Gagne, *Soundpieces 2*, p. 525.

71 Gagne, *Soundpieces 2*, pp. 530–31.

72 Quoted in McClary, *Conventional Wisdom*, p. 150.

73 McClary, *Conventional Wisdom*, pp. 150–51.

74 Gagne, *Soundpieces 2*, p. 534.

75 Gann, "Electronic Music, Always Current," p. 24.

76 Gann, *American Music in the Twentieth Century*, p. 354.

77 Jerrold Levinson, *Music in the Moment* (Ithaca: Cornell University Press, 1997), p. xi.

78 *Ibid.*, pp. 13–14.

79 *Ibid.*, p. ix.

80 *Ibid.*

81 *Ibid.*, p. x.

82 Anthony Tommasini, "Music, Minus Those Pesky Composers," *New York Times*, 6 August 2000, Arts and Leisure, p. 28.

83 "In the Center of American Music" (interview with Frank J. Oteri conducted on 21 November 2000), *New Music Box*, no. 21 (II, no. 9): www.newmusicbox.org/first-person/jan01/5.html.

84 Alex Ross, "The Harmonist," *The New Yorker*, 8 January 2001, p. 46.

85 Robert Commanday, "'Klinghoffer' Soars Into S.F.," *San Francisco Chronicle*, 1 November 1992, Datebook, p. 42.

86 R. Taruskin, "The Golden Age of Kitsch," *The New Republic*, 21 March 1994, p. 38; rpt. in R. Taruskin, *The Danger of Music*, p.260

87 Philip Glass, "A Bridge Between the Past, the Present, and the Future," booklet essay accompanying Glass, *Symphony No. 5: Requiem, Bardo, Nirmanakaya*, Nonesuch Records 79618-2 (2000).

88 David Brooks, *Bobos in Paradise: The New Upper Class and How They Got There* (New York: Simon and Schuster, 2000), p. 40.

89 *Ibid.*, p. 242.

90 *Ibid.*, pp. 206–7.

91 John Maynard Keynes, *Tract on Monetary Reform* (1923).

Art Credits

Figure 1-1 © CORBIS.

1-2 1931, Carnegie Institute, Mount Wilson Observatory, Pasadena, Calif. AKG Images.

1-3 Cartography by Bill Nelson.

1-4 © Karlheinz Stockhausen.

1-5 Music Division, New York Public Library for the Performing Arts, Astor, Lenox, and Tilden Foundations.

1-6 From the "Horpartitur" of *Artikulation* (by Ligeti, published by Schott, 1970; p. 54). © 1970 by Schott Music International, copyright renewed, all rights reserved.

2-1 Rendered by A Good Thing, Inc.

2-2 In Glenn Watkins, *Soundings: Music in the Twentieth Century*, Schirmer, New York, and Collier-Macmillan, London, 1988, p. 587.

2-3 Marcel Duchamp, 1917, replica 1964. Tate Gallery, London, © Tate Gallery, London, Art Resource, NY. © 2004 Artists Rights Society (ARS), New York/ADAGP, Paris/Succession Marcel Duchamp.

2-4 Image courtesy EMF Archives.

2-5a In Marc Treib, *Space Calculated in Seconds: The Philips Pavilion, Le Corbusier, Edgard Varèse*, Princeton University Press, Princeton, NJ, © 1996 by Marc Treib, p. 16.

2-5b Model of Philips Pavilion. In Bálint András Varga, *Conversations with Iannis Xenakis*, London, Faber and Faber, 1996.

2-5c Iannis Xenakis, *MetastaseisB*, Full Score, Boosey and Hawkes Music Publishers, London and New York, 1953–1954, mm. 309–317.

2-5d Philips Company Archives. In Marc Treib, *Space Calculated in Seconds: The Philips Pavilion, Le Corbusier, Edgard Varèse*, Princeton University Press, Princeton, NJ, © 1996 by Marc Treib, jacket illustration and facing p. 1.

2-6 In *Scratch Music*, ed. Cornelius Cardew, MIT Press, Cambridge, MA, 1972, pp. 114ff.

2-7 Luigi Nono, *Ein Gespenst geht um in der Welt*, 1971, manuscript.

2-08a La Monte Young, *Composition 1960 #7*. Copyright © La Monte Young 1963, renewed 1991. All rights reserved.

2-8b Photograph by Brigitte Hellgoth, 1976, Kölnischer Kunstverein, Cologne. AKG Images/Brigitte Hellgoth.

2-9   "December 1952," by Earle Brown. © 1961(renewed) by Associated Music Publishers, Inc. (BMI). International Copyright secured. All Rights Reserved. Reprinted by permission.

2-10 Score page from Eric Salzman, *The Nude Paper Sermon*, manuscript. Collection of the author.

2-11 Sylvano Bussotti, "New Year's Greeting," reproduced in John Cage, *Notations*, Something Else Press, New York, 1969, unpaginated. © 1969 by John Cage.

2-12 Earle Brown, Available Forms I. Copyright © 1961 (Renewed) by Associated Music Publishers, Inc. (BMI). International Copyright Secured. All Rights Reserved. Reprinted by Permission.

2-13 Music Division, New York Public Library for the Performing Arts, Astor, Lenox, and Tilden Foundations.

2-14 © 1962 by C.F. Peters Corporation.

3-1   *The New York Times.*

3-2   Washington, D.C., January 1953, © Bettmann/ CORBIS.

3-3   Mary Ann Sullivan, Bluffton University.

3-4   Paul Sacher Foundation, Igor Stravinsky Collection, Basel.

3-5   Howard Sochurek, Moscow, August 1, 1958 (Igy Conference). Time Life Pictures/Getty Images.

4-1   Russolo, *Il risveglio di una città* (1914). In Glenn Watkins, *Soundings: Music in the Twentieth Century*, Schirmer, New York, and Collier-Macmillan, London, 1988, p. 240.

4-2   December 14, 1927, Paris, © Bettmann/CORBIS.

4-3   © Bettmann/CORBIS.

4-4   LIDO DOC INA-GRM/SIPA.

4-5   © Karlheinz Stockhausen.

4-6   Columbia-Princeton Electronic Music Studio Archives, image courtesy of Robert Moog.

4-7a Philips Company Archives.

4-7b Philips Company Archives.

5-1   Lotte Jacobi, Long Island, 1939. AKG Images.

5-2   Photograph by Angus McBean, Harvard Theatre Collection. Courtesy of the Metropolitan Opera.

5-3   San Francisco Opera, 1997. Photograph courtesy of Marty Sohl.

6-1   AKG Images/Marion Kalter.

6-2   From David Schiff, *The Music of Elliott Carter*, Cornell University Press, Ithaca, NY, p. 48.

7-1   National Archives.

7-2   Library of Congress, *New York World-Telegram & Sun* Collection.

7-3   Library of Congress, *New York World-Telegram & Sun* Collection.

7-4   London, February 22, 1964. © Hulton-Deutsch Collection/ CORBIS.

7-5   Bruce BecVar, 1973–1974. Metropolitan Museum of Art, Gift of Arthur N. BecVar, 1980 (1980.544).

7-6   Music Division, New York Public Library for the Performing Arts, Astor, Lenox, and Tilden Foundations.

7-7   Courtesy of BMI Archives.

8-1   Pandit Pran Nath accompanied by La Monte Young and Marian Zazeela, 1971. Photograph by Robert Adler. Copyright © Pandit Pran Nath Musical Composition Trust.

8-2   © Sabine Matthes.

8-3   Photograph by Richard Landry. In Steve Reich, *Writings on Music 1965–2000*, ed. and intro. Paul Hillier, Oxford University Press, Oxford and New York, 2002, pp. 30–31.

8-4   Photograph by Gian Franco Gorgoni. In Steve Reich, *Writings on Music 1965–2000*, ed. and intro. Paul Hillier, Oxford University Press, Oxford and New York, 2002, p. 67.

8-5   Byrd Hoffman Water Mill Foundation. Photograph: Babette Mangolte.

8-6   February 8, 1957. Library of Congress, *New York World-Telegram & Sun* Collection.

9-1   © Sabine Matthes.

9-2   © 1970 by C.F. Peters Corporation, New York. All rights reserved. Used by permission.

9-3   Al Ravenna, 1955. Library of Congress, *New York World-Telegram & Sun* Collection.

9-4   Photograph by Robin Holland, used by permission of David Del Tredici.

9-5   *New York Times*, photograph by Teresa Zabala.

9-6   Paul Sacher Foundation, Sofia Gubaidulina Collection, Basel.

10-1   © Bruce Davidson/Magnum Photos.

10-2   © 1981 by Edition Peters, London. All rights reserved. Used by permission.

10-3   Courtesy of BMI Archives.

10-4   Houston Grand Opera.

10-5   Photograph by Deborah Feingold. Hulton Archive by Getty Images.

10-6   From *Computer Music: Synthesis, Composition, and Performance*, 2nd ed., by Charles Dodge and Thomson A. Jerse, p. 331. © 1997. Reprinted with permission of Wadsworth, a division of Thomson Learning.

10-7   From *IAGA Bulletin* by permission of IAGA.

10-8   © Peter Menzel/www.menzelphoto.com.

10-9   Courtesy of the Metropolitan Opera.

10-10   AKG Images/Marion Kalter.

10-11   Houston Grand Opera.

Further Reading

The Twentieth Century

General Sources

Adorno, Theodor W. *Quasi una Fantasia: Essays on Modern Music*, trans. Rodney Livingstone. New York: Norton, 1994.

Albright, Daniel. *Untwisting the Serpent: Modernism in Music, Literature, and Other Arts.* Chicago: University of Chicago Press, 2000.

Antokoletz, Elliott. *Twentieth-Century Music.* Englewood Cliffs, N.J.: Prentice Hall, 1992.

Austin, William W. *Music in the Twentieth Century.* New York: Norton, 1966.

Battcock, Gregory, ed. *Breaking the Sound Barrier: A Critical Anthology of the New Music.* New York: E. P. Dutton, 1981.

Burbank, Richard. *Twentieth-Century Music: A Chronology.* London: Thames and Hudson, 1984.

Cope, David H. *New Directions in Music.* 5th ed., Dubuque, Iowa: William C. Brown, 1989.

Gann, Kyle. *American Music in the Twentieth Century.* New York: Schirmer, 1997.

Hitchcock, H. Wiley. *Music in the United States.* 4th ed., Englewood Cliffs, N.J.: Prentice Hall, 1999.

Kallin, Anna, and Nicolas Nabokov, eds. *Twentieth-Century Composers.* 3 vols. Vol. I: Virgil Thomson, *American Music since 1910*; Vol. II: Hans Heinz Stuckenschmidt, *Germany and Central Europe*; Vol. III: Humphrey Searle and Robert Layton, *Britain, Scandinavia and the Netherlands.* New York: Holt, Rinehart and Winston, 1971–72.

Mitchell, Donald. *The Language of Modern Music.* London: Faber and Faber, 1963.

Morgan, Robert P. *Twentieth-Century Music.* New York: Norton, 1991.

Salzman, Eric. *Twentieth-Century Music: An Introduction.* 4th ed., Englewood Cliffs, N.J.: Prentice Hall, 2001.

Schwartz, Elliott, and Barney Childs, eds. *Contemporary Composers on Contemporary Music.* New York: Holt, Rinehart and Winston, 1967. Expanded ed., New York: Da Capo, 1998.

Schwartz, Elliot, and Daniel Godfrey, eds. *Music since 1945: Issues, Materials, and Literature.* New York: Schirmer, 1993.

Sheppard, W. Anthony. *Revealing Masks: Exotic Influences and Ritualized Performance in Modernist Music Theater.* Berkeley and Los Angeles: University of California Press, 2001.

Simms, Bryan R. *Music of the Twentieth Century: Style and Structure.* New York: Schirmer, 1986.

Simms, Bryan R., ed. *Composers on Modern Musical Culture*. New York: Schirmer, 1999.

Slonimsky, Nicolas. *Music since 1900*. 4th ed., New York: Scribners, 1971.

_____. *Supplement to Music since 1900*. New York: Scribners, 1986.

Vinton, John, ed. *Dictionary of Contemporary Music*. New York: E. P. Dutton, 1971.

Watkins, Glenn. *Pyramids at the Louvre: Music, Culture, and Collage from Stravinsky to the Postmodernists*. Cambridge: Harvard University Press, 1994.

_____. *Soundings: Music in the Twentieth Century*. New York: Schirmer, 1988.

Whittall, Arnold. *Exploring Twentieth-Century Music: Tradition and Innovation*. Cambridge: Cambridge University Press, 2003.

_____. *Musical Composition in the Twentieth Century*. Oxford: Oxford University Press, 1999.

Yates, Peter. *Twentieth-Century Music*. New York: Pantheon Books, 1967.

Chapter 1   Starting from Scratch

Adorno, Theodor W. *Philosophy of Modern Music*, trans. Anne G. Mitchel and Wesley V. Blomster. New York: Seabury Press, 1973.

Bandur, Markus. *Aesthetics of Total Serialism*. Basel: Birkhäuser, 2001.

Boulez, Pierre. *Boulez on Music Today*, trans. Susan Bradshaw and Richard Rodney Bennet. Cambridge: Harvard University Press, 1971.

_____. *Orientations: Collected Writings*, ed. Jean-Jacques Nattiez, trans. Martin Cooper. Cambridge: Harvard University Press, 1986.

_____. *Stocktakings from an Apprenticeship*, trans. Stephen Walsh. Oxford: Clarendon Press, 1991.

Brindle, Reginald Smith. *The New Music*. Oxford: Oxford University Press, 1974.

_____. *Serial Composition*. New York: Oxford University Press, 1966.

Carroll, Mark. *Music and Ideology in Cold War Europe*. Cambridge: Cambridge University Press, 2003.

Cott, Jonathan. *Stockhausen: Conversations with the Composer*. New York: Simon and Schuster, 1975.

Glock, William, ed. *Pierre Boulez: A Symposium*. London: Eulenburg Books, 1986.

Grant, M. J. *Serial Music, Serial Aesthetics: Compositional Theory in Postwar Europe*. Cambridge: Cambridge University Press, 2001.

Griffiths, Paul. *Boulez*. London: Oxford University Press, 1978.

_____. *Modern Music: The Avant-Garde since 1945*. London: J. M. Dent, 1981.

Harvey, Jonathan. *The Music of Stockhausen*. Berkeley and Los Angeles: University of California Press, 1975.

Henze, Hans Werner. *Bohemian Fifths: An Autobiography*, trans. Stewart Spencer. London: Faber & Faber, 1998.

_____. *Music and Politics: Collected Writings, 1953–81*, trans. P. Labanyi. London: Faber & Faber, 1982.

Hodeir, André. *Since Debussy: A View of Contemporary Music*, trans. Noel Burch. New York: Grove Press, 1961.

Koblyakov, Lev. *Pierre Boulez: A World of Harmony*. Milton Park: Taylor & Francis, 1990.

Kurtz, Michael. *Stockhausen: A Biography*, trans. Richard Toop. New York: Farrar Straus & Giroux, 1993.

Leibowitz, René. *Schoenberg and His School: The Contemporary Stage of the Language of Music*, trans. Dika Newlin. New York: Philosophical Library, 1949. Reprint, New York, Da Capo, 1975.

Maconie, Robin. *Stockhausen on Music: Lectures and Interviews*. London: Marion Boyars, 1989.

_____. *The Works of Karlheinz Stockhausen*. London: Oxford University Press, 1976.

Stacy, Peter F. *Boulez and the Modern Concept*. Lincoln: University of Nebraska Press, 1987.

Tannenbaum, Mya. *Conversations with Stockhausen*. Oxford: Oxford University Press, 1987.

Williams, Alastair. *New Music and the Claims of Modernity*. Aldershot, U.K.: Ashgate, 1997.

Wörner, Karl Heinrich. *Stockhausen: Life and Work*, trans. G. W. Hopkins. London: Faber & Faber, 1973.

Chapter 2   Indeterminacy

Bailey, Derek. *Improvisation: Its Nature and Practice in Music*. Ashebourne, Derbyshire: Moorland, 1980.

Bois, Mario. *Iannis Xenakis, the Man and His Music: A Conversation wth the Composer and a Description of His Works*. London: Boosey & Hawkes, 1967.

Cage, John. *A Year from Monday*. Middletown, Conn.: Wesleyan University Press, 1967.

_____. *Empty Words: Writings, 1973–78*. Middletown, Conn.: Wesleyan University Press, 1979.

_____. *For the Birds: In Conversation with Daniel Charles*. London: Boyars, 1981.

_____. *M: Writings, 1967–73*. Middletown, Conn.: Wesleyan University Press, 1973.

_____. *Silence*. Middletown, Conn.: Wesleyan University Press, 1961.

Cage, John, ed. *Notations*. New York: Something Else Press, 1969.

Cardew, Cornelius. *Stockhausen Serves Imperialism and Other Essays*. London: Latimer, 1974.

Cardew, Cornelius, ed. *Scratch Music*. Cambridge, Mass.: MIT Press, 1974.

Cole, Hugo. *Sounds and Signs: Aspects of Musical Notation*. Oxford: Oxford University Press, 1974.

DeLio, Thomas. *Circumscribing the Open Universe: Essays on Cage, Feldman, Wolff, Ashley and Lucier*. Washington, D.C.: Rowman and Littlefield, 1984.

DeLio, Thomas, ed. *The Music of Morton Feldman*. Westport, Conn.: Greenwood Press, 1996.

Feldman, Morton. *Essays*, ed. Walter Zimmerman. Kerpen: Beginner Press, 1985.

Gena, Peter, ed. *A John Cage Reader*. New York: C. F. Peters, 1982.

Kaprow, Allan. *Assemblage, Environments, and Happenings*. New York: Abrams, 1966.

Karkoschka, Erhard. *Notation in New Music*. New York: Praeger, 1972.

Kostelanetz, Richard, ed. *Conversing with Cage*. New York: Limelight Editions, 1987.

_____. *John Cage*. New York: Praeger, 1970.

_____ . *John Cage: Writer*. New York: Limelight Editions, 1993.

Nattiez, Jean-Jacques, ed. *The Boulez-Cage Correspondence*, trans. R. Samuels. Cambridge: Cambridge University Press, 1993.

Pritchett, James. *The Music of John Cage*. Cambridge: Cambridge University Press, 1993.

Revill, David. *The Roaring Silence: John Cage, A Life*. New York: Arcade, 1992.

Stone, Kurt. *Music Notation in the Twentieth Century*. New York: Norton, 1980.

Varga, Bálint András. *Conversations with Iannis Xenakis*. New York: Farrar, Straus and Giroux, 1996.

Xenakis, Iannis. *Arts, Sciences: Alloys*, trans. Sharon Kanach. New York: Pendragon Press, 1985.

_____ . *Formalized Music: Thought and Mathematics in Composition*. Bloomington: Indiana University Press, 1971.

Chapter 3   The Apex

Babbitt, Milton. *Words about Music*, ed. Stephen Dembski and Joseph N. Straus. Madison: University of Wisconsin Press, 1987.

Boretz, Benjamin, and Edward T. Cone. *Perspectives on American Composers*. Princeton: Princeton University Press, 1971.

_____ . *Perspectives on Contemporary Music Theory*. New York: Norton, 1972.

_____ . *Perspectives on Notation and Performance*. New York: Norton, 1976.

_____ . *Perspectives on Schoenberg and Stravinsky*. Princeton: Princeton University Press, 1968.

Copland, Aaron, and Vivian Perlis. *Copland: Since 1943*. New York: St. Martin's Press, 1989.

Craft, Robert. *Stravinsky: Chronicle of a Friendship, 1948–1971*. Rev. ed., Nashville: Vanderbilt University Press, 1994.

Forte, Allen. *The Structure of Atonal Music*. New Haven: Yale University Press, 1973.

Krenek, Ernst. *Horizons Circled: Reflections on My Life in Music*. Berkeley and Los Angeles: University of California Press, 1974.

Lang, Paul Henry, ed. *Problems of Modern Music*. New York: Norton, 1962.

Mead, Andrew W. *An Introduction to the Music of Milton Babbitt*. Princeton: Princeton University Press, 1994.

Nabokov, Nicolas. *Bagazh: Memoirs of a Russian Cosmopolitan*. New York: Atheneum, 1975.

Peles, Stephen, et al., eds. *The Collected Essays of Milton Babbitt*. Princeton: Princeton University Press, 2003.

Perspectives of New Music, Vol. XIV/2 and XV/1 (1976), special issue.

Straus, Joseph N. *Stravinsky's Late Music*. Cambridge: Cambridge University Press, 2001.

Sravinsky, Igor, and Robert Craft. *Conversations with Igor Stravinsky*. Garden City, N.Y.: Doubleday, 1959.

Werth, Alexander, ed. *Musical Uproar in Moscow*. London: Turnstile Press, 1949. Reprint, Westport, Conn.: Greenwood Press, 1973.

Wuorinen, Charles. *Simple Composition*. New York: Longman, 1979.

Chapter 4   The Third Revolution

Appleton, Jon, and Ronald Perera, eds. *The Development and Practice of Electronic Music.* Englewood Cliffs, N.J.: Prentice Hall, 1974.

Chadabe, Joel. *Electric Sound: The Past and Promise of Electronic Music.* Upper Saddle River, N.J.: Prentice Hall, 1997.

Ernst, David. *The Evolution of Electronic Music.* New York: Schirmer, 1977.

Heikinheimo, Seppo. *The Electronic Music of Karlheinz Stockhausen: Studies of the Esthetical and Formal Problems of Its First Phase,* trans. Brad Absetz. Helsinki: Suomen Musikkitieteellinin Seura, 1972.

Howe, Hubert S., Jr. *Electronic Music Synthesis.* New York: Norton, 1975.

Jacobson, Bernard. *A Polish Renaissance.* London: Phaidon Press, 1996.

Mirka, Danuta. *The Sonoristic Structuralism of Krzysztof Penderecki.* Katowice: Akademia Muzyczna, 1997.

Ouellette, Fernand. *A Biography of Edgard Varèse,* trans. D. Coltman. New York: Orion Press, 1966.

Robinson, Ray. *Krzysztof Penderecki: A Guide to His Work.* Princeton: Prestige, 1983.

Robinson, Ray, and Allen Winold. *A Study of the Penderecki St Luke Passion.* Celle, N.J.: Warner Bros., 1983.

Steinitz, R. *György Ligeti: Music of the Imagination.* Boston: Northeastern University Press, 2003.

Schwartz, Elliott. *Electronic Music: A Listener's Guide.* New York: Praeger, 1972.

Stucky, Steven. *Lutoslawski and His Music.* Cambridge: Cambridge University Press, 1981.

Thomas, Adrian. *Górecki.* Oxford: Oxford University Press, 1997.

Toop, Richard. *György Ligeti.* London: Phaidon Press, 1999.

Van Solkema, Sherman, ed. *The New Worlds of Edgard Varèse: A Symposium.* Brooklyn, N.Y.: Institute for Studies in American Music, 1979.

Chapter 5   Standoff (I)

Banks, Paul, ed. *The Making of Peter Grimes.* Woodbridge: Boydell Press/Britten-Pears Library, 1995.

Brett, Philip, ed. *Benjamin Britten: Peter Grimes.* Cambridge: Cambridge University Press, 1983.

Britten, Benjamin. *On Receiving the First Aspen Award.* London: Faber & Faber, 1964.

Carpenter, Humphrey. *Benjamin Britten: A Biography.* New York: Simon and Schuster, 1993.

Cooke, Mervyn. *Britten and the Far East: Asian Influences in the Music of Benjamin Britten.* Woodbridge: Boydell Press/Britten-Pears Library, 1998.

———. *Britten: War Requiem.* Cambridge: Cambridge University Press, 1996.

Cooke, Mervyn, ed. *The Cambridge Companion to Benjamin Britten.* Cambridge: Cambridge University Press, 1999.

Cooke, Mervyn, and Philip Reed, eds. *Benjamin Britten: Billy Budd.* Cambridge: Cambridge University Press, 1993.

Evans, Peter. *The Music of Benjamin Britten*. Rev. ed., Oxford: Oxford University Press, 1995.

Howard, Patricia, ed. *Benjamin Britten: The Turn of the Screw*. Cambridge: Cambridge University Press, 1985.

Howes, Frank. *The English Musical Renaissance*. London: Secker and Warburg, 1966.

Hughes, Meirion, and Robert Stradling. *The English Musical Renaissance, 1840–1940: Constructing a National Music*. 2nd ed., Manchester: Manchester University Press, 2001.

Kennedy, Michael. *Britten*. London: J. M. Dent, 1981.

Kildea, Paul. *Selling Britten: Music and the Market Place*. Oxford: Oxford University Press, 2002.

Mitchell, Donald. *Benjamin Britten: Death in Venice*. Cambridge: Cambridge University Press, 1987.

———. *Britten and Auden in the Thirties: The Year 1936*. Seattle: University of Washington Press, 1981.

Mitchell, Donald, and Hans Keller, eds. *Benjamin Britten: A Commentary on His Works from a Group of Specialists*. London: Rockliff, 1952.

Mitchell, Donald, and Philip Reed, eds. *Letters from a Life: Selected Letters and Diaries of Benjamin Britten*. Berkeley and Los Angeles: University of California Press, 1991.

Palmer, Christopher, ed. *The Britten Companion*. London: Faber and Faber, 1984.

Pirie, Peter J. *The English Musical Renaissance*. London: Victor Gollancz, 1979.

White, Eric Walter. *Benjamin Britten: His Life and Operas*. 3rd ed., London: Faber and Faber, 1983.

Wilcox, Michael. *Benjamin Britten's Operas*. Bath: Absolute Press, 1997.

Chapter 6 Standoff (II)

Carter, Elliott. *Collected Essays and Lectures, 1937–1995*, ed. Jonathan W. Bernard. Rochester, N.Y.: University of Rochester Press, 1997.

Edwards, Allen. *Flawed Words and Stubborn Sounds: A Conversation with Elliott Carter*. New York: Norton, 1971.

Pollack, Howard. *Harvard Composers: Walter Piston and His Students, from Elliott Carter to Frederic Rzewski*. Metuchen, N.J.: Scarecrow Press, 1992.

Rosen, Charles. *The Musical Languages of Elliott Carter*. Washington, D.C.: United States Government Printing Office, 1984.

Schiff, David. *The Music of Elliott Carter*. London: Eulenburg Books, 1983. 2nd ed., Ithaca, N.Y.: Cornell University Press, 1998.

Stone, Kurt, and Else Stone, eds. *The Writings of Elliott Carter: An American Composer Looks at Modern Music*. Bloomington: Indiana University Press, 1977.

Chapter 7 The Sixties

Berio, Luciano. *Two Interviews*, ed. and trans. David Osmond-Smith. London: Marion Boyars, 1985.

Davis, Edward E., ed. *The Beatles Book*. New York: Cowles, 1968.

Davis, Jerome. *Talking Heads.* New York: Vintage Books, 1986.

DeLio, Thomas, ed. *Contiguous Lines: Issues and Ideas in the Music of the Sixties and Seventies.* Lanham, N.Y.: University Press of America, 1985.

Eisen, Jonathan, ed. *The Age of Rock: Sounds of the American Cultural Revolution.* New York: Vintage Books, 1969.

Friedlander, Paul. *Rock and Roll: A Social History.* Boulder: Westview Press, 1996.

Frith, Simon. *Sound Effects: Youth, Leisure and the Politics of Rock 'n' Roll.* New York: Random House, 1981.

Frith, Simon, and Andrew Goodwin, eds. *On Record: Rock, Pop, and the Written Word.* New York: Random House, 1990.

Gitlin, Todd. *The Sixties: Years of Hope, Days of Rage.* New York: Bantam Books, 1987.

Hamm, Charles, Bruno Nettl, and Ronald Byrneside. *Contemporary Music and Music Cultures.* Englewood Cliffs, N.J.: Prentice Hall, 1975.

Haskell, Barbara. *Blam! The Explosion of Pop, Minimalism, and Performance, 1958–1964.* New York: Norton, 1984.

Kozinn, Allan. *The Beatles.* London: Phaidon Press, 1995.

Macdonald, Ian. *Revolution in the Head: The Beatles' Records and the Sixties.* Rev. ed., London: Fourth Estate, 1994.

Marcus, Greil. *Mystery Train: Images of American Rock 'n' Roll Music.* New York: E. P. Dutton, 1975.

Moore, A. F. *The Beatles: Sgt. Pepper's Lonely Hearts Club Band.* Cambridge: Cambridge University Press, 1997.

Osmond-Smith, David. *Berio.* Oxford: Oxford University Press, 1991.

_____. *Playing with Words: A Guide to Luciano Berio's Sinfonia.* London: Royal Musical Association, 1985.

Rockwell, John. *All American Music: Composition in the Late Twentieth Century.* New York: Knopf, 1983.

Tamm, Eric. *Brian Eno: His Music and the Vertical Color of Sound.* New York: Farrar Straus & Giroux, 1989.

Thomson, Elizabeth, and David Gutman, eds. *The Lennon Companion.* Rev. ed., New York: Da Capo Press, 2004.

Chapter 8   A Harmonious Avant-Garde?

Battcock, Gregory, ed. *Minimal Art: A Critical Anthology.* New York: E. P. Dutton, 1968.

Haydon, Geoffrey. *John Tavener: Glimpses of Paradise.* London: Victor Gollancz, 1994.

Hillier, Paul. *Arvo Pärt.* Oxford: Oxford University Press, 1997.

Jones, Robert T., ed. *Music by Philip Glass.* New York: Harper & Row, 1987.

Kostelanetz, Richard, ed. *Writings on Glass: Essays, Interviews, Criticism.* New York: Schirmer, 1998.

Mertens, Wem. *American Minimal Music.* New York: Alexander Broude, 1983.

Potter, Keith. *Four Musical Minimalists.* Cambridge: Cambridge University Press, 2000.

Reich, Steve. *Writings about Music.* New York: Oxford University Press. 2002.

Schwarz, K. Robert. *Minimalists.* London: Phaidon, 1996.

Strickland, Edward. *Minimalism: Origins*. Bloomington: Indiana University Press, 1993.

Tavener, John, with Mother Thekla, and Ivan Moody. *Ikons: Meditations in Words and Music*. London: HarperCollins, 1995.

_____. *The Music of Silence: A Composer's Testament*, ed. Brian Keeble. London: Faber & Faber, 1999.

Young, La Monte, and Marian Zazeela. *Selected Writings*. Munich: Heiner Friedrich, 1969.

Chapter 9   After Everything

Attali, Jacques. *Noise: The Political Economy of Music*, trans. Brian Massumi. Minneapolis: University of Minnesota Press, 1985.

Gillespie, Don, ed. *George Crumb: Profile of a Composer*. New York: C. F. Peters, 1985.

Griffiths, Paul. *Modern Music and After: Directions since 1945*. Oxford: Oxford University Press, 1995.

_____. *Peter Maxwell Davies*. London: Robson, 1982.

Ivashkin, Alexander. *Alfred Schnittke*. London: Phaidon, 1996.

Kaczynski, Tadeusz. *Conversations with Witold Lutoslawski*, trans. Yolanta May. London: J. & W. Chester, 1984.

Lochhead, Judy, and Joseph Auner, eds. *Postmodern Music/Postmodern Thought*. New York: Routledge, 2002.

Meyer, Leonard B. *Music, the Arts, and Ideas*. 2nd ed., Chicago: University of Chicago Press, 1994.

Nyman, Michael. *Experimental Music: Cage and Beyond*. New York: Schirmer, 1974.

Penderecki, Krzysztof. *Labyrinth of Time: Five Addresses for the End of the Millennium*, ed. Ray Robinson, trans. William Brand. Chapel Hill, N.C.: Hinshaw Music, 1998.

Pruslin, Stephen, ed. *Peter Maxwell Davies: Studies from Two Decades*. London: Boosey & Hawkes, 1970.

Reynolds, Roger. *Mind Models: New Forms of Music Experience*. New York: Praeger, 1975.

Rochberg, George. *The Aesthetics of Survival: A Composer's View of Twentieth-Century Music*, ed. William Bolcom. Ann Arbor: University of Michigan Press, 1984.

Seabrook, Mike. *Max: The Life and Music of Peter Maxwell Davies*. London: Trafalgar Square, 1994.

Shepherd, John, Phil Virden, Graham Vulliamy, and Trevor Wishart. *Whose Music? A Sociology of Musical Languages*. London: Latimer New Dimensions, 1977.

Slobin, Mark. *Subcultural Sounds: Micromusics of the West*. Middletown, Conn.: Wesleyan University Press, 1993.

Small, Christopher. *Musicking*. Middletown, Conn.: Wesleyan University Press, 1998.

Willis, Brian. *Art after Modernism: Rethinking Representation*. Boston: Godine, 1984.

Chapter 10   Millennium's End

Anderton, Craig. *MIDI for Musicians*. New York: Amsco, 1986.

Biggs, Hayes, and Susan Orzel, eds. *Musically Incorrect: Conversations about Music at the End of the Twentieth Century*. New York: C. F. Peters, 1998.

Boom, Michael. *Music through MIDI*. Redmond, Wash.: Microsoft Press, 1987.

Born, Georgina. *Rationalizing Culture: IRCAM, Boulez, and the Institutionalization of the Avant-Garde*. Berkeley and Los Angeles: University of California Press, 1995.

Brentano, Robyn. *Outside the Frame: Performance and the Object: A Survey History of Performance Art in the USA since 1950*. Cleveland: Cleveland Center for Contemporary Art, 1994.

DeFuria, Steve. *The MIDI Book*. Milwaukee: Hal Leonard Books, 1988.

Dodge, Charles, and Thomas A. Jerse. *Computer Music: Synthesis, Composition, and Performance*. New York: Schirmer, 1985.

Ferneyhough, Brian. *Collected Writings*, ed. James Boros and Richard Toop. London: Routledge, 1995.

Gilmore, Bob. *Harry Partch: A Biography*. New Haven: Yale University Press, 1998.

Goldberg, Roselee. *Performance Art: From Futurism to the Present*. Rev. ed., New York: Thames & Hudson, 2001.

Howell, John. *Laurie Anderson*. New York: Thunder's Mouth Press, 1992.

Jabobson, Linda, ed. *Cyberarts: Exploring Art and Technology*. San Francisco: Backbeat Books, 1992.

Kornick, Rebecca H. *Recent American Opera*. New York: Columbia University Press, 1991.

Manning, Peter. *Electronic and Computer Music*. Oxford: Clarendon Press, 1985.

Mathews, Max. *The Technology of Computer Music*. Cambridge, Mass.: MIT Press, 1985.

Partch, Harry. *"Bitter Music": Collected Journals, Essays, Introductions, and Librettos*, ed. Thomas McGeary. Urbana: University of Illinois Press, 1991.

———. *Genesis of a Music*. 2nd ed., Madison: University of Wisconsin Press, 1974.

Roads, Curtis, ed. *The Music Machine*. Cambridge, Mass.: MIT Press, 1989.

Roads, Curtis, and John Strawn, eds. *Foundations of Computer Music*. Cambridge, Mass.: MIT Press, 1985.

Roth, Moira. *Amazing Decade: Women and Performance Art, 1970–1980*. Hollywood, Calif.: Astro Artz, 1984.

Index

Page numbers in *italics* indicate illustrations.